BIRDS OF MEXICO

COLLARED ARAÇARI
(*Pteroglossus torquatus*)

BIRDS OF MEXICO

A Guide
for Field Identification

By

EMMET REID BLAKE

Illustrated by

DOUGLAS E. TIBBITTS

THE UNIVERSITY OF CHICAGO PRESS

CHICAGO & LONDON

A Contribution of the Field Museum of Natural History

International Standard Book Number: 0–226–05640–6
Library of Congress Catalog Card Number: 53–8737

THE UNIVERSITY OF CHICAGO PRESS, CHICAGO 60637

The University of Chicago Press, Ltd., London

To

EUGENE H. BLAKE

Who held the light and pointed out the way

and to

ERNEST G. HOLT

Who introduced me to the fascinating world

of tropical birds

PREFACE

THE phenomenal growth of bird study in the United States since the early part of the century can be attributed largely to the stimulus provided by the publication of manuals emphasizing field identification. Recognition is the first step toward a fuller appreciation of a species, its habits, and its place in nature. With the first step, one gains the key to a vast literature and can participate to the limit of one's interest or ability in a field once virtually closed to all except the specialist. While many study birds for recreation alone, those who become familiar with scientific procedure as well as proficient in field identification may make important contributions to ornithology.

In recent years an increasing number of Americans have looked to the tropics for new experiences in bird watching. Many ask museum ornithologists to recommend suitable guides for the areas to be visited. Unfortunately, few nontechnical birdbooks have yet been published for any of the tropical regions of the world. Several of these treat South American birds, but until recently a single guide, Sturgis' *Field Book of Birds of the Panama Canal Zone* (1928), has had to serve the whole of Middle America north to our southern border. Sutton's *Mexican Birds, First Impressions* (1951) is an important addition to bird literature of Latin America. While not a field guide, it nevertheless serves as an introduction to the Mexican fauna and will be of interest to all bird watchers who visit the country.

Ornithologists have long been aware of the need for a comprehensive Mexican bird guide. No other country lying partly within the tropics is so readily accessible to Americans, and few offer so much of interest to the bird student. A trip to Mexico often means the realization of an ambition to become acquainted with a large new fauna, and especially to see exotic tropical birds in their natural habitat. Such an experience loses much of its meaning unless one knows at least the names of the birds as a basis for further study. This handbook is designed to meet that fundamental need for identification. Its purpose will have been wholly realized if it also stimulates a wider interest in Mexican birds.

Any comprehensive field guide to a large fauna is, of necessity, the product of many workers. In preparing this handbook I have drawn freely from the reports of others who have worked in Mexico or in adjacent areas.

The monumental *Biologia Centrali-Americana* of Salvin and Godman, published between 1879 and 1904, is the great landmark of Mexican and Middle American ornithology. In recent years important contributions to our knowledge of this fauna have been made by Pierce Brodkorb, Thomas D. Burleigh, John Davis, L. Irby Davis, Miguel Alvarez del Toro, Ernest P. Edwards, Ludlow Griscom, Harold C. Hanson, Robert B. Lea, A. Starker Leopold, Frederick W. Loetscher, George H. Lowery, Alden H. Miller, Robert T. Moore, Robert J. Newman, Raymond A. Paynter, Jr., Allan R. Phillips, Frank A. Pitelka, A. J. van Rossem, Alexander F. Skutch, Charles G. Sibley, Robert W. Storer, George M. Sutton, Richard E. Tashian, Melvin A. Traylor, Josselyn Van Tyne, Helmuth O. Wagner, Alexander Wetmore, and others too numerous to mention.

Peterson's well-known field guides, Hoffmann's *Birds of the Pacific States*, and similar regional guides have been important sources of information relating to the field characters of various species that range north of Mexico. I am indebted to Dr. Alexander Wetmore for permission to use the new, and as yet unpublished, English names that have been chosen for certain North American species by the nomenclatural committee of the American Ornithologists' Union. Dr. Eugene Eisenmann has given generously of his time in helping to select the most suitable name for species south of the area covered by the A.O.U. check-list; in fact, it is largely through his unflagging efforts that some consistency in this respect has finally been achieved for Mexican and Middle American birds. I am indebted to Dr. Herbert Friedmann, Dr. Alden H. Miller, the late Dr. James L. Peters, Dr. Josselyn Van Tyne, and Dr. John T. Zimmer for the loan of museum specimens needed for examination. I also owe much to my colleagues at the Chicago Natural History Museum. Dr. Karl P. Schmidt and Dr. Austin L. Rand have been unfailing sources of encouragement from the very inception of the project, while also advising me on various aspects of the work. Mr. Melvin A. Traylor has verified my information regarding certain Veracruz and Yucatán birds with which he has had field experience. All illustrations are by Douglas E. Tibbitts, staff artist of Chicago Natural History Museum. Miss Ruth Johnson typed the entire manuscript and prepared the Index. Her efficient execution of these largely thankless chores is deeply appreciated.

I assume full responsibility for all errors, whether of commission or of omission. While I have endeavored to make the list of species and subspecies complete and to summarize our present knowledge of their distribution accurately, mistakes would seem almost inevitable in a work of this scope. Many changes in present taxonomic and geographic concepts are also to be expected as additional specimens and intensive research gradually refine our knowledge of Mexican birds. Each year new subspecies are described from Mexico, and doubtless scores of others are yet to be discovered. Birds long considered distinct must sometimes be relegated to synonomy, others "split" or re-evaluated, and specialists often differ in details of nomenclature. These, however, are essentially technical matters chiefly of concern to taxonomists. Their final solution will not seriously affect the usefulness of a book, such as this, that is intended to serve primarily as a guide to field identification and only secondarily as a check-list.

EMMET R. BLAKE
Associate Curator of Birds

CHICAGO NATURAL HISTORY MUSEUM

CONTENTS

CONTENTS   xiii

LIST OF ILLUSTRATIONS

INTRODUCTION

MEXICO is today the most fertile new field for a comprehensive handbook of birds. Its rich avifauna is only partially duplicated to the northward. With the opening of the Pan-American Highway, a Mexican vacation has become commonplace for Americans from every walk of life. Each year an increasing number of American automobiles enter the country, accounting for some hundreds of thousands of adult visitors annually. Additional thousands go by train, plane, and ship.

Mexico offers much of interest and beauty for every taste. Its archeological treasures, pleasant climate, and hospitality to visitors have been widely proclaimed. For many, one of the leading attractions of a Mexican trip will be the extraordinary variety and, above all, novelty of the bird life. This far exceeds in number of forms that of the United States and Canada combined and accounts for about one-fifteenth of the world's total.

Almost a thousand species of birds representing eighty-nine families have been found within the political boundaries of Mexico. Subspecies swell the list to some two thousand named forms, making its fauna the richest of any country lying largely in temperate regions. This impressive total includes more than seven hundred and fifty resident species and about two hundred winter visitants and transients of regular occurrence. While many of the residents are also represented in the United States and Canada, more than eighty species are endemic to Mexico, and some four hundred others do not range beyond its northern border.

This great association of bird life stems only in part from the fortunate circumstance of Mexico's geographic position. Tropical Middle and South America as well as the temperate north have contributed heavily to the fauna, and the number of species and families represented is strongly influenced by the remarkable diversity of Mexico's climate and topography. Much of the interior of the country consists of a high triangular plateau, with a temperate climate, bounded on the east and west by great mountain ranges that converge toward the south, where are to be found a dozen or more of the highest peaks. The coastal plains vary from twenty-five miles to more than a hundred miles in width. The Pacific slope is largely desert; the Caribbean decidedly humid, especially in the south.

Mexican birds have been studied intensively for many years. Specimens numbered in the scores of thousands are preserved in museums the world over as material for further research, and each year marks the discovery of more new forms. While progress has been made toward a fuller understanding of the origin and relationships of the fauna as a whole, little more is known about Mexican birds today than was known about those of the United States three-quarters of a century ago. This applies especially to the local distribution, habits, and life-histories of the birds, of which our knowledge is still inadequate.

SCOPE OF THE WORK

This handbook treats briefly, in nontechnical terms, all the 967 species that have been recorded from the Mexican mainland (including Baja California), the adjacent waters, and associated islands. Although intended primarily as a guide for Mexico, and hence arbitrarily limited to the birds of that country, it will serve almost equally well in Guatemala and elsewhere in northern Middle America.

The scope and content of the book are suggested by the title. Its primary objective is the sight identification of birds in their natural habitat. Emphasis is placed on the more conspicuous diagnostic characters, and attention is often directed to those aspects of distribution, habitat, or song that serve to facilitate or corroborate the identification. The Mexican distribution of each species is briefly outlined, this being further elaborated in a separate paragraph when there are two or more subspecies to be considered.

The Mexican avifauna, far greater than that of the entire United States and Canada, obviously is much too large to permit of extended biographical sketches. The addition of notes on the habits, song, nest, eggs, etc., of almost a thousand species would have expanded the book much beyond the practical limits of a field guide. There is, accordingly, need for regional guides, each treating in greater detail the birds of a relatively small area, as has been the trend in birdbooks for the United States. A guide to Mexican birds that do not occur in the United States is projected by Edward L. Chalif, and popular guides to other components of the avifauna will almost certainly appear during the next few years.

METHOD OF TREATMENT

The eighty-nine families of birds represented in Mexico are treated as independent sections, their sequence being that of Wetmore (1951), the recognized standard. Each family having more than one Mexican representative is provided with a dichotomous key, which, by reference to readily discernible field characters, usually assures identification at species level. Verification is provided by the text description and other components of the species account. Field identification of birds below species level (i.e., subspecies or "races") is usually unsatisfactory, if not wholly impossible. Emphasis, therefore, is placed on the "species" per se, the geographical varieties or "races" thereof being merely listed without diagnosis, and their respective ranges in Mexico briefly outlined.

NOMENCLATURE

The authoritative *Distributional Check-List of the Birds of Mexico*, Part I, by Friedmann, Griscom, and Moore (1951), is the source of the scientific names of most of the species comprising the families Tinamidae (Tinamous)—Trochilidae (Hummingbirds). The nomenclature of the remainder is derived from other standard sources, especially Peters (*Birds of the World*), Hellmayr (*Birds of the Americas*), the A.O.U. *Check-List of North American Birds* (4th ed. and its supplements), and various authoritative revisions of more recent date.

English or "common" names are designated for species alone, in keeping with a fairly recent but desirable practice. Virtually all birds of the Western Hemisphere have been given English names, but unanimity of usage has been achieved only for those of the A.O.U. check-list area. To the southward, in Mexico and tropical America generally, different names have often been applied to the same form by different writers, and not infrequently new names are coined to replace the old. Since this has led to much confusion, English names used in this guide have been selected with the utmost care in the hope that they will meet with general approval. Virtually all the names are the unanimous choice of several students of tropical American birds who have devoted much thought to this neglected aspect of ornithology. While no attempt has been made to erect a rigid system of vernacular nomenclature, generic relationships and natural groups have been respected whenever possible, and names that are at least in part descriptive usually have been given preference over patronymics and those with geographic implications. When two or more names are available in the literature, the one that best characterizes the *species as a whole* is used, even though it may be less appropriate for the Mexican representative than some other. Inevitably a few wholly incongruous, if not ridiculous, names are retained, some by virtue of being already in very general use and others because the only suitable names are preoccupied, in some instances, by South American species.

Few English names have been coined, and these only to replace those that are conspicuously inappropriate. New names for certain northern species, if approved by the nomenclatural committee of the American Ornithologists' Union for use in the forthcoming check-list, have been accepted, although replacing others long familiar to bird watchers in the United States and Canada. While the authoritative A.O.U. check-list has been followed closely, the names of several essentially tropical birds treated therein have been replaced by names considered more suitable for the species complex. In any case, alternate common names of long standing are listed under "Remarks" and also appear in the Index.

SEASONAL STATUS

The seasonal status of each species and race is shown by the presence or absence of an asterisk (*) before its name. Nonresident birds, whether migrant winter visitants, transients, or "accidentals," are indicated by a single asterisk. Birds that breed in Mexico, but winter elsewhere, are indicated by two asterisks. A species is considered to be a resident if represented in Mexico throughout the year by at least one race. It should be emphasized that the status of many Mexican birds is still uncertain, and radical changes in present concepts are to be expected as field work continues.

The actual headings used for each species, and a brief explanation of treatment follow.

Description.—The approximate length (in inches) of every species is indicated by a numeral (or by inclusive numerals) preceding the general description. These measurements are not absolute but rather a suggestion of the average length of the adult bird for purposes of comparison. The description provides details of color and pattern that are useful in verifying a tentative identification and is designed to convey a general impression of the species as represented in Mexico and adjacent areas. The breeding plumage of the male is emphasized, since this is most distinctive and usually is acquired even by winter visitants while still in Mexico. Females are described when notably unlike males, and immature birds only when quite distinct from either parent. The colors of the "soft parts" (iris, bill, legs, etc.) and the anatomical features are not mentioned unless useful in identification.

Distribution.—This section outlines in broad terms the over-all Mexican distribution of the species. The guide area alone is considered, since extra-limital ranges usually are of no immediate concern to one while in the field. States are listed from north to south and from west to east. A brief reference to habitat is included in the statement of distribution whenever practicable, this element often serving to eliminate from consideration birds that are superficially similar but normally of a different habitat. Technical ecological terminology of the specialist is avoided, since a reference to coastal marshes, arid lowlands, heavy tropical forest, humid mountain forest, etc., conveys to the general student a much clearer picture of the habitat. The distribution of many species is given in terms of altitude above sea-level. Designated altitudes and geographical boundaries should not be taken too literally, however, since the distribution of many Mexican birds is yet poorly known. For some years to come bird watchers in Mexico can expect to find almost any species far beyond its "book range."

Races.—Many species are represented in Mexico by two or more geographical varieties, subspecies, or "races." While usually indistinguishable except from the critical examination of series of specimens, the ranges of many are sufficiently well known that the geographic implication permits an arbitrary identification. Identification on the grounds of probability is *always* tentative but, even so, may be of value when correlated with other observations.

Travelers in Mexico will be aware of conspicuous changes in the flora and fauna from place to place. These denote distinct biotic provinces, of which some eighteen have been identified in the country as a whole. Subspecies reflect environmental differences and are of the utmost importance in the study of evolution. While variations in plumage are the·usual criteria of subspecies, students should also be alert to other evidence of environmental influence as revealed by the habits and life-histories of the birds. In this book the various races are designated by their scientific names alone, appended to the paragraph on distribution.

Remarks.—A brief characterization of the species and life-history notes that facilitate or corroborate its identification are combined under this heading. Attention is directed to the more conspicuous diagnostic characters, and comparisons are often made with birds that are superficially similar. In practice, most species that are identified tentatively from the keys can be verified by reference to this section alone. If still uncertain, read the detailed description of plumages.

ILLUSTRATIONS

Three hundred and twenty-nine birds, or more than a third of the species recorded in Mexico, are portrayed, either wholly or in part, to show field characters that are of diagnostic value. Each picture serves a dual purpose, in that it both identifies a species and also helps to illustrate the range of variation within the family. Breeding plumage is generally featured, since this best shows the distinctive characters and usually is acquired even by migrants while still in Mexico.

The temptation to portray only birds that do not occur in the United States, disregarding several hundred others that are no less a part of the Mexican fauna, has been dismissed in favor of a more representative selection. While many bird watchers in the United States are highly skilled in the art of field identification, the majority concentrate on the birds of a single region, and few will profess equal competence in all parts of the country. Many common eastern and western species that range into Mexico are therefore illustrated, in keeping with the objectives of a comprehensive field guide intended both for the regional expert and for the acknowledged novice.

SUGGESTIONS FOR THE USER OF THIS BOOK

You are interested in birds and are planning a trip to Mexico. You have a comprehensive field guide that will enable you to identify any species likely to be seen anywhere in the country at any season of the year. How should the book be used?

The first step in identifying a bird is to determine its family. If one is familiar with the birds of the United States, one will recognize most of the families that occur in Mexico. Only sixteen of the eighty-nine families represented in the country do not range north of its border. Even a novice usually knows many more bird families than he realizes. Almost everyone can recognize herons, ducks, hawks, pigeons, parrots, owls, hummingbirds, woodpeckers, jays, wrens, thrushes, sparrows, and probably many other kinds of birds. These form a working nucleus to which other families can be added from time to time. Pictures are very useful aids to family recognition. All the tropical bird families in Mexico and most that are well known in the north are illustrated in this guide with line drawings that reveal family characteristics far better than do lengthy nontechnical descriptions.

Having allocated a bird as to family, turn to the appropriate "key" for help in identifying the species. The dichotomous keys emphasize physical characters most likely to be seen in the field. Each unit of the key presents only two choices. For example, if the bird is not in agreement with 1*a*, it must be 1*b*. The number following 1*b* indicates the next set of choices, and so on until the proper category followed by a name is reached. Even the longer keys are easily used, since most birds will "key out" after a very few steps.

The success of any trip undertaken for a specific purpose is best insured by careful planning and thoughtful preparation. Before going to Mexico in the interest of bird study, leaf through the guide and compile a list of species known to occur in the areas to be visited. Identification by elimination is an important aspect of competent field work, especially if one is in a new region with a strange fauna. A list of "possibles," therefore, will contribute much to your success in the field, whether you intend to study birds in a single locality or while traveling from place to place.

As with any tool, a field guide becomes increasingly serviceable as one gains experience in its use. Browse through the guide at leisure. Read some of the descriptions and statements of distribution. Learn the sequence of families and study the pictures, in order to recognize families with which you are unfamiliar. Check through several of the keys and note which "characters" or kinds of field marks seem to be most significant. While their relative values vary from family to family, some are mentioned repeatedly, and one soon learns which ones to note particularly. In brief, familiarize yourself with every aspect of the book, so that it can be used with facility. The time thus spent in preparation will be amply repaid by the added enjoyment of your trips afield in a country noted for the remarkable diversity of its bird life.

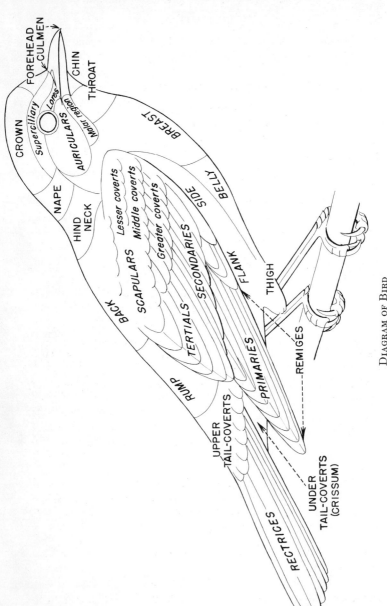

DIAGRAM OF BIRD

Family TINAMIDAE. Tinamous

GREAT TINAMOU. *Tinamus major.*—15. Above mainly dark olive, the back and wing-coverts spotted and barred with black; throat white; neck pale cinnamon, minutely speckled with brown; breast and sides tinged with olive; belly and thighs whitish, barred with black.

Distribution.—Dense lowland forests of southeastern Mexico.

Races.—*T. m. robustus* (Veracruz, northern Oaxaca, and northern Chiapas). *T. m. percautus* (southern Veracruz, Tabasco, southern Campeche, and adjacent parts of Quintana Roo).

Remarks.—A shy, solitary, forest species easily distinguished from other Mexican tinamous by its *large size and olive color*. While most active at dawn and dusk, its call—a long, tremulous note followed by three or four shorter notes in the same key—may be heard at any hour. Six or eight glossy blue, spheroidal eggs are laid in a depression, usually between the roots of a large tree.

LITTLE TINAMOU. *Crypturellus soui meserythrus.*—9. Crown and cheeks slaty gray; mantle and upper back rich brown, becoming brighter, more rufescent posteriorly; throat white; chest and sides grayish brown, the latter often washed with cinnamon; breast and abdomen ochraceous or rufous.

Distribution.—Lowland forests of Veracruz, northern Oaxaca, Tabasco, and Campeche.

Remarks.—This diminutive tinamou prefers thickets, second-growth woodlands, or forest edge. Although very furtive and not easily seen, it is abundant locally and may be heard at all hours, but especially at night. Its usual call is a tremulous whistle consisting of steadily ascending notes of diminishing length. The two glossy, clay-colored eggs apparently are attended by the male alone.

SLATY-BREASTED TINAMOU. *Crypturellus boucardi boucardi.*—11. Crown, neck, and mantle blackish or dusky brown, becoming rich chestnut on back and rump; wing-coverts and posterior upperparts faintly barred with black; throat gray; anterior underparts brownish gray or dusky, this washed with dull cinnamon posteriorly; sides, abdomen, and crissum more or less barred with bright cinnamon.

Distribution.—Humid lowland forests of southern Veracruz, Tabasco, Oaxaca, and Chiapas.

Remarks.—Darkest of the Mexican tinamous, appearing all-black from a short distance. It inhabits heavily forested areas and is not readily observed, although often common locally.

Rufescent Tinamou

RUFESCENT TINAMOU. *Crypturellus cinnamomeus* (Illus. p. 2).— 11. Above mainly dull chestnut, becoming darker posteriorly, the back and rump finely barred with black or pale buff; secondaries, tertials, and wing-coverts brownish black, boldly barred with buff; throat white; cheeks, neck, and breast cinnamomeus; sides and abdomen paler and boldly barred with brownish black posteriorly.

Distribution.—Central Sinaloa and southern Tamaulipas southward in lowland forests and foothills, ranging locally to an altitude of about 4,500 feet.

Races.—*C. c. occidentalis* (Pacific slope from central Sinaloa to Guerrero). *C. c. mexicanus* (eastern Mexico from San Luis Potosí and southern Tamaulipas to northern Puebla and northern Veracruz). *C. c. sallaei* (southern Puebla, southern Veracruz, southern and eastern Oaxaca, and the Pacific side of the Isthmus of Tehuantepec south to Tonalá, Chiapas). *C. c. goldmani* (Yucatán and Quintana Roo). *C. c. soconuscensis* (Soconusco district, Chiapas). *C. c. vicinior* (interior valleys of Chiapas). *C. c. intermedius* (Tabasco and southern Campeche).

Remarks.—Rufescent Tinamous inhabit scrubby thickets and the undergrowth of dense forests. Brightest and most widespread of the Mexican species, it is easily distinguished by its *conspicuous buff bars* and plaintive monotone whistles. Four or five glossy, purplish red eggs are deposited on the ground as with other tinamous.

Family GAVIIDAE. Loons

KEY TO THE SPECIES (WINTER PLUMAGE)

1a. More than 28 inches long; bill stout, virtually straight

Common Loon, p. 4

 b. Less than 28 inches long; bill relatively slender, sometimes upturned   2

2a. Above speckled; bill slightly upturned   . .   Red-throated Loon, p. 3

 b. Above not speckled; bill not upturned . . . . . .   Arctic Loon, p. 3

*RED-THROATED LOON. *Gavia stellata.*—22–26. *Breeding plumage:* Head and sides of neck gray; underparts mainly dark brown, the hind-neck and mantle green-tinted, and streaked with white; underparts white except for a conspicuous chestnut throat-patch. *Winter plumage:* Above gray, thickly speckled with white; below white.

Distribution.—Rare winter visitant to the Gulf of California and adjacent parts of Baja California (San Felipe) and Sonora (Tiburón Island, Sargent Point).

Remarks.—The *chestnut throat-patch* is diagnostic. In winter this loon is best distinguished from the following by its somewhat *upturned bill and white-speckled back*, the latter appearing pale at a distance. In Mexico, small loons are most likely to be the following species.

*ARCTIC LOON. *Gavia arctica pacifica* (Illus. p. 4).—22–26. *Breeding plumage:* Crown, nape, and hind-neck gray; chin and sides of neck black, the latter white-streaked; throat purplish black; wings and back brownish black, the latter boldly white-spotted; underparts white. *Winter plumage:* Above dark gray or blackish, the feathers sometimes edged with lighter, but never white-spotted; below white.

Distribution.—Baja California and Sonora, in winter and spring only. Common.

Remarks.—The loon most likely to be seen in Mexican waters. Common Loons are also unspotted in winter, but they are much larger birds, and have relatively short, thick bills.

Arctic Loon (winter)

*COMMON LOON. *Gavia immer elasson.*—28–34. *Breeding plumage:* Head and neck glossy black, the latter with an incomplete white collar; upperparts, including wings, black, conspicuously spotted with white; below white. *Winter plumage:* Above dark grayish brown or black; below white.

Distribution.—Rare winter visitant on the coasts of Baja California and Sonora, and possibly not uncommon off Tiburón Island.

Remarks.—When in breeding plumage the *wholly black head* is diagnostic. Immature birds and winter adults are best distinguished from Arctic Loons by their larger size and heavier bills.

Family COLYMBIDAE. Grebes

1a. More than 20 inches long; neck notably long and slender
Western Grebe, p. 6

  b. Less than 15 inches long; neck not notably long and slender . . 2

2a. Bill thick, mainly pale; wings without white patch
Pied-billed Grebe, p. 6

  b. Bill slender, wholly black; a white winged-patch conspicuous in
flight 3

3a. Sides of head with a white or colored patch . . . Eared Grebe, p. 6

  b. Sides of head uniform . . . . Least Grebe, p. 5

LEAST GREBE. *Colymbus dominicus* (Illus. p. 5).—9. Above mainly dark glossy brown, the neck and head slate-gray; throat-patch black

LEAST GREBE

(summer) or whitish (winter); below dingy white or mottled, the breast and sides strongly tinged with brown; white wing-patch prominent in flight; bill black, slender, and pointed.

Distribution.—Ponds and lagoons at moderate elevations throughout Mexico.

Races.—*C. d. dominicus* (Cozumel Island, Quintana Roo). *C. d. brachyp-terus* (virtually ubiquitous in lowland fresh-water lagoons). *C. d. bangsi* (arid lowlands of Baja California and Sonora).

Remarks.—This diminutive species is readily distinguished from the Pied-billed Grebe, a superficially similar bird, by its *slender black bill and white wing-patch*. It is the only grebe that may be found commonly in summer.

EARED GREBE. *Colymbus caspicus californicus.*—11–13. *Breeding plumage:* Head, neck, chest, and upperparts mainly black, the crown crested and sides of head with a conspicuous golden-buff tuft; flanks rich chestnut, the underparts otherwise white; wing-patch (white) prominent in flight; bill black, slender, slightly upturned. *Winter plumage:* Above grayish black; neck and underparts mainly whitish, a patch of same usually behind auriculars.

Distribution.—Breeds casually in northern Baja California and Chihuahua. Winters commonly from Baja California and Nuevo León south, locally, to Jalisco, Mexico, and Veracruz.

Remarks.—The breeding plumage is unmistakable. Winter birds resemble Least Grebes, but are much larger and have a *pale patch behind each cheek.*

*WESTERN GREBE. *Aechmophorus occidentalis.*—22–28. Above black; below, including cheeks and sides of neck, immaculate white; wing-patch (white) very conspicuous in flight; bill yellow and, like neck, decidedly long.

Distribution.—Winters commonly in Baja California and locally from Sonora and Chihuahua south to Puebla.

Remarks.—Totally unlike any other grebe in having a very *long, slender neck,* and boldly contrasting *black-and-white plumage.*

PIED-BILLED GREBE. *Podilymbus podiceps* (Illus. p. 7).—11–13. *Breeding plumage:* Above dark brown; below mainly whitish or brownish gray, the throat with a conspicuous black patch; bill bright yellow, stout, and with a vertical black band. *Winter plumage:* Similar, but neck and breast washed with cinnamon, and bill without a vertical band.

Distribution.—Widespread and generally abundant in winter, occasionally breeding in Baja California and Guanajuato. Common resident in west-central Mexico.

Races.—*P. p. podiceps* (as above except where replaced in summer by the following form). *P. p. antillarum* (resident in Colima, Jalisco, Mexico—perhaps elsewhere).

Remarks.—A compact, ducklike bird with a *pale, thick bill* having a conspicuous vertical band in summer. The other two small grebes of Mexico have slender, *black bills, and white wing-patches* easily seen in flight. Pied-billed Grebes have been recorded as far south as Yucatán and may be expected in winter wherever ponds and lagoons are found.

Pied-billed Grebe (summer)

Family DIOMEDEIDAE. Albatrosses

Key to the Species

1a. Head and body white or mainly white 2

   b. Head and body extensively brown or sooty 3

2a. Entire body white; head tinged with buff; bill pinkish; feet pale bluish . . . . Short-tailed Albatross (adult), p. 7

   b. Mainly white, the back dark brown, like wings; bill gray; feet pinkish . . . . Laysan Albatross, p. 8

3a. Uniformly deep chocolate-brown bill and feet pink
Short-tailed Albatross (immature), p. 7

   b. Mainly sooty, the forepart of the head (sometimes rump and abdomen) whitish; bill dark reddish brown, feet black
Black-footed Albatross, p. 8

*SHORT-TAILED ALBATROSS. *Diomedea albatrus.*—33–37. *Adult:* Head and body white, the former tinged with yellowish buff; wings and tips of tail dark brown; bill pinkish; feet bluish white. *Immature:* Deep chocolate-brown, the bill and feet pinkish.

Distribution.—Casual or accidental visitant to the coastal waters of Baja California, where formerly possibly not uncommon locally. Unreported in recent years.

Remarks.—This albatross approaches extinction and today is not likely to be found in our area. The *white back* of the adult is diagnostic. Immature birds can be distinguished from other uniformly dusky albatrosses by their *pale* (flesh-colored) bills and feet.

*BLACK-FOOTED ALBATROSS. *Diomedea nigripes.*—26–34. *Adult:* Above dusky or sooty brown, the forehead and upper tail-coverts conspicuously white; throat and sides of head (anteriorly) whitish, shading to sooty on the neck, breast, sides, and flanks; abdomen and crissum whitish; bill deep reddish brown; feet black. *Immature:* Dark sooty, palest below, the area adjacent to bill sometimes whitish.

Distribution.—Recorded as a casual visitant in the vicinity of the Revilla Gigedo Islands and off the Pacific Coast of Baja California, where now rare to uncommon.

Remarks.—This species ranges the north Pacific when not breeding and is the albatross most likely to be seen in Mexican waters. From a distance there is little to distinguish it from an immature Short-tailed Albatross; a closer view reveals the *white face* (and sometimes *rump*), *dark bill, and black feet.*

*LAYSAN ALBATROSS. *Diomedea immutabilis.*—28–32. Extensively white, the back, wings, and ends of tail dark sooty brown; a sooty area in front of eye; bill gray; feet pinkish.

Distribution.—Formerly a casual visitant off the Pacific Coast of Baja California (San Geronimo, Guadalupe, and San Martín Islands), but not reported in recent years.

Remarks.—A *white* albatross with a *dark back*. Unmistakable. While long unrecorded off Mexico, individuals may yet wander to our area; a possibility not to be forgotten.

Family PROCELLARIIDAE. Shearwaters, Fulmars, Petrels

KEY TO THE SPECIES

1*a*. Above and below dusky brown or *pale* grayish brown 2

   b. Below white, the upperparts extensively pearl gray, dusky brown, or black 5

2*a*. Pale grayish brown; bill yellowish, rather short and thick
                  Northern Fulmar (dark phase), p. 9

   b. Dusky or dark brown (appearing blackish at a distance); bill rather long and slender 3

3*a*. Tail moderately long and distinctly wedge-shaped; bill pale reddish
              Wedge-tailed Shearwater (dark phase), p. 10

   b. Tail not long or wedge-shaped; bill blackish 4

4*a.* Larger (16–18 inches); underside of wings mottled with white

Sooty Shearwater, p. 10

   b. Smaller (14 inches); underside of wings mottled with gray

Short-tailed Shearwater, p. 11

5*a.* Above extensively pale gray or silvery 6

   b. Above dark brown, sooty, or black 7

6*a.* Larger (16–18 inches); bill yellowish

Northern Fulmar (light phase), p. 9
Antarctic Fulmar, p. 9

   b. Smaller (11–12); bill black; in flight, a conspicuous black mark across
wings and back . . . . Blue-footed Petrel, p. 11

7*a.* Tail wedge-shaped and rather long; bill reddish

Wedge-tailed Shearwater (light phase), p. 10

   b. Tail not as in 7*a;* bill pinkish or black 8

8*a.* Larger (18 inches); underside of wings mottled with gray; bill and
feet pinkish . . . . Pink-footed Shearwater, p. 10

   b. Smaller (13–15); underside of wings white; bill black

Common Shearwater, p. 11
Revilla Gigedo Shearwater, p. 11

---

*NORTHERN FULMAR. *Fulmarus glacialis rodgersii.*—16–18. *Light phase:* Head, neck, and underparts white; back and scapulars pale gray, the wings somewhat darker (grayish brown), becoming dusky toward tips, but without black markings; bill strongly hooked, decidedly short and thick, mainly yellowish; feet whitish. *Dark phase:* Uniform pale grayish brown, the wings above sometimes mottled with white.

Distribution.—Winters casually off the Pacific Coast of northern Baja California; a single record for Sinaloa.

Remarks.—Fulmars in light plumage resemble various gulls superficially but are easily distinguished by their shorter and thicker bills and by the absence of black on the wing-tips. Their *gliding flight* on stiffened wings is a characteristic shared by no gull. Dark-plumaged individuals are considerably paler than Sooty Shearwaters and resemble no other sea bird.

*ANTARCTIC FULMAR. *Priocella antarctica.*—17–18. Above mainly pearl gray, palest on head; primaries slaty black, the inner webs extensively white toward base; forehead, sides of head, and underparts immaculate white; bill rather short and thick, mainly pink or yellowish, the ridge and tip black; feet pinkish.

Distribution.—Accidental; a single record for Sinaloa (Mazatlán).

Remarks.—Also known as Silver-gray Fulmar and Slender-billed Fulmar.

*PINK-FOOTED SHEARWATER. *Puffinus creatopus.*—18. Above dusky brown; below white, the sides of the head, flanks, and undersurface of wings mottled with gray; bill and feet pinkish, the former black-tipped and rather long.

Distribution.—Sometimes common, but of irregular occurrence off the Pacific Coast of Baja California (Guadalupe Island; Los Coronados Islands; off Santa Domingo Point).

Remarks.—Largest of the white-breasted shearwaters with *dark brownish upperparts.* The *pink* bill and feet at once distinguish it from the three smaller, but somewhat similar, species that breed in our area.

WEDGE-TAILED SHEARWATER. *Puffinus pacificus chlororhynchus.*—15–16. *Light phase:* Above deep sooty brown, darkening to blackish on the primaries and rectrices; tail rather long and distinctly wedge-shaped; below white, the sides grayish, darkening to dusky on the crissum; bill decidedly long and slender, pale reddish, tipped with black; feet pale yellowish pink. *Dark phase:* Underparts grayish brown, palest on the throat.

Distribution.—Breeds commonly on San Benedicto Island of the Revilla Gigedo group, and occasionally recorded elsewhere off the Pacific Coast (Cape San Lucas, Baja California; off Nayarit).

Remarks.—Also known as Pacific Shearwater. *See* Revilla Gigedo Shearwater.

*SOOTY SHEARWATER. *Puffinus griseus.*—16–18. Dusky brown, palest below, the underside of the wings with more or less white; bill blackish, decidedly long and rather slender; feet slate gray.

Distribution.—Occurs commonly off the Pacific Coast of Baja California from March until August; occasionally recorded in the Gulf of California and along the coast of Sonora.

Remarks.—Most shearwaters ordinarily remain well offshore when not breeding and are not likely to be seen from land. The Sooty is an exception, often being found abundantly in coastal waters. While resembling both the Short-tailed and the resident Wedge-tailed Shearwater (dark phase), it leaves Mexican waters before the arrival of the first and is distinguished from the second by its larger size, relatively *short tail, and black bill.*

*SHORT-TAILED SHEARWATER. *Puffinus tenuirostris.*—14. Dusky brown or sooty, palest below, the underside of the wings mottled with grayish; bill blackish, rather short and slender; feet gray.

Distribution.—Apparently a rare or accidental visitant, recorded but once off the coast of Baja California (Los Coronados Islands).

Remarks.—Also known as Slender-billed Shearwater. This species ranges the north Pacific in summer, appearing off the California coast in fall and early winter. At that season strays are most likely to be found in Mexican waters. While resembling both Sooty and Wedge-tailed Shearwaters (dark phase) in color, they are much smaller than the former and lack the reddish bill and long, wedge-shaped tail of the latter.

COMMON SHEARWATER. *Puffinus puffinus opisthomelas.*—13–15. Above deep sooty brown, darkening to black on the rump, wing-tips, and tail; below (including underside of wings) mainly white, the sides of the head and neck mottled with grayish; flanks and crissum sooty brown; bill blackish, rather long, and very slender; feet extensively pinkish.

Distribution.—Breeds on various islands off the west coast of Baja California (Guadalupe, San Martín, San Benito, and Natividad), and recorded off the coast of Sonora.

Remarks.—This race, best known as the Black-vented Shearwater, was long considered a distinct species. *See* Revilla Gigedo Shearwater.

REVILLA GIGEDO SHEARWATER. *Puffinus auricularis.*—13. Above black, the sides of the neck somewhat mottled; underparts (including underside of wings) immaculate white, the crissum dusky; bill and feet black.

Distribution.—Breeds on Clarión, San Benedicto, and Socorro Islands, off the Pacific Coast; a questionable record for Cape San Lucas, Baja California.

Remarks.—Also known as Townsend Shearwater. Nearest a Common Shearwater in size and color, but smaller, *jet black* (not dusky or brownish) above, and with uniform *white under wing-coverts.* A third breeding shearwater of the area (*P. pacificus*) also has white underparts (light phase), but it is sooty brownish above and has a relatively *long, wedge-shaped tail.*

*BLUE-FOOTED PETREL. *Pterodroma cookii orientalis.*—11–12. Above pale gray, darkening on lower back, rump, and wings, the last mainly black, but inner webs of the primaries extensively white; tail rather long, the outer feathers white; forehead, lores, malar area, and underparts, including lining of wings, immaculate white; bill black, rather short and thick; feet blue.

Distribution.—Accidental. A single record at sea between the Revilla Gigedo Islands and Cape San Lucas, Baja California.

Remarks.—Also known as Cook Petrel. This species is believed to breed on islands off the Chilean coast and in summer or autumn may occasionally stray into our area. A gray-and-white bird, it will be recognized in flight by the black band, like an inverted **W**, that extends across its wings and back.

Family HYDROBATIDAE. Storm Petrels

Key to the Species

1a. Upper tail-coverts conspicuously white; one race of Leach Petrel
      (*O. l. socorroensis*) with grayish coverts 2

  b. Upper tail-coverts not white or grayish 4

2a. Tail forked; feet black (West Coast) 3

  b. Tail not forked; feet partly yellow (East Coast) . Wilson Petrel, p. 12

3a. Larger (7–8 inches); tail deeply forked; rump-patch *white or grayish*
                                                      Leach Petrel, p. 13

  b. Smaller (6 inches); tail moderately forked; rump-patch white
                                                      Wedge-rumped Petrel, p. 13

4a. Larger ($7\frac{1}{2}$–9 inches); tail deeply forked 5

  b. Smaller ($5\frac{3}{4}$ inches); tail rounded or wedge-shaped
                                                      Least Petrel, p. 14

5a. Sooty gray, the under wing-coverts whitish; "fluttery flight"
                                                      Ashy Petrel, p. 13

  b. Blackish; without white on underside of wings; ternlike flight
                                                      Black Petrel, p. 13

*WILSON PETREL. *Oceanites oceanicus oceanicus.*—7. Mainly sooty black, palest on the greater wing-coverts; upper tail-coverts immaculate white, the flanks and crissum partly so; tail square-tipped; legs and toes black, the inner webs of the feet bright yellow.

Distribution.—Recorded off the Caribbean coast (Veracruz), where possibly a casual summer visitant.

Remarks.—A blackish, swallow-sized sea bird with a *square-tipped tail* and very conspicuous rump-patch. The Atlantic race of Leach Petrel, not yet recorded from Mexican waters, has a *forked tail*, all-black feet, and notably erratic flight quite unlike the *skimming* movements of this species.

*WEDGE-RUMPED PETREL. *Oceanodroma tethys kelsalli.*—6. Similar to a Wilson Petrel but smaller, tail moderately forked, and feet without yellow.

Distribution.—Rare or casual in summer, being recorded occasionally at sea off the Pacific Coast (west of southernmost Baja California, Jalisco, and Guerrero).

Remarks.—Also known as Storm Petrel.

LEACH PETREL. *Oceanodroma leucorhoa.*—7–8. Sooty black, the greater wing-coverts somewhat paler, nearer grayish brown; upper tail-coverts *white or grayish;* sides of rump often with a white or gray patch; tail deeply forked.

Distribution.—The Pacific Coast of Baja California, breeding on various offshore islands.

Races.—*O. l. willetti* (breeds on Los Coronados Islands, off northern Baja California). *O. l. chapmani* (breeds on the San Benito Islands, off central Baja California). *O. l. socorroensis* (breeds on Guadalupe Island; recorded from the Revilla Gigedo group).

Remarks.—The only resident pale-rumped petrel. The Guadalupe form has a *grayish rump* that appears sooty at a distance. Usually it can be distinguished from any of the black-rumped petrels by its more erratic, or "bouncing," flight, which suggests that of a nighthawk.

GUADALUPE PETREL. *Oceanodroma macrodactyla.*

Remarks.—A white-rumped petrel very similar to the preceding. It formerly bred on Guadalupe Island, off Baja California, but is now believed to be extinct. Last reported in August, 1912.

BLACK PETREL. *Oceanodroma melania.*—9. Sooty brown or blackish, the greater wing-coverts usually somewhat paler; tail deeply forked.

Distribution.—Coastal waters of Baja California, breeding commonly on various offshore islands (Consag Rock, San Luís Islands, Partida Island). Also recorded off the coast of Sonora (San Estebán Island), Nayarit, and Guerrero.

Remarks.—Largest, and perhaps the most abundant, of the all-back petrels. While resembling the following species in plumage, Black Petrels differ in flight, their wing-beats being slower and more regular, as with terns.

ASHY PETREL. *Oceanodroma homochroa.*—7½. Sooty grayish, appearing black at a distance, the underside of the wings with more or less whitish; tail deeply forked.

Distribution.—The Pacific Coast of Baja California, breeding (at least casually) on Los Coronados, San Benito, and (possibly) Guadalupe Islands.

Remarks.—The Ashy Petrel's *fluttery flight* is perhaps its most useful field character. Other petrels of similar appearance either "bounce" erratically (*O. l. socorroensis*) or have relatively slow wing-beats (*O. melania*). The *whitish* under wing-coverts are distinctive, but not likely to be seen.

LEAST PETREL. *Halocyptena microsoma.*—$5\frac{3}{4}$. Sooty brown or blackish, the greater wing-coverts usually paler; tail rounded or somewhat wedge-shaped.

Distribution.—Coastal waters of Baja California and off the Pacific Coast of Mexico, breeding abundantly on the San Benito Islands and in the northern portion of the Gulf of California.

Remarks.—A sooty, *sparrow-sized sea bird* with a wedge-shaped tail. Unmistakable. Least Petrels winter at sea, principally to the southward. They return in numbers during April, and casuals are to be expected at any season.

Family PHAËTHONTIDAE. Tropic-birds

Key to the Species

1*a*. Bill reddish; long central tail feathers white, attenuated
Red-billed Tropic-bird, p. 14

b. Bill yellowish; long central tail feathers red, wirelike
Red-tailed Tropic-bird, p. 15

RED-BILLED TROPIC-BIRD. *Phaëthon aetherus mesonauta* (Illus. p. 15).—26–40. *Adult:* Mainly silky white, the tertials and outer webs of the outer primaries black; a conspicuous black stripe passing through the eye; back and rump finely barred with black; tail white, the middle feathers attenuated and greatly elongated; bill coral-red. *Immature:* Similar to adult, but more heavily barred, and without elongated central tail feathers.

Distribution.—Coastal waters of Baja California and the Pacific Coast south to Guerrero.

Remarks.—The only tropic-bird likely to be seen in Mexican waters. It is fairly common in the Gulf of California and off the Pacific Coast. Some of the precipitous islands are utilized by small breeding colonies throughout most of the year.

*RED-TAILED TROPIC-BIRD. *Phaëthon rubricauda rothschildi.*—
20–34. Superficially similar to the resident tropic-bird, but with a *yellowish*
bill and *red, wirelike, middle tail feathers.*

Distribution.—Apparently very rare in Mexican waters, but occasionally reported off the Pacific Coast during the warmer months.

RED-BILLED TROPIC-BIRD

Family PELECANIDAE. Pelicans

KEY TO THE SPECIES

1*a*. Mainly white . . . . American White Pelican, p. 15
  b. Mainly brown . . . . Brown Pelican, p. 15

*AMERICAN WHITE PELICAN. *Pelecanus erythrorhynchos.*—50–65.
Mainly white, but with black primaries, yellowish orange bill and pouch,
and reddish feet.

Distribution.—Winters in the lagoons and bays of both coasts, occurring
locally in the interior.

Remarks.—When flying at great heights, this pelican can be distinguished from other large, mainly white birds (Snow Goose, Wood
Ibis) by its retracted head and characteristic flight pattern, in which
wing-beats alternate with sailing. Unlike Brown Pelicans, this species
feeds by scooping fish from the water while swimming.

BROWN PELICAN. *Pelecanus occidentalis* (Illus. p. 16).—48–55.
Breeding plumage: Head white, the crown tinged with yellow; neck mainly

rich velvety brown; upperparts gray or silvery and usually streaked with brown; primaries and underparts dark brown; sides more or less white-streaked. *Winter plumage:* Similar, but head and neck white. *Immature:* Above grayish brown; below mainly white, the breast and sides often brown-streaked.

Distribution.—Common resident along the Atlantic Coast, and on the Pacific Coast south to Nayarit and the Tres Marías Islands; in winter south to Oaxaca, including offshore islands.

BROWN PELICAN

Races.—*P. o. occidentalis* (casual visitant at Contoy Island and Puerto Morelos, Quintana Roo). *P. o. carolinensis* (Atlantic slope). *P. o. californicus* (Gulf of California and the Pacific Coast south to Nayarit; winters to Oaxaca and on offshore islands).

Remarks.—Perhaps the most conspicuous bird in coastal waters. Brown Pelicans are deliberate, but masterful, fliers and feed by diving expertly from a considerable height. Their breeding colonies are usually on outlying islands and may include several thousand birds.

Family SULIDAE. Boobies, Gannets

*NORTHERN GANNET. *Morus bassanus.*—35–40. *Adult:* Mainly white, the head and neck tinged with pale yellow; primaries sooty black; bare skin of throat bluish black; bill yellowish; feet black. *Immature:* Above dark brown, minutely spotted or speckled with white; below white, generously mottled with brown; tail sooty brown.

Distribution.—Recorded in winter from Veracruz; probably occurs casually elsewhere on the Caribbean coast as a winter vagrant.

BLUE-FOOTED BOOBY. *Sula nebouxii.*—30–34. *Adult:* Mainly cinnamon brown, the head, neck, and chest usually mottled with white; lower breast and abdomen white; bare skin of throat slate-color; feet blue. *Immature:* Similar, but breast and abdomen mottled with dusky brownish.

Distribution.—Coasts of Baja California and numerous islands in the Gulf of California; Revilla Gigedo and Tres Marías Islands.

Remarks.—An abundant species, best distinguished by its *bright blue feet*. It differs also from the adults of other boobies in appearing more or less *mottled above*.

BLUE-FACED BOOBY. *Sula dactylatra.*—30–34. *Adult:* Mainly white, the flight feathers, greater wing-coverts, and tail dark brown or blackish; bare skin of face and throat dark blue; color of bill and feet variable, but *never red or bright* blue. *Immature:* Head and neck dark brown, concolor with back and wings; breast paler, passing into whitish on the abdomen.

Distribution.—Both coasts, locally, breeding on offshore islands.

Races.—*S. d. dactylatra* (Matamoros, Tamaulipas, and the Alacrán Reefs, off northern Yucatán). *S. d. californica* (Pacific Coast, breeding on Clarión and San Benedicto Islands, and probably on Alijos Rocks, Baja California).

Remarks.—Also known as White Booby and Masked Booby. Where the two occur together, this species can be distinguished from the following (adults) by its larger size, more extensively black wings, and darker tail. Immature birds resemble immature *S. nebouxii*, but are paler below and never have bright blue feet.

RED-FOOTED BOOBY. *Sula sula websteri.*—26–28. *Adult:* (White phase). Mainly white, faintly washed with yellow; primaries sooty black; tail pale brown or grayish brown; bill pale blue, the base reddish; bare skin of throat black; area around eye bluish; feet bright red. (Brown phase). Mainly pale brown, lightest on head and tail. *Immature:* Above and below dull brown; feet pink or yellowish.

Distribution.—Coast of Sinaloa and Nayarit, breeding on various offshore islands (Tres Marías, Clarión, and San Benedicto Islands, the last two of the Revilla Gigedo group).

Remarks.—The only Mexican booby with *bright red feet*. Adults in flight somewhat resemble *S. dactylatra*, a considerably larger bird, but differ in having *only the primaries black*.

BROWN BOOBY. *Sula leucogaster.*—26–30. *Adult:* Mainly rich chocolate-brown, the abdomen, sides, and flanks white; bill and legs yellowish; bare skin of face and throat yellowish or blue. *Immature:* Mainly brownish, the underparts lightest and somewhat mottled; primaries and tail sooty black; legs yellow.

Distribution.—Coasts of Baja California, Gulf of California, and numerous Pacific islands, occurring occasionally along the Pacific Coast. Also reported off the Yucatán Peninsula.

Races.—*S. l. leucogaster* (recorded off Campeche, Yucatán, and Quintana Roo). *S. l. brewsteri* (coasts of Baja California, Sonora, and Sinaloa, where abundant offshore, and numerous islands south to the Revilla Gigedo group). *S. l. nesiotes* (Clipperton, Tres Marías, and Isabel Islands; accidental or casual at Manzanillo, Colima).

Remarks.—Also known as White-bellied Booby. The sharply defined brown-and-white underparts (adults) are unmistakable. Immature birds are not easily distinguished from those of other species, but usually are considerably darker, and appear almost black at a distance.

Family PHALACROCORACIDAE. Cormorants

KEY TO THE SPECIES

1*a*. Bill notably slender; throat-pouch reduced, dull red
Pelagic Cormorant, p. 21

  b. Bill not notably slender; throat-pouch conspicuous, not dull red   .   2

2*a*. Base of bill and throat-pouch orange
Double-crested Cormorant, p. 19

  b. Base of bill and throat-pouch not orange 3

3*a*. Throat-pouch blue (breeding season), bordered by a buffy band
Brandt Cormorant, p. 21

  b. Throat-pouch dull yellow, bordered (breeding season) with white
Olivaceous Cormorant, p. 20

DOUBLE-CRESTED CORMORANT. *Phalacrocorax auritus.*—28–34. *Adult:* Glossy black, the feathers of the back and wing-coverts with brown centers; bill mainly black, the base yellowish; bare throat-pouch orange. During the breeding season earlike tufts are developed, and white tufts appear briefly above and behind each eye. *Immature:* Mainly dusky brown, the underparts palest and sometimes whitish; bill and throat dark to orange color.

Distribution.—Resident on the Pacific Coast and some offshore islands; recorded from Quintana Roo in winter.

Races.—*P. a. floridanus* (Atlantic Coast, locally, in winter only). *P. a. albociliatus* (coasts of Baja California, Gulf of California, and coastal Sonora south locally to Guerrero; also the Revilla Gigedo Islands).

Remarks.—This species gets its name from the earlike tufts that are borne during the breeding season. At all seasons it can be distinguished by its conspicuous *orange throat-pouch*, and the yellowish patch at the base of the bill.

OLIVACEOUS CORMORANT. *Phalacrocorax olivaceus* (Illus. p. 20).
—24–28. *Adult:* Mainly glossy black, the back and wing-coverts brownish;
bill uniform brownish; throat-pouch dull yellow—not orange as in *auritus*.
During the breeding season the pouch is bordered with white, and a tuft of
white filaments adorns the cheeks. *Immature:* Mainly brownish, lightest
below.

OLIVACEOUS CORMORANT

Distribution.—Common resident of lowland rivers, lagoons, and coastal
bays.

Races.—*P. o. mexicanus* (Pacific lowlands from Jalisco southward, and
eastern Mexico generally, in suitable habitat). *P. o. chancho* (Pacific
coastal areas south to Colima; sometimes to Guerrero).

Remarks.—Also known as Common Cormorant. Very similar to a
Double-crested Cormorant in winter, but much smaller and with a *dull*

yellow throat-pouch. This form is even more gregarious than are the other cormorants, and not so restricted to coastal areas.

BRANDT CORMORANT. *Phalacrocorax penicillatus.*—28–33. *Breeding plumage:* Mainly glossy greenish black, the head and neck tinged with purplish; bare throat-pouch blue, bordered by a conspicuous buffy band; sides of head, neck, and scapular area adorned with long cream-colored filaments; bill blackish. *Winter:* Similar, but without filaments, and pouch not conspicuously blue. *Immature:* Mainly brownish, palest below.

Distribution.—Guadalupe Island and islands off the coasts of Baja California.

Remarks.—The *blue throat-pouch* (breeding season) and its *buffy border* are the best field marks. In good light, Brandt Cormorants appear much glossier than either of the preceding species, but duller than the Pelagic.

PELAGIC CORMORANT. *Phalacrocorax pelagicus resplendens.*—25–30. *Breeding plumage:* Above and below mainly glossy black, the head and neck with purplish reflections, the body with greenish; throat-pouch small, coral-red; neck with white filament-like feathers; flanks near base of tail conspicuously white; bill very slender, blackish. *Winter:* Similar to the breeding plumage, but without filaments on the neck, and lacking white patches at base of tail. *Immature:* Dark brown, appearing dusky black at a distance.

Distribution.—Northern portion of the Pacific Coast of Baja California.

Remarks.—This strictly maritime cormorant is notable for its *very slender bill* and remarkably iridescent plumage. During the breeding season it is easily identified, especially in flight, by a *white patch on each flank* near the base of the tail. Its distinctive *red throat-patch* is less prominent than in other cormorants, and immature birds are generally much darker.

Family ANHINGIDAE. Snake-birds

ANHINGA. *Anhinga anhinga leucogaster* (Illus. p. 22).—28–36. *Male:* Mainly glossy black, the wing-coverts immaculate white; tertials and upper back respectively streaked and spotted with white; tail buff-tipped. *Female:* Similar to male, but smaller and with head, neck, and upper breast buff-colored. *Immature:* Mainly brownish.

Distribution.—Widespread in the vicinity of sluggish rivers, lagoons, and swamps.

Remarks.—Anhingas are also known as Water-turkeys and Darters. They resemble cormorants superficially and have much the same habits. Anhingas will always be known by their extremely *long, snakelike necks* and straight, *pointed bills*. In flight they alternately flap and sail, and commonly soar for long periods above swampy areas.

ANHINGA

Family FREGATIDAE. Frigate-birds

KEY TO THE SPECIES

1*a.* Mainly black; head and back with purplish gloss

Magnificent Frigate-bird, p. 23

b. Similar, but head and back with greenish gloss

Great Frigate-bird, p. 22

GREAT FRIGATE-BIRD. *Fregata minor palmerstoni.*—39–41. *Male:* Mainly black, the head and back lightly glossed with green; wing-coverts and inner secondaries brown; underparts brownish black; tail deeply forked; throat-pouch red. *Female:* Similar, but hind-neck with a brown collar; throat and fore-neck whitish; chest, breast, and sides white. *Immature:* Above mainly brownish black; head, neck, and underparts whitish, usually tinged with buff or pale rufous.

Distribution.—Breeds on the Revilla Gigedo Islands; casual elsewhere off the Pacific Coast.

Remarks.—Also known as Lesser Man-o'-war-bird and Bar-winged Frigate-bird. Adult males cannot be distinguished in flight from the following species. Females differ in having a *white throat and underparts;* immature birds by the *rusty coloring* of the white areas. Under favorable conditions, adults show a brown wing band that is lacking in Magnificent Frigate-birds.

MAGNIFICENT FRIGATE-BIRD. *Fregata magnificens rothschildi* (Illus. p. 23).—38–40. *Male:* Above and below mainly black, the head and

MAGNIFICENT FRIGATE-BIRD

back lightly glossed with violet or purple; tail deeply forked; throat-pouch red. *Female:* Similar to male, but much less glossy, and wing-coverts brownish, not black; breast and sides white. *Immature:* Similar to female, but head and neck also white.

Distribution.—Common resident on both coasts, breeding locally on offshore islands.

Remarks.—Also known as Magnificent Man-o'-war-bird. The frigate-bird commonly seen over Mexican coastal waters. Like all members of the family, it is a master of flight and is most often seen soaring on motionless wings. Recent reports suggest that frigate-birds sometimes cross the Isthmus of Tehuantepec.

Family ARDEIDAE. Herons, Bitterns

The fifteen species of herons and bitterns found in Mexico are grouped below in five major categories (numbered I–V) based upon conspicuous recognition characters. Each category is provided with an independent key. Several species having a combination of the designated characters appear in more than one category.

KEY TO THE SPECIES

I. Above and below immaculate white, or sometimes (immature Little Blue Heron) more or less spotted and blotched with bluish or slate color; primaries and secondaries often largely pale slate.   *See* page 24

II. Above extensively bluish, bluish slate, or gray, the underparts (except neck) either similar or essentially white. Plumage of neck often vinaceous, reddish, maroon, or chestnut.   *See* page 25

III. Underparts (breast only in immature Chestnut-bellied Herons) broadly striped, or more or less uniform pale buff; if the latter, very small (11–13 inches) and with a prominent buff wing-patch.   *See* page 25

IV. Liberally spotted, barred, or vermiculated with buff (or chestnut) and black; throat and abdomen sometimes immaculate white or dull cinnamon.   *See* page 26

V. Neck or abdomen (sometimes both) with conspicuous vinaceous, cinnamon, chestnut, or maroon.   *See* page 26

CATEGORY I

1a. More than 28 inches; bill yellow or flesh-colored 2

b. Less than 24 inches; bill black or bluish 4

2a. More than 48 inches; bill and legs yellow

Great White Heron, p. 27

b. Less than 40 inches; legs black or bluish 3

3*a*. Smaller (28–32 inches). Bill flesh-colored, conspicuously tipped with black . . . . Reddish Egret (immature), p. 28

b. Larger (34–40 inches). Bill yellow . . . . . . Common Egret, p. 29

4*a*. Bill and legs black; *feet yellow* . . . . Snowy Egret, p. 29

b. Bill bluish tipped with black; legs and feet greenish
Little Blue Heron (immature), p. 28

Category II

1*a*. More than 40 inches; underparts boldly streaked with black and white . . . . Great Blue Heron, p. 27

b. Less than 35 inches; underparts mainly dusky, bluish slate, or white   2

2*a*. Below entirely or mainly white 3

b. Not as in 2*a*. 4

3*a*. Underparts white or pearl gray; back and crown black
Black-crowned Night Heron (adult), p. 32

b. Posterior underparts immaculate white; neck (sometimes breast) mainly bluish (adult) or chestnut (immature)
Tricolored Heron, p. 30

4*a*. Head and throat mainly black, the crown and cheeks white or pale yellowish . . . . Yellow-crowned Night Heron (adult), p. 33

b. Not as in 4*a*. 5

5*a*. More than 28 inches; bill flesh-colored, boldly tipped with black
Reddish Egret (adult), p. 28

b. Less than 24 inches; bill dusky or partly yellowish 6

6*a*. More than 20 inches; head and neck uniform maroon
Little Blue Heron (adult), p. 28

b. Less than 17 inches; crown and occipital crest black; neck mainly chestnut, the underside white . . . . . Green Heron (adult), p. 27

Category III

1*a*. More than 20 inches; top of head, neck, and back uniform 2

b. Less than 17 inches; crown dusky or glossy greenish black—not concolor with neck 4

2*a*. Above mainly tawny; sides of neck with a very conspicuous black stripe . . . . American Bittern, p. 36

b. Not as in 2*a*. 3

3*a*. Head, neck (except median underside), and back dull chocolate-brown; breast (only) streaked
Chestnut-bellied Heron (immature), p. 31

b. Above grayish brown, the underparts very boldly streaked with white and brownish   Yellow-crowned Night Heron (immature), p. 33
Black-crowned Night Heron (immature), p. 32

4a. Underparts and wing-coverts pale buff, the former sometimes dimly streaked . . . . Least Bittern, p. 35

 b. Underparts boldly streaked; no wing-patch; coverts more or less spotted or streaked . . . . Green Heron (immature), p. 27

Category IV

1a. Upperparts boldly spotted or barred with buff and black 2

 b. Upperparts narrowly barred or vermiculated with chestnut (or ochraceous) and black 3

2a. Above and below liberally spotted with buff and black; throat and belly immaculate white . . . Banded Tiger-Heron (immature), p. 33

 b. Above and below liberally barred with buff and black; throat and belly not white . . . . Bare-throated Tiger-Heron (immature), p. 33

3a. Head, neck, and breast deep chestnut, narrowly barred with black
Banded Tiger-Heron (adult), p. 33

 b. Crown black, the neck and breast ochraceous-buff narrowly barred with black . . . . Bare-throated Tiger-Heron (adult), p. 33

Category V

1a. More than 26 inches 2

 b. Less than 24 inches 5

2a. Neck, back, and wings narrowly barred or vermiculated 3

 b. Not as in 2a. 4

3a. Throat feathered; neck chestnut and black, the median underside boldly streaked with white . . . Banded Tiger-Heron (adult), p. 33

 b. Throat bare; neck tawny and black, the median underside buffy
Bare-throated Tiger-Heron (adult), p. 33

4a. Back and wings dark glossy green, the underparts mainly rich chestnut . . . . Chestnut-bellied Heron (adult), p. 31

 b. Back and wings grayish slate, the underparts similar but paler
Reddish Egret (adult), p. 28

5a. Mainly bluish, the head and neck maroon
Little Blue Heron (adult), p. 28

 b. Not as in 5a. 6

6a. Below extensively white, the neck and upper back mainly chestnut
Tricolored Heron (immature), p. 30

 b. Not as in 6a. 7

7a. Smaller (11–13 inches). With very prominent buffy wing-patches
Least Bittern, p. 35

 b. Larger (15–17 inches). Without wing-patches . . Green Heron, p. 27

GREAT BLUE HERON. *Ardea herodias.*—40–50. *Adult:* Throat and median crown white, the latter bordered with black; neck gray or grayish lavender streaked below with black and white; back and wings extensively bluish gray; whitish plumes on back and neck; underparts boldly streaked with black and white; thighs and forward edge of wings chestnut; bill yellowish; legs black. *Immature:* Similar to adult, but crown black; without white plumes; upperparts more or less brownish, the underparts streaked with same.

Distribution.—Resident in northwestern, north-central, and southern Mexico. Occurs extensively elsewhere in winter.

Races.—*A. h. hyperonca* (northwestern Baja California and offshore islands, wintering south to Guadalupe Island). *A. h. treganzai* (mainly northwestern Mexico south to Colima and Hidalgo; possibly to Jalisco). *A. h. sanctilucae* (coasts and islands of southern Baja California and Sonora). **A. h. herodias* (winters in eastern and southeastern Mexico). **A. h. wardi* (winter visitant; distribution uncertain, but probably widespread). *A. h. lessonii* (north-central and southern Mexico).

Remarks.—A very large, mainly bluish heron unlike any other Mexican species. Great Blue Herons are especially common in winter and at that season occur in suitable habitats throughout the country. The geographical races usually are not separable in the field, and their respective ranges are poorly known.

GREAT WHITE HERON. *Ardea occidentalis.*—48–55. Immaculate white, the bill and legs yellowish.

Distribution.—Apparently rare on the coast of the Yucatán Peninsula (recorded from Rio Lagartos, Yucatán; Ascensión Bay, Quintana Roo; Chinchorro Bank, near Cozumel Island).

Remarks.—This heron equals or exceeds the Great Blue in size and is much larger than any other all-white heron. Its distinctive *yellow bill, legs,* and feet are conspicuous at a distance. Common Egrets have black legs and are considerably smaller. Some authorities consider this form a local color phase of the Great Blue Heron.

GREEN HERON. *Butorides virescens.*—15–17. *Adult:* Crown and occipital crest black glossed with green; neck mainly chestnut, the throat and underside of neck white; back and wings greenish or bluish green, the coverts edged with white; underparts brownish gray; bill dusky above, yellowish below; legs greenish yellow or orange. *Immature:* Similar to adult, but less brightly colored (browner), and with *boldly streaked underparts.*

Distribution.—Resident in Baja California, northern, central, and eastern Mexico; virtually country-wide in winter.

Races.—*B. v. anthonyi* (northern Baja California, northwestern Sonora, north-central Sinaloa, and northwestern Durango; winters eastward to Tamaulipas and south on the Pacific Coast to Chiapas). *B. v. frazari* (Baja California south of San Ignacio, latitude 27°21′ N.). *B. v. eremonomus* (central Chihuahua and northwestern Durango south to Guanajuato; winters to western Michoacán). *B. v. virescens* (eastern Mexico south to Tabasco and Chiapas; widespread elsewhere in winter). *B. v. maculatus* (Chinchorro Bank, Quintana Roo, chiefly in mangroves).

Remarks.—A small dark heron with pale *greenish yellow or orange legs*. Its bluish green upperparts and *rich chestnut neck* are conspicuous only under favorable conditions. Immature birds are rather drab and heavily streaked below. Common, especially near streams and ponds.

LITTLE BLUE HERON. *Florida caerulea caerulea.*—20–24. *Adult:* Head and neck maroon; breast and back dark slaty blue, the feathers considerably elongated; wings slaty blue or dull black; abdomen blackish; bill, legs, and feet dusky. *Immature:* Wholly white or, when molting, more or less striped and mottled with slaty blue and white; bill bluish, tipped with black; legs dull greenish.

Distribution —Common resident along both coasts; casual and local in the interior.

Remarks.—Adults appear black rather than blue at a distance. White immature birds often show some blue or slate blotches, and also differ from other white herons in color of bill and legs. *See* Snowy Egret.

REDDISH EGRET. *Dichromanassa rufescens* (Illus. p. 29).—28–32. *Dark phase:* Head and neck vinaceous-rufous, the feathers notably elongated and loose; wings and body slaty gray, lightest below; scapular plumes straight but prominent, extending beyond end of tail; bill *flesh-colored*, and with a conspicuous *black tip;* legs bluish. *White phase:* Plumage entirely white, the bill and legs as in the dark phase.

Distribution.—Resident in Baja California and locally in the lowlands of both coasts; casual elsewhere, especially in winter.

Races.—*D. r. dickeyi* (Baja California and Sonora south at least to Sinaloa; southward along the Pacific Coast in winter). *D. r. rufescens* (eastern Mexico; perhaps elsewhere in winter). *D. r. colorata* (coasts of the Yucatán Peninsula and adjacent islands).

Remarks.—A dark, medium-sized heron with notably "shaggy" plumage, especially about the neck. No other Mexican heron has a *flesh-colored bill* with a conspicuous *black tip;* an excellent field character for distinguishing immature birds from Common Egrets.

COMMON EGRET. *Casmerodius albus egretta.*—34–40. Immaculate white, the bill yellow and legs black. During the breeding season conspicuous scapular plumes extend beyond the tail.

Distribution.—Common coastal resident, occurring locally in the interior.

Remarks.—Also known as American Egret. The five white herons found in Mexico have distinctively colored bills and legs. Of the five,

REDDISH EGRET (DARK PHASE)

this species is exceeded in size only by the Great White Heron of coastal Yucatán and Quintana Roo. Both have yellow bills. The egret's *black legs* are diagnostic. *See* Little Blue Heron, Reddish Egret, and Snowy Egret.

SNOWY EGRET. *Leucophoyx thula* (Illus. p. 30).—18–24. Immaculate white, the bill and legs black, the *feet yellow*. Breeding birds have delicate scapular plumes with conspicuous recurved ends.

Distribution.—Widespread and locally abundant, especially in lowland areas.

Races.—*L. t. brewsteri* (Baja California, Sonora, and northern Chihuahua south on the Pacific Coast at least to Guerrero). *L. t. thula* (northern and eastern Mexico southward, except where occupied by *brewsteri;* the proper designation for the birds of many areas is still uncertain).

SNOWY EGRET (SPRING)

Remarks.—The only white heron with *yellow feet* and contrasting *black legs.* Immature Little Blue Herons are about the same size, but have pale *greenish legs and feet,* and are often blotched with blue or slate. Their bills are *bluish* at the base. Snowy Egrets, alone, customarily shuffle their feet when feeding.

TRICOLORED HERON. *Hydranassa tricolor ruficollis* (Illus. p. 31).—22–26. *Adult:* Mainly dark blue, the throat whitish or chestnut, and neck tinged with lilac; rump, abdomen, and under wing-coverts immaculate white; bill and legs yellowish. Breeding birds have a white occipital crest and pale scapular plumes. *Immature:* Above dull brown or bluish; neck bright chestnut; throat and abdomen white.

Distribution.—Coastal lowlands and the interior of southern Mexico locally (Morelos, Hidalgo, Puebla, etc.)

Remarks.—This heron is distinguished from all others in Mexico by its conspicuously *contrasting white belly.* In flight the undersides of its

TRICOLORED HERON

wings show extensive white patches. Otherwise, at a distance, it somewhat resembles an adult Little Blue Heron. Both nest in colonies in trees and bushes, and frequent swamps, marshes, and tidal mud flats.

CHESTNUT-BELLIED HERON. *Agamia agami* (Illus. p. 32).— 26–30. *Adult:* Above mainly deep glossy green, the scapulars partly chestnut; forehead and crown blackish, becoming slaty blue on the long occipital feathers; auriculars black; neck, median line of throat, and underparts mainly bright chestnut, the breast slaty blue; feathers of lower neck recurved and with bluish centers; iris and bare skin of face yellow. *Immature:* Neck and upperparts brownish, the wings and tail faintly glossed with green; top of head and hind-neck blackish; throat and underparts mainly creamy white, the breast and sides striped with dusky brown; iris orange; legs olive-green.

Distribution.—Lowlands of Veracruz, Tabasco, and Chiapas. Seldom recorded in Mexico.

Remarks.—Also known as Agami Heron. A medium-sized, chestnut-and-glossy-green heron with a bluish crest and breast. Perhaps the most colorful heron in our area. The rather nondescript immatures appear wholly *dull chocolate-brown* above, with boldly streaked brown-and-white breasts. This heron has a notably long, straight bill and rather short legs.

CHESTNUT-BELLIED HERON

BLACK-CROWNED NIGHT HERON. *Nycticorax nycticorax hoactli.*— 22–26. *Adult:* Forehead white; crown and back black, faintly glossed with green; wings and tail ashy or bluish gray; underparts immaculate white; bill black; legs yellow. *Breeding plumage:* Similar, but with two long slender occipital plumes. *Immature:* Above grayish brown, streaked and spotted with white; below white, boldly streaked with brown; bill and legs greenish.

Distribution.—Resident in Baja California, Sonora, Sinaloa, and Veracruz. Virtually country-wide in winter. A breeding colony in Mexico City.

Remarks.—A *black-backed* heron with *pale wings* and white under-parts. Night herons appear very stocky and seem to have shorter legs than other herons. Immature birds of both night herons are very similar but the Black-crowned has a smaller bill and is somewhat lighter and less spotted above than the Yellow-crowned. Its legs are shorter and greener. Both species are most active at dusk or after nightfall. During the day they roost quietly in trees, usually near swamps or water.

YELLOW-CROWNED NIGHT HERON. *Nyctanassa violacea.*—20–24. *Adult:* Head and throat extensively black, the crown and cheeks white or pale yellow; plumage otherwise mainly bluish gray, the back and wings streaked with dark brown; bill black; legs yellowish. *Immature:* Mainly brown, but boldly streaked and spotted with buff; throat and lower abdomen whitish; bill and legs greenish.

Distribution.—Resident in the coastal lowlands and on Socorro Island, off the Pacific Coast. Elsewhere (locally) in winter.

Races.—*N. v. violacea* (eastern and southern Mexico). *N. v. bancrofti* (Baja California and Sonora southward on the Pacific Coast, including off-shore islands). *N. v. gravirostris* (Socorro Island, Revilla Gigedo Group).

Remarks.—*See* Black-crowned Night Heron.

BANDED TIGER-HERON. *Tigrisoma lineatum lineatum.*—26–30. *Adult:* Head, neck (except median underside), and sides of breast rich chestnut or cinnamon, obscurely spotted and barred with black; upperparts mainly dusky olive minutely vermiculated and barred with ochraceous-buff, the flight feathers grayish slate, narrowly tipped with white; tail glossy greenish black; throat, underside of neck, and median breast white, with broad brown or cinnamon streaks; abdomen ochraceous-buff or grayish. *Immature:* Head, neck, and upperparts very boldly spotted with buff and black; throat and median underparts mainy white, this more or less liberally spotted with black.

Distribution.—Rare or accidental. One record for Chiapas.

Remarks.—Banded and Bare-throated Tiger-Herons are much alike, but the former has a feathered throat and very conspicuous *chestnut* on its head and neck. Immature birds appear boldly spotted and are essentially white below. Not likely to be seen except in the humid lowlands of the extreme south.

BARE-THROATED TIGER-HERON. *Heterocnus mexicanus* (Illus. p. 34).—28–32. *Adult:* Crown and hind-neck black; neck (except median underside) and mantle narrowly barred with black and buff; upperparts mainly brownish olive, minutely vermiculated and barred with buff, the flight feathers sooty black; tail glossy greenish; throat bare; a narrow buffy white line on underside of neck, this more or less streaked with black; abdomen buffy or dull yellowish cinnamon. *Immature:* Above and below very boldly barred with buff and brown; flight feathers and tail blackish, narrowly barred with white.

Distribution.—Coastal slopes from southern Sonora, San Luis Potosí, and southern Tamaulipas southward.

BARE-THROATED TIGER-HERON

Races.—*H. m. mexicanus* (Jalisco and southern Tamaulipas southward). *H. m. fremitus* (fresh-water streams of southern Sonora and Sinaloa; doubtfully distinct from *mexicanus*).

Remarks.—Also known as Cabanis Tiger-Heron or Tiger-Bittern. Tiger-herons are solitary in habits and customarily frequent wooded swamps and the banks of lowland streams and ponds. They take flight only as a last resort, and, when disturbed, usually steal quietly away in the undergrowth. This species, the only tiger-heron likely to be seen in Mexico, occurs extensively in the lowlands and can hardly be confused with any other heron of our area except perhaps a Banded Tiger-Heron in immature plumage. The *bare throat* is diagnostic and can be seen at a considerable distance. *See* Banded Tiger-Heron.

LEAST BITTERN

LEAST BITTERN. *Ixobrychus exilis* (Illus. p. 35).—11–13. *Male:* Crown and back glossy greenish black; sides of head, neck, and a patch on each wing bright chestnut; greater wing-coverts tawny buff; underparts, including throat and median line of neck, buffy white; bill mainly yellow; legs greenish. *Female:* Similar to male, but dull brown above, the underparts broadly streaked with buff.

Distribution.—Baja California, Pacific and Atlantic slopes, and locally in winter in the interior of the south.

Races.—*I. e. hesperis* (Baja California, wintering southward on the Pacific slope). *I. e. pullus* (coastal mangrove swamps of southern Sonora; winter range uncertain). *I. e. exilis* (eastern Mexico generally; perhaps elsewhere in winter).

Remarks.—A diminutive heron with black upperparts and a prominent *buff-colored wing-patch*. Least Bitterns are notably furtive and usually will be seen only when flushed from dense marsh grass or reeds. Probably more abundant than present records indicate.

*AMERICAN BITTERN. *Botaurus lentiginosus.*—23–26. Above mainly brown and tawny, the back and wing-coverts minutely streaked, speckled, and vermiculated; throat white; a conspicuous black patch on each side of upper neck; underside of neck and plumage below pale buff, broadly streaked with tawny; bill and legs yellowish green.

Distribution.—Widespread in winter, occurring principally in Baja California and in the coastal slopes generally. Casual elsewhere in suitable habitats.

Remarks.—A stout-bodied, essentially *tawny* heron with broadly striped underparts. No other heron has a black patch on the sides of its neck. Bitterns are solitary in habits, and frequent grassy swamps and marshes. When disturbed, they usually freeze in position with the bill up-turned until danger has passed. Few large birds are so inconspicuous and so capable of avoiding detection unless actually flushed from cover.

Family COCHLEARIIDAE. Boat-billed Herons

BOAT-BILLED HERON. *Cochlearius cochlearius zeledoni* (Illus. p. 37).—18–20. *Adult:* Forehead white; crown, long occipital crest, and upper back black; wings and lower back bluish gray; sides of head, throat, and mantle similar, but washed with buff; below mainly vinaceous or dull chestnut, the sides black; bill remarkably broad and flattened. *Immature:* Much like adult, but without crest, and upperparts more rufous; below whitish, washed with cinnamon.

Distribution.—Southern Sinaloa and southern Tamaulipas southward, mainly in humid lowland forests and swamps.

Remarks.—This remarkable bird suggests a Black-crowned Night Heron at a distance, but has a *broad, flattened bill* unlike that of any other heron. It is solitary in habit and will usually be found in dense jungle growth near fresh-water lagoons and sluggish streams.

BOAT-BILLED HERON

Family CICONIIDAE. Storks

KEY TO THE SPECIES

1a. Primaries and tail black; bill depressed toward tip   Wood Ibis, p. 37
  b. Primaries and tail not black; bill notably thick, the underside some-
       what upturned . . . . Jabiru, p. 37

WOOD IBIS. *Mycteria americana* (Illus. p. 38).—34–38. *Adult:* Head and neck featherless, gray or blackish; plumage mainly white, the tail and remiges glossy black; bill depressed near tip, dusky. *Immature:* Similar to adult, but head and neck more or less feathered, whitish.

Distribution.—Coastlands (common locally), and occasionally else-where in suitable habitat.

Remarks.—Wood Ibises are very gregarious, and large flocks some-times may be seen soaring at great heights above the ground. Unlike herons, they fly with the neck extended and, when not soaring on set wings, usually flap and sail alternately. No heron has a decurved bill. White Pelicans have black primaries and a similar flight pattern, but retract their heads while in flight. White Ibises are much smaller and have only the primaries tipped with black.

JABIRU. *Jabiru mycteria.*—48–55. *Adult:* Head and neck featherless, mainly black, the lower third of the neck red or bright orange; plumage im-maculate white; bill notably heavy, virtually straight or slightly upturned. *Immature:* Mainly brownish gray.

Distribution.—Humid southern lowlands, where apparently uncommon or rare. One record for southern Veracruz (Cosamaloapam), and occasionally seen in Chiapas.

Remarks.—Jabirus are among the largest of flying birds and can hardly be mistaken for any other species in Mexico. No other heron-

WOOD IBIS

like bird of our area has so massive a bill or a naked black neck with *bright orange or red* toward its base.

Family THRESKIORNITHIDAE. Ibises, Spoonbills

KEY TO THE SPECIES

1*a.* Bill long and notably flattened, the tip spoonlike

Roseate Spoonbill, p. 40

  b. Bill long, slender, and decurved 2

2*a*. Mainly white (adult), or with white underparts . . White Ibis, p. 39
  b. Mainly dark; without conspicuous white below . . Glossy Ibis, p. 39

GLOSSY IBIS. *Plegadis falcinellus mexicana* (Illus. p. 39).—18–22. *Adult:* Border around naked parts of face and base of bill usually white; head, neck, upper back, and underparts purplish chestnut; wings, lower back, and tail bronzy green; bill long, slender, and decurved. *Immature:* Mainly grayish brown, the head and neck finely streaked with white.

GLOSSY IBIS

Distribution.—Locally abundant in the coastlands and in the vicinity of marshes, lakes, and streams of the interior. Tres Marías Islands.

Remarks.—A dark heron-like bird with a long *decurved bill*. This ibis appears blackish at a distance, but, in good light, the remarkable metallic quality of its plumage may be seen. Immature birds are much duller than adults and lack the whitish underparts of immature White Ibises.

WHITE IBIS. *Eudocimus albus.*—22–24. *Adult:* Plumage mainly white, the tips of the outer primaries black; bill, bare skin of face, and legs red, the first long, slender, and decurved. *Immature:* Head, neck, chest, and up-perparts grayish brown, more or less streaked anteriorly; breast and posterior underparts white.

Distribution.—Marshes, lagoons, and mud flats, mainly in the coastlands.

Remarks.—White Ibises commonly associate with herons, but even at a distance are easily distinguished by their *decurved bills, red faces,* and *black-tipped primaries.* Highly gregarious, they nest in large colonies and often can be seen soaring in the manner of Wood Ibises. The latter is much larger and shows far more black on its wings. Immature Glossy Ibises are *wholly dark*—not white-bellied, as with this species.

ROSEATE SPOONBILL. *Ajaia ajaja.*—28–32. *Adult:* Head and throat featherless; plumage extensively pink, the neck, breast, and upper back white; lesser wing-coverts and tail-coverts carmine; tail buff; bill notably flattened, the tip spoonlike. *Immature:* Head and throat feathered; plumage mainly pink, without carmine or buff.

Distribution.—Resident in the coastlands, occurring locally in the interior, especially in winter.

Remarks.—The tropics afford few sights more memorable than that of a flock of Spoonbills in their natural habitat. They frequent mud flats, coastal lagoons, and mangrove thickets with herons and ibises, but are unmistakable at any distance.

Family PHOENICOPTERIDAE. Flamingos

AMERICAN FLAMINGO. *Phoenicopterus ruber* (Illus. p. 40).—40–48. *Adult:* Mainly rosy-vermilion and pink, palest below; remiges black. *Immature:* Mainly brownish gray, more or less tinged with pink.

AMERICAN FLAMINGO

Distribution.—Yucatán, locally, wandering to Campeche, Cozumel Island, and central Quintana Roo in winter. A colony of more than 3,000 birds has been reported on the Rio de Celestun, northwestern Yucatán during the dry season. It apparently moves to Laguna Lagartos for breeding purposes toward the middle of June. Casual in southern Veracruz.

Family ANATIDAE. Ducks, Geese, Swans

KEY TO ADULT MALES[1]

1a. Swans, geese, and goose-sized ducks (i.e., Muscovy) 2

  b. Ducks 7

2a. White; wings sometimes black-tipped 3

  b. Not essentially white 4

3a. Wing-tips black; head and breast sometimes stained with rust
Snow Goose, p. 44
Ross Goose, p. 44

  b. Wings without black; neck notably long . . . Whistling Swan, p. 44

4a. Above and below black; a conspicuous white wing-patch
Muscovy Duck, p. 48

  b. Not as in 4a. 5

5a. Head, neck, and upperparts grayish brown; a white patch at base of pink bill . . . . White-fronted Goose, p. 45

  b. Head and neck mainly black, this sometimes extending to the upper back and chest; white-collared or with a white cheek-patch   6

6a. Black restricted to head and neck; throat and cheeks white
Canada Goose, p. 46
Cackling Goose, p. 46

  b. Black not restricted to head and neck; a white collar on upper neck
Black Brant, p. 45

7a. Bill long, narrow, and virtually cylindrical; head black, and usually with a conspicuous crest 8

  b. Bill more or less flattened, the base sometimes notably swollen; head sometimes round and pufflike, but usually not distinctly crested 10

8a. Crested 9

  b. Not crested; bill and feet red; extended wings mainly white, the tips black . . . . Common Merganser, p. 60

9a. Crest fanlike, extensively white; neck black; extended wings mainly dark, the speculi white . . . . Hooded Merganser, p. 60

[1] Species of regular occurrence.

    b. Crest scraggly, without white; neck white; a reddish chest-band; extended wings mainly white, the tips black

Red-breasted Merganser, p. 61

10*a.* Above and below black; or head, neck, and chest essentially black, the belly white 11

    b. Not as in 10*a.* 14

11*a.* Virtually all black; bill red and orange, the base notably swollen; a white wing-patch, or two white patches on head 12

    b. Breast and belly white; back black or whitish; bill pale bluish, sometimes ringed with white; iris yellow 13

12*a.* A white patch on forehead and nape . . . . . . Surf Scoter, p. 58

    b. A white wing-patch . . . . White-winged Scoter, p. 58

13*a.* Bill with two white rings; back and scapulars black, the wing-patches ashy gray . . . . Ring-necked Duck, p. 55

    b. Bill not ringed; back, scapulars, and wing-patches (speculi) white

Lesser Scaup, p. 56

14*a.* Upper wing-coverts pale blue, thus forming a large patch on the forepart of the wing; bill sometimes notably long and spoonlike . 15

    b. Not as in 14*a.* 17

15*a.* Bill spoonlike; head and neck glossy blackish; chest white, the belly chestnut . . . . Northern Shoveller, p. 53

    b. Not as in 15*a.* 16

16*a.* Head, neck, and body cinnamon-red . . . . Cinnamon Teal, p. 49

    b. Head and neck dark gray, the underparts reddish; a white crescentic patch between bill and eye . . . . . Blue-winged Teal, p. 49

17*a.* Head and neck essentially reddish, this in sharp contrast with the buff or black of the chest 18

    b. Not as in 17*a.* 20

18*a.* Smaller (13–15 inches); a broad greenish stripe behind each eye; chest liberally spotted; speculi glossy green . . Common Teal, p. 50

    b. Larger (17–22 inches); sides of head uniform reddish; chest and upper back black; speculi ashy gray 19

19*a.* Forehead abrupt, the crown high and rounded; back and scapulars grayish . . . . Redhead, p. 55

    b. Forehead and crown sloping to the bill; back and scapulars essentially white . . . . Canvasback, p. 54

20*a.* Conspicuously crested, or head notably pufflike; if the latter, with a round white spot at base of bill, or with a white patch extending from cheeks to back of crown 21

    b. Not as in 20*a.* 23

21a. A prominent, white-patterned crest; throat white, the breast purplish . . . . Wood Duck, p. 53

   b. A round, pufflike head; throat dark, the chest white like belly; extended wings largely white 22

22a. Larger (16–22 inches); head and throat iridescent greenish black; a round white spot in front of each eye . Common Goldeneye, p. 57

   b. Smaller (13–15 inches); head and throat black, with violet and green reflections; a white patch extending from cheeks to back of head . . . . Bufflehead, p. 57

23a. Small, to very small and stocky, short-necked ducks with fanlike tails, these often held erect; reddish above, or brownish with a white face-patch 24

   b. Not as in 23a. 25

24a. Forepart of head black, the hindpart reddish like neck and back; a white wing-patch . . . . Masked Duck, p. 59

   b. A conspicuous white face-patch; crown black, the neck and back either bright reddish or essentially brown; wings without white
Ruddy Duck, p. 60

25a. Long-legged and rather long-necked ducks, usually gangling in appearance; in flight the feet trail behind the tail; partly arboreal . 26

   b. Not as in 25a. 27

26a. Head and underparts tawny; back and wings essentially black; a white V-shaped patch on rump . . . . Fulvous Tree-Duck, p. 46

   b. Sides of head, upper back, and breast grayish; the belly and rump black; back reddish; a large white wing-patch
Black-bellied Tree-Duck, p. 47

27a. Speculum iridescent blue, this bordered in front and behind with white; breast chestnut, or underparts brown-mottled 28

   b. Speculum white, greenish black, or bronzy; wing-coverts chestnut, white, or gray; neck and middle tail feathers sometimes notably long 29

28a. Head glossy green; a conspicuous white collar; breast chestnut, the belly whitish . . . . Mallard, p. 48

   b. Above and below brown-mottled, palest on sides of head and neck; bill greenish yellow . . . . Mexican Duck, p. 49

29a. Neck and middle tail feathers notably long; head and throat uniform brown; underside of neck and breast gleaming white.
Common Pintail, p. 51

   b. Not as in 29a. 30

30a. Head brownish, darkest above; chest scalloped black and white; wing-coverts chestnut, the speculi white . . . . . . Gadwall, p. 52

b. Head grayish or speckled, the crown white; a green patch behind eye; wing-coverts white; chest and sides pinkish

American Widgeon, p. 51

*WHISTLING SWAN. *Olor columbianus.*—45–55. *Adult:* Plumage white, the head and neck sometimes stained with rusty; bill and legs black, the base of the former usually with a yellowish spot. *Immature:* Pale ashy gray, darkest on the head; bill and legs reddish or dusky.

Distribution.—Winters casually in extreme northern Baja California.

Remarks.—Swans are distinguished from other waterfowl by their all-white plumage and very long necks. In flight the slender neck is fully extended and accounts for about half the bird's length. White Pelicans, Wood Ibises, White Ibises, and Snow Geese, while largely white, have conspicuous *black wing-tips* and various other distinguishing characters. Egrets lack dark wing-tips, but fly with their necks retracted and legs trailing behind.

*TRUMPETER SWAN. *Olor buccinator.*—65. Similar to a Whistling Swan, but considerably larger, and without yellow on the bill. Immature birds have dull yellowish brown feet.

Distribution.—A single Mexican record—Matamoros, Tamaulipas, January 21, 1909.

Remarks.—*See* Whistling Swan.

*SNOW GOOSE. *Chen hyperborea hyperborea.*—25–30. *Adult:* Mainly white, the primaries black; head and breast often stained with rusty; bill and feet pink or reddish; a black area on the cutting edge of the bill. *Immature:* Pale ashy gray, more or less mottled with dusky or brownish, the flight feathers blackish; bill and feet dusky.

Distribution.—Winters in Baja California, and in Mexico south (locally) to Oaxaca and Tabasco.

Remarks.—A medium-sized, *white or grayish* goose with *black wing-tips.* Ross Geese, while very similar, are about the size of Mallards and have notably short, stubby bills. They winter in Chihuahua; the Snow Goose ranges extensively elsewhere.

*ROSS GOOSE. *Chen rossii.*—22–26. *Adult:* Mainly white, the primaries black; bill notably short and stubby, carmen-red or pale purplish, the upper mandible corrugated and with warty protuberances near the base; feet dull reddish. *Immature:* Similar, but less immaculate white, the head, line through eye, and upper back with more or less grayish brown; bill greenish or pinkish, like the feet, and without protuberances.

Distribution.—Winters casually on Bustilles Lake, Chihuahua.

Remarks.—*See* Snow Goose.

*WHITE-FRONTED GOOSE. *Anser albifrons frontalis* (Illus. p. 45).
—26–30. *Adult:* Forehead and band at base of bill white, the head and neck uniform grayish brown, this darkening on the back; remiges, rump, and tail sooty brown, the last white-tipped; upper tail-coverts white; chest pale grayish brown, lightening posteriorly, the breast and abdomen more or less blotched or barred with black, or sometimes virtually all-black; bill pink; legs yellowish. *Immature:* Similar, but without a white face-patch and usually much paler below, the underparts with little or no black; bill and legs yellow.

BLACK BRANT   WHITE-FRONTED GOOSE   CANADA GOOSE

Distribution.—Winters in Baja California, and in Mexico south at least to Oaxaca, Puebla, and Veracruz.

Remarks.—A medium-sized, grayish brown goose with *white* tail-coverts, and a *white band at the base of the bill* (adult); in flight, black-and-white markings on the breast and abdomen conspicuous. These are lacking in immature birds. No other goose of our area has *yellow legs*.

*BLACK BRANT. *Branta bernicla orientalis* (Illus. p. 45).—22–26. *Adult:* Head, neck, chest, and upper back black, the upper neck with a black-streaked, white collar; back and scapulars deep sooty brown, this darkening on the remiges, rump, and tail; tail-coverts white; body sooty brown below, the sides and flanks barred with white; lower abdomen and crissum white; bill and legs black. *Immature:* Similar, but more grayish, and without a white collar; sides and flanks not barred.

Distribution.—Winters commonly on the west coast of Baja California south at least to Magdalena Bay.

Remarks.—A strictly maritime species, resembling both Canada and Cackling Geese in general appearance, but with *black cheeks* and a *white collar*. Immature birds and adults at a distance show no collar. However, they are much darker than either of the geese, and lack their contrasting necks and breasts.

*CANADA GOOSE. *Branta canadensis* (Illus. p. 45).—28–35. Head and neck black, the throat and cheeks white; back, scapulars, and wing-coverts brownish gray, this darkening on the remiges; rump and tail black, the tail-coverts white; breast pale ashy gray, shading to white on the lower abdomen and crissum; sides brownish gray; bill and feet black.

Distribution.—Winters in extreme northeastern Baja California and northern Mexico south, in the east, at least to Veracruz.

Races.—*B. c. leucopareia* (as above; records from Sonora, Jalisco, and Guanajuato require verification). *B. c. parvipes* (Veracruz—the type specimen; probably winters in northern Mexico west to Chihuahua).

Remarks.—The only other black-headed goose with *white cheeks and throat* is the Cackling Goose, one race of which (*minima*) is Mallard-sized, the other (*hutchinsii*) somewhat larger. Relative size and the Canada's lower-pitched voice serve to distinguish the two species when found together.

*CACKLING GOOSE. *Branta hutchinsii.*—23–30. Similar to a Canada Goose, but somewhat smaller, one race (*minima*) being hardly larger than a Mallard.

Distribution.—Winters south (locally) to Jalisco; a single record for Baja California.

Races.—*B. h. hutchinsii* (recorded from Chihuahua, Tamaulipas, and Jalisco). *B. h. minima* (recorded near San Quintín, Baja California, November 3, 1934).

Remarks.—*See* Canada Goose.

FULVOUS TREE-DUCK. *Dendrocygna bicolor helva.*—18–20. Crown reddish brown; sides of head buffy brown, shading to buffy white on the throat; a broad black stripe on hind-neck; upperparts mainly black, the back and scapulars barred with buffy brown; tail-coverts creamy white; a chestnut patch on the upper wing; breast yellowish brown, shading to pale cinnamon posteriorly, the long feathers on the sides white-striped; bill bluish black; legs deep bluish gray.

Distribution.—Baja California, and Mexico south locally to Jalisco (Lago de Chapala), and the Valley of Mexico. Winters south at least to Guerrero and Tabasco. Apparently absent from Chihuahua and Coahuila.

Remarks.—Tree-ducks are unlike other ducks in having legs of such length that the feet trail behind the tail in flight. The wing-beat is less rapid than that of most ducks, and in flight the head and neck droop below the level of the back. When alighting, tree-ducks stretch the neck downward sharply, the bill almost touching the feet. Both species frequent cover on the borders of ponds and lagoons, and in Mexico will often be found feeding in cornfields. This species is distinguished by its *tawny brown underparts;* the Black-bellied by its *white wing-patch* and *black* belly. The Fulvous has a long, squealing whistle; the Black-bellied a peculiarly shrill whistle.

BLACK-BELLIED TREE-DUCK. *Dendrocygna autumnalis* (Illus. p. 47).—20–22. Crown reddish brown; sides of head and neck ashy gray,

BLACK-BELLIED TREE-DUCK

fading to white on the throat; a black stripe on hind-neck; lower neck, back, and breast rich cinnamon; wings, rump, tail, abdomen, and sides black, the first with a very large white patch; bill reddish; legs pink.

Distribution.—Both coastal slopes and Cozumel Island, in the vicinity of ponds and lagoons. Absent from Baja California.

Races.—*D. a. fulgens* (Tamaulipas). *D. a. lucida* (lowlands generally, in suitable habitats).

Remarks.—The *long, heavy legs* mark this species as a tree-duck; the *black* belly and *white wing-patch* distinguish it from the Fulvous. Unmistakable.

MUSCOVY DUCK. *Cairina moschata.*—Male 30–35; female 23–28. Mainly deep sooty brown or black, the back and rump with purplish reflections; wings glossed with green, the wing-coverts and wing-linings white.

Distribution.—Tropical lowlands from Sinaloa and Tamaulipas southward; also Cozumel Island.

Remarks.—A black, goose-sized duck with very conspicuous *white wing-patches*. The purple and green reflections on the upperparts cannot be seen at a distance. The White-winged Scoter, a winter visitor in Baja California, is the only other *black* duck of our area with white wing-patches.

*MALLARD. *Anas platyrhynchos platyrhynchos.*—22–26. *Male:* Head and neck glossy green; a narrow white collar; upperparts mainly brownish, the scapulars buffy white; rump and tail-coverts glossy black, the middle upper coverts with recurved tips; a glossy purplish blue speculum, this bordered with *two* white bars; breast deep chestnut, the abdomen, sides, and flanks pale grayish; bill yellow. *Female:* Mottled brown, palest below, the speculum white-bordered as in the male; wing-linings of both sexes immaculate white.

Distribution.—Winters in Baja California, and south at least to Michoacán, Mexico, and Veracruz.

Remarks.—The green-headed, ruddy-breasted male offers no problem, especially if its *white collar* can be seen. Females differ from most other brown-mottled ducks in having a *yellow bill*, white wing-linings, and a white bar on *both* sides of the speculum. Mexican Ducks, while very similar, are much darker than Mallards, and show no white on their tails.

*HAWAIIAN DUCK. *Anas wyvilliana.*

Remarks.—Accidental. A single record for Mazatlán, Sinaloa, prior to 1859.

MEXICAN DUCK. *Anas diazi.*—20–22. Resembles a female Mallard, but considerably darker, and without white or conspicuously pale edgings on the tail feathers. Males have *greenish yellow bills.*

Distribution.—Northern Chihuahua and the highlands of central Mexico.

Races.—*A. d. diazi* (highlands of central Mexico). *A. d. novimexicana* (extreme northern Chihuahua).

Remarks.—Only the female Mallard, a winter visitor, is likely to be confused with this common resident. Other brown-mottled ducks lack the distinctive *white-bordered speculum,* and most are white below.

CINNAMON TEAL. *Anas cyanoptera septentrionalium.*—15–17. *Male:* Mainly cinnamon-red, the rump and tail dusky blackish, the back scalloped with same; wing-coverts pale blue, the speculum glossy green; bill black; iris orange. *Female:* Above sooty brown, the upper wings with a large, conspicuous blue patch, as in male; sides of head, neck, and underparts tawny brown, the breast and sides spotted with darker.

Distribution.—Northern Baja California, Chihuahua, Tamaulipas, and Jalisco, occurring extensively elsewhere in winter. As yet unrecorded in Durango, Querétaro, and the Yucatán Peninsula.

Remarks.—A small *reddish* duck with prominent *blue wing-patches.* Female Cinnamon and Blue-winged Teals are virtually indistinguishable in the field. Female Shovellers are very similar, but have notably large, spoon-shaped bills.

*BLUE-WINGED TEAL. *Anas discors* (Illus. p. 49).—14–16. *Male:* Head and neck deep gray, darkest on crown and throat; a conspicuous white

BLUE-WINGED TEAL

crescent in front of each eye; upperparts deep sooty brown, the feathers of the back and scapulars edged with buff; upper wing-coverts pale blue, the speculum glossy green; below pale reddish cinnamon, liberally spotted with black; wing-linings and axillars white; a white patch on each flank near tail. *Female:* Similar to a female Cinnamon Teal, the two usually not separable in the field.

Distribution.—Virtually country-wide in winter. Abundant.

Remarks.—No other duck has a *white, crescent-shaped patch* in front of each eye. Females lack this distinctive mark but, in common with the Cinnamon Teal and Shoveller, have white wing-linings and a *large blue patch on the upper wing.*

*COMMON TEAL. *Anas crecca carolinensis* (Illus. p. 50).—13–15. *Male:* Head and upper neck chestnut, the former with a glossy green stripe

COMMON TEAL

behind the eye; lower neck, back, rump, and sides pale gray, finely vermiculated with black; a vertical white bar in front of wing; speculum iridescent green; below buffy white, the breast liberally spotted with black; crissum black, with a buffy patch at each side. *Female:* Above blackish, the back and scapulars more or less spotted with buff; a glossy green speculum; below whitish, the breast, sides, and flanks much spotted and mottled with brown.

Distribution.—Widespread in winter, but as yet unrecorded in the Yucatán Peninsula.

Remarks.—Also known as Green-winged Teal. This, the smallest of teals, lacks the blue wing-patch of the Cinnamon and Blue-winged. A green patch on each side of the head distinguishes the male. When at rest it also shows a *white bar* in front of each wing. Females, while rather nondescript, are the only *small* ducks with green speculi in the absence of blue wing-patches.

*COMMON PINTAIL. *Anas acuta tzitzihoa.*—22–28. *Male:* Head and hind-neck dark brown, this shading into the gray of the back, where finely vermiculated; scapulars and tertials very long, black edged with gray; wing-coverts pale brownish gray; speculum bronzy green, appearing black at a distance; middle rectrices black, very narrow, and greatly elongated; neck (below) and underparts white, the sides and flanks vermiculated with black; crissum black. *Female:* Above sooty brown, liberally streaked and spotted with buff; speculum usually obscure; sides of head tawny, minutely streaked with dusky; below whitish, more or less mottled with tawny, or brown-spotted.

Distribution.—Abundant in winter; recorded from every state except Querétaro.

Remarks.—The drake is unmistakable; a strikingly handsome, *long-necked* duck with a brown head, white underparts, and very *long, pointed tail.* Females resemble female Mallards, but seem much trimmer, and lack a white bar before and behind the speculum.

*EUROPEAN WIDGEON. *Mareca penelope.*—16–20. *Male:* Somewhat like an American Widgeon, but with a *reddish brown* head, *buffy crown,* and *grayish* (not brownish) upperparts. *Female:* Resembles a female American Widgeon, the two not usually separable in the field, Both sexes have pale *mottled wing-linings and axillaries,* while these are virtually white in American Widgeons.

Distribution.—Recorded but once in our area (Descanso, northern Baja California).

*AMERICAN WIDGEON. *Mareca americana* (Illus. p. 52).—17–21. *Male:* Forehead and median crown white; a glossy green stripe behind eye; head and throat otherwise buffy white, very liberally speckled with black, the whole appearing gray at a distance; back and scapulars pinkish brown, minutely vermiculated with black, the rump and tail sooty; a large white patch on the upper wing; speculum glossy green, broadly margined with black; chest, sides, and flanks purplish pink, the wing-linings, breast, and abdomen white; crissum black; a white patch at each side of tail. *Female:* Head and upper neck grayish (i.e., white speckled with dusky); above sooty brown, the feathers edged with tawny; a white or pale patch on the upper wing; speculum black; chest, sides, and flanks tawny brown, the breast and abdomen white.

Distribution.—Virtually country-wide in winter.

Remarks.—Also known as Baldpate. In flight both sexes show a large white area on the *forepart* of the wings. When swimming, the male's *white forehead, dark eye-patch,* and white flank-patch are con-

AMERICAN WIDGEON

spicuous marks. Females resemble female Gadwalls when swimming, but usually have paler (less brownish) heads and necks.

*GADWALL. *Anas strepera* (Illus. p. 52).—18–22. *Male:* Head brown, darkest above, the cheeks and throat tawny or buffy; upperparts mainly

GADWALL

sooty brown, the back, scapulars, sides, and flanks vermiculated with buff and dusky; tail-coverts black; a large chestnut patch on the upper wing, this followed by black; a conspicuous white speculum; chest blackish, more or less scalloped with buff or white; breast and abdomen white. *Female:* Dark brown, more or less mottled with tawny, the head and neck palest; a conspicuous white speculum; breast and abdomen white, the former often brown-spotted.

Distribution.—Winters in Baja California, and south at least to Guerrero, Puebla, and Tabasco.

Remarks.—The *white speculum* is a good field mark. In flight it shows as a white patch on the *hindpart* of the wing. A Widgeon's wing-patch is on the *forepart*. Swimming Gadwalls suggest Mexican Ducks, but are somewhat paler, and usually show some white on their wings. Mexican Ducks are more uniform. Gadwalls have black tail-coverts that contrast with the paler rump and flanks.

NORTHERN SHOVELLER. *Spatula clypeata.*—18–20. *Male:* Head and neck black glossed with green; back, rump, and middle rectrices sooty, the lateral tail feathers largely white; scapulars white, the longer feathers partly blue; a blue patch on the upper wing; speculum glossy green, this bordered in front with white; chest white; breast, abdomen, and sides chestnut; a white patch on each flank near tail; iris yellow; bill black, much longer than the head, and broadening toward the tip. *Female:* Brown-mottled, darkest above, the wings and shape of bill as in male.

Distribution.—Winters extensively and often in abundance. Not yet reported from the Yucatán Peninsula.

Remarks.—The very *long, spoon-shaped bill,* unique among ducks, is at all times the best field character for either sex. In flight the added length of the oversized bill gives an unbalanced appearance. Swimming Shovellers rest low in the water, with the *bill pointed downward.*

*WOOD DUCK. *Aix sponsa.*—16–18. *Male:* Conspicuously crested, the crown, crest, and sides of head iridescent green and purplish; throat, postocular stripe, and line above eye white; back bronzy, this becoming black posteriorly, where much glossed with blue and violet; breast purplish chestnut; abdomen white; sides and flanks tawny, boldly barred with black and white. *Female:* Head and neck grayish brown, the crown and modified crest darkest and glossed with green; a pale area around the eyes, the eyelids bright yellow; throat white; above bronzy brown, the secondaries white-tipped and largely iridescent blue; breast, sides, and flanks mottled with brown and tawny, the abdomen whitish.

Distribution.—Winters casually in northern Mexico (Sonora), and south at least to Distrito Federal.

Remarks.—No description and few pictures do justice to the drake, which is unequaled among American ducks in brilliance of plumage and beauty of pattern. The relatively drab female will be known by its *modified crest, white eye-ring,* and sharply outlined white throat. In flight both sexes appear large-headed and very short-necked.

*CANVASBACK. *Aythya valisineria* (Illus. p. 54).—18–22. *Male:* Head and neck dark reddish chestnut, the crown and throat dusky; chest and upper back black; back and scapulars white, finely vermiculated with

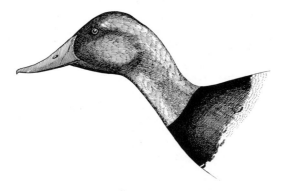

CANVASBACK

dusky; rump and tail-coverts black; below mainly white; bill as long as head, black, the upper mandible sloping into the flattened forehead. *Female:* Head, neck, chest, and upper back yellowish brown, the upperparts otherwise essentially brown; a pale, obscure stripe through eye; throat, breast, and abdomen whitish, the sides and flanks brown; profile of bill and forehead as in male.

Distribution.—Winters in northern Baja California, and in western Mexico south to Michoacán and Distrito Federal; also, the Atlantic slope south to Veracruz.

Remarks.—A large *white-bodied duck* with a dark head, neck, and chest. The pattern of the female is not sharply defined, but vaguely suggests that of the male. Both sexes are distinguished from ducks of similar pattern (Redheads, and female Ring-necks, Scaups, and Golden-eyes) in having *long bills that slope into a flattened forehead.*

*REDHEAD. *Aythya americana* (Illus. p. 55).—17–21. *Male:* Head and upper neck bright reddish chestnut; lower neck, upper back, and chest black; back, scapulars, sides, and flanks finely vermiculated with white and dusky, the whole appearing gray at a distance; speculum pearly gray; rump and tail-coverts black; lower breast and abdomen white; iris yellow; bill shorter than head, pale bluish tipped with black. *Female:* Similar to a female Canvasback, but with a relatively short bill, high-domed head, and pearly gray speculum; bill as in male, but paler.

REDHEAD

Distribution.—Winters in northern Baja California and from northern Mexico south to Michoacán, Mexico, and Tamaulipas.

Remarks.—Redheads resemble Canvasbacks superficially, but in profile show a *short bill, abrupt forehead,* and *high-domed* head. Male Redheads appear *gray-backed* at a distance; the Canvasback *white.* Female Redheads, Ring-necks, and Scaups are troublesome at a distance. Under favorable conditions the Ring-neck shows a *white eye-ring* and *white-ringed bill;* the Scaup a *distinct white face-patch.* Of the three, Scaups alone show a *white* (not gray) *wing-stripe* in flight.

*RING-NECKED DUCK. *Aythya collaris* (Illus. p. 56).—16–18. *Male:* Head and neck glossy purplish black, the posterior crown slightly tufted; an obscure chestnut collar on the lower neck; chest and upperparts mainly black, the speculi ashy gray; breast and abdomen white, the sides and flanks minutely vermiculated with white and dusky; iris yellow; bill bluish, black-tipped, and with two white rings—one subterminal, the second at the base. *Female:* Similar to a female Redhead, but with a distinct white eye-ring and two white rings on the bill.

Distribution.—Widespread in winter. Reported in abundance in southeastern Veracruz as late as April 16.

Remarks.—The only duck of our area with a *white-ringed bill.* Swimming drakes also show a white barlike patch in front of each wing and, unlike Redheads and Scaups, are *black* (not gray) *above.* The chestnut collar is usually a poor field character. Female Ring-necks and Redheads both have a pale area on the forepart of the head, but this is not sharply defined, as in female Scaups.

LESSER SCAUP (*left and right*); RING-NECKED DUCK (*center*)

*GREATER SCAUP. *Aythya marila nearctica.*—17–20. Similar to a Lesser Scaup, but somewhat larger, the head in profile rounder, and the white wing-stripe usually notably longer, in most birds extending well across the inner primaries. In good light the drake's head shows *greenish* (not purplish) *reflections.*

Distribution.—Accidental or casual winter visitor in Baja California (one record) and northwestern Mexico (Sinaloa, two records).

*LESSER SCAUP. *Aythya affinis* (Illus. p. 56).—15–17. *Male:* Head, neck, chest, and upper back black, the first showing purplish reflections in certain light; lower neck sometimes with a vague brownish collar; back and scapulars white, coarsely vermiculated with black, the whole appearing whitish at a distance; a white wing-stripe, this usually restricted to the secondaries; rump and tail-coverts black; breast and abdomen white; iris yellow; bill grayish blue, tipped with black. *Female:* Area at base of bill usually white, this rather sharply defined; plumage elsewhere mainly brownish, the breast and abdomen white; a conspicuous white wing-stripe; bill as in male.

Distribution.—Widespread in winter.

Remarks.—The only scaup likely to be seen in Mexico. At a distance the drake appears white, with a black head, neck, chest, and tail. Male Ring-necks are similar in part, but have *black backs* and *white-ringed bills*. In flight the conspicuous *white wing-stripe* distinguishes scaups of both species and sexes from all similar ducks. Females, unlike female Redheads and Ring-necks, also have a *well-defined* white area bordering the bill.

*COMMON GOLDENEYE. *Bucephala clangula americana.*—16–22. *Male:* Head and upper neck glossy black, this showing strong green reflections in certain light; a large round white spot between the eye and bill; back, rump, tail, primaries, and wing-linings black, the plumage otherwise immaculate white; iris yellow; bill black. *Female:* Head deep chocolate-brown; a white collar and white wing-patch; upper back, chest, sides, and flanks grayish, the back, scapulars, rump, and tail sooty black; breast, abdomen, and crissum white; bill dusky or (sometimes) yellowish.

Distribution.—Winters casually in Baja California and possibly elsewhere in northwestern Mexico. Recorded once in Sinaloa and in Durango.

Remarks.—A stocky, short-necked duck with a notably large black or brown head. Drakes, black-headed and white-bodied, are the only ducks with a conspicuous white spot between the eye and bill. The brown-headed female has a *white collar* and *grayish* chest and upperparts. In flight both sexes show *black wing-linings*, and *white wing-patches*.

*BUFFLEHEAD. *Bucephala albeola.*—13–15. *Male:* Head and upper neck mainly glossy black, this showing strong green, purple, and violet reflections in certain lights; a large white patch extending from the auriculars to the hind-crown; lower neck, body, wing-coverts, and secondaries immaculate white, the back, rump, scapulars, and primaries black. *Female:* Head, neck, and upperparts sooty brown, the first with a large white cheek-patch; a white speculum; chest, sides, and flanks pale grayish, the breast and abdomen white.

Distribution.—Winters in Baja California, and south at least to Jalisco Mexico, and Tamaulipas. Generally uncommon to rare.

Remarks.—A very stocky, teal-sized duck with a notably "puffy" head. The male's white triangular head-patch is virtually diagnostic. Male Hooded Mergansers show a similar head-patch, but have *long slender bills* and much less white on their bodies. In flight a merganser appears streamlined; a Bufflehead decidedly chubby. Female Buffleheads suggest diminutive female Goldeneyes, but lack a white collar, and have a white cheek-patch.

*WHITE-WINGED SCOTER. *Melanitta fusca dixoni.*—20–23. *Male:* Black, shading to sooty brown on breast and abdomen, the speculum white; a small white spot below each eye; iris white or pale gray; bill mainly red and orange, the swollen base black. *Female:* Similar to male, but the black replaced with deep sooty brown, this appearing black at a distance; sides of head with two pale patches; bill mainly dusky, the sides sometimes pinkish.

Distribution.—Winters in northern Baja California.

Remarks.—Scoters will be recognized as large, thickset ducks, black (or sooty) of plumage, with swollen bills and very short necks. Both species are largely coastal while in Mexico. Males of each are at all times virtually unmistakable. The females are much alike while on the water, but in flight this species shows a white speculum. Muscovies, the only other *black* ducks with white wing-patches in our area, have the white restricted to the *coverts* or forepart of the wings.

*SURF SCOTER. *Melanitta perspicillata* (Illus. p. 58).—18–20. *Male:* Mainly black, the forehead and nape white; iris white; bill much swollen, essentially red and orange, but with a round black spot at base of upper mandible. *Female:* Sooty brown, palest below, the breast and abdomen

SURF SCOTER

usually grayish or mottled; two pale patches on sides of head; bill dusky, the base with a black spot on each side.

Distribution.—Winters in northern Baja California and commonly on the coast of Sonora.

Remarks.—*See* White-winged Scoter.

MASKED DUCK. *Oxyura dominica* (Illus. p. 59).—12–14. *Male:* Forepart of head black, the hindpart reddish cinnamon, this extending to the rump, breast, and flanks; back and scapulars streaked or spotted with black; a large white wing-patch; tail black, fan-shaped, the feathers much stif-

MASKED DUCK

fened; abdomen tawny; bill pale blue. *Female:* Above deep sooty brown or blackish, the hind-neck, back, and scapulars liberally spotted and barred with buff; sides of head buffy, this scored by two dark stripes; below whitish, the neck and chest black-spotted, and usually tinged with rust; wings and tail as in male.

Distribution.—Resident, locally, in Nayarit, Jalisco, Colima, Tamaulipas, and Veracruz.

Remarks.—A small reddish duck with a *black face and white wing-patches;* the female a diminutive brownish duck with *white wing-patches and two conspicuous face-stripes.* Drakes are reddish at all seasons; the male Ruddy brightly colored only in summer.

RUDDY DUCK. *Oxyura jamaicensis rubida.*—14–16. *Male (summer)*: Crown and nape black; sides of head below eye white; throat, neck, and upperparts mainly reddish chestnut, the rump, remiges, and fanlike tail sooty brown or blackish; below essentially whitish or silvery; bill bright blue; (*winter*): Crown black, the upperparts otherwise dark brown finely vermiculated with ashy, this often flecked with reddish; a white face-patch; throat and neck pale grayish brown; below as in summer, the chest often tinged with tawny; bill dusky. *Female:* Essentially like winter male, but without a clear white face-patch; crown brown (not black) like back; sides of head buffy white, this scored by a single brown stripe; bill dusky.

Distribution.—South very locally to central Baja California and the Valley of Mexico, occurring extensively elsewhere in winter.

Remarks.—The small sized, chubby proportions, and rather long tail, with its graduated, spikelike feathers, distinguish Ruddy and Masked Ducks from all other Mexican waterfowl. They leave the water with difficulty, but, once air-borne, fly rapidly, if somewhat jerkily. Drakes of both species characteristically hold the fanlike tail erect while swimming. Male Ruddies, unlike Masked Ducks, lose their bright plumage in winter, but show conspicuously *white cheeks* at all seasons. Female Ruddies have only *one cheek-stripe* and lack white wing-patches.

*HOODED MERGANSER. *Lophodytes cucullatus.*—16–19. *Male:* Head, neck, and upperparts mainly black or deep sooty brown, the first with a conspicuous white fanlike crest; inner remiges white-streaked; two black bars in front of each wing; chest, breast, and abdomen white, the sides and flanks brownish; iris yellow; bill black, cylindrical, and shorter than head. *Female:* Mainly grayish brown, the crest reddish brown, the breast and abdomen white; a white wing-patch; bill dusky above, orange below.

Distribution.—A rare winter visitor. One record each for Baja California and Veracruz and three for Distrito Federal.

Remarks.—*See* Red-breasted Merganser.

COMMON MERGANSER. *Mergus merganser americanus.*—22–26. *Male:* Not crested. Head and upper neck metallic greenish black; back and scapulars black, the rump and tail gray; primaries sooty, the wings otherwise essentially white; lower neck and underparts white; bill red, notably long and slender; iris reddish brown. *Female:* Head and upper neck reddish brown, the first with a prominent occipital crest; chin and upper throat white, this sharply defined; hind-neck and upperparts ashy gray; a white speculum; below white; bill dull red.

Distribution.—Resident, but very local in the mountains of Chihuahua, winters casually elsewhere in the north (Baja California, Sonora, and Tamaulipas), and south to state of Mexico.

Remarks.—Drakes, black-headed and black-backed, show more white than any other large duck. The absence of a crest is unique among mergansers of either sex. Females are best distinguished from female Red-breasted Mergansers by their more conspicuous crests and very *distinct throat-patch.*

*RED-BREASTED MERGANSER. *Mergus serrator* (Illus. p. 61).— 18–23. *Male:* Head crested, black glossed with green; back and scapulars black; wings extensively white, the primaries black; rump and tail gray, the former finely vermiculated with white; neck and underparts white, the chest

RED-BREASTED MERGANSER

with a broad rusty band, the sides and flanks vermiculated with dusky; bill bright red, long and slender; iris red. *Female:* Head and occipital crest reddish brown; throat whitish, this shading to brownish on the lower neck and chest; above dusky brown or grayish, the speculum white; breast and abdomen white; bill dull red; iris red or yellowish.

Distribution.—Winters fairly commonly in Baja California and Sonora.

Remarks.—The only merganser likely to be seen in Mexico. All three species are fish-eaters, and as a group are easily distinguished from other ducks by their long cylindrical bills. In flight, mergansers appear decidedly streamlined, and carry the bill, neck, and body on a horizontal line. The drakes of each are virtually unmistakable. Female Red-breasted and American Mergansers are much alike, but the former's throat shows as a whitish area that *shades into the brown* of the cheeks and neck; not as a gleaming white patch with definite borders.

Family CATHARTIDAE. New World Vultures

Key to the Species

KING VULTURE. *Sarcoramphus papa* (Illus. p. 63).—28–32; wingspread about 6½ feet. *Adult:* Mainly creamy white, this tinged with pinkish on the back and shoulders, the remiges, rump, and tail black; a dusky ruff on the lower neck; bare skin of head and upper neck patterned with orange, red, and blue; bill orange and black, the cere with a conspicuous wrinkled caruncle; iris white. *Immature:* Mainly sooty brown or blackish, the underparts usually with more or less white; fleshy caruncle on cere reduced or lacking.

Distribution.—Hot lowlands, from Sinaloa and Veracruz southward.

Remarks.—This magnificent white-and-black vulture is especially abundant in the forested lowlands of the south, where large flocks are likely to be attracted by any decaying carcass. Its soaring flight is much like that of a Turkey Vulture. Immature birds resemble the latter, but have broader tails and usually show some white on their underparts.

BLACK VULTURE. *Coragyps atratus.*—22–26; wingspread about 4½ feet. Uniform dull black, the bill and bare skin of the head and neck sooty; underside of wings near base of primaries whitish or silver gray, this forming a conspicuous pale area, as seen in flight from below; tail rather short and broad.

Distribution.—Baja California (Cerralus Island), Tres Marías Islands, and Mexico generally, probably occurring abundantly in the lowlands of every state.

KING VULTURE

Remarks.—This vulture is the one likely to be seen in the greatest numbers in and about lowland towns and villages. Its *blackish* bill, head, and neck at once distinguish it from *adult* Turkey Vultures, a larger species with a *white bill* and *reddish head*. In flight, the very *short, broad tail* of the Black, unlike that of the Turkey Vulture, extends little beyond the edge of its wings. Black Vultures flap frequently; the Turkey soars almost continuously. A pale patch on the underside of the wing at the base of the primaries also serves to identify Black Vultures at a distance when in flight.

TURKEY VULTURE. *Cathartes aura.*—28–30; wingspread about 6 feet. *Adult:* Mainly sooty brown or blackish, the feathers of the upperparts with bluish reflections; bare skin of head and neck dull purplish red; bill whitish; tail rather long and narrow. *Immature:* Similar, but browner and without bluish reflections on the upperparts; bare skin of head and neck blackish, the bill sometimes dusky.

Distribution.—Country-wide, occurring at all altitudes; also Tres Marías and Cozumel Islands.

Races.—*C. a. aura* (lowlands and foothills, exclusive of Baja California; also Tres Marías and Cozumel Islands). *C. a. teter* (Baja California, and the Mexican plateau generally, occurring elsewhere during migration).

Remarks.—Points of dissimilarity between the Turkey and Black Vulture have been discussed under the latter. Where eagles and large black hawks also occur, a soaring Turkey Vulture can be distinguished by its relatively inconspicuous head and narrower tail. From below, the remiges appear paler than the wing-linings and body. *See* Solitary Eagle, Golden Eagle, and Bald Eagle.

YELLOW-HEADED VULTURE. *Cathartes burrovianus.*—24–28. Plumage wholly black, the upperparts faintly glossed with greenish; bare skin of head and neck mainly yellowish, the forecrown red, the midcrown bluish gray; bill creamy buff; iris red.

Distribution.—Lowlands of southern Veracruz southward. Probably common, but in the past usually mistaken for the Turkey Vulture.

Remarks.—The only all-black vulture with a distinctly *yellowish head.* Although originally described from Veracruz, this common tropical American species was until recently considered a variant of the Turkey Vulture. It is tamer than a Turkey Vulture and, in flight, shows a whitish patch much like that of a Black Vulture, in addition to the silvery underwings.

CALIFORNIA CONDOR. *Gymnogyps californianus.*—45–55; wingspread 9–10½ feet. *Adult:* Sooty brown or blackish, the wing-linings white; bare skin of head and neck orange; bill yellowish. *Immature:* Similar, but without white on the wings; head, neck, and bill dusky.

Distribution.—Formerly resident in northern Baja California. No Mexican records in recent years, and now apparently limited to south-central California.

Remarks.—While not likely to be found in our area today, a condor would, in any case, be recognized by its size alone. Adults have a prominent white strip along the *forward edge* of the wing-lining.

Families ACCIPITRIDAE, PANDIONIDAE, FALCONIDAE

Hawks, Ospreys, Falcons, and Allies

The diurnal birds of prey form a relatively homogeneous group that is not likely to be mistaken for any other. However, the identification of many species is often troublesome, even for the expert, and allocation of individual birds is frequently impossible under field conditions.

Many hawks are very similar, especially when in immature plumage, and most species acquire a variety of intermediate plumages before reaching maturity, usually after several years. To complicate their identification still more, some hawks normally have two color phases which may vary more or less with age. To these difficulties may be added the fact that birds of prey are likely to be wary and are usually seen soaring far overhead or perched at a distance. Nevertheless, their identification can be mastered with perseverance, and one should not be discouraged by initial failure or uncertainty.

More than half the birds of prey recorded from Mexico also occur in the United States and Canada, a circumstance that should lessen the difficulties of American bird students. The 21 species that do not range north of Mexico are principally tropical forms that are largely restricted to the southern portion of the country. Many occur only in humid lowland forests, and several are extremely rare. While, obviously, no field key to so large a fauna of hawks can be entirely satisfactory, a clue to the identification of each will be found in the following arbitrary categories and their respective keys. Species with diverse plumages (or color phases) may appear in two or more keys.

KEY TO THE SPECIES

I. Eagle-sized, or very small birds of prey. *See* page 66

II. Underparts entirely, or very extensively, gleaming white, creamy white, or *pale* buffy white. Usually without bars, streaks, or spots, unless on wings or tail. If present elsewhere, the bars, spots, or streaks either inconspicuous or largely restricted to the flanks, thighs, or lower abdomen. *See* page 67

III. Black, dark slate, or deep chocolate-brown, appearing black at a distance. Underparts not appreciably paler than the back. Tail and underside of wings often conspicuously barred. Rump or lower abdomen and crissum sometimes immaculate white. *See* page 69

IV. Underparts uniform *pale* grayish slate (sometimes pearly gray, or minutely vermiculated, but appearing uniform at a distance), cinnamon-rufous, or rich tawny cinnamon. *See* page 70

V. Underparts either generously streaked, or lower breast, upper abdomen, and sides black. If *streaked* below, the *wings long and pointed.*
See page 70

VI. Underside of body more or less extensively barred, the bars often inconspicuous at a distance, or sometimes restricted to the abdomen, flanks, and thighs. *See* page 71

CATEGORY I

1a. More than 25 inches long 2

b. Less than 15 inches long 7

2a. Mainly white below, or head and tail (only) immaculate white . 3

b. Black, or deep sooty brown, the throat and chest sometimes white 4

3a. Underparts extensively white, the tail broadly barred; head pale gray; a conspicuous nuchal ruff . . . . Harpy Eagle, p. 88

b. Underparts blackish, the head and tail white
Bald Eagle (adult), p. 90

4a. Rather slender, the tail decidedly long and with several conspicuous bars (humid tropical forests) . . . . . . Black Eagle-Hawk, p. 90

b. Very sturdy; tail expansive, but not notably long; tail unbarred or with a single conspicuous bar, this sometimes terminal (Pacific coastlands and interior mountains) 5

5a. Smaller (26–28 inches). Slaty black, the tail narrowly white-tipped and with a gray median bar . . . . Solitary Eagle, p. 87

b. Larger (30–35 inches). Deep chocolate-brown, the tail either uniform or pale (sometimes white) basally 6

6a. Tail uniform; wing-linings paler than remiges
Bald Eagle (immature), p. 90

b. Tail not uniform, the terminal portion conspicuously darker than the base; wing-linings darker than remiges . . Golden Eagle, p. 90

7a. Wings long and pointed 8

b. Wings broad and rounded 12

8a. Extensively grayish or slate-colored; primaries virtually unbarred, but with rufous on their inner webs 9

b. Not as in 8a. 10

9a. Head and terminal portion of secondaries pearly gray; tail uniformly black . . . . Mississippi Kite (adult), p. 75

b. Head and underparts concolor; tail with two white bars
Plumbeous Kite (adult), p. 75

10a. Back and tail reddish . . . . Sparrow Hawk, p. 99

b. Back and tail not reddish 11

  b. Underparts boldly patterned, but not streaked; a broad black band
across abdomen

                              Orange-breasted Falcon, p. 96
                              Bat Falcon, p. 97

12a. Tail broad and rounded; inner webs of remiges extensively rufous
                              Roadside Hawk, p. 81

  b. Tail rather long and narrow; underparts often barred with russet
or cinnamon

                              Double-toothed Kite, p. 75
                              Sharp-shinned Hawk, p. 78

Category II

9*a*. Head and hind-neck pearly gray like back and wings, the latter long and narrow; tail inconspicuously barred
Marsh Hawk (adult male), p. 91

   b. Head and hind-neck pale bluish slate, sharply distinct from the black wings and back; wings short and broad; tail boldly barred
Gray-headed Kite (adult), p. 73

10*a*. With very broad wings, and a broad, rounded tail 11

   b. Not as in 10*a*. 16

11*a*. Tail with one or more conspicuous bars, these sometimes (Short-tailed Hawk) not evident on the upper surface 12

   b. Tail uniformly pale below, or inconspicuously barred 14

12*a*. Large (20–24 inches). Tail gleaming white, with a broad subterminal bar . . . . White-tailed Hawk, p. 78

   b. Small (15–17 inches). Tail boldly barred, this always evident on the underside 13

13*a*. Tail (above and below) and underside of remiges very conspicuously barred . . . . Hook-billed Kite (immature), p. 74

   b. Tail notably short, the underside barred; wing-linings and base of remiges immaculate white
Short-tailed Hawk (light phase adult), p. 83

14*a*. Tail reddish above; wing-linings darker than underside of remiges; lower abdomen sometimes with a broad band of streaks
Red-tailed Hawk (light phase), p. 79

   b. Not as in 14*a*. 15

15*a*. A conspicuous dark band across the chest; underside of tail and remiges darker than wing-linings
Swainson Hawk (light phase), p. 81

   b. Underparts, including wings and tail, mainly white, the thighs deep russet; wing-coverts and scapulars extensively reddish
Ferruginous Hawk (light phase), p. 79

16*a*. With short, rounded wings and a long, rounded tail, the latter boldly barred above and below; a narrow white or buff nuchal collar 17

   b. Wings very long and narrow, and with a dark patch on the underside near the bend; a conspicuous subterminal tail-bar; chest sparsely spotted . . . . Osprey, p. 92

17*a*. Large (20–24 inches). Tail notably graduated
Collared Forest-Falcon (adult), p. 93

   b. Small (14–16 inches). Tail not notably graduated
Bicolored Hawk (immature), p. 77

Category III

Category IV

1*a*. Below gray or pale slate, distinctly lighter than the upperparts .   2

  b. Not gray 5

2*a*. Falcon-like, the wings long and pointed 3

  b. Not falcon-like, the wings short and rounded, the tail rather long   4

3*a*. Head and hind-neck pearly white, the secondaries broadly tipped
    with same; tail uniform black . . . . Mississippi Kite, p. 75

  b. Head and hind-neck concolor with underparts; secondaries uniform
    black; tail with two narrow white bars, these usually not visible
    from above . . . . Plumbeous Kite, p. 75

4*a*. Large (20–24 inches). A conspicuous gray superciliary stripe;
    underparts minutely vermiculated (mountain forests)
                                Northern Goshawk, p. **77**

  b. Small (14–16 inches). Underparts uniform pearly gray or pale
    slate, the thighs chestnut; without pale superciliaries (tropical
    forests) . . . . Bicolored Hawk, p. **77**

5*a*. Above and below mainly cinnamon-rufous, the head creamy white;
    a black patch on chest . . . . Black-collared Hawk, p. 86

  b. Under parts rich tawny cinnamon; a white patch on rump
                             Marsh Hawk (female), p. 91

Category V

1*a*. Streaked below 2

  b. Not streaked below, the lower breast, sides, and abdomen exten-
    sively black 4

2*a*. More than 15 inches
                              Prairie Falcon, p. 96
               Peregrine Falcon (immature), p. 96

  b. Less than 12½ inches 3

3*a*. Back and tail reddish, narrowly barred with dusky
                      Sparrow Hawk (female), p. 99

  b. Back and tail not reddish, the latter barred with white
                            Pigeon Hawk, p. 99

4*a*. Wings long and pointed; tail black, and usually conspicuously
    barred with white 5

  b. Wings not pointed; throat, breast, hind-neck, and tail white, the
    last black terminally . . . . Crested Caracara (adult), p. 94

5*a*. Upperparts pale bluish slate; a narrow reddish nuchal collar; pos-
    terior underparts tawny buff . . . . . . Aplomado Falcon, p. 98

  b. Upperparts uniform black; posterior underparts chestnut 6

6*a*. Larger (13–15 inches). A broad band of rufous across the fore-breast; tail conspicuously barred . . . Orange-breasted Falcon, p. 96

b. Smaller (9½–11½ inches). Throat and chest buffy white; tail very narrowly barred . . . . Bat Falcon, p. 97

CATEGORY VI

1*a*. Barred below with gray, black, or sooty brown 2

b. Barred below with russet, cinnamon, or reddish brown, the under-parts sometimes appearing at a distance pinkish, tawny, or mottled 8

2*a*. Wings long and pointed; throat and breast immaculate creamy white . . . . Peregrine Falcon (adult), p. 96

b. Not as in 2*a*. 3

3*a*. Underparts narrowly barred 4

b. Underparts boldly barred 6

4*a*. Wings short and rounded, the tail relatively long and notably graduated . . . . Barred Forest-Falcon, p. 93

b. Wings and tail broad, the latter moderately rounded 5

5*a*. Larger (15–17 inches). Above mainly pale slaty gray
Gray Hawk, p. 83

b. Smaller (12–13 inches); above brown; throat white, with a median stripe . . . . Double-toothed Kite (male), p. 75

6*a*. Conspicuously crested; hind-neck, auriculars, and sides of breast rufous . . . . Ornate Eagle-Hawk (adult), p. 88

b. Not as in 6*a*. 7

7*a*. Above brown, the underparts evenly barred with brown and whitish; tail notably graduated
Collared Forest-Falcon (immature), p. 93

b. Above bluish slate, the underparts irregularly barred with slate and white . . . . . . Hook-billed Kite (male gray phase), p. 74

8*a*. Wings short and rounded; tail relatively long
Cooper Hawk, p. 77
Sharp-shinned Hawk, p. 78

b. Wings and tail broad 9

9*a*. Above dark brown, usually more or less mottled, or upperparts uniform grayish brown 10

b. Above sooty black; sometimes with a white or cinnamon nuchal collar 12

10*a.* More than 18 inches; underparts extensively tawny reddish, the
barring often indistinct; a rufous patch on shoulders

Red-shouldered Hawk, p. 80

b. Less than 17 inches 11

11*a.* Upperparts, throat, and chest uniform grayish brown, the posterior
underparts barred with rufous; inner webs of remiges reddish

Roadside Hawk, p. 81

b. Upperparts dark brown, mottled with paler; underparts boldly
barred with white and reddish brown; remiges largely white on
inner webs . . . . Broad-winged Hawk, p. 81

12*a.* More than 15 inches; underparts white or buffy, conspicuously
barred with brown or cinnamon . . Hook-billed Kite (female), p. 74

b. Less than 14 inches; underparts mainly rufous, narrowly barred
with white . . . . Double-toothed Kite (female), p. 75

Family ACCIPITRIDAE. Hawks, Eagles, and Allies

WHITE-TAILED KITE. *Elanus leucurus majusculus.*—15–16. *Adult:*
Above pale gray, the wing-coverts extensively black; forehead, sides of head,
underparts, and tail white; bill black, iris orange-rufous; feet yellowish.
Immature: Similar, but head and breast with more or less rusty; tail pearl
gray.

Distribution.—Recorded from northern Baja California (not since
1903), Nuevo León, Tamaulipas, Veracruz, Tabasco, and Campeche. Breeds
locally, but everywhere uncommon to rare.

Remarks.—A very pale, falcon-like hawk with a *white tail.* The conspicuous *black patch* near the bend of its wings is also a good field mark.
Kites lack the dash and aggressiveness of many birds of prey and, to
their detriment, are more trusting than most. In buoyancy of flight this
species strongly suggests a gull. It apparently delights to soar in a high
wind. When hunting, it often hovers above its prey like a Sparrow
Hawk.

SWALLOW-TAILED KITE. *Elanoïdes forficatus* (Illus. p. 73).—
23–25. Head, hind-neck, patch on lower back, and underparts immaculate
white; upperparts (except head) slaty black, more or less glossed with greenish, the upper back and scapulars sometimes with purplish maroon reflections; wings and tail notably long and slender, the latter deeply forked and
scissor-like.

Distribution.—Migratory in eastern Mexico, but undoubtedly resident
in the extreme south.

Races.—*E. f. forficatus* (recorded as a migrant in Nuevo León, Veracruz, Distrito Federal, and Oaxaca). *E. f. yetapa* (Campeche and Chiapas, where presumably resident).

Remarks.—One of the most distinctive and graceful of the birds of prey. Swallow-tails occur in the Caribbean lowlands during migration

SWALLOW-TAILED KITE

and may be found in the southern portion of the country at all seasons. They prefer swampy areas adjacent to sluggish tropical rivers and sometimes associate in loose flocks. Swallow-tails prey chiefly on large insects and small reptiles, which are deftly caught on the wing.

GRAY-HEADED KITE. *Leptodon cayanensis.*—18–19. *Adult:* Crown and hind-neck bluish slate gray, lightening on sides of head, the upperparts otherwise mainly black; tail broad, narrowly white-tipped, and with two whitish bars; below immaculate white, the undersides of wings and tail black, boldly barred with white. *Immature:* Orbital area, posterior portion of crown, back, wings, and tail deep sooty brown, the last either barred, as in adult, or with pale brown bars; head (except back of crown), hind-neck, and underparts creamy white.

Distribution.—The Caribbean slope, from southern Tamaulipas southward.

Remarks.—Also known as Cayenne Kite. Gray-headed Kites frequent humid lowland forests and the vicinity of marshes. They are rather uncommon and of very local occurrence. Adults are distinguished by their *bluish slate heads* which contrast sharply with the black upper parts. Immature birds have a very conspicuous *dark patch toward the back of the white head*. Both are white below and have *broadly barred tails*. *See* Black-and-White Eagle-Hawk.

HOOKED-BILLED KITE. *Chondrohierax uncinatus.*—15–17. *Male* (*gray phase*): Above dark bluish slate. Tail mainly black, narrowly white-tipped, and with two broad white or gray bars; below pale bluish slate, the breast, abdomen, and flanks sometimes barred with white, buff, or cinnamon; bill black; iris white; legs orange; (*dark phase*): Deep sooty black, glossed with purplish bronze, the hind-neck with more or less white; a single broad white tail-bar. *Female* (*brown phase*): Sides of head and forehead bluish slate, becoming sooty black on nape; a cinnamon band across hind-neck, the upperparts otherwise mainly sooty black or deep brown; tail black, narrowly tipped with pale grayish brown and with two broad bands of same; sides of neck and underparts very broadly barred with buffy white and cinnamon. *Immature:* Above sooty brown or blackish, the tail black, narrowly white-tipped, and with three to four brownish bars; a whitish or pale buff nuchal collar; sides of head and underparts white, the flanks and thighs sometimes narrowly barred with brown or dusky.

Distribution.—Pacific and Caribbean lowlands, ranging to an altitude of 3,000 feet locally (southern Sinaloa).

Races.—*C. u. uncinatus* (southern Sinaloa, Mexico, and Guerrero, chiefly below 3,000 feet altitude). *C. u. aquilonis* (lowlands of the eastern and southern portions of the country).

Remarks.—Hooked-billed Kites are remarkably variable, and individuals may have any combination of the characters mentioned. Any medium-sized, broad-winged hawk, with one or several very conspicuous tail-bands and *heavily barred* (slate or cinnamon) *underparts*, is likely to be this species. No similar hawk has a *white iris*. Humid lowland forests and marshlands.

DOUBLE-TOOTHED KITE. *Harpagus bidentatus fasciatus.*—12–14. *Male:* Sides of head and crown bluish slate, the upperparts otherwise deep sooty brown; inner webs of tail with three narrow white bars; below white, the throat with a dusky median stripe, the remainder narrowly barred with grayish brown or russet; sides of neck and adjacent barring usually reddish; bill black, the upper mandible with a double notch. *Female:* Upperparts and throat as in male, the underparts very extensively russet, more or less barred with white. *Immature:* Deep sooty brown above, the top and sides of the head narrowly streaked with white; below creamy white, the throat with a conspicuous black median stripe, the remainder with numerous pear-shaped spots.

Distribution.—Humid lowland forests of Oaxaca and Veracruz; uncommon, but to be expected elsewhere in the extreme southern portion of the country.

Remarks.—Also known as Double-toothed Hawk. A *small* forest hawk with a *narrowly barred tail* and russet, or russet-barred, underparts. No similar bird has a white throat with a *single dusky median stripe.*

*MISSISSIPPI KITE. *Ictinia misisippiensis.*—14. *Adult:* Head, hind-neck, upper back, and secondaries pale pearly gray, this darkening on the underparts; lower back, scapulars, and wing-coverts slaty black; wings long and pointed (falcon-like), the median portion of the primaries streaked or spotted with chestnut; tail square-tipped and wholly black. *Immature:* Similar to adult above, the underparts boldly brown-streaked; tail somewhat barred below.

Distribution.—Winters casually in the eastern and southern portions of the country. Not reported in the Yucatán Peninsula.

Remarks.—A dark, falcon-like hawk with a *pearl-gray head* and uniform *black tail.* A contrasting, *pale gray patch* on the hind edge of the wing usually shows in flight. This kite resembles the more abundant Plumbeous Kite superficially, but the latter—apparently a summer visitant—has two white tail-bars, considerable rufous on its primaries, and lacks a pale wing-patch.

**PLUMBEOUS KITE. *Ictinia plumbea.*—14–15. *Adult:* Head and underparts uniform bluish gray, this darkening on hind-neck and back, where passing into slaty black on the scapulars, wings, and tail; wings notably long and pointed; inner webs of the primaries (except tips) largely rufous; tail black, square-tipped, the inner webs of the lateral feathers with two conspicuous white bars; bill black; iris reddish; feet reddish orange. *Immature:* Head, hind-neck, and underparts white or buffy white, boldly streaked with black; upperparts mainly black, the back, scapulars, and wing-coverts minutely barred with white; remiges white-tipped, the primaries extensively rufous medially; tail as in adult.

Distribution.—Eastern Mexico, ranging from southern Tamaulipas and San Luis Potosí southward, including the Yucatán Peninsula. Not reported in winter.

Remarks.—Much like a Mississippi Kite, but with *two white tail-bars* (as seen from below) and a prominent rufous patch on the extended wing. Any grayish or dusky, falcon-like hawk seen in summer is likely to be this species; if in winter, it is probably the preceding.

SNAIL KITE. *Rostrhamus sociabilis major* (Illus. p. 76).—17–19. *Male:* Sooty black, the tail white-tipped and extensively white toward base; bill black, notably slender, the bare loral area and cere bright red, like the eyes

SNAIL KITE

and legs. *Female:* Deep brown, the underparts very broadly streaked with whitish, buff, or cinnamon; a conspicuous white line over each eye; a patch of white at base of tail; bill black; cere and legs bright orange.

Distribution.—Veracruz and Campeche, principally in fresh-water marshes.

Remarks.—This marsh-dweller is a geographical variety of Florida's Everglade Kite. While resembling Marsh Hawks in size, general proportions, and habit of hovering above their prey, Snail Kites nevertheless are easily distinguished by their much darker plumage and more labored flight. The *slender bill* is often conspicuous at a distance.

NORTHERN GOSHAWK. *Accipiter gentilis atricapillus.*—20–24. *Adult:* Crown and sides of head slaty black; a broad white line above eye; upperparts mainly bluish slate, the tail narrowly white-tipped, decidedly long, and slightly rounded; below whitish, minutely vermiculated with gray, the throat and breast with fine black shaft-streaks; bill bluish black, the cere yellow; iris red; legs yellow. *Immature:* Above brown, much intermixed with buff or whitish, the tail with four to five broad, pale brownish bars; below creamy white, conspicuously streaked and spotted with brown.

Distribution.—Mountains of northwestern Mexico (south to Jalisco), wintering casually to Guerrero.

Remarks.—The members of this genus have short, *rounded wings* and relatively *long tails.* They are bold hunters, dashing in flight, and notably adept in following the evasive movements of their prey. They are essentially woodland birds, this species being limited to the highlands. Goshawks can usually be distinguished from other accipitrine species by their superior size. Immature birds have plumage much like that of Sharp-shinned and Cooper Hawks, but are paler above (where usually *mottled*) and have *whitish superciliaries.* Adults are unmistakable: *bluish slate above*, pearly gray below, and with very prominent white superciliaries.

BICOLORED HAWK. *Accipiter bicolor.*—14–16. *Adult:* Crown and hind-neck black, the upperparts otherwise extensively bluish slate; wings and tail sooty brown or blackish, the latter with three or four rather obscure bars; below immaculate pearly gray or pale slate, the thighs chestnut-rufous. *Immature:* Above deep sooty brown, darkest on crown, the feathers of the back, scapulars, and wing-coverts narrowly tipped with rufous; a conspicuous buff or white nuchal collar; tail white-tipped, and with three or four white bars; underparts pale tawny, ochraceous, or buff.

Distribution.—Lowlands of eastern and southeastern Mexico.

Races.—*A. b. fidens* (southern Tamaulipas, Veracruz, and Oaxaca). *A. b. bicolor* (Yucatán and Quintana Roo).

Remarks.—A small short-winged forest hawk, either *pale gray below*, with *rufous* thighs, or *tawny below*, and with a conspicuous *nuchal collar.* Not likely to be mistaken for any other bird of its area.

COOPER HAWK. *Accipiter cooperii.*—14–18. *Adult:* Above bluish slate, darkest on crown; wings short and rounded; tail rather long, slightly rounded, and with three or four broad grayish bars; underparts essentially dull cinnamon, more or less spotted and barred with white. *Immature:* Above deep brown, the feathers of head, back, and wing-coverts edged with tawny or rufous; tail as in adult; underparts white or tinged with buff anteriorly, the whole boldly streaked with sooty brown; thighs spotted and barred with brown.

Distribution.—Breeds in Baja California and in the northwestern portion of the country east to Nuevo León; widespread elsewhere in winter.

Remarks.—A trim, medium-sized hawk with *short wings* and a *long, rounded tail.* At a distance adults appear dull rufous or pinkish below, the white spots and bars being inconspicuous. Sharp-shinned Hawks are similar, but considerably smaller (sex for sex), and have *square-tipped tails.* Both prefer wooded areas and do not so habitually soar in the open as do buteos. Their usual flight is rapid and direct, consisting of several quick wing-beats followed by a short sail.

SHARP-SHINNED HAWK. *Accipiter striatus.*—10–14. Similar to a Cooper Hawk, but much smaller, and with a *square-tipped tail.* Adult males are less bluish above, and immature birds usually have narrower and paler stripes.

Distribution.—Highlands generally, chiefly in the pine-oak belt, occurring extensively elsewhere in winter.

Races.—*A. s. striatus* (virtually country-wide in winter). *A. s. suttoni* (breeds in the pine-oak belt; extent of winter range uncertain). *A. s. madrensis* (Sierra Madre del Sur, Guerrero, and probably Oaxaca west of the Isthmus of Tehuantepec). *A. s. chionigaster* (northwestern Chiapas southward).

Remarks.—*See* Cooper Hawk.

WHITE-TAILED HAWK. *Buteo albicaudatus hypospodius.*—20–24. *Adult:* Sides of head and upperparts mainly slate gray; wings darker, decidedly long, and with an extensive rufous patch on the lesser coverts and scapulars; rump and tail white, the latter narrowly barred with dusky, and with a very conspicuous subterminal band; below immaculate white, the malar area and sides of chest slate gray. *Immature:* Mainly deep sooty brown, the median underparts (except throat) with more or less white; a patch of rufous on the lesser wing-coverts; tail whitish or mottled with gray, the subterminal bar usually lacking. Birds in more advanced plumage are similar to adults, but have slate-colored throats.

Distribution.—Mexico generally, exclusive of Baja California, occurring principally in open, grassy country, and areas of mesquite growth.

Remarks.—The *white* tail, with its *conspicuous subterminal bar,* is virtually diagnostic. Immature birds are largely blackish, but have pale tails, white blotches on the median underparts, and *dark winglinings* that contrast with the flight feathers.

*FERRUGINOUS HAWK. *Buteo regalis.*—20–24. *Adult (light phase)*: Above dark brown, more or less streaked (anteriorly) with white; wing-coverts extensively tawny or dull rufous; tail whitish, unbarred, the tips sometimes edged with cinnamon buff; below white, or narrowly barred on abdomen and sides, the thighs usually reddish and narrowly barred with darker; legs fully feathered; *(dark phase)*: Deep chocolate-brown, more or less tinged with rufous anteriorly; underside of flight feathers virtually immaculate white, the tail (below) whitish and without bars.

Distribution.—Uncommon winter visitant. Recorded from Baja California, Durango, Coahuila, Zacatecas, Guanajuato, and Hidalgo.

Remarks.—Also known as Ferruginous Rough-legged Hawk. From below birds in light plumage appear almost uniformly white. The russet thighs show as a dark **V** in adults. When in dark plumage, the conspicuously *whitish* flight feathers and very *pale, unbarred* tail are good field marks. Immature White-tailed Hawks are somewhat similar, but have *dark wing-linings* and whitish or blotched underparts. Most likely to be seen over open country.

RED-TAILED HAWK. *Buteo jamaicensis.*—18–23. *Adult:* Above dark chocolate-brown, this sometimes much intermixed with white, or mottled with rufous; tail (above) either reddish, or white-tipped .and narrowly barred with sooty; a conspicuous dusky malar streak; underparts white or whitish, the lower abdomen often with a broad band of brown streaks; thighs pinkish or barred with chestnut; underside of tail uniformly pale or obscurely barred with grayish. *Immature:* Above dark brown, generously mottled with buff or pale rufous, tail pale brownish, narrowly barred with dusky; throat and breast creamy white, boldly streaked with brown, the underparts otherwise densely spotted and barred with white and brown; tail pale below, and sometimes obscurely barred with grayish.

Distribution.—Virtually country-wide.

Races.—**B. j. borealis* (winters south at least to Michoacán and Guanajuato). *B. j. calurus* (Baja California and northwestern Mexico, occurring extensively elsewhere in winter). **B. j. kriderii* (recorded in winter from Durango and Zacatecas). *B. j. fuertesi* (Chihuahua, Coahuila, and Nuevo León; a winter record for Sonora). *B. j. fumosus* (Tres Marías Islands). *B. j. socorroensis* (Socorro Island). *B. j. cóstaricensis* (highlands generally, except where occupied by *calurus* and *fuertesi*).

Remarks.—Red-tails exemplify the more conspicuous buteonine characters, i.e., broad wings and a rounded, expansive tail of moderate length. The reddish tail (above) of adults is diagnostic. From below, the *broad band of abdominal stripes* shown by several forms is a useful field mark. Resident races of the mainland occur chiefly in the highlands. In winter Red-tails range the whole of Mexico but are uncommon in the Yucatán Peninsula and adjacent lowlands.

ZONE-TAILED HAWK. *Buteo albonotatus albonotatus.*—18–22. *Adult:* Mainly black, the tail with two conspicuous white bars and a third partly concealed by the crissum, the relative widths of the three decreasing basally; a small white area at base of upper mandible. *Immature:* Deep sooty brown, appearing black at a distance, the underparts more or less white-spotted; underside of tail mainly whitish, black-tipped, and with numerous blackish bars.

Distribution.—Baja California and locally elsewhere, breeding principally in highland pine forests. Recorded from Baja California, Sonora, Sinaloa, Coahuila, Zacatecas, Mexico, Puebla, and Veracruz.

Remarks.—Zone-tails have rather long wings and tails for buteos. Their flight silhouette is much like that of a Turkey Vulture, but they are more likely to be confused with Common and Great Black Hawks. The first has a *single*, very broad, white tail-bar. Great Black Hawks resemble Zone-tails in barring, but have *white upper tail-coverts.*

RED-SHOULDERED HAWK. *Buteo lineatus.*—18–22. *Adult:* Above dark brown, the feathers (especially anteriorly) more or less margined with buff, ochraceous, or rufous; a rufous patch on the shoulders; remiges and tail sooty brown, conspicously notched (primaries) and barred (tail) with white on the upper surface; below variable: usually pale ochraceous-buff, generously barred with pinkish cinnamon posteriorly, or irregularly streaked and spotted with brown, cinnamon, and buff; underside of tail grayish, narrowly barred with paler. *Immature:* Above brown, the crown much streaked with buff or cinnamon, the tail narrowly barred with grayish brown; below pale buffy white, boldly spotted and streaked with brown.

Distribution.—Baja California and northeastern Mexico south to the Valley of Mexico and Veracruz. Occurs elsewhere, locally, in winter.

Races.—*B. l. elegans* (northeastern Baja California, ranging south to Sinaloa in winter). **B. l. lineatus* (recorded from Nuevo León, where apparently accidental). *B. l. texanus* (northeastern portion of the country south to the Valley of Mexico and Veracruz). **B. l. alleni* (a single winter record for Jalisco).

Remarks.—Much like the Red-tail in form, but with a less expansive tail, and this *distinctly barred* above and below. The *reddish* underparts (adults) suggest Cooper and Sharp-skinned Hawks, but these have short, rounded wings and relatively long tails. A pale patch at the base of the primaries (as seen from below) is a good flight mark in any plumage.

SWAINSON HAWK. *Buteo swainsoni.*—19–21. *Adult:* Above dark brown, the primaries uniform blackish; tail narrowly barred with grayish brown; a pale patch at base of tail, this sometimes very conspicuous; below mainly white, the breast extensively brown or dull chestnut, contrasting sharply with the throat and abdomen, the latter often barred with rusty; underside of tail pale grayish, faintly barred with darker. *Immature:* Mainly deep chocolate-brown, the underparts more or less streaked and spotted with buff.

Distribution.—Breeds in Baja California, Sonora, Chihuahua, and Durango. Virtually country-wide (except Yucatán Peninsula) during migration, and occasionally recorded in winter (Nuevo León).

Remarks.—A large, sluggish hawk with rather narrow, pointed wings as compared with a Red-tail. The *pale wing-linings* usually contrast conspicuously with the *darker flight feathers.* White-bellied adults have a broad, *reddish brown band across the breast.* Look for a white patch near the base of the pale tail. Swainson Hawks prefer open country. Unlike most birds of prey, they commonly migrate in loose flocks. Not likely to be found in winter.

*BROAD-WINGED HAWK. *Buteo platypterus platypterus.*—15–17. *Adult:* Above dark brown, the nape often mottled with cinnamon; tail conspicuously barred with black and white, the bars about equal in width; throat white, streaked with dusky; sides of neck and breast reddish brown, more or less spotted with white, the abdomen and flanks white, irregularly barred with rusty. *Immature:* Similar to adult above, but tail-bars narrower and dimmer; below white, conspicuously streaked and spotted with brown.

Distribution.—Common migrant, wintering locally. Recorded only from Sinaloa, Jalisco, Colima, Guerrero, Oaxaca, Chiapas, and Veracruz.

Remarks.—A crow-sized hawk with a stocky flight silhouette like that of a Red-tail. Undersides of the wings uniformly pale, but without a contrasting light patch at the base of the primaries as in Red-shouldered Hawks. In adults the tail is *evenly barred* with black and white, an excellent corroborative character. As with Swainson Hawks, Broadwings customarily migrate in loose flocks that may number scores of individuals.

ROADSIDE HAWK. *Buteo magnirostris* (Illus. p. 82).—14–16. *Adult:* Above dull grayish brown; inner webs of remiges reddish, tipped and barred with brown; underside of wings pale buff; tail with four or five brown and pale bars of about equal width; sides of head, throat, and breast dull grayish brown, the posterior underparts whitish, narrowly barred with cinnamon, and sometimes tinged with gray; thighs buff, very narrowly barred with rufous. *Immature:* Similar to adult above, but crown and hind-neck streaked with tawny buff; below pale tawny, the throat and breast conspicuously streaked with brown, the abdomen and flanks more or less barred with tri-angular reddish brown spots.

Distribution.—Pacific and Caribbean slopes, from Colima and central Tamaulipas southward, and islands off the Yucatán Peninsula. Very common.

ROADSIDE HAWK

Races.—*B. m. xantusi* (Colima to Guerrero and Oaxaca). *B. m. griseo-couda* (Caribbean slope, from central Tamaulipas southward, exclusive of the Yucatán Peninsula). *B. m. petersi* (southeastern Oaxaca and south-western Chiapas). *B. m. conspectus* (Yucatán Peninsula). *B. m. gracilis* (Cozumel, Meco, Holbox, and Mujeres Islands). *B. m. direptor* (south-eastern Chiapas).

Remarks.—Also known as Large-billed Hawk, Tropical Broad-winged Hawk, and Insect Hawk. One of the most abundant of tropical hawks, suggesting a northern Broad-winged somewhat in size and proportions, but with brighter underparts of a different pattern. The rufous portions of the primaries and secondaries are not usually visible. Roadside Hawks prefer open country, second-growth woods, and forest edge. In Mexico they commonly perch near roads and are easily approached.

SHORT-TAILED HAWK. *Buteo brachyurus.*—15–17. *Adult (light phase)*: Sides of head and upperparts black, the forehead white near base of bill; below, including wing-linings and inner webs of the primaries (toward base), immaculate white; tail whitish below, darkening toward tip, where usually barred with dusky; *(black phase)*: Either wholly black, or deep sooty brown, the underside of the flight feathers whitish, barred with dusky. *Immature (light phase)*: Above dark brown, more or less streaked with white, the tail with several pale bands; below, including underside of wings, creamy white, the chest, abdomen, and flanks brown-spotted; *(black phase)*: Deep sooty brown, the underparts more or less streaked with white.

Distribution.—Chiefly eastern and southern Mexico, but decidedly rare and of local occurrence.

Remarks.—A small, compactly formed buteo, either immaculate white below, or almost wholly black (including the wing-linings), but with a distinctly barred tail. When in black plumage, the white patch at base of bill is a good field mark. Immature birds are extremely variable, but usually appear essentially like one or the other of the two adult phases.

GRAY HAWK. *Buteo nitidus* (Illus. p. 84).—15–17. *Adult:* Above pale grayish slate, this lightening on the throat and breast, where obscurely barred with white; tail sooty black, with three very conspicuous white bars; lower breast and posterior underparts narrowly barred with gray and white. *Immature:* Above deep sooty brown, the hind-neck, back, and wing-coverts much intermixed with cinnamon-buff; tail (above) with numerous pale brownish bars, the underside whitish barred with dusky; breast, sides, and abdomen whitish (or pale buffy), boldly spotted and streaked with sooty brown, the thighs narrowly barred with same.

Distribution.—Lowlands and foothills (locally to an altitude of about 7,500 feet), exclusive of Baja California.

Races.—*B. n. maximus* (northern portion of the country south, possibly, to Durango; doubtfully distinct from the following). *B. n. plagiatus* (coastal slopes from Nayarit, Jalisco, southern Tamaulipas, and Puebla southward, locally). *B. n. micrus* (Tabasco, Campeche, Chiapas, and the Yucatán Peninsula, where not occupied by the preceding).

Remarks.—Also known as Mexican Goshawk. At a distance, this very common lowland hawk appears almost uniformly gray, but with a *white-barred, black tail*. On closer view, one can see the evenly barred underparts. No other medium-sized species of buteonine proportions is

GRAY HAWK

barred in this manner. Chiefly open country and second-growth woods, especially where well watered.

BAY-WINGED HAWK. *Parabuteo unicinctus.*—18–22. *Adult:* Deep chocolate-brown, the shoulders and thighs rich chestnut; tail white-tipped and with an extensive white patch toward base, the two light areas separated by a broad subterminal band. *Immature:* Sides of head and upperparts deep chocolate-brown, more or less intermixed with tawny cinnamon, the shoulders extensively chestnut; underparts rich tawny or buff, very boldly streaked and spotted with brown, the thighs narrowly barred with russet; white of tail tinged with buff.

Distribution.—Widespread, but of local occurrence; found chiefly in open country, especially savannahs.

Races.—*P. u. superior* (Baja California and northwestern Mexico). *P. u. harrisi* (the Pacific slope from Nayarit to Oaxaca; northeastern Mexico south to Guanajuato and Veracruz).

Remarks.—Also known as Ring-tailed Hawk and One-banded Hawk. The eastern race is usually called Harris Hawk. A sluggish, buteo-like hawk, appearing entirely black except for the tail. This is *white, with a single broad black subterminal band.* Not to be confused with the Common Black Hawk, which has a *black tail* with a single *white bar.* The *reddish* shoulders, wing-linings, and thighs are useful field marks under favorable conditions.

WHITE HAWK. *Leucopternis albicollis ghiesbreghti* (Illus. p. 85).— 19–22. *Adult:* Immaculate white, the primaries very broadly black-tipped;

WHITE HAWK

tail with a narrow black subterminal band. *Immature:* Similar, but wings extensively black, the secondaries black with white tips, the coverts more or less streaked with black; a broad subterminal tail-band.

Distribution.—Lowland forests of southern Veracruz, Tabasco, Oaxaca, and Chiapas.

Remarks.—An "albino" Red-shouldered Hawk, or so this magnificent species might be considered at first sight. White Hawks are one of the most beautiful birds of prey, and certainly one of the most distinctive. They prefer the seclusion of humid lowland forests and are rather uncommon in Mexico.

GREAT BLACK HAWK. *Hypomorphnus urubitinga ridgwayi.*—20–24. *Adult:* Mainly black, the upper tail-coverts white, and thighs often white-barred; tail black, narrowly white-tipped, and with two conspicuous white bands—one narrow and one very broad. *Immature:* Above deep chocolate-brown, the head and hind-neck much streaked with tawny, the wings dimly barred with pale brownish; tail narrowly barred with brown and buffy white; upper tail-coverts mainly buff; below rich tawny, boldly streaked with brown, the thighs narrowly barred with same; underside of wings and tail pale buff, narrowly barred with brown.

Distribution.—Coastal lowlands from Sonora and southern Tamaulipas southward. Common.

Remarks.—Also known as Urubitinga. A very large black hawk, distinguished from all similar species by its *white rump* and *two white tail-bars*. Zone-tailed and Common Black Hawks have dark rumps, and the latter a *single* white band across the middle of the tail. Common and Great Black Hawks show a small pale area near the wing-tips. Both are decidedly sluggish and often soar at length in true buteonine fashion. They are most abundant in the hot lowlands, especially near water.

COMMON BLACK HAWK. *Buteogallus anthracinus.*—18–22. Similar to a Great Black Hawk, but adults with black upper tail-coverts and a single broad white band across the middle of the tail. Immature birds of both species are much alike, but the Great Black has a longer tail with less distinct barring.

Distribution.—Lowlands generally, except Baja California. Common.

Races.—*B. a. anthracinus* (as above, except where replaced by the following). *B. a. subtilis* (coastal Chiapas, chiefly in mangrove swamps).

Remarks.—Also known as Crab Hawk and Mexican Black Hawk *See* Zone-tailed Hawk and Great Black Hawk.

BLACK-COLLARED HAWK. *Busarellus nigricollis nigricollis* (Illus. p. 87).—18–20. *Adult:* Head and throat creamy white or pale ochraceous, the crown and nape narrowly streaked with black; a large black patch on chest, the plumage otherwise extensively bright cinnamon or rufous; primaries black, the secondaries broadly tipped with same; tail rather short, reddish basally, the terminal half black. *Immature:* Mainly deep chocolate-brown, the head and median underparts with more or less buffy white; lesser wing-coverts and remiges (basally) russet, the underside of the wings extensively tawny, narrowly barred with black; thighs chestnut.

Distribution.—Recorded from Sinaloa, Guerrero, Chiapas, Veracruz, Tabasco, and Campeche.

Remarks.—Also known as Fishing Hawk. A *reddish hawk with a pale head* and black chest-patch. The black-tipped wings are very broad, and the black tail rather short. Adults are unmistakable. Immature

BLACK-COLLARED HAWK

birds are virtually so, being quite unlike any other hawk of their area. Restricted to the hot lowlands, where usually found near marshes and placid rivers.

SOLITARY EAGLE. *Urubitornis solitaria.*—26–28. *Adult:* Mainly slate-colored, darkest on head and neck; a short nuchal crest; upper tail-coverts narrowly white-tipped and usually mottled with gray; wings notably broad; tail rather short, narrowly white-tipped, and with a broad white or grayish median bar. *Immature:* Deep chocolate-brown, the forehead, superciliaries, and median underparts pale buff; primaries black, the inner webs tawny basally; inner webs of outer rectrices (above) tawny, flecked with dusky, the underside pale basally, darkening terminally.

Distribution.—Northwestern and southern Mexico, locally. Very rare.

Races.—*U. s. sheffleri* (mountains of extreme southeastern Sonora, near the Chihuahua boundary). *U. s. solitaria* (recorded only from Los Hesos, Jalisco, and Tehuantepec, Oaxaca).

Remarks.—A blackish eagle-sized hawk with a very broad median tail-bar. Great Black Hawks are much smaller and have *two* conspicuous white tail-bars. *See* Golden Eagle, Bald Eagle, and Turkey Vulture.

HARPY EAGLE. *Harpia harpyja.*—34–36. *Adult:* Head pale gray, the long occipital feathers forming a prominent erectile crest and ruff; upperparts mainly black, the tail white-tipped and with several broad gray bars; chest black, the underparts otherwise mainly white; thighs narrowly barred with black; cere and bill bluish black; legs and claws notably thick and powerful. *Immature:* Crown pale gray, the occipital crest blackish tipped with white; back, wings, etc., pale gray, more or less mottled with black, the tail with a black subterminal bar; sides of head and underparts mainly white.

Distribution.—Heavy lowland forests of southern Mexico. Reported only from Oaxaca, Chiapas, Veracruz, Tabasco, and Campeche, the last a sight record 50 miles east of the city.

Remarks.—Harpy Eagles frequent dense tropical forests and are uncommon in Mexico. Powerful birds, as may be judged by the remarkable development of their legs and claws, they apparently prey almost entirely on large birds and medium-sized forest mammals.

BLACK-AND-WHITE EAGLE-HAWK. *Spizastur melanoleucus.*—22–24. *Adult:* Head, neck, and underparts (including the wing-linings) mainly white, the lores, orbital area, and patch on back of crown black; back and scapulars black, the wings deep sooty brown; tail evenly barred with black and pale grayish brown; legs fully feathered; cere and basal half of bill reddish orange, the tip black; iris yellow. *Immature:* Similar to adult, but black areas largely replaced by brown; wing-coverts white-tipped.

Distribution.—Heavy lowland forests of Oaxaca, Chiapas, Veracruz, and Yucatán.

Remarks.—A large forest hawk with *gleaming white head, neck, and underparts.* Immature birds resemble immature Gray-headed Kites superficially, but are much larger. Both have a conspicuous dark patch behind the crown, as in adult Eagle-Hawks. *See* Ornate Eagle-Hawk.

ORNATE EAGLE-HAWK. *Spizaëtus ornatus vicarius* (Illus. p. 89).—23–25. *Adult:* Above mainly black or deep brown, the rump narrowly barred with white; a conspicuous black occipital crest; tail rather long, evenly barred with black and pale grayish brown, the underside with four or five prominent blackish and pale bars; auriculars, hind-neck, and sides of breast tawny rufous; throat and median breast immaculate white, the first bordered with a broad black stripe; flanks, abdomen, and legs boldly barred with black and white, the tarsi fully feathered; bill black; iris orange-yellow. *Immature:* Head, neck, and underparts mainly white, the sides, flanks, and legs barred with black; occipital crest and upperparts generally dark brown, the tail with several black bars separated by broad pale bands.

ORNATE EAGLE-HAWK

Distribution.—Humid lowland forests (occasionally to an altitude of about 5,000 feet) of Tamaulipas, Veracruz, Yucatán, Oaxaca, and Chiapas.

Remarks.—Also known as Crested Eagle-Hawk. Eagle-Hawks have rather broad wings, long rounded tails, and feathered tarsi. Retiring in habits, they frequent heavy forests, chiefly in the lowlands, and are not likely to be seen soaring in the open. This form, the most colorful of the three Mexican species, is unmistakable when in adult plumage. Immature birds resemble immature Black-and-White Eagle-Hawks, but have *barred* flanks and legs and a much more conspicuous occipital crest.

BLACK EAGLE-HAWK. *Spizaëtus tyrannus serus.*—25–28. *Adult:* Mainly black, the basal portions of the long occipital feathers white and often conspicuous; tail long, somewhat rounded, and with four or five black and grayish brown bars of equal width; thighs and crissum narrowly barred with white, the abdomen sometimes white-spotted; legs fully feathered; bill black; iris orange-yellow. *Immature:* Mainly sooty brown, the forehead, superciliary area, throat, and breast creamy white, the last usually black-streaked; auriculars and sides of throat black; legs, crissum, and tail white-barred, as in adult.

Distribution.—Heavily forested lowlands and foothills of southeastern and southern Mexico. Reported in San Luis Potosí, Puebla, Veracruz, Campeche, Yucatán, Oaxaca, and Chiapas.

Remarks.—Also known as Tyrant Eagle-Hawk. *See* Ornate Eagle-Hawk.

GOLDEN EAGLE. *Aquila chrysaëtos canadensis.*—30–35. *Adult:* Deep chocolate-brown, the nape and hind-neck often tawny or golden brown; tail grayish basally, the terminal portion sooty brown; legs feathered to feet. *Immature:* Similar, but basal portion of tail largely white, and with a pale area at the base of the primaries as seen from below.

Distribution.—Mountainous areas, including Baja California, south to Durango, Guanajuato, Hidalgo, and Nuevo León.

Remarks.—In flight, at a distance, a Golden Eagle might conceivably be mistaken for a Turkey Vulture. The latter, however, has narrower wings and a much less ample tail, with no suggestion of paleness at its base. A vulture's head is inconspicuous at a distance, and, when soaring, its wings are held somewhat above the horizontal. *See* Solitary Eagle and Bald Eagle.

BALD EAGLE. *Haliaeetus leucocephalus leucocephalus.*—30–34. *Adult:* Head and tail creamy white, the plumage otherwise deep chocolate-brown. *Immature:* Deep chocolate-brown, appearing black at a distance.

Distribution.—Coasts of Baja California, where of local occurrence and rather uncommon

Remarks.—Adults are unmistakable at any distance. Immature birds are wholly dusky, resembling a Golden Eagle superficially, but lacking its two-toned tail and pale patch at the base of the primaries. Turkey Vultures have relatively inconspicuous heads and much less ample tails. In flight, Bald Eagles usually soar less continuously than either the vulture or the Golden Eagle.

MARSH HAWK. *Circus cyaneus hudsonius.*—18–20. *Male:* Sides of head and upperparts pale gray, the remiges broadly tipped with dusky; a conspicuous white patch on the rump; throat and chest pale gray, the underparts otherwise white, lightly spotted, and barred with rufous. *Female:* Sides of head and upperparts dark brown, more or less intermixed with cinnamon anteriorly; a conspicuous white patch on the rump; below tawny cinnamon, the throat and breast narrowly streaked with brown. *Immature:* Similar to female above, the underparts paler, nearer buffy white, and boldly streaked with brown.

Distribution.—Resident in northern Baja California and perhaps elsewhere; virtually country-wide in winter and migration.

Remarks.—Also known as Common Harrier. The common hawk of meadows, savannahs, and grassy marshes. Marsh Hawks customarily fly within a few feet of the ground, alternately sailing and flapping with graceful ease, and usually can be distinguished by their slender structure and the white rump-patch. White-tailed and Snail Kites frequent the same habitat, but the first has *black shoulders* and a *white tail*, while Snail Kites (males) are much darker and have a more labored flight. The white rump-patch is a good field mark in any plumage.

BLACKISH CRANE-HAWK. *Geranospiza nigra.*—18–20. *Adult:* Dull slaty black, the tail with two evenly spaced white bars; bill black; iris crimson; legs orange. *Immature:* Similar to adult, but forehead, superciliaries, and throat whitish, the sides of the head and hind-crown white-streaked; tail barred as in adults, but white toward base; abdomen, flanks, and thighs more or less barred with buff.

Distribution.—The Pacific and Caribbean slopes, chiefly in lowland forests.

Races.—*G. n. livens* (recodred only from Alamos and Guirocoba, Sonora). *G. n. nigra* (Sinaloa, Nayarit, Colima, Oaxaca, Chiapas, Tamaulipas, Veracruz, Puebla, and Yucatán).

Remarks.—Also known as Frog Hawk. A rather large, long-legged black hawk with *two very broad, evenly spaced white tail-bars.* No similar species has red eyes and bright orange legs. Great Black Hawks are much sturdier, and have *two* white tail-bars—one narrow and one very broad. Heavily wooded lowlands, usually near water.

Family PANDIONIDAE. Ospreys

OSPREY. *Pandion haliaëtus.*—20–24. *Adult:* Above deep sooty brown, the head extensively white, the crown and hind-neck with more or less blackish; a conspicuous dusky postocular stripe; underparts white, the chest usually somewhat spotted with pale rufous; underside of tail with five to seven dusky bars. *Immature:* Similar to adult, but feathers of the upper parts narrowly edged with white, and chest more boldly spotted.

Distribution.—Resident in the Tres Marías Islands, Baja California, and south on the Pacific Coast at least to Sinaloa; also resident on the coast of Yucatán and Quintana Roo. Winters extensively on both coasts.

Races.—*P. h. carolinensis* (as above, except Yucatán and Quintana Roo, where found only in winter and as a common migrant). *P. h. ridgwayi* (coasts of Yucatán and Quintana Roo).

Remarks.—The only *large* coastal raptor with *gleaming white underparts.* Ospreys have very long, narrow wings as compared with those of eagles and other hawks of similar size. When in flight, a dark area usually shows on the underside of the wing near the bend.

Family FALCONIDAE. Falcons, Caracaras

LAUGHING FALCON. *Herpetotheres cachinnans chapmani* (Illus. p. 92).—18–22. Crown, hind-neck, and underparts pale buff or creamy white,

LAUGHING FALCON

the first with black shaft-streaks; sides of head mainly black, this continuing behind the nape as a conspicuous band; back, scapulars, and wings deep chocolate-brown, the inner webs of the remiges extensively buff; tail rounded and very conspicuously barred with black and white.

Distribution.—Wooded portions of the Pacific and Caribbean coastal lowlands, exclusive of Baja California; locally in the interior.

Remarks.—Also known as Laughing Hawk. The only white-headed hawk with a very conspicuous *black mask* and *pale nuchal collar*. Laughing Falcons prefer heavily forested areas but also occur in second growth and about clearings. They are generally phlegmatic and seldom soar in the open. The English name is derived from the characteristic call, a series of loud, varied notes most often heard at dawn or late in the afternoon, and sometimes delivered as a rather musical medley by two birds.

COLLARED FOREST-FALCON. *Micrastur semitorquatus naso.*—20–24. *Adult:* Above sooty black, the hind-neck with a white collar joining the white of the throat; a white wedge extending through the auriculars from below; tail rather long and fanlike, white-tipped, and with several white bars; below immaculate white, the underside of the remiges more or less barred. There are two other phases, i.e., a *tawny phase*, in which the collar and underparts are buff, and a *dark phase*, in which the underparts are concolor with the back, the abdomen sometimes barred with white. *Immature:* Similar to adult above, the underparts pale buffy white, very boldly barred with deep sooty brown.

Distribution.—Wooded portions of the Pacific and Caribbean coastal slopes from Sinaloa, San Luis Potosí, and central Tamaulipas southward, including the Yucatán Peninsula. Rather rare.

Remarks.—Also known as Pied Forest Hawk. A large, slender hawk of lowland forests and thickets. The *pale nuchal collar* and *long, rounded tail* are good field characters. Forest-Falcons seldom leave dense cover. They often pounce on their prey from a perch, but are capable of speedy, darting flight when in pursuit.

BARRED FOREST-FALCON. *Micrastur ruficollis guerilla* (Illus. p. 94).—13–14. *Adult:* Above slaty brown, the tail long and rounded, and with three or four very narrow white bars; sides of head and throat pale sooty gray, the underparts otherwise whitish, very narrowly and evenly barred with slaty black. *Immature:* Similar to adult above, but browner and with a narrow buffy white nuchal collar; throat whitish, the underparts otherwise tawny buff, narrowly barred with brown, especially on the breast.

Distribution.—Tropical forests of Puebla, Veracruz, Campeche, Yucatán, Oaxaca, and Chiapas.

Remarks.—Also known as Small Forest Hawk. The only small blackish hawk with *finely barred underparts*. If *buffy* below, look for a

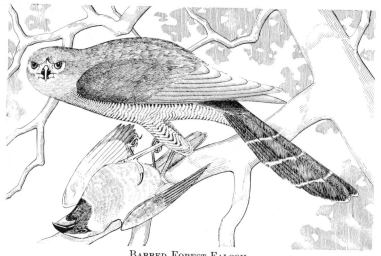

BARRED FOREST-FALCON

distinct nuchal collar. The long rounded tail is also a good character. Dense lowland forests and thickets. Rather uncommon.

RED-THROATED CARACARA. *Daptrius americanus guatemalensis.*—20–22. Mainly black, the abdomen, crissum, and thighs immaculate white; bare skin of throat and face deep vermilion; iris deep red; legs vermilion.

Distribution.—Humid lowland forests of Chiapas (Mapastepec and Esperanza).

Remarks.—Also known as Carrion Falcon. A glossy black hawk with a *bare red throat* and *gleaming white belly*. Dense tropical forests, where usually found in pairs or in small flocks, rarely singly. The call is loud and disagreeable and has been likened to the word *cacao*, with the first syllable repeated several times.

CRESTED CARACARA. *Caracara cheriway* (Illus. p. 95).—20–24. *Adult:* Crown, occipital crest, and upperparts generally, deep brownish black, the hind-neck creamy white, barred with black; a pale band across the primaries; tail creamy white basally, where narrowly barred with dusky, the terminal portion black; throat, sides of neck, and breast creamy white, the last narrowly barred; abdomen, sides, flanks, and thighs black; crissum creamy white; bare portion of face bright orange. *Immature:* Essentially like adult, but with deep chocolate-brown replacing the black plumage; hind-neck, breast, and abdomen streaked with creamy white.

Distribution.—Tres Marías Islands, Baja California, and lowlands generally, chiefly in dry open country; locally in humid forests.

Races.—*C. c. audubonii* (as above, except the Tres Marías Islands). *C. c. pallidus* (Tres Marías Islands).

CRESTED CARACARA

Remarks.—Also known as Mexican Buzzard. Caracaras are capable of powerful flight and sometimes soar in the manner of vultures. This species, an inveterate scavenger, is often found in the vicinity of carrion. Its *black crest*, long pale neck, and long legs are prominent when standing. In flight the *contrasting* white throat and breast, black belly, and white-and-black tail are distinctive. No other bird of prey has very conspicuous *pale patches* on the wing-tips.

GUADALUPE CARACARA. *Caracara lutosus.*

Remarks.—Extinct. Formerly resident on Guadalupe Island, off the west coast of Baja California. ENDEMIC.

PRAIRIE FALCON. *Falco mexicanus.*—16–18. Forehead and super-ciliary stripe whitish; upperparts grayish brown, the feathers of the crown with dark shaft-streaks, the remainder margined with tawny; a conspicu-ous brown postocular and malar streak; primaries long and pointed, the inner webs deeply notched with buffy white; tail rather long, grayish brown, the inner webs of the outer rectrices dimly notched with pale buff; throat white, the underparts otherwise pale buffy white, boldly streaked with sooty brown.

Distribution.—Resident (locally) in Baja California. Winters from northern Mexico south to Zacatecas, Hidalgo, and Oaxaca.

Remarks.—The *long, pointed wings* and relatively long, *narrow tail* identify this bird as one of the seven "true" falcons known to Mexico. While differing considerably in size and color, all have similar propor-tions and rapid flight characterized by *deep, decisive* wing-strokes. Prairie Falcons resemble Peregrine Falcons, but are much paler above and show a dark patch at the base of the wings (underside) when in flight. They inhabit deserts and mountainous wastelands but may be found elsewhere in winter.

PEREGRINE FALCON. *Falco peregrinus.*—15–20. *Adult:* Above bluish slate, darkening to sooty black on the head and primaries; a very conspicu-ous mystacial stripe; wings long and pointed; tail narrow and dimly barred; below creamy white, often tinged with pinkish on the breast, the lower breast, abdomen, flanks, and thighs narrowly barred with black. *Immature:* Above deep chocolate-brown, the crown more or less intermixed with buff, the feathers elsewhere narrowly margined with buff or pale rufous; a black postocular and mystacial stripe; underparts rich buff, often pinkish on the breast, the whole boldly streaked with sooty brown.

Distribution.—Resident in northern Baja California and on islands off the coast of Sonora; migrates and winters on both coasts, ranging inland casually.

Races.—*F. p. anatum* (as above). **F. p. pealei* (a single winter record for northern Baja California).

Remarks.—Also known as Duck Hawk. Adult Peregrines resemble Prairie Falcons but are *slaty black* (not brown) above and have narrowly *barred* (not streaked) *underparts*. They lack pale superciliaries. Imma-ture birds are less distinctive, although notably darker (brown) above than Prairie Falcons. The latter is essentially a bird of the dry interior, while Peregrines are more likely to be found in coastlands.

ORANGE-BREASTED FALCON. *Falco deiroleucus.*—13–15. *Adult:* Sides of head and upperparts black, the feathers of the back, wing-coverts, rump, and upper tail-coverts edged with bluish slate; tail mainly black, narrowly white-tipped, and with several narrow white bars; throat white, or faintly tinged with buff; breast, lower abdomen, and thighs chestnut; a broad black band across the median underparts, this conspicuously barred with buff. *Immature:* Similar to adult in pattern, but paler, the black areas replaced by deep sooty brown, and the chestnut by pale buff; thighs barred with black.

Distribution.—A single record for Veracruz (Tecolutla). Probably of casual occurrence elsewhere in southern Mexico.

Remarks.—Also known as Temminck Falcon. Much like a Bat Falcon, but notably larger and more prominently barred on the tail and underparts. The *reddish breast and black belly* in combination are diagnostic.

BAT FALCON. *Falco albigularis* (Illus. p. 97).—$9\frac{1}{2}$–$11\frac{1}{2}$. *Adult:* Sides of head, crown, and hind-neck black, this becoming bluish slate posteriorly;

Bat Falcon

primaries and tail black, the latter very narrowly barred with bluish slate (above) and white (below); median throat, sides of neck, and chest buffy white, tinged with tawny laterally; breast, upper abdomen, and sides sooty black, very narrowly barred with white; lower abdomen, crissum, and thighs chestnut. *Immature:* Similar to adult, but less slaty above, and duller below, the breast and upper abdomen sooty brown.

Distribution.—The Pacific and Caribbean slopes, south through southern Mexico, including the Yucatán Peninsula.

Races.—*F. a. petrophilus* (arid foothills of extreme southeastern Sonora to Sinaloa; doubtfully distinct). *F. a. albigularis* (as above, except where occupied by *petrophilus*).

Remarks.—Also known as White-throated Falcon. A very small, sturdy falcon, *mainly black below*, but with a *whitish* throat and chest and rich chestnut belly. Orange-breasted Falcons are much larger, and will be known by their reddish chests, tawny bellies, and more prominent tail-barring.

APLOMADO FALCON. *Falco femoralis septentrionalis* (Illus. p. 98).— 15–17. Above pale bluish slate, darkest on head, the crown bordered by a conspicuous buff or tawny stripe originating above the eye; a black postoc-

APLOMADO FALCON

ular and malar stripe; primaries long and pointed, mainly dusky, the inner webs deeply notched with white; tail blackish, white-tipped, and with six or seven conspicuous white bars; throat and breast pale buffy white, the posterior edge forming a deep semicircle; sides, flanks, and band across abdomen dull black, the feathers narrowly white-tipped; lower abdomen, thighs, and crissum tawny buff or ochraceous.

Distribution.—Both coastal slopes from Sinaloa, Chihuahua, and Tamaulipas southward. Casual elsewhere, especially in arid regions.

Remarks.—A pale, medium-sized falcon with a *whitish breast, black sides,* and *narrow* black abdominal band. At close range the pale superciliaries and rusty nuchal collar serve to eliminate all similar raptors. *See* Bat Falcon.

*PIGEON HAWK. *Falco columbarius.*—11–12½. *Male:* Above bluish gray or bluish slate, the feathers with black shaft-streaks; sides of head pale, more or less streaked with darker; primaries long and pointed, the inner webs deeply notched with white; tail white-tipped, and with a broad subterminal and several lesser black bars; below whitish, generously streaked with brown or rusty, the whole sometimes tinged with buff. *Female* and *immature:* Similar to male, but brown or sooty above, and with the underparts less heavily streaked.

Distribution.—Winter visitor and common migrant, chiefly in the coastal plains, but occurring elsewhere casually.

Races.—*F. c. columbarius* (chiefly coastal, including the Tres Marías and Cozumel Islands; casual elsewhere). *F. c. bendirei* (virtually countrywide, including Baja California and the Yucatán Peninsula). *F. c. richardsonii* (recorded from Sonora, Tamaulipas, and Zacatecas).

Remarks.—A small falcon, about the size of a Sparrow Hawk, but with uniformly dark upperparts and prominent ventral stripes. Cooper and Sharp-shinned Hawks are also bluish slate above (adult) or striped below (immature), but are distinguished by their short, *rounded wings* and *long tails.*

SPARROW HAWK. *Falco sparverius.*—10½. *Male:* Crown, wingcoverts, and secondaries bluish gray, the first with a chestnut median patch; primaries long and pointed, mainly black, the inner webs deeply notched with white; hind-neck, back, scapulars, rump, and tail rufous, the last white-tipped and with a broad, black subterminal band; a few black bars on back and scapulars; throat and sides of head whitish, the latter with two vertical black stripes; breast tawny rufous, shading to pale buffy white on abdomen and flanks, where sparsely spotted with black. *Female:* Above dull rufous, evenly barred with dusky, the crown very narrowly streaked with same; sides of head with two vertical stripes as in male; below pale buffy white, broadly streaked with rusty.

Distribution.—Resident in Baja California and the western portion of the country south to Guerrero; virtually country-wide in winter.

Races.—*F. s. sparverius* (as above except where occupied by the following). *F. s. peninsularis* (Baja California north to latitude 28°, and the lowlands of Sonora and Sinaloa). *F. s. tropicalis* (the Grand Valley of Chiapas southward).

Remarks.—The only *small* hawk with a *reddish back and tail.* Sparrow Hawks prefer fairly open country and prey chiefly on insects and small rodents. They fly with rapid wing-beats, seldom soaring, but, when hunting, customarily hover briefly above their prey. This characteristic shared by no other small hawk.

Family CRACIDAE. Curassows, Guans, Chachalacas

KEY TO THE SPECIES

1*a*. Larger (30–38 inches). Turkey-like; white-streaked below; conspicuously crested, or with a bare red "horn"   2

  b. Smaller (20–25 inches). Pheasant-like; brownish olive above, mainly black, or generously barred with black and cinnamon-rufous . . .   4

2*a*. Throat bare; underparts boldly streaked with white
                                                    Crested Guan, p. 101

  b. Throat mainly or entirely feathered; underparts not white-streaked   3

3*a*. With a very prominent crest; plumage mainly black (male) or cinnamon-rufous (female) . . . . . .   Great Curassow, p. 100

  b. Not crested; crown with bare spikelike red horn; a broad white tail-bar . . . .   Horned Guan, p. 104

4*a*. Upperparts brownish olive; median line of throat feathered . . .   5

  b. Mainly black, or generously barred with black and cinnamon-rufous . . . .   Black Chachalaca, p. 103

5*a*. Abdomen and tail-tips chestnut . Rufous-bellied Chachalaca, p. 102

  b. Abdomen and tail-tips whitish or pale brownish
                                                    Plain Chachalaca, p. 102

GREAT CURASSOW. *Crax rubra* (Illus. p. 101).—30–38. *Male:* Mainly black, the head very conspicuously crested; abdomen and crissum white; bill dusky, the base of the upper mandible with a prominent yellow nob. *Female:* Considerably smaller than male and without nob at base of bill; head and neck black, thickly spotted with white, the crest boldly barred with same; upperparts otherwise mainly cinnamon-rufous or chestnut (often blackish anteriorly), the remiges and tail usually finely mottled with black; chest dusky chestnut shading to cinnamon on breast and sides; abdomen and crissum buffy.

Distribution.—Tropical forests of eastern and southern Mexico.

Races.—*C. r. rubra* (San Luis Potosí and southern Tamaulipas southward, except Cozumel Island). *C. r. griscomi* (Cozumel Island).

Remarks.—A large, black or cinnamon-rufous, *turkey-like bird with a very conspicuous crest.* Curassows inhabit heavily forested areas and usually are found singly or in pairs; less commonly in small flocks. While mainly terrestrial, they roost in trees and often feed on berries and fruit

GREAT CURASSOW

among the lower branches. The call is a low, soft "grunt," repeated at intervals.

CRESTED GUAN. *Penelope purpurascens purpurascens.*—34–36. Area about eye and entire throat bare, the former blue, the latter mainly reddish orange; plumage mainly brownish olive or glossy bronze-green, the mantle, wing-coverts, and breast more or less boldly white-streaked; abdomen and flanks brownish.

Distribution.—Tropical forests of both coastal slopes from Sinaloa and southern Tamaulipas southward.

Remarks.—A common resident of dense lowland forests. Guans and Curassows are much hunted for food, but where not frequently disturbed they are fairly tame. Guans are more arboreal than Curassows, and rather gregarious. When certain trees are in fruit, a number of guans sometimes congregate to feed, and at that time may easily be approached.

RUFOUS-BELLIED CHACHALACA. *Ortalis wagleri.*—25.

Area around eye and throat (except median line) bare, the former red and blue, the latter reddish; upperparts, fore-neck, and chest mainly brownish olive, the head and upper neck grayish; lower breast and abdomen rich chestnut; tail large, fanlike, greenish bronze broadly tipped with chestnut.

Distribution.—Wooded areas and dense chaparral of western Mexico from southern Sonora and Chihuahua south to Jalisco. ENDEMIC.

Races.—*O. w. griseiceps* (southern Sonora, southern Chihuahua, and northern Sinaloa; doubtfully distinct from the following form). *O. w. wagleri* (central Sinaloa and western Durango south, locally, to Jalisco).

Remarks.—Also known as Wagler Chachalaca. Chachalacas are rather drab, pheasant-like birds, with large fan-shaped tails and bare throats feathered along the median line. This species usually frequents lowland thickets, especially where swampy, but also occurs in the wooded mountains of western Durango to an altitude of about 5,500 feet. *See* Plain Chachalaca.

PLAIN CHACHALACA. *Ortalis vetula* (Illus. p. 103).—20–25.

Area around eye and throat (except median line) bare, blue, and reddish, respectively; head and upper neck grayish; plumage otherwise mainly brownish olive, the lower breast and posterior underparts either dingy white or uniform pale buffy brown; tail large and rounded, greenish bronze broadly tipped with whitish or buff.

Distribution.—Wooded lowlands of eastern and southern Mexico and the Pacific slope from Colima (probably Jalisco) southward.

Races.—*O. v. mccalli* (southeastern San Luis Potosí, Nuevo León, Tamaulipas, and northern Veracruz). *O. v. poliocephala* (southern and western Mexico to an altitude of about 4,000 feet). *O. v. vetula* (Veracruz, Puebla, Tabasco, southern Campeche, eastern Oaxaca, and northwestern Chiapas). *O. v. intermedia* (Campeche and Quintana Roo; doubtfully distinct from the following form). *O. v. pallidiventris* (drier parts of the Yucatán Peninsula, including offshore islands; northern and eastern Campeche). *O. v. leucogastra* (southeastern Chiapas). *O. v. vallicola* (interior valleys of Chiapas).

Remarks.—Also known as Common Chachalaca. A gregarious, thicket-dwelling bird, much given to clamorous vocalization, especially at dawn and during the late afternoon. Its call, somewhat suggestive of the vernacular name, is repeated with resounding emphasis, often by several birds in unison. Abundant locally. *See* Rufous-bellied Chachalaca.

PLAIN CHACHALACA

BLACK CHACHALACA. *Penelopina nigra nigra.*—23–25. *Male:* Orbital area and throat bare, the first bluish, the throat red like bill and legs; plumage mainly black, the lower breast and posterior underparts sometimes brownish. *Female:* Above and below cinnamon or cinnamon-rufous, liberally barred with black.

Distribution.—Humid mountain forests of Chiapas.

HORNED GUAN. *Oreophasis derbianus* (Illus. p. 104).—35. Crown with a round (featherless), vermilion-colored "spike" or casque; plumage mainly black, the anterior parts strongly glossed with greenish; below (including underside of neck) mainly white, minutely streaked with black, the lower abdomen, flanks, and thighs dusky brownish; tail large, fanlike, mainly black, but with a broad white band across the median portion; bill bright yellow; iris white.

HORNED GUAN

Distribution.—Humid mountain forests of Chiapas (Volcán de Tacaná and near Pinabete).

Remarks.—Also known as Derby Mountain Guan. A magnificent black-and-white, turkey-like bird, with a conspicuous *vermilion "horn" and white-barred tail*. As with the Great Curassow of lowland forests, this guan is mainly terrestrial, but roosts and often feeds in trees. It is moderately gregarious except when breeding, and not especially wary unless frequently disturbed.

Family PHASIANIDAE. Quails, Partridges

   b. Below mainly grayish and olive-brown (posteriorly), the breast
     and sides streaked with chestnut
                       Long-tailed Wood-Partridge (male), p. 107

10*a.* Throat and area below eye deep chestnut or bright tawny cinnamon 11
   b. Throat, etc., not chestnut or cinnamon 12

11*a.* Throat and flanks chestnut, the latter broadly white-barred; crown,
     mantle, and breast bluish slate (Baja California)
                          Mountain Quail, p. 108
   b. Sides of head and throat tawny cinnamon, the plumage otherwise
     essentially olive-brown; breast and sides with pale shaft-streaks
                       Singing Quail (male), p. 114

12*a.* Throat buff or pale yellowish buff; breast liberally scalloped, or un-
     derparts with irregular brown barring 13
   b. Throat white (or whitish), or conspicuously speckled with black
     and white 14

13*a.* A tufted crest; superciliaries not distinct; hind-neck and breast
     scalelike, the feathers gray, narrowly edged with black
                         Scaled Quail, p. 108
   b. Not crested; superciliaries conspicuous (tawny buff); above
     mottled and spotted; underparts whitish, irregularly barred with
     brown . . . . Common Bobwhite (female), p. 112
               Black-throated Bobwhite (female), p. 113

14*a.* Throat white (or essentially white), sometimes tinged with vio-
     laceous, or very lightly streaked with dusky 15
   b. Throat conspicuously speckled with black and white; a tawny or
     dusky crest; underparts extensively white-spotted, the wings of
     the male with considerable chestnut . . . . Elegant Quail, p. 111

15*a.* Crested; above mainly grayish (unpatterned), or breast, sides, and
     flanks evenly barred with black and white 16
   b. Not crested; not grayish above; if barred below, the throat im-
     maculate white and with a conspicuous black border 18

16*a.* Brownish above, the breast, sides, and flanks prominently barred
     (southern highlands) . . . . Banded Quail, p. 112
   b. Grayish above and on breast; abdomen scalloped or extensively
     whitish 17

17*a.* Sides and flanks grayish brown, streaked with white; abdomen con-
     spicuously scalloped (Los Coronados Islands and Baja California)
                    California Quail (female), p. 109
   b. Sides and flanks chestnut, streaked with white; abdomen whitish
                    Desert Quail (female), p. 110

18a. More than 12 inches; forehead and superciliaries white; hind-neck and breast gray, broadly streaked with chestnut (mountain forests of Chiapas) . . . . Buffy-crowned Wood-Partridge, p. 108

  b. Less than 10 inches; hind-neck and breast not as in 18a. 19

19a. Throat bordered with black, this sometimes extending over the breast; underparts liberally barred or mainly cinnamon
                    Common Bobwhite (males of several races), p. 112

  b. Throat not black-bordered; underparts mainly olive-brown or pinkish cinnamon 20

20a. Above buff-streaked; below pinkish cinnamon, the throat usually not immaculate white . . . . . Harlequin Quail (female), p. 115
                    Ocellated Quail (female), p. 116

  b. Above olive-brown, blotched with black; breast, sides, and flanks tawny cinnamon-brown, the abdomen rich buff or buffy white
                    Singing Quail (female), p. 114

BEARDED WOOD-PARTRIDGE. *Dendrortyx barbatus.*—10–11½. Forehead, crown, and auriculars buffy brown, darkest posteriorly; hind-neck and upper back chestnut, broadly streaked with gray; lower back, scapulars, rump, and upper tail-coverts olive-brown, barred, mottled, and blotched with black and buff; wings and tail essentially dusky russet, vermiculated and obscurely barred with black; sides of neck gray and chestnut, the malar area, throat, and chest plain gray; breast and upper abdomen bright cinnamon, shading to cinnamon-buff posteriorly; sides, flanks, and lower abdomen olive-brown, faintly barred with buff; bare area around eye, bill, and legs red.

Distribution.—Humid mountain forests of Veracruz (Jalapa, Orizaba, Jico). ENDEMIC.

Remarks.—Rare and little known, this large partridge inhabits heavily forested mountains and is not likely to be mistaken for any other bird of its area. *See* Long-tailed Wood-Partridge.

LONG-TAILED WOOD-PARTRIDGE. *Dendrortyx macroura.*—9½– 10½. Head (and throat) essentially black or blackish, the superciliary and malar stripes sometimes white, heavily suffused with brownish; occipital crest with more or less russet; sides of neck, hind-neck, and upper back russet or chestnut, the feathers broadly edged with gray; scapulars and folded wing olive-brown, mottled and spotted with tawny buff and black; chest, breast, and sides pale gray, sometimes conspicuously spotted or streaked with russet, the flanks and posterior underparts essentially olive-brown; iris, bare skin around eye, bill, and legs bright red.

Distribution.—Highland forests, from Jalisco, the state of Mexico, and Veracruz south to Guerrero and eastern Oaxaca. ENDEMIC.

Races.—*D. m. macroura* (mountains above the Valley of Mexico, and highlands of Veracruz). *D. m. griseipectus* (oak forests of the Pacific slope of the Cordillera, in Mexico, Distrito Federal, and Morelos). *D. m. diversus* (highland forests of northwestern Jalisco). *D. m. striatus* (highland forests of southern Jalisco and Michoacán, and above 8,000 feet in the Cordillera of Guerrero). *D. m. oaxacae* (mountain forests of eastern Oaxaca, from Cerro San Felipe to Mount Zempoaltepec).

Remarks.—A *black-throated*, rather dingy-plumaged, highland wood-partridge with a *bright red bill*. The Bearded Wood-Partridge, a much rarer bird, also has a red bill and very similar upperparts, but is readily distinguished by its *gray* throat and *cinnamon* breast.

BUFFY-CROWNED WOOD-PARTRIDGE. *Dendrortyx leucophrys leucophrys.*—12–13. Forepart of crown and superciliaries creamy white or pale buff; remainder of crown and hind-neck dull chestnut, the latter white-streaked; upper back bright russet, the feathers broadly edged with gray; upperparts otherwise essentially olive-brown, more or less vermiculated with black and buff, the folded wing extensively cinnamon; throat white; sides of head dull slate, this becoming paler on the sides of the neck and breast, where broadly streaked with russet; belly olive-brown, the sides and flanks streaked with russet; bill black above, orange below; bare skin around eye, and legs orange-red.

Distribution.—Wooded highlands of Chiapas (Sierra Madre de Chiapas).

Remarks.—Also known as Highland Partridge. Largest of the Mexican partridges, and the only forest-dwelling highland species with a pale *buff or white forehead and throat*. Heavy undergrowth of thick mountain forests.

MOUNTAIN QUAIL. *Oreortyx picta confinis.*—10–11. Crown, mantle, breast, and upper abdomen clear bluish slate, the first with a long, slender black plume; back, rump, tail, and wings grayish olive-brown, the inner webs of the innermost remiges edged with white; throat and flanks bright chestnut, the first with a white lateral margin, the flanks very broadly white-barred.

Distribution.—Mountains of Baja California south to the Sierra Juárez and Sierra San Pedro Mártir.

Remarks.—The *chestnut* throat and *long, slender plume* are unmistakable. One of the most handsome of all quails. Fairly common on the brush-covered slopes of the higher mountains.

SCALED QUAIL. *Callipepla squamata* (Illus. p. 109).—10–11. Above mainly pale grayish brown, the median crown with a short tufted crest;

mantle, breast, and sides conspicuously scalloped, the feathers pale bluish gray, narrowly tipped with black; flanks white-streaked, mainly grayish or pale olive-brown; abdomen tawny, pale buff, or whitish, liberally barred, and sometimes with a chestnut median patch.

Distribution.—Arid open country south to Jalisco and Morelos.

Races.—*C. s. pallida* (northern Sonora, northern Chihuahua, and northwestern Coahuila). *C. s. castanogastris* (eastern Coahuila, northern Nuevo León, and Tamaulipas). *C. s. squamata* (southern Chihuahua, southern

SCALED QUAIL

Coahuila, San Luis Potosí, and Nuevo León south through south-central Mexico).

Remarks.—A pale, desert or dry-country species with conspicuously "scaled" plumage. The *white-tipped, tufted crest* is also a good field mark.

CALIFORNIA QUAIL. *Lophortyx californica.*—9½–10½. *Male:* Forehead pale olive-buff, the posterior portion white like the superciliaries; median crown and nape dull brown; an erect, fanlike black plume; hind-neck and mantle bluish slate, the first white-speckled, the latter narrowly scalloped with black; back and wings grayish brownish, the inner remiges edged with buff; cheeks and throat black, bordered behind with white, the breast clear bluish gray or grayish drab; sides and flanks olive-brown, streaked with white; abdomen whitish or pale buff, conspicuously scalloped with black, and with a chestnut median patch. *Female:* Similar to male, but head not conspicuously patterned, the forehead and crown grayish brown; sides of head and throat whitish, lightly streaked with black; plume much reduced; abdomen without a chestnut patch.

Distribution.—Los Coronados Islands and Baja California, chiefly in open chaparral country.

Races.—*L. c. plumbea* (Los Coronados Islands and northwestern Baja California south, locally, to about 30° N.). *L. c. decolorata* (Baja California from about latitude 30° N. south to latitude 25° N.). *L. c. achrustera* (Baja California south of latitude 25° N.).

Remarks.—Also known as Valley Quail. This species and the following are superficially similar, the males of both having *black throats* and erect (somewhat recurved) *fanlike plumes*. In Baja California such a bird is most likely to be a California Quail, and one should look for its distinctive, *scalloped abdomen*.

DESERT QUAIL. *Lophortyx gambelii* (Illus. p. 110).—10–11. *Male:* Forehead, area below eye, and throat black, bordered behind with white;

DESERT QUAIL

crown (from level of eyes) reddish brown, the posterior superciliaries white; an erect, fanlike black plume; above mainly bluish gray, the back sometimes tinged with olive; a broad band of gray across the chest; lower breast and abdomen buffy white, the median portion with a large black patch; sides and flanks chestnut, prominently stripped with white. *Female:* Similar to male, but head mainly grayish brown, the throat and malar area whitish, lightly streaked with darker; plume much reduced; abdomen pale buff or whitish and without a black patch.

Distribution.—Desert portions of northeastern Baja California, Sonora, and Sinaloa; also Tiburón Island, Gulf of California.

Races.—*L. g. gambelii* (northeastern Baja California south to central Sonora). *L. g. fulvipectus* (southwestern Sonora). *L. g. friedmanni* (coastal Sinaloa from Río Fuerte south to Río Culiacán). *L. g. pembertoni* (Tiburón Island, Gulf of California).

Remarks.—Also known as Gambel Quail. Much like a California Quail, but with a *reddish* crown (male), white-striped, *chestnut flanks, and pale abdomen.*

ELEGANT QUAIL. *Lophortyx douglasii* (Illus. p. 111).—9–10. *Male:* Head essentially white, but very liberally streaked (crown) and speckled

ELEGANT QUAIL

(cheeks and throat) with black; a tawny cinnamon crest; hind-neck and upper back bluish gray, the former spotted with rufous; back, rump, and folded wing mainly olive-brown, the scapulars extensively rufous, boldly spotted with white; underparts largely gray, the abdomen and flanks conspicuously white-spotted, the breast sometimes faintly streaked with reddish. *Female:* Top of head, hind-neck, scapulars, and wing-coverts deep brown, conspicuously streaked and spotted with pale brown or buff; feathers of crest sooty brown; back and rump grayish olive-brown; underparts mainly whitish, the throat black-streaked, the remainder very liberally barred and striped with brown.

Distribution.—Dry western portion of the country, from Sonora and Chihuahua south to northwestern Jalisco, and possibly Colima. ENDEMIC.

Races.—*L. d. bensoni* (Sonora, south to Guaymas and San Javier). *L. d. douglasii* (extreme southern Sonora, Sinaloa, and northwestern Durango). *L. d. languens* (known only from Trompa, Chihuahua). *L. d. impedita* (Nayarit). *L. d. teres* (northwestern Jalisco).

Remarks.—Also known as Douglas Quail. The only quail with a *speckled throat.* Males are decidedly colorful, having a *tawny* crest, chestnut-streaked hind-neck, and considerable rufous on their wings. Both sexes are white-spotted below.

BANDED QUAIL. *Philortyx fasciatus.*—8–8½. *Adult:* Above mainly buffy olive-brown, the scapulars and inner remiges boldly spotted with sooty brown, this narrowly barred with pale buff; black-plumed (median crown), the feathers chestnut-tipped; throat dull white, the chest buffy brown; breast, sides, and flanks evenly barred with black and white, the abdomen usually immaculate. *Immature:* Similar to adult, but forehead, sides of head, and throat black.

Distribution.—Southern highlands, in the states of Colima, Michoacán, Guerrero, Mexico, Morelos, and Puebla. ENDEMIC.

Remarks.—Also known as Barred Quail. This diminutive species is restricted to the southern part of the country, where it occurs in open country at high altitudes. No Mexican relative is *broadly barred with black and white* on the sides and flanks.

COMMON BOBWHITE. *Colinus virginianus.*—8–10. *Male:* Extremely variable, especially on the head and underparts. Above either sooty and blackish, the hind-neck, scapulars, and wings minutely spotted with white, or mantle distinctly reddish, the hind-neck streaked with black and white, the upperparts otherwise extensively mottled, barred, and streaked with brown, gray, and buff; lores, superciliaries, and throat white, the last bordered with black, or throat (sometimes the entire head and breast) black, the underparts otherwise either extensively cinnamon (or chestnut) or mainly whitish, liberally barred with black. *Female:* Lores, superciliaries, and throat pale tawny buff; upperparts essentially as in male, the underparts whitish or buffy white, conspicuously barred with black or brown; flanks sometimes streaked with tawny cinnamon.

Distribution.—Virtually country-wide, exclusive of Baja California and the Yucatán Peninsula. Not found in heavy forests and deserts. Sea-level to an altitude (locally) of about 7,500 feet.

Races.—*C. v. ridgwayi* (northern to south-central Sonora). *C. v. texanus* (northeastern Coahuila, Nuevo León, and central Tamaulipas). *C. v. maculatus* (southeastern San Luis Potosí and southeastern Tamaulipas south to central-north Veracruz). *C. v. aridus* (southeastern San Luis Potosí to central and central-western Tamaulipas). *C. v. graysoni* (tableland from southeastern Nayarit and southern Jalisco to the Valley of Mexico, Morelos, central-southern San Luis Potosí, and southern Hidalgo). *C. v. nigripectus* (southern half of the states of Mexico, Morelos, and Puebla). *C. v. pectoralis* (central Veracruz, up to 5,000 feet on the eastern slope of the Cordillera). *C. v. godmani* (lowlands of Veracruz, and possibly Tabasco). *C. v. minor* (northeastern Chiapas and adjacent portion of Tabasco). *C. v. insignis* (western boundary of Chiapas at an altitude of 3,000–6,000 feet). *C. v. salvini* (coastal plains of southern Chiapas). *C. v. coyolcos* (Pacific slope of Oaxaca and Chiapas, from city of Tehuantepec to Tonalá). *C. v. thayeri* (northeastern Oaxaca). *C. v. atriceps* (Putla area of Oaxaca, possibly ranging into Guerrero). *C. v. nelsoni* (known only from Chicomuselo, Chiapas).

Remarks.—Students who think of the bobwhite in terms of our well-known American bird will be much surprised by the appearance of most Mexican varieties. Except for *texanus*, the males of all are extensively hazel, cinnamon, or chestnut below, and several have *black* throats. Females (and males above) are much like our northern bird.

BLACK-THROATED BOBWHITE. *Colinus nigrogularis.*—7½–8½. *Male:* Superciliaries and throat black; malar stripe, forehead, and a narrow stripe above the superciliaries white, the crown itself brown and dusky; hind-neck, mantle, sides, and flanks rusty or cinnamon, spotted and streaked with white, the scapulars and inner flight feathers black-spotted; breast and abdomen very conspicuously scaled, the feathers white, with broad black edgings. *Female:* Superciliaries, malar area, and throat tawny buff, the upperparts very similar to the male, but without cinnamon on the hind-neck and mantle; below white, the feathers barred with black and rusty.

Distribution.—Yucatán Peninsula.

Races.—*C. n. caboti* (Campeche and Yucatán, exclusive of the Progreso region). *C. n. persiccus* (arid northern portion of the Yucatán Peninsula).

Remarks.—Also known as Black-throated Quail. A "Bobwhite" with a *black throat and heavily scalloped underparts*. Females resemble female Common Bobwhites, but the latter do not occur in the Yucatán Peninsula. Fields and forest edge.

SPOTTED WOOD-QUAIL. *Odontophorus guttatus* (Illus. p. 114).—
10–11½. *Male:* Crown sooty blackish, the lateral and posterior portion of
the occipital crest bright cinnamon-buff; a broad chestnut postocular stripe;
upperparts mainly dusky olive-brown (olive phase) or reddish olive-brown
(red phase); in either case, the scapulars and inner flight feathers with large
black spots, and the plumage more or less mottled and streaked with buff;
throat black, narrowly streaked with white, the underparts otherwise olive-
brown, liberally spotted with white. *Female:* Similar to male, but smaller
and darker, and without cinnamon on the crest.

Distribution.—Humid forests of Oaxaca, Chiapas, Veracruz, Tabasco,
and Campeche.

SPOTTED WOOD-QUAIL

Remarks.—Spotted Wood-Quails live in heavily wooded areas from
sea-level to an altitude of at least 7,000 feet. While very shy, they are
not uncommon in suitable habitats. No similar bird has a *striped* throat
or *white spots below*. The nuchal crest, partly cinnamon in the male, is
also a good character.

SINGING QUAIL. *Dactylortyx thoracicus.*—8–9. *Male:* Above olive-
brown, more or less mottled with grayish, the scapulars and inner remiges
with large black spots and narrowly streaked with buff; an obscure black
nuchal collar; superciliaries, sides of head, and throat bright tawny cinnamon; breast, sides, and flanks olive-brown or buffy brown, the feathers with

pale shaft-streaks; abdomen whitish. *Female:* Similar to male above; superciliaries and sides of head whitish or grayish brown, the throat white or tinged with vinaceous; breast, sides, and flanks tawny cinnamon-brown, the abdomen rich buff or buffy white.

Distribution.—Mountain forests (principally) of the Pacific and Gulf slopes from Jalisco and southern Tamaulipas southward.

Races.—*D. t. thoracicus* (wooded mountain slopes from San Luis Potosí and southern Tamaulipas to Puebla and Veracruz). *D. t. sharpei* (Campeche and Yucatán). *D. t. devius* (mountain forests from Jalisco south to Guerrero). *D. t. lineolatus* (wooded mountain slopes of southeastern Oaxaca and western Chiapas). *D. t. chiapensis* (central Chiapas). *D. t. fuscus* (eastern half of the Sierra Madre of Chiapas).

Remarks.—Also known as Long-toed Partridge. A medium-sized, olive-brown partridge occurring chiefly at high altitudes in dense humid forests. No similar species has a *tawny cinnamon throat*. A timid bird, it is likely to be overlooked unless accidentally flushed. The song consists of a series of musical whistles initiated by a note repeated several times with increasing force.

HARLEQUIN QUAIL. *Cyrtonyx montezumae* (Illus. p. 115).—8–9½. *Male:* Median portion of crown brown, the short expansive nuchal crest tawny buff; area around eye white, the sides of the head conspicuously patterned with black; chin and median throat black, bordered posteriorly (except in *merriami*) and laterally with a very broad white band; back and

HARLEQUIN QUAIL

scapulars reddish brown, narrowly streaked with buff, the folded wing pale grayish or brown, much spotted or barred with black; sides of breast, sides, and flanks bluish slate, very liberally spotted with white; flanks sometimes chestnut-spotted; median breast and median abdomen chestnut, this forming a broad ventral stripe. *Female:* Above reddish brown, intermixed with grayish, and more or less barred with black, the mantle, back, and scapulars prominently streaked with white or buff; a short, buff-colored nuchal crest; chin and median throat white or buffy, the underparts otherwise pinkish cinnamon, vinaceous, or fawn, sparsely streaked with black.

Distribution.—Foothills and highlands south to Oaxaca.

Races.—*C. m. mearnsi* (northwestern portion of the country, exclusive of Baja California). *C. m. montezumae* (northern Coahuila, Nuevo León, and west-central Tamaulipas south to Michoacán, Puebla, and Oaxaca). *C. m. merriami* (eastern slope of Mount Orizaba, Veracruz). *C. m. sallei* (Michoacán south to east-central Oaxaca).

Remarks.—Also known as Montezuma Quail. *See* Ocellated Quail.

OCELLATED QUAIL. *Cyrtonyx ocellatus ocellatus.*—8–9½. *Male:* Crown blackish slate or dull olive; a short, expansive nuchal crest; area around eye white, the sides of the head conspicuously patterned with black and bluish slate; chin and median throat black, margined laterally and posteriorly with a very broad white band, this followed by a black band; upperparts mainly grayish, tinged with olive, the mantle, back, and scapulars more or less blotched, the wings spotted and barred with black, and the whole conspicuously streaked with buff or chestnut; underparts mainly ochraceous (breast) and bright chestnut, the sides of the breast grayish, spotted with buff. *Female:* Similar to a female Harlequin Quail, but darker above, and with buff-colored (never white) dorsal streaks.

Distribution.—Dry highlands of eastern Oaxaca and Chiapas.

Remarks.—A magnificent bird of more open country above an altitude of about 5,000 feet. The head of the male is very similar to that of *C. montezumae*, but its underparts are *ochraceous* (breast) *and bright chestnut*, without the white spotting of the Harlequin.

Family MELEAGRIDAE. Turkeys

Key to the Species

1*a.* Tail reddish, the feathers tipped with pale cinnamon-brown, buffy, or white; chest of male with a long tufted "beard"

  b. Tail grayish, the feathers tipped with metallic coppery bronze; rump, upper tail-coverts, and tail with metallic blue "eyespots"; crown of male with a rounded protuberance

COMMON TURKEY. *Meleagris gallopavo.*—Male 45–50; female 30–36. Similar to the domestic turkey.

Distribution.—Wooded portions of the Sierra Madre Occidental and Sierra Madre Oriental and coastal plains of the northeast.

Races.—*M. g. merriami* (mountains of northeastern Sonora, where now uncommon). *M. g. onusta* (western slope of the Sierra Madre Occidental, from southeastern Sonora and southwestern Chihuahua south at least to east-central Sinaloa). *M. g. mexicana* (Chihuahua east of the Cordillera, Durango, northern Jalisco, and possibly Hidalgo). *M. g. intermedia* (Coahuila, Nuevo León, Tamaulipas, and San Luis Potosí). *M. g. gallopavo* (Michoacán to Veracruz; in prehistoric times probably south to Oaxaca).

Remarks.—Recent studies indicate that turkeys still occupy most of their original range, although extirpated locally, or sometimes existing as isolated populations. They occur principally in pine and oak woods of the highlands and hence are directly affected by lumbering operations, as well as by hunting. Domestic turkeys are the descendants of birds from the south of Mexico.

OCELLATED TURKEY. *Agriocharis ocellata.*—Resembles a Common Turkey superficially, but tail grayish (not reddish), the feathers of the rump, upper tail-coverts, and tail with bright metallic coppery bronze tips and a metallic blue subterminal "eyespot." Males lack a "beard" on the chest, but have an erect, rounded protuberance on the crown and a conspicuous white patch on the secondaries.

Distribution.—Extreme eastern Chiapas, Tabasco, Campeche, Yucatán, and Quintana Roo, chiefly in savannahs and brushy forest edge.

Remarks.—This magnificent lowland turkey is distinguished by its bronze-tipped *gray tail* and metallic *blue "eyespots."* It frequents open country and is fairly common locally in the vicinity of cornfields.

Family GRUIDAE. Cranes

KEY TO THE SPECIES

1*a.* Larger (50). Mainly white, with black primaries
  b. Smaller (35–48). Mainly ashy gray, with slate-colored primaries

*WHOOPING CRANE. *Grus americana.*—50. *Adult:* Crown, sides of head (lores and malar area), and narrow strip extending along each side of neck bare, reddish; plumage mainly white, the primaries and their coverts black; iris yellow; legs and feet black. *Immature:* Head, etc., fully feathered, somewhat dusky; plumage otherwise mainly whitish as in adult, but more or less extensively blotched with cinnamon-buff or brownish.

Distribution.—Formerly wintered south at least to Jalisco, Guanajuato, and Tamaulipas. Few recent Mexican records.

*SANDHILL CRANE. *Grus canadensis.*—35–48. *Adult:* Forepart of crown and lores unfeathered, reddish; plumage mainly ashy-gray, palest below and often more or less extensively washed with rusty or dark ochraceous; primaries and their coverts slate-color; iris bright red; legs and feet dusky greenish. *Immature:* Similar to adult, but body with more or less brown, especially above. Younger birds have the entire head feathered.

Distribution.—Winters southward (locally) to Jalisco, Mexico, and Quintana Roo.

Races.—*G. c. canadensis* (winters in Baja California and Sonora south to Jalisco, Distrito Federal, and San Luis Potosí). *G. c. tabida* (winters in Baja California, Sonora, and elsewhere eastward and southward, locally, to Mexico, Quintana Roo, and Cozumel Island).

Remarks.—Also known as Brown Crane. The two races of this species that winter in Mexico are known respectively as the "Little Brown" and the "Sandhill" Crane. The former can be distinguished by its smaller size and shorter bill. Although somewhat heron-like in appearance, a crane's *bald, reddish forehead* is unmistakable. Cranes fly with both the neck and the legs extended, while herons retract the neck when in flight.

Family ARAMIDAE. Limpkins

LIMPKIN. *Aramus guarauna dolosus* (Illus. p. 119).—26–28. Above brownish olive, the underparts dull chocolate-brown; head and neck narrowly streaked with white and elsewhere generously spotted with same; bill mainly black, the lower mandible yellowish toward base.

Distribution.—Lowlands from Oaxaca and Veracruz southward, including Cozumel Island.

Remarks.—Large rail-like birds, drably colored, but *liberally streaked and spotted with white.* Limpkins frequent swamps and marshes difficult of access and are not easily observed, although often heard. Their calls are notably discordant and far-reaching, but virtually indescribable.

LIMPKIN

Family RALLIDAE. Rails, Gallinules, Coots

KEY TO THE SPECIES

1*a*. Large (12–18 inches) 2

  b. Small (5½–9½ inches) 7

2*a*. Bill rather long; underparts extensively ochraceous, cinnamon, or chestnut 3

  b. Bill short; underparts slate-colored or deep purplish 5

3*a*. Back streaked; abdomen and flanks barred with white

King Rail, p. 120
Clapper Rail, p. 120

  b. Back not streaked; abdomen and flanks uniform black 4

4*a*. Head and chest gray . . . . Gray-necked Wood-Rail, p. 122

  b. Head and chest chestnut . . . . Rufous-necked Wood-Rail, p. 123

5*a*. Head, neck, and underparts deep violet purple

Purple Gallinule, p. 126

  b. Head, neck, and underparts blackish slate 6

6*a*. Frontal shield and bill bright red, the latter green-tipped

Common Gallinule, p. 125

  b. Frontal shield chestnut; bill conspicuously whitish

American Coot, p. 126

7a. Underparts uniform slate-colored or median throat and chest black   8
  b. Not as in 7a.   9
8a. Back and scapulars white-speckled; underparts uniform slate-
   colored . . . . Black Rail, p. 124
  b. Back and scapulars white-streaked; median throat black
                                                      Sora, p. 123
9a. Back and scapulars streaked 10
  b. Not as in 9a; underparts uniform chestnut or bright russet . . . 12
10a. Underparts spotted and barred with black and white
                                                Spotted Rail, p. 121
  b. Not as in 10a. 11
11a. Larger (9 inches). Bill long; breast cinnamon   Virginia Rail, p. 121
  b. Smaller (6½–7 inches). Bill short; breast tawny   Yellow Rail, p. 125
12a. Larger (8 inches). Crown and back concolor   Uniform Crake, p. 122
  b. Smaller (5½–6 inches). Head slate-colored, not concolor with back
                                                Ruddy Crake, p. 124

*KING RAIL. *Rallus elegans elegans.*—15–18. Above dark brown, liberally streaked with tawny olive; a pale line above lores to eye; throat white; cheeks, lower neck, breast, and upper abdomen rich ochraceous-buff or cinnamon, the underparts otherwise sooty black, boldly barred with white; iris reddish brown; bill long, the lower mandible mainly reddish orange.

Distribution.—A rare or accidental winter visitant, of which there are but three records (Guanajuato, Veracruz).

CLAPPER RAIL. *Rallus longirostris.*—13–16. Above grayish brown or olive-brown, rather obscurely streaked with gray or olive-gray; a whitish line above lores to eye; throat white; malar area, lower neck, breast, and upper abdomen ochraceous-buff or cinnamon-buff, the underparts otherwise grayish brown, boldly barred with white; iris reddish brown or pale yellow; bill long, the lower mandible mainly yellowish.

Distribution.—The Pacific Coast (including Baja California) south to Nayarit; fresh-water marshes of Distrito Federal and Tlaxcala; arid coastal region (locally) of the Yucatán Peninsula.

Races.—*R. l. levipes* (salt marshes of northwestern Baja California south, in winter, to San Quintín Bay). *R. l. magdalenae* (tidal lagoons of the Pacific Coast of Baja California from Magdalena Bay north at least to Scammon Lagoon; winters south to latitude 23°27′ N.). *R. l. beldingi* (mangrove swamps of the gulf coast of extreme southern Baja California). *R. l. rhizophorae* (coastal marshes of southern Sonora). *R. l. nayaritensis* (San Blas, Nayarit). *R. l. tenuirostris* (fresh-water marshes of Distrito Federal and Tlaxcala). *R. l. pallidus* (Río Lagartos, Yucatán, and possibly coastal Campeche locally). *R. l. grossi* (Chinchorro Reef, Quintana Roo; doubtfully distinct).

Remarks.—Clapper Rails are characteristic of salt-water marshes, tidal lagoons, and mangrove swamps and are seldom found elsewhere. King and Virginia Rails have very similar plumage, but the first is not likely to be seen in Mexico, the second is notably smaller, and both prefer fresh-water marshes.

VIRGINIA RAIL. *Rallus limicola limicola* (Illus. p. 121).—9. *Adult:* Above rich sooty brown, liberally streaked with tawny olive, the upper wing-coverts cinnamon-rufous; a pale line above lores to eye; sides of head

VIRGINIA RAIL

gray; throat white; lower neck, breast, and upper abdomen cinnamon, the underparts otherwise mainly black, conspicuously barred with white; iris bright red; bill long, dusky above, reddish below. *Immature:* Mainly dull black, the upper wing-coverts rufous; median breast and abdomen often extensively white.

Distribution.—Baja California and possibly Sonora; a resident colony also in Distrito Federal. Winters locally elsewhere, but generally overlooked. A single record for Yucatán (June 23).

Remarks.—Except for the rare and very distinctive Spotted Rail, this fresh-water, marsh inhabitant is the only *small rail with a long slender bill*. Easily distinguished from rails of similar plumage (King and Clapper) by its diminutive size.

SPOTTED RAIL. *Pardirallus maculatus insolitus.*—9½. Mainly deep rich brown or sooty, the upperparts (especially the scapulars, wing-coverts, and upper back) conspicuously streaked with white, the underparts very liberally spotted (anteriorly) and barred with same; iris dark red; bill long, mainly yellowish olive, becoming orange near base.

Distribution.—Known only from two specimens (Tuxtla Gutiérrez, Chiapas, and British Honduras).

Remarks.—The only rail with *spotted and barred underparts.* Unmistakable.

UNIFORM CRAKE. *Amaurolimnas concolor guatemalensis.*—8. Above deep reddish olive-brown; below rich tawny or bright russet, the throat usually much paler than lower neck and breast; iris yellow; bill rather short, mainly yellowish green.

Distribution.—Swampy lowland forests of Oaxaca. Extremely rare, but to be expected elsewhere in suitable habitats.

Remarks.—Nearest a Ruddy Crake in general appearance, but without the latter's black head, and occupying a different habitat.

GRAY-NECKED WOOD-RAIL. *Aramides cajanea* (Illus. p. 122).—14–17. Forehead (to middle of crown), hind-neck, mantle, and chest clear

GRAY-NECKED WOOD-RAIL

slate gray, the back of the head washed with brownish; upperparts otherwise mainly dull olive, the wings extensively cinnamon-rufous; throat white; breast, upper abdomen, and sides tawny cinnamon, the lower underparts black; an inverted **V**-shaped band of white sometimes separating the black and cinnamon areas; bill moderately long, the basal half reddish, like iris and legs.

Distribution.—Central and southern Mexico, chiefly in swampy lowland forests and mangrove jungles.

Races.—*A. c. mexicana* (southern Tamaulipas, Hidalgo, Distrito Federal, Veracruz, Tabasco, Oaxaca, and Chiapas locally). *A. c. vanrossemi* (Chiapas). *A. c. albiventris* (eastern Chiapas and the Yucatán Peninsula, including Cozumel Island).

Remarks.—A brightly colored, chicken-sized rail with a *gray head* and uniform *black abdomen and flanks*. Wood-Rails inhabit more or less inaccessible swamplands, but are much less elusive than most of their relatives. Of the two species in Mexico, this is the one most likely to be seen.

RUFOUS-NECKED WOOD-RAIL. *Aramides axillaris.*—12. Head (except throat), neck, breast, and sides of abdomen rich chestnut; upper back clear slate gray, shading to dull olive posteriorly, the rump and tail black; primaries cinnamon-rufous; median throat white; abdomen, flanks, and crissum black; bill rather short, yellowish green; legs reddish.

Distribution.—Coastal lagoons and mangrove swamps from Sinaloa and Yucatán southward. Uncommon to rare.

SORA. *Porzana carolina* (Illus. p. 123).—7–8. Median crown, lores, and median line of throat (to chest) dull black; sides of crown and upper-

SORA RAIL

parts essentially olive-brown; hind-neck, upper back, and scapulars with more or less black, the last two narrowly white-streaked; sides of head and breast grayish, fading to dull white on the abdomen and crissum; sides and flanks sooty brown, conspicuously barred with white; iris reddish; bill short, mainly pale yellowish green, like legs.

Distribution.—Widespread resident of fresh-water marshes, but generally overlooked.

Remarks.—The *short yellow bill and black throat-patch* are diagnostic. As with other small rails, Soras are more likely to be heard than seen. They have a variety of calls, the most characteristic being a plaintive two-syllable whistle with a rising inflection and descending "whinny."

BLACK RAIL. *Laterallus jamaicensis coturniculus.*—5½. Crown and sides of head black, shading to deep slate gray on the underparts; abdomen, flanks, and crissum minutely barred with white; hind-neck and upper back deep chestnut brown, becoming sooty brown (less rufescent) posteriorly, where white-speckled; iris red; bill short and black; legs greenish yellow.

Distribution.—Coastal marshes of northwestern Baja California (San Quintín, San Ramón).

Remarks.—A slaty, sparrow-sized rail with a *short black bill*. The *white-speckled* back and wing-coverts distinguish it from all other small marsh birds.

RUDDY CRAKE. *Laterallus ruber* (Illus. p. 124).—5½–6. Head (except throat) blackish slate; hind-neck, sides of neck, and upper back bright

RUDDY CRAKE

chestnut, becoming duller, less rufescent posteriorly, where rich chocolate-brown; below mainly cinnamon, palest on throat and abdomen, the flanks and crissum washed with chestnut; iris reddish brown; bill short and black; legs olive-green.

Distribution.—Marshes of the Atlantic slope from southern Tamaulipas southward.

Races.—*L. r. tamaulipensis* (southern Tamaulipas, Veracruz, Oaxaca, and Campeche). *L. r. ruber* (Yucatán Peninsula and Cozumel Island).

Remarks.—Also known as Red Rail. The only small reddish rail with a *black head*. Not uncommon, but exceedingly difficult to observe.

YELLOW RAIL. *Coturnicops noveboracensis goldmani.*—6½–7. Above deep brown, the back, scapulars, and wing-coverts minutely barred with white and very broadly streaked with cinnamon-buff; sides of head (except lores), throat, and breast mainly ochraceous-buff or pale tawny, fading to buffy white on the median abdomen; lower abdomen and flanks blackish, minutely barred with white; iris yellowish brown or reddish; bill short, mainly yellowish.

Distribution.—Known only from Lerma (Valley of Toluca), state of Mexico.

COMMON GALLINULE. *Gallinula chloropus cachinnans* (Illus. p. 125). —12–14. Head, neck, and upper back blackish slate, the underparts bluish

COMMON GALLINULE

slate; plumage elsewhere mainly brownish olive, the median abdomen and crissum white; flanks with broad white stripes; iris reddish; frontal shield and bill bright red, the latter green-tipped and rather short; legs pale greenish.

Distribution.—Virtually country-wide in marshes and similar habitats.

Remarks.—Also known as Florida Gallinule. Gallinules are accomplished swimmers and are quite as likely to be found in open water as skulking in the adjacent marshes. Both species resemble ducks when swimming at a distance and have the same pumping motion of the head and neck. No duck has a red chicken-like bill. The *red frontal shield* and *white flank-patch* at once distinguish this species. Purple Gallinules will always be known by their *bluish* shields.

PURPLE GALLINULE. *Porphyrula martinica.*—12–14. Head and underparts deep violet-purple, the lower abdomen and crissum white; hindneck bright violet-blue; upperparts mainly greenish olive-brown, the remiges extensively greenish blue; iris brown; frontal shield pale bluish, the bill short, bright red, tipped with yellowish; legs greenish yellow.

Distribution.—Virtually country-wide in marshes and similar habitats.

Remarks.—*See* Common Gallinule.

AMERICAN COOT. *Fulica americana americana.*—13–16. Mainly deep slaty gray, the head and neck darkest; crissum white; iris red; frontal shield chestnut; bill short, either white or pale yellowish; legs and toes greenish, the latter lobed.

Distribution.—Virtually country-wide in fresh-water ponds and lagoons, but of very local occurrence.

Remarks.—A compact, slate-colored, ducklike bird with a *short white bill* and reddish frontal shield. Coots are more aquatic than either of the gallinules and are usually to be found swimming well offshore. They dive readily, and characteristically "run" across the water for some distance before taking flight.

Family HELIORNITHIDAE. Sun-grebes

SUN-GREBE. *Heliornis fulica* (Illus. p. 126).—11–12. Crown, hindneck, and broad postocular stripe glossy black, the last bordered above by

Sun-grebe

a conspicuous white superciliary stripe; upperparts mainly brownish olive, the fan-shaped tail dusky brown tipped with white; cheeks cinnamon-buff or white; sides of neck with a white stripe bordered below (posteriorly) by black; underparts essentially white, the breast and sides washed with pale brown or buff; legs short, yellow like toes, the latter boldly barred with black.

Distribution.—Heavily forested lowland streams and ponds of Oaxaca, Chiapas, southern Veracruz, and Campeche.

Remarks.—Also known as Finfoot. Sun-grebes are highly aquatic and probably never stray beyond the banks of sluggish tropical streams. They apparently are quite rare in Mexico and little is known of their habits.

Family EURYPYGIDAE. Sun-bitterns

SUN-BITTERN. *Eurypyga helias major* (Illus. p. 127).—18. Head blackish, the throat white; neck, chest, and upper back brownish or dull

SUN-BITTERN

cinnamon, finely vermiculated with black, the dorsal plumage essentially gray or grayish buff with black barring; wings with bright chestnut and buff patches; expansive tail liberally vermiculated, and with two broad black-and-chestnut bars; breast and abdomen buffy white; bill and legs orange; iris red.

Distribution.—Humid lowlands of Chiapas and Tabasco in the vicinity of forest streams and ponds.

Remarks.—Sun-bitterns frequent rank undergrowth of tropical riverbanks and swamps and are semiaquatic in habits. They are among the most beautiful of Mexican birds when displaying with extended wings and tail—a posture sometimes held for several minutes. Solitary, retiring, and apparently uncommon in our area.

Family JACANIDAE. Jaçanas

AMERICAN JAÇANA. *Jacana spinosa spinosa* (Illus. p. 128).—8–9. *Adult:* Head, neck, upper back, and chest glossy black; above and below otherwise mainly maroon or deep chestnut, the remiges greenish yellow, narrowly edged or tipped with brown; bill and frontal shield yellow, the two separated by a reddish area; underside of wings near bend with a yellow

AMERICAN JAÇANA

spur; legs and feet greenish, the toes very long and with notably long, slender claws. *Immature:* Frontal shield much reduced; above mainly grayish brown; sides of head (except black postocular stripe) and underparts white or blotched, the breast sometimes buffy.

Distribution.—Ponds and marshes of the Pacific and Atlantic slopes. Locally elsewhere, including Cozumel Island.

Remarks.—The brightly colored adult is unmistakable, and usually is one of the most conspicuous birds of its habitat. Immature birds somewhat resemble Wilson Phalaropes, but are easily distinguished from all shore birds by their remarkably long toes and claws and *rounded wings.*

Family HAEMATOPODIDAE. Oystercatchers

OYSTERCATCHER. *Haematopus ostralegus* (Illus. p. 129).—16–18. Head, neck, and chest black; plumage otherwise either dusky brownish

OYSTERCATCHER

(*bachmani*), or upperparts (except head, etc.) mainly grayish olive-brown, the upper tail-coverts and band across wings white—in this event the posterior underparts also white (*palliatus*) or mainly white, the breast and sides sometimes boldly spotted (*frazeri*). Bill blunt, compressed laterally, and mainly red; iris yellow; legs pale.

Distribution.—Coasts of Baja California, the Pacific and Atlantic coasts (locally), and various offshore (Pacific) islands.

Races.—*H. o. bachmani* (coasts of Baja California, breeding only in the northern half of the Pacific side). *H. o. frazeri* (coasts of Baja California, Sonora, Sinaloa, and on the Revilla Gigedo and Tres Marías Islands; elsewhere southward in winter). *H. o. palliatus* (coasts of Oaxaca, Chiapas, Veracruz, Yucatán, and Cozumel Island; presumably coastwise elsewhere).

Remarks.—Large, stocky shore birds with very *heavy red bills, yellow eyes,* and pale legs. Oystercatchers may be either wholly black (*bachmani*) or mainly white below (breast and abdomen), with an extensive white patch on the wings and base of tail. They frequent seashores, especially where rocky.

Family CHARADRIIDAE. Plovers and Allies

KEY TO THE SPECIES

1a. Above conspicuously mottled, spotted, or speckled; underparts black or mottled (spring), or neck and breast lightly streaked with brown (fall) 2

  b. Above virtually uniform; underparts mainly white or whitish, unstreaked, but often with a black collar 3

2a. Tail boldly barred with brown and white; axillaries black; in spring plumage the lower abdomen and crissum white
Black-bellied Plover, p. 131

  b. Tail dark, not conspicuously barred; axillaries not black; in spring plumage the abdomen and crissum black like breast
American Golden Plover, p. 132

3a. With a black or brown band (sometimes two) across the chest . . 4

  b. Without a black or brown pectoral band; sometimes with a conspicuous patch on each side of breast 7

4a. A double pectoral band or collar; rump and base of tail buffy cinnamon . . . . Killdeer, p. 133

  b. A single pectoral band or collar; rump and base of tail brown, like back 5

5a. Smaller (5½–6 inches); a *broad* black patch bordering the white forehead; crown and sides of neck with more or less rufous
Collared Plover, p. 133

  b. Larger (6½–9½ inches); a *narrow* black band bordering the white forehead in spring plumage only; head and neck without rufous . 6

6a. More than 8 inches; bill black, rather long, and decidedly sturdy
Thick-billed Plover, p. 134

  b. Less than 7½ inches; bill notably small, orange tipped with black
Ringed Plover, p. 132

7a. Larger (8–9½ inches); above buffy brown, the tail without conspicuous white; sides of head and breast suffused with buff
Mountain Plover, p. 134

b. Smaller (6–7 inches); above pale grayish brown, the tail with conspicuous white; a black or brown patch on each side of breast

Snowy Plover, p. 132

*BLACK-BELLIED PLOVER. *Squatarola squatarola.* (Illus. p. 131).—
10½–12. *Spring:* Forehead, stripe above eye, and sides of neck white, the median crown and nape more or less mottled with brown; hind-neck, back, and wings (except primaries) deep sooty brown, boldly mottled with white; primaries blackish; rump white; tail barred with brown and white; sides of head and underparts (including the axillaries) mainly black, the lower ab-

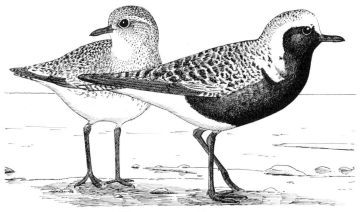

BLACK-BELLIED PLOVER

FALL   SPRING

domen and crissum white. *Fall:* Above brown, extensively mottled, spotted, or speckled with buffy white; below whitish, the sides of the head, lower neck, breast, and flanks lightly streaked with brown, this appearing *mottled* at a distance; axillaries black.

Distribution.—Winters commonly on both coasts, arriving in late July and migrating northward in June.

Remarks.—A *large*, stocky plover, quite unlike any other shore bird except the very rare Golden Plover. The two are easily separated when in spring plumage. The Black-bellied then has a *whitish rump and tail*, and immaculate *white belly* and under tail-coverts. In fall and winter, when both are extensively streaked (or mottled) below, a black patch below the wing near the body (axillaries) distinguishes this species.

*AMERICAN GOLDEN PLOVER. *Pluvialis dominica.*—9½–10½. Similar to a Black-bellied Plover in comparable plumage, but somewhat smaller and much darker, especially above, the upperparts (including the rump) extensively spotted with golden buff; tail dark (not conspicuously barred with brown and white); axillaries pale brownish (not black). In spring the lower abdomen is black, like the throat and breast.

Distribution.—Occasionally recorded on both coasts, and on Clarión Island of the Revilla Gigedo group during migration. Also reported in Puebla, Tlaxcala, and the interior of Veracruz.

Races.—*P. d. dominica* (as above, except Clarión Island). *P. d. fulva* (accidental straggler to Clarión Island, where recorded May 21, 1897, and April 30, 1925).

Remarks.—*See* Black-bellied Plover.

*RINGED PLOVER. *Charadrius hiaticula semipalmatus.*—6½–7½. *Spring:* Forehead, narrow nuchal collar, and underparts, except for a black band across the chest, white; upperparts mainly brown, the white forehead and nuchal collar bordered behind with black; tail dusky brown, the lateral feathers conspicuously white-tipped; bill decidedly short, orange-yellow tipped with black; legs orange-yellow. *Fall:* As in spring, but the black of the plumage replaced with brown. Immature birds have wholly dark bills.

Distribution.—Infrequently recorded, but probably a common migrant and winter resident on both coasts.

Remarks.—Also known as Semipalmated Plover. The relatively *slight* bill, *yellowish at the base* in adults, is unmistakable. In other respects much like a Snowy Plover, but much darker above, and with a very conspicuous band extending *entirely* across the chest.

SNOWY PLOVER. *Charadrius alexandrinus.*—6–7. *Spring:* Forehead white, followed by a patch of black, the upperparts otherwise very pale grayish brown; primaries sooty; lateral tail feathers white; a black patch on each side of breast, the underparts immaculate white; bill black and rather slender; legs dusky. *Fall:* As in spring, but the black of the plumage replaced with brown.

Distribution.—Common resident in Baja California, wintering south to Nayarit. Migratory and wintering (?) on the east coast, possibly breeding in northeastern Tamaulipas.

Races.—*C. a. nivosus* (as above, except the east coast). **C. a. tenuirostris* (the east coast, probably chiefly as a migrant).

Remarks.—A small, *very pale* plover with *dark bill and legs.* The conspicuous chest-band of other small plovers is represented in the Snowy by a dark patch on each side of its breast.

COLLARED PLOVER. *Charadrius collaris* (Illus. p. 133).—5½–6. *Adult:* Above mainly pale grayish brown, becoming dusky on the primaries; forehead white, the forepart of the crown black, this followed by a pale rufous area extending behind the eyes and along the sides of the neck; a black stripe from bill to eye; underparts white, the chest with a broad black band; bill black, rather long, and slender; legs flesh-color. *Immature:* Similar to adult, but without a black crown-patch; loral stripe brown or obsolete; band across chest dull blackish, this usually incomplete medially.

Distribution.—Essentially coastal, occurring from Sinaloa and Veracruz southward.

COLLARED PLOVER

Remarks.—Also known as Azara Plover. Smallest of the Mexican species. Much darker above than the larger Snowy, from which it differs also in having a *conspicuous chest-band and pale legs.* No other Mexican plover has rufous on its head and neck.

KILLDEER. *Charadrius vociferus vociferus.*—8½–10. Above mainly grayish brown, the rump and upper tail-coverts buffy cinnamon; forehead, patch above and behind the eye, narrow band across hind-neck, and underparts white; lower neck and chest each with a black band; a black bar across the forepart of the crown; primaries blackish, the inner webs extensively white; a white stripe across the extended wing; tail rounded, very expansive, the feathers white-tipped and with a black subterminal area, this becoming ochraceous toward the base.

Distribution.—Resident in Baja California and south to Guerrero, Guanajuato, and Tamaulipas, occurring extensively elsewhere in winter.

Remarks.—A medium-sized "shore bird" with *two black collars*, one bordering the lower throat and a second, narrower, across the chest. Killdeers are easily distinguished in flight, even at a distance, by their brightly colored rumps and very ample, white-tipped tails.

THICK-BILLED PLOVER. *Charadrius wilsonia.*—7–8. *Spring:* Above mainly pale grayish brown, the primaries sooty; forehead, spot behind eye, and underparts white, the chest with a very broad black band; a black band across the forepart of the crown (above the eyes), and a blackish stripe from bill to eye; bill black, rather long, and decidedly sturdy; legs grayish flesh color. *Fall:* As in spring, but black portions of plumage replaced with brown.

Distribution.—Common resident on the Pacific Coast (including Baja California) and recorded as a migrant on the east coast, where also probably breeding.

Races.—*C. w. beldingi* (Pacific Coast; accidental at Tacolutla, Veracruz). *C. w. wilsonia* (migratory on the east coast, probably breeding locally).

Remarks.—Also known as Wilson Plover. The decidedly *large, jet-black bill* and flesh-gray legs set this plover apart from all other "ringed" shore birds. Ringed Plovers have *yellowish* legs and notably short bills.

*MOUNTAIN PLOVER. *Eupoda montana* (Illus. p. 134).—8–9½. *Spring:* Above mainly pale grayish brown, more or less suffused with buff,

MOUNTAIN PLOVER (FALL)

the primaries and tail sooty; forepart of crown and line from bill to eye black; forehead, superciliary stripes, and underparts white, the breast faintly washed with buff; bill black, rather slender; legs pale brownish yellow. *Fall:* As in spring, but without a black crown-patch and loral stripe.

Distribution.—Winters fairly commonly in northwestern Baja California (casually to La Paz), and recorded from Sonora, Zacatecas, Coahuila, Nuevo León, and Tamaulipas. To be expected locally elsewhere in northern Mexico.

Remarks.—Mountain Plovers, like Killdeers, are essentially birds of the interior. The *absence* of a breast-band and the *uniform buffy brown upperparts* serve to identify this rather undistinguished species. In flight the wings show a pale bar, and the tail a dark subterminal band.

Family SCOLOPACIDAE. Snipe, Sandpipers, and Allies

KEY TO THE SPECIES

1a. Bill distinctly curved 2

  b. Bill usually straight; in several *small* species the bill *slightly* curved   4

2a. Bill downcurved, sickle-like 3

  b. Bill upcurved; plumage tawny brown and buff
Marbled Godwit, p. 140

3a. Larger (22–26 inches); bill notably long; underparts buffy
Long-billed Curlew, p. 139

  b. Smaller (15–17 inches); bill moderately long; underparts not essentially buffy . . . .   Whimbrel, p. 138

4a. Rump (and sometimes lower back) white, or essentially whitish .   5

  b. Rump and lower back dark, the tail sometimes paler 13

5a. With a distinct, and usually conspicuous, white wing-stripe . . .   6

  b. Without a white wing-stripe; bill appreciably longer than head   . 11

6a. Larger (14–16 inches); bill much longer than head; a notably conspicuous wing-stripe   . . . . Willet, p. 142

  b. Smaller (7–11 inches); bill not longer than head; wing-stripe normal, or upperparts strikingly patterned as seen in flight   . .   7

7a. Above strikingly patterned; lower back and tail extensively white; a black bar across the rump   8

  b. Not as in 7a. 9

8a. Head, back, and breast essentially uniform black or blacklish; legs dusky   . . . .   Black Turnstone, p. 145

b. Head and neck notably patterned, the throat white; above extensively reddish in spring; legs orange . Ruddy Turnstone, p. 144

9*a.* Smaller (7–8 inches); bill decidedly slender
White-rumped Sandpiper, p. 150

b. Larger (10–11 inches); bill short and sturdy, or long and tapered 10

10*a.* Bill short, yellowish basally; rump and base of tail white, the latter broadly black-tipped; breast grayish brown, or underparts liberally barred and spotted . . . . Surf-bird, p. 144

b. Bill long, uniformly black; rump barred, the tail grayish; underparts cinnamon-rufous or white . . . . Knot, p. 147

11*a.* Snipelike, the bill about twice the length of the head and decidedly sturdy; below reddish in spring . . . . Dowitcher, p. 145

b. Not as in 11*a.* 12

12*a.* Smaller (8–9 inches); bill slightly downcurved; underparts white (fall and winter) or liberally barred (spring); tail pale, without bars; legs greenish . . . . Stilt Sandpiper, p. 151

b. Larger (9½–14½ inches); bill straight or slightly upcurved; below white, the breast streaked (spring) or tinged with gray (fall); tail barred; legs yellow . . . . Lesser Yellow-legs, p. 140
Greater Yellow-legs, p. 141

13*a.* With a distinct white wing-stripe 14

b. Without a white wing-stripe 18

14*a.* Bill considerably longer than head, the tip decidedly downcurved; in spring, reddish above and with a black belly . . Dunlin, p. 151

b. Bill straight; never much longer than head 15

15*a.* Above olive-brown, the underparts spotted in spring; base of bill yellowish; habitually "teeters" the body while standing
Spotted Sandpiper, p. 141

b. Not as in 15*a.* 16

16*a.* Wing-stripe notably conspicuous; head, neck, and back largely rusty in spring, the plumage decidedly pale in fall and winter
Sanderling, p. 147

b. Wing-stripe and plumage not as in 16*a.* Sparrow-sized sandpipers or "peeps". 17

17*a.* Sides of head, neck, and breast conspicuously buffy
Baird Sandpiper, p. 150

b. Not as in 17*a.* . . . . Semipalmated Sandpiper, p. 148
Western Sandpiper, p. 148
Least Sandpiper, p. 150

18a. Above uniform slate gray, or underparts pale buff 19

 b. Not as in 18a. 20

19a. Larger (10–11 inches); bill appreciably longer than head; above gray, the underparts white, or conspicuously barred (rocky seashores) . . . . Wandering Tattler, p. 143

 b. Smaller (7½–8½ inches); bill shorter than head; above tawny and black, the underparts pale buff (mainly prairies, marshes, the sides of ponds, etc.) . . . . Buff-breasted Sandpiper, p. 152

20a. Bill twice as long as head; scapulars boldly streaked with buff, the chest mottled with brown (wet meadows, boggy woodlands, etc.)
Common Snipe, p. 146

 b. Bill about as long as head; breast not mottled, but sometimes pale buff streaked with black 21

21a. Larger (11–12 inches); above tawny and blackish, the tail barred with same (prairies, grassy hillsides, etc.) . . Upland Plover, p. 137

 b. Smaller (7½–9½ inches); plumage and habitat not as in 21a. . . . 22

22a. Above virtually uniform, or minutely spotted with white; sides of tail very conspicuously barred with black and white
Solitary Sandpiper, p. 141

 b. Above not uniform or speckled; tail not white or barred; a very distinct buffy band across the breast . . Pectoral Sandpiper, p. 150

*UPLAND PLOVER. *Bartramia longicauda* (Illus. p. 138).—11–12. *Adult:* Crown blackish, the median stripe and superciliaries pale buff, this continuing over the sides of the head and neck, where generously streaked; upperparts deep sooty brown, the feathers conspicuously margined with buff; primaries uniform blackish; tail rather long, distinctly barred, the outer feathers palest and with more or less white and ochraceous; throat and abdomen immaculate white, the neck and breast pale buff, distinctly streaked with blackish, the flanks and wing-linings conspicuously barred; bill shorter than head, dark above and yellowish below; legs yellowish. *Immature:* Similar to adult, but buff areas much darker, and streaks less distinct.

Distribution.—Widespread migrant, occurring principally in April, August, and September. Not recorded from Baja California or the Yucatán Peninsula.

Remarks.—A large shore bird of the prairies, fields, and grassy hillsides. The *short bill*, rather long neck and tail, and conspicuously streaked neck and breast are unmistakable. Unlike most shore birds,

UPLAND PLOVER

this species often perches on posts and has a habit of elevating its wings briefly upon alighting. Its short, stiff wing-strokes suggest the flight of a Spotted Sandpiper.

*ESKIMO CURLEW. *Numenius borealis.*

Remarks.—Eskimo Curlews resemble Whimbrels superficially. Now probably extinct, they may once have been casual transients in Mexico, although but two specific records are known (Lake Palomas, Chihuahua, April 8, 1892, and "Mexico," about 1896).

*WHIMBREL. *Numenius phaeopus hudsonicus* (Illus. p. 139).—15–17. Crown dull brown, the median stripe and superciliaries buffy white, generously streaked with brown; a dark stripe through the eye; upperparts grayish brown, somewhat obscurely mottled with paler, the primaries uniformly sooty; throat, abdomen, and crissum immaculate white, the malar area, neck, and breast buffy white, distinctly streaked with brown; flanks and wing-linings pale buff, barred with brown; bill very long (3–4 inches) and distinctly curved (depressed) toward the tip.

Distribution.—Winters commonly on the Pacific Coast (including Baja California and the Revilla Gigedo Islands), where recorded from July

WHIMBREL

to May 15. To be expected regularly on the Atlantic Coast, but thus far reported only in northeastern Tamaulipas and Tabasco.

Remarks.—Also known as Hudsonian Curlew. *See* Long-billed Curlew.

*LONG-BILLED CURLEW. *Numenius americanus.*—22–26. Mainly pale buff (spring) or pinkish buff (fall), the upperparts generously streaked and barred with sooty brown; throat white, the neck and chest narrowly streaked with brown; bill notably long (5–8 inches), and conspicuously *downcurved.*

Distribution.—A regular winter visitor, occurring on both coasts, and locally in the interior. To be expected from July to May.

Races.—*N. a. americanus* (as above). *N. a. parvus* (as above).

Remarks.—Curlews are the only large shore birds with very *long, downcurved bills.* They often fly in **V**-shaped flocks, sometimes quite high or well offshore, and are likely to be shy. Salt marshes, mud flats, estuaries, and grassy prairies are their usual habitats. The Long-billed is easily distinguished from a Whimbrel (Hudsonian Curlew) by its superior size, notably longer bill, and much buffier plumage. It lacks a dark eye-streak.

*MARBLED GODWIT. *Limosa fedoa.*—16–20. *Spring:* Above mainly brown, liberally streaked, barred, and spotted with pale buff or whitish; wing-coverts and inner remiges pale cinnamon or pinkish buff; throat immaculate white, the underparts otherwise pale buff, conspicuously barred or "marbled" with brown on the breast, sides, and flanks; bill very long (3½–5 inches) and usually distinctly upcurved at the end. *Fall:* As in spring, but much buffier; underparts virtually immaculate.

Distribution.—Winters on both coasts, locally in abundance, arriving in August and migrating northward in May. Nonbreeding individuals sometimes pass the summer.

Remarks.—The large size and long, slightly *upcurved bill* distinguished godwits from most other shore birds. Avocets have very slender upturned bills and are boldly patterned with black and white. Curlews are buff-plumaged like godwits, and frequent the same habitats, but have bills that curve *downward*. The Hudsonian Godwit, a decidedly smaller species, was sighted at Salina Cruz on the Pacific side of the Isthmus of Tehuantepec in July, 1952 (Irby Davis, Richard Herbert), and is to be expected as a transient on both coasts. Its *black-and-white ringed tail* and *blackish underwings*, as seen in flight, are good field marks. Hudsonians have reddish breasts in spring, but are whitish-breasted and gray-backed in fall.

*LESSER YELLOW-LEGS. *Tringa flavipes.*—9½–10½. *Spring:* Above sooty brown or blackish, liberally speckled and barred with white and gray; rump white; tail barred with white and brown; primaries uniformly sooty; underparts white, the sides of the head, neck, and breast heavily streaked, the flanks barred with dusky brown; bill black, a little longer than the head; legs bright yellow. *Fall and immature:* As in spring, but more uniform grayish brown above, and underparts but lightly streaked; neck and chest essentially grayish.

Distribution.—Eastern coastal lowlands during migration and in winter (July to May), also occurring regularly in suitable parts of the interior. Much less common in Baja California and on the Pacific Coast.

Remarks.—Of the several *white-rumped* sandpipers with pale tails and dark, unpatterned wings, only this species and the following have conspicuously *bright yellow legs*. Both prefer flooded meadows and the muddy banks of shallow ponds to the sandy beaches that attract most sandpipers. Yellow-legs differ considerably in size, and the Lesser has a relatively *short, straight bill*, while that of the Greater is almost twice the length of its head, and is perceptibly upturned at the end. *See* Stilt Sandpiper.

*GREATER YELLOW-LEGS. *Tringa melanoleuca.*—$12\frac{1}{2}$–$14\frac{1}{2}$. Very similar to a Lesser Yellow-legs, but considerably larger, and with a proportionately longer and slightly upturned bill.

Distribution.—Common transient and winter visitant (July 26 to April 26) in the coastal lowlands, occurring inland regularly during migration.

Remarks.—*See* Lesser Yellow-legs.

*SOLITARY SANDPIPER. *Tringa solitaria.*—$7\frac{1}{2}$–$8\frac{1}{2}$. *Spring:* Above sooty brown, the head and hind-neck white-streaked, the back and scapulars speckled with same; primaries uniform blackish; tail dark medially, the lateral feathers very conspicuously barred with black and white; underparts mainly white, the neck and chest narrowly streaked with dark brown; bill blackish, about the length of the head; legs olive greenish. *Fall and immature:* As in spring, but more grayish and uniform above, the head often without streaks; underparts virtually unstreaked, the neck and chest usually dull grayish brown.

Distribution.—Coastal lowlands in migration and winter, occurring locally in the interior.

Races.— *T. s. solitaria* (principally eastern and southern portions of the country, occasionally straggling to Baja California). *T. s. cinnamomea* (Baja California and the lowlands of both coasts).

Remarks.—A medium-sized sandpiper with *unpatterned wings, dark rump, and boldly barred outer tail feathers*. Swift and erratic in flight, often rising to a considerable height, the Solitary customarily jerks and nods its head like a Yellow-legs when standing, and, like it, usually avoids sandy beaches.

*SPOTTED SANDPIPER. *Actitis macularia.*—7–8. *Spring:* Above olive-brown, obscurely streaked (head) and barred (back) with dusky; superciliaries white; lateral rectrices white-tipped, the outermost barred with white and dusky; a white stripe across the extended wing; underparts white, boldly spotted with blackish; bill black, the lower mandible yellowish basally; legs olive or dull yellowish. *Fall and immature:* As in spring, but uniformly olive-brown above, and immaculate white below.

Distribution.—A common migrant, both on the coast and in suitable parts of the interior, occurring also on various offshore islands (Socorro

Island, Chinchorro Reef, etc.). Winters commonly in the coastal lowlands; to be expected from late July until the middle of May.

Remarks.—The only small sandpiper with *spotted underparts* (breeding plumage). White-bellied winter adults and immature birds are easily distinguished from other small, nondescript shore birds by their habit of "teetering," or bobbing the entire body while standing. In flight the wings are held stiffly, and the stroke is conspicuously short.

WILLET. *Catoptrophorus semipalmatus* (Illus. p. 142).—14–16. *Spring:* Above grayish brown, more or less conspicuously streaked (head and hindneck) and barred (back and scapulars) with dusky; wings blackish, the

WILLET

remiges with a very broad white band at all seasons; upper tail-coverts white; underparts white, the cheeks and neck narrowly streaked, and the breast and flanks irregularly barred with brown; bill rather long and decidedly sturdy, mainly blackish; legs grayish. *Fall and immature:* As in spring, but without streaks and bars, the upperparts uniform grayish brown, the neck and chest tinged with grayish.

Distribution.—Breeds locally in Tamaulipas; winters commonly on the Pacific Coast, where nonbreeding stragglers also pass the summer, and at least casually on the Atlantic side (Tampico, Tamaulipas; Yucatán Peninsula; Cozumel Island).

Races.—*C. s. inornatus* (as above; a breeding bird from Tepehuaje, Tamaulipas, about 80 miles north of Tampico, has been assigned to this form). **C. s. semipalmatus* (winters commonly on the coast of Tamaulipas and probably southward; to be expected breeding in the northern portion).

Remarks.—*Large grayish* shore birds with *long, straight bills.* Willets are rather nondescript when at rest, but in flight the black-and-white patterned wing-tips are unmistakable. Coastal beaches and grassy flats are their usual habitat.

*WANDERING TATTLER. *Heteroscelus incanus* (Illus. p. 143).—10–11. *Spring:* Above uniform slate gray; superciliaries, sides of head, and neck white, the last two narrowly streaked with slate; underparts very closely

WANDERING TATTLER (SPRING)

barred with white and slate; bill dusky, a little longer than the head; legs yellowish. *Fall:* Above as in spring, but underparts mainly white, without streaks or bars, the head, neck, breast, and flanks tinged with gray.

Distribution.—Winters regularly on the Pacific Coast, including Baja California and the Revilla Gigedo Islands, where often abundant. Stragglers are sometimes reported in summer.

Remarks.—Tattlers habitually frequent rocky seashores and are likely to be found with Surf-birds, Black Turnstones, or Spotted Sandpipers. The *long* black bill and *uniform slaty gray upperparts* are excellent field characters at all seasons; the conspicuously *barred, underparts* are distinctive in spring.

*SURF-BIRD. *Aphriza virgata.*—10. *Spring:* Above mainly sooty black, the head and neck streaked with grayish, the feathers elsewhere broadly edged with paler; upper tail-coverts and base of tail white, the terminal half of the tail black, narrowly tipped with white; a broad white stripe across the flight feathers; underparts white, the neck streaked, the remainder conspicuously barred and spotted with dusky; bill about as long as the head, decidedly sturdy, yellowish tipped with black; legs yellowish. *Fall:* Grayish brown, the throat, abdomen, and flanks immaculate white, or but sparsely streaked; wings, tail, and upper tail-coverts as in spring.

Distribution.—The Pacific Coast in migration, possibly wintering locally.

Remarks.—Surf-birds, like Wandering Tattlers and Black Turnstones, are usually found on rocky shores washed by the tides. The *short bill* (yellowish at the base), *yellowish legs,* conspicuous wing-stripe, and *single* large white patch at the base of the tail are distinctive in combination. Surf-birds in fall plumage resemble Black Turnstones superficially, but the latter have *slender, all-black bills, dusky legs,* white extending over the lower back, and a *broad black bar across the rump.*

*RUDDY TURNSTONE. *Arenaria interpres* (Illus. p. 144).—8½–9½. *Spring:* Head extensively white, but very boldly patterned with black, this joining the black of the neck and breast; upper back, scapulars, and wing-coverts largely russet, intermixed with black; a white stripe across the extended wing; lower back, rump, and upper tail-coverts white, the latter

RUDDY TURNSTONE (SPRING)

with a broad black bar; terminal half of tail black, narrowly tipped with white; throat and posterior underparts white; bill black, rather short, and slightly upturned; legs orange. *Fall:* Wings, rump, and tail as in spring, the head, neck, and breast essentially dark brown; back, scapulars, etc., blackish, variegated with white and buff; legs orange.

Distribution.—Migratory on both coasts and on some offshore islands, wintering casually in Baja California.

Races.—*A. i. interpres* (Revilla Gigedo Islands, Baja California, and the Pacific Coast generally). *A. i. morinella* (recorded from Chiapas and the coast of the Yucatán Peninsula, including Mujeres and Cozumel Islands; accidental in Sonora).

Remarks.—Both turnstones show a startling harlequin pattern on the wings, back, and tail when in flight. This species is the more colorful of the two, especially when in its red-backed, white-headed breeding plumage. The *white* throat and *orange* legs are good field marks at all times. Mud flats and sandy beaches are its usual habitats.

*BLACK TURNSTONE. *Arenaria melanocephala.*—9. *Spring:* Head, neck, breast, and upperparts mainly sooty black, the forehead, superciliaries, and auriculars usually white-streaked; lores white; a white stripe across the extended wing; lower back, rump, and upper tail-coverts white, the last with a broad black bar; terminal half of tail black, narrowly tipped with white; posterior underparts white; bill black, rather short, and slightly upturned; legs dusky. *Fall:* As in spring, but without white on the head, and the dark portions of the plumage much lighter (browner).

Distribution.—Winters commonly on the coast of Baja California and Sonora (July to April), occurring principally on rocky shores.

Remarks.—*See* Surf-bird and Ruddy Turnstone.

*DOWITCHER. *Limnodromus griseus* (Illus. p. 146).—10½–12. *Spring:* Above, except the lower back, rump, and tail, dark brown, liberally streaked and barred with buff and rufous; a pale superciliary streak; lower back immaculate white, the rump, upper tail-coverts, and tail barred with black and white; underparts cinnamon-rufous, lightly spotted (throat and breast) and barred or spotted (flanks) with black; bill blackish, about twice the length of the head; legs olive. *Fall:* Above grayish brown, the lower back, rump, upper tail-coverts, and tail as in spring; superciliaries and abdomen whitish, the underparts otherwise pale brownish gray, more or less mottled on the breast; flanks lightly barred with dusky.

Distribution.—A winter resident and fairly common migrant, occurring locally in the interior as well as on both coasts. To be expected from August until early June. Distribution of the two races in Mexico is not yet fully established.

Races.—*L. g. scolopaceus* (principally Baja California and the Pacific Coast, but also recorded from Chihuahua, Tamaulipas, the interior of Jalisco, and Guanajuato). *L. g. griseus* (probably most abundant on the Atlantic Coast, but also recorded from Baja California and Sonora, and doubtless to be found in the interior).

Remarks.—A snipelike shore bird with a *white* lower back and a *whitish rump and tail*. No other sandpiper has both a *very long* bill and

DOWITCHER (SPRING)

rich cinnamon underparts—the latter largely grayish in winter. Beaches, mud flats, and marshes.

COMMON SNIPE. *Capella gallinago delicata.*—10–11. Crown, back, and scapulars deep sooty brown, the first with a pale median stripe, the scapulars broadly striped with buff; superciliaries pale buff; a dusky stripe from bill to eye; wing-coverts white-spotted, the primaries uniformly sooty; rump and upper tail-coverts barred with sooty and buff; tail black basally, broadly tipped with rufous, and with a narrow black subterminal bar; chin whitish, the lower throat, neck, and breast mottled with brown and buff; abdomen white, the flanks barred with brown; bill about twice the length of the head, greenish gray, tipped with black; legs pale grayish.

Distribution.—Breeds in Jalisco and Guanajuato, and probably in mountains of northern Baja California. Virtually country-wide in winter except desert areas.

Remarks.—Also known as Wilson Snipe. Wet meadows, boggy woodlands, and the muddy banks of small streams and marshes are the characteristic haunts of snipe. The *long, straight bill*, buff-streaked brown plumage, and erratic, zigzag flight distinguish snipes from all other birds of this habitat.

*KNOT. *Calidris canutus rufa* (Illus. p. 147).—10–11. *Spring:* Above extensively streaked (crown and hind-neck) and mottled with black and gray, the back and scapulars with patches of pale cinnamon; primaries dusky, the extended wing showing a white stripe; rump and upper tail-coverts barred with black and white, the tail pale grayish; superciliaries, sides of head, and underparts cinnamon-rufous; bill and legs black, the former about as long as the head. *Fall:* Above pale brownish gray, the rump, upper tail-coverts, and tail as in spring; superciliaries and underparts white, very lightly streaked with dusky.

Distribution.—Coastwise in migration, probably wintering casually. Reported from Baja California, Sonora, Sinaloa, and Veracruz.

KNOT (SPRING)

Remarks.—A stocky, medium-sized shore bird with a rather *short, sturdy bill* and a *whitish* rump and tail. Dowitchers, also reddish below when in breeding plumage, have very long, snipelike bills, and white extending far up the back at all seasons. Knots and Lesser Yellow-legs might be confused when in winter plumage, but the latter has a longer, much slenderer bill, *yellow* (not black) legs, and a white rump-patch.

*SANDERLING. *Crocethia alba* (Illus. p. 148).—7–8. *Spring:* Above cinnamon-rufous, conspicuously streaked (head and hind-neck) and spotted (back and scapulars) with black, many of the feathers with white tips; primaries blackish, the extended wing showing a very broad white stripe; sides of rump white, and the lateral rectrices very pale; throat, neck, and sides of breast pale cinnamon, lightly streaked and spotted with dusky, the underparts otherwise immaculate white; bill and legs black, the former about as long as the head. *Fall:* Above pale gray, narrowly streaked and boldly spotted with black; wings and tail as in spring, the forehead, sides of head, and underparts immaculate white.

Distribution.—Winters extensively on both coasts, remaining from August until the middle of May.

Remarks.—Whitest of the smaller sandpipers in fall and winter. Best distinguished in spring by the rusty coloring of the head, neck, breast, and upperparts. Sanderlings have a notably conspicuous wing-

SANDERLING

FALL　　　　　　　　　　　　　SPRING

stripe, and in flight suggest Northern Phalaropes. Sandy seashores and coastal mud flats.

*SEMIPALMATED SANDPIPER. *Ereunetes pusillus.*—5½–6½. *Spring:* Above dark brown, liberally streaked with pale gray and buff; primaries blackish, the extended wing showing a narrow pale stripe; upper tail-coverts and tail blackish medially, the lateral feathers pale gray; superciliaries and underparts white, the sides of the head, neck, and broad band across breast faintly streaked with brownish; bill and legs blackish, the former about as long as the head and rather sturdy. *Fall:* As in spring, but much browner above, and the underparts either wholly white or breast faintly tinged with brown.

Distribution.—Probably winters on both coasts, but thus far recorded only from Quintana Roo and Cozumel Island.

Remarks.—*See* Western Sandpiper.

*WESTERN SANDPIPER. *Ereunetes mauri* (Illus. p. 149).—6–6¾. *Spring:* Very similar to a Semipalmated Sandpiper in coloration, but crown, back, and scapulars with more or less cinnamon-rufous, breast more boldly streaked, and sides also usually with dark markings; bill black, perceptibly longer than the head, and rather slender; legs black. *Fall:* Above pale brownish gray, the feathers with dark shaft-streaks; forehead and underparts usually immaculate white, the breast sometimes minutely streaked.

Distribution.—Both coasts in migration and winter; probably common, but definitely recorded only from Baja California (July 1–April 25), Sonora, Sinaloa, Nayarit, Oaxaca, Chihuahua, Veracruz, and Cozumel Island.

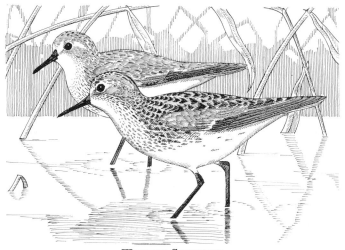

WESTERN SANDPIPER

FALL   SPRING

Remarks.—Sparrow-sized sandpipers of several species are often lumped together as "peeps," the term usually being applied to the Semipalmated, Western, Least, and Baird. While rather nondescript and very similar in all plumages, each has distinctive characters that simplify its identification, especially when two or more are seen together. Largest of the four "peeps," and perhaps the most distinctive, is the Baird. It can always be recognized by its *buffy brown head* and rather conspicuous *buffy breast-band.* The diminutive Least Sandpiper has a notably *slender* bill, and *yellowish green* (not blackish) *legs.* The Semipalmated and Western, both black-legged, are more difficult when found separately. The first has an appreciably shorter bill (sometimes hardly as long as the head) that appears relatively thick. Its breast is usually *faintly washed with buff* in fall and winter, but this does not form a distinct band, as in the Baird. By contrast, the Western's bill is a little longer than its head. It often has rather conspicuous rufous on the upperparts, but lacks buff on the breast.

*LEAST SANDPIPER. *Erolia minutilla.*—5¼–6. Very similar to a Semipalmated Sandpiper, but a little smaller, more heavily streaked on the breast (spring plumage), and with a decidedly thinner bill, and *yellowish green* (not blackish) *legs.*

Distribution.—Winters commonly on both coasts (late July to early June), and less abundantly in the interior, where recorded from Chihuahua, Coahuila, San Luis Potosi, Guanajuato, Querétaro, Mexico, and Puebla.

Remarks.—*See* Western Sandpiper.

*WHITE-RUMPED SANDPIPER. *Erolia fuscicollis.*—7–8. *Spring:* Above grayish brown, streaked and spotted with blackish, the crown, back, and scapulars with more or less rusty; superciliaries white; primaries sooty, the extended wing showing a pale stripe; upper tail-coverts immaculate white, the tail dusky; underparts white, the malar area, neck, breast, and sides very distinctly streaked with brown; bill dusky, about as long as the head; legs greenish. *Fall:* Superciliaries, wings, rump, and tail as in spring, the upperparts otherwise mainly brownish gray; below white, the breast tinged with pale brownish and very lightly streaked.

Distribution.—A transient, thus far recorded only from Yucatán and Cozumel Island. To be expected in spring.

Remarks.—A peeplike sandpiper, resembling the Baird, but with a very conspicuous *white rump, and greenish* (not black) *legs.*

*BAIRD SANDPIPER. *Erolia bairdii.*—7–7¾. Resembles Least and Semipalmated Sandpipers, but larger than either, and upperparts much buffier; a pale buff band across the breast, this obscurely streaked with dusky, especially when in spring plumage; bill black, rather slender, and about as long as the head; legs greenish or slate color.

Distribution.—Apparently a regular migrant, occurring on both coasts, and recorded from widely separated localities in the interior.

Remarks.—*See* Western Sandpiper.

*PECTORAL SANDPIPER. *Erolia melanotos.*—8½–9½. Above deep sooty brown, the feathers conspicuously edged with buff and rusty; superciliaries pale; rump, upper tail-coverts, and median portion of tail sooty black, the lateral rectrices grayish; primaries sooty, the extended wing without a pale stripe; throat and posterior underparts white, the sides of the head, neck, and breast buffy brown, distinctly streaked with blackish; bill about as long as the head, greenish yellow toward the base, the terminal portion black; legs greenish yellow.

Distribution.—A regular migrant, occurring both on the coast and in the interior. To be expected from late July to late October and in March and April.

Remarks.—The *buffy, black-streaked band* extending across the lower neck and breast in *sharp contrast* with the immaculate white throat and abdomen is the hallmark of this species. Least Sandpipers are similar when in breeding plumage, but are decidedly smaller and have *black bills*. The Baird, also smaller and with a black bill, is not so distinctly streaked on the breast and has *black legs*.

*DUNLIN. *Erolia alpina pacifica.*—7½–8½. *Spring:* Above grayish brown, streaked with dusky, the back, scapulars, and upper tail-coverts more or less extensively cinnamon or rusty; superciliaries pale but obscure; primaries sooty, the extended wing showing a conspicuous white stripe; tail grayish, the median portion darkest; underparts mainly white, the sides of the head, neck, and breast streaked with dusky; a large black patch on the abdomen; bill black, considerably longer than the head, and slightly down-curved toward the tip; legs dusky olive. *Fall:* Above grayish brown; below white, the neck and breast grayish, lightly streaked with brown, this forming an indistinct pectoral band.

Distribution.—Winters commonly on the coasts of Baja California and Sonora. To be expected in northeastern Tamaulipas.

Remarks.—Also known as Red-backed Sandpiper. A smallish sandpiper with a decidedly *long, downcurved bill*. In spring the *black belly and reddish back* are unmistakable. The long, *curved* bill is the best field character in fall and winter.

*STILT SANDPIPER. *Micropalama himantopus.*—8–9. *Spring:* Median crown blackish, the lateral portions, nape, and auriculars cinnamon; a conspicuous white superciliary stripe; hind-neck, back, and scapulars sooty black, more or less streaked and barred with buffy white; wing-coverts pale brownish gray, the primaries uniformly sooty; extended wing without a pale stripe; rump and upper tail-coverts white, barred with dusky, the tail uniformly grayish; underparts white, very conspicuously barred with dusky; bill black, considerably longer than the head; legs greenish. *Fall:* Above pale grayish brown, the wings, rump, and tail as in spring; below white, the sides of the head, neck, and breast faintly tinged with grayish buff and obscurely streaked with brown.

Distribution.—Migratory on both coasts (sparingly in the interior), apparently wintering casually.

Remarks.—Totally unlike any other small sandpiper in spring, when barred below and with a cinnamon band across the cheeks. Resembles a Lesser Yellow-legs in fall and winter, but smaller and with a longer, heavier bill that tapers appreciably and appears to droop slightly at the tip. The conspicuous *white superciliaries and greenish* (not yellow) *legs* are also good characters.

*BUFF-BREASTED SANDPIPER. *Tryngites subruficollis.*—$7\frac{1}{2}$-$8\frac{1}{2}$. *Adult:* Above grayish buff or pale tawny, boldly streaked and spotted with black; middle tail feathers blackish, the lateral feathers paler, white-tipped, and with black subterminal bar; primaries sooty, the inner webs (and under coverts) marbled with black and white; sides of head and underparts pinkish buff or buffy cinnamon, obscurely mottled with white; bill blackish, a little shorter than the head; legs yellowish. *Immature:* Similar to adult, but somewhat paler and with narrow white edgings on the black feathers.

Distribution.—A rare migrant recorded from Tamaulipas (August and September) and Guanajuato.

Remarks.—The only small sandpiper with *pale buffy underparts.* Immature birds appear very scaly above; the adults buffy brown, boldly marked with black. To be expected on prairies and the shores of streams and ponds, as well as in marshes and on the seashore.

Family RECURVIROSTRIDAE. Avocets, Stilts

KEY TO THE SPECIES

1*a*. Above uniform brown or glossy black; tip of bill slightly upturned

  b. Above boldly patterned; bill very slender, the tip conspicuously upturned . . . .

BLACK-NECKED STILT. *Himantopus mexicanus* (Illus. p. 153).—14. *Male:* Above mainly glossy black, the tail pale gray; forepart of head, spot behind eye, and underparts immaculate white; bill slightly recurved; iris red; legs bright pink, notably long and slender. *Female:* Similar to male, but back and scapulars brownish, appearing black at a distance.

Distribution.—Coastal lowlands generally; elsewhere locally.

Remarks.—A large, black-and-white wader with extraordinarily *long, slender red legs.* Stilts abound in fresh and salt-water marshes and on the grassy banks of lagoons and lowland streams. Unmistakable.

BLACK-NECKED STILT

AMERICAN AVOCET. *Recurvirostra americana.*—17–20. *Breeding plumage:* Head, neck, and breast pale cinnamon or pinkish; scapulars and wings black and white; plumage otherwise immaculate white, bill very long and slender and distinctly recurved; legs bluish, notably long and slender. *Winter plumage:* Similar to breeding plumage, but without cinnamon, the head, neck, and breast white, or faintly tinged with bluish gray.

Distribution.—Widespread in winter, especially coastwise, and reported breeding locally in San Luis Potosí. To be expected principally from August to the middle of May.

Remarks.—Few waders surpass Avocets in beauty and grace. They frequent the same habitats as Stilts and are easily identified by their extremely *slender, upturned bills* and boldly patterned dorsal plumage, the latter especially conspicuous in flight.

Family PHALAROPODIDAE. Phalaropes

KEY TO THE SPECIES

1*a*. Neck or underparts with cinnamon, cinnamon-rufous, or chestnut 2

  b. Without cinnamon, cinnamon-rufous, or chestnut 4

2*a*. Underparts mainly or wholly cinnamon

                           Red Phalarope (spring), p. 154

  b. Underparts mainly white 3

3*a*. A prominent wing-stripe; plumage above dull slate color, sometimes
streaked with buff . . . . . . Northern Phalarope (spring), p. 155

  b. No wing-stripe; crown and hind-neck pale gray or whitish
                      Wilson Phalarope (spring), p. 154

4*a*. A conspicuous wing-stripe; upper tail-coverts mainly dark 5

  b. No wing-stripe; upper tail-coverts white
                      Wilson Phalarope (fall), p. 154

5*a*. Bill fairly heavy; back mainly pale bluish gray
                      Red Phalarope (fall), p. 154

  b. Bill very slender; back dark and more or less streaked
                      Northern Phalarope (fall), p. 155

*RED PHALAROPE. *Phalaropus fulicarius.*—$7\frac{1}{2}$–$8\frac{1}{2}$. *Female* (*breeding
plumage*): Sides of head white, the crown, hind-neck, and chin black; upperparts mainly black, conspicuously striped with buff; wings dusky and with
a broad white stripe; neck and underparts deep chestnut; bill rather stout,
yellowish tipped with black; legs yellowish. *Male* (*breeding plumage*): Similar
to female, but smaller and much duller; crown and hind-neck streaked with
ochraceous; cheeks less extensively white and underparts mottled with same.
Adults in winter: Forehead and sides of head (except dusky postocular
streak) white like underparts; plumage above mainly bluish gray.

    Distribution.—Regular migrant off the Pacific Coast of Baja Cali-
fornia; recorded once off the Revilla Gigedo Islands (May 12, 1925) and
at sea off Sonora.

    Remarks.—Essentially maritime in migration and winter, and not
likely to be seen from land. *See* Northern Phalarope and Sanderling.

    *WILSON PHALAROPE. *Steganopus tricolor.*—$7\frac{1}{2}$–9. *Female* (*breeding
plumage*): Top of head pale grayish, passing into white on hind-neck; sides
of head mainly black, shading into rich chestnut on sides of neck, this
continuing as a broken line over the scapulars and merging with the cinnamon of the lower throat, neck, and chest; back mainly bluish gray, but
interrupted by chestnut of the scapulars; upper throat, breast, belly, and
crissum white; bill black, needle-like; legs yellowish. *Male* (*breeding plumage*): Similar to female, but smaller, much duller, and without a sharply
contrasting pattern. *Adults in winter:* Above mainly pale gray, shading to
grayish brown on the wings; forehead, sides of head, and upper tail-coverts
white like underparts.

    Distribution.—Migrates principally along the Pacific Coast, but some-
times also recorded in the interior (northern borders of Chihuahua and
Coahuila, San Luis Potosí, Puebla, and Quintana Roo).

Remarks.—The only shore bird with a broad black-and-chestnut stripe on each side of the neck. In fall and winter Wilson Phalaropes will be recognized by their very *slender black bills,* pale gray backs, and *white rumps.* Other phalaropes show a conspicuous wing-stripe when in flight.

*NORTHERN PHALAROPE. *Lobipes lobatus.*—6½–7½. *Female* (*breeding plumage*): Upperparts, including sides of head, mainly sooty brown or slate color; back and scapulars striped with brownish red; wings broadly barred with white; below mainly white, the sides of neck and chest bright cinnamon-rufous; bill and legs black, the first notably slender. *Male* (*breeding plumage*): Similar to female, but smaller and duller, and usually without cinnamon-rufous on chest. *Winter plumage:* Above mainly gray, or streaked with buff and white; forehead and sides of head (except dusky postocular streak) white like underparts; sides of breast grayish.

Distribution.—Common migrant along the Pacific Coast, principally offshore, and twice recorded in the interior (Sonora and San Luis Potosí).

Remarks.—When in breeding plumage, the *sooty* or *slate-colored head* and brownish rufous neck-patch are diagnostic. Migrants (usually in winter plumage) resemble Red Phalaropes but can be distinguished by their smaller size, *slender black bills,* and *black* (not yellowish) *feet.* Wilson Phalaropes also have very slender black bills, but lack white wing-bars.

Family BURHINIDAE. Thick-knees

DOUBLE-STRIPED THICK-KNEE. *Burhinus bistriatus bistriatus* (Illus. p. 156).—20. Crown and hind-neck dusky, especially laterally, the median portion finely streaked with buff; broad white superciliaries; head and neck largely buffy, finely streaked with brown, this shading to pale grayish buff on the breast, where minutely streaked; upperparts dusky brown, more or less boldly streaked with buff; tail mainly white, black-tipped, and virtually concealed by the upper coverts; belly white; bill rather short and thick, mainly black, the base of the lower mandible greenish like legs; iris and eyelids yellow.

Distribution.—Oaxaca, Chiapas, Veracruz, and Tabasco, chiefly in savannahs having brush cover.

Remarks.—Also known as Mexican Thick-knee and American Thick-knee. Thick-knees inhabit more or less open country and are fairly abundant in some localities. They are essentially terrestrial and nocturnal in habits but may be flushed by day and are capable of rather swift flight.

DOUBLE-STRIPED THICK-KNEE

Family STERCORARIIDAE. Jaegers

KEY TO THE SPECIES

1*a*. More than 20 inches long; projecting middle rectrices broad and
twisted . . . . Pomarine Jaeger, p. 156

b. Less than 20 inches long; projecting middle retrices attenuated
Parasitic Jaeger, p. 156

*POMARINE JAEGER. *Stercorarius pomarinus.*—20–22. Very similar
to a Parasitic Jaeger, plumage for plumage, but with *broad, twisted middle
tail feathers*.

Distribution.—Migrates and winters off both coasts, but only twice
recorded in Mexican waters ("off west coast," October 8; off Contoy Island,
Quintana Roo, August 3, 1930).

*PARASITIC JAEGER. *Stercorarius parasiticus.*—15–20. *Adult* (*light
phase*): Above mainly deep sooty brown, darkening on "cap"; base of
primaries and base of tail appear whitish in flight; sides of head and neck
pale yellowish; below mainly white, usually more or less shaded with grayish brown posteriorly; middle retrices pointed and several inches longer than
outer tail feathers; (*dark phase*): Mainly dusky brown; a pale patch at base
of tail and primaries. *Immature:* Above and below mottled with brown,
buff, and white; middle rectrices pointed, but usually not longer than
adjacent feathers.

Distribution.—Migrates and winters off both coasts. Occasionally reported at sea off Baja California (July 10–April 19).

Remarks.—Jaegers are aggressive, hawklike sea birds with rather narrow wings that show a flash of white at the base of the primaries. Adults are distinguished from all similar birds by their *projecting middle tail feathers*. They winter at sea and are not likely to be seen from land, and but rarely in Mexican waters. Long-tailed Jaegers have not yet been reported in our area, but are to be expected. They suggest Parasitics, but have more distinct black caps, paler backs, brighter cheeks, and less white on their primaries. The middle rectrices of many individuals project 8 or 10 inches, as compared with 4 inches or less, in Parasitic Jaegers.

Family LARIDAE. Gulls, Terns

KEY TO THE SPECIES

1a. Gulls 2

Superficially like terns, but averaging larger and with proportionately broader wings (the tips often patterned), usually a square-tipped tail (this deeply notched in the Sabine Gull), and a relatively sturdy bill that is slightly hooked at the end. Gulls are less graceful than terns and fly with the bill extended on a level with the body, not depressed, as with terns. They feed from or near the surface of the water, often while swimming, and never dive headforemost, as do terns. Some gulls are black-headed in summer plumage, but none has a conspicuous black cap. The term "mantle," often used in describing gulls, refers to the back and wingcoverts.

b. Terns 26

Often mistaken for gulls by the novice, but easily distinguished from them by their relatively slender, *sharply pointed bills*, narrower, more pointed wings, more graceful flight, and forked (or deeply notched) tails, this being rounded only in the Noddy. Terns characteristically fly with the bill pointed downward. They dive for their food, a technique not employed by gulls. Most terns have a conspicuous black cap when in summer plumage, but none are black-headed unless also black below.

2a. Head immaculate white, or essentially white, the mantle uniform pearly gray or bluish slate 3

b. Head not immaculate white, or essentially white. Mantle usually pearly gray in summer plumage, but often liberally mottled with white and pale grayish brown in winter. Above and below sometimes deep sooty brown or pale brownish gray 14

3a. Tail black; underparts pale ashy gray, the mantle bluish slate
Heermann Gull (summer), p. 162

   b. Tail and underparts white; mantle uniformly pearly gray or bluish
slate 4

4a. Primaries without black; pearly gray like mantle
Glaucous-winged Gull (summer), p. 165

   b. Primaries black, or the outer feathers conspicuously black-tipped;
often with white spots or "windows" toward the ends 5

5a. Black of the four outer primaries *cut straight across*, and without
white spots or "windows"; posterior crown and nape pearly gray;
bill greenish yellow; legs black
Black-legged Kittiwake (adult), p. 167

   b. Not as in 5a. 6

6a. Tail black-tipped; a black nuchal collar, and conspicuous patch
of black on forward edge of extended wing near body
Black-legged Kittiwake (immature), p. 167

   b. Not as in 6a. 7

7a. Notably large (18–25 inches); head immaculate white; bill decidedly sturdy, yellow, sometimes with a black ring or reddish spot
near the tip 8

   b. Small or medium-sized (13–17 inches); nape and sides of head more
or less smudged or mottled with dusky or brownish; bill rather
slender, dull reddish, blackish, or yellow tipped with black . . . 11

8a. Mantle bluish slate, appearing very dark at a distance; a reddish
spot near tip of lower mandible; legs flesh color
Western Gull (adult), p. 164

   b. Mantle pearly gray; bill ringed, or with a reddish spot near tip
of lower mandible 9

9a. With a dusky ring near tip of bill; a white subterminal spot on two
outermost primaries of each wing   Ring-billed Gull (summer), p. 162

   b. Bill not ringed; a reddish spot near tip of lower mandible; primaries
white-tipped, and with a white "window" on two outermost
feathers 10

10a. With pale eyes and flesh-colored legs
Herring Gull (summer), p. 163

   b. With dark eyes and greenish yellow legs
California Gull (summer), p. 163

11a. Orbital area, auriculars, and nape blackish or dingy; a distinct
black band across the white wing-tips   Franklin Gull (winter), p. 166

   b. Not as in 11a. 12

22*a*. Underparts uniform ashy gray, the mantle bluish slate (winter adult), or above and below deep sooty brown (immature)

Heermann Gull, p. 162

b. Above and below extensively pale grayish brown, more or less mottled with white 23

23*a*. Less than 17 inches; abdomen and crissum immaculate white, unlike throat and breast; a broad black subterminal tail-bar

Laughing Gull (immature), p. 165

b. More than 18 inches; abdomen and crissum not immaculate white, but more or less mottled like throat and breast 24

24*a*. Remiges and tail uniform pale grayish brown; plumage sparsely mottled . . . . Glaucous-winged Gull (winter), p. 165

b. Primaries black or deep sooty; tail blackish or with a broad subterminal bar; plumage extensively mottled 25

25*a*. A black subterminal tail-bar   Ring-billed Gull (immature), p. 162

b. Tail dusky or blackish, without a distinct subterminal bar

Herring Gull (immature), p. 163
California Gull (immature), p. 163
Western Gull (immature), p. 164

26*a*. Mainly black or deep sooty brown 27

b. Immaculate white, or with white underparts 28

27*a*. Head and underparts black, the upperparts dark slate

Black Tern (summer), p. 168

b. Deep sooty brown; forehead and crown pearly gray

Brown Noddy, p. 173

28*a*. Uniform white; bill black . . . . White Tern, p. 174

b. Not entirely white, the upperparts largely black, slate color, or pearly gray 29

29*a*. Above black, or mainly dark slate gray 30

b. Above pearly gray, the crown or hind-neck sometimes black or dusky; tail usually deeply forked 32

30*a*. Upperparts (except forehead) uniformly black; or above deep sooty brown, barred and speckled with whitish   Sooty Tern, p. 171

b. Essentially as in 24*a*, but with a white band across the hind-neck 31

31*a*. Very small (9–10 inches); forehead extensively white, the posterior crown, nape, and patch behind eye dusky; tail *notched* (not deeply forked) . . . . Black Tern (winter), p. 168

b. Medium-sized (13–15 inches); crown and stripe from bill to eye black; or crown and nape streaked and mottled; tail deeply forked, the outer feathers extensively white . . . . . Bridled Tern, p. 171

32*a.* Notably large (19–22 inches); bill decidedly sturdy, orange or red
Caspian Tern, p. 169
Royal Tern, p. 172

 b. Very small, or medium-sized (8–17 inches); bill relatively slender,
sometimes orange or red, but often black 33

33*a.* Less than 10 inches long; if black-capped, with a yellow bill
Least Tern, p. 171

 b. More than 13 inches long; if black-capped, the bill orange, red,
or black 34

34*a.* With a uniform black cap extending from bill to hind-neck . . . 35

 b. Not black-capped; forehead and median crown more or less whitish,
the nape and hind-neck usually with some dusky or black . . . 38

35*a.* With a conspicuous nuchal crest; bill reddish orange, or black
tipped with white 36

 b. Not crested; bill black, or red tipped with black 37

36*a.* Bill reddish orange (Pacific Coast) Elegant Tern (summer), p. 173

 b. Bill black, tipped with yellow (East Coast)
Sandwich Tern (summer), p. 173

37*a.* Bill wholly black, rather short and sturdy
Gull-billed Tern (summer), p. 168

 b. Bill red, tipped with black, and rather slender
Common Tern (summer), p. 170
Forster Tern (summer), p. 170

38*a.* With a conspicuous nuchal crest, this mainly black; bill orange, or
black tipped with yellow 39

 b. Not crested; bill black or dusky reddish 40

39*a.* Bill orange (Pacific Coast) . . . . . Elegant Tern (winter), p. 173

 b. Bill black, tipped with yellow (East Coast)
Sandwich Tern (winter), p. 173

40*a.* Bill wholly black, rather short and sturdy; crown white, lightly
streaked with black; a dusky patch behind eye
Gull-billed Tern (winter), p. 168

 b. Bill dusky reddish; nape and hind-neck dusky, or with a broad
black stripe through eye 41

41*a.* Back of head extensively dusky; a dusky patch on forward edge
of the extended wing near body . . Common Tern (winter), p. 170

 b. A conspicuous black stripe through eye; nape usually somewhat
dusky . . . . Forster Tern (winter), p. 170

HEERMANN GULL. *Larus heermanni* (Illus. p. 162).—16–18. *Adult* (*summer*): Head and neck white; hind-neck, upper tail-coverts, and underparts pale gray, darkening to slate on the mantle; secondaries tipped with white; primaries and tail black, the latter narrowly white-tipped; bill red, tipped with black; legs black; (*winter*): As in summer, but head mottled with grayish brown. *Immature:* Deep sooty brown, the wings and tail darkest; bill and feet black, the former reddish toward base.

Distribution.—The Pacific Coast (including the Gulf of California), breeding commonly on numerous offshore islands.

HEERMANN GULL

ADULT   IMMATURE

Remarks.—The only *dark gray* gull with a *white* head and *black* tail. Hardly less distinctive are immature birds with their *uniformly sooty brown plumage.*

*RING-BILLED GULL. *Larus delawarensis.*—18–19. *Adult* (*summer*): Mainly white, the mantle pearly gray; outer primaries black, the two outermost feathers with a white subterminal spot; iris pale yellow, the eye-ring red; bill greenish yellow, with a *complete* black ring near tip; legs yellowish; (*winter*): Head and hind-neck streaked with dusky. *Immature:* Grayish brown above, the underparts whitish, more or less mottled with brown; outer primaries uniform black; a narrow subterminal tail-bar; bill pinkish, the terminal half black; legs gray or pinkish.

Distribution.—Winters commonly on the Pacific Coast, occurring locally in the interior south to Jalisco, Zacatecas, and Guanajuato. To be expected on the Gulf Coast.

Remarks.—The *complete black ring* near the tip of the bill (of adults) is virtually diagnostic. In other respects this common wintering species most closely resembles the California Gull, a somewhat larger bird with more white on the primaries. Immature Ring-bills differ from all other large gulls in having a relatively *narrow* (but conspicuous) *subterminal tail-bar.*

*HERRING GULL. *Larus argentatus smithsonianus.*—22–25. *Adult* (*summer*): Mainly white, the mantle pearly gray; outer primaries extensively black, tipped with white, the two outermost feathers with a white subterminal spot; iris white or pale yellow; bill yellow with a reddish spot near tip of lower mandible; legs flesh color; (*winter*): Head and hind-neck streaked with dusky. *Immature:* Grayish brown, more or less mottled and streaked with grayish white, the wings and tail blackish; bill blackish, paler at base; legs flesh color.

Distribution.—Winters on both coasts, but in greatest abundance on the Caribbean side. Uncommon or casual in the interior.

Remarks.—No other large *pearly-backed* gull with *black* primaries has *pale eyes and flesh-colored legs.* Immature birds are very similar to Western and California Gulls in comparable plumage, the three usually being virtually indistinguishable in the field. However, several distinctive characters can be observed under ideal conditions. Immature Herring Gulls tend to be browner than either the Western or the California, and usually have paler heads. California Gulls have *relatively* small bills that are *extensively flesh-colored basally.* The lower mandible of Western Gulls has a notably *deep angle.*

*CALIFORNIA GULL. *Larus californicus.*—20–23. *Adult* (*summer*): Mainly white, the mantle pearly gray; outer primaries black, tipped with white, the second feather with a conspicuous white subterminal spot; iris brown, the eye-ring red; bill yellow, with a red spot near tip of lower mandible; legs greenish yellow; (*winter*): Head and neck streaked with dusky; a red-and-black spot on the lower mandible; legs greenish gray. *Immature:* Profusely mottled with grayish brown and grayish white, the primaries and tail blackish; bill black-tipped, the basal half pinkish.

Distribution.—Winters commonly on the coasts of Baja California, south on the Pacific Coast to Oaxaca, and much less abundantly on the Gulf Coast to Veracruz. Casual in the interior—Chihuahua, Durango, Guanajuato, Mexico, Nuevo León. Reported in Sonora as late as June 16.

Remarks.—The *red* (or red-and-black) *spot* on the lower mandible, and *greenish yellow* (or greenish gray) *legs* distinguish adult California Gulls from other large *pearly-backed* species with *black, patterned wing-tips. See* Herring Gull.

WESTERN GULL. *Larus occidentalis* (Illus. p. 164).—21–24. *Adult:* Mainly white, the mantle bluish slate; secondaries broadly white-tipped, the primaries slaty black, tipped with white, the outermost feather with a white subterminal spot; iris brown, the eye-ring red; bill deep yellow, with red spot near tip of lower mandible; legs pale flesh color. *Immature:* Dark

WESTERN GULL

IMMATURE   ADULT

grayish brown, profusely mottled with paler, the remiges and tail sooty black; bill black or broadly black-tipped; legs pale flesh color.

Distribution.—Baja California, the Gulf of California, and the coast of Sonora, wintering southward perhaps to Nayarit.

Races.—*L. o. wymani* (Pacific side of Baja California, breeding commonly on the coastal islands; a sight record for Sonora). *L. o. livens* (Gulf of California and the adjacent coasts, wintering south to Nayarit and perhaps to the Revilla Gigedo Islands).

Remarks.—A large white gull with a *dark gray* (slate-colored) mantle, *black, white-tipped primaries, and flesh-colored legs.* No similar gull has an immaculate white head and neck at all seasons. Immature birds resemble California Gulls in comparable plumage, but have *larger*, essentially *black bills* with a deep angle on the underside near tip.

*GLAUCOUS-WINGED GULL. *Larus glaucescens.*—22–25. *Adult* (*summer*): Mainly white, the mantle pearly gray; outer primaries similar, or faintly dusky (never black), tipped with white; bill pale yellow, the lower mandible with a red spot near tip; legs flesh color; (*winter*): Head, neck, and breast mottled with dusky. *Immature:* Pale brownish gray, profusely mottled with gray or buffy; bill pinkish basally, the terminal half black.

Distribution.—Winters commonly in Baja California; casual to Sonora.

Remarks.—Readily distinguished by the absence of black on the primaries, these being essentially concolor with the mantle in all plumages.

*NELSON GULL. *Larus nelsoni.*—22–25. *Adult* (*summer*): Mainly white, the mantle pearly gray; secondaries and inner primaries broadly white-tipped, the five outermost primaries *brownish gray* tipped with white; bill deep yellow, tipped with whitish, the lower mandible with a large red subterminal spot. *Immature:* Similar to immature Glaucous-winged Gulls, but tail deeper brown.

Distribution.—Apparently an accidental winter visitor in the vicinity of Baja California (San Geronimo Island, March 18, 1897).

Remarks.—This rare gull, known from but five specimens, may prove to be a hybrid of the Glaucous and Vega Gulls, the latter a far-northern and Asiatic race of the Herring Gull.

LAUGHING GULL. *Larus atricilla* (Illus. p. 166).—15–17. *Adult* (*summer*): Head and primaries black; mantle dark bluish gray, the secondaries white-tipped; hind-neck, rump, tail, and underparts white; iris brown, the eyelids and bill red; legs reddish brown; (*winter*): Head white, more or less mottled with grayish brown; bill blackish. *Immature:* Above extensively grayish brown, more or less mottled with paler; remiges sooty black, the secondaries white-tipped; rump and upper tail-coverts white, the tail with a black subterminal bar; throat and breast grayish brown, the posterior underparts white; bill black; legs brownish.

Distribution.—Breeds on the coast of Sinaloa and off the coasts of Campeche (Arcas Keys) and Yucatán (Alacrán Reef). Winters commonly on both coasts (August 7 to May 17), occurring occasionally on lakes of the interior.

Remarks.—The only resident black-headed gull. Adults are readily distinguished at all seasons from other small gulls by the *dark gray mantle* and *black, unpatterned primaries* that blend into the mantle at a little distance. Immature birds are much darker than other small gulls

LAUGHING GULL (SPRING)

in comparable plumage, and have *pale brownish or mottled* (not white) necks and breasts.

*FRANKLIN GULL. *Larus pipixcan.*—13–15. *Adult (summer):* Head black; mantle and remiges bluish gray, the latter white-tipped; a conspicuous black subterminal bar on each of the five outer primaries; hind-neck, rump, tail, and underparts white, the latter usually with a rosy flush; bill dark red; legs reddish brown; *(winter):* Head more or less white, the orbital area, auriculars, and hind-neck blackish. *Immature:* Forehead whitish, the crown, sides of head, hind-neck, and mantle grayish brown; primaries black, the inner feathers and secondaries white-tipped; rump and tail white, the latter with a broad black subterminal bar; underparts white; bill and legs brownish.

Distribution.—A common transient on both coasts (late April; August and September). Possibly casual in winter.

Remarks.—An irregular, but very *distinct, black band* that crosses the *white wing-tips* serves to identify adults. Immature birds lack the brownish neck and breast of young Laughing Gulls, and differ from immature Bonaparte Gulls in having *uniformly black primaries.*

*EUROPEAN BLACK-HEADED GULL. *Larus ridibundus.*—15. *Adult* (*summer*): Head deep chocolate-brown; a narrow white eye-ring interrupted in front; mantle very pale pearly gray, the plumage otherwise mainly white; primaries black-tipped and with a black margin on the inner webs; secondaries pale gray like mantle; bill and legs deep red; (*winter*): Head mainly white or smudged with dusky; bill red, as in summer. *Immature:* Above grayish brown, more or less intermixed with pale gray; primaries white medially, the tips and margins black; a sooty brown subterminal tail-bar; legs dull reddish yellow.

Distribution.—Accidental winter visitor on the Gulf Coast. Thus far recorded but once in our area—Gulf of Campeche, near Veracruz, in February, 1912.

Remarks.—In winter plumage this common Old World species might be mistaken for a Bonaparte Gull with a black-tipped, *yellow bill.* Its wing pattern, somewhat like that of a Bonaparte, readily distinguishes it from both Franklin and Laughing Gulls, the only small species that occur commonly on the east coast.

*BONAPARTE GULL. *Larus philadelphia.*—13–14. *Adult* (*summer*): Head slaty black; a narrow white crescent above and below the eye; mantle pale pearly gray; outer primaries white, conspicuously tipped with black, the inner remiges pearly gray; hind-neck, rump, tail, and underparts white; bill black; legs red; (*winter*): Head white, with a dusky spot behind the eye; legs orange or flesh-color. *Immature:* Above extensively grayish brown, more or less intermixed with pearly gray; primaries mainly black, the inner webs extensively white; a dusky spot behind the eye; underparts, rump, and tail white, the last with a narrow black subterminal bar.

Distribution.—Winters fairly commonly on the coasts of Baja California, Sonora, Sinaloa, and probably at least casually on the Atlantic Coast (Tampico, Tamaulipas, March 1, 1951). Recorded inland in Jalisco and Guanajuato.

Remarks.—A small gull, black-headed in breeding plumage, with *black-tipped, white outer primaries.* The dusky spot behind the eye of white-headed winter birds is a useful corroborative field mark.

*BLACK-LEGGED KITTIWAKE. *Rissa tridactyla pollicaris.*—15–17. *Adult* (*summer*): Mainly white, the mantle and remiges pearly gray, the outer primaries black-tipped; bill pale greenish yellow; legs black; (*winter*): Posterior crown and nape pearly gray; a dusky spot behind the eye; bill dusky, the terminal half pale yellow. *Immature:* Mainly white, the mantle pearly gray; a black crescent across the hind-neck; shoulders and outer primaries black, the latter with white inner margins; tail narrowly black tipped; bill black; legs dusky.

Distribution.—Winters off the west coast of Baja California, occurring regularly in the vicinity of the Los Coronados Islands and San Geronimo Island.

Remarks.—Also known as Common Kittiwake. This species and the following, unlike other gulls, are most likely to be seen well offshore. In breeding plumage the wing-tips appear to have been "dipped in ink," so straight is the line of demarkation between the black and gray. Immature birds will be recognized at a distance by their dark nuchal bar, black primaries, and boldly patterned shoulders.

*SABINE GULL. *Xemia sabini woznesenskii.*—12–14. *Adult (summer):* Head slaty black; back, scapulars, and wing-coverts pearly gray; primaries mainly black, but white-tipped and extensively white on the inner webs; hind-neck, secondaries, rump, underparts, and tail white, the last deeply notched; bill black basally, the terminal half yellow; legs black; *(winter):* Head mainly white, the hind-neck (at least) more or less grayish; bill black. *Immature:* Above grayish brown; primaries mainly black, the secondaries white; underparts and tail white, the latter broadly black-tipped; bill black.

Distribution.—Casual in migration to Baja California, where recorded from July 31 to August 20.

Remarks.—The only gull with a *notched tail*. At a distance, Sabine Gulls appear to have *all-black primaries* and a triangular white patch extending across the hind edge of the wings.

*BLACK TERN. *Chlidonias niger surinamensis.*—9–10. *Adult (summer):* Head and underparts black; back, wings, and tail slate gray, the latter deeply notched; under tail-coverts white; bill black; legs dusky; *(winter):* Forehead, hind-neck, and underparts white; posterior crown and nape dusky; a blackish patch behind the eye; back, wings, and tail dark gray. Birds in changing plumage may be extensively mottled. *Immature:* Similar to winter adult, but more or less brownish above.

Distribution.—A widespread and rather common transient, especially in the coastal lowlands. Recorded in Mexico from July to October and from April to June. Winters in South America.

Remarks.—The only *small tern* with dusky or *slate-colored* (not pearly gray) *upperparts*. During migration individuals may be either black-bodied, pied, or white below. The diminutive Least Tern is also white below, but much paler above, and has a *whitish tail*.

GULL-BILLED TERN. *Gelochelidon nilotica* (Illus. p. 169).—13–14. *Adult (summer):* Crown and nape of neck black; back and wings pale pearly gray, the primaries dusky silver terminally; underparts and tail white, the latter moderately forked; bill black, decidedly sturdy. *Immature* and *winter adult:* Head whitish, the crown streaked with black; a dusky patch behind the eye.

Distribution.—Resident on the Pacific Coast, including Baja California, occurring also on the Gulf Coast in winter.

Races.—*G. n. vanrossemi* (Baja California, islands in the Gulf of California, and the Pacific Coast of Mexico, breeding locally in the northern portion). **G. n. aranea* (winters casually on the Gulf Coast, possibly breeding locally).

Remarks.—The only medium-sized, *pearly-backed tern* with a rather *stout bill* that is *wholly black* at all seasons. Common and Forster

GULL-BILLED TERN

Terns in winter plumage have dusky reddish bills that appear black at a distance, but each has distinctive head markings. *See* Common Tern.

CASPIAN TERN. *Hydroprogne caspia.*—19–22. *Adult* (*summer*): Crown and long nuchal feathers black; back and wings pale pearly gray, the primaries becoming dusky silver terminally; underparts and tail white, the latter moderately forked; bill notably sturdy, deep coral-red, tipped with orange; legs black; (*winter*): Forehead, crown, and nape white, conspicuously streaked with black, especially posteriorly; bill orange-red. *Immature:* Forehead pale grayish, the upperparts more or less spotted with brownish black; outer primaries largely dusky; bill dull orange, tipped with dusky.

Distribution.—Baja California and both coasts of Mexico, breeding locally on the Pacific side (Scammon's Lagoon, Baja California; Isla Larición, Sinaloa).

Remarks.—A very large, orange-billed tern, resembling the Royal superficially, but with a much *less deeply forked tail* and darker primaries as seen from below. In winter the Caspian's forehead is more or less streaked, while that of the Royal is largely white. When at rest a Caspian's wing-tips, unlike those of a Royal Tern, extend well beyond the tip of the tail.

*COMMON TERN. *Sterna hirundo hirundo.*—13–15. *Adult (summer):* Crown and nape black; back and wings pearly gray, the outer webs of the primaries dusky silver; underparts, rump, and tail white or pearly gray, the latter very deeply forked; bill red, broadly tipped with black; legs reddish; *(winter):* Crown extensively white, the nape, hind-neck, and postocular area black; bill dusky reddish. *Immature:* Forehead pale gray, the upperparts extensively brownish; a patch of blackish on the nape and shoulders; bill brownish, becoming reddish toward base; legs pinkish.

Distribution.—Winters on the Pacific Coast; migratory in Baja California and along the Gulf Coast.

Remarks.—This species and the following are often confused, but there are several dependable characters by which they can be distinguished. The primaries of a Common Tern are somewhat dusky, and therefore darker than the mantle, while the wing-tips of a Forster are slightly paler than the rest of its wing. Common Terns have a white or very pale tail that contrasts with the back. These parts are virtually uniform in Forster Terns. There should be little difficulty with juveniles or with birds in winter plumage. Common Terns have a blackish hind-crown and a dusky patch along the forward edge of the upper wing; the Forster a very conspicuous black stripe through its eye. Sandwich Terns have yellow-tipped black bills and black legs.

*FORSTER TERN. *Sterna forsteri.*—14–15. *Adult (summer):* Very similar to a Common Tern, the two often indistinguishable in the field; *(winter):* Crown white; a conspicuous *black patch through the eye;* hind-neck marked with dusky. *Immature:* Forehead white, the upperparts with more or less pale grayish brown; a broad *black patch through the eye.*

Distribution.—Migrates and winters commonly on the Pacific Coast (including Baja California), and probably casually on the Gulf Coast. May breed in northeastern Tamaulipas.

Races.—*S. f. forsteri* (Baja California and the Pacific Coast in migration and winter). *S. f. litoricola* (a spring record for northern Veracruz; may breed in northeastern Tamaulipas, and to be expected southward as a transient or winter visitor).

Remarks.—*See* Common Tern.

*ROSEATE TERN. *Sterna dougallii dougallii.*—14–17. Much like a Common Tern in breeding plumage, but larger, paler above, and with a *black bill*, this sometimes reddish basally. Tail very deeply forked, the tips extending *far beyond* the folded wings.

Distribution.—Accidental. Recorded on the Pacific Coast of Oaxaca prior to 1876 (Ventosa Bay, Isthmus of Tehuantepec).

*BRIDLED TERN. *Sterna anaetheta nelsoni.*—13½–15. *Adult (summer)*: Forehead, superciliaries, hind-neck, and underparts white, the latter faintly tinged with gray; crown, nape, and stripe in front of eye black, the upperparts otherwise dark slaty gray; tail deeply forked, the outermost feathers mainly white; bill and legs black; *(winter)*: Crown and nape streaked and mottled with white. *Immature:* Similar to adult in winter, but crown and hind-neck mainly pale gray or dusky, the upperparts otherwise extensively brownish.

Distribution.—Known only from Sihuatanejo, Guerrero, and off the coast of Panama. Breeding range unknown.

Remarks.—A little-known Pacific representative of the common Caribbean Bridled Tern. *See* Sooty Tern.

SOOTY TERN. *Sterna fuscata.*—15–16½. *Adult:* Forehead, superciliaries (to level of eye), and underparts white, the latter sometimes tinged with gray; crown, nape, and broad stripe from bill to eye jet-black, this becoming deep sooty black posteriorly; tail deeply forked, the outermost feathers white, but tinged with dusky terminally; bill and legs black. *Immature:* Above deep sooty brown, the back, scapulars, and wing-coverts more or less barred or speckled with whitish; bill dusky brown.

Distribution.—Breeds on various Pacific islands and very locally off the Yucatán Peninsula. Largely pelagic at other seasons.

Races.—*S. f. fuscata* (coast of Yucatán and Quintana Roo, breeding on various reefs and keys). *S. f. crissalis* (breeds on the Revilla Gigedo and Tres Marías Islands, and Isabella Island, Nayarit; casual elsewhere, but principally at sea).

Remarks.—The only *white-bellied tern with black upperparts* likely to be seen in our area. Bridled Terns, thus far unrecorded on the east coast, are superficially similar, but have a white nuchal collar (hind-neck) and *slate-colored upperparts*. At a distance this conspicuously black-and-white tern might be mistaken for a Black Skimmer. However, it has a *brightly colored, "undershot" bill* and strip of white along the hinder edge of the extended wing.

LEAST TERN. *Sterna albifrons.*—8–9. *Adult (summer)*: Forehead (to level of eyes) and underparts white, the latter sometimes faintly tinged with gray; crown, hind-neck, and stripe from bill to eye black; upperparts pale pearly gray, the two or three outer primaries dusky, margined with white on the inner webs; tail deeply forked; bill yellow, tipepd with black; legs orange; (*winter*): Lores, forehead, and crown grayish; a blackish occipital crescent extending forward to the eyes; bill dusky; legs dull yellow. *Immature:* Similar to winter adult, but crown, back, and scapulars streaked or marked with dusky; primaries and forward edge of the extended wing (near body) dusky.

Distribution.—Migratory and at least casual in winter on both coasts. Breeds locally in northern Baja California (two small colonies of undetermined affinity) and probably elsewhere on the Pacific Coast. Allocation of many Mexican records is uncertain, since the subspecific characters of this tern appear only in the breeding plumage.

Races.—*S. a. browni* (Pacific Coast, apparently breeding in northern Baja California). *S. a. mexicana* (recorded from Sonora and Sinaloa). *S. a. staebleri* (recorded from the mouth of the Río Cahuacán, Chiapas). **S. a. antillarum* (recorded from the Río Lagartos, Yucatán; a Tamaulipas record probably is referable to this form). **S. a. athalassos* (to be expected on the Gulf Coast).

Remarks.—A swallow-sized tern with *pale upperparts and whitish tail*. Unmistakable. The black cap and yellow of the bill are lost in winter. Black Terns are larger and much darker above (slate-colored) in all plumages.

ROYAL TERN. *Thalasseus maximus maximus* (Illus. p. 172).—19–21. *Adult* (*summer*): Crown and nuchal feathers black, the latter notably long

ROYAL TERN (SPRING)

and pointed; back and wings pale pearly gray, the primaries dusky margined with white on the inner webs; underparts and tail white, the latter *deeply forked;* bill decidedly sturdy, reddish orange; legs black; (*winter*): Forehead and median crown white, the posterior crown, nuchal feathers, and postocular stripe black, more or less mixed with white; bill orange. *Immature:* Without elongated occipital feathers; upperparts mainly white, spotted with brown, the tail dusky, tipped with white.

Distribution.—Common resident on both coasts, including Baja California and numerous associated islands.

Remarks.—*See* Caspian Tern.

ELEGANT TERN. *Thalasseus comatus.*—16–17. Very similar to a Royal Tern, but considerably smaller, the two not readily distinguishable in the field without direct comparison of size.

Distribution.—Baja California and the Pacific Coast generally, breeding locally.

Remarks.—*See* Royal and Forster Terns.

SANDWICH TERN. *Thalasseus sandvicensis acuflavidus.*—14–16. Very similar to a Royal Tern in plumage, but much smaller, and with a *slender, yellow-tipped, black bill.* Feet black.

Distribution.—Resident in the southern portion of the Gulf Coast, breeding very locally. Recorded from Veracruz (winter), Yucatán (breeds on Alacrán Reef), and Quintana Roo (Cozumel Island).

Remarks.—Also known as Cabot Tern and Yellow-nibbed Tern. No other tern has a jet-black, *yellow-tipped bill.* At a distance the conspicuous nuchal crest is often a useful field mark, especially in winter, when three other pearly-backed terns of the east coast also have black or blackish bills. *See* Common, Forster, and Gull-billed Terns.

BROWN NODDY. *Anoüs stolidus* (Illus. p. 174).—14–15. *Adult:* Forehead and crown pearly gray, darkening on the hind-neck, the plumage otherwise deep sooty brown, darkest on the wings and tail and appearing uniformly blackish at a distance; tail rounded; bill and legs black. *Immature:* Similar to adult, but paler and browner; crown grayish brown; a narrow white line above the eye.

Distribution.—Breeds commonly on various islands off both coasts; largely pelagic in winter.

Races.—*A. s. stolidus* (breeds on Mujeres and Contoy Islands off the coast of Quintana Roo; pelagic in winter). *A. s. ridgwayi* (breeds on the Revilla Gigedo Islands; Tres Marías Islands; Isabella Island, Nayarit; and Tres Marietas Islands, Jalisco. Recorded off the coast of Guerrero).

Remarks.—Also known as Common Noddy and Noddy Tern. A deep brown medium-sized sea bird, with a *whitish or pearly gray forehead and crown*. No other Mexican tern has a *rounded tail*.

BROWN NODDY

WHITE TERN. *Gygis alba candida.*—11–12. *Adult:* Immaculate white, the primaries and rectrices sometimes with dusky shafts; tail deeply forked; bill black, becoming blue at base; legs black, the toes with yellowish webs. *Immature:* Similar to adult, but with a black postocular spot; remiges and tail with black shafts.

Distribution.—The Revilla Gigedo group, off the Pacific Coast (Oneal Rock, near Socorro Island).

Remarks.—Also known as Fairy Tern. The only *wholly white* tern in our area. White Terns inhabit scattered islets of the tropical seas and are not likely to be found near the mainland.

Family RYNCHOPIDAE. Skimmers

BLACK SKIMMER. *Rynchops nigra nigra* (Illus. p. 175).—16–18. *Breeding plumage:* Above sooty black, the secondaries and inner primaries white-tipped, forming (in flight) a more or less conspicuous white margin along posterior edge of wing; tail moderately forked, mainly white; forehead, sides of head, and underparts immaculate white; bill knifelike, the lower mandible much longer than upper, and both bright red toward base. *Winter plumage:* Similar, but upperparts duller, more brownish, and hind-neck with a broad white collar.

Distribution.—Pacific and Atlantic coasts, breeding locally in considerable abundance.

Remarks.—The brightly colored, peculiarly "undershot," *knifelike bill* is unmistakable. Skimmers commonly feed by plowing the surface of the water with the long lower mandible, a custom that has given rise to the vernacular name. Except for their distinctive bills, skimmers

BLACK SKIMMER

might be mistaken at a distance for Sooty Terns, the only member of its family that is all-black above and white below.

Family ALCIDAE. Auklets and Allies

KEY TO THE SPECIES

1a. Throat, neck, chest, and sides dusky or brownish gray 2

  b. Underparts mainly white, the throat sometimes black 3

2a. Larger (14 inches). Bill dull orange and sometimes with a small "horn" near base; adults in breeding plumage with conspicuous facial plumes . . . . Rhinoceros Auklet, p. 176

  b. Smaller (8 inches). Bill mainly black; without "horn" or facial plumes . . . . Cassin Auklet, p. 176

3a. Bill black, slender; upperparts uniformly dark

Xantus Murrelet, p. 176

  b. Bill pale, rather thick; upperparts not uniform, the crown darker than back; throat black in breeding plumage

Ancient Murrelet, p. 176

XANTUS MURRELET. *Endomychura hypoleuca.*—8½–10. Above *uniformly* blackish; below mainly white, the sides and flanks (sometimes sides of breast) more or less washed with gray; bill black, rather slender, and sharply pointed.

Distribution.—Guadalupe Island, Baja California, and islands in the Gulf of California, breeding locally.

Races.—*E. h. hypoleuca* (breeds only on Guadalupe Island; stragglers reported about southern Baja California). *E. h. scrippsi* (Baja California south to Natividad Island). *E. h. craveri* (breeds on islands of the Gulf of California; winters off the Pacific Coast of Baja California).

Remarks.—Any murrelet (in our area) having extensively *white underparts* is most likely to be this species. It resembles the Ancient Murrelet, a rare winter straggler in Mexican waters, but can be distinguished by its *uniform upperparts* and *black bill.*

*ANCIENT MURRELET. *Synthliboramphus antiquus.*—9½–10½. *Winter plumage:* Head extensively black, the throat dusky; back bluish slate, in distinct contrast with crown; *sides of neck and underparts white,* the flanks dusky; bill pale, rather short and thick.

Distribution.—Winter straggler to Baja California (Ensenada, December 25, 1927).

Remarks.—*See* Xantus Murrelet.

CASSIN AUKLET. *Ptychoramphus aleuticus.*—8. Above dusky grayish or brownish slate; sides of head, throat, and neck (sometimes chest) dull brownish gray; underparts otherwise mainly white, the sides washed with pearl gray; bill rather thick, mainly black, the lower portion yellowish near base; iris white.

Distribution.—Various islands adjacent to the western coast of Baja California.

Races.—*P. a. aleuticus* (breeds on San Geronimo and San Martín Islands, off northern Baja California; winters at sea). *P. a. australis* (San Benito Islands south to San Roque Island, Baja California).

Remarks.—Only one other Mexican alcid (Rhinoceros Auklet) appears wholly black while swimming. Cassin Auklets are easily distinguished by their diminutive size, yellowish patch near base of lower mandible, and white iris.

*RHINOCEROS AUKLET. *Cerorhinca monocerata.*—14. *Winter plumage:* Above sooty black; throat, breast, sides, and flanks dull grayish brown, appearing sooty at a distance, the underparts otherwise white; bill decidedly thick, mainly dull orange or yellowish.

Distribution.—Uncommon winter visitant off the Pacific Coast of northern Baja California.

Remarks.—*See* Cassin Auklet.

Family COLUMBIDAE. Pigeons, Doves

KEY TO THE SPECIES

ROCK DOVE. *Columba livia.*—12–13½. Typically as follows, but subject to radical variation under domestication. Mainly clear grayish or bluish gray, the neck and forebreast with more or less metallic green, this appearing violet in certain lights; wing-coverts usually black-barred; rump white; tail moderately rounded, the feathers very broad and tipped with black.

Distribution.—An introduced species. Common in and about most Mexican towns, usually in a semiferal state.

Remarks.—Also known as Domestic Pigeon. At a distance, some Rock Doves suggest Band-tailed Pigeons, but these lack whitish rumps and obviously are *wild* birds. *See* Red-billed Pigeon.

WHITE-CROWNED PIGEON. *Columba leucocephala.*—13. Crown white, bordered behind by a deep maroon crescent; hind-neck extensively metallic bronze-green, the feathers edged with black and appearing squamate; plumage otherwise bluish slate, the abdomen somewhat paler than breast; iris white; bill reddish, tipped with greenish; legs bright red.

Distribution.—Cozumel Island, occurring casually on the adjacent mainland, where recorded once at La Vega, Yucatán. Accidental at Salina Cruz, on the Pacific side of the Isthmus of Tehuantepec.

Remarks.—A very dark slate-colored pigeon with a *conspicuous white crown.* Not likely to be seen in our area except on Cozumel Island, off the coast of Quintana Roo.

RED-BILLED PIGEON. *Columba flavirostris.*—13–14. Head, neck, breast, and lesser wing-coverts rich vinaceous or purplish; back, scapulars, greater wing-coverts, and remiges (partly) grayish brown; plumage otherwise bluish gray or slate, the tail appearing black below; iris orange or reddish, the eyelids bright'red; bill reddish tipped with yellow; legs pink or red.

Distribution.—Arid regions (exclusive of Baja California and northern Sonora), mainly below 3,500 feet; also Tres Marías Islands.

Races.—*C. f. flavirostris* (as above, exclusive of the Tres Marías Islands). *C. f. madrensis* (María Madre, María Magdalena, and Cleofas Islands of the Tres Marías group).

Remarks.—In the southern portion of its range this very common species is best distinguished from a Pale-vented Pigeon, a much rarer bird, by its *red bill,* uniform *vinaceous* head, neck, and breast, and much *darker abdomen and tail.* Red-billed Pigeons usually inhabit woodlands, but may also be found near houses, often with Rock Doves.

PALE-VENTED PIGEON. *Columba cayennensis pallidicrissa.*—12–13. *Male:* Forepart of crown, neck, upper back, scapulars, lesser wing-coverts, and breast rich vinaceous or purplish; hind portion of crown and nape metallic bronze-green, shading to grayish on cheeks; flight feathers and tail mainly grayish brown; rump and upper tail-coverts bluish slate; throat white; abdomen and crissum pale grayish or whitish; iris orange-red; bill black; legs red. *Female:* Similar to male, but duller and much less extensively vinaceous or purplish.

Distribution.—Humid lowland forests of southern Veracruz, Tabasco, Campeche, and eastern Chiapas. Uncommon, but to be expected elsewhere in southeastern Mexico.

Remarks.—Also known as Rufous Pigeon. A large purplish-breasted pigeon with a *black bill* and pale *grayish throat and abdomen.* Likely to be confused only with a Red-billed Pigeon, which, however, is virtually restricted to dry regions.

BAND-TAILED PIGEON. *Columba fasciata* (Illus. p. 180).—13½–15. Head and underparts pale grayish, more or less tinged with vinaceous, the crissum whitish; a white band across the nape; hind-neck metallic greenish

BAND-TAILED PIGEON

bronze, somewhat squamate in appearance; back, scapulars, and upper wing-coverts grayish brown, becoming bluish gray on the greater coverts and secondaries; tail very broad, moderately rounded, mainly grayish, and usually with a broad dusky subterminal band; iris pale yellow, the eyelids red; bill and legs yellow, the former black-tipped.

Distribution.—Highlands generally, chiefly above 5,000 feet.

Races.—*C. f. monilis* (northern Baja California). *C. f. vioscae* (mountains and foothills of southern Baja California). *C. f. fasciata* (mountain forests, exclusive of Baja California).

Remarks.—Band-tailed Pigeons resemble Rock Doves at a distance, especially in flight, but are readily distinguished by their *dark* (not whitish) rumps and *pale grayish tail-tips.* The *yellow bill and white* *nuchal collar* are diagnostic. They subsist principally on acorns and are largely restricted to mountain oak forests.

SCALED PIGEON. *Columba speciosa* (Illus. p. 181).—12. *Male:* Head purplish chocolate-brown, shading to pale vináceous on chin and upper throat; hind-neck, sides of neck, lower throat, and breast metallic purplish black, liberally and very conspicuously spotted with white; upper back purplish black, this spotted with cinnamon; upperparts otherwise mainly chestnut, the flight feathers and tail respectively sooty and glossy black; lower breast pale vinaceous, fading to white on lower abdomen and crissum, each feather being conspicuously margined with dusky purplish; bill bright

Scaled Pigeon

red; legs lavender. *Female:* Similar to male, but back, rump, and scapulars grayish brown; underparts without vinaceous tinge.

Distribution.—Humid lowland forests of southeastern Mexico (Veracruz, Oaxaca, Campeche, and Yucatán).

Remarks.—A magnificent forest-dwelling pigeon usually found among the upper branches of large trees. Rather uncommon in Mexico, but unmistakable.

SHORT-BILLED PIGEON. *Columba nigrirostris.*—11–12. Mainly deep purplish, more or less distinctly tinged with vinaceous, the wings, tail, back, and rump glossy sooty brownish; iris pink; bill black; legs reddish.

Distribution.—Humid lowland forests of southeastern Mexico (southern Veracruz, Tabasco, Oaxaca, Chiapas, Yucatán, and Quintana Roo).

Remarks.—Short-billed Pigeons prefer dense lowland rain forests, but sometimes range to about 5,000 feet above sea-level. They usually appear dusky or blackish, the purplish coloring being evident only in strong light.

*PASSENGER PIGEON. *Ectopistes canadensis.*

Remarks.—Passenger Pigeons formerly wintered with certainty in Distrito Federal, Puebla, southern Veracruz, and Tabasco. Now extinct, the species probably once ranged (at least casually) throughout the eastern portion of the country.

MOURNING DOVE. *Zenaidura macroura.*—$11\frac{1}{2}$–$12\frac{1}{2}$. Above mainly pale grayish brown, the nape with a more or less distinct gray patch; sides of neck often glossy metallic purplish violet; usually with a small black spot below the auriculars; wings grayish, the inner portion black-spotted; tail rather long, decidedly pointed (when closed) or fanlike (when spread), with broad white tips; throat whitish buff, shading through vinaceous fawn on breast and sides to buff on the abdomen and crissum; bill black; legs pink.

Distribution.—Virtually country-wide, including various offshore islands.

Races.—*Z. m. marginella* (resident in Baja California, Pacific Mexico, and the central plateau, occurring extensively elsewhere in winter). **Z. m. carolinensis* (winters commonly on the central plateau, occurring widely elsewhere in less abundance). *Z. m. tresmariae* (Tres Marías Islands). *Z. m. clarionensis* (Clarión Island).

Remarks.—The long tail and graceful form are good field characters. Otherwise, Mourning Doves suggest birds of the genus *Leptotila* at a distance. Look for the black wing-spots and clear *gray primaries*. Fields, open country, and second-growth woods, where especially abundant in winter.

SOCORRO DOVE. *Zenaidura graysoni.*—12. Much like a Mourning Dove, but with reddish cinnamon underparts.

Distribution.—Limited to Socorro Island of the Revilla Gigedo group.

ZENAIDA DOVE. *Zenaida aurita yucatanensis.*—10–11. Above mainly grayish brown or fawn color, the head brighter (brownish cinnamon) and hind-neck usually distinctly grayish, this bordered laterally by an area of metallic purplish violet; a conspicuous black spot or streak below (a second sometimes above) the auriculars; wings dusky, the scapulars black-spotted and secondaries broadly white-tipped; tail rather short, the outer feathers broadly white-tipped and with a black subterminal band; underparts mainly russet or deep vinaceous fawn; flanks bluish gray; bill black; legs reddish.

Distribution.—Yucatán, Quintana Roo, and various offshore islands (Cozumel, Holbox, and Mujeres).

Remarks.—A "Mourning Dove" with a *short* tail and *white-tipped secondaries*. White-winged Doves show far more white on their wings and have longer tails.

WHITE-WINGED DOVE. *Zenaida asiatica* (Illus. p. 183).—10–11. Mainly grayish brown or fawn color, the crown and hind-neck tinged with

WHITE-WINGED DOVE

violaceous; a black spot or streak below the auriculars; primaries blackish toward base, the greater wing-coverts largely white; tail moderately rounded, the lateral feathers bluish slate, very broadly tipped with whitish and with a black subterminal band; throat and breast buffy fawn, shading to pale bluish gray posteriorly; iris red; bill black; legs reddish.

Distribution.—Virtually country-wide, from sea-level to an altitude of about 7,000 feet; occasionally higher.

Races.—*Z. a. mearnsi* (chiefly Baja California, islands of the Gulf of California, and the western portion of the country). *Z. a. clara.*(cape region of Baja California). *Z. a. asiatica* (chiefly eastern and southeastern Mexico).

Remarks.—The only Mexican dove with a *very conspicuous white wing-patch*. Mourning Doves lack this, and have notably *rounded* tails. Zenaida Doves have only the secondaries white-tipped.

INCA DOVE. *Scardafella inca* (Illus. p. 184).—7½–8. Above pale grayish brown, liberally scalloped with dusky; primaries extensively chestnut, tipped and edged with sooty; tail notably long, the three outer feathers

Inca Dove

with very broad white tips; underparts pale gray, faintly tinged with vinaceous, the feathers (especially posteriorly) more or less conspicuously tipped with dusky; iris orange or red; bill dusky; legs pink.

Distribution.—Virtually country-wide below 7,000 feet. Not yet reported in Tlaxcala, Tabasco, Campeche, and Yucatán.

Remarks.—Also known as Scaled Dove. Inca Doves, like the following three "ground-doves," prefer open country and are essentially terrestrial. While all four show a flash of chestnut on the wings when in flight, the Inca alone has *scaled plumage* and a *long, white-tipped tail*. Very tame and decidedly abundant in suitable habitat.

COMMON GROUND-DOVE. *Columbigallina passerina*.—6–6½. *Male:* Forehead, sides of head, wing-coverts, and underparts mainly pinkish, shading to gray on the flanks; lower throat and breast more or less distinctly black-spotted; abdomen and crissum whitish; crown and hind-neck bluish gray, the back, scapulars, and rump grayish brown; extended wings partly chestnut, the coverts boldly spotted with purplish violet; tail rather short and square-tipped, the lateral feathers mainly black, narrowly tipped with whitish; bill and iris reddish, the former black-tipped; legs pink. *Female:* Mainly grayish olive or fawn color, palest below, the lower throat and breast vaguely spotted or scalloped with darker; wings and tail essentially like male, but wing-coverts often chestnut-spotted.

Distribution.—Arid regions generally, but less common on the central plateau. Also resident on numerous islands off both coasts.

Races.—*C. p. pallescens* (as above, except Socorro Island). *C. p. socorroensis* (Socorro Island, off the west coast).

Remarks.—Three sparrow-sized doves occur in Mexico and may be found together over a large portion of the country. Each has a *short, square-tipped tail* and shows a flash of rufous on the wings when in flight. This species alone has a *spotted breast.* Its crown and hind-neck appear lightly scaled under favorable conditions.

RUDDY GROUND-DOVE. *Columbigallina talpacoti.*—6–7. *Male:* Forehead pale gray, darkening on crown and hind-neck; upperparts otherwise mainly cinnamon, the remiges extensively chestnut, tipped with black; scapulars black-spotted; tail rather short and square-tipped, the three outer feathers black, narrowly tipped with cinnamon; underparts deep vinaceous, the crissum chestnut; bill dusky; iris reddish; legs pink. *Female:* Above mainly grayish brown, shading to pale brownish gray on the underparts; wings and tail essentially like male, but the coverts without cinnamon.

Distribution.—Lowlands of western and southeastern Mexico.

Races.—*C. t. eluta* (southern Sinaloa south to northern Guerrero). *C. t. rufipennis* (southern Tamaulipas and San Luis Potosí southward, including the Yucatán Peninsula and Cozumel Island).

Remarks.—Also known as Talpacoti Dove. Any diminutive, *cinnamon-backed* dove is of this species. Females lack the breast-spots and faintly scaled crown of a Common Ground-Dove. Ruddies are larger than Plain-breasted Ground-Doves and have much more chestnut on their wings. A further distinction is the wing-spotting; conspicuous in a Ruddy, obscure or sparse in a Plain-breasted Ground-Dove.

PLAIN-BREASTED GROUND-DOVE. *Columbigallina minuta interrupta.*—5½–6. *Male:* Forehead pale bluish gray, darkening on the crown and nape where tinged with grayish brown; upperparts otherwise mainly grayish brown, the wings (inner webs) extensively chestnut; coverts tinged with vinaceous, and sparsely spotted with metallic blue-black; tail rather short and rounded, mainly grayish and sooty, the outermost feathers white-tipped; sides of head, neck, and underparts immaculate vinaceous; iris pink; legs pale. *Female:* Upperparts and breast pale grayish olive; throat and posterior underparts whitish; wings and tail similar to male.

Distribution.—Lowlands of Veracruz, Tabasco, Campeche, and the Pacific side of Chiapas.

Remarks.—*See* Common and Ruddy Ground-Doves.

BLUE GROUND-DOVE. *Claravis pretiosa.*—7½–8. *Male:* Bluish gray, the forehead, sides of head, and underparts much paler than plumage above; remiges dusky, the coverts boldly black-spotted; tail square-tipped, the lateral feathers black; iris red, pink, or yellow; bill grayish olive; legs pale. *Female:* Above mainly pale olive-brown or buffy brown, shading to russet on the upper tail-coverts and middle rectrices; wing-coverts spotted or barred with chestnut; throat white; breast tawny brown; abdomen pale gray; crissum russet.

Distribution.—Lowlands of southwestern Mexico north to southern San Luis Potosí and southern Tamaulipas.

Remarks.—This colorful ground-dove prefers heavily forested areas, but may be found elsewhere. The *pale bluish gray* males are unmistakable. With females, the *russet tail* and *chestnut wing-bars* are useful field marks.

MAROON-CHESTED GROUND-DOVE. *Claravis mondetoura.*—8–8½. *Male:* Above mainly slate gray, palest on forehead; wing-coverts and adjacent secondaries broadly banded with violet-black; tail moderately rounded, the lateral feathers very broadly white-tipped; sides of head pale gray, passing into white on the throat; lower neck and breast purplish chestnut; abdomen grayish, fading to white on the crissum. *Female:* Above mainly olive-brown, the forehead and tail-coverts deep cinnamon; wing-coverts and adjacent secondaries broadly banded with purplish; throat pale cinnamon, shading to dusky olive-brown on lower neck and breast; posterior underparts whitish or buffy white.

Distribution.—Mountain forests of Veracruz and southeastern Chiapas. Apparently rare and of very local occurrence.

Races.—*C. m. ochoterena* (Veracruz, locally; recorded only from Jalapa, Omealca, Jocuila, and Orizaba). *C. m. salvini* (recorded only from Santa Rosa and Volcán de Tacaná, southeastern Chiapas).

Remarks.—Also known as Mondetoura Dove.

WHITE-TIPPED DOVE. *Leptotila verreauxi.*—11. Forehead whitish, or pale vinaceous, darkening on the crown and hind-neck, where strongly tinged with metallic bronze or violet; upperparts otherwise mainly grayish brown or olive-brown, the inner webs of the remiges margined with rufous toward base; tail moderately rounded, the lateral feathers blackish, conspicuously tipped with white; sides of head, neck, and breast pale vinaceous, the posterior underparts whitish or tinged with pale buff; iris yellowish; bill black; legs red.

Distribution.—Virtually country-wide from sea-level to an altitude of 6,000–7,000 feet. Not recorded from Baja California.

Races.—*L. v. angelica* (northern and eastern Mexico—except Baja California and northern Sonora—south to western Chiapas, Puebla, and northern Veracruz). *L. v. capitalis* (Tres Marías Islands). *L. v. fulviventris* (southern Veracruz, Tabasco, eastern Chiapas, Campeche, and Yucatán). *L. v. bangsi* (Socunusco district of Chiapas).

Remarks.—Also known as White-fronted Dove. Members of this genus are distinguished by their *vinaceous* necks and breasts, *whitish* or *buff-colored* abdomens, and *rounded, white-tipped tails* (lateral feathers only). All have cinnamon wing-linings; an excellent field mark as the bird flies overhead. The four Mexican species are superficially similar and not always separable in areas where two or more occur. This species has the most conspicuous tail-tips.

CARIBBEAN DOVE. *Leptotila jamaicensis gaumeri.*—10–10½. Forepart of crown white, this shading to gray on the median crown and nape, where tinged with purplish; neck metallic bronzy purple or violet; upperparts mainly grayish olive-brown, the inner webs of the flight feathers extensively rufous; tail moderately rounded, the lateral feathers white-tipped; throat, abdomen, and crissum white, the breast pale vinaceous; bill black; legs reddish.

Distribution.—Yucatán (locally) and Quintana Roo, including various offshore islands (Holbox, Mujeres, and Cozumel).

Remarks.—Also known as Jamaican Dove and White-bellied Dove. *See* White-tipped Dove.

GRAY-HEADED DOVE. *Leptotila plumbeiceps plumbeiceps.*—9–10. Forepart of crown pale gray darkening to bluish slate gray on the hindneck; upperparts otherwise mainly olive-brown, the remiges partly rufous toward base of inner webs; tail moderately rounded, the lateral feathers blackish, tipped with white; chin, median throat, abdomen, and crissum white; sides of head and sides of throat buff, becoming vinaceous or faintly pinkish on the breast, sides, and flanks; bill black; legs red.

Distribution.—Eastern San Luis Potosí and southern Tamaulipas south in humid lowland forests (chiefly) to Oaxaca, northeastern Chiapas, and Tabasco. Rare.

Remarks.—A *small*, forest-dwelling Leptotila with a *bluish-slate crown. See* White-tipped Dove and Gray-chested Dove.

GRAY-CHESTED DOVE. *Leptotila cassinii cerviniventris.*—10–10½. Above mainly warm olive-brown or deep chocolate, the forehead very pale gray or whitish; hind-neck and sides of neck grayish, the former often faintly bronzy posteriorly; inner webs of flight feathers margined with rufous toward base; tail moderately rounded, the lateral feathers blackish, tipped with white; sides of head and sides of throat pale grayish, darkening on the breast, where tinged with vinaceous; median throat, abdomen, and crissum white or whitish, the sides and flanks brownish olive; iris yellowish; bill black; legs red.

Distribution.—Humid lowland forests of Tabasco (Tenosique, Santa Tomás) and Chiapas (Santa Rosa, Comitán).

Remarks.—Also known as Cassin Dove. This species is the most distinctive of the Mexican Leptotilas. Darkest of the four, it usually has a conspicuously *gray* neck and chest, and *brownish flanks. See* White-tipped Dove and Gray-headed Dove.

RUDDY QUAIL-DOVE. *Geotrygon montana montana.*—8–9. *Male:* Above bright chestnut, the hind-neck and back usually reddish purple; tail rather short, very broad, and moderately rounded; throat pale pinkish cinnamon, shading to vinaceous on the breast; abdomen and crissum pale buffy cinnamon; iris variable; bill and legs red or purplish. *Female:* Above deep brownish olive, the forehead and sides of head dull cinnamon; throat, abdomen, and crissum pale buffy white; breast dusky brownish olive, becoming buffy cinnamon medially and posteriorly.

Distribution.—Apparently absent from the central plateau, but fairly abundant from southern Sinaloa and central Tamaulipas (Río Sabina) southward, occurring chiefly in wooded areas below 3,000 feet.

Remarks.—Quail-doves are essentially terrestrial forest birds. Short-tailed and stocky, they suggest quails at first glance. Although fairly tame and sometimes abundant locally, quail-doves usually will be seen but briefly when flushed from the undergrowth or deep shadows of the forest floor. This species is the only one of its group likely to be found in wooded lowlands and foothills. It is usually recognizable even when the light is too dim to reveal the beauty of its *rich chestnut* (or deep olive) *plumage.*

PURPLISH-BACKED QUAIL-DOVE. *Geotrygon lawrencii carrikeri.*—10. Crown, nape, and hind-neck mainly dull grayish green, the forehead (to level of eyes) grayish white; back and scapulars deep purplish; wing-coverts, rump, and upper tail-coverts olive-brown; tail rather short, broad, and moderately rounded, mainly dusky, but narrowly tipped with grayish; throat and area below eye white, the two separated by a very conspicuous black stripe; lower throat and breast bluish gray; abdomen and crissum buffy white, the flanks brown; iris red; bill red, tipped with black; legs red.

Distribution.—Humid mountain forests of southeastern Veracruz (Cerro de Tuxtla and Volcán San Martín, Sierra de Tuxtla).

Remarks.—Also known as Lawrence Quail-Dove. A white-faced, gray-breasted quail-dove restricted to mountain "cloud-forests." The *black submalar streak* is diagnostic. See Ruddy Quail-Dove, the characteristic lowland representative.

WHITE-FACED QUAIL-DOVE. *Geotrygon albifacies.*—11–12½. Forepart of crown pale grayish or bluish gray, the posterior portion and hindneck brownish, violaceous brown, or bluish slate; upperparts otherwise deep chestnut, the upper back usually glossed with metallic greenish, blue, or purplish; sides of head, throat, median abdomen, and crissum pale buff, the first often tinged with gray; breast brownish cinnamon, this sometimes faintly washed with gray; sides and flanks brownish or cinnamon; iris orange or red; bill black; legs red.

Distribution.—Humid mountain forests from Guerrero and Veracruz southward.

Races.—*G. a. rubida* (Sierra Madre del Sur, Guerrero). *G. a. anthonyi* (the Chiapas Highlands—Triunfo, Volcán de Tacaná, Santa Rosa). *G. a. albifacies* (Veracruz, Oaxaca, and east-central Chiapas).

Remarks.—The only Mexican dove with *cinnamon underparts.* White-faced Quail-Doves are restricted to mountain "cloud forests," chiefly from 6,000 to 9,000 feet above sea-level. Their habits are much like those of the Ruddy Quail-Dove.

Family PSITTACIDAE. Parrots, Macaws

Key to the Species

19a. More than 13 inches; wings with red patch . Mealy Parrot, p. 201

  b. Less than 11 inches; wings without red patch

Yellow-lored Parrot (female), p. 198

MILITARY MACAW. *Ara militaris* (Illus. p. 191).—27–30. Mainly green or yellowish olive-green, the forehead and lores bright red; remiges (above), middle and greater wing-coverts purplish blue like tips of tail; rump and tail-coverts cerulean blue; tail very long and pointed, the basal half deep red above, the underside uniform yellowish olive-green like underside of wings; bare sides of head pinkish; iris yellow.

Military Macaw

Distribution.—Arid and semiarid regions generally, occurring both in the coastal slopes and up to 8,000 feet altitude in the pine and oak forests.

Races.—*A. m. sheffleri* (southeastern Sonora, northeastern Sinaloa, and southwestern Chihuahua; doubtfully distinct from *militaris*). *A. m. militaris* (absent in the Caribbean lowlands, but widely distributed elsewhere).

Remarks.—Also known as Green Macaw. A very large, mainly green, *long-tailed parrot with a red forehead.* Replaces the Scarlet Macaw in the mountains and arid lowlands. Much larger than a Thick-billed Parrot and with a proportionately longer tail conspicuously *red* toward the base.

SCARLET MACAW. *Ara macao.*—34–38. Extensively scarlet or vermilion, the wing-coverts rich chrome-yellow, the remiges deep purplish blue; lower back, rump, and tail-coverts azure-blue; tail very long, pointed, and mainly red; bare sides of head pinkish; iris yellow.

Distribution.—Humid lowland forests of southern Tamaulipas, Veracruz, Tabasco, Campeche, Oaxaca, and Chiapas.

Remarks.—Largest and most brilliantly colored of the Mexican parrots. This species is often conspicuously common in humid lowland forests, where it entirely replaces the more widespread Military Macaw.

GREEN PARAKEET. *Aratinga holochlora.*—10–12. Mainly bright greenish, the underparts paler and more yellowish than plumage above; tail rather long, the feathers graduated and pointed.

Distribution.—Socorro Island, off the Pacific Coast; western and eastern parts of the mainland except in humid lowland forests.

Races.—*A. h. brevipes* (Socorro Island, Revilla Gigedo group). *A. h. brewsteri* (Sonora, Sinaloa, and Chihuahua, chiefly from 4,000 to 6,000 feet above sea-level). *A. h. holochlora* (foothills and mountains of eastern and southern Mexico). *A. h. strenua* (Pacific lowlands of Oaxaca and Chiapas).

Remarks.—A medium-sized, *wholly green* parrot with a *long pointed tail*. Olive-throated and Orange-fronted Parakeets are similar, but both have considerable blue on their wings, and the latter a brightly colored forehead. All three are decidedly abundant locally and form large noisy flocks when not breeding. Green Parakeets are most abundant in the lowlands and at medium altitudes, but also range as much as 7,000 feet above sea-level.

OLIVE-THROATED PARAKEET. *Aratinga astec.*—9–10. Above mainly bright green, the nasal tufts yellowish or orange; remiges deep blue basally, tipped and edged (inner webs) with black; throat and breast brownish olive, shading to yellowish green on abdomen; tail rather long and pointed, the outer feathers graduated; iris yellow, the bare orbital ring whitish.

Distribution.—Atlantic slope from central Tamaulipas southward.

Races.—*A. a. vicinalis* (central Tamaulipas south to northeastern Veracruz). *A. a. astec* (humid lowlands from Veracruz and northern Oaxaca southward).

Remarks.—Also known as Aztec Parakeet. No other parrot in eastern Mexico has bluish wings in the absence of red. The *orange-colored nasal tufts* are distinctive, but not always conspicuous. From below this parakeet appears *brownish olive*, not clear yellowish green, as with Green Parakeets.

ORANGE-FRONTED PARAKEET. *Aratinga canicularis* (Illus. p. 196).—9. *Adult:* Above mainly bright green; forehead extensively orange or yellowish orange, bordered behind by a more or less distinct bluish area; remiges extensively blue, the tips and inner webs broadly edged with black; throat and breast pale olive-green, shading to yellowish green on the abdomen; tail long and pointed; iris and bare orbital ring yellow. *Immature:* Similar to adult, but orange of forehead reduced to a small patch.

Distribution.—Pacific slope from Sinaloa southward.

Races.—*A. c. clarae* (Sinaloa and western Durango south to Colima and central Michoacán). *A. c. eburnirostrum* (arid lowlands from eastern Michoacán south to Oaxaca). *A. c. canicularis* (Pacific slope of the Isthmus of Tehuantepec and Chiapas).

Remarks.—A diminutive sharp-tailed parrot with a *yellowish orange forehead*. This character is considerably reduced in immature birds. They are best distinguished from Green Parakeets by the deep blue on their flight feathers.

THICK-BILLED PARROT. *Rhynchopsitta pachyrhyncha* (Illus. p. 193).—15–16. Mainly dull olive-green; forehead, lores, and stripe extending

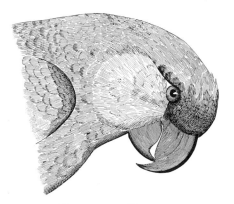

THICK-BILLED PARROT

along sides of crown deep red—this repeated on the bends of the wings and on thighs; tail long and pointed, the outer feathers graduated. In flight a bright yellow patch on the under wing-coverts is conspicuous. Bill black and notably thick; iris reddish.

Distribution.—Mountain forests of Sierra Madre Occidental and southward over the central plateau to Michoacán; occasionally east to Veracruz.

Remarks.—Thick-billed Parrots range over a large part of western and central Mexico and are especially characteristic of highland pine forests. They occur locally in the foothills and occasionally wander northward to the mountains of southern Arizona. *See* Military Macaw and Maroon-fronted Parrot.

MAROON-FRONTED PARROT. *Rhynchopsitta terrisi.*—16–17. Much like a Thick-billed Parrot, but larger and much darker green; forehead and superciliaries brownish maroon (not deep red), the latter more or less abbreviated; patch on under wing-coverts dark brownish gray, not chrome yellow, as in *pachyrhyncha*.

Distribution.—Highlands (locally) of the Sierra Madre Oriental in central-west Nuevo León (Sierra Potosí and mountains southeast of Galeana). ENDEMIC.

Remarks.—This species, unlike the preceding, is decidedly rare and occupies a very limited range. The *maroon-colored forehead* and dark wing-linings are diagnostic. In flight Thick-billed Parrots show a *yellowish* patch on the undersides of the wings.

BARRED PARAKEET. *Bolborhynchus lineola lineola* (Illus. p. 194).— 6½. Mainly yellowish green, the hind-neck, back, and flanks more or less

BARRED PARAKEET

conspicuously barred with dusky; upper wing-coverts entirely black (or broadly black-tipped), forming a prominent patch; primaries largely blackish, the outer webs deep green; tail rather short, moderately graduated, and with sharply pointed feathers.

Distribution.—Humid mountain forests of southern Mexico (Veracruz, Guerrero, and Chiapas).

Remarks.—The only very small Mexican parrot with *narrowly barred plumage*. At a distance the *black patch* on each shoulder is the most useful field character. A rare bird in Mexico, this species occurs only in dense forests at high altitudes.

BLUE-RUMPED PARROTLET. *Forpus cyanopygius.*—5–5½. *Male:* Forehead and sides of head bright yellowish green; above otherwise mainly dull green, the greater wing-coverts, lower back, and rump bright turquoise or cerulean blue; plumage below mainly pale greenish blue, the under wing-coverts bright turquoise or cerulean like rump; tail very short and sharply pointed, the underside yellowish green tinged with blue; bill pale and notably thick; iris yellow. *Female:* Similar to male, but blue plumage replaced with bright green.

Distribution.—Arid lowlands and foothills of northwestern Mexico and the Tres Marías Islands off the coast of Nayarit. ENDEMIC.

Races.—*F. c. pallidus* (southeastern Sonora, locally, and northern Sinaloa; doubtfully distinct from the following). *F. c. cyanopygius* (arid lowlands, mainly below 4,000 feet altitude, from Sinaloa and Durango south to Colima and Zacatecas). *F. c. insularis* (Tres Marías Islands).

Remarks.—Also known as Mexican Parrotlet. A sparrow-sized parrot with a *short pointed tail*. The brightly colored, *blue-rumped* males are unmistakable; the females hardly less so because so small. Parrotlets are a conspicuous element of the arid lowland fauna of western Mexico, especially as they range the countryside in flocks when not breeding.

ORANGE-CHINNED PARAKEET. *Brotogeris jugularis jugularis.*— 6½–7. Crown and posterior upperparts bluish green; back and scapulars distinctly brownish olive, but not sharply defined from adjacent areas; wings mainly yellowish green (greater coverts) and bluish green, the lesser and middle coverts essentially brown, this forming a prominent patch; chin orange; sides of head pale bluish green shading to yellowish green on the underparts; tail rather short, graduated, the feathers sharply pointed.

Distribution.—Arid Pacific lowlands of Guerrero, Oaxaca, and Chiapas.

Remarks.—Also known as Tovi Parakeet. The *orange-colored chin* is diagnostic. No other small sharp-tailed parrot has a brownish wing-patch. Very abundant and usually conspicuous.

Orange-fronted Parakeet

BROWN-HOODED PARROT. *Pionopsitta haematotis haematotis*
(Illus. p. 197).—8–8½. Crown and hind-neck essentially dull olive, shading
to grayish on the malar area, the whole appearing dusky at a distance; a
small red ear-patch; edge of wing at shoulder bright blue, the primaries
deep purplish basally; breast tawny olive, the belly and thighs bright green;
a bright red patch on sides beneath wings; tail short, square-tipped, the
lateral feathers largely red basally.

Distribution.—Lowland forests of southern Veracruz and Campeche.

Remarks.—Also known as Red-eared Parrot. A very stocky short-
tailed parrot with a *dusky head* and *brownish olive breast*. The red ear-
patch is usually inconspicuous. In flight the wings appear bluish below,
and a red patch shows on each side of the body. This species is fairly
abundant locally but usually feeds quietly in the tops of large forest
trees and is easily overlooked.

BROWN-HOODED PARROT

WHITE-CROWNED PARROT. *Pionus senilis senilis* (Illus. p. 197).—
9–9½. Forehead, median crown, and throat white, the head otherwise deep
blue; back and rump dark green; remiges purplish blue and black, the
coverts mainly bronzy brown; tail short and virtually square, the lateral
feathers reddish basally; breast and abdomen green, usually more or less
scalloped with deep blue; under tail-coverts dull red; iris orange, the bare
skin around the eyes deep red.

WHITE-CROWNED PARROT

Distribution.—Lowlands of southeastern Mexico from San Luis Potosí and southern Tamaulipas southward, including the Yucatán Peninsula.

Remarks.—No other white-topped parrot has a *white throat* and *reddish under tail-coverts*. While female Yellow-lored and White-fronted Parrots also lack red on their wings, they have little or no white on their foreheads, and usually have a suggestion of yellow or red on the lores.

YELLOW-LORED PARROT. *Amazona xantholora* (Illus. p. 198).— 9–10. *Male:* Forepart of crown white; lores yellow, the orbital area bright red; auriculars black; a bright red wing-patch; remiges largely deep purplish blue; tail short, virtually square, the lateral feathers red (basally) and

YELLOW-LORED PARROT

yellowish green; above and below otherwise deep green, heavily scalloped with black. *Female:* Similar to male, but less colorful. Crown essentially blue (not white); auriculars with less black, and red of head and wings replaced with green.

Distribution.—Yucatán, especially the eastern and central parts, and Cozumel Island.

Remarks.—The only medium-sized parrot in our area with *yellow lores*. Males have bright red primary coverts and a very conspicuous white crown-patch. Note the boldly scalloped plumage. Females could be mistaken for White-crowned Parrots except for their *blue* crowns and yellowish lores. White-fronted Parrots of both sexes show some white on their foreheads and have *red lores*. They are not so liberally scalloped as this species.

WHITE-FRONTED PARROT. *Amazona albifrons.*—9½–10. Much like a Yellow-lored Parrot, but with bright red lores, much less white on the forepart of the crown, and with more uniform (less scalloped) green plumage. Females lack a red wing-patch.

Distribution.—Chiefly arid portions of the Pacific and Atlantic lowlands from southern Sonora and southeastern Veracruz southward.

Races.—*A. a. saltuensis* (southern Sonora, Sinaloa, and western Durango). *A. a. albifrons* (arid Pacific lowlands from Nayarit southward). *A. a. nana* (arid portions of southeastern Veracruz, Tabasco, Yucatán Peninsula, and northeastern Chiapas).

Remarks.—No other small or medium-sized, short-tailed parrot has a white forehead and a large red patch extending to the base of the bill. Very common in dry parts of both coastal slopes. Often kept as a pet and trained to talk. *See* Yellow-lored and White-crowned Parrots.

RED-CROWNED PARROT. *Amazona viridigenalis.*—12. Forehead, lores, and crown bright red; patch behind eye and above auriculars violet, the latter very bright green; above and below otherwise mainly dark green, the hind-neck more or less boldly scalloped; outer webs of secondaries vermilion, the primaries broadly tipped with black or deep blue; tail rather short, somewhat rounded, and broadly tipped with yellowish green.

Distribution.—Nuevo León, Tamaulipas, San Luis Potosí, and northeastern Veracruz, mainly at moderate elevations. ENDEMIC.

Remarks.—The only short-tailed parrot with a *red crown*. A noisily conspicuous bird wherever found, this species is rather common in northeastern Mexico. Not likely to be overlooked by even a casual observer.

RED-LORED PARROT. *Amazona autumnalis autumnalis* (Illus. p. 200).—12–13. *Adult:* Similar to a Red-crowned Parrot, but crown and hind-neck mainly pale lavender, the forehead and lores alone bright red; a chrome-yellow patch below the eye from base of lower mandible, the patch often more or less intermixed with red, but essentially yellow. Old birds usually have some red on the chin. *Immature:* Similar to adult, but cheeks green (not yellow), and forehead less extensively red.

Distribution.—Humid lowlands of eastern and southern Mexico (Tamaulipas, San Luis Potosí, Puebla, Oaxaca, Chiapas, Tabasco, and Campeche).

Remarks.—Also known as Yellow-cheeked Parrot. A large, *red-fronted* parrot with *yellow cheeks*. Common in the moist lowlands of eastern Mexico.

RED-LORED PARROT

LILAC-CROWNED PARROT. *Amazona finschi.*—11½–12½. Much like a Red-lored Parrot, but without red or yellow on sides of head; red of forehead more restricted and much deeper and duller; hind-neck and underparts more or less conspicuously scalloped.

Distribution.—Wooded foothills and mountains (locally to an altitude of about 7,000 feet) from southeastern Sonora and southwestern Chihuahua south to Oaxaca. ENDEMIC.

Races.—*A. f. woodi* (as above, south to northeastern Sinaloa). *A. f. finschi* (southern Sinaloa and Durango south to Oaxaca).

Remarks.—Also known as Finsch Parrot. The *deep maroon* forehead and *pale purplish* crown are unmistakable. Sometimes found at sea-level, but more abundant in the mountains.

YELLOW-HEADED PARROT. *Amazona ochrocephala* (Illus. p. 201). —13–15. *Adult:* Head either wholly yellow (*oratrix* and *tresmariae*) or essentially green, with a yellow crown-patch and bright yellow band across hind-neck; a large red wing-patch; tail square-tipped, the lateral feathers red basally; bill buffy white, or dusky with a pale patch near base; iris orange. *Immature:* Head wholly green; wings without red or yellow.

Distribution.—Tres Marías Islands, off the coast of Nayarit, and both coastal slopes from Colima and Tamaulipas southward.

Races.—*A. o. tresmariae* (Tres Marías Islands). *A. o. oratrix* (Colima and Guerrero on the west coast; Atlantic slope from Nuevo León and central Tamaulipas southward except where occupied by the following). *A. o. auro-palliata* (Oaxaca and Chiapas).

Remarks.—Individuals, as well as the geographical representatives vary considerably in the amount of yellow on their heads. While adults are virtually unmistakable, immature birds can easily be mistaken for other members of the genus when in immature plumage. Of these, only four species approach Yellow-headed Parrots in size.

YELLOW-HEADED PARROT

MEALY PARROT. *Amazona farinosa guatemalae.*—14–15. Mainly dull grayish green, palest below, the crown and hind-neck pale bluish; tail broadly tipped with greenish yellow; a conspicuous red wing-patch.

Distribution.—Humid lowland forests of Veracruz, Oaxaca, and Chiapas.

Remarks.—Also known as Blue-crowned Parrot. Largest of the square-tailed species in Mexico, and probably the least common. Rather nondescript, but with a *bluish crown* and *two-toned tail*, the terminal half appearing distinctly yellowish. At a distance, note the *dull grayish green* plumage; unpatterned immature birds of other species appear much brighter.

Family CUCULIDAE. Cuckoos

KEY TO THE SPECIES

1a. Wholly black; bill compressed laterally, the ridge notably arched and knifelike 2

b. Not black; bill not as in 1a. 3

2*a.* Larger (14 inches). Bill smooth . . . . . Smooth-billed Ani, p. 205

  b. Smaller (11½–12 inches). Upper mandible with parallel grooves
Groove-billed Ani, p. 205

3*a.* Upperparts conspicuously streaked 4

  b. Upperparts not streaked 6

4*a.* Mainly terrestrial; above greenish bronze, narrowly streaked with
white 5

  b. Arboreal; above ochraceous or buff, broadly streaked with black
Striped Cuckoo, p. 206

5*a.* Larger (20–23 inches). Underparts dull whitish, the median breast
streaked . . . . Greater Road-runner, p. 207

  b. Smaller (17–20 inches). Underparts distinctly buff, the median
breast unstreaked . . . . Lesser Road-runner, p. 208

6*a.* Below wholly or mainly white, the breast sometimes spotted . . 7

  b. Below not white; throat and breast immaculate 9

7*a.* Breast spotted; tail broad and notably fanlike
Pheasant Cuckoo, p. 207

  b. Underparts immaculate 8

8*a.* Lower mandible yellowish; extended wings with conspicuous
rufous; tail broadly white-tipped . . Yellow-billed Cuckoo, p. 203

  b. Bill wholly black; wings and tail not as in 8*a.*
Black-billed Cuckoo, p. 202

9*a.* Above chestnut or rufous; tail much longer than head and body
Squirrel Cuckoo, p. 204

  b. Above not chestnut or rufous; tail not notably long 10

10*a.* Below rich tawny ochraceous or cinnamon
Rufous-rumped Ground-Cuckoo, p. 207

  b. Below buff or buffy white . . . . . . Mangrove Cuckoo, p. 203

*BLACK-BILLED CUCKOO. *Coccyzus erythropthalmus.*—11. Above
uniform brownish olive or bronze, the remiges somewhat rufescent near
base; tail long and notably graduated, the feathers (except middle pair)
narrowly tipped with whitish, and with a dusky subterminal bar; lores,
malar area, throat, and chest pale grayish or grayish buff, shading to dull
white posteriorly, the flanks and crissum faintly washed with buff; *bill black*,
slender, and moderately curved; eye-ring red.

Distribution.—Widespread during migration, but infrequently reported. Winters in northwestern South America. A single winter record for
San Luis Potosí (Tamazunchale, Febraury, 26, 1951).

Remarks.—This species and the following are the only Mexican cuckoos that are uniform above, and *immaculate white* (or whitish) *below*. Both are rather slender, smoothly plumaged birds of retiring habits, and may easily be overlooked. While superficially similar, this species is distinguished by its *black bill, red eye-ring,* and uniformly colored wings. To be expected in April, and in September and October.

**YELLOW-BILLED CUCKOO. *Coccyzus americanus.*—10½–11. Above grayish brown, faintly glossed with bronze posteriorly; remiges (especially the inner webs of the primaries) extensively cinnamon-rufous; tail long, notably graduated, the feathers (except middle pair) black, conspicuously tipped with white, the outermost with white outer webs; underparts dull white, the breast faintly gray-tinged; flanks and crissum often pale buff; bill black above, mainly yellowish below, rather slender and curved.

Distribution.—Breeds in northern Mexico, and widespread elsewhere in migration. Winters in South America.

Races.—*C. a. americanus* (breeds in Nuevo León, Tamaulipas, and probably south to mountains of Veracruz; migrates principally through eastern Mexico, including Yucatán). *C. a. occidentalis* (breeds in northwestern Mexico, including Baja California; migrates principally west of the central plateau, but also recorded from Tabasco).

Remarks.—A solitary and furtive bird, the Yellow-billed Cuckoo breeds locally in northern Mexico, but is known principally as a migrant. Its conspicuous *white-tipped tail* and flash of *rufous* on the wings are prime recognition characters when in flight. The *yellowish lower mandible* is also a good field mark.

MANGROVE CUCKOO. *Coccyzus minor.*—11½–12½ (Illus. p. 203).— Above mainly grayish brown, faintly glossed with bronze posteriorly; tail long, notably graduated, the middle feathers like back, but with dusky tips; lateral rectrices black with broad white tips; stripe behind eye black-

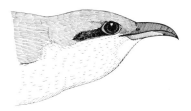

MANGROVE CUCKOO

ish, the bare orbital ring yellow; underparts mainly ochraceous or pale buff, the throat usually palest and sometimes whitish; bill black above, yellowish below, curved and rather stout.

Distribution.—Coastlands, and locally to an altitude of about 4,000 feet; also Tres Marías and Cozumel Islands.

Races.—*C. m. palloris* (Tres Marías Islands and the Pacific Coast from central Sinaloa southward). *C. m. continentalis* (Caribbean lowlands, including islands off the coast of Yucatán, and the interior of Chiapas locally). *C. m. cozumelae* (Cozumel Island).

Remarks.—Also known as Black-eared Cuckoo. This common resident cuckoo resembles a Yellow-billed, but has *yellowish-buff underparts* and lacks rufous on its wings. The conspicuous *black patch behind each eye* is a good field character. Partial to mangrove thickets of the coastlands, but to be expected elsewhere.

SQUIRREL CUCKOO. *Piaya cayana* (Illus. p. 204).—17–19. Above chestnut or cinnamon-rufous, the tone darkening posteriorly; tail notably

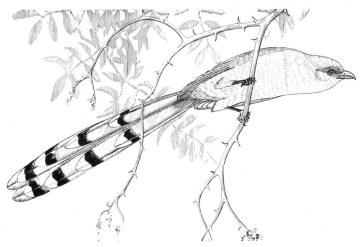

SQUIRREL CUCKOO

long and graduated, the feathers white-tipped and either with a broad sub-terminal black area, or mainly dusky chestnut, tipped with white; in this event, the underside distinctly dusky; sides of head, throat, and forebreast pinkish buff or pale cinnamon, the underparts otherwise grayish or dusky; crissum sometimes black; bill and bare orbital ring pale greenish, the former distinctly curved; iris crimson.

Distribution.—Southern Sonora, Chihuahua, and Tamaulipas southward, from sea-level to 7,800 feet locally; racial boundaries largely undefined.

Races.—*P. c. mexicana* (principally the drier portions of western and interior Mexico from southern Sonora and Chihuahua southward). *P. c. thermophila* (eastern San Luis Potosí and Tamaulipas southward, mainly below 5,000 feet; also the Pacific Coast of Oaxaca south of the Isthmus).

Remarks.—Squirrel Cuckoos resemble no other Mexican bird. They are unform chestnut or rufous above and have *very long, white-tipped tails*. The abdomen of the eastern form is decidedly dusky; that of the western more nearly pearl gray. Both are solitary and rather furtive birds, found principally in thickets or at medium heights in woodlands.

SMOOTH-BILLED ANI. *Crotophaga ani.*—14. Wholly glossy black, the upperparts, throat, and breast with greenish or violet reflections in strong light; tail blue-black, rather long, and with rounded tip; bill black, notably deep and compressed laterally, the ridge (culmen) distinctly arched and knifelike.

Distribution.—Holbox and Cozumel Islands off the coast of Quintana Roo.

Remarks.—Two species of ani are found on Holbox and Cozumel Islands. This form is considerably larger than a Groove-billed and has a perfectly smooth bill as seen under favorable conditions. Both are quite unlike any other Mexican bird.

GROOVE-BILLED ANI. *Crotophaga sulcirostris* (Illus. p. 206).—11½–12. Similar to *C. ani*, but considerably smaller, less glossy, and upper mandible with several curved grooves and ridges.

Distribution.—Cape district of Baja California (formerly) and widespread elsewhere, especially in lowland areas.

Races.—*C. s. pallidula* (formerly the lowlands of southern Baja California; now possibly extinct). *C. s. sulcirostris* (Mexico generally, especially in the lowlands, and islands off the coast of Yucatán; occasionally found up to 6,000 feet altitude).

Remarks.—Anis are wholly black, loosely feathered, and decidedly graceless birds, with arched, keel-like bills. They are conspicuously abundant in suitable habitats throughout their range and almost invariably are found in small flocks along hedgerows, the edges of thickets, and brushy open country. On Holbox and Cozumel Islands, off the coast of Yucatán, a larger species with a *smooth* bill also occurs commonly.

GROOVE-BILLED ANI

STRIPED CUCKOO. *Tapera naevia excellens* (Illus. p. 206).—11–12. Crown and occipital crest dull cinnamon, boldly streaked with black; upperparts otherwise mainly grayish buff or cinnamon-ochraceous, the back and scapulars broadly streaked, and wing-coverts spotted with sooty black; tail rather long, graduated, mainly brownish edged with buff or cinnamon; superciliaries pale, the auriculars and narrow malar stripe dusky; throat, breast, and crissum pale buff, the abdomen and sides white.

STRIPED CUCKOO

Distribution.—Wooded lowlands of Veracruz, Tabasco, Oaxaca, and Chiapas.

Remarks.—The only *small* cuckoo with *streaked upperparts.* A shy bird, it is fairly common locally, and usually is found on or near the ground in scrubby woods or thickets.

RUFOUS-RUMPED GROUND-CUCKOO. *Morococcyx erythropygus.*
—10–11. Above grayish brown or olive-brown, the crown usually streaked with paler and bordered by buff-colored superciliaries; wings glossy green-ish bronze; lower back and rump sooty, the feathers tipped with buff or reddish brown; tail bronzy, tipped with buff or whitish, and usually with black subterminal bar; underparts mainly tawny ochraceous or cinnamon-buff, the crissum dusky; bill cruved, black above and yellowish below; bare orbital area blue and yellow.

Distribution.—Arid Pacific lowlands (occasionally to an altitude of about 4,000 feet) from southern Sinaloa southward.

Races.—*M. e. dilutus* (southern Sinaloa to Jalisco and Colima). *M. e. simulans* (Michoacán, Guerrero, and Puebla, breeding up to about 4,000 feet). *M. e. mexicanus* (Oaxaca, west of the Isthmus of Tehuantepec). *M. e. erythropygus* (arid Pacific lowlands from the Isthmus of Tehuantepec south-ward).

Remarks.—Also known as Lesser Ground-Cuckoo and Lesson Ground-Cuckoo. At first glance this bird might be mistaken for a Mangrove Cuckoo with very bronzy wings and tail, and deeply colored underparts. No similar bird has a *reddish* rump. It is rather incon-spicuous and lives almost exclusively on or near the ground in thickets and second-growth woods.

PHEASANT CUCKOO. *Dromococcyx phasianellus rufigularis.*—14–15. Crown and hind-neck rusty brown, somewhat crested, and usually bright-est posteriorly; superciliaries white; a dusky postocular streak; upperparts mainly dusky brownish or glossy purplish bronze; wing-coverts edged with white or buff, the primaries tipped with same; tail long, fanlike, and white-tipped, the basal half covered by filmy coverts with white tips; under-parts mainly white, the throat and chest spotted with sooty brown; bill blackish, rather slender, and moderately curved; iris variable—white, yel-low, or brownish.

Distribution.—Lowlands (mainly) of extreme southern Mexico, includ-ing the Yucatán Peninsula.

Remarks.—A rare and little-known ground-cuckoo with an *expan-sive, fanlike tail* and conspicuous white underparts. Usually found on or near the ground in dry thickets and scrubby woods.

GREATER ROAD-RUNNER. *Geococcyx californianus.*—20–23. Crown, hind-neck, and upper back blue-black, spotted and streaked with tawny or whitish; lower back, scapulars, and wings mainly greenish bronze, boldly streaked with white; tail slender and graduated, the feathers (except middle pair) broadly white-tipped and usually edged with same; throat white or pale buff; malar area, neck, and chest ochraceous buff narrowly streaked with black; breast and posterior underparts pale buffy white; iris yellow or orange, the bare orbital area bright blue.

Distribution.—Baja California eastward and southward over the central plateau, where found up to 8,000 feet altitude in the drier portions.

Remarks.—Road-runners are characteristic of the drier portions of Mexico and commonly occur both at sea-level and in the mountains. Although almost exclusively terrestrial and very speedy afoot, they usually nest a few feet above the ground and, when necessary, can fly strongly for short distances. This species is best distinguished from the following by its generously streaked neck and forebreast.

LESSER ROAD-RUNNER. *Geococcyx velox.*—17–20. Similar to a Greater Road-runner above, but with extensively buff-colored underparts; underside of neck and median breast without stripes; crissum dusky or dull cinnamon, and much darker than the abdomen.

Distribution.—Arid lowlands and mountains (up to 8,000 feet locally) of western and central Mexico south to Chiapas and Yucatán.

Races.—*G. v. melanchima* (western Mexico, from southern Sonora to the lower mountains of Nayarit; intergrades extensively elsewhere with the following races). *G. v. velox* (moderate elevations in the vicinity of Mount Orizabo, Veracruz, and Mount Zempoaltepec, Oaxaca; intergrades with the preceding form in the southern portion of the central plateau). *G. v. affinis* (Yucatán and Chiapas, intergrading with *melanchima* near the Pacific Coast).

Remarks.—*See* Greater Road-runner.

Family TYTONIDAE. Barn Owls

BARN OWL. *Tyto alba pratincola* (Illus. p. 209).—14–15. Above mainly ochraceous buff intermixed with gray and finely speckled with black and white; remiges and tail usually obscurely barred; facial disks and underparts white or buff (sometimes ochraceous), the latter minutely spotted with dusky brown; eyes black.

Distribution.—Virtually all of Mexico, including many islands off the Pacific Coast and in the Gulf of California.

Remarks.—A large hornless owl with very *distinct facial disks* and *minutely spotted* white or buff underparts. Barn Owls often frequent old buildings, but usually are so retiring as to be easily overlooked.

BARN OWL

Family STRIGIDAE. Owls

KEY TO THE SPECIES

1a. Small to very small owls (5–10 inches) 2

  b. Medium-sized to very large owls (13–23 inches) 6

2a. Horned. Plumage essentially gray or reddish, the underparts (at least) streaked and finely vermiculated

Screech-Owl, spp., pp. 211–13

  b. Not horned. 3

3a. Legs notably long; above spotted, the underparts barred; open country, where essentially terrestrial . . . Burrowing Owl, p. 217

  b. Not as in 3a. 4

4a. Underparts distinctly striped 5

  b. Underparts not striped, the pattern obscure; sparrow-sized (deserts only) . . . . Elf Owl, p. 217

5a. Tail rather long and usually held at an angle with the back; head round, but not pufflike; ventral stripes sharply defined

Pygmy-Owl, spp., pp. 215–16

   b. Tail short, inconspicuous, and held in line with the back; head notably large and pufflike; ventral stripes very broad, but not sharply defined (mountain forests only)

Saw-whet Owl, spp., pp. 223–24

6a. Ear-tufts notably long, and usually conspicuous 7

   b. Ear-tufts lacking, or short and very inconspicuous (as in *A. flammeus*) 11

7a. Ear-tufts and brows white; underparts finely vermiculated, appearing uniform (tawny brownish) at a distance

Crested Owl, p. 214

   b. Ear-tufts not white; underparts boldly patterned 8

8a. Larger (18–23 inches). Below liberally barred, the upperparts mottled with brown, gray, and tawny; a white throat-patch

Great Horned Owl, p. 215

   b. Smaller (13–17 inches). Below either striped, or striped and barred 9

9a. Above deep sooty brown (blackish), more or less intermixed with tawny, the buffy underparts striped, barred, and blotched with blackish (mountain forests) . . . . Stygian Owl, p. 222

   b. Not as in 9a. 10

10a. Face and throat white; underparts distinctly striped

Striped Owl, p. 221

   b. Face tawny, the throat dark; underparts liberally barred and striped . . . . Long-eared Owl, p. 221

11a. Tawny buff, liberally striped above and below with brown (open country in grassy fields and marshes; winter only)

Short-eared Owl, p. 222

   b. Not as in 11a. 12

12a. Above mainly black or uniformly deep sooty brown; if the latter, with a broad blackish breast-band 13

   b. Above white-spotted, barred with white or tawny, or virtually uniform; if the last, with striped underparts 14

13a. Band across hind-neck, and underparts barred with black and white . . . . Black-and-White Owl, p. 219

   b. A very conspicuous breast-band; posterior underparts tawny buff, this sometimes narrowly barred . . . . . . Spectacled Owl, p. 215

14a. Above conspicuously barred or spotted; breast barred, or underparts essentially spotted 15

    b. Above virtually uniform or finely dotted and vermiculated with gray or buff; below (including breast) boldly striped

                                             Mottled Wood-Owl, p. 218

15*a.* Upperparts distinctly white-spotted; below irregularly barred, appearing white-spotted at a distance . . . . . . Spotted Owl, p. 220

    b. Upperparts and breast barred, the posterior underparts broadly striped 16

16*a.* Ground color of plumage white; feet and toes feathered.

                                             Barred Owl, p. 220

    b. Ground color of plumage tawny and buffy; toes naked

                                             Fulvous Owl, p. 220

SCOPS OWL. *Otus scops flammeolus.*—6–7. Resembles a small Screech-Owl superficially, but with brown eyes, very rudimentary rounded ear-tufts, and naked toes, these even lacking bristles. A brown and rufous color phase, the former usually with some reddish or tawny on the head and scapulars.

Distribution.—High mountains of Michoacán, Mexico, Distrito Federal, and Veracruz. Apparently rare and of very local occurrence, but to be expected northward at high altitudes.

Remarks.—Also known as Flammulated Owl. No other small highland owl has *brown eyes.* The absence of conspicuous ear-tufts also sets the Scops apart from other Mexican representatives of this distinctive genus. Its characteristic call is a low-pitched mellow note repeated regularly at intervals of several seconds.

COMMON SCREECH-OWL. *Otus asio* (Illus. p. 212).—7–10. *Gray phase:* Ear-tufts prominent; plumage above brownish gray, mottled and minutely vermiculated with dusky, the crown, hind-neck, back, scapulars, and wing-coverts black-streaked; outer scapulars white, the greater wing-coverts white-tipped; below essentially white, this more or less streaked with black, and liberally barred (or vermiculated) with dusky or reddish; iris yellow; toes featherless, but bearing bristles. *Rufous phase:* Ground color cinnamon-rufous or reddish, the pattern as in the gray phase. This plumage occurs only in the eastern races.

Distribution.—Baja California and northern Mexico south on the central plateau to Hidalgo.

Races.—*O. a. quercinus* (northwestern Baja California south to latitude 31°). *O. a. cardonensis* (Pacific slope of Baja California from latitude 31° south to latitude 28°). *O. a. xantusi* (southern Baja California north to latiude 27°30′). *O. a. yumanensis* (northeastern Baja California and extreme northern Sonora). *O. a suttoni* (recorded from Durango, Aguascalientes,

Querétaro, and Hidalgo). *O. a. sortilegus* (Jalisco). *O. a. mccallii* (northern Nuevo León and Tamaulipas). *O. a. semplei* (vicinity of Monterrey, Nuevo León).

Remarks.—Small, conspicuously tufted owls with mottled gray or reddish plumage. The five species that fit this general description are so lacking in really obvious field marks that sight identification below generic level should not be attempted except under ideal conditions.

COMMON SCREECH-OWL

Generally the call of each is quite distinctive and dependable. Eastern races of this species have a characteristic quavering call that follows a descending scale; the western races a series of distinct, mellow notes that follow with increasing rapidity, and finally merge into a tremolo.

VINACEOUS SCREECH-OWL. *Otus vinaceus.*—8. Resembles a Common Screech-Owl, the two usually not separable in the field. In *vinaceus* the ground color of the upperparts is buffy pink, and the outer scapulars are largely buff-colored, without dusky bars or mottling; legs *finely* mottled or vermiculated, not immaculate or coarsely barred.

Distribution.—Pacific Coast from southwestern Sonora to Guerrero. Endemic, and apparently rare.

Races.—*O. v. sinaloensis* (southwestern Sonora and northwestern Sinaloa). *O. v. vinaceus* (extreme northeastern Sinaloa and western Chihuahua). *O. v. seductus* (Michoacán and Guerrero, in the watershed of the Río Balsas).

Remarks.—Possibly a race of the Common Screech-Owl.

PACIFIC SCREECH-OWL. *Otus cooperi chiapensis.*—8½. Essentially like a Common Screech-Owl, but with the feathering of the lower leg ending abruptly.

Distribution.—Arid Pacific lowlands of Chiapas (Mazatán), where apparently uncommon. A questionable record for the Isthmus of Tehuantepec (Cacoprieto).

Remarks.—Also known as Cooper Screech-Owl. While the screech-owls of southern Mexico are virtually indistinguishable in the field, this form alone is at present known to occur in the arid Pacific lowlands south of Guerrero.

SPOTTED SCREECH-OWL. *Otus trichopsis.*—6½-8. Similar to a Common Screech-Owl in general appearance, but with several distinctive characters that may be seen under exceptional circumstances: bristly tips of the face feathers greatly elongated; hind-neck buff-spotted, this forming two more or less distinct broken bands; above and below rather broadly streaked with black.

Distribution.—Highlands south to Oaxaca, chiefly in pine forests.

Races.—*O. t. aspersus* (northern Mexico south to Durango, Guanajuato, and San Luis Potosí). *O. t. pinosus* (known from a single immature bird taken near Las Vegas, Veracruz; doubtfully distinct from the following). *O. t. trichopsis* (highlands of west-central Mexico south at least to Oaxaca).

Remarks.—Also known as Whiskered Owl. A mottled-gray screech-owl with two irregular bands of *buffy spots across the hind-neck*. Its usual call consists of four hollow notes, the first three given rapidly, the fourth following a brief pause.

VERMICULATED SCREECH-OWL. *Otus guatemalae.*—8-9. Essentially like a Common Screech-Owl, but with totally naked feet and toes, and somewhat darker plumage above; upperparts more or less liberally spotted with black, and usually unstreaked. A brown and rufous color phase.

Distribution.—Western, central, and southern Mexico. Absent from Baja California.

Races.—*O. g. tomlini* (arid foothills and highlands of southeastern Sonora, eastern Sinaloa, and Durango). *O. g. hastatus* (southwestern Sinaloa and Jalisco, at low altitudes). *O. g. cassini* (humid mountains of Veracruz and probably southwestern Tamaulipas). *O. g. fuscus* (humid lowlands in the vicinity of Mount Orizaba, Veracruz). *O. g. guatemalae* (mountains of southeastern Veracruz, Oaxaca, and Chiapas). *O. g. thompsoni* (arid parts of Campeche and Yucatán).

Remarks.—Also known as Middle American Screech-Owl. The only screech-owl of our area with *completely bare feet and toes*. While this character is not likely to be visible under field conditions, it is often possible to see the *small dusky spots above* that more or less replace the dorsal streaks of other Mexican relatives.

CRESTED OWL. *Lophostrix cristata stricklandi* (Illus. p. 214).—17. Ear-tufts and superciliaries mainly white, the former very long and con-

CRESTED OWL

spicuous; crown deep sooty brown, becoming cinnamon-brown posteriorly, where minutely vermiculated with dusky; wing-coverts white-spotted, the primaries notched or barred with white or buff; a chestnut patch below and behind each eye; underparts essentially tawny, this finely vermiculated with darker; iris yellow or reddish brown; toes naked.

Distribution.—Lowland forests of southern Veracruz, Oaxaca, and Chiapas. Apparently very rare and local.

Remarks.—A large *white-tufted* owl with *bright chestnut cheeks*. The only tufted owl of our area without streaks, spots, or bars on the underparts.

GREAT HORNED OWL. *Bubo virginianus.*—18–23. Ear-tufts very prominent, mainly black; above liberally mottled and vermiculated with black and gray, this more or less intermixed with tawny; a conspicuous white throat-patch; below essentially tawny or white, conspicuously barred with dusky; iris bright yellow; feet and toes fully feathered.

Distribution.—Virtually country-wide.

Races.—*B. v. pacificus* (northwestern Baja California). *B. v. elachistus* (cape district of Baja California north to latitude 30°; Espirutu Santo Island). *B. v. pallescens* (Vizcaino Desert Province of Baja California; northern and western Mexico south to Nayarit). *B. v. mayensis* (eastern, central, and southern Mexico).

Remarks.—A notably *large "eared" owl* with conspicuously *barred underparts*. In Mexico Great Horned Owls are not limited to forested areas; they also occur in arid wastelands far from woods.

SPECTACLED OWL. *Pulsatrix perspicillata saturata.*—17–20. Hornless. Above uniform deep sooty brown or blackish, this extending across the breast as a broad band; feathers in front of eyes, and narrow superciliary stripe white; a white crescentic chest-patch, this inclosing a black throat-patch; abdomen, sides, and flanks tawny buff, sometimes barred with dusky.

Distribution.—Lowland forests of Veracruz, Oaxaca, and Chiapas. Common locally.

Remarks.—A large "earless" owl, wholly black above, tawny below, and with a *broad black chest-band*. Spectacled Owls are characteristic of heavy tropical forests. Their usual call has been likened to a prolonged, rapid tapping of a woodpecker. Sometimes two birds perform a duet, in which the notes of each have a slightly different tone.

NORTHERN PYGMY-OWL. *Glaucidium gnoma* (Illus. p. 223).—6½–7. *Adult:* Hornless. Above mainly grayish brown or reddish brown; top of head and hind-neck liberally dotted with white or buff, the back, scapulars, and sides of breast more or less boldly spotted with same; a black-and-white collar across the lower hind-neck, this often obscure or represented by a black patch at each side of neck; tail rather long, and with five to eight pale bars; a brown or reddish throat-band; below mainly white, the breast, sides, and flanks boldly striped with sooty brown or cinnamon-brown. *Immature:*

Similar to adult, but top of head immaculate gray, in sharp contrast with the back, the forehead only sparsely dotted or finely streaked.

Distribution.—Mountains of middle and southern Baja California and the highlands of Mexico generally, chiefly above an altitude of 6,000 feet.

Races.—*G. g. hoskinsii* (mountains of Baja California north to latitude 27°). *G. g. gnoma* (widespread in highland areas, occasionally ranging as low as 4,000 feet).

Remarks.—The common pygmy-owl of higher altitudes. Least Pygmy-Owls are essentially birds of the lowlands and foothills, but may also be found locally at moderate elevations in mountains. Adults of both differ from Ferruginous Pygmy-Owls, the common lowland species, in having pale *dots* (not fine streaks) on the top of the head. Some authorities consider the Northern and Least to be merely zonal representatives of a single species. The former, however, has a longer, more liberally barred tail and rather conspicuous back-spots. In the higher mountains caution must be exercised as regards saw-whet owls. While also hornless, and very small, they differ from all pygmy-owls in having notably *large heads*, short, *inconspicuous tails*, and very *broadly streaked* (almost blotched) *underparts*. The saw-whet's tail is held in line with its back; the pygmy's usually forms an angle with the back.

LEAST PYGMY-OWL. *Glaucidium minutissimum.*—5½–6. Similar to a Northern Pygmy-Owl, but back, scapulars and sides of breast unspotted; tail relatively short and usually with only three or four pale bars.

Distribution.—Western, east-central, and southern Mexico, occurring locally to an altitude of about 7,000 feet.

Races.—*G. m. oberholseri* (dry lowlands and foothills of central and southern Sinaloa). *G. m. palmarum* (southeastern Sinaloa and western Nayarit). *G. m. griscomi* (arid lowlands and foothills of southwestern Morelos and northeastern Guerrero). *G. m. occultum* (known only from the lower slopes of Mount Zempoaltepec, eastern Oaxaca, and the vicinity of Palenque, Chiapas). *G. m. sanchezi* (southern San Luis Potosí, at moderate elevations).

Remarks.—*See* Northern Pygmy-Owl.

FERRUGINOUS PYGMY-OWL. *Glaucidium brasilianum.*—6½. *Adult:* Hornless. Above mainly brown or cinnamon-rufous; top of head and hind-neck finely streaked with white or buff; an imperfect black-and-white band across the lower hind-neck; outer scapulars and wing-coverts more or less white-spotted; tail rather long, variable in color and pattern, but usually either immaculate reddish or mainly brown, with six or more white or reddish bars; below white or tinged with buff, the breast, sides, and flanks boldly streaked with brown or reddish. *Immature:* Similar to adult, but top of head without streaks.

Distribution.—Lowlands generally, and the central plateau locally, chiefly below an altitude of 4,000 feet. Not recorded from Baja California.

Races.—*G. b. cactorum* (northern and western Mexico south to Colima and Michoacán; rare on the central plateau). *G. b. ridgwayi* (southern portion of the country, including the Yucatán Peninsula).

Remarks.—Also known as Streaked Pygmy-Owl. The common pygmy-owl of the lowlands. Look for fine pale *streaks* on the top of the head. Least Pygmy-Owls have dotted crowns, and only *three or four* tail-bars.

ELF OWL. *Micrathene whitneyi.*—5–6. Hornless. Above mainly grayish brown, minutely spotted with buff; superciliaries white; a white collar across the lower hind-neck; outer scapulars partly white, the wing-coverts, primaries, and tail more or less spotted with white or buff; below essentially white, this much intermixed with gray and tawny.

Distribution.—Socorro Island of the Revilla Gigedo group and the desert portions of southern Baja California, northwestern, and south-central Mexico.

Races.—*M. w. sanfordi* (Baja California south of latitude 23°40'). *M. w. whitneyi* (as above, exclusive of Socorro Island and Baja California; recorded from Sonora, Guanajuato, Mexico, Distrito Federal, and Puebla). *M. w. graysoni* (Socorro Island off the Pacific Coast).

Remarks.—A sparrow-sized desert owl, hornless, white-browed, and lacking a distinct pattern below. Usually common in areas with giant cactus.

BURROWING OWL. *Speotyto cunicularia* (Illus. p. 218).—9. *Adult:* Hornless. Above reddish brown, liberally spotted with white and buff; throat and chest white, the two separated by a dark band; below essentially white, this liberally spotted and barred with reddish brown, the whole often tinged with buff; legs notably long. *Immature:* Similar, but unpatterned below.

Distribution.—Virtually country-wide in plains and barren open country. Also many islands off the Pacific Coast.

Races.—*S. c. hypugaea* (as above, except where occupied by the following). *S. c. rostrata* (Clarión Island of the Revilla Gigedo group).

BURROWING OWL

Remarks.—A small *terrestrial owl*, spotted above, barred below, and with very *long conspicuous legs*. Common in suitable habitats and often seen in daytime, usually standing on some eminence near its burrow.

MOTTLED WOOD-OWL. *Ciccaba virgata* (Illus. p. 219).—13–15. Hornless. Above deep sooty brown, usually liberally dotted or vermiculated with gray or buff, but appearing blackish at a distance; loral region and superciliaries grayish or tawny; tail rather long, very dark, and with four or five narrow white bars; below either white or tawny, boldly streaked with deep brown, the sides of the breast somewhat mottled; toes naked; iris brown.

Distribution.—Forested regions, from sea-level to an altitude of about 8,000 feet.

Races.—*C. v. squamulata* (southern Sonora and Chihuahua south to Guerrero, Morelos, and Mexico). *C. v. tamaulipensis* (southern Nuevo León and

Tamaulipas). *C. v. centralis* (eastern and southern Mexico, including the Yucatán Peninsula).

Remarks.—Also known as Squamulated Owl. The most abundant of the larger tropical owls. This species frequents thick forests and is not likely to be seen unless decoyed by imitating its peculiar guttural

MOTTLED WOOD-OWL

hoot. No other large owl with *striped* underparts is virtually uniform above.

BLACK-AND-WHITE OWL. *Ciccaba nigrolineata* (Illus. p. 220).— 14–16. Hornless. Face and upperparts mainly black, the superciliaries white-spotted, the hind-neck white-barred; tail white-tipped, and with four narrow white bars; below white, very liberally barred with black; feet and toes naked; iris brown, reddish, or yellow.

Distribution.—Lowland forests of southern Veracruz, Oaxaca, and Chiapas. Apparently rare.

BLACK-AND-WHITE OWL

SPOTTED OWL. *Strix occidentalis lucida.*—19. Hornless. Above reddish brown, liberally spotted with white, the tail white-barred; face pale grayish; below spotted and barred with white and brown, the whole more or less intermixed with buff; feet and toes heavily feathered; iris dark.

Distribution.—Mountain forests of Sonora, Chihuahua, and Nuevo León south to Guanajuato and Michoacán. Apparently very rare and local.

Remarks.—Much like a Barred Owl superficially, but with white *spots* replacing the latter's bars. Both have similar calls: rather high-pitched hooting, the notes usually in groups of three or four.

BARRED OWL. *Strix varia sartorii.*—19. Hornless. Above grayish brown, liberally barred with white; face pale gray; below essentially white, the breast barred with brown, the posterior underparts boldly striped with same; feet and toes fully feathered; iris blackish.

Distribution.—Wooded portions of the central plateau from Durango to Oaxaca and Veracruz.

Remarks.—Large, round-headed, hornless owls with *heavily barred upperparts*. From below look for the *barred* breast and *striped* belly. Fulvous Owls are similar in pattern, but their ground color is *tawny* (not white), and the barring not so distinct.

FULVOUS OWL. *Strix fulvescens.*—17. Hornless. Above dark reddish brown, liberally barred with buff or tawny; face grayish; below tawny ochraceous, the breast barred with reddish brown, the posterior underparts boldly striped with same; toes naked; iris black.

Distribution.—Humid mountain forests of Oaxaca (Totontepec) and Chiapas (Teopisca, Volcán de Tacaná, Cerro Ovancho).

Remarks.—Also known as Guatemalan Barred Owl. Possibly a race of *Strix varia. See* Barred Owl.

STRIPED OWL. *Rhinoptynx clamator forbesi* (Illus. p. 221).—13–15. Horns prominent. Above essentially tawny ochraceous, boldly striped with sooty brown, the flight feathers and tail barred with same; face and throat white, bordered behind with black; below brown-streaked, the ground color white or buffy; feet and toes feathered; iris brown.

Distribution.—Lowland forests of southern Veracruz (Presidio, Potrero Viejo) and Chiapas. Apparently very rare north of Panama.

STRIPED OWL

Remarks.—Also known as Striped Horned Owl. This little-known owl suggests a Long-eared, but is totally without bars below. Its white face and throat are corroborative field marks.

LONG-EARED OWL. *Asio otus wilsonianus.*—14–16. Horns prominent. Above deep brown, more or less mottled with tawny, the primaries and tail barred with same; crown, back, and secondaries usually much vermiculated with grayish; face largely tawny buff, this bordered behind with black; breast ochraceous, broadly barred with brown; abdomen and flanks essentially white, this boldly streaked and barred with brown; feet and toes feathered; iris bright yellow.

Distribution.—Resident in northwestern Baja California, where not uncommon locally. Winters locally, but fairly commonly in wooded areas south at least to Jalisco and Puebla.

Remarks.—Long-eared and Great Horned Owls might conceivably be confused. The former, comparatively small and slender, has *close-set ear-tufts* and a *tawny* face. It lacks the white "collar" that is so conspicuous in Horned Owls, and from below shows *both streaks and bars*. Its usual call is a low, mellow hooting that is almost pigeon-like. Sometimes, when alarmed, catlike calls.

STYGIAN OWL. *Asio stygius.*—15–17. Horned. Above deep sooty brown or blackish, this sometimes much intermixed with buff; tail liberally barred with tawny; face essentially blackish, the rim grayish or buffy; below buffy white, the breast blotched with sooty, the remainder very liberally streaked and barred with same; feet and toes naked.

Distribution.—Mountain forests of Sinaloa, Durango, Chiapas, and Veracruz. Apparently rare and of very local occurrence.

Races.—*A. s. lambi* (known only from the mountains of northeastern Sinaloa and northwestern Durango). *A. s. robustus* (reported only from the upper slopes of Volcán de Tacaná, Chiapas, and Mirador, Veracruz).

Remarks.—A fairly large, blackish "horned" owl with mottled black-and-buff underparts. The nearest thing to an all-black owl in our area.

*SHORT-EARED OWL. *Asio flammeus flammeus* (Illus. p. 222).— 14–16. Horns very short and inconspicuous. Essentially tawny buff, palest

SHORT-EARED OWL

below, the whole very liberally striped with deep brown, the primaries and tail boldly notched and barred; feet and toes feathered; iris bright yellow, the eyes broadly encircled with black.

Distribution.—Winters in Baja California, on various offshore islands, and extensively elsewhere in open grassy country and marshes. Not yet recorded in the Yucatán Peninsula.

Remarks.—The brown-streaked, tawny plumage is unlike that of any other owl. Largely diurnal in habits, the Short-eared could be mistaken for a female Marsh Hawk as it hunts back and forth over a field or marsh. The relatively large head, shorter tail, erratic flight, and buffy wing-patches should distinguish the owl at any distance.

NORTHERN SAW-WHET OWL. *Aegolius acadicus acadicus.*—7–8. Hornless. Above essentially reddish brown; forehead and facial rim white-

NORTHERN PYGMY-OWL

streaked; hind-neck and scapulars more or less blotched with white, the primaries white-notched; tail dusky brown, white-tipped, and with two or three narrow white bars; below white, very broadly streaked with reddish; feet and toes feathered; iris lemon-yellow.

Distribution.—Mountain forests south locally to Oaxaca, Puebla, and Veracruz. Apparently absent in Baja California.

Remarks.—Much like a pygmy-owl, but with a very large head and short, *inconspicuous tail*. The saw-whet's ventral stripes are notably broad, somewhat reddish, and soft-appearing; those of a pygmy are narrower and more distinct. Pygmy-owls, unlike saw-whets, usually hold the tail at an angle with the body.

UNSPOTTED SAW-WHET OWL. *Aegolius ridgwayi tacanensis.*—7. Very similar to a Northern Saw-whet Owl, and possibly conspecific, but lacking white spots or bars on the wings and tail, and with toes partly bare.

Distribution.—Known from a single male collected on the upper slopes of Volcán de Tacaná, Chiapas. The species ranges south to Costa Rica.

Family NYCTIBIIDAE. Potoos

COMMON POTOO. *Nyctibius griseus mexicanus* (Illus. p. 225).—14. Grayish brown, more or less mottled and vermiculated with cinnamon, gray, and black; crown broadly black-streaked, the back, scapulars, and underparts with narrow streaks; median breast usually with several black spots; bill rather strong, notched near tip, the gape remarkably broad; iris bright yellow.

Distribution.—Sinaloa, San Luis Potosí, and southern Tamaulipas southward, chiefly in the lowlands. Probably more general than present records indicate.

Remarks.—Potoos resemble out-sized Caprimulgids, but differ anatomically. They feed on insects and are essentially nocturnal in habits. Potoos characteristically perch bold-upright on a post or stub during the day and are very difficult to detect unless disturbed accidentally.

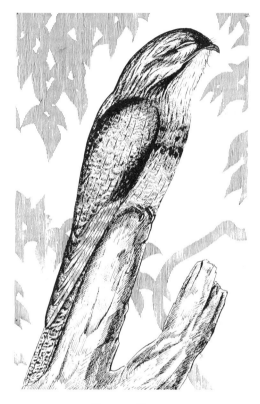

COMMON POTOO

Family CAPRIMULGIDAE. Nightjars and Allies

KEY TO THE SPECIES

1a. Primaries with a *single* white or buff bar 2

   b. Primaries never white-barred; sometimes liberally barred with buff or tawny 3

2a. Usually seen in flight; chin and throat white; wings notably long; tail proportionately short, generously barred, and with a white subterminal band . . . . Lesser Nighthawk, p. 226

Common Nighthawk, p. 227

  b. Usually flushed from ground; a white crescent across *lower* throat; tail rather long, white-tipped (female), or with several white feathers . . . . Pauraque, p. 228

3*a.* Smaller (7–7½ inches). Lateral rectrices (male) with less than ¾ inches of white on terminal portion 4

  b. Larger (8½–12 inches). Lateral rectrices with more than 1½ inches of white or tawny on terminal portion 6

4*a.* Nuchal collar conspicuous; scapulars and throat buff-spotted
Spot-tailed Nightjar, p. 232

  b. Nuchal collar absent or obscure; scapulars and throat not buff-spotted 5

5*a.* Essentially rufous; feathers of chest elongated, forming an erectile "apron" . . . . Eared Poor-will, p. 230
Yucatán Poor-will, p. 230

  b. Essentially grayish; without an erectile "apron"
Common Poor-will, p. 229

6*a.* A conspicuous nuchal collar 7

  b. Without a distinct nuchal collar 8

7*a.* Larger (10 inches). Nuchal collar rufous
Tawny-collared Nightjar, p. 231

  b. Smaller (8½–9 inches). Nuchal collar tawny or buff
Buff-collared Nightjar, p. 231

8*a.* Larger (11–12 inches). Essentially dusky rufous; inner webs of lateral rectrices mainly white (above) or tawny (below)
Chuck-will's-widow (male), p. 230

  b. Smaller (9–9½ inches). Essentially grayish brown; tail not as in 8*a.*
Whip-poor-will, p. 232

LESSER NIGHTHAWK. *Chordeiles acutipennis* (Illus. p. 227).—7½–8½. *Male:* Above grayish; extensively mottled, vermiculated, streaked, and spotted with dusky and buff; wings very long and mainly sooty, the *four* outermost primaries with a broad white band; tail vermiculated and narrowly black-barred, the feathers (except middle pair) with a conspicuous white subterminal bar; throat mainly white, the underparts otherwise buff, *narrowly* barred with dusky. *Female:* Similar to male, but wing-bar buffy, and tail without a white subterminal bar.

  Distribution.—Virtually country-wide.

  Races.—*C. a. inferior* (southern two-thirds of Baja California). *C. a. texensis* (breeds in northern Baja Califronia and northern portions of the country south to southern Sinaloa, Puebla, and Veracruz; winters from central Sinaloa and Guanajuato southward). *C. a. micromeris* (arid lowlands of southern Mexico).

Remarks.—Also known as Trilling Nighthawk and Texas Nighthawk. This common resident resembles the following species, but usually is buffier below, grayer (less dusky) above, and has only *four* primaries conspicuously barred. Its best field character appears during flight, when it can be seen that the wing-bar is nearer the tips of the primaries than in *C. minor.* While feeding, it usually flies closer to the ground than does *minor*, and breeding birds have a nasal, mewing note,

LESSER NIGHTHAWK

followed by a purring sound quite unlike the characteristic "spee-ick" note of the latter. *See* Common Nighthawk.

**COMMON NIGHTHAWK. *Chordeiles minor.*—8½–9. Similar to a Lesser Nighthawk, but larger and usually much darker (less grayish and buffy) above; crown and forebreast extensively sooty or grayish, and often intermixed with ochraceous; underparts whitish, or buffy white, rather *boldly barred* with dusky, the lower abdomen and crissum sometimes immaculate white; wings long, mainly sooty, the *five* outermost primaries of both sexes with a broad white bar.

Distribution.—Mainly migratory, but breeds in Sonora, Chihuahua, Tamaulipas, and Durango. The four races known only as migrants probably occur far more generally in spring and fall than present records indicate. Undetermined examples of this species have been recorded as migrants in San Luis Potosí, Zacatecas, Puebla, Nuevo León, and Tamaulipas.

Races.—*C. m. minor* (migratory in Nayarit, Nuevo León, and Campeche). *C. m. chapmani* (migratory in Campeche and Yucatán). **C. m. ascrriensis* (breeds in Tamaulipas; migratory in Guanajuato and Campeche). *C. m. howelli* (migratory in Campeche). **C. m. henryi* (breeds in Sonora, Chihuahua, and Durango; migratory in Tamaulipas, Jalisco, Oaxaca, and Campeche). *C. m. hesperis* (migratory in Campeche).

Remarks.—This species winters south of Mexico and is known to breed in but four of the northern states. Nighthawks seen during the migratory periods, and in the northern portions of the country in summer, may be either *acutipennis* or *minor*. *See* Lesser Nighthawk.

PAURAQUE. *Nyctidromus albicollis* (Illus. p. 228).—10–12. *Male:* Above grayish, brown, and ochraceous, more or less vermiculated with

PAURAQUE

dusky, the crown boldly black-streaked; scapulars mainly black, the outer feathers gray, edged with ochraceous, and having a black subterminal spot; wings moderately long, the primaries extending to middle of tail, and with a broad white bar; tail decidedly long, the four inner feathers grayish, vermiculated with dusky, the outermost all-black, the others mainly white, or with white inner webs; auriculars chestnut; chin and throat more or less dusky, the lower portion with a conspicuous white crescent; underparts otherwise tawny ochraceous, narrowly and irregularly barred with sooty, the abdomen sometimes immaculate. *Female:* Similar to male, but primaries with a pale buff (not white) bar, and tail notched with buff, the tips (only) of several feathers white.

Distribution.—Tres Marías Islands, lowlands of the mainland generally (except Baja California and Sonora), and islands off the Yucatán Peninsula.

Races.—*N. a. insularis* (Tres Marías Islands). *N. a. nelsoni* (western Mexico from Sinaloa southward, intergrading with *yucatanensis* in southern Michoacán and in the interior of Guerrero). *N. a. yucatanensis* (Morelos and southern Tamaulipas southward, including Mujeres and Cozumel Islands). *N. a. merrilli* (Nuevo León, Tamaulipas, San Luis Potosí, and Puebla, wintering south to Veracruz).

Remarks.—Also known as Parauque. Except for nighthawks, Pauraques are perhaps the best known of the Mexican nightjars. Inhabitants of woodlands and of open countryside, they are most likely to be flushed accidentally on a forest path or seen at night when blinded by automobile lights. Their large size, *white chest and wing-bars*, and long tail aid in identification. Note the *chestnut auriculars*. At night, in the lowlands, one can hardly fail to hear their distinctive and oft-repeated call—"Who are you?" *See* Tawny-collared Nightjar.

COMMON POOR-WILL. *Phalaenoptilus nuttallii.*—7–7½. *Male:* Above mainly gray or grayish brown, the median crown usually dusky; scapulars and wing-coverts black-spotted; flight feathers alternately barred with black and ochraceous, the primaries extending to or near the tip of the tail; middle tail feathers like back, the others mainly sooty, broadly white-tipped, and obscurely barred with buff or grayish; sides of head and chin dusky; lower throat white; chest dusky or blackish, the underparts otherwise whitish or buffy (sometimes dusky grayish), vaguely barred with black. *Female:* Similar to male, but throat and tips of tail pale buff.

Distribution.—Baja California and northern Mexico (except Nuevo León and Tamaulipas) south to Guanajuato.

Races.—*P. n. nuttallii* (breeds in Sonora and Coahuila; also reported in Guanajuato). *P. n. californicus* (northeastern Baja California south to latitude 30°). *P. n. dickeyi* (southern Baja California north to latitude 30°). *P. n. adusta* (Sonora, locally). *P. n. hueyi* (Colorado delta in extreme northeastern Baja California, and probably northwestern Sonora). *P. n. centralis* (known only from Durango, Jalisco, and Guanajuato).

Remarks.—This poor-will lacks the conspicuous white wing-bar of nighthawks (*Chordeiles*) and has a *white-tipped tail*. The extensive *white throat-patch* (buff in females) and *blackish chest* are good field characters, as is its small size. Poor-wills normally obtain their food by making short leaps from the ground; rarely if ever by "hawking."

EARED POOR-WILL. *Otophanes mcleodii.*—7½. *Male:* Crown, back, and rump brownish or dusky, the first minutely mottled, and with long lateral feathers forming erectile "ear-tufts"; hind-neck sometimes with a more or less distinct buffy bar; scapulars boldly black-spotted, the upper wing-coverts with rounded whitish spots; primaries banded with pale rufous; middle tail feathers concolor with back, the lateral rectrices white-tipped, and obscurely barred with rufous toward base; lower throat white; feathers of chest elongated, forming an erectile "apron"; abdomen and crissum tawny or buff; rictal bristles notably long and *incurved* terminally. *Female:* Essentially like male, but much more extensively rufescent and tawny.

Distribution.—Mountains of extreme southern Sonora, western Chihuahua, Jalisco, and Guerrero. Known from only eight specimens and presumed to be very rare. ENDEMIC.

Races.—*O. m. mcleodii* (as above, except Guerrero). *O. m. rayi* (vicinity of Chilpancingo, Guerrero).

YUCATÁN POOR-WILL. *Otophanes yucatanicus.*—7½. *Male:* Above and below mainly chestnut-brown and grayish, the crown black-streaked, the plumage elsewhere much vermiculated and mottled with dusky; a series of angular black spots on the scapulars; wings rather short, the primaries hardly extending to middle of tail, and generously barred or spotted with cinnamon and dusky; middle rectrices concolor with back, the others similar at base, but white-tipped and with a subterminal dusky area; a conspicuous white band across the lower throat; feathers of the chest elongated, forming an erectile "apron"; abdomen and crissum grayish buff, finely vermiculated with dusky; rictal bristles notably long and *slender*, the terminal portion usually *straight*. *Female:* Essentially like male, but more rufescent, and tail more narrowly white-tipped.

Distribution.—Yucatán Peninsula (Campeche and Yucatán), where apparently very rare.

*CHUCK-WILL'S-WIDOW. *Caprimulgus carolinensis.*—11–12. *Male:* Mainly dusky rufous or cinnamon-buff, generously vermiculated and mottled with black, the upperparts rather broadly streaked with same; wings boldly spotted, notched, and mottled with cinnamon-buff, the primaries quite long and extending to or near tip of tail; tail tawny, elaborately vermiculated and vaguely barred with black, the inner webs of the three outer feathers mainly immaculate white (above) or tawny (below); throat tawny or cinnamon, generously barred with dusky; chest with a buffy white, ill-defined band; breast minutely vermiculated, considerably darker and more rufescent than posterior underparts, where distinctly barred. *Female:* Similar to male, but tail without white or immaculate tawny; rectrices uniformly mottled and vermiculated.

Distribution.—Eastern Mexico, mainly as a migrant, but possibly wintering casually. Recorded from Nuevo León, San Luis Potosí, Veracruz, Oaxaca, and Quintana Roo (Cayo Culebra).

Remarks.—A very large, dusky-rufescent goatsucker. The inner webs of the three outer tail feathers (male) are chiefly white (above) or tawny (below). Unmistakable.

TAWNY-COLLARED NIGHTJAR. *Caprimulgus salvini.*—10. *Male:* Above rich sooty brown, or grayish brown, extensively mottled and vermiculated with gray, the crown and scapulars much paler than back, and both streaked (or spotted) with black; a conspicuous tawny rufous nuchal collar; wings rather long, the primaries extending beyond middle of tail and notched or barred with cinnamon; tail fanlike, mainly sooty like back, the three outer feathers with very broad white tips, these having *oblique* anterior edges; throat sooty, minutely barred with cinnamon, the feathers of the lower portion white-tipped, forming an indistinct collar; underparts otherwise extensively sooty brown intermixed with whitish, the crissum tawny, sparsely barred with brown; rictal bristles prominent and notably thick at base. *Female:* Similar to male, but tail without white, the three outer feathers narrowly buff-tipped.

Distribution.—Lowlands of eastern and southeastern Mexico. Rather uncommon and of local occurrence.

Races.—*C. s. salvini* (lowlands of Nuevo León, Tamaulipas, San Luis Potosí, and Veracruz). *C. s. badius* (Yucatán).

Remarks.—Also known as Salvin Whip-poor-will. This forest nightjar is between a Chuck-will's-widow and Whip-poor-will in size. It is much *duskier* (less rufescent or grayish) than either, and has a very distinct nuchal collar. The *oblique* forward edge of the white tail-tips (males) is found in no other Mexican species. *See* Pauraque.

BUFF-COLLARED NIGHTJAR. *Caprimulgus ridgwayi ridgwayi.*— 8½–9. *Male:* Above grayish brown, minutely vermiculated and mottled with dusky, the crown and back more or less streaked or spotted with black; hindneck with a narrow tawny or buff collar extending behind the auriculars; wings rather long, the primaries reaching beyond middle of tail and distinctly notched and barred with ochraceous; tail essentially like back, the three outer feathers broadly tipped (mainly on inner webs) with whitish or buff; throat dusky, minutely spotted or barred with buff; a white or buffy white chest-band, the underparts otherwise pale tawny or whitish, more or less extensively barred with sooty. *Female:* Similar to male, but tail narrowly buff-tipped.

Distribution.—Chiefly lowlands and foothills (sometimes to 6,000 feet) from Sonora, Sinaloa, and Durango south through the western and south-central portions of the central plateau to Oaxaca and Chiapas. Winters at lower elevations.

Remarks.—Also known as Ridgway Whip-poor-will. Nearest a Whip-poor-will in general appearance, but readily distinguished by the *conspicuous nuchal collar*. Several nightjars have this character, but each differs notably in other respects. *See* Pauraque and Spot-tailed Nightjar.

WHIP-POOR-WILL. *Caprimulgus vociferus.*—9–9½. *Male:* Mainly grayish brown, mottled and vermiculated with darker, the median crown and back streaked with black; scapulars black-spotted and often dotted with buff; wings rather long, the primaries reaching beyond middle of tail and generously notched or barred with ochraceous; tail mainly grayish, vermiculated and obscurely barred with black, the three outermost feathers very broadly white-tipped; throat sooty brown, minutely barred with ochraceous, and bordered posteriorly by a narrow white band; underparts more or less mottled, becoming pale grayish buff posteriorly, where obscurely barred. *Female:* Similar to male, but band across chest and tips of tail pale buff.

Distribution.—Virtually country-wide, but apparently absent in Baja California and in the Yucatán Peninsula.

Races.—**C. v. vociferus* (winters in the eastern and southern portions of the country). *C. v. arizonae* (Sonora and Chihuahua south to northern Guanajuato, wintering at least to Michoacán). *C. v. oaxacae* (eastern, southern, and southwestern Mexico; a variable race, apparently intermediate between *arizonae* and *chiapensis*, and with no distinct boundaries). *C. v. chiapensis* (mountains of Chiapas).

Remarks.—A widespread and often common resident. Whip-poor-wills are much more likely to be heard than seen. Their characteristic call is a vigorous repetition of the vernacular name.

*SPOT-TAILED NIGHTJAR. *Caprimulgus maculicaudus.*—7–7½. *Male:* Crown, malar area, and scapulars black, the last with large buff or ochraceous spots; hind-neck with a distinct ochraceous or rufous collar, the upperparts otherwise ochraceous buff, vermiculated with black; wings sooty, the coverts buff-tipped, and primaries notched with ochraceous rufous; middle rectrices concolor with back, the remainder mainly black, but conspicuously white-tipped and with two to three large white oval spots on the inner webs; median throat and chest ochraceous or pale buff, this area appearing scalloped or spotted; breast cinnamon-buff, minutely barred with black, the posterior underparts immaculate buff or ochraceous. *Female:* Similar to male, but tail without white, the lateral feathers barred and notched with ochraceous or cinnamon.

Distribution.—A widespread South American species recently discovered in the vicinity of Tutla, Oaxaca (January 1–April 2, 1941), and Santa Julia, Ocozocoautla, Chiapas (April 24, 1949).

Remarks.—Also known as Spot-tailed Whip-poor-will. Apparently a winter visitant from South America. This rare and little-known species is readily distinguished from other small nightjars by its *black crown, richly colored nuchal collar,* buff-spotted scapulars, and *general rufescence.* The clearly defined *oval spots* on the inner webs of its tail are diagnostic. *See* Buff-collared Nightjar.

Family APODIDAE. Swifts

Key to the Species

WHITE-COLLARED SWIFT. *Streptoprocne zonaris mexicana.*—8. Mainly black, the neck encompassed by a narrow white collar, this broadening over the chest; tail moderately forked, the feather shafts barely exposed terminally.

Distribution.—Southern Mexico (San Luis Potosí, Guerrero, Oaxaca, Chiapas, Veracruz, and Tabasco), breeding in the mountains but at other seasons sometimes ranging to sea-level.

Remarks.—The *white collar* is diagnostic and can be seen from a considerable distance. White-naped Swifts are *wholly* blackish below. Both are characteristic of mountainous areas and usually will be seen feeding on the wing in swirling flocks.

WHITE-NAPED SWIFT. *Streptoprocne semicollaris.*—9. Head, neck, and chest grayish, the throat with darker shaft streaks; a conspicuous white band across the hind-neck; above and below otherwise blackish, or very dark sooty, the upperparts faintly glossed with greenish; tail moderately forked.

Distribution.—Mountains (chiefly) of Sinaloa, Chihuahua, Morelos, Hidalgo, and Mexico. Known only from eight specimens and presumed to be rare. ENDEMIC.

Remarks.—The only swift with a white nuchal band or *incomplete collar.* When flying overhead, it might easily be mistaken for a Black Swift, a smaller bird with *uniform black underparts.* The white nape is the only dependable field mark at a distance. *See* Black Swift.

*CHIMNEY SWIFT. *Chaetura pelagica.*—5. Above fuscous, palest posteriorly; underparts mainly sooty, the throat and chest paler, or distinctly grayish; tail inconspicuous, the feather shafts notably exposed (spinelike) terminally.

Distribution.—Migratory in the eastern portion of the country, where recorded only from April 1 to May 6 (San Luis Potosí, Tamaulipas, Veracruz, and Cozumel Island).

Remarks.—*See* Vaux Swift and Chestnut-collared Swift.

VAUX SWIFT. *Chaetura vauxi* (Illus. p. 235).—3¾–4. Very similar to a Chimney Swift, but considerably smaller and somewhat paler below, the two not readily separable in the field.

Distribution.—Breeds in eastern and southern Mexico, and widespread elsewhere during migration. Winters extensively in the southern portion of the country.

Races.—**C. v. vauxi* (migratory in western Mexico, wintering in the southern part of the country). *C. v. tamaulipensis* (breeds in Tamaulipas, San Luis Potosí, and adjacent parts). *C. v. richmondi* (Veracruz, Oaxaca, and Chiapas, presumably intergrading with the following in Tabasco and Campeche). *C. v. gaumeri* (Yucatán, Quintana Roo, and Cozumel Island).

Remarks.—Except during spring migration (April and May), any uniformly sooty and apparently tail-less swift is most probably this form. All other resident species have comparatively prominent tails, and

VAUX SWIFT

most are conspicuously patterned above or below. *See* Chimney Swift and Chestnut-collared Swift.

CHESTNUT-COLLARED SWIFT. *Chaetura rutila.*—5½. *Male:* Mainly dark sooty brown or dark sooty grayish; hind-neck, auriculars, lower throat, and breast rich chestnut-rufous; tail moderately long, square-tipped, the feather shafts slightly exposed terminally. *Female:* Similar to male, but without a rufous collar.

Distribution.—Mountains of western and southern Mexico.

Races.—*C. r. griseifrons* (Nayarit, Jalisco, Durango, and Zacatecas). *C. r. brunneitorques* (Oaxaca, Chiapas, Mexico, Puebla, and Veracruz).

Remarks.—The only Mexican swift in which the sexes differ in plumage. Females can be distinguished in flight from Chimney and Vaux Swifts by their much *darker* (less grayish) *underparts* and relatively *conspicuous tails;* Black Swifts are much larger than any of the three, and have *notched* tails.

BLACK SWIFT. *Cypseloides niger.*—6½. Sooty black, the forehead and lores usually more or less grayish; wings and tail faintly glossed with greenish, the latter broad, moderately forked when spread, and feather tips without exposed shafts, as in Chestnut-collared, Vaux, and Chimney Swifts.

Distribution.—Highlands of western and southern Mexico, chiefly as a migrant or winter visitant, but breeding locally.

Races.—*C. n. borealis* (breeds in Nayarit, Puebla, and Veracruz; recorded as a migrant in Baja California, Durango, San Luis Potosí, Mexico, and Oaxaca; to be expected extensively elsewhere). *C. n. costaricensis* (Sierra Madre de Chiapas).

Remarks.—Largest and darkest of the four unpatterned swifts. Look for its grayish forehead and broad, slightly forked tail. Rather common in many localities, especially in winter. *See* White-naped Swift.

WHITE-THROATED SWIFT. *Aëronautes saxatalis* (Illus. p. 236).— 5¾–6. Above sooty blackish, the secondaries usually pale-tipped and some-

WHITE-THROATED SWIFT

times forming a conspicuous wing-patch; throat, breast, median abdomen, and patch on each side of rump white, the underparts otherwise black; tail rather long and slightly forked, the feathers pointed, but without exposed terminal shafts.

Distribution.—Highlands generally (including Baja California), but apparently of local occurrence.

Races.—*A. s. saxatalis* (mountainous areas south to south-central Mexico). *A. s. nigrior* (recorded in Michoacán and Chiapas; to be expected elsewhere in southern Mexico).

Remarks.—The boldly patterned, black-and-white underparts are diagnostic. White-throated Swifts nest in cliffs and canyons difficult of access and are not likely to be seen except at a distance while feeding on the wing. They often associate with Violet-green Swallows while nesting, but the two have very different flight silhouettes, and the swift a more rapid wing-beat.

GREAT SWALLOW-TAILED SWIFT. *Panyptila sancti-hieronymi.*— 7–8. Similar to a Lesser Swallow-tailed Swift, but decidedly larger.

Distribution.—Common in the vicinity of Tuxtla Gutierrez, Chiapas, in spring and summer. Presumably resident.

Remarks.—Until recently this large swallow-tailed species was known only from the mountains of Guatemala. It is most active after rains and has a call-note suggesting that of a domestic chick. Its *deeply forked tail* distinguishes it at a glance from all but the following species, a notably smaller bird.

LESSER SWALLOW-TAILED SWIFT. *Panyptila cayennensis verae-crucis.*—5. Mainly velvet-black, the lores, throat, chest, sides of neck, and patch on each flank white; hind-neck with a narrow whitish or brownish collar; *tail deeply forked*, the outer feathers attenuated, but without exposed terminal shafts.

Distribution.—The Mexican race is known from a single specimen collected at Presidio, Veracruz, in June. Presumably resident. A related form is found from Honduras to Brazil.

Family TROCHILIDAE. Hummingbirds

Fifty-nine of the sixty hummingbirds recorded from Mexico meet the specifications of one or more of the six arbitrary categories listed below, and appear in their respective keys. One endemic species, the Dusky Hummingbird (*Cynanthus sordidus*) of western and southern Mexico is described in the text, as are females that lack distinctive field marks.

I. With a glittering or bright metallic gorget unlike the color of the adjacent underparts. Gorget conspicuous when viewed in suitable light, and usually extending over the entire throat (or throat and breast), but sometimes limited to the median or lower throat.
See page 238

II. Crown or forehead and forepart of crown bright metallic, varying in color, but never like the back. *See* page 241

III. Underparts wholly or very extensively cinnamon-buff or cinnamon-rufous. *See* page 241

IV. Underparts wholly or very extensively green, greenish bronze, or bronze-green; throat often with a colorful gorget and tail sometimes notably forked or scissor-like. *See* page 242

V. Underparts, or abdomen and tail only, mainly immaculate white. Median throat and chest sometimes with a prominent black stripe. The numerous hummingbirds (especially females) having underparts better designated as "whitish," grayish white, pale grayish, etc., or with more or less cinnamon on the flanks, are not included here.
See page 243

VI. Very large, or notably small hummingbirds. *See* page 244

KEY TO CATEGORY I

1*a*. Gorget (and sometimes breast) bright metallic green or emerald-green 2

b. Gorget not green 11

2*a*. Crown, or forehead to middle of crown, metallic violet-purple or dark metallic blue 3

b. Not as in 2*a*. 5

3*a*. Forepart of crown dark metallic blue; tail purplish black, rather long and deeply forked . . . Common Wood-Nymph (male), p. 253

b. Crown only, or forepart of head (including chin and malar area) deep metallic violet-purple 4

4*a*. Larger (4½–5 inches). Crown purple; bill black
Magnificent Hummingbird (male), p. 260

b. Smaller (3½ inches). Forehead and chin purple; bill reddish tipped with black . . . . White-eared Hummingbird (male), p. 253

5*a*. Tail mainly cinnamon-rufous, or purplish chestnut edged with bronze 6

b. Tail not as in 5*a*. 10

6*a*. Very small (2½ inches). Conspicuously crested 7

b. Medium-sized (3½–4 inches). Without a crest 8

7a. Crest cinnamon-buff; abdomen dusky
Rufous-crested Coquette (male), p. 251

b. Crest dark green; abdomen spotted with coppery bronze
Black-crested Coquette (male), p. 251

8a. Forepart of head black; a conspicuous white postocular streak
Black-fronted Hummingbird (male), p. 253

b. Entire head and breast green; postocular streak lacking 9

9a. Abdomen brownish gray . . . Rufous-tailed Hummingbird, p. 256

b. Abdomen cinnamon-buff . . . Fawn-breasted Hummingbird, p. 256

10a. Bill long; breast and median underparts mainly white
Green-throated Mountain-gem (male), p. 259

b. Bill very short; breast black; abdomen dusky
Emerald-chinned Hummingbird (male), p. 250

11a. Gorget bright metallic blue, greenish blue, or violet-blue 12

b. Gorget not as in 11a. 14

12a. Gorget violet-blue; chest white; outer tail feathers very long, sharply pointed, tipped and barred with white
Sparkling-tailed Hummingbird (male), p. 262

b. Not as in 12a. 13

13a. Large (5–5¼ inches). Gorget blue or violet-blue; outer tail feathers broadly white-tipped . . Blue-throated Hummingbird (male), p. 258
Violet Sabre-wing (female), p. 248

b. Small (3½–4 inches). Gorget greenish blue; tail without white
Broad-billed Hummingbird (male), p. 252

14a. Gorget bright metallic purple or violet-purple 15

b. Gorget not as in 14a. 20

15a. Lateral feathers of gorget very long, forming distinct streamers . 16

b. Gorget without lateral steamers 17

16a. Crown concolor with back; sides and flanks partly buff
Lucifer Hummingbird (male), p. 263
Beautiful Hummingbird (male), p. 263

b. Crown metallic purple or violet-purple like gorget
Costa Hummingbird (male), p. 265

17a. Tail deeply forked (scissor-like), the outer feathers very long and narrow . . . . Slender Shear-tail (male), p. 261

b. Tail not scissor-like or otherwise unusual 18

18a. More than 4 inches long. Rump and tail blackish; underparts mainly sooty . . . Amethyst-throated Hummingbird (male), p. 259

b. Less than 3½ inches long. Rump and tail metallic bronze-green or coppery 19

19a. Rump and tail bronze-green; upper throat black
>>> Black-chinned Hummingbird (male), p. 264

b. Rump and tail coppery; upper throat not black
>>> Blue-throated Golden-tail, p. 254

20a. Gorget bright metallic rose-red, reddish purple, or reddish violet . 21

b. Gorget not as in 20a. 29

21a. Lateral feathers of gorget very long, sometimes forming distinct streamers 22

b. Gorget without lateral streamers 25

22a. Crown metallic rose-red, like gorget
>>> Anna Hummingbird (male), p. 264

b. Crown bronze-green, like back 23

23a. Tail cinnamon-rufous at base, the outer feathers white-tipped
>>> Bumblebee Hummingbird (male), p. 266
>>> Wine-throated Hummingbird (male), p. 266

b. Tail without cinnamon; not white-tipped 24

24a. Gorget uniformly colored, the lateral streamers rounded at ends; bill black . . . . Broad-tailed Hummingbird (male), p. 267

b. Gorget streaked with white, the lateral streamers pointed at ends; bill pinkish below . . . . . Calliope Hummingbird (male), p. 265

25a. Tail deeply forked (scissor-like), the outer feathers notably long
>>> Mexican Shear-tail (male), p. 262

b. Tail not scissor-like or otherwise unusual 26

26a. Outer tail feathers white-tipped; rump with a white streak or patch 27

b. Tail not white-tipped 28

27a. Crown bright metallic green or bluish green
>>> Long-billed Star-throat (male), p. 261

b. Crown and back concolor Plain-capped Star-throat (male), p. 260

28a. Wing-coverts and wings extensively chestnut; breast metallic blue
>>> Garnet-throated Hummingbird (male), p. 260

b. Wings without chestnut; breast not blue
>>> Amethyst-throated Hummingbird (male), p. 259

29a. Gorget bright metallic ruby-red; tail black
>>> Ruby-throated Hummingbird (male), p. 263

b. Gorget bright metallic scarlet or orange-red; tail mainly cinnamon-rufous 30

30a. Back and rump rufous, concolor with tail
>>> Rufous Hummingbird (male), p. 267

b. Back and rump not rufous . . . Allen Hummingbird (male), p. 268

KEY TO CATEGORY II

1a. With a brightly colored metallic gorget (as viewed in suitable light)   2

  b. Without a gorget, the underparts extensively white or pale grayish   7

2a. Gorget green; chin and malar area sometimes violet-purple, like forehead 3

  b. Gorget not green 5

3a. Tail distinctly purplish; deeply forked
Common Wood-Nymph (male), p. 253

  b. Tail mainly bronze; especially above; not deeply forked 4

4a. Larger (4½–5 inches). Bill black; entire crown violet-purple
Magnificent Hummingbird (male), p. 260

  b. Smaller (3½ inches). Bill mainly reddish; forehead (only) and chin violet-purple . . . . . . White-eared Hummingbird (male), p. 253

5a. Crown bright metallic violet-purple or rose-red like gorget, the latter with lateral streamers 6

  b. Crown bright metallic bluish green, unlike gorget, the latter without lateral streamers . . . . Long-billed Star-throat (male), p. 261

6a. Crown and gorget brilliant metallic rose-red
Anna Hummingbird (male), p. 264

  b. Crown and gorget brilliant metallic violet-purple
Costa Hummingbird (male), p. 265

7a. Underparts mainly uniform grayish Wedge-tailed Sabre-wing, p. 247

  b. Underparts entirely or extensively immaculate white 8

8a. Crown bright metallic greenish blue Red-billed Azure-crown, p. 255

  b. Crown bright metallic violet-blue or indigo-blue
Violet-crowned Hummingbird, p. 257
Green-fronted Hummingbird (male), p. 257

KEY TO CATEGORY III

1a. Entire underparts uniform cinnamon-buff or cinnamon-rufous . . 2

  b. Throat and chest not as in 1a. 7

2a. Lateral tail feathers mainly cinnamon-rufous; not white-tipped . 3

  b. Lateral tail feathers boldly white-tipped or mainly bronze . . . 5

3a. Middle tail feathers cinnamon-rufous tipped with bronze
Cinnamon Hummingbird, p. 256

  b. Middle tail feathers metallic greenish bronze 4

4a. More than 4½ inches in length (Chiapas only)
Rufous Sabre-wing, p. 247

    b. Less than 3½ inches in length (Baja California only)
Black-fronted Hummingbird (female), p. 253

5*a.* Auriculars dusky, forming a district patch; rump chestnut; tail not
    white-tipped . . . .   Little Hermit, p. 247

    b. Lateral tail feathers conspicuously white-tipped; auriculars and
    rump not as in 5*a.* 6

6*a.* Sides of rump with a conspicuous buff patch
Sparkling-tailed Hummingbird (female), p. 262

    b. Without a buff patch on sides of rump
Slender Shear-tail (female), p. 261

7*a.* Throat and chest bright metallic green 8

    b. Gorget, bright metallic scarlet or orange-red, the chest white . . 9

8*a.* Forepart of head (including chin) black; a white postocular stripe
Black-fronted Hummingbird (male), p. 253

    b. Entire head greenish; without a postocular stripe
Fawn-breasted Hummingbird, p. 256

9*a.* Back cinnamon-rufous, concolor with tail
Rufous Hummingbird (male), p. 267

    b. Back metallic bronze-green, not concolor with tail
Allen Hummingbird (male), p. 268

KEY TO CATEGORY IV

1*a.* With a brilliant metallic gorget (as viewed in suitable light) . . 2

   b. Without a distinct gorget 7

2*a.* Tail notably long, scissor-like 3

   b. Tail neither notably long nor deeply forked 4

3*a.* Tail boldly white-barred; gorget violet-blue
Sparkling-tailed Hummingbird (male), p. 262

   b. Tail uniform black; gorget violet-purple
Slender Shear-tail (male), p. 261

4*a.* Gorget green 5

   b. Gorget bluish or greenish blue, never purely green
Broad-billed Hummingbird (male), p. 252

5*a.* Conspicuously crested, the occipital feathers cinnamon-buff
Rufous-crested Coquette (male), p. 251

   b. Not crested 6

6*a.* Forehead and chin violet-purple; bill mainly reddish
White-eared Hummingbird (male), p. 253

   b. Forehead and chin green; bill black, notably short
Emerald-chinned Hummingbird (male), p. 250

7a. Notably small (2½ inches). Forepart of head cinnamon
Rufous-crested Coquette (female), p. 251

  b. Not as in 7a. 8

8a. Tail deep chestnut or mainly violet 9

  b. Tail not as in 8a. 11

9a. Flight feathers (and coverts) extensively chestnut, like tail
Berylline Hummingbird, p. 255

  b. Wings and coverts without chestnut 10

10a. Median throat black; tail mainly violet
Green-breasted Mango (male), p. 250

  b. Throat and breast uniformly metallic green; tail chestnut
Rufous-tailed Hummingbird, p. 256

11a. Wing-coverts cinnamon-buff or coppery 12

  b. Wing-coverts green 13

12a. Wing-coverts cinnamon-buff; outer tail feathers extensively white
Stripe-tailed Hummingbird (male), p. 257

  b. Wing-coverts coppery, like rump; tail without white
Blue-tailed Hummingbird, p. 255

13a. Larger (4½ inches). Sides of head with a conspicuous blue patch
Green Violet-ear, p. 249

  b. Smaller (3¼ inches). Sides of head uniformly green
Fork-tailed Emerald (male), p. 251

KEY TO CATEGORY V

1a. Tail white . . . . White-necked Jacobin (male), p. 248

  b. Tail not white, but sometimes white-tipped 2

2a. Crown bright metallic bluish; not concolor with back 3

  b. Crown and back more or less concolor 5

3a. Crown greenish blue; crissum grayish brown
Red-billed Azure-crown, p. 255

  b. Crown violet-blue or indigo-blue; crissum white 4

4a. Crown violet-blue . . . . . Violet-crowned Hummingbird, p. 257

  b. Crown indigo-blue . . . Green-fronted Hummingbird (male), p. 257

5a. Large (4¼ inches). Median throat with a conspicuous black stripe,
the flanks extensively metallic bronze
Green-breasted Mango (female), p. 250

  b. Small (3¼ inches). Throat and most of underparts immaculate white
White-bellied Emerald, p. 254

Key to Category VI

1a. 4½ inches or more in length 2

  b. 3 inches or less in length 17

2a. With a brilliant metallic gorget 3

  b. Without a distinct gorget. Underparts sometimes extensively
metallic bluish violet or violet-blue 8

3a. Lateral tail feathers white-tipped 4

  b. Tail without white 7

4a. Gorget blue or violet-blue; outer tail feathers very extensively
white-tipped 5

  b. Gorget metallic purplish red or reddish purple; tail moderately
white-tipped 6

5a. Bill curved; middle tail feathers bronze-green
                              Violet Sabre-wing (female), p. 248

  b. Bill straight; middle tail feathers black
                         Blue-throated Hummingbird (male), p. 258

6a. Crown bright metallic green or bluish green
                          Long-billed Star-throat (male), p. 261

  b. Crown not as in 6a. . . . . Plain-capped Star-throat, p. 260

7a. Gorget green; crown metallic violet-purple
                    Magnificent Hummingbird (male), p. 260

  b. Gorget violet-purple or reddish purple; crown concolor with back
          Amethyst-throated Hummingbird (male), p. 259

8a. Tail white, or the lateral feathers conspicuously white-tipped . . 9

  b. Tail without white 14

9a. Underparts extensively metallic bluish violet or violet-blue . . . 10

  b. Underparts mainly dusky, grayish, or pale buff 11

10a. Abdomen and tail immaculate white; a white bar across the hind-
neck . . . . White-necked Jacobin (male), p. 248

  b. Not as in 10a . . . . Violet Sabre-wing (male), p. 248

11a. Below mainly buff; bill markedly curved and middle tail feathers
notably long . . . . Long-tailed Hermit, p. 246

  b. Not as in 11a. 12

12a. Underparts, especially the throat, conspicuously scalloped
                White-necked Jacobin (female), p. 248

  b. Underparts uniform grayish or dusky 13

13a. Middle tail feathers metallic bronze-green
                Magnificent Hummingbird (female), p. 260

  b. Tail mainly black . . Blue-throated Hummingbird (female), p. 258

LONG-TAILED HERMIT. *Phaethornis superciliosus* (Illus. p. 246).—
6–6½. Crown brownish, shading to metallic greenish bronze on hind-neck
and back; rump and upper tail-coverts buff or ochraceous, barred with
dusky; tail black, white-tipped, the middle feathers attenuated and notably
longer than the outer; superciliaries and malar area buff or whitish; underparts mainly dingy buff or pale brownish, the median throat clear buff
margined laterally with dusky; bill very long and decidedly curved.

LONG-TAILED HERMIT

Distribution.—Southern Mexico, principally at lower altitudes.

Races.—*P. s. mexicanus* (Pacific slope from Nayarit to western Oaxaca)
P. s. veraecrucis (Atlantic slope from Veracruz through eastern Oaxaca to
Tabasco and northeastern Chiapas, where intergrading with the following).
P. s. longirostris (Tabasco and southeastern Chiapas).

Remarks.—A large curve-billed hummingbird with very long,
white-tipped middle tail feathers. Unmistakable.

LITTLE HERMIT. *Phaethornis longuemareus adolphi.*—3¾. Crown brownish, or metallic greenish bronze, like hind-neck, back, and scapulars; rump and upper tail-coverts chestnut; tail decidedly graduated and fanlike, mainly greenish bronze tipped with buff or chestnut; malar area and superciliaries whitish, the latter incomplete anteriorly; auriculars dusky; underparts cinnamon-rufous or ochraceous, palest on throat and chest; bill very long and moderately curved, black above and yellow below toward base.

Distribution.—Humid lowland forests of the Atlantic slope from Veracruz to Yucatán.

Remarks.—Also known as Longuemare Hermit. The *dusky* auriculars, *chestnut rump*, and sharply graduated, *chestnut-tipped tail* are good field characters. A fairly common bird below 4,000 feet altitude.

WEDGE-TAILED SABRE-WING. *Campylopterus curvipennis.*—5–5½. *Male:* Crown metallic violet-blue, the upperparts otherwise bright metallic green or greenish bronze; wings blackish, faintly glossed with purple, the outer primaries with remarkably thickened shafts; tail fanlike, purplish below, the lateral feathers purple-tipped; sides of head mainly dusky, a distinct white spot behind each eye; underparts gray, the crissum often brownish; bill moderately long, rather sturdy, and slightly curved. *Female:* Similar to male, but crown duller and lateral rectrices very broadly gray-tipped; shafts of primaries not thickened.

Distribution.—Wooded lowlands of eastern Mexico.

Races.—*C. c. curvipennis* (southwestern Tamaulipas southward, in eastern San Luis Potosí, northeastern Puebla, Veracruz, eastern Oaxaca, and northeastern Chiapas). *C. c. excellens* (Sierra de Tuxtla and Jesús Carranza, southern Veracruz; possibly a distinct species). *C. c. pampa* (Yucatán Peninsula).

Remarks.—The *violet-blue crown* and uniform *grayish* (not white) *underparts* are diagnostic. A forest- and thicket-dwelling bird found principally at lower altitudes, this hummer sometimes ranges up to about 4,000 feet in the mountains. The eastern race, *excellens*, may represent a distinct species.

RUFOUS SABRE-WING. *Campylopterus rufus.*—5. *Male:* Forepart of crown brownish, the upperparts otherwise mainly bright metallic green, becoming distinctly greenish bronze on the four inner rectrices; tail very broad, the lateral feathers mainly cinnamon-rufous, but with a conspicuous subterminal blackish band (inner webs only of the outermost feathers); wings sooty, the shafts of the outer primaries greatly thickened; underparts ochraceous cinnamon; bill long, rather sturdy, and slightly curved. *Female:* Similar to male, but shafts of primaries not thickened.

Distribution.—Highlands of Chiapas (Cerro Brujo and eastern part of Sierra Madre), where locally abundant in second-growth woods and more open country.

VIOLET SABRE-WING. *Campylopterus hemileucurus hemileucurus.*— 5¼. *Male:* Crown blackish, the hind-neck and upper back bright metallic bluish violet like underparts; lower back, rump, and middle rectrices dull bluish green; wings blackish, the outer primaries with very thick shafts; tail broad, mainly purplish black, the three outermost feathers white-tipped for half their length; bill moderately long, rather sturdy, and markedly curved. *Female:* Crown brownish or bronze, the upperparts otherwise mainly bright metallic greenish bronze; lateral rectrices very broadly white-tipped, as in male; primary shafts normal; throat bluish violet; malar area, auriculars, and median underparts grayish, the sides and flanks washed with glittering green.

Distribution.—Humid mountain forests of southern Mexico (Guerrero, Oaxaca, Chiapas, Tabasco, and Veracruz).

Remarks.—Also known as De Lattre Sabre-wing. From a distance, or in poor light, this hummer (male) appears all-black except for the broadly white-tipped outer tail feathers. Females are much like male Blue-throated Hummingbirds, but have *bronzy* (not black) middle rectrices, the lateral feathers much more broadly white-tipped, and lack a white postocular stripe.

WHITE-NECKED JACOBIN. *Florisuga mellivora mellivora* (Illus. p. 249).—4½. *Male:* Head, hind-neck, throat, and breast dark violet-blue, the lower hind-neck with a crescent-shaped white bar; back, rump, upper tail-coverts, sides of breast, and flanks bright metallic green; abdomen white; tail very broad, immaculate white, but narrowly tipped with black; bill black, moderately long and straight. *Female:* Upperparts and sides of neck bright metallic greenish bronze, the outermost rectrices white-tipped, the remainder bluish toward ends, but usually with very narrow white tips; throat, breast, and sides dusky or bronzy, the feathers (especially anteriorly) very conspicuously scalloped with whitish; abdomen white; crissum white-tipped, the feathers with a subterminal blue band.

Distribution.—Humid lowland forests of Oaxaca, Chiapas, and Veracruz.

Remarks.—The only hummingbird with an immaculate *white tail* (male) or conspicuously *scalloped throat* (female). Generally uncommon.

WHITE-NECKED JACOBIN

GREEN VIOLET-EAR. *Colibri thalassinus thalassinus* (Illus. p. 249).—
$4\frac{1}{4}$-$4\frac{3}{4}$. *Male:* Above mainly bright metallic bronze-green, the crown dullest
and somewhat brownish; tail blue-tipped, and with a broad, subterminal

GREEN VIOLET-EAR

dusky band; auriculars, sides of neck, and median breast metallic violet-
blue; the underparts otherwise mainly bright metallic green; crissum paler,
the feathers edged with buff; bill black, rather short, and slightly curved.
Female: Smaller and somewhat duller than male, especially below, the
median breast often lacking a bluish patch.

Distribution.—Mountain forests (mainly temperate zone) of southern Mexico from Jalisco and San Luis Potosí southward.

Remarks.—A characteristic and very abundant resident of highland oak forests. The conspicuous *violet-blue patch* on each side of its head is diagnostic.

GREEN-BREASTED MANGO. *Anthracothorax prevostii prevostii* (Illus. p. 250).—4¼. *Male:* Above bright metallic greenish bronze; middle rectrices blackish, like wings, the others dark violet, narrowly edged with black; median throat velvety black, shading to metallic bluish green on breast, the underparts otherwise mainly bright metallic greenish bronze; crissum dull violet; bill black, rather long, and sightly curved. *Female:* Similar to male above, but tail mainly bluish or bronze, the lateral feathers white-tipped; throat and median underparts whitish, the former with a black median stripe sometimes extending to median breast and abdomen; sides of breast and flanks metallic bronze-green.

GREEN-BREASTED MANGO (FEMALE)

Distribution.—Lowlands of eastern Mexico from southern Tamaulipas southward, including islands off the Yucatán Peninsula.

Remarks.—Also known as Prevost Mango. Males are easily distinguished from other mainly green species by their *black throats* and deep *violet tails;* females by the very conspicuous *black stripe* extending through the white of the median underparts.

EMERALD-CHINNED HUMMINGBIRD. *Abeillia abeillei abeillei.*— 3. *Male:* Above bright metallic bronze-green, the tail (except four inner feathers) blue-black toward tips, where narrowly edged with gray; throat glittering green; chest and breast velvety black, the underparts otherwise mainly greenish bronze, becoming dusky on abdomen; bill black, decidedly short, and needle-like. *Female:* Similar to male above, the underparts extensively dusky grayish.

Distribution.—Humid mountain forests of Veracruz, Oaxaca, and Chiapas.

Remarks.—Also known as Abeille Hummingbird.

RUFOUS-CRESTED COQUETTE. *Lophornis delattrei brachylopha.*—
2½. *Male:* Forehead and long feathers of crest rufous; crown, hind-neck, and back greenish bronze, the last bordered posteriorly by a narrow buff bar; rump dull purplish bronze; tail mainly cinnamon-rufous, the feathers edged with bronze; throat, malar area, and auriculars brilliant metallic green, the median breast with a few white feathers; underparts otherwise dull greenish, tinged with grayish buff on abdomen; bill short, straight, and needle-like, mainly pale, tipped with black. *Female:* Not crested. Forepart of crown and throat rufous; a pale buff bar across rump; lateral rectrices rufous-tipped and with a broad black subterminal band; belly grayish brown, the crissum cinnamon.

Distribution.—Known only from two males collected at San Vicente de Benitez (altitude 1,500 feet), southwestern Guerrero. The species ranges to northern South America.

Remarks.—Also known as De Lattre Hummingbird. A notably small species with a *rufous crest* or rufous forehead and throat. Its reddish tail and *buffy rump-patch* are also good field characters. Apparently very rare in Mexico.

BLACK-CRESTED COQUETTE. *Paphosia helenae.*—2½. *Male:* Crown and long occipital crest dark metallic green, the upperparts otherwise mainly metallic bronze-green; a narrow white bar across lower back, the upper tail-coverts black; tail mainly chestnut, the feathers edged with bronze; throat bright metallic green bordered posteriorly by a patch of velvety black; a tuft of feathers on each side buff-colored; crissum cinnamon; bill short and needle-like, mainly pale, tipped with dusky. *Female:* Above similar to male, but without an occipital crest; tail mainly bronze and black tipped with chestnut; throat pale buff, minutely speckled with bronze, the underparts otherwise like male.

Distribution.—Humid lowlands of Veracruz, Oaxaca, and Chiapas.

Remarks.—Also known as Princess Helena Coquette. Smallest of Mexican hummingbirds. The *spotted abdomen* is diagnostic.

FORK-TAILED EMERALD. *Chlorostilbon canivetii.*—3¼. *Male:* Above metallic bronze-green; below glittering emerald-green; tail blue-black, rather long, and very deeply forked; bill moderately long, needle-like, red tipped with black. *Female:* Above similar to male; below uniform grayish; tail moderately forked, mainly blue-black, the lateral feathers gray-tipped.

Distribution.—Sinaloa, San Luis Potosí, and southern Tamaulipas southward, including islands off the coast of Yucatán.

Races.—*C. c. auriceps* (western Mexico from Sinaloa and Durango to Guerrero). *C. c. canivetii* (eastern, south-central, and southern Mexico, including the Yucatán Peninsula). *C. c. forficatus* (Holbox, Mujeres, and Cozumel Islands).

Remarks.—Also known as Canivet Emerald and Common Emerald. A very common species known by its *deeply forked, blue-black tail* and glittering *emerald* underparts (male). While females usually cannot be identified in the field with certainty, their tail characters serve to eliminate most similar hummers.

DUSKY HUMMINGBIRD. *Cynanthus sordidus.*—3½. *Male:* Above dull metallic greenish bronze, the crown and rump usually duller and browner than back; a whitish postocular spot or streak; underparts dusky grayish, palest on the abdomen; bill mainly reddish, straight, and rather long. *Female:* Similar to male, but the four outer tail feathers vaguely gray-tipped and with a broad subterminal band.

Distribution.—Western and southern Mexico (Jalisco, Michoacán, Guerrero, Distrito Federal, Morelos, Hidalgo, and Puebla) to an altitude of about 8,000 feet. ENDEMIC.

Remarks.—A medium-sized, drably colored hummingbird with a *reddish bill.* Notably undistinguished in appearance and often abundant in towns and gardens.

BROAD-BILLED HUMMINGBIRD. *Cynanthus latirostris.*—3½–4. *Male:* Above metallic bronze-green; tail moderately forked, mainly blue-black, the four inner feathers often gray-tipped; throat bright metallic greenish blue or bluish green, the underparts otherwise mainly metallic green; crissum dusky and sometimes edged with white; bill moderately long, slightly curved, and mainly red. *Female:* Similar to male above; underparts uniformly sooty grayish; bill dusky above, reddish below toward base. Differs from all similar hummingbirds in the lack of throat-speckling.

Distribution.—Virtually country-wide (exclusive of Baja California and the Yucatán Peninsula), including the Tres Marías Islands.

Races.—*C. l. magicus* (northwestern Mexico from Sonora and Chihuahua south to Jalisco). *C. l. propinquus* (central Mexico from Guanajuato to northern Michoacán). *C. l. latirostris* (eastern Mexico from Nuevo León and Tamaulipas south to Morelos and northern Veracruz). *C. l. toroi* (southwestern Michoacán and northern Guerrero). *C. l. nitida* (Pacific slope of the Sierra Madre del Sur of Guerrero, southern Oaxaca, and Chiapas). *C. l. doubledayi* (Puebla and northern Oaxaca). *C. l. lawrencei* (María Madre and Cleofa Islands, of the Tres Marías group).

Remarks.—Common locally from sea-level to an altitude of about 8,000 feet. The several forms differ as to the shade and intensity of the throat-patch, but otherwise are very similar. *See* White-eared Humming-bird.

COMMON WOOD-NYMPH. *Thalurania furcata ridgwayi.*—4. *Male:* Forehead to middle of crown dark metallic blue, the posterior crown dull bluish green; hind-neck and upperparts otherwise mainly metallic bronze-green; tail glossy purplish black, long, and deeply forked; throat and chest brilliant metallic green; underparts otherwise mainly dull blackish, the sides washed with metallic green; bill black, moderately long. *Female:* Above metallic bronze-green, the underparts pale gray; tail white-tipped and with a broad subterminal band.

Distribution.—Known from a single specimen collected near San Sebastián, in the humid lowlands of western Jalisco. The species ranges to Bolivia and southeastern Brazil.

BLACK-FRONTED HUMMINGBIRD. *Hylocharis xantusii.*—$3\frac{1}{4}$-$3\frac{1}{2}$. *Male:* Forehead, chin, and malar area velvety black; upperparts mainly bright metallic bronze-green, the upper tail-coverts edged with cinnamon; tail deep chestnut, the middle feathers edged with bronze; a conspicuous white postocular stripe; throat and chest glittering emerald-green, the underparts otherwise mainly cinnamon; bill rather short, reddish tipped with black. *Female:* Crown brownish; back and middle tail feathers metallic bronze-green, the lateral feathers cinnamon-rufous, with a black subterminal spot or bar; underparts ochraceous-buff; bill dusky above, mainly reddish below.

Distribution.—Southern Baja California casually north to latitude 29° ENDEMIC.

Remarks.—Also known as Xantus Hummingbird. The *black face* (male) and conspicuous *white postocular streak* are unmistakable. Most abundant in the Cape region.

WHITE-EARED HUMMINGBIRD. *Hylocharis leucotis* (Illus. p. 253). —$3\frac{1}{2}$ *Male:* Forepart of head (including chin) metallic violet-purple; postocular streak white, very conspicuous; crown and back metallic bronze-green, becoming greenish bronze on rump and middle rectrices, the lateral feathers

WHITE-EARED HUMMINGBIRD

black; throat glittering emerald-green, the underparts otherwise extensively bronze-green; crissum edged with buff; bill rather short, reddish, tipped with black. *Female:* Lores and chin buff, shading to brownish on crown; postocular streak white, the area below brown; upperparts mainly metallic bronze-green, the lateral rectrices blackish toward ends and gray-tipped; throat, median breast, and abdomen whitish, the first speckled with bronze-green and sides washed with same; bill dusky above, reddish below toward base.

Distribution.—Highlands generally, especially in pine forests above 4,000 feet.

Races.—*H. l. borealis* (Sonora, Sinaloa, Chihuahua, Tamaulipas, and Durango). *H. l. leucotis* (temperate zone, except where occupied by the *borealis*).

Remarks.—This species is the one most likely to be seen in mountain pine forests. The purple-faced, white-eared males are unmistakable. Females are less distinctive, but differ from all others in having buffy foreheads and a *brownish patch below a white postocular streak.* Broad-bills lack this conspicuous streak and females are *grayish* (not essentially white) *below.*

BLUE-THROATED GOLDEN-TAIL. *Hylocharis eliciae.*—$3\frac{1}{4}$. Above mainly metallic bronze-green, the upper tail-coverts bright coppery bronze; tail burnished golden-bronze; throat, malar area, and chest bright metallic violet-purple; breast and sides bronze-green; abdomen and crissum grayish brown washed with cinnamon; bill reddish tipped with dusky.

Distribution.—Humid lowlands of Veracruz and Chiapas.

Remarks.—Also known as Elicia Golden-tail. A *blue-throated* hummer with a *bright coppery rump.* Rare.

WHITE-BELLIED EMERALD. *Amazilia candida candida.*—$3\frac{1}{4}$. Above extensively metallic bronze-green, shading to greenish bronze posteriorly; lateral rectrices gray-tipped and with a dusky subterminal patch; median underparts immaculate white, the sides of the neck emerald-green, becoming greenish bronze on the flanks; bill rather long, black above and pink below.

Distribution.—Humid lowlands and lower mountains (up to 4,500 feet altitude) of eastern Mexico from southern San Luis Potosí and Veracruz southward, including the Yucatán Peninsula.

Remarks.—Very similar to Red-billed Azure-crowns of the adjacent highlands, but easily distinguished by the uniformity of its upperparts and *white crissum.* Abundant.

RED-BILLED AZURE-CROWN. *Amazilia cyanocephala cyanocephala.*—3¾–4. Crown bright metallic greenish blue, the upperparts otherwise mainly bronze-green; rump and tail more purely bronze, the latter sometimes with an obscure dusky subterminal patch; throat, median breast, and abdomen immaculate white; sides and flanks metallic greenish bronze; crissum grayish brown edged with white; bill rather long, dusky above and reddish below.

Distribution.—Mountains (chiefly) of eastern and southern Mexico (southern Tamaulipas, San Luis Potosí, Veracruz, Oaxaca, and Chiapas). Accidental in Quintana Roo (Camp Mengel).

Remarks.—A very common inhabitant of mountain pine forests. No other hummingbird of its area has a *bluish crown* and *immaculate white underparts. See* White-bellied Emerald.

BERYLLINE HUMMINGBIRD. *Amazilia beryllina.*—3½–4. *Male:* Above metallic green, passing into dull bronze on the rump; tail purplish chestnut with violet reflections; wings more or less extensively chestnut, especially basally; below mainly glittering emerald-green, the crissum chestnut edged with white; bill moderately long, dusky above and reddish below. *Female:* Similar to male, but abdomen usually extensively grayish buff or dull cinnamon.

Distribution.—Virtually country-wide, exclusive of northern Mexico, Baja California, and the Yucatán Peninsula.

Races.—*A. b. viola* (western Mexico from southeastern Sonora and southern Chihuahua south to Guanajuato and Guerrero). *A. b. beryllina* (eastern and south-central Mexico). *A. b. devillei* (Pacific slope of Chiapas). *A. b. lichtensteini* (mountains of central Chiapas).

Remarks.—A glittering green hummingbird with a glossy purplish chestnut tail and conspicuous *chestnut* on its wings. Ranges from sea-level to about 9,000 feet altitude in the mountains. Usually abundant wherever found.

BLUE-TAILED HUMMINGBIRD. *Amazilia cyanura guatemalae.*—3¾. Entire head and underparts (except crissum) bright emerald-green, the wing-coverts and rump coppery bronze; remiges mainly dusky purplish, the secondaries largely chestnut toward base; tail-coverts and tail deep bluish; bill rather short, dark above and reddish below.

Distribution.—Pacific slope of Chiapas (Huehuetán and Cacahoatán)

Remarks.—The *coppery rump* and *blue-black tail* are diagnostic. A bird of arid lowlands and foothills.

CINNAMON HUMMINGBIRD. *Amazilia rutila.*—$3\frac{3}{4}$–$4\frac{1}{4}$. Above mainly metallic greenish bronze, the tail deep cinnamon-rufous or chestnut, edged (lateral feathers) and tipped with bronze; below cinnamon-rufous; bill reddish, tipped with dusky.

Distribution.—Arid lowlands (principally) of western and southern Mexico, occurring also on Tres Marías, Holbox, and Mujeres Islands.

Races.—*A. r. rutila* (Pacific Coast from Sinaloa to Guerrero, ranging eastward through Oaxaca to the Yucatán Peninsula; Holbox and Mujeres Islands). *A. r. graysoni* (María Madre and Cleofa Islands of the Tres Marías group, off the Pacific Coast). *A. r. corallirostris* (Pacific slope of southern Chiapas).

Remarks.—Also known as Cinnamomeous Hummingbird. The only hummingbird of its area with *uniform* cinnamon underparts and *deep chestnut tail.*

FAWN-BREASTED HUMMINGBIRD. *Amazilia yucatanensis.*—$3\frac{3}{4}$. Above mainly metallic greenish bronze, the lateral rectrices either deep cinnamon-rufous or chestnut, edged and tipped with bronze; throat and breast glittering emerald-green, shading to bronze on the flanks; abdomen cinnamon-buff; bill reddish, tipped with dusky.

Distribution.—Arid lowlands of eastern and southern Mexico.

Races.—*A. y. chalconota* (northeastern Mexico). *A. y. cerviniventris* (San Luis Potosí, Veracruz, Puebla, Chiapas, and Campeche). *A. y. yucatanensis* Chiapas, Tabasco, and the Yucatán Peninsula).

Remarks.—Also known as Yucatán Hummingbird and Buff-bellied Hummingbird. This form replaces the Cinnamon Hummingbird in eastern Mexico. It might be mistaken for a Rufous-tailed Hummingbird of the same general area, but differs in having a *buffy* (not brownish gray) *abdomen.*

RUFOUS-TAILED HUMMINGBIRD. *Amazilia tzacatl tzacatl.*—$3\frac{1}{2}$–$3\frac{3}{4}$. Above metallic greenish bronze, becoming deep chestnut on the upper tail-coverts and tail, the latter broadly edged and tipped with purplish violet; throat and breast glittering emerald-green shading to bronze on the flanks; abdomen grayish; crissum chestnut; bill rather long, reddish, tipped with dusky.

Distribution.—Humid lowlands (principally) of eastern Mexico from southern Tamaulipas south to Yucatán and Chiapas.

Remarks.—Also known as Rieffer Hummingbird. Much like a Fawn-breasted Hummingbird, but with a *grayish* (not buffy) *belly.* Both are very common in the eastern lowlands, but this species occurs principally in humid districts, while the Fawn-breasted prefers dry country.

VIOLET-CROWNED HUMMINGBIRD. *Amazilia violiceps.*—$3\frac{3}{4}$–$4\frac{1}{4}$. Crown and hind-neck metallic violet-blue, the upperparts otherwise mainly olive-bronze or greenish bronze; tail olive-bronze or glossy violet margined with bronze; entire underparts immaculate white; bill reddish, tipped with dusky.

Distribution.—Western and south-central Mexico southward, chiefly at moderate elevations. ENDEMIC.

Races.—*A. v. ellioti* (Sonora and southwestern Chihuahua south to Michoacán; winters east to Hidalgo, accidental in Arizona). *A. v. violiceps* (southern Michoacán and Morelos to Chiapas).

Remarks.—The *gleaming white underparts* distinguish this common species from all others over most of its range. From Guerrero southward, however, it might be mistaken for a Green-fronted Hummingbird.

GREEN-FRONTED HUMMINGBIRD. *Amazilia viridifrons.*—4. *Male:* Forehead and median crown dark indigo-blue; sides of crown, auriculars, hind-neck, and upper back dusky bronze-green; lower back and rump bronzy olive, becoming coppery bronze on upper tail-coverts and tail, the latter buff-tipped; underparts immaculate white, the sides grayish glossed with bronze; bill reddish, tipped with dusky. *Female:* Similar to male, but forehead and crown dull green, and tail without buff tips.

Distribution.—Central Guerrero and central Oaxaca to Chiapas. ENDEMIC.

Remarks.—*See* Violet-crowned Hummingbird.

STRIPE-TAILED HUMMINGBIRD. *Eupherusa eximia* (Illus. p. 258). —$3\frac{1}{4}$–$3\frac{1}{2}$. *Male:* Above bright metallic green, becoming glittering emerald-green below; wings mainly dusky purplish, and with a very conspicuous patch of cinnamon-rufous near the base; tail extensively dusky bronze, the inner webs of the two outer feathers (except tips) immaculate white, like crissum; bill moderately long, dull black. *Female:* Similar to male above, the underparts grayish, and abdomen tinged with pale buff.

Distribution.—Southern Mexico, exclusive of the Yucatán Peninsula. Uncommon to rare, occurring principally from 1,000 to 4,000 feet above sea-level.

Races.—*E. e. poliocerca* (Guerrero and Oaxaca, chiefly on the Pacific slope). *E. e. nelsoni* (Veracruz, Puebla, and Oaxaca, chiefly on the Atlantic slope). *E. e. eximia* (Chiapas).

STRIPE-TAILED HUMMINGBIRD

Remarks.—The only hummingbird with a sharply defined and very conspicuous patch of *cinnamon* at the base of the wings. From below its tail appears *white* with a broad black tip. Unmistakable.

BLUE-THROATED HUMMINGBIRD. *Lampornis clemenciae.*—5–5¼. *Male:* Above extensively metallic bronze-green, the crown and rump somewhat olive-bronze, shading to dusky bronze on upper tail-coverts; tail glossy black, the lateral feathers broadly white-tipped; a narrow but conspicuous white stripe behind eye; throat bright metallic blue or violet-blue, the underparts otherwise sooty gray; crissum margined with white; bill dull black. *Female:* Similar to male, but throat grayish.

Distribution.—Highlands generally, especially above 6,000 feet altitude.

Races.—*L. c. bessophilus* (Sonora, Sinaloa, Chihuahua, and Durango). *L. c. clemenciae* (central plateau and the Sierra Madre Oriental south to Chiapas).

Remarks.—The very broadly white-tipped lateral tail feathers distinguish this species from the following. Both are characteristic of the higher mountains. *See* Magnificent Hummingbird and Violet Sabrewing.

AMETHYST-THROATED HUMMINGBIRD. *Lampornis amethystinus* (Illus. p. 259).—4¼–5. *Male:* Above metallic greenish bronze, becoming duller posteriorly, where more or less dusky; tail very broad, mainly black, the outermost feathers obscurely gray-tipped; postocular stripe white; throat bright metallic violet-purple or reddish purple, the underparts otherwise grayish brown or dusky; bill moderately long, dull black. *Female:* Similar to male, but without purple gorget, the throat being buff, ochraceous, or dusky, like breast.

AMETHYST-THROATED HUMMINGBIRD

Distribution.—Nayarit, San Luis Potosí, and southern Tamaulipas southward in the mountains, chiefly above 6,000 feet.

Races.—*L. a. brevirostris* (Nayarit, Jalisco, Colima, Michoacán, and northwestern portion of the state of Mexico). *L. a. amethystinus* (San Luis Potosí and southern Tamaulipas south in the mountains to Chiapas). *L. a. margaritae* (mountains of Guerrero and western Oaxaca). *L. a. salvini* (Volcán de Tacaná, southeastern Chiapas).

Remarks.—Also known as Cazique Hummingbird. No other large hummingbird of the area with very dusky underparts lacks white on its tail. *See* Blue-throated Hummingbird and Magnificent Hummingbird.

GREEN-THROATED MOUNTAIN-GEM. *Lampornis viridi-pallens.* —4–4½. *Male:* Crown bright metallic green, becoming greenish bronze on hind-neck and back; rump coppery bronze; upper tail-coverts and tail black; postocular streak white, the area below bronze or coppery; throat metallic emerald-green, the feathers edged with white, causing a closely spotted appearance; chest and median underparts white or whitish, the sides washed with metallic greenish; bill rather short, dull black. *Female:* Similar to male, but more or less uniform bright metallic green (less bronzy) above, and without a green gorget, the throat being buffy whitish; tail bronze-green tipped with dusky, the outermost feathers mainly gray.

Distribution.—Highlands of Chiapas.

Races.—*L. v. ovandensis* (upper slopes of Mount Ovando). *L. v. viridi-pallens* (Atlantic and Pacific slopes of Chiapas, up to 10,000 feet altitude).

GARNET-THROATED HUMMINGBIRD. *Lamprolaima rhami rhami.*—4¼. *Male:* Above bright metallic green or bronze-green; wings extensively chestnut or rufous, the tips dusky purplish; tail very deep violet-purple; median throat glittering reddish purple, the gorget bordered with velvety black; chest and median breast deep metallic violet-blue; underparts otherwise blackish, the sides glossed with greenish bronze; bill black, rather short. *Female:* Similar to male, but outer rectrices gray-tipped and underparts dusky brownish, the throat and chest not colorful as in males.

Distribution.—Mountains of Guerrero, Mexico, Veracruz, Oaxaca, and Chiapas, chiefly above 5,000 feet.

Remarks.—One of the most colorful of Mexican hummingbirds. A very common species with *chestnut wings*. From below the male's *reddish gorget* and metallic *blue breast* are good field marks.

MAGNIFICENT HUMMINGBIRD. *Eugenes fulgens.*—4½–5. *Male:* Crown metallic violet-purple; upperparts otherwise mainly bright metallic greenish bronze, the wing-coverts, rump, and middle rectrices sometimes more or less coppery; lateral rectrices narrowly gray-tipped; throat glittering emerald-green; chest and median breast black more or less glossed with metallic bronze, the posterior underparts dusky; bill rather long, black. *Female:* Above metallic bronze-green, the lateral rectrices broadly gray-tipped; below grayish, the feathers of the throat with brownish centers.

Distribution.—Widespread at high altitudes, chiefly above 5,000 feet.

Races.—*E. f. fulgens* (highlands generally, exclusive of Baja California and Chiapas). *E. f. viridiceps* (mountains of Chiapas).

Remarks.—Also known as Rivoli Hummingbird. The only Mexican hummer with a *purplish* crown and *green* gorget. Females are somewhat like female Blue-throated and Amethyst-throated Hummingbirds, but are distinguished by their grayer (less dusky) underparts and greenish middle rectrices. Blue-throats of both sexes have *conspicuously white-tipped tails*.

PLAIN-CAPPED STAR-THROAT. *Heliomaster constantii.*—4½. *Male:* Above metallic bronze, the rump with a white median stripe or patch; tail blackish toward end, the lateral feathers white-tipped; postocular and malar stripes whitish and rather conspicuous; chin and upper throat blackish or dusky gray; lower throat bright metallic red or purplish red; underparts extensively dusky or brownish gray, fading to whitish on the abdomen and crissum; bill black, very long, and rather sturdy. *Female:* Similar to male, but red of throat less extensive; chin and throat sometimes entirely dusky or blackish.

Distribution.—Arid lowlands (to about 4,500 feet altitude) of western Mexico from southern Sonora southward.

Races.—*H. c. pinicola* (western slope of the Sierra Madre Occidental from extreme southern Sonora to western Jalisco). *H. c. leocadiae* (Pacific slope from east-central Michoacán and Guerrero southward).

Remarks.—Also known as Constant Star-throat. *See* Long-billed Star-throat.

LONG-BILLED STAR-THROAT. *Heliomaster longirostris pallidiceps.* —4½. *Male:* Crown metallic green or bluish green; hind-neck coppery bronze; upperparts otherwise mainly bright metallic greenish bronze, the rump with an elongated white median patch; tail black toward end, the lateral feathers conspicuously white-tipped; postocular spot and malar streak white; chin black; gorget metallic reddish purple, scalloped behind; breast and median underparts ash gray fading to white on the abdomen; sides and flanks metallic green, the latter bearing a conspicuous white tuft; crissum black, tipped with white; bill black, decidedly long. *Female:* Similar to male, but without brightly colored crown and throat, these being, respectively, bronze and black (or black-streaked), the throat sometimes fringed behind with metallic purple.

Distribution.—Lowland forests of Guerrero, Oaxaca, Chiapas, Veracruz, and Tabasco.

Remarks.—The colorful male, with its metallic *bluish green crown* and *reddish gorget*, is unmistakable. Females resemble female Plain-capped Star-throats of the dryer lowlands, but have a *black crissum* conspicuously tipped with white.

SLENDER SHEAR-TAIL. *Doricha enicura.*—3–4¼. *Male:* Above metallic bronze-green or golden-bronze; tail notably long and deeply forked, the lateral feathers dusky purplish and often more than 2 inches in length; chin and sides of head bronze-green; throat extensively bright violet-purple; a broad buff or whitish breast-band; underparts otherwise mainly metallic green, the abdomen whitish; bill black, rather long, and slightly curved. *Female:* Above metallic bronze-green; tail of normal length, not forked, the basal half cinnamon-rufous, followed by a black band, the two outer feathers white-tipped; postocular spot buff; underparts uniform cinnamon-rufous.

Distribution.—Highlands of Chiapas, where locally abundant.

Remarks.—*See* Sparkling-tailed Hummingbird.

MEXICAN SHEAR-TAIL. *Doricha eliza.*—3½–4. *Male:* Above metallic bronze-green; tail long and very deeply forked, the three outer feathers sooty bronze or purplish, edged with pale cinnamon toward base of inner webs; throat bright metallic purple-violet; chest, median breast, and posterior underparts dull white, the sides and flanks metallic bronze-green; bill black, long, and moderately curved. *Female:* Similar to male above, but tail short, pale cinnamon toward base, the two outer feathers gray-tipped and with a subterminal black area; throat and median underparts whitish tinged with buff, the sides and flanks glossed with bronze-green.

Distribution.—Dry parts of southeastern Mexico from Veracruz (where rare) to Yucatán and Holbox Island. ENDEMIC.

Remarks.—*See* Sparkling-tailed Hummingbird.

SPARKLING-TAILED HUMMINGBIRD. *Tilmatura dupontii dupontii* (Illus. p. 262).—2½–3½. *Male:* Above metallic bronze-green, the sides of the rump with a conspicuous white patch; tail long and very deeply forked (scissor-like), the outer feathers pointed, purplish black tipped and barred with white; throat metallic violet-blue; chest and sides of neck

SPARKLING-TAILED HUMMINGBIRD

whitish; underparts otherwise extensively bronze-green; bill black, moderately long. *Female:* Above metallic bronze-green, the sides of the rump with a conspicuous buff patch; tail fan-shaped, mainly black tipped with white; underparts uniform cinnamon-rufous.

Distribution.—Highlands (principally) of south-central and southern Mexico (Jalisco, Colima, Michoacán, Guerrero, Mexico, Distrito Federal, Morelos, Veracruz, and Chiapas).

Remarks.—Also known as Dupont Hummingbird. A diminutive hummingbird with a very long *white-barred, scissor-like tail* and *violet-blue* throat. Male Shear-tails also have long forked tails, but of uniform color. Their gorgets are more distinctly *violet* (less blue) than in this species. Females of all three are very similar, but each has a different range.

LUCIFER HUMMINGBIRD. *Calothorax lucifer.*—3¾. *Male:* Above metallic bronze-green or golden-green; tail mainly dusky bronze or blackish, the lateral feathers notably narrow and all sharp-tipped; a white postocular spot; gorget brilliant metallic violet-purple or purplish violet, the lateral feathers considerably elongated; chest, median breast, abdomen, and crissum dull white, the sides and flanks metallic green mixed with buff; bill black, slightly curved. *Female:* Above similar to male, but rectrices much broader, the three outermost pale cinnamon at base, followed by a black area; two outermost feathers broadly white-tipped; postocular spot or streak buff; underparts pale cinnamon-buff, fading to whitish on the abdomen and crissum.

Distribution.—Fairly common at moderate elevations (4,000–7,500 feet) in eastern and central Mexico (rarer in west) south to Chiapas and Veracruz; migratory in northern part of range.

Remarks.—A small purple-throated hummer with a slightly *curved* bill and *rusty* sides. Costa Hummingbirds are similar, but have *purplish foreheads*, straight bills, and *greenish* sides. *See* Beautiful Hummingbird.

BEAUTIFUL HUMMINGBIRD. *Calothrax pulcher.*—3¾. Very similar to a Lucifer Hummingbird, but males have much longer tails, with broader, round-tipped feathers. Adult females resemble female Lucifers, but are *buffy grayish* (not cinnamon-buff) *below.*

Distribution.—Southern Mexico (exclusive of the Yucatán Peninsula) from Guerrero, Distrito Federal, and Puebla to Chiapas. ENDEMIC.

*RUBY-THROATED HUMMINGBIRD. *Archilochus colubris.*—3¼. *Male:* Above metallic bronze-green; tail forked, purplish black, the outer feathers with pointed tips; throat bright metallic ruby-red; chest and crissum grayish white, the latter with dusky centers; median underparts otherwise dusky grayish, the sides and flanks metallic green; bill black, slightly curved, and moderately long. *Female:* Above metallic bronze-green, the tail white-tipped, mainly black or with a broad subterminal black band; underparts uniform whitish, the throat sometimes minutely speckled with dusky.

Distribution.—Widespread as a migrant and winter visitant, ranging from sea-level to almost 10,000 feet in the highlands. Unreported in Baja California, Sonora, and a few other states.

Remarks.—Male Ruby-throats resemble Broad-tailed Hummingbirds, but have *flame-colored* gorgets quite unlike the latter's *reddish violet* throat. Females are virtually indistinguishable in the field. Ruby-throats, Rufous, and Allen Hummingbirds have very similar gorgets, but differ notably in other respects.

BLACK-CHINNED HUMMINGBIRD. *Archilochus alexandri.*—3¼. *Male:* Above metallic bronze-green, the crown dullest and often greenish bronze; tail deep purplish, broadly edged with bronze, the feathers with pointed tips; chin, upper throat, and malar area velvety black; lower throat bright metallic purplish violet; chest and crissum grayish white, the underparts otherwise dusky brownish glossed with green; bill black, moderately long, and slightly curved. *Female:* Above metallic bronze-green; below dull grayish white, fading to pure white on the crissum; tail (except middle feathers) white-tipped, mainly purplish black, or with a black subterminal band.

Distribution.—Breeds in northern Baja California, Sonora, and Tamaulipas. Widespread elsewhere (except the Yucatán Peninsula) in winter.

Remarks.—A small hummer with an apparently *black* throat bordered below with white. In favorable light the *lower throat* shows brilliant purplish. Females are almost identical with female Costas. *See* Costa Hummingbird.

ANNA HUMMINGBIRD. *Calypte anna.*—3½. *Male:* Forehead, crown, sides of head (except white postocular stripe), and throat brilliant metallic rose-red, the lateral feathers of the gorget forming streamers; upperparts extensively metallic bronze-green; tail dusky blackish; underparts (except gorget) dusky grayish, more or less washed with metallic green; bill black, rather short. *Female:* Above metallic bronze-green; below dingy grayish, the median throat often with a few metallic purplish red feathers; lateral rectrices white-tipped and with a black subterminal band.

Distribution.—Northwestern Baja California, ranging to northern Sonora in winter. Recorded from Guadalupe, Cedros, and Los Coronados Islands.

Remarks.—Much like a Costa Hummingbird, but with a *"flame-colored"* or bright rose-red (not violet-purple) crown, face, and throat. Females resemble female Black-chinned and Costa Hummingbirds, but usually have more throat-spotting and sometimes a distinct median throat-patch.

COSTA HUMMINGBIRD. *Calypte costae.*—3¼. Forehead, crown, and throat brilliant metallic violet or violet-purple, the lateral feathers of the gorget forming very distinct streamers; upperparts extensively metallic bronze-green, the lateral rectrices sooty, tipped with black; lower throat, chest, and crissum grayish, the underparts otherwise dusky washed with metallic green; bill black, straight, and moderately long. *Female:* Above metallic greenish bronze, the crown often dull brownish; below mainly dingy whitish, the malar area, throat, and chest often tinged with buff; tail extensively purplish black, the lateral feathers boldly white-tipped.

Distribution.—Resident in Baja California, Sonora, and various offshore islands. Ranges to Sinaloa in winter.

Remarks.—The brilliant *violet or violet-purple* crown, face, and throat are distinctive. Anna Hummingbirds have a similar pattern, but their heads and gorgets appear bright *rose-red* in suitable light. Lucifers have similar gorgets, but lack purple on the face and crown. *See* Black-chinned Hummingbird.

CALLIOPE HUMMINGBIRD. *Stellula calliope* (Illus. p. 265).—2¾. *Male:* Above metallic bronze-green; tail purplish black or dusky, inconspicuously tipped with brownish gray, the bases of the middle feathers

Calliope Hummingbird

(sometimes others) edged with cinnamon; feathers of the gorget long, narrow, bright reddish purple, the throat appearing conspicuously streaked with reddish and white; underparts mainly whitish strongly tinged with buff laterally, the sides and flanks glossed with metallic greenish; crissum white, washed with buff; bill rather short, dusky above, pinkish below toward base. *Female:* Above metallic bronze-green; middle rectrices bronzy, tipped with black, the lateral feathers boldly white-tipped and with a broad sub-terminal band; throat and chest whitish, the former minutely speckled with dusky bronze; underparts otherwise whitish washed with pale buff, especially on the flanks and crissum.

Distribution.—Resident in mountains of northern Baja California and Guerrero. Winters in the highlands of western and south-central Mexico (Guanajuato and Distrito Federal).

Races.—*S. c. calliope* (as above, except Guerrero). *S. c. lowei* (mountains of Guerrero).

Remarks.—No other hummingbird has a red throat *streaked with white*. Females resemble female Broad-tails but are much smaller. Female Rufous Hummingbirds have *reddish* rumps and conspicuous cinnamon on their tails. Female Black-chins have *grayish* (not buff) *sides*.

BUMBLEBEE HUMMINGBIRD. *Atthis heloisa.*—2¾. *Male:* Above metallic bronze-green; lateral rectrices white-tipped, conspicuously cinnamon-rufous at base, this followed by a broad band of black; gorget brilliant metallic reddish purple, the lateral feathers forming streamers; chest and median underparts whitish, the sides and flanks tinged with buff and glossed with bronze-green; bill dusky, rather short, and slightly curved. *Female:* Above metallic greenish bronze; tail mainly cinnamon-rufous, the lateral feathers buff-tipped and with a broad subterminal black band; throat, median breast, and abdomen whitish, the first minutely speckled with bronze; sides, flanks, and crissum cinnamon-buff.

Distribution.—Mountains of southeastern Sinaloa, southwestern Chihuahua, Nuevo León, and Tamaulipas south to Oaxaca and Veracruz. ENDEMIC.

Races.—*A. h. margarethae* (both slopes of the Sierra Madre Occidental from extreme southwestern Chihuahua and southeastern Sinaloa to eastern Michoacán and western part of the state of Mexico). *A. h. heloisa* (mountains of eastern Mexico south to Oaxaca and Veracruz; accidental in Arizona).

Remarks.—Also known as Heloise Hummingbird. Much like a Calliope Hummingbird, but with an *unstreaked* gorget and conspicuous *cinnamon* at the base of the *white-tipped tail*. Female Calliopes have white tail-tips but lack the Bumblebees' cinnamon. *See* Broad-tailed and Rufous Hummingbirds.

WINE-THROATED HUMMINGBIRD. *Atthis ellioti ellioti.*—2¾. Very similar to a Bumblebee Hummingbird, but occupying a different area.

Distribution.—Mountains of Chiapas (Tumbalá, Santa Rosa).

Remarks.—Also known as Elliot Hummingbird. Possibly a race of the Bumblebee Hummingbird and by many so considered.

BROAD-TAILED HUMMINGBIRD. *Selasphorus platycercus.*—3¾. *Male:* Above metallic bronze-green; tail (except middle feathers) purplish black; throat bright metallic reddish purple, the lateral feathers elongated; lower neck white, shading to grayish on the median underparts, the flanks (especially) and sides tinged with buff and more or less glossed with bronze; crissum white streaked with buff; bill black, moderately long. *Female:* Above metallic bronze-green; tail cinnamon-rufous at base, the lateral feathers white-tipped and with a broad black subterminal band; underparts mainly pale grayish, the throat usually minutely speckled with bronze; sides and crissum washed with buff.

Distribution.—Widespread in the highlands, mainly from 7,000 to 12,000 feet above sea-level.

Races.—*S. p. platycercus* (highlands generally, exclusive of Baja California and Chiapas). *S. p. guatemalae* (recorded once from Teopisca, Chiapas).

Remarks.—Male Broad-tails resemble Ruby-throats but are larger and have bright *reddish purple* (not flame-colored) gorgets. Females are almost identical with female Calliopes except in size. A patch of rufous on the sides of the spread tail (near base) distinguishes them from female Black-chinned and Costa Hummingbirds. *See* Rufous and Allen Hummingbirds.

*RUFOUS HUMMINGBIRD. *Selasphorus rufus.*—3¼–3½. *Male:* Crown metallic bronze-green; stripe through eye, auriculars, hind-neck, and upperparts uniform rufous, the tail with black-tipped, sharply pointed feathers; throat extensively bright metallic scarlet or orange-red; lower neck and chest white, the underparts otherwise essentially rufous; bill black, moderately long. *Female:* Above metallic greenish bronze; tail rufous at base, the middle feathers terminating in bronze, the remainder white-tipped and with a blackish subterminal bar; throat, breast, and abdomen white, the first speckled with metallic scarlet (glitters only in suitable light); sides, flanks, and crissum buff.

Distribution.—Winters south to Baja California, Guerrero, state of Mexico, and Veracruz, chiefly from 1,100 to 8,000 feet above sea-level.

Remarks.—A *rufous-backed* hummer with a bright-red gorget. Male Allen Hummingbirds have rufous auriculars and tails, but are green-backed. The two are similar below and females are quite indistinguishable in the field. Both resemble female Broad-tailed Humming-birds, but have more reddish on their tails.

*ALLEN HUMMINGBIRD. *Selasphorus sasin sasin* (Illus. p. 268).—
3¼. *Male:* Similar to a Rufous Hummingbird, but upperparts (except tail and coverts) wholly metallic bronze-green. *Female:* Virtually identical with a female Rufous Hummingbird, the two not separable in the field.

ALLEN HUMMINGBIRD

Distribution.—Winters in Baja California and northwestern Mexico south to Aguascalientes, Guanajuato, and Distrito Federal, chiefly from 1,100 to 8,000 feet above sea-level.

Remarks.—*See* Rufous Hummingbird.

Family TROGONIDAE. Trogons

KEY TO THE SPECIES

1a. Underparts with red or pink, this sometimes confined to the lower belly and under tail-coverts 2

   b. Underparts with conspicuous yellow 10

2a. Tail (three outer rectrices) with more or less white or whitish, this always conspicuous from below 3

   b. Tail without white . . . . Slaty-tailed Trogon, p. 270

3a. Outer rectrices wholly white or boldly barred with black; wing-coverts conspicuously curved; upper tail-coverts at least as long as the rectrices; male crested . . . . Quetzal, p. 270

   b. Not as in 3a. 4

4a. Middle rectrices deep metallic blue, the terminal third of the outer feathers immaculate white . . . . Eared Trogon, p. 270

   b. Not as in 4a. 5

5a. Middle rectrices metallic green or bluish green 6

   b. Middle rectrices reddish brown or bright coppery 7

6a. Outer rectrices black, with square white tips
Mountain Trogon (male), p. 271

   b. Outer rectrices black, narrowly barred with white
Bar-tailed Trogon (male), p. 273

7a. Chest and upperparts metallic green or golden-bronze, the middle rectrices bright coppery, tipped with black; three outer tail feathers white, *finely* vermiculated with black
Elegant Trogon (male), p. 272

   b. Chest and upperparts brown, the middle rectrices dull reddish brown, tipped with black 8

8a. Lower breast and belly white, the flanks and under tail-coverts pink; a white ear-patch . . . . . Elegant Trogon (female), p. 272

   b. Abdomen, flanks, and under tail-coverts bright red; breast usually with a distinct white band 9

9a. Outer webs of three outer rectrices white, evenly barred with black
Mountain Trogon (female), p. 271

   b. Outer rectrices dusky silvery, narrowly white-tipped, and with a narrow black subterminal bar . . Bar-tailed Trogon (female), p. 273

10a. Outer rectrices evenly barred with black and white, the tips immaculate; wing-coverts grayish, or narrowly barred with white
Violaceous Trogon, p. 273

   b. Outer rectrices black, with square white tips; wings wholly black
Citreoline Trogon, p. 271

QUETZAL. *Pharomachrus mocino mocino.*—14–15. *Male:* Head, upperparts, and breast bright metallic green or golden-green; remiges and inner tail feathers black, the three outer rectrices immaculate white; a prominent crest; wing-coverts long and curved; upper tail-coverts remarkably elongated and filmy, the inner pair often attaining a length of more than 2 feet; abdomen and under tail-coverts bright red, the tail below (outer feathers) wholly white; bill yellow. *Female:* Above metallic green, the head, breast, and abdomen brownish; lower belly and crissum red; wings and tail sooty, the outer rectrices barred with white; not crested; upper tail-coverts extending to tips of rectrices; bill blackish.

Distribution.—Humid mountain forests of extreme eastern Oaxaca and Chiapas, chiefly above 4,500 feet.

Remarks.—The Quetzal, national bird of Guatemala, was venerated as a religious symbol by the ancient Aztecs. Perhaps the most striking member of a notably colorful family, it is considered by many the most beautiful bird of the Western Hemisphere. Although now protected, Quetzals were long hunted for the millinery trade and today occur only locally in humid mountain forests, where once probably abundant. Males will be recognized by their crests and long, filmy upper tail-coverts; females by their brownish heads and underparts.

EARED TROGON. *Euptilotis neoxenus.*—13–14. *Male:* Head and throat black glossed with green, the breast and upperparts mainly metallic green or golden-green, this shading to blue-green on the upper tail-coverts; tail deep metallic blue, the three outer feathers broadly white-tipped; abdomen and under tail-coverts bright red. *Female:* Crown and sides of head essentially slate gray, shading to grayish brown on the throat, breast, and upper abdomen; plumage otherwise as in male.

Distribution.—Mountain forests of Chihuahua, Zacatecas, Nayarit, and Michoacán. ENDEMIC.

Remarks.—This trogon receives its name from the long feathers of the ear-coverts and their terminating filaments. The best field character for both sexes is the tail. From below, the *broad, overlapping white tips* of the outer feathers make it appear about *equally* black and white, *not barred* with black and white.

SLATY-TAILED TROGON. *Trogon massena massena.*—13–14. *Male:* Breast and upperparts metallic green or golden-green; wing-coverts finely vermiculated with black and white, the primaries and outer rectrices uniform black; sides of head and throat black; abdomen and under tail-coverts bright red, the tail below wholly black; iris yellow; bill orange.

Female: Dull slate, the lower abdomen and under tail-coverts bright red; bill black above, orange below.

Distribution.—Humid lowland forests of Veracruz, Campeche, and Oaxaca southward.

Remarks.—Also known as Massena Trogon. The only Mexican trogon without white on its tail. As seen from below, the *wholly blackish tail* is diagnostic. Most trogons usually show little, if any, white from behind. This species is the largest of our lowland representatives. While generally phlegmatic, its movements when plucking fruit on the wing are graceful and decidedly quick.

CITREOLINE TROGON. *Trogon citreolus.*—10½. *Male:* Head, breast, and wings dull black; back and scapulars metallic green or purplish green, shading to rich violet-blue on the upper tail-coverts; inner tail feathers black-tipped, but essentially like back, the three outer rectrices with broad white tips; belly and crissum bright yellow or yellowish, the lower breast partly white; iris yellow. *Female:* Similar to male, but upperparts uniform dull black; white tips of outer rectrices almost square.

Distribution.—Coastal plains and foothills from Sinaloa and southern Tamaulipas southward.

Races.—*T. c. citreolus* (Pacific slope south to western Oaxaca). *T. c. sumichrasti* (coastal plain from central Oaxaca to central Chiapas). *T. c. melanocephala* (Caribbean slope from southern Tamaulipas southward).

Remarks.—The only yellow-bellied trogon in western Mexico. In the eastern and southern lowlands, where Violaceous Trogons also occur, this species is readily distinguished by the pattern of its three outer rectrices. These are uniform black, with almost *square white tips*.

MOUNTAIN TROGON. *Trogon mexicanus* (Illus. p. 272).—11½–12½. *Male:* Face and throat black, the chest and upperparts mainly metallic green or greenish bronze; wings sooty, the coverts and secondaries finely vermiculated; middle rectrices glossy green, the three outer feathers black with almost square white tips; a white band across breast, the belly and crissum bright red. *Female:* Face and throat blackish, the upperparts, breast, and upper abdomen mainly brown; wing-coverts finely vermiculated; middle rectrices reddish brown, narrowly tipped with black, the adjacent pairs wholly black; three outer rectrices barred with black and white on outer webs, the tips white; belly and crissum bright red or pink.

Distribution.—Highlands of western Chihuahua, Zacatecas, San Luis Potosí, and central Tamaulipas southward in mountain forests.

Races.—*T. m. clarus* (western Chihuahua). *T. m. mexicanus* (Zacatecas, San Luis Potosí, and central Tamaulipas southward in the mountains).

Remarks.—Also known as Mexican Trogon. A characteristic mountain species, occurring principally above 4,000 feet. Especially common in oak forests. While resembling Elegant and Bar-tailed Trogons superficially, the tail pattern of each is distinctive, especially as seen from below. Of the three, Mountain Trogons alone have the

MOUNTAIN TROGON

outer rectrices either conspicuously tipped with white, or their *outer webs evenly barred* with black and white.

ELEGANT TROGON. *Trogon elegans.*—11–12. *Male:* Forepart of head and throat black, the breast and upperparts mainly metallic green or golden-bronze; wing-coverts and secondaries finely vermiculated with black and white; inner tail feathers metallic coppery, tipped with black; three outer rectrices extensively white, liberally speckled and vermiculated with black, the tips immaculate; a broad white breast-band; abdomen, flanks, and crissum bright red. *Female:* Face and throat dusky, the chest and upperparts mainly brown; a white ear-patch; outer rectrices essentially as in male, the inner feathers dull reddish brown; lower breast and abdomen white or whitish, the flanks and crissum bright pink.

Distribution.—Tres Marías Islands, off the Pacific Coast, and the mainland south to Guerrero and Puebla, chiefly in the foothills and mountains.

Races.—*T. e. goldmani* (María Madre and María Magdalena Islands of the Tres Marías group). *T. e. canescens* (Sonora, western Chihuahua, northern Sinaloa). *T. e. ambiguus* (Durango, Zacatecas, Nuevo León, and Tamaulipas south to Guerrero and Puebla).

Remarks.—This widespread species, known also as the Coppery-tailed Trogon, is the only member of its family to reach the United States, where it occurs locally in the mountains of southern Arizona and extreme southern Texas. In both sexes the underside of the tail is the best field character: essentially *white or silvery, with fine vermiculations and immaculate tips.* Brown-backed females might be mistaken for female Bar-tailed Trogons, but are largely *white below*, with *pink* flanks and under tail-coverts.

BAR-TAILED TROGON. *Trogon collaris puella.*—10. *Male:* Face and throat black; chest and upperparts mainly bright metallic green; wings black, the coverts with narrow white bars; three outer tail feathers black, narrowly barred (at regular intervals) with white; a white band across the lower breast; abdomen and under tail-coverts bright red. *Female:* Green of male replaced with brown; wing-coverts brownish; three outer tail feathers dusky or silvery, white-tipped, and with a narrow black subterminal bar.

Distribution.—San Luis Potosí and Veracruz south through the Yucatán Peninsula and Oaxaca, chiefly at moderate elevations.

Remarks.—Also known as Collared Trogon. Smallest of the six red-bellied trogons of our area. Males have evenly barred tails, as seen from below, and are virtually unmistakable. Females resemble female Elegant Trogons superficially, but are mainly bright red below, with only a *band of white across the breast.* Female Mountain Trogons have conspicuous black and white bars on their *outer* rectrices.

VIOLACEOUS TROGON. *Trogon violaceous braccatus.*—9½. *Male:* Head and throat black, the hind-neck and breast violet-blue; above mainly metallic green, the inner rectrices black-tipped; three outer tail feathers evenly barred with black and white, the tips immaculate; wings black, the coverts grayish; lower breast, abdomen, and under tail-coverts rich golden-yellow. *Female:* Throat, breast, and upperparts mainly dull black, the wing-coverts narrowly barred with white; three outer rectrices black, the outer webs barred as in males; belly and crissum bright yellow.

Distribution.—Eastern San Luis Potosí and southern Tamaulipas south through Puebla, Oaxaca, and the Yucatán Peninsula.

Remarks.—Also known as Gartered Trogon. The only other yellow-bellied species in our area (Citreoline) has *black* outer tail feathers with square white tips. Both are essentially lowland birds, but Violaceous Trogons may also be found as much as 4,500 feet above sea-level. Their call is a clear distinct whistle, unlike that of any other American species.

Family ALCEDINIDAE. Kingfishers

KEY TO THE SPECIES

1*a*. Above blue 2
 b. Above dark glossy green 3
2*a*. Underparts mainly rufous . . . . Ringed Kingfisher, p. 274
 b. Underparts mainly white . . . . Belted Kingfisher, p. 274
3*a*. Notably small (5½ inches); underparts mainly rufous
Pygmy Kingfisher, p. 275
 b. Not notably small (8–11½ inches); underparts mainly white . . . 4
4*a*. Smaller (8 inches); folded wings spotted and barred with white
Green Kingfisher, p. 275
 b. Larger (10½–11½); folded wings uniform green
Amazon Kingfisher, p. 275

RINGED KINGFISHER. *Ceryle torquata torquata.*—15–16. *Male:* Above blue, the hind-neck with a more or less conspicuous white collar; inner webs of remiges edged and notched with white, the tail narrowly barred with same; throat and crissum white; breast and abdomen rufous. *Female:* Similar to male, but with a broad blue band across the chest.

Distribution.—Coastal slopes from southern Sinaloa, Nuevo León, and central Tamaulipas southward.

Remarks.—The only *large* kingfisher with a *chestnut belly*. Our only other blue-backed kingfisher, the Belted, is considerably smaller and has a white belly. It will not be found in summer. Lowland rivers and lagoons.

*BELTED KINGFISHER. *Ceryle alcyon.*—11–12. *Male:* Blue above, with a white nuchal collar; inner webs of remiges edged and notched with white, the tail narrowly barred with same; below white, the chest with a broad blue band. *Female:* Similar to male, but with a rufous band across the belly and with rufous flanks.

Distribution.—Winters in Baja California, western Mexico south to Durango, and extensively on the Atlantic slope.

Races.—*C. a. caurina* (Baja California and western Mexico south to Sinaloa and Durango). *C. a. alcyon* (Atlantic slope).

Remarks.—A blue-backed kingfisher with a *white* belly. Females have rufous flanks and a rufous band across the abdomen. The next two species are superficially similar below, but both have glossy green upperparts. Chiefly lowlands, but ranging locally to an altitude of about 5,000 feet.

AMAZON KINGFISHER. *Chloroceryle amazona mexicana.*—$10\frac{1}{2}$–$11\frac{1}{2}$. *Male:* Above dark glossy green, the inner webs of the remiges and lateral rectrices notched with white; a white nuchal collar; throat and belly white, the breast-band rufous. *Female:* Similar to male, but breast-band glossy green, this often incomplete medially.

Distribution.—Southern Sinaloa, Puebla, and southern Tamaulipas southward in the lowlands.

Remarks.—Largest of the three green-backed kingfishers in our area. Likely to be mistaken only for the Green Kingfisher, a much smaller bird, which shows considerable white on its wings, even when at rest. Female Greens have two narrow bands below; the female Amazon a single broad band, or a large green patch on each side of the chest.

GREEN KINGFISHER. *Chloroceryle americana.*—8. *Male:* Above dark glossy green; a white nuchal collar; wings spotted and barred with white, the lateral rectrices notched and patterned with same; throat and abdomen white, the breast-band rufous; sides and flanks spotted with green. *Female:* Similar to male, but rufous of breast-band replaced with two green bands.

Distribution.—Lowlands generally, ranging to an altitude of at least 5,000 feet locally.

Races.—*C. a. hachisukai* (northwestern and north-central Mexico south to Nayarit). *C. a. septentrionalis* (eastern and southern Mexico, chiefly in the lowlands).

Remarks.—Green Kingfishers might be mistaken for Amazons at a distance when their smaller size is not evident. Look for the Green's *white wing-spots;* the Amazon's folded wing is wholly green. Female Green Kingfishers have two narrow green bands below; the female Amazon a single broad band, or a green patch on each side of its chest. Common in suitable habitat.

PYGMY KINGFISHER. *Chloroceryle aenea stictoptera* (Illus. p. 276).— $5\frac{1}{2}$. *Male:* Above dark glossy green, the flight feathers and outer tail feathers more or less white-spotted; throat pale buffy orange, shading to bright rufous on the breast, sides, and flanks; belly and under tail-coverts white. *Female:* Similar to male, but with a green band across the breast.

Distribution.—Oaxaca, Veracruz, and the Yucatán Peninsula southward in the lowlands.

Remarks.—Also known as Least Green Kingfisher. A diminutive green kingfisher with bright rufous underparts. Unmistakable. It frequents lowland forest streams and the shaded borders of tropical ponds

PYGMY KINGFISHER

and lagoons. Unlike its relatives, the Pygmy subsists largely on insects, which are captured expertly on the wing.

Family MOMOTIDAE. Motmots

KEY TO THE SPECIES

1*a.* Larger (13–17 inches). Middle tail feathers notably elongated and usually with a conspicuous terminal racket 2

  b. Smaller (7–11 inches). Tail graduated, but middle feathers without a terminal racket; throat blue or whitish 5

2*a.* A conspicuous blue or turquoise stripe above eye, the crown and hind-neck greenish olive, like back; throat sometimes with a black triangular patch 3

  b. Crown and hind-neck not greenish olive; without distinct bluish superciliaries, but crown sometimes fringed all around with blue; throat never black 4

3a. Superciliaries turquoise-blue; a black triangular throat-patch, this bordered with blue laterally . . . Turquoise-browed Motmot, p. 278

  b. Superciliaries bright blue; throat and chest pale olive-green or tinged with rufous . . . . Keel-billed Motmot, p. 278

4a. Top of head and hind-neck uniform rufous; underparts pale greenish blue . . . . Russet-crowned Motmot, p. 280

  b. Top of head wholly blue, or middle of crown black, broadly fringed with blue; below greenish olive or extensively russet

                        Blue-crowned Motmot, p. 280

5a. Smaller (7 inches). Top of head and hind-neck cinnamon, the back greenish; throat white; tail rather short . . . Tody Motmot, p. 277

  b. Larger (11 inches). Top of head and back uniform greenish olive; throat pale blue; tail decidedly long . . Blue-throated Motmot, p. 278

TODY MOTMOT. *Hylomanes momotula* (Illus. p. 277).—7. Crown and hind-neck rufous, the back, scapulars, and rump green; superciliary spot

TODY MOTMOT

turquoise; a black patch behind eye; lores and stripe below auriculars buffy white; sides of throat and abdomen white; median throat and breast buffy olive, this usually tinged with green; flanks largely tawny or tinged with greenish; tail rather short, the feathers notably graduated.

Distribution.—Wooded coastal slopes from Chiapas and Veracruz southward, exclusive of the Yucatán Peninsula.

Races.—*H. m. chiapensis* (Pacific slope of Chiapas). *H. m. momotula* (Caribbean slope from Veracruz southward).

Remarks.—This diminutive motmot frequents the undergrowth of humid lowland forests. A phlegmatic and usually silent bird, it is easily overlooked in the deep shadows. Its small size and *reddish cap* contrasting with a green back assure its identification.

BLUE-THROATED MOTMOT. *Aspatha gularis.*—10–11. Mainly greenish olive, palest below, the throat pale blue; orbital area bright cinnamon, the auriculars with a conspicuous black patch; a black chest-spot; tail rather long and notably graduated, the middle feathers bluish terminally.

Distribution.—Mountain forests of Chiapas.

Remarks.—The only motmot with a *blue throat*. Like the Tody, this species lacks the racket-tipped tail that so enhances the appearance of other motmots. Blue-throats spend much of the day in their nesting holes, which are dug into earthen banks, and are likely to be missed except when they emerge to feed at dawn and in the late afternoon.

KEEL-BILLED MOTMOT. *Electron carinatum.*—13–15. Above mainly greenish olive, the forehead reddish; superciliaries bright blue; lores, orbital area, auriculars, and elongated chest-spot black; below pale olive-green, darkening posteriorly, and more or less tinged with cinnamon; tail decidedly long, essentially bluish, the middle feathers racket-tipped; bill notably broad and flattened, the curved ridge keel-like.

Distribution.—Humid lowland forests of the Caribbean slope from southern Veracruz and Tabasco southward, exclusive of the Yucatán Peninsula. Apparently rare.

Remarks.—The peculiarly broadened bill, with its keel-like ridge, is unlike that of any other Mexican motmot. At a distance look for the *green cap* and racket-tipped tail. The following species also has both, but shows a *blue-bordered, black throat-patch,* and bluish remiges with black tips.

TURQUOISE-BROWED MOTMOT. *Eumomota superciliosa* (Illus. p. 279).—13. Above mainly greenish olive, the back tinged with rufous;

a broad turquoise-blue stripe above each eye; lores and long feathers behind eye black; remiges and tail greenish blue above, but black-tipped, the middle rectrices notably elongated and with spatulate tips; a conspicuous triangular throat-patch, this bordered laterally with turquoise-blue; sides of throat and breast greenish olive shading to rufous on the posterior underparts.

TURQUOISE-BROWED MOTMOT

Distribution.—Lowlands of southern Mexico and various offshore islands.

Races.—*E. s. bipartita* (Veracruz, Oaxaca, and Chiapas). *E. s. superciliosa* (Tabasco, Campeche, and northern half of the Yucatán Peninsula; also Cozumel and Meco Islands).

Remarks.—The striking contrast between the greenish back and light blue wings and tail is a good field character at any distance. From below look for the *blue-bordered, triangular patch* of the throat and chest. A strikingly beautiful motmot, most likely to be found in dry woodlands and second growth. *See* Keel-billed Motmot.

RUSSET-CROWNED MOTMOT. *Momotus mexicanus.*—11½–12½. Crown and upper back reddish brown, passing into grayish green posteriorly; lores and long feathers behind eye black; flight feathers and tail above greenish blue, the middle rectrices terminating in small black-tipped rackets; below pale greenish blue, the median breast of adults with several black feathers forming an elongated spot.

Distribution.—Arid lowlands and foothills of western Mexico, ranging from extreme southern Sonora and western Chihuahua southward.

Races.—*M. m. vanrossemi* (extreme southern Sonora and probably adjacent parts of Chihuahua and Sinaloa). *M. m. mexicanus* (Sinaloa and Durango south to Guerrero and Puebla). *M. m. saturatus* (Oaxaca and Chiapas).

Remarks.—Also known as Mexican Motmot. The only *large* motmot with a *reddish cap* and pale blue underparts. Common locally, especially at lower altitudes.

BLUE-CROWNED MOTMOT. *Momotus momota.*—15½–17. Crown either wholly blue, narrowly bordered with black (*M. m. coeruliceps*), or with a large black median patch broadly margined with blue; lores and cheeks black; above and below essentially greenish olive, the upper back and underparts sometimes strongly tinged with rufous; a black chest-spot; middle rectrices racket-tipped.

Distribution.—Northeastern Mexico south through the Yucatán Peninsula, Oaxaca, and Chiapas, chiefly in humid lowland forests.

Races.—*M. m. coeruliceps* (Nuevo León and central Tamaulipas south to Puebla and northern Veracruz). *M. m. goldmani* (southern Veracruz, Tabasco, and Oaxaca). *M. m. exiguus* (Campeche and Yucatán). *M. m. lessonii* (lowland and humid mountain forests of Chiapas).

Remarks.—This large motmot frequents the lower branches and deep shadows of heavy forests. It is essentially a lowland bird, but ranges into the foothills and mountains locally. *Coeruliceps* alone has an all-blue crown; the more southern forms have a conspicuous blue fringe around a black crown-patch. Chiapas birds are notably rufous below, especially on the breast.

Family GALBULIDAE. Jacamars

RUFOUS-TAILED JACAMAR. *Galbula ruficauda melanogenia* (Illus. p. 281).—9–9½. *Male:* Breast, sides of head, and upperparts bright metallic green; tail notably graduated, the three outer pairs of feathers tawny rufous; chin sometimes dusky; throat white, this forming a conspicuous triangular patch; abdomen, sides, flanks, and crissum tawny rufous; bill black, straight, notably long and sharply pointed. *Female:* Similar to male, but throat pale buff.

Distribution.—Humid lowland forests of Veracruz and Chiapas.

RUFOUS-TAILED JACAMAR

Remarks.—Also known as Black-faced Jacamar. Jacamars, at first glance, might be mistaken for out-sized hummingbirds, the illusion being heightened by their *slender*, sharply pointed bills, coppery green plumage, and posture while resting. They inhabit densely wooded areas of the humid lowlands, and customarily perch silently on exposed twigs from which passing insects may be captured by swift, darting flight.

Family BUCCONIDAE. Puffbirds

KEY TO THE SPECIES

1*a*. Black above, white below, the abdomen with a broad black band,
    bill notably large, wholly black . . . . White-necked Puffbird, p. 282

  b. Brownish above, the underparts reddish or buffy white; plumage at
    base of bill white-streaked and notably shaggy

                        White-whiskered Puffbird, p. 283

WHITE-NECKED PUFFBIRD. *Notharcus macrorhynchos hyperryn-chus* (Illus. p. 282).—9½. Above mainly black; forehead and nuchal collar white, the latter sometimes concealed; sides of head and underparts white,

WHITE-NECKED PUFFBIRD

the upper abdomen crossed by a broad black band; flanks sooty, narrowly barred with white; bill black, notably large and strongly hooked; iris purplish or red.

Distribution.—Humid lowland forests of Oaxaca, Chiapas, and Campeche.

Remarks.—Puffbirds are insectivorous and often dart after food in the manner of flycatchers. This species frequents treetops and is most likely to be seen on an exposed perch high above the ground. From below the *black abdominal band* is very conspicuous at any distance. No similar bird has a white forehead and black upperparts.

WHITE-WHISKERED PUFFBIRD. *Malacoptila panamensis inornata* (Illus. p. 283).—8. *Male:* Sides of head and upperparts reddish brown, shading to chestnut on the rump; cheeks streaked with reddish buff, the back and scapulars finely spotted with same; long erectile feathers of malar region tawny or white; below essentially reddish tawny or ochraceous, the breast and sides sometimes vaguely streaked; bill moderately large, dark

WHITE-WHISKERED PUFFBIRD

above, yellowish below; iris reddish. *Female:* Similar to male in pattern, but less reddish above (grayish brown), the underparts essentially buffy white; breast and sides more or less streaked with dusky.

Distribution.—Humid lowland forests of Tabasco and Chiapas.

Remarks.—A small, puff-headed forest bird with shaggy, white-streaked feathers about the base of the bill. Males are usually dull reddish below; females essentially buffy white, with some streaks on the breast. Heavy forests, usually near the ground.

Family RAMPHASTIDAE. Toucans

KEY TO THE SPECIES

1*a*. Wholly green, palest below . . . . Emerald Toucanet, p. 284

  b. Black above, the underparts with more or less yellow 2

2*a*. Throat and chest bright yellow, the breast and abdomen black; a white rump-patch . . . . Keel-billed Toucan, p. 285

  b. Below essentially greenish yellow, the abdomen with a scarlet-and-black band . . . . Collared Araçari, p. 284

EMERALD TOUCANET. *Aulacorhynchus prasinus.*—12–14. Above bright green, the anterior portions more or less tinged with olive; throat dull white, passing into pale emerald-green posteriorly, the flanks usually yellowish green; crissum and tips of rectrices chestnut; bill mainly bright yellow above, black below, the base narrowly bordered with yellow.

Distribution.—Humid mountain forests (principally) of southwestern and extreme southern Mexico.

Races.—*A. p. wagleri* (Guerrero and western Oaxaca). *A. p. prasinus* (mountains of Veracruz and adjacent parts of San Luis Potosí, Hidalgo, and Oaxaca). *A. p. stenorhabdus* (Sierra Madre, Chiapas). *A. p. virescens* (Quintana Roo).

Remarks.—Emerald Toucanets are characteristic of the moist "cloud forests" of the higher southern mountains, but may be found locally in wooded foothills. As with all toucans, they nest in hollow trees, the two white eggs being deposited in March or April. When not breeding, toucanets are usually found in small flocks that range the forest crown in quest of fruit and berries. Able mimics, they nevertheless have a variety of unmusical, but characteristic, calls.

COLLARED ARAÇARI. *Pteroglossus torquatus* (Illus. p. 285).—14–16. Head, throat, and back glossy black; the upperparts otherwise glossy bottle-green; underparts greenish yellow, more or less washed with scarlet anteriorly, the median breast often with a conspicuous black patch; a scarlet band across the abdomen, this much intermixed with black medially; thighs chestnut; upper mandible pale yellowish, the ridge extensively black; lower mandible all-black, the bill narrowly margined with yellow at base; iris yellow or orange.

Distribution.—Lowland forests of southern Mexico.

Races.—*P. t. torquatus* (lowlands of Veracruz and Oaxaca southward, except where occupied by the following). *P. t. erythrozonus* (Yucatán Peninsula).

Remarks.—Araçaris are the most abundant of the Mexican tuocans and are usually found in small flocks except while breeding. They prefer the upper branches of large forest trees and might easily escape detection but for their noisy activity while feeding.

COLLARED ARAÇARI

KEEL-BILLED TOUCAN. *Ramphastos sulfuratus sulfuratus* (Illus. p. 286).—18–20. Mainly black, the throat, sides of neck, and chest bright lemon-yellow; hind-neck more or less tinged with maroon; upper tail-coverts white, the lower coverts bright red; bill notably large and colorful, extensively yellow, the terminal portion orange and reddish.

Distribution.—Humid lowland forests of southeastern Mexico, from Puebla, Oaxaca, and Veracruz southward.

Remarks.—One of the most characteristic birds of dense tropical forests, but less abundant in Mexico than the Collared Araçari. Both toucans have similar habits and are likely to be found together in fruit-bearing trees. This species is instantly recognized by its large size, brightly colored bill, and *yellow throat*. In flight, from behind, the white

Keel-billed Toucan

patch at the base of the tail is a useful field mark. A monotonous, froglike croak of considerable volume is its most characteristic call.

Family PICIDAE. Woodpeckers

Key to the Species

1*a*. Back and wings liberally barred, spotted, or broadly streaked with black and white 2

  b. Upperparts not barred, spotted, or streaked with black and white 10

2*a*. Underparts virtually unmarked; lower abdomen chrome-yellow or red 3

  b. Not as in 2*a*. 7

3*a*. Upper tail-coverts (sometimes rump) immaculate white; tail mainly black 4

  b. Rump, upper tail-coverts, and tail conspicuously barred 6

4*a*. Sides of head and sometimes crown largely black

                                Black-cheeked Woodpecker, p. 298

  b. Head without black; auriculars concolor with throat 5

5*a.* More than 8 inches long. Nape (sometimes crown) and abdomen yellow, orange, or red . . . . Golden-fronted Woodpecker, p. 296

b. Less than 7 inches long. Nape (sometimes median crown) and abdomen red . . . . Red-vented Woodpecker, p. 297

6*a.* Nuchal area with conspicuous yellow

Golden-cheeked Woodpecker, p. 296

b. Head without yellow; nape brownish like auriculars

Gray-breasted Woodpecker, p. 295

7*a.* Throat and median breast concolor with abdomen, either white or pale brownish gray 8

b. Throat and median breast not pale, not concolor with abdomen . 9

8*a.* Sides of breast (sometimes flanks) rather boldly spotted

Nuttall Woodpecker, p. 300

b. Sides of breast (sometimes flanks) minutely spotted or streaked

Ladder-backed Woodpecker, p. 301

9*a.* Throat red or white; wings (greater coverts) with a conspicuous white patch . . . . Yellow-bellied Sapsucker, p. 298

b. Throat not red or white; wings without a prominent white patch

Williamson Sapsucker (female), p. 299

10*a.* Above and below essentially black, chestnut, or tawny olive . . 11

b. Not essentially black, chestnut, or tawny olive 13

11*a.* More than 20 inches long. Mainly black, the wings with conspicuous white . . . . Imperial Woodpecker, p. 304

b. Less than 10 inches long. Wings without white 12

12*a.* Mainly chestnut, the crown ochraceous or tawny

Chestnut-colored Woodpecker, p. 291

b. Mainly tawny olive-brown, the crown red or dusky

Smoky-brown Woodpecker, p. 299

13*a.* Upperparts largely black; median back, rump, or tail-coverts sometimes white or brown 14

b. Not mainly black above 19

14*a.* Median back and entire underparts white or brown

Hairy Woodpecker, p. 300

b. Back and wings essentially black; underparts not uniform . . . 15

15*a.* Upper tail-coverts immaculate white; abdomen white or yellow . 16

b. Upper tail-coverts not white; abdomen either pink or liberally barred 17

16*a.* Crown black, concolor with back

Williamson Sapsucker (male), p. 299

  b. Crown extensively red, not concolor with back
                                 Acorn Woodpecker, p. 294

17*a.* Scapulars partly white, or back with **V**-shaped white mark originating on sides of neck; underparts boldly barred 18

  b. Scapulars and back glossy greenish black; underparts largely pinkish . . . . Lewis Woodpecker, p. 293

18*a.* Head either wholly red, or crown, throat, and neck black
                                 Pale-billed Woodpecker, p. 303

  b. Auriculars (sometimes forehead) extensively black; chin and median throat spotted or streaked with black and white
                                 Lineated Woodpecker, p. 292

19*a.* Above and below with conspicuous green or olive; underparts liberally barred 20

  b. Not greenish or olive; upperparts mainly brown, sometimes liberally barred with black; underparts spotted or striped 22

20*a.* Crown slate color; nape (sometimes border of crown) bright red . 21

  b. Crown and hind-neck pale gray (without red)
                                 Gray-crowned Woodpecker, p. 289

21*a.* Crown bordered all around with red; underparts evenly barred
                                 Golden-olive Woodpecker, p. 290

  b. Crown not entirely bordered with red; underparts with irregular bars . . . . Bronze-winged Woodpecker, p. 290

22*a.* Upperparts liberally barred; chest with a conspicuous black crescent 23

  b. Upperparts essentially uniform, or back and rump with more or less white; chest without a black crescent 24

23*a.* Feather shafts and underside of wings and tail reddish orange
                                 Red-shafted Flicker, p. 288

  b. Feather shafts and underside of wings and tail bright yellow
                                 Gilded Flicker, p. 289

24*a.* Median back and rump barred or spotted with white; underparts distinctly streaked . . . . . . Brown-barred Woodpecker, p. 303

  b. Back and rump without white; underparts boldly spotted
                                 Brown-backed Woodpecker, p. 302

RED-SHAFTED FLICKER. *Colaptes cafer.*—11½–13. *Male:* Lores, crown, and hind-neck grayish brown or cinnamon; if brown, the back, scapulars, and folded wings similar but barred with black; if cinnamon, the back, etc., paler between the bars; extended wings mainly blackish above, the shafts reddish orange and outer webs notched or barred with grayish brown or cinnamon-buff; underside of wings pinkish orange, becoming dusky toward tips; rump and upper tail-coverts white, the latter barred with black; tail above black, the feathers (except middle pair) with reddish orange shafts; underside of tail reddish orange, broadly tipped with black; sides of head (except lores) and throat gray; malar streak red; underparts (except wings and tail) whitish, pinkish, or buffy white, the chest with a conspicuous black crescent and elsewhere generously spotted (barred posteriorly) with black. *Female:* Similar to male, but malar streak either lacking or cinnamon, like crown.

Distribution.—Guadalupe Island (formerly) and wooded highlands of the mainland generally.

Races.—*C. c. rufipileus* (Guadalupe Island off Baja California; now extinct). *C. c. collaris* (western slopes of Sierra San Pedro Mártir and Sierra Juárez, Baja California, and northwestern Mexico south to Zacatecas). *C. c. nanus* (northeastern Mexico south to San Luis Potosí). *C. c. mexicanus* (central highlands south to Oaxaca). *C. c. mexicanoïdes* (Chiapas).

Remarks.—The black-crescented chest and boldly spotted underparts are characteristic of all flickers. Their flight is undulating, as with other woodpeckers, but the conspicuous *white rump-patch* serves to distinguish them from most species, even at a distance. Although primarily arboreal, flickers spend much time on the ground in search of ants, an important element of their diet. This species occurs commonly in oak and pine forests above 5,000 feet. *See* Gilded Flicker.

GILDED FLICKER. *Colaptes chrysoïdes.*—10–11. Superficially similar to a Red-shafted Flicker, but smaller and usually paler (never cinnamon) above; feather shafts of wings bright yellow (not reddish orange) and wings below largely creamy yellow; basal half of tail below yellow (not reddish orange), the remainder black.

Distribution.—Baja California, Tiburón Island, Sonora, and northern Sinaloa.

Races.—*C. c. mearnsi* (northwestern Baja California, Tiburón Island, and northern Sonora). *C. c. brunnescens* (central Baja California, between latitude 28° and 30° N.). *C. c. chrysoïdes* (Baja California south of latitude 28° N.). *C. c. tenebrosus* (central Sonora south to northern Sinaloa).

Remarks.—This species resembles the common flicker of eastern United States (*C. auratus*), but lacks a red nuchal patch. The malar stripe of the male is *bright red*, not black. Where their ranges overlap, Gilded and Red-shafted Flickers are readily distinguished by the different coloring of the undersides of their wings and tails.

GRAY-CROWNED WOODPECKER. *Piculus auricularis.*—8½. *Male:* Crown and hind-neck uniform pale gray; upperparts mainly light olive-

green, the wings somewhat brighter than back, and both rump and upper
tail-coverts usually narrowly barred with yellowish white; sides of head
dull buff or brownish white; malar stripe bright red; throat whitish, more
or less flecked or barred with gray; underparts mainly greenish olive, irregularly (but sharply) barred with pale yellowish. *Female:* Similar to male, but
without red; malar area streaked with dull grayish.

Distribution.—Western Mexico (exclusive of Baja California) south to
Guerrero. ENDEMIC.

Races.—*P. a. sonoriensis* (southeastern Sonora and possibly the adjacent parts of Chihuahua and Sinaloa). *P. a. auricularis* (southern Sinaloa,
Jalisco, and Guerrero).

Remarks.—Also known as Western Green Woodpecker and Godman Woodpecker. The only conspicuously greenish and olive-colored
woodpecker found in the western parts of the country. It is a resident of
the highland pine and oak forests and can be mistaken for no other bird
of its area. Note the *gray* crown.

BRONZE-WINGED WOODPECKER. *Piculus aeruginosus.*—9–10.
Male: Crown slate gray, bordered laterally (from eye) and behind with
bright crimson; back, scapulars, rump, and upper tail-coverts clear olive-
green, the last two narrowly barred with yellowish; wings (when folded)
golden brownish olive, the underside yellow; tail similar but broadly tipped
with dusky; loral area pale buff passing to grayish white on auriculars;
malar stripe crimson; throat grayish white narrowly streaked with dusky;
breast and posterior underparts greenish olive *irregularly* barred with pale
yellowish white. *Female:* Similar to male, but malar area grayish streaked
with darker; sides of crown not bordered with crimson.

Distribution.—Southern Nuevo León, southern Tamaulipas, San Luis
Potosí, northern Veracruz, and Puebla. ENDEMIC.

Remarks.—Also known as Lichtenstein Woodpecker. A fairly
common species of the lowlands and foothills to an altitude of about
5,000 feet in the mountains. No other greenish woodpecker of its area
has contrasting bronzy wings. In flight the wings show *yellow below*.

GOLDEN-OLIVE WOODPECKER. *Piculus rubiginosus* (Illus. p. 291).
—8–9. Much like a Bronze-winged Woodpecker, but with a slate-colored
crown bordered all around with bright crimson; back and scapulars yellowish olive-green or orange-olive; sides of head (except malar area) mainly
pale buff, the auriculars minutely barred posteriorly with dusky; lower
neck and chest yellowish olive, narrowly (but sharply) barred with pale
yellow.

Distribution.—Southeastern and extreme southern Mexico, mainly in lowland areas.

Races.—*P. r. yucatanensis* (Caribbean lowlands from southern Veracruz southward). *P. r. maximus* (mountains of Chiapas).

Remarks.—Also known as Green Woodpecker and Swainson Woodpecker. This species replaces Bronze-winged Woodpeckers in southern

GOLDEN-OLIVE WOODPECKER

Mexico. It has similar habits but is more decidedly a bird of the lowlands. Its flicker-like call note can safely be used for identification.

CHESTNUT-COLORED WOODPECKER. *Celeus castaneus* (Illus. p. 292).—8½–9½. Bill pale yellowish; head and long occipital crest either wholly tawny (female) or with dull red lores and malar stripes (male); above and below otherwise mainly chestnut, the rump usually somewhat yellowish; tail and wings broadly tipped with black or dusky; back, scapulars, upper wing-coverts, and underparts (except throat and yellow under wing-coverts) with numerous **V**-shaped black bars.

Distribution.—Lowlands of southeastern Mexico.

Remarks.—A medium-sized, essentially chestnut woodpecker with a tawny head and occipital crest. This species frequents heavy forests and is uncommon to rare throughout its range. Not likely to be mistaken for any other Mexican species.

CHESTNUT-COLORED WOODPECKER

LINEATED WOODPECKER. *Dryocopus lineatus* (Illus. p. 293).—11–12½. *Male:* Crown, occipital crest, and malar stripe bright red; lores and auriculars slate color, sometimes bordered below by a narrow creamy white line extending to sides of neck; upperparts mainly black, the scapulars partly white, this forming a prominent bar along each side of back; chin (sometimes throat) whitish, minutely spotted or streaked with black; lower neck (sometimes throat) and breast black, the underparts otherwise pale buffy white, generously barred with black; bill whitish; iris yellow or white. *Female:* Similar to male, but forehead, forepart of crown, and malar area black.

Distribution.—Widespread in forested lowlands, exclusive of Baja California.

Races.—*D. l. obsoletus* (southern Sonora, northern Sinaloa, and probably adjacent parts of Chihuahua). *D. l. scapularis* (southern Sinaloa to Guerrero). *D. l. petersi* (Tamaulipas, Nuevo León, San Luis Potosí, and probably northern Veracruz). *D. l. similis* (southern Veracruz southward).

Remarks.—Also known as White-billed Woodpecker. Wooded lowlands and foothills, ranging locally to an altitude of about 5,000 feet. Lineated Woodpeckers prefer heavily forested districts and are especially attracted to areas in which large trees have been "ringed" and left standing. They resemble Pale-billed Woodpeckers superficially, but differ in head pattern.

LINEATED WOODPECKER

*LEWIS WOODPECKER. *Asyndesmus lewis.*—10–10½. Forehead, lores, chin, malar area, and anterior auriculars deep red; upperparts otherwise mainly glossy greenish black, the hind-neck with a narrow but conspicuous silvery collar connecting with the silvery breast; throat black, like posterior auriculars; lower neck and entire breast silvery gray, the latter becoming intermixed with pink on the sides and flanks; abdomen essentially pinkish red; crissum greenish black.

Distribution.—Winters in northern Baja California and (casually) northern Sonora.

Remarks.—The glossy black upperparts, silvery collar and breast, and pink abdomen are unmistakable. To the usual woodpecker diet Lewis Woodpeckers add both fruit and insects, the latter skilfully captured in mid-air. Their flight is strong and direct and quite unlike the undulating flight of other woodpeckers.

ACORN WOODPECKER. *Melanerpes formicivorus* (Illus. p. 294).—
$7\frac{1}{2}$–$8\frac{1}{4}$. *Male:* Nasal tufts black like chin and upper throat; forehead white
or pale yellowish, a line of same extending downward across lores and continuing across the lower throat as a broad band; crown and hind-neck
bright red; upperparts (including orbital area and auriculars) mainly glossy
purplish or greenish black, the wings with a broad white band prominently
displayed in flight; breast glossy purplish black, more or less spotted or
streaked with white posteriorly; underparts essentially white, the sides,
flanks, and crissum (sometimes abdomen) boldly streaked with black.

ACORN WOODPECKER

Female: Similar to the male, but red of crown greatly reduced and separated
from the pale forehead by a black band.

Distribution.—Pine and oak forests, principally in highland areas.

Races.—*M. f. martirensis* (Baja California, mainly on the western
slopes of the Sierra San Pedro Mártir south to latitude 31° N.). *M. f.
angustifrons* (cape district of Baja California). *M. f. formicivorus* (highlands
generally, south to Oaxaca, Puebla, and Veracruz). *M. f. lineatus* (southern
Chiapas; probably identical with *M. f. albeolus* of British Honduras).

Remarks.—Also known as Ant-eating Woodpecker. Characteristic
of oak and pine forests, and hence one of the most abundant and widespread of all highland woodpeckers. Acorn Woodpeckers are rather
noisy, conspicuous birds, of very distinctive appearance. The broad,
yellowish white forehead and throat-patch, streaked underparts, and

white wing-patch are useful field marks. This species feeds largely on acorns and commonly stores them, sometimes in vast numbers, by pounding each into a small pit dug into a tree-trunk.

GRAY-BREASTED WOODPECKER. *Centurus hypopolius* (Illus. p. 295).—8–9½. *Male:* Forehead dull white, grayish buff, or pale brownish; median crown with more or less red; head (otherwise), hind-neck, and underparts (except posterior portion) deep grayish brown or buffy brown; back, scapulars, wings, rump, and tail (middle and outer feathers) very con-

GRAY-BREASTED WOODPECKER

spicuously barred with white; lower abdomen yellow; flanks and crissum white, boldly barred with black. *Female:* Similar to male, but without a red crown-patch; head wholly pale grayish brown, like underparts.

Distribution.—Dry parts of western and southwestern Mexico generally, including Baja California and Tiburón Island.

Races.—*C. h. cardonensis* (central part of Baja California north on the east side to about latitude 32°). *C. h. brewsteri* (Baja California south of latitude 28°30′). *C. h. tiburonensis* (Tiburón Island, off the coast of Sonora). *C. h. uropygialis* (northern and central Sonora). *C. h. albescens* (northeastern Baja California and northwestern Sonora). *C. h. fuscescens* (southwestern Sonora, northern Sinaloa, and southwestern Chihuahua). *C. h. sulfuriventer* (Sinaloa and Durango south to Jalisco and Aguascalientes). *C. h. hypopolius* (Mexico, Morelos, Puebla, Guerrero, and Oaxaca).

Remarks.—Also known as Desert Woodpecker and Gila Woodpecker. Five of the Mexican "ladder-backed" woodpeckers have unmarked brownish gray throats and breasts. Usually the cheeks are similar. Of this group, only the Gray-breasted *lacks a bright* (red or yellow) *nuchal patch.* Except for the Golden-cheeked Woodpecker, all related species have a more or less immaculate *white rump-patch* that is very conspicuous in flight. Widespread and common, especially in deserts and arid districts.

GOLDEN-FRONTED WOODPECKER. *Centurus aurifrons.*—8½–9¾. *Male:* Nasal tufts chrome-yellow, orange, or red; center of crown or entire crown and hind-neck bright red, this sometimes separated from the nasal tufts by a white or grayish band; hind-neck either yellowish orange or red, like crown; back and wing-coverts liberally barred with black and white; rump and upper tail-coverts white; tail mainly black, the outermost feathers white-barred near tips; sides of head and underparts essentially grayish or pale brownish gray, the abdomen chrome-yellow, pink, or bright red; flanks and crissum whitish barred with black. *Female:* Similar to male, but crown without red.

Distribution.—Northern and eastern Mexico southward.

Races.—*C. a. incanescens* (northeastern Chihuahua and northern Coahuila). *C. a. aurifrons* (northeastern Coahuila south to Jalisco, Michoacán, Mexico, and central Tamaulipas). *C. a. grateloupensis* (eastern Mexico from southern Tamaulipas and southeastern San Luis Potosí south to central Veracruz and eastern Puebla). *C. a. veraecrucis* (southeastern Veracruz south to northern Chiapas and western Campeche). *C. a. dubius* (eastern Campeche and Yucatán southward). *C. a. leei* (Mecos and Cozumel Islands; perhaps Mujeres Island). *C. a. polygrammus* (Pacific slope from southeastern Oaxaca to western Chiapas). *C. a. frontalis* (Chiapas, except extreme western and northern parts). *C. a. santacruzi* (southwestern Chiapas).

Remarks.—Golden-fronted Woodpeckers vary considerably from place to place, especially as to the boldness of their dorsal barring. Some races have red and others orange on their napes and bellies. They prefer dry districts with sparse or second-growth timber. Often fairly abundant in towns as well as in rural areas.

GOLDEN-CHEEKED WOODPECKER. *Centurus chrysogenys* (Illus. p. 297).—7¾–8¾. *Male:* Forehead pale buff, the nasal tufts often orange-yellow; crown more or less extensively bright red, passing abruptly to deep chrome-yellow or yellowish orange on hind-neck; lores, malar area, auriculars (at least anteriorly), and sometimes chin dull yellowish; orbital area black, especially above posteriorly; upperparts, including wings and tail, conspicuously barred with black and white; below pale brownish gray, the abdomen dull yellowish; flanks and crissum whitish barred with black. *Female:* Similar to male, but without red crown-patch; top of head brownish gray like underparts.

Distribution.—Western Mexico from Sinaloa south to Oaxaca. ENDEMIC.

Races.—*C. c. chrysogenys* (Sinaloa and Nayarit). *C. c. flavinuchus* (Jalisco, Colima, Morelos, Guerrero, and Oaxaca).

Remarks.—Adults have distinctive golden-yellow cheeks. A black area around, and especially above, the eye is often a useful field mark.

GOLDEN-CHEEKED WOODPECKER

The *barred rump* eliminates all other ladder-backed woodpeckers except the Gray-breasted.

RED-VENTED WOODPECKER. *Centurus rubricapillus.*—6½. *Male:* Nasal tufts (sometimes chin) yellow; forehead whitish, this extending on sides of crown where shading to color of auriculars and throat; center of crown and nape bright red; back and wing-coverts narrowly barred with black and white, the rump and upper tail-coverts immaculate white; tail mainly black, the outer webs of the outer feathers notched with white; sides of head, throat, and breast pale brownish gray; abdomen pink to bright red; flanks and crissum whitish barred with black. *Female:* Similar to male, but crown without red.

Distribution.—Northern part of the Yucatán Peninsula and Cozumel Island.

Races.—*C. r. rubricomus* (northern part of the Yucatán Peninsula). *C. r. pygmaeus* (Cozumel Island).

Remarks.—Also known as Swainson Woodpecker. This species has a very limited distribution in Mexico and is not likely to be mistaken for any other woodpecker of its area. Fairly abundant in dry thickets and second-growth timber. Usually found within a few feet of the ground. *See* Golden-fronted Woodpecker.

BLACK-CHEEKED WOODPECKER. *Centurus pucherani perileucus* (Illus. p. 298).—7¼-7¾. *Male:* Forehead yellow; crown and hind-neck bright red; orbital and auricular areas black, the former inclosing a white postocular spot; upperparts (except white rump and upper tail-coverts) mainly black, the back, scapulars, wing-coverts, and secondaries narrowly barred with white; tail black, this more or less white-barred basally; lores, malar area, and throat pale brownish gray, shading to dull yellowish brown on the

BLACK-CHEEKED WOODPECKER

breast; sides, flanks, and crissum similar, but paler, and extensively barred with black; abdomen bright red. *Female:* Similar to male, but crown mainly black, the nape only being red.

Distribution.—Veracruz, Puebla, and Oaxaca southward.

Remarks.—Also known as Pucheran Woodpecker and White-barred Woodpecker. The only Mexican member of the genus having black on the sides of its head. Females also have black crowns and a red nuchal patch. Chiefly humid lowland forests.

*YELLOW-BELLIED SAPSUCKER. *Sphyrapicus varius.*—7½-8 *Male:* Head, throat, and breast either virtually wholly red (*daggetti*), or top of head and throat red, the lower neck and breast black. If black-breasted, the auriculars largely black and sides of head with two conspicuous pale yellowish stripes originating, respectively, at base of bill and above eye; malar region sometimes black (*varius*), and nape either white (*varius*) or red (*nuchalis*). Both sexes of all races essentially black above, where boldly spotted and streaked with white or pale yellowish; upper tail-coverts white; greater wing-coverts white, forming a very conspicuous wing-patch; lower breast, belly, and crissum dingy yellow. *Female:* Essentially like male, but black-breasted races either white-throated (*varius*) or with a red patch below the white chin and upper throat; top of head sometimes glossy black.

Distribution.—Virtually country-wide in migration and winter.

Races.—*S. v. daggetti* (Pacific side of Baja California south to latitude 30°). *S. v. nuchalis* (Baja California and northwestern Mexico south to Jalisco and western San Luis Potosí; casually to Guatemala). *S. v. varius* (southern Sinaloa, southern Durango, eastern Coahuila, Nuevo León, and Tamaulipas southward).

Remarks.—This distinctive woodpecker will be recognized by its very conspicuous white wing-patches and red or black breast. The three races are known, respectively, as Red-breasted, Red-naped, and Yellow-bellied Sapsuckers. The first occurs only in northwestern Baja California and is quite unmistakable. Male Yellow-bellied Sapsuckers are distinguished from male Red-napes by their *black malar stripes* and *white* napes; females by their *wholly* white throats. The two may be found together in the southern portion of the Red-nape's range.

*WILLIAMSON SAPSUCKER. *Sphyrapicus thyroideus.*—8½–9. *Male:* Nasal tufts and narrow line extending below auriculars white like the postocular streak; upperparts glossy purplish black (adult) or dusky (immature); wing-coverts and rump white; chin and median throat bright red (adult) or white (immature); breast black, the abdomen bright yellow or pale yellowish white; sides, flanks, and crissum white, more or less striped, barred, or spotted with black. *Female:* Head brownish, the posterior portion somewhat streaked or barred with black; above and below liberally barred with black and whitish; median breast sometimes glossy black; belly yellowish.

Distribution.—Winters in northern Baja California and western Mexico south to Durango and Jalisco.

Races.—*S. t. thyroideus* (winters in northern Baja California). *S. t. nataliae* (winters in western Mexico south to Durango and Jalisco).

Remarks.—Also known as Black-crowned Sapsucker. Unlike most woodpeckers, the sexes of this species are strikingly distinct. At a distance males appear mainly black, but have very conspicuous white wing-patches and rumps. Brown-headed, yellow-bellied females are profusely barred. They might be mistaken for Gray-breasted Woodpeckers if seen from behind, but have *barred* (not immaculate) *rumps.*

SMOKY-BROWN WOODPECKER. *Veniliornis fumigatus.*—6–6½. *Male:* Crown and hind-neck bright red, the former more or less intermixed with sooty; nasal tufts and sides of head (except malar area) pale buff or creamy white; throat and malar area grayish or dusky; above and below essentially yellowish tawny olive, the back sometimes intermixed with reddish orange; remiges and tail sooty brown. *Female:* Similar to male, but crown and hind-neck dusky.

Distribution.—Eastern Mexico from San Luis Potosí and northern Veracruz southward, including the Yucatán Peninsula.

Races.—*V. f. oleagineus* (San Luis Potosí, northern Veracruz, Mexico, and Puebla). *V. f. sanguinolentus* (Oaxaca and southern Veracruz southward).

Remarks.—Also known as Smoke-colored Woodpecker and Oleaginous Woodpecker. Perhaps the most drab and nondescript of Mexican woodpeckers. While rather uncommon in our area, this species occurs at least casually in wooded areas at all altitudes.

HAIRY WOODPECKER. *Dendrocopos villosus.*—7–9. *Male:* Nasal tufts and narrow band extending below auriculars white, buff, or pale brownish; crown black (with more or less red in immature birds), like auriculars, the two separated by a white or brownish line originating above eye; nape bright red; upperparts mainly black, the back and rump with more or less white or brownish, and outer webs of primaries liberally spotted with same; four inner tail feathers black, the others wholly or mainly immaculate white or pale brown; underparts white, dingy whitish, or brown; sides of the breast usually moderately spotted or streaked with black. *Female:* Similar to male, but without a red nuchal patch.

Distribution.—Wooded highlands generally.

Races.—*D. v. hyloscopus* (northern Baja California, in the Sierra Juárez and the Sierra San Pedro Mártir). *D. v. icastus* (eastern Sonora and western Chihuahua south to Jalisco and Zacatecas). *D. v. intermedius* (Nuevo León, Tamaulipas, San Luis Potosí, and Hidalgo). *D. v. jardinii* (highlands of southern Mexico from Jalisco south to Oaxaca). *D. v. sanctorum* (highlands of Chiapas).

Remarks.—The Hairy Woodpeckers of Mexico present a remarkable diversity of appearance, since the white plumage (median back, wing-spots, and underparts) of the more northern races is replaced by various shades of brown in the south. All are restricted to the highlands and are rather common in pine and oak forests.

NUTTALL WOODPECKER. *Dendrocopos nuttallii.*—7–7½. *Male:* Forehead black, in autumn and winter finely streaked with white; crown and nape bright red; sides of head and malar area mainly black, the orbital area and auriculars broadly bordered with white; upperparts essentially black, the back, scapulars, wings, and rump broadly barred with white; below mainly whitish, often tinged with pale buff, the sides of the breast, flanks, and crissum liberally spotted with black. *Female:* Similar to male, but head without red.

Distribution.—Northwestern Baja California.

Remarks.—At first glance this species might be mistaken for a Ladder-backed Woodpecker. Ladder-backs have much smaller spots on their sides and flanks, and males show less black on their foreheads. They occur principally in very arid country and deserts—habitats usually avoided by Nuttalls.

LADDER-BACKED WOODPECKER. *Dendrocopos scalaris* (Illus. p. 301).—$5\frac{1}{2}$–$7\frac{1}{2}$. *Male:* Nasal tufts pale brownish; crown more or less extensively red, the forepart usually minutely speckled with white; auriculars

LADDER-BACKED WOODPECKER

and orbital area black, broadly bordered with whitish and hence not confluent with black of hind-neck; a black malar stripe; upperparts conspicuously barred with black and white; underparts dingy whitish or buffy white, the sides of the breast and sides streaked or spotted with black; flanks whitish, vaguely barred with black. *Female:* Similar to male, but entire crown and hind-neck black.

Distribution.—Virtually country-wide in arid districts, including various islands off the Pacific Coast.

Races.—*D. s. graysoni* (Tres Marías Islands). *D. s. eremicus* (northern Baja California from about latitude 32° on the Pacific side south to about latitude 29°). *D. s. lucasanus* (Baja California from tip of peninsula north to about latitude 28°31′, and numerous neighboring islands). *D. s. cactophilus* (northeastern Baja California, Sonora, Chihuahua, and northern Durango; Tiburón Island). *D. s. sinaloensis* (southern Sonora and Sinaloa). *D. s. centrophilus* (Nayarit, southern Durango, Jalisco, western Zacatecas, and western Michoacán). *D. s. azelus* (west-central Michoacán, southwestern Puebla, Guerrero, and west-central Oaxaca). *D. s. symplectus* (northern Coahuila, Nuevo León, and Tamaulipas). *D. s. giraudi* (southern Coahuila, San Luis Potosí, Guanajuato, Hidalgo, Puebla, and Mexico). *D. s. scalaris* (northeastern Veracruz). *D. s. ridgwayi* (coastal parts of southeastern Veracruz). *D. s. parvus* (northern part of the Yucatán Peninsula; Cozumel Island). *D. s. percus* (Chiapas).

Remarks.—Also known as Cactus Woodpecker. A small to medium-sized "ladder-backed" species with a black or mainly red crown and hind-neck and *pale brownish underparts*. Note the *small spots* on the sides and flanks. Ladder-backs can be confused with Nuttall Woodpeckers in northern Baja California, but elsewhere are virtually unmistakable. They inhabit drier parts of the country and may be found at all altitudes.

BROWN-BACKED WOODPECKER. *Dendrocopos arizonae.*—7–8. *Male:* Above deep sooty brown, the nuchal area bright red; outer webs of primaries spotted with white, and the two outer rectrices white-barred; auriculars and malar stripes sooty brown, the sides of the head otherwise white or grayish, like underparts; plumage below boldly spotted with sooty brown. *Female:* Similar to male, but without red on nape.

Distribution.—Highlands of western Mexico south to Michoacán.

Races.—*D. a. arizonae* (northeastern Sonora east to northern and central Chihuahua). *D. a. fraterculus* (southeastern Sonora and adjacent parts of Chihuahua south to Michoacán).

Remarks.—Also known as Arizona Woodpecker. No other Mexican woodpecker is virtually *uniform* sooty brown above, with *boldly spotted* *underparts*. A highland form, occurring extensively in the oak and pine forests of western Mexico.

BROWN-BARRED WOODPECKER. *Dendrocopos stricklandi*.—7–7½. Superficially similar to a Brown-backed Woodpecker, but median back and rump boldly barred or spotted with white; anterior underparts and sides distinctly streaked (not spotted) with sooty brown; three outer rectrices white-barred; nuchal patch of males more extensive.

Distribution.—Highlands of central and eastern Mexico. ENDEMIC.

Races.—*D. s. aztecus* (Michoacán, Mexico, and Distrito Federal). *D. s. stricklandi* (Veracruz and Puebla above 9,000 feet).

Remarks.—Also known as Strickland Woodpecker. This species replaces Brown-backed Woodpeckers in the higher mountains of central and eastern Mexico. It is rather uncommon and little is known of its habits.

PALE-BILLED WOODPECKER. *Phloeoceastes guatemalensis* (Illus. p. 303).—13–14. *Male:* Head and occipital crest bright red; upperparts mainly black or sooty; sides of neck with a white or pale yellowish stripe extending to the scapulars; lower neck and chest (sometimes entire breast) black, the underparts otherwise boldly barred with black and white or pale

PALE-BILLED WOODPECKER (FEMALE)

yellowish buff. *Female:* Similar to male, but forehead, median crown, inner feathers of occipital crest, and throat black.

Distribution.—Chiefly heavily wooded areas below 6,000 feet. Absent from Baja California and the central plateau.

Races.—*P. g. dorsofasciatus* (Sonora, Sinaloa, and Nayarit). *P. g. regius* (Tamaulipas, San Luis Potosí, Veracruz, and Mexico). *P. g. nelsoni* (western Mexico from Jalisco south to western Oaxaca). *P. g. guatemalensis* (Chiapas, Tabasco, and the Yucatán Peninsula).

Remarks.—Also known as Flint-billed Woodpecker and Guatemalan Ivory-billed Woodpecker. Fairly common locally in wooded areas from sea-level to an altitude of 5,000–6,000 feet. Pale-billed and Lineated Woodpeckers are much alike, but either the former's head is *wholly red,* or the crown and throat are black. Both species are thin-necked like a Pileated Woodpecker. When feeding, a Pale-billed Woodpecker drums with a characteristic "double rap" that is quite unlike the drumming cadence of the Lineated.

IMPERIAL WOODPECKER. *Campephilus imperialis.*—20–22. *Male:* Mainly glossy blue-black, the nape and long recurved feathers of the occipital crest bright red; secondaries and inner webs of primaries largely white; a prominent white V-shaped pattern on back. *Female:* Similar to male, but head without red, and crest much more recurved.

Distribution.—Sierra Madre, in states of Sonora, Chihuahua, Durango, Zacatecas, Jalisco, and Michoacán. ENDEMIC.

Remarks.—One of the largest and most magnificent of all woodpeckers. No other Mexican species has a *recurved occipital crest.* In flight the conspicuous *white wing-patches* are good field marks. Imperials require extensive stands of large trees and are now uncommon and of very local occurrence. Like the American Ivory-billed, they probably face extinction unless steps are taken to preserve their habitat.

Family DENDROCOLAPTIDAE. Woodcreepers

KEY TO THE SPECIES

1*a.* Crown, hind-neck (sometimes back), and underparts with conspicuous streaks, spots, or bars; bill usually long and slightly decurved 2

 b. Upperparts without streaks, spots, or bars; underparts usually uniform, the breast sometimes spotted; bill not decurved or notably long 8

TAWNY-WINGED WOODCREEPER. *Dendrocincla anabatina* (Illus. p. 306).—7–7½. Head (except throat), back, and scapulars olive-brown brightening posteriorly, the tail rufous; wings tawny, the coverts brownish and tips dusky; underparts essentially dull brown, the throat buffy and chest minutely spotted with same; bill moderately long and rather sturdy.

Distribution.—Lowland forests of southeastern Mexico.

Races.—*D. a. anabatina* (Veracruz, Tabasco, Oaxaca, and Quintana Roo). *D. a. typhla* (Campeche and Yucatán).

Remarks.—Also known as Northern Dendrocincla. Tawny-winged and Ruddy Woodcreepers frequent dense tropical forests and are often found together. In dim light they might be mistaken for rather drab short-tailed thrushes with long bills. This species shows a large *tawny wing-patch* in flight.

TAWNY-WINGED WOODCREEPER

RUDDY WOODCREEPER. *Dendrocincla homochroa homochroa.*—7½. Mainly cinnamon-rufous, the wings and tail chestnut; bill moderately long and rather sturdy.

Distribution.—Lowland forests of Oaxaca, Campeche, and Yucatán.

Remarks.—Also known as Ruddy Dendrocincla. A reddish brown woodcreeper with unpatterned plumage. Dendrocinclas are less active than their relatives, but search for food in much the same manner. Their tail-tips are stiffened, but lack the conspicuous spines of many woodcreepers. *See* Tawny-winged Woodcreeper.

OLIVACEOUS WOODCREEPER. *Sittasomus griseicapillus* (Illus. p. 307).—6–6½. Head, upper back, and underparts dull olive; lower back, scapulars, rump, and tail rufous, the last rather long, notably graduated and tipped with decurved spines; wings mainly dusky, the inner secondaries rufous, the remainder broadly tipped with same; a transverse tawny wing-patch; bill moderately long and slender.

Distribution.—Lowland forests of Jalisco and southeastern Mexico.

OLIVACEOUS WOODCREEPER

Races.—*S. g. jaliscensis* (Jalisco). *S. g. sylvioides* (Veracruz, Tabasco, Oaxaca, and Chiapas). *S. g. gracileus* (extreme eastern Tabasco and the Yucatán Peninsula).

Remarks.—The only woodcreeper with *uniform dull olive head and underparts*. It resembles a Wedge-bill superficially, but the latter has a *buffy throat*, spotted breast, and peculiarly *upturned lower mandible*. Both frequent lowland forests and are easily overlooked.

WEDGE-BILL. *Glyphorhynchus spirurus pectoralis.*—6. Crown sooty brown, shading to russet on back, scapulars, and wings; a transverse tawny wing-patch; superciliaries pale buff; sides of head more or less streaked with buffy white; rump rufous; tail chestnut, rather long, the feathers notably graduated and with conspicuously decurved terminal shafts; underparts tawny olive, the throat buff-colored; whitish triangular breast-spots; bill rather short, wedge-shaped.

Distribution.—Veracruz.

Remarks.—A small buff-throated woodcreeper with pale breast-spots. One of the furnariids, the Plain Xenops, has a similar wedge-shaped bill but lacks tail-spines. Its white submalar stripe is a good distinguishing mark. Wedge-bills feed like other woodcreepers, using their spine-tipped tails for support. Their tawny wing-patches are often conspicuous in flight. *See* Olivaceous Woodcreeper.

STRONG-BILLED WOODCREEPER. *Xiphocolaptes promeropirhynchus.*—$11\frac{1}{2}$–$12\frac{1}{2}$. Crown, hind-neck, and sides of head dusky brown, narrowly streaked with buff; back and wing-coverts uniform brown, the upper back sometimes finely streaked with whitish; wings (except coverts), rump, and tail mainly cinnamon-rufous or chestnut; upper throat whitish; underparts dull brown, the lower throat, breast, and sides (sometimes upper abdomen) very narrowly streaked with whitish; bill long, slightly decurved, and notably sturdy.

Distribution.—Mountains of southern Mexico, chiefly at high altitudes in pine forests.

Races.—*X. p. omiltemensis* (Sierra Madre del Sur, Guerrero). *X. p. sclateri* (Veracruz and Oaxaca). *X. p. emigrans* (mountains of Chiapas).

Remarks.—Also known as Great-billed Woodhewer. A very large, *heavy-billed* woodcreeper with *pale shaft-streaks* on head, neck, breast, and sides. Unmistakable.

BARRED WOODCREEPER. *Dendrocolaptes certhia sancti-thomae* (Illus. p. 309).—10–$11\frac{1}{2}$. Crown and hind-neck russet, the feathers with black, crescent-like bars; back and wing-coverts olive-brown, the former obscurely barred; wings cinnamon-rufous; rump and tail chestnut; chin whitish, faintly barred with dusky; sides of head and underparts mainly brownish buff or buffy cinnamon, conspicuously barred with black; bill long and rather sturdy.

Distribution.—Lowland forests from central Veracruz south through Campeche.

Remarks.—Also known as Barred Woodhewer. The only Mexican woodcreeper with conspicuous *bars*.

BARRED WOODCREEPER

IVORY-BILLED WOODCREEPER. *Xiphorhynchus flavigaster* (Illus. p. 309).—9–9½. Crown and hind-neck sooty black with numerous tear-shaped, buffy spots; back and scapulars brown, the feathers with broad buff streaks narrowly edged with black; wings, rump, and tail mainly chestnut or cinnamon-rufous; throat and chest creamy buff, the feathers of the latter edged with dusky; underparts otherwise brownish, broadly streaked with pale buff, the latter often edged with dusky; bill pale, long, and rather sturdy.

IVORY-BILLED WOODCREEPER

Distribution.—Pacific and Caribbean slopes, principally in dry, open woodlands.

Races.—*X. f. tardus* (extreme southeastern Sonora). *X. f. mentalis* (western Mexico south to Michoacán). *X. f. flavigaster* (Guerrero and western Oaxaca). *X. f. saltuarius* (southern Tamaulipas, southeastern San Luis Potosí, and northern Veracruz). *X. f. eburneirostris* (southeastern Mexico, exclusive of the Yucatán Peninsula). *X. f. yucatanensis* (Yucatán Peninsula; Meco Island).

Remarks.—Also known as Ivory-billed Woodhewer. Five of the twelve Mexican woodcreepers have *broad stripes* above or below. Of these, only the Ivory-billed, Stripe-throated, and Streak-headed are boldly marked on the *back*. The next species is superficially similar to this, but has a *streaked throat*. Both are larger than Streak-headed Wood-creepers and have much heavier bills.

STRIPE-THROATED WOODCREEPER. *Xiphorhynchus striatigularis.*—9. Similar to an Ivory-billed Woodcreeper, but throat black-striped, buff streaks of the breast margined with a chainlike streak of blackish, and wing-coverts streaked with black and buff.

Distribution.—Known from a single specimen (female) collected at Altamira, southern Tamaulipas.

SPOTTED WOODCREEPER. *Xiphorhynchus erythropygius* (Illus. p. 310).—8–8½. Crown and hind-neck dark olive, finely streaked or spotted with pale buff; upper back and scapulars olive-brown, conspicuously

Spotted Woodcreeper

spotted with buff; wings, lower back, rump, and tail mainly chestnut or cinnamon-rufous; sides of head, throat, and forebreast yellowish buff, the feathers olive-tipped; underparts otherwise mainly buffy olive, boldly spotted with yellowish buff; bill moderately long and sturdy.

Distribution.—Humid mountain forests of southern Mexico.

Races.—*X. e. erythropygius* (Veracruz, Guerrero, and Oaxaca). *X. e. parvus* (Chiapas).

Remarks.—Also known as Spotted Woodhewer. No other Mexican woodcreeper is boldly *spotted above and below*.

WHITE-STRIPED WOODCREEPER. *Lepidocolaptes leucogaster* (Illus. p. 311).—9. Crown, hind-neck, and sides of neck blackish, the forehead spotted, the remainder streaked with pale buff, these streaks sometimes extending to the upper back, where narrowly edged with black; back and scapulars buffy olive-brown; wings, rump, and tail mainly chestnut; sides of head and throat white, the former usually streaked or shaded with dusky; underparts creamy white, the feathers broadly edged with grayish olive, resulting in a boldly striped pattern; bill long, decidedly slender, and decurved.

Distribution.—Western and south-central portions of the country. ENDEMIC.

Races.—*L. l. umbrosus* (southeastern Sonora and adjacent parts of Chihuahua and Sinaloa south probably to northern Jalisco). *L. l. leucogaster* (southwestern and south-central Mexico south to Oaxaca).

Remarks.—Members of this genus have relatively *slender, curved bills*. This species is distinguished by its *creamy white* (not buffy) throat and ventral stripes. *See* Streak-headed Woodcreeper.

WHITE-STRIPED WOODCREEPER

STREAK-HEADED WOODCREEPER. *Lepidocolaptes souleyetii.*— 7½–8. Crown and hind-neck sooty black, becoming cinnamon-brown on upper back and scapulars, the whole more or less generously streaked with pale buff, this narrowly edged with black; wings, rump, and tail mainly chestnut; sides of head and neck pale buff, streaked with blackish; throat and chest pale buff, the latter faintly scalloped with dusky; underparts otherwise grayish brown, the breast and sides of upper abdomen rather boldly steaked with pale buff; bill long, slender, and somewhat decurved.

Distribution.—Southern Mexico, principally in lowland forests.

Races.—*L. s. guerrerensis* (Sierra Madre del Sur, Guerrero). *L. s. insignis* (lowlands of Veracruz, Oaxaca, Tabasco, northern Chiapas, and southwestern Campeche). *L. s. compressus* (southwestern Chiapas).

Remarks.—Also known as Thin-billed Woodhewer. An essentially lowland species replaced in mountain forests by the following. Its *back* is essentially uniform, as with *leucogaster*, but its throat and the *broad stripes* of its underparts are *buff-colored* rather than creamy white. *See* Ivory-billed Woodcreeper and White-striped Woodcreeper.

SPOT-CROWNED WOODCREEPER. *Lepidocolaptes affinis.*—$7\frac{1}{2}$–8. Crown, back, and scapulars brown, the anterior portion minutely spotted with pale buff, the upper back often with pale shaft-streaks; wings, rump, and tail mainly chestnut; sides of head and neck pale buff, streaked with black; throat pale buff, the underparts otherwise brownish with pale buff streaks, these narrowly margined with black; bill long, rather slender, and decurved.

Distribution.—Highlands of western Tamaulipas and southern Mexico.

Races.—*L. a. lignicida* (arid hills north and west of Ciudad Victoria, western Tamaulipas). *L. a. affinis* (mountain forests of Hidalgo, Veracruz, Puebla, Mexico, Guerrero, Oaxaca, and Chiapas).

Remarks.—Also known as Allied Woodhewer. The woodcreeper most likely to be found in the higher mountains. Not to be confused with the Strong-billed, a much larger bird with a decidedly heavy bill and *pale shaft-streaks.*

Family FURNARIIDAE. Spinetails, Ovenbirds, and Allies

KEY TO THE SPECIES

1*a*. Above and below almost wholly uniform dusky brown; bill long and slender 2

  b. Not as in 1*a*. 3

2*a*. Throat whitish . . . . Scaly-throated Leaf-scraper, p. 316

  b. Throat not whitish . . . . Tawny-throated Leaf-scraper, p. 315

3*a*. Lower mandible upturned; a conspicuous white submalar stripe
Plain Xenops, p. 315

  b. Lower mandible not upturned; without a white submalar stripe 4

4*a*. Breast chestnut; not concolor with abdomen
Rufous-breasted Spinetail, p. 313

    b. Breast and abdomen uniform; sometimes cinnamon-rufous, but never chestnut 5

5*a.* Throat buffy; superciliary stripes very conspicuous
                          Buff-throated Foliage-gleaner, p. 314

    b. Throat not buffy; superciliary stripes inconspicuous or lacking . . 6

6*a.* More than 7 inches. Underparts cinnamon-rufous
                          Ruddy Foliage-gleaner, p. 314

    b. Less than 7 inches. Underparts pale buffy brown
                          Scaly-throated Foliage-gleaner, p. 314

RUFOUS-BREASTED SPINETAIL. *Synallaxis erythrothorax* (Illus. p. 313).—5¾–6. Crown, sides of head, and back brown, shading to rufous on tail, the latter as long as body, notably graduated, and with tips usually

RUFOUS-BREASTED SPINETAIL

conspicuously frayed; wings mainly dusky brown, the coverts and outer webs of remiges (except tips) rufous; throat slate gray or minutely streaked and speckled with white; breast and sides bright rufous; abdomen pale grayish, the flanks and crissum reddish brown or olive-brown.

    Distribution.—Lowlands of extreme southern and southeastern Mexico.

    Races.—*S. e. furtiva* (Veracruz, Tabasco, and probably Oaxaca). *S. e. erythrothorax* (Yucatán Peninsula). *S. e. pacifica* (Pacific lowlands of Chiapas).

Remarks.—A small, chestnut-breasted bird with a rather long, frayed tail. Spinetails frequent thickets and forest undergrowth and are likely to be abundant in the brush beside lowland streams. Their remarkably bulky nests are constructed with large twigs and have the entrance at one side.

SCALY-THROATED FOLIAGE-GLEANER. *Anabacerthia striaticollis variegaticeps.*—6¼. Crown and hind-neck grayish olive, minutely streaked with whitish; back, scapulars, and rump rich brown; wings mainly dusky, the outer webs like back, or russet-brown; tail chestnut; lores dusky; superciliaries and eye-ring buff; malar stripe and auriculars dusky or brownish; throat and chest creamy white, the feathers of the chest obscurely edged with dusky; underparts otherwise pale buffy brown, darkest on the flanks.

Distribution.—Guerrero and Veracruz southward in mountain forests.

Remarks.—Also known as Scaly-throated Tree-hunter. The conspicuous *buff-colored eye-ring* and postocular streak, and pale, faintly *scalloped throat and chest* are good field characters. Characteristically feeds among the twigs and leaves of the outer branches in the manner of a warbler.

RUDDY FOLIAGE-GLEANER. *Automolus rubiginosus.*—7½–8. Above rich chestnut-brown, brightest on rump and tail; throat and chest rufous or tawny ochraceous, shading to rich brown on sides and flanks; crissum cinnamon.

Distribution.—Humid mountain forests of southern Mexico.

Races.—*A. r. guerrerensis* (Guerrero and western Oaxaca). *A. r. rubiginosus* (Veracruz). *A. r. umbrinus* (Chiapas).

Remarks.—Also known as Ruddy-throated Automolus and Ruddy Ovenbird. Largest of Mexican furnariids, and the only species with *bright rufous-and-tawny underparts.* Ruddies occur only at high altitudes and are found principally in the undergrowth of dense forests. Although fairly common locally, they are easily overlooked. Little is known of their habits.

BUFF-THROATED FOLIAGE-GLEANER. *Automolus ochrolaemus cervinigularis* (Illus. p. 315).—7–7½. Upperparts mainly dark olive-brown, brightening to russet on wings; rump and tail chestnut; crown and hind-neck sooty brown; sides of head and throat mainly tawny buff or creamy white; a dusky postocular streak; median breast and abdomen rich buff, shading to olive-brown on sides and flanks; crissum cinnamon.

Distribution.—Lowland forests of Veracruz, Tabasco, Oaxaca, and Chiapas.

Remarks.—Also known as Buff-throated Automolus. The representative ovenbird of tropical lowland forests. Distinguished from a Ruddy Foliage-gleaner by its *creamy buff* throat and conspicuous superciliary stripes. A shy and little-known species found principally in dense undergrowth.

BUFF-THROATED FOLIAGE-GLEANER

PLAIN XENOPS. *Xenops minutus mexicanus* (Illus. p. 315).—$4\frac{1}{2}$-$4\frac{3}{4}$. Crown olive-brown, shading through cinnamon on back to rufous on rump and tail; two black feathers between inner and outer rectrices; wings sooty, the remiges with a reddish transverse band; pale superciliaries; a con-

PLAIN XENOPS

spicuous white submalar stripe; throat pale buff or whitish; chest white-streaked, becoming olive-brown or faintly rufous posteriorly; bill short and wedge-shaped, the lower mandible conspicuously upturned.

Distribution.—Humid lowlands from Oaxaca and Veracruz southward.

Remarks.—Also known as Little Xenops. The *wedge-shaped bill*, upturned below, and prominent *white submalar stripes* are conspicuous field marks. Wings and tail appear patched in flight. *See* Wedge-bill.

TAWNY-THROATED LEAF-SCRAPER. *Sclerurus mexicanus mexicanus.*—6. Above mainly deep sooty brown, the rump and upper tail-coverts chestnut; tail black; throat and chest rich tawny rufous, shading to rich dusky brown posteriorly; bill long, very slender, black above and pale below.

Distribution.—Humid lowland forests of Veracruz, Mexico, and Chiapas.

Remarks.—Also known as Mexican Leaf-scraper. Leaf-scrapers are slender-billed, dusky olive-brown birds of dense tropical undergrowth. The thin bill and short tail eliminate all thrushes. Both Mexican species are very similar in appearance and have much the same range. This form has a distinctly *chestnut rump* and *reddish throat*. Scaly-throated Leaf-scrapers are much rarer in our area. Their very pale, faintly streaked, and mottled throats are distinctive.

SCALY-THROATED LEAF-SCRAPER. *Sclerurus guatemalensis guatemalensis* (Illus. p. 316).—6½. Above deep rich brown, the rump and upper tail-coverts somewhat brighter than back; tail black; throat whitish,

SCALY-THROATED LEAF-SCRAPER

more or less streaked or mottled with dusky brown; underparts otherwise much like plumage above, the chest usually brightest and finely streaked with pale tawny; bill long, very slender, and mainly blackish.

Distribution.—Humid lowland forests of Veracruz, Tabasco, and Chiapas.

Remarks.—Also known as Guatemalan Leaf-scraper. *See* Tawny-throated Leaf-scraper.

Family FORMICARIIDAE. Antbirds

KEY TO THE SPECIES

1*a*. More than 7 inches 2
   b. Less than 6 inches 4

2a. Below tawny ochraceous; tail notably abbreviated

  b. Not as in 2a. 3

3a. Above black or chestnut, the underparts white

  b. Above deep brown, the underparts dusky or grayish .

4a. Conspicuously barred with black and white

  b. Not barred 5

5a. Wholly or extensively slate gray or black 6

  b. Underparts not slate-colored or black 8

6a. Wholly slate gray; wings without bars

  b. Upperparts essentially slate gray or black; wings sometimes barred 7

7a. Above slate gray . . . .

  b. Above black . . . .

8a. Larger ($5\frac{1}{2}$–6 inches). 9

  b. Smaller (4–$4\frac{1}{2}$ inches). 11

9a. Crown chestnut; sides of head and hind-neck black-streaked

  b. Not as in 9a. 10

10a. Below tawny ochraceous . . . . .

   b. Below pale yellowish or brownish yellow, the back sometimes with
      a cinnamon patch . . . .

11a. Underparts rich chestnut; wings conspicuously barred

   b. Not as in 11a. 12

12a. Underparts pale yellowish or grayish olive

   b. Underparts mainly brownish . . .

GREAT ANTSHRIKE. *Taraba major melanocrissus* (Illus. p. 318).—
$7\frac{1}{2}$–8. *Male:* Above mainly black, the wings white-barred, and back with a concealed white patch; below white, the lower flanks and crissum dusky; iris red; bill black, notably sturdy, and strongly hooked. *Female:* Rufous above, white below. Wings without bars.

Distribution.—Lowlands of Veracruz and Tabasco.

Remarks.—No other Mexican antbird has sharply contrasting black-and-white or rufous-and-white plumage. It is fairly common locally, but frequents thickets and underbrush, where difficult to observe. Its song consists of a series of softly rising and falling notes.

GREAT ANTSHRIKE

BARRED ANTSHRIKE. *Thamnophilus doliatus* (Illus. p. 318).—6. *Male:* Above and below very conspicuously barred with black and white; feathers of the crown considerably elongated, forming an erectile crest;

BARRED ANTSHRIKE

iris white or pale yellow. *Female:* Crown chestnut, the upperparts otherwise mainly cinnamon-rufous; cheeks and narrow nuchal collar buff streaked with black; throat pale buff, sometimes minutely black-streaked, and shading to ochraceous buff posteriorly.

Distribution.—Caribbean slope, including the Yucatán Peninsula and adjacent islands. Also the Pacific slope of Chiapas.

Races.—*T. d. intermedius* (Tamaulipas, southern San Luis Potosí, Puebla, Veracruz, Tabasco, Oaxaca, and Chiapas). *T. d. yucatanensis* (Yucatán Peninsula; Meco and Cozumel Islands).

Remarks.—The boldly *barred* male is unmistakable. Females, while much less distinctive, are easily recognized by their *chestnut* crowns, and *black-streaked cheeks* and hind-necks. While not especially shy, this common antbird frequents undergrowth and thickets and is likely to be known best by its repertoire of harsh, staccato calls and musical whistles.

RUSSET ANTSHRIKE. *Thamnistes anabatinus anabatinus.*—6. *Male:* Above mainly tawny brown, becoming chestnut on the upper tail-coverts and tail; median back with a more or less concealed patch of pale cinnamon; throat and breast pale tawny, shading to grayish yellow posteriorly, the sides darker and tinged with pale grayish brown. *Female:* Similar to male, but without a concealed dorsal patch.

Distribution.—Humid lowlands of Tabasco.

Remarks.—Also known as Tawny Bush Bird. No other Mexican antbird has a *bright patch* on its back. This usually is difficult to see, but the *contrasting* tawny back and chestnut tail are also good field marks. A very rare and little-known species.

PLAIN ANTVIREO. *Dysithamnus mentalis septentrionalis.*—4½. *Male:* Crown, hind-neck, and auriculars slate gray, the back, wings, and tail dull grayish olive; upper wing-coverts black, minutely tipped with white; throat and breast pale gray, darkening on the sides; abdomen tinged with pale yellow. *Female:* Crown and hind-neck dull rufous, the wings and tail similar but paler; back and rump dull olive; throat whitish, the breast and sides tinged with pale grayish olive; abdomen pale yellow.

Distribution.—Reported only at Pacaitún, southwestern Campeche.

Remarks.—A diminutive antbird with a slate-colored or dull rufous cap and dull olive back. There are only two Mexican records of this common Central American form.

SLATY ANTWREN. *Myrmotherula schisticolor schisticolor.*—4. *Male:* Mainly slate gray, the wing-coverts black, like throat and breast; white wing-bars. *Female:* Above brownish olive, brightening to russet on wings and tail; throat buffy white; breast and abdomen tawny buff, the sides and flanks often tinged with olive.

Distribution.—Lowlands of Chiapas (Santa Rosa and Comitán).

Remarks.—Males suggest male Dot-winged Antwrens, but are slaty above (not black) and have no white on their tails. Females are brown above and have tawny underparts.

DOT-WINGED ANTWREN. *Microrhopias quixensis boucardi.*—4½. *Male:* Mainly black, the median back with an extensive (but usually concealed) white patch; wing-coverts and lateral tail feathers conspicuously white-tipped; sides, flanks, and lower abdomen slate-colored. *Female:* Above mainly dusky slate, the wing-coverts and tail white-tipped as in males; below chestnut, darkest on throat and breast.

Distribution.—Humid lowlands of Veracruz, Tabasco, and Oaxaca.

Remarks.—Unlike most formicariids, this species usually feeds well above the ground. It is rather common in suitable habitats, but easily overlooked. Both sexes are well-marked, the female, especially, being quite unlike any other Mexican member of the family; slaty above, chestnut below.

DUSKY ANTBIRD. *Cercomacra tyrannina crepera.*—5½–6. *Male:* Mainly slate-colored, the underparts lightest and washed with grayish brown posteriorly; wing-coverts blackish, minutely tipped with white; a concealed white patch on back. *Female:* Above mainly grayish olive or brownish, the wings brighter and somewhat rufescent; below tawny ochraceous, the flanks and crissum tinged with grayish olive.

Distribution.—Humid lowlands of Veracruz, Tabasco, southwestern Campeche (Pacaitún), and Chiapas.

Remarks.—Dusky Antbirds frequent thickets and forest undergrowth, usually in pairs, and are quite common locally, a circumstance more easily corroborated by sound than by direct observation. The male will be recognized by its generally *slate-colored* plumage; the female by its *tawny* underparts.

BLACK-FACED ANTTHRUSH. *Formicarius analis* (Illus. p. 321).—7–7½. Above deep reddish brown, the crown often sooty like tail; a chestnut nuchal collar; lores, malar area, and throat black; auriculars and narrow band across chest rufous; breast dusky, shading to dull white on abdomen; under tail-coverts reddish brown or tawny.

Distribution.—Lowlands of southeastern Mexico.

Races.—*F. a. moniliger* (Veracruz, Tabasco, Oaxaca, and Chiapas). *F. a. pallidus* (Yucatán Peninsula).

Remarks.—Also known as Chestnut-collared Antbird. Essentially terrestrial and much like a thrush, but with a shorter tail. The chestnut collar and black face and throat are good field marks. This antbird frequents thickets and forest undergrowth and usually is very wary. Its song has a ventriloquial quality and consists of a series of ascending notes.

BLACK-FACED ANTTHRUSH

SCALED ANTPITTA. *Grallaria guatimalensis* (Illus. p. 321).—7½. Crown grayish slate; upperparts essentially olivaceous, the whole distinctly scalloped; wings brown, the feathers edged with russet; sides of head and throat olive-brown, usually streaked or spotted with dusky; breast and abdomen tawny ochraceous; tail strikingly abbreviated.

Distribution.—Humid forests of southwestern and southern Mexico, chiefly at high altitudes.

SCALED ANTPITTA

Races.—*G. g. ochraceiventris* (Jalisco, Guerrero, and Morelos). *G. g. guatimalensis* (Veracruz, Tabasco, and Chiapas).

Remarks.—Antpittas frequent dense humid forests at high altitudes and are almost wholly terrestrial in habits. Although fairly common locally, they are very shy and difficult to observe. Look for them on or near the ground in heavy forest undergrowth.

Family COTINGIDAE. Cotingas

KEY TO THE SPECIES

1*a*. Upperparts bright blue, or blackish speckled with white
Lovely Cotinga, p. 323

  b. Not as in 1*a*. 2

2*a*. Throat rose-colored . . . . . Rose-throated Becard (male), p. 325

  b. Throat not rose-colored 3

3*a*. Throat and breast streaked . . . . . Bright-rumped Attila, p. 323

  b. Throat and breast not streaked 4

4*a*. Above mainly cinnamon 5

  b. Above not cinnamon 9

5*a*. Crown black or blackish 6

  b. Crown not black or blackish 7

6*a*. Underparts yellowish; crown glossy black
Gray-collared Becard (female), p. 325

  b. Underparts tawny buff; crown dull black or dusky
Rose-throated Becard (female), p. 325

7*a*. Virtually concolor above and below 8

  b. Underparts buff; much lighter than upperparts
Cinnamon Becard, p. 325

8*a*. Larger (9–9½ inches) . . . . Rufous Piha, p. 324

  b. Smaller (8–8½ inches) . . . . Rufous Mourner, p. 324

9*a*. Upperparts mainly dull brown, the crown sometimes black . . . 10

  b. Upperparts not dull brown 11

10*a*. Crown black . . . . Black-capped Tityra (female), p. 327

  b. Crown not black . . . . Masked Tityra (female), p. 326

11*a*. Mainly whitish or pearl gray, the wings black 12

  b. Not mainly whitish or pearl gray; wings not wholly black
Gray-collared Becard (male), p. 325

12*a*. Crown extensively black . . . Black-capped Tityra (male), p. 327

  b. Forehead and sides of head black . . Masked Tityra (male), p. 326

LOVELY COTINGA. *Cotinga amabilis* (Illus. p. 323).—7½. *Male:* Mainly bright blue, the throat, malar area, and abdomen rich purple; wings and tail black, the wing-coverts and secondaries edged with blue. *Female:* Above sooty or dark grayish brown, dappled or speckled with gray; sides of head and underparts pale gray, the throat generously speckled, and breast and sides boldly spotted with brown.

Distribution.—Lowland forests of southeastern Mexico north to Oaxaca and Veracruz.

Remarks.—The male of this species is the only brilliantly colored cotinga in Mexico. Females are decidedly drab, but will be known by their dappled upperparts.

LOVELY COTINGA

BRIGHT-RUMPED ATTILA. *Attila spadiceus* (Illus. p. 324).—7½–8½. Crown brownish olive streaked with black anteriorly; back and tail olive-green or brown tinged with chestnut; rump and tail-coverts chrome-yellow or ochraceous tawny; wings dark brown, the coverts edged with buffy brown; underparts mainly pale gray, the throat and chest brown-streaked; breast, flanks, and lower abdomen often tinged with olive or yellowish buff.

Distribution.—Sinaloa and Veracruz southward in lowland forests.

Races.—*A. s. pacificus* (Pacific slope, from Sinaloa to western Oaxaca). *A. s. flammulatus* (southeastern lowlands except where occupied by the following). *A. s. gaumeri* (Campeche and Yucatán; also Holbox, Meco, and Mujeres Islands). *A. s. cozumelae* (Cozumel Island).

Remarks.—Also known as Polymorphic Attila and Mexican Attila. An obscurely colored bird, usually shy and easily overlooked, this cotinga nevertheless is fairly common locally. While suggesting a fly-catcher, the bright *yellow rump* and *streaked* throat and chest are distinctive. Its song is a musical trill notably difficult to trace.

BRIGHT-RUMPED ATTILA

RUFOUS MOURNER. *Rhytipterna holerythra holerythra.*—8–8½. Cinnamon-brown, the underparts somewhat paler and brighter than plumage above.

Distribution.—Recorded only from Oaxaca (Tutla) and extreme southern Veracruz, where common locally. To be expected elsewhere in humid lowland forests of the extreme south.

Remarks.—This tropical species resembles a Cinnamon Becard superficially, but is much larger, and virtually uniform above and below. The becard is *redder* (less dusky) *above* and has *tawny buff* (not rufous) underparts. Its bill is shorter and heavier, and the crown somewhat *darker* than the back, the two not concolor as in the Mourner. *See* Rufous Piha.

RUFOUS PIHA. *Lipaugus unirufus unirufus.*—9–9½. Cinnamon-brown, the underparts somewhat paler and brighter than plumage above.

Distribution.—Humid lowlands of southeastern Mexico (Veracruz, Tabasco, Chiapas).

Remarks.—A solitary, thrushlike bird, distinguished from the Rufous Mourner by its much larger size, and from any of the thrushes by its uniform cinnamon color. An inhabitant of deep forest shade, this species is much more likely to be heard than seen. When disturbed, it usually announces its presence by several emphatic, but musical, whistles.

CINNAMON BECARD. *Pachyramphus cinnamomeus.*—5½–6. Above cinnamon or rufous, darkest on the crown; below rich tawny buff, palest on throat and abdomen.

Distribution.—Lowland forests of Tabasco and Chiapas. Uncommon.

Races.—*P. c. cinnamomeus* (Tabasco). *P. c. fulvidior* (Chiapas).

Remarks.—Becards appear rather large-headed and thick-billed, and have relatively weak legs. This species is *wholly* reddish above, lacking the black cap of female Gray-collared and Rose-throated Becards. *See* Rufous Mourner.

GRAY-COLLARED BECARD. *Pachyramphus major.*—5½–6. *Male:* Crown *glossy* black; forehead, nape, sides of head, and underparts clear gray; back and rump grayish brown to ash gray, in contrast to the white scapulars; wings and their coverts dusky black, conspicuously edged with white; tail rounded and prominently white-tipped. *Female:* Crown *glossy* black; back and tail bright cinnamon; sides of head and hind-neck buff; underparts mainly yellowish, the throat palest, and both abdomen and crissum tinged with buff.

Distribution.—Western and eastern Mexico from sea-level to an altitude of about 8,000 feet.

Races.—*P. m. uropygialis* (Sinaloa and Guerrero). *P. m. major* (Nuevo León and Tamaulipas south to Oaxaca and Veracruz). *P. m. australis* (Tabasco). *P. m. itzensis* (Yucatán and Quintana Roo).

Remarks.—Also known as Black-capped Becard and Mexican Becard. This cotinga has a remarkably extensive vertical range but is much less abundant than the following. In some areas it is largely confined to oak and pine forests between 3,000 and 5,000 feet above sea-level. Both sexes are black-capped, as with Rose-throated Becards, but this species alone has a *distinct nuchal collar* concolor with the underparts. Males are further distinguished by their *wholly* gray underparts and *white-patterned* wings and tail-tips.

ROSE-THROATED BECARD. *Platypsaris aglaiae* (Illus. p. 326).—6½. *Male:* Above all-black, or crown black, the back and tail gray; below mainly pale gray or dusky, the throat rosy or rich purple. *Female:* Crown dark gray or blackish, the upperparts otherwise mainly uniform cinnamon or grayish brown; sides of head and nuchal collar (when present) buff-colored like underparts.

Distribution.—Virtually country-wide, exclusive of Baja California.

Races.—*P. a. richmondi* (Sonora and probably Chihuahua). *P. a. albiventris* (Pacific slope from Sinaloa to Oaxaca). *P. a. insularis* (Tres Marías Islands). *P. a. gravis* (northeastern Mexico south to Morelos and northern Veracruz). *P. a. aglaiae* (highlands of central Veracruz and northern Oaxaca). *P. a. sumichrasti* (southern Veracruz, Tabasco, Campeche, and Chiapas). *P. a. yucatanensis* (Yucatán; also Holbox and Cozumel Islands).

Remarks.—The only member of the family represented in the United States (southern Arizona and Texas). Individuals as well as geographical races of this species vary widely in color tone, but all are

ROSE-THROATED BECARD

MALE   FEMALE

fundamentally alike in pattern. The *red-throated* males are unmistakable; females, lacking the distinctive throat-patch, might be mistaken for Gray-collared Becards except for their *buffy* (not yellowish) underparts and *dull* crowns. They lack a distinct nuchal collar.

MASKED TITYRA. *Tityra semifasciata* (Illus. p. 327).—7½–8. *Male:* Mainly pearl gray, darkest above, where somewhat bluish gray; forehead, sides of head, chin, wings, and tail mainly black, the latter white-tipped; iris, bare area around eye, and basal half of bill reddish, the latter otherwise black. *Female:* Similar to male, but head without black, the upperparts and cheeks mainly drab brown; remiges and tail blackish, the latter white-tipped; bill as in male.

Distribution.—Pacific and Caribbean slopes from Sonora and southern Tamaulipas southward.

Races.—*T. s. hannumi* (Sonora). *T. s. griseiceps* (Pacific slope from Sinaloa to Chiapas). *T. s. personata* (Caribbean slope from southern Tamaulipas southward, exclusive of the Yucatán Peninsula). *T. s. deses* (Yucatán).

Remarks.—The only cotinga with a *bicolored bill* and extensively *bare orbital area*. Masked Tityras nest in abandoned woodpecker holes or similar sites, and when not breeding usually forage through the tree-tops in small bands. Their characteristic call is a peculiar grunting note.

MASKED TITYRA

BLACK-CAPPED TITYRA. *Tityra inquisitor fraserii.*—7–7½. *Male:* Mainly pearl gray, darkest above, where somewhat bluish gray; entire crown and loral area black; flight feathers and tail mainly black, the latter white-tipped; bill black. *Female:* Crown, flight feathers, and tail mainly black; sides of head chestnut; back brown, the upperparts otherwise brownish gray; plumage below pale grayish white faintly washed with brown.

Distribution.—Caribbean slope from Veracruz southward, including the Yucatán Peninsula.

Remarks.—This species (male) resembles the more abundant Masked Tityra superficially, but has a *wholly black bill and crown*. The *chestnut* cheeks and *black* crown of the female are also diagnostic. Both species inhabit wooded areas of moderate elevation and have very similar habits.

Family PIPRIDAE. Manakins

1a. Mainly greenish 2

  b. Not greenish; sometimes brownish olive, or largely black and white 4

2a. Abdomen yellow . . . . . White-collared Manakin (female), p. 330

  b. Abdomen not yellow 3

3a. Larger (4½ inches). Middle rectrices elongated
                          Long-tailed Manakin (female), p. 329

  b. Smaller (4 inches). Tail square   Red-capped Manakin (female), p. 328

4a. Thrush-like; mainly brownish olive . .   Thrush-like Manakin, p. 331

  b. Not as in 4a. 5

5a. Head bright red . . . .   Red-capped Manakin (male), p. 328

  b. Head not red 6

6a. Back bright blue; middle rectrices notably elongated
                          Long-tailed Manakin (male), p. 329

  b. Back not blue; belly yellow   White-collared Manakin (male), p. 330

RED-CAPPED MANAKIN. *Pipra mentalis mentalis* (Illus. p. 329).—4. *Male:* Mainly black, the head and mantle extensively orange-vermilion; chin, underside of wings, and thighs pale yellow. *Female:* Mainly dull green, the throat and abdomen somewhat yellowish.

Distribution.—Caribbean lowlands from Veracruz southward.

Remarks.—Also known as Yellow-thighed Manakin. An unmistakable and usually common inhabitant of forest undergrowth. The greenish females resemble immature Long-tailed Manakins superficially, but are smaller and somewhat duller above. The colorful males are much more likely to be seen; in any case their characteristic, and remarkably loud, wing-snapping during courtship will be heard during the breeding season.

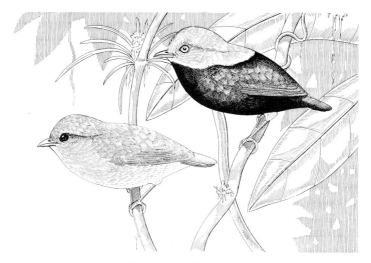

RED-CAPPED MANAKIN

LONG-TAILED MANAKIN. *Chiroxiphia linearis* (Illus. p. 330).—4½ inches—exclusive of the long middle tail feathers. *Male:* Mainly black, the back and scapulars clear azure-blue; a patch of elongated crimson feathers in median crown; middle rectrices black, very narrow, and notably long; legs bright orange. *Female:* Above bright olive-green shading to paler, more grayish green below; middle rectrices green, narrow, and considerably elongated; legs bright orange.

Distribution.—Arid lowlands (principally) of Oaxaca and Chiapas.

Remarks.—Immature females lack the elongated middle tail feathers of adults and resemble female Red-capped Manakins. Males perform a courtship dance much like that of White-collared Manakins, but apparently never snap their wings audibly.

LONG-TAILED MANAKIN

WHITE-COLLARED MANAKIN. *Manacus candei* (Illus. p. 331).—4½.
Male: Crown, wings (except upper coverts) and tail black, the hind-neck and
upper back white like throat and breast; lower back, rump, and upper tail-
coverts green, becoming bright yellow on abdomen and crissum; legs bright
orange. *Female:* Mainly dull green shading to bright greenish yellow on the
abdomen; legs bright orange.

Distribution.—Humid lowland forests of the Caribbean slope from
Veracruz southward.

Remarks.—Also known as Candé Manakin. Females of this species
can be distinguished from those of *Pipra mentalis*, a common bird of the
same area, by their decidedly *yellowish* abdomens. This manakin per-
forms a remarkable courtship dance (always near the ground in forest

undergrowth) in which the male jumps back and forth between two twigs, the dancer usually landing facing its previous perch, and each jump initiated by a loud "snap" of the wings.

WHITE-COLLARED MANAKIN

THRUSH-LIKE MANAKIN. *Schiffornis turdinus verae-pacis.*—6½. Mainly brownish olive, the underparts (abdomen and sides) paler, more purely olive than above; wings and tail russet.

Distribution.—Veracruz southward in humid lowland forests.

Remarks.—Also known as Brown Manakin. In dim light this manakin might be mistaken for an obscurely colored thrush. A shy bird, it inhabits forest undergrowth and is not easily observed. Its song is a short series of warbling notes.

Family TYRANNIDAE. Tyrant Flycatchers

With a single exception, all the flycatchers recorded in Mexico meet the specifications of one or more of the eight arbitrary categories listed below and appear in their respective keys. The Paltry Tyrannulet (*Tyranniscus vilissimus*), a small, undistinguished flycatcher of Chiapas, is described in the text.

I. Species with one or more of the following prominent characters: a notably long, scissor-like tail; striped, or wholly white underparts; mainly black above and below; or with conspicuous vermilion or pink coloring.   *See* page 333

II. Small to medium-sized flycatchers having underparts with more or less conspicuous buff, tawny, cinnamon, or brownish coloring. When crested, the crest either fan-shaped and brightly colored when erect, or pointed and almost concolor with the back; bills variable, and rictal bristles sometimes strikingly developed.   *See* page 333

III. Underparts wholly or extensively *bright* chrome- or lemon-yellow. If yellow is limited to the abdominal area, the head is grayish, not concolor with the back, and both tail and wings are without rufous edgings.   *See* page 334

IV. Medium-sized or large flycatchers (6–9 inches) with pale gray or grayish white throat and forebreast; crown and hind-neck essentially concolor with the back (sometimes darker, but never distinctly gray); abdomen pale yellow or yellowish white; wings and tail with more or less conspicuous cinnamon or buff (lacking in Thick-billed Kingbird).   *See* page 335

V. Grayish brown or dull grayish olive above, and with little or no bright yellow below (except Yellow-bellied Elaenia). Underparts usually with more or less *pale* yellowish white and dull grayish olive, the latter most pronounced on breast and sides; underparts sometimes either entirely whitish (Beardless Flycatcher) or grayish olive (Greater Pewee). Wing-bars and eye-ring usually lacking or obscure. Sometimes distinctly crested (Greater Pewee), or with a concealed *white* crown-patch (Yellow-bellied and Caribbean Elaenias).

See page 335

VI. Small or medium-sized ($4\frac{1}{2}$–$5\frac{1}{2}$ inches), greenish, or greenish olive flycatchers. Usually with olive and yellowish underparts, but sometimes grayish and white below. Wing-bars and eye-ring conspicuous.

See page 336

VII. Conspicuously greenish or greenish olive flycatchers with more or less *bright* yellow on underparts. Wing-bars usually lacking; when present, the bars either bright *yellow* or *buffy*, and crown slate color or brownish olive, not concolor with the back.   *See* page 336

VIII. Notably small flycatchers (3–4 inches), for the most part inhabiting thickets and the undergrowth of humid lowland forests. One species, Northern Beardless Flycatcher, is a representative of the *arid* tropical fauna.   *See* page 336

3*a.* Underparts essentially tawny or russet . Tufted Flycatcher, p. 357

  b. Underparts not as in 3*a*. Sometimes with a conspicuous cinnamon
  pectoral band . . . .   Pileated Flycatcher, p. 357
                                           Belted Flycatcher, p. 357

4*a.* More than 6½ inches. Throat, breast, and upperparts (except tail)
  grayish . . . . Say Phoebe, p. 337

  b. Less than 5½ inches. Breast never grayish; upperparts usually
  olive or olive-brown 5

5*a.* Throat immaculate white (unlike breast), or with a yellow rump   6

  b. Throat sometimes pale, but never white; rump not yellow . . . 7

6*a.* Throat white; bill strikingly broad, spadelike; tail notably short
                                White-throated Spade-bill, p. 359

  b. Throat not white; rump conspicuously yellow; bill and tail normal
                                Sulphur-rumped Flycatcher, p. 358

7*a.* Underparts more or less uniform buffy white or tawny buff
                                Buff-breasted Flycatcher, p. 356

  b. Throat and breast grayish olive; posterior underparts buffy ochre
                                Ochre-bellied Flycatcher, p. 365

Category III

1*a.* Very small (3–4¼ inches). Underparts uniformly bright yellow . 2

  b. Large (7–9½ inches). Throat white or gray, unlike posterior underparts 3

2*a.* With conspicuous superciliaries; bill and tail short
                                Yellow-bellied Tyrannulet, p. 364

  b. Without a superciliary stripe; bill long and flattened; tail rather
  long and notably graduated . . Common Tody-Flycatcher, p. 360

3*a.* Head (except throat) mainly black or blackish, the crown
  bordered with white 4

  b. Head (including throat) gray or grayish; crown not bordered with
  white 6

4*a.* Smaller (7–7½ inches). Bill rather small; white border of crown
  usually not closed behind . Vermilion-crowned Flycatcher, p. 345

  b. Larger (9–9½ inches). Bill very large; white border of crown
  usually closed behind 5

5*a.* Feathers of wings and tail conspicuously edged with cinnamon-
  rufous . . . . Great Kiskadee, p. 346

  b. Wings and tail without conspicuous cinnamon-rufous
                                Boat-billed Flycatcher, p. 345

6a. Tail (like wings) dusky brownish   . . .   Tropical Kingbird, p. 342

 b. Tail (unlike wings) mainly black   7

7a. Outer webs of outermost rectrices white

Western Kingbird, p. 341

 b. Outer webs of outermost rectrices pale brownish (never white),
the tail usually tipped with same . . . . . Cassin Kingbird, p. 341

CATEGORY IV

1a. Large (9 inches). Wings and tail without cinnamon or buff

Thick-billed Kingbird, p. 343

 b. Size variable; wings and tail (usually) edged with conspicuous
cinnamon or buff   2

2a. Upper tail-coverts broadly edged with cinnamon

Flammulated Flycatcher, p. 350

 b. Upper tail-coverts without cinnamon (*Myiarchus* spp.)   3

3a. Inner webs of rectrices entirely or mainly (more than half)
cinnamon; wings usually with two more or less distinct bars

Great-crested Flycatcher, p. 347
Ash-throated Flycatcher, p. 347
Pale-throated Flycatcher, p. 348
Ometepe Flycatcher, p. 348
Brown-crested Flycatcher, p. 348

 b. Cinnamon of the tail reduced to less than half of the inner webs
(sometimes lacking in Dusky-capped Flycatcher); wing-coverts
sometimes tipped with cinnamon, but without conspicuous wing-
bars . . . .   Yucatán Flycatcher, p. 349

Dusky-capped Flycatcher, p. 349

CATEGORY V

1a. Moderately crested   2

 b. Not crested   4

2a. Underparts dingy, grayish olive   . . . . .   Greater Pewee, p. 352

 b. With a *white* crown-patch, and yellow or whitish abdomen . . .   3

3a. Abdomen yellow . . . . Yellow-bellied Elaenia, p. 362

 b. Abdomen whitish . . . .   Caribbean Elaenia, p. 363

4a. Bill entirely black; crown distinctly darker than back

Eastern Phoebe, p. 337

 b. Bill pale below; crown not distinctly darker than back   5

5a. Larger (5–7 inches). Underparts not uniform; with more or less
grayish olive   6

 b. Smaller (4 inches). Underparts essentially pale yellowish white

Northern Beardless Flycatcher, p. 364

6a. Throat, median breast, and abdomen pale yellowish white
Olive-sided Flycatcher, p. 350

b. Throat (often), breast, and sides with more or less grayish olive
Eastern Wood Pewee, p. 351
Western Wood Pewee, p. 351
Tropical Pewee, p. 352

Category VI

1a. Wing-bars and bend of wing (sometimes under wing-coverts) buffy

b. Wing-bars, etc., not buffy . . . . . . *Empidonax* spp., pp. 352–56

2a. Throat dull white; under wing-coverts and *thighs* buff
White-throated Flycatcher, p. 356

b. Underparts bright greenish yellow and yellowish olive; thighs not buff . . . . Yellowish Flycatcher, p. 355

Category VII

1a. With conspicuous wing-bars 2

b. Without wing-bars 3

2a. Wing-bars bright yellow; crown slate color
Slate-headed Tody-Flycatcher, p. 361

b. Wing-bars buff; crown brownish olive
Sepia-capped Flycatcher, p. 365

3a. With a bright *yellow* crown-patch . . . Greenish Elaenia, p. 363

b. Without a crown-patch 4

4a. Above and below bright olive-green . . Eye-ringed Flat-bill, p. 360

b. Not as in 4a. 5

5a. Smaller (4 inches). Throat and breast gray; bill arched
Northern Bent-bill, p. 362

b. Larger (5 inches). Throat and breast not conspicuously gray; bill flat . . . . Yellow-olive Flycatcher, p. 360

Category VIII

1a. Underparts bright yellow 2

b. Underparts not bright yellow 3

2a. Bill and tail short; superciliaries conspicuous
Yellow-bellied Tyrannulet, p. 364

b. Bill and tail long, the former notably flattened; without distinct superciliaries . . . . Common Tody-Flycatcher, p. 360

3a. Throat and breast whitish or conspicuously gray; not concolor with the abdomen 4

b. Throat and breast not gray 5

4a. Crown and hind-neck slate color; bill black, decidedly flat

Slate-headed Tody-Flycatcher, p. 361

  b. Crown and hind-neck not slate color; bill brownish, the ridge decidedly arched . . . .   Northern Bent-bill, p. 362

5a. Bill notably broad; underparts largely brownish

White-throated Spade-bill, p. 359

  b. Bill very small; underparts dull white

Northern Beardless Flycatcher, p. 364

*EASTERN PHOEBE. *Sayornis phoebe.*—6¼. Crown, hind-neck, and sides of head sooty brown, the first usually distinctly darker than back; back and scapulars grayish olive; wings and tail mainly brownish, the wing-coverts usually edged with paler but not distinctly barred; underparts dull yellowish white (more yellowish in winter), the throat often whitish and sides of breast tinged with grayish olive; bill black.

Distribution.—Winters south to Oaxaca and Veracruz.

Remarks.—This phoebe resembles a Wood Pewee superficially, but lacks distinct wing-bars and has a *black* bill. Its crown appears darker than its back even at a distance, whereas the two are concolor in pewees. Phoebes have a habit of twitching their tails while perching and often can be distinguished by this charcteristic alone.

BLACK PHOEBE. *Sayornis nigricans.*—6¼. Mainly dull black or blackish slate, the abdomen immaculate white; remiges and outer rectrices edged with white or whitish; bill black.

Distribution.—Virtually country-wide, exclusive of the Caribbean lowlands and Yucatán Peninsula.

Races.—*S. n. salictaria* (northern Baja California, in willow associations). *S. n. brunnescens* (Cape San Lucas district of Baja California). *S. n. semiatra* (Pacific coastal area). *S. n. nigricans* (north-central Mexico southward). *S. n. aquatica* (a Central American form reported only from Ocosingo, Chiapas).

Remarks.—No other Mexican flycatcher has a *black head and breast*. Black Phoebes, like the Eastern, usually are found near water and generally place their grass and mud-lined nests against a rock or beam having an overhanging projection. Common and virtually unmistakable.

SAY PHOEBE. *Sayornis saya.*—7. Upperparts and sides of head grayish brown, darkest anteriorly; wings brownish edged with paler; tail dull black; throat and breast similar to plumage above, but somewhat paler and faintly tinged with buff; abdomen, flanks, and crissum dull cinnamon-buff; bill black.

Distribution.—Northern portion of the country, wintering southward on the central plateau to Puebla and Veracruz.

Races.—*S. s. quiescens* (northern Baja California and perhaps northwestern Sonora; extent of winter range unknown). *S. s. saya* (northern Mexico, wintering southward on the central plateau to Puebla and Veracruz).

Remarks.—The grayish brown upperparts, *blackish* tail, and *buffy* abdomen are good field marks. In common with other phoebes, this species habitually twitches its tail while perching, and by this custom alone the three are distinguished even at a distance from similar flycatchers.

VERMILION FLYCATCHER. *Pyrocephalus rubinus* (Illus. p. 338).— 5–5½. *Male:* Crown and underparts bright red, the latter palest and sometimes tinged with orange; sides of head and upperparts mainly brownish, the

VERMILION FLYCATCHER

remiges edged with grayish; tail dull black, the outer feathers narrowly edged with whitish; bill black. *Female:* Above mainly brownish gray, the auriculars dusky brown, and crown faintly streaked with same; tail blackish, the outer feathers edged with gray; throat and breast whitish, the latter narrowly but distinctly streaked with dusky; abdomen and crissum pale salmon color. *Immature:* Similar to female, but abdomen yellowish.

Distribution.—Drier portions of the country.

Races.—*P. r. flammeus* (Pacific slope from Sonora to Nayarit). *P. r. mexicanus* (Baja California and Mexico generally, except the Pacific slope and where occupied by the following). *P. r. blatteus* (southern Veracruz, Tabasco, northern Chiapas, the Yucatán Peninsula, and Cozumel Island).

Remarks.—No one will mistake the brilliantly colored male. Females are drab by comparison, but easily recognized by their *faintly streaked* breasts and *pinkish* abdomens. One of the most characteristic birds of the drier regions.

*SCISSOR-TAILED FLYCATCHER. *Muscivora forficata.*—11–14. *Male:* Crown and hind-neck pearl gray, the median crown with a concealed reddish patch; back and scapulars grayish, tinged with pink or yellowish; upper tail-coverts and wings mainly dusky, the lesser coverts with a vermilion patch; tail very long, "scissor-like," the three outer feathers greatly elongated, mainly white tinged with salmon, and broadly black-tipped, the remainder black and much shorter; throat and breast white or pale gray, the sides of the latter usually with a vermilion patch; abdomen and crissum pale salmon. *Female:* Similar to male, but usually without a crown-patch; tail much shorter, and posterior underparts paler, often orange-buff.

Distribution.—A common migrant and winter visitant occurring in the eastern and southern portions of the country.

Remarks.—Two flycatchers with notably long, scissor-like tails are found in Mexico. This species is distinguished by its *gray head*, mainly *white* outer tail feathers, and pinkish abdomen. A bird of the more open countryside, it often congregates in large numbers during migration.

FORK-TAILED FLYCATCHER. *Muscivora tyrannus monachus* (Illus. p. 340).—13–16. *Adult:* Crown, hind-neck, and sides of head black, the first with a large concealed yellow patch; back and scapulars pale gray, darkening on the rump; tail black, notably long, and "scissor-like," the outer feathers edged with white toward base; wings dusky brown, the feathers margined with paler; underparts immaculate white. *Immature:* Similar to adult, but black of head replaced by sooty brown, and crown without yellow patch; tail usually much shorter, its coverts and those of the wings margined with cinnamon.

Distribution.—Lowlands of southeastern Mexico (Veracruz, Tabasco, and Oaxaca).

Remarks.—Also known as Swallow-tailed Flycatcher. Rather uncommon, but to be found locally at all seasons. The *black crown and tail*, and *white* underparts at once distinguish it from the Scissor-tail, a common winter visitant in the same area.

FORK-TAILED FLYCATCHER

*EASTERN KINGBIRD. *Tyránnus tyránnus.*—7½–8. Crown and sides of head black, the former with a concealed orange patch; back, scapulars, and rump grayish slate; wings dusky, the coverts and remiges conspicuously edged with white; tail intensely black, broadly tipped with white; underparts mainly white, the breast, sides, and flanks usually more or less tinged with gray.

Distribution.—Ranges through eastern Mexico during migration, wintering in the southern portion of the country.

Remarks.—The *slaty black* upperparts, contrasting *white* underside, and conspicuously *white-tipped tail* are the best field marks. The members of this genus vary considerably in color, but all are large, well-proportioned birds with strongly hooked bills, and a concealed crown-patch of red, orange, or yellow. They prefer rather open countryside to forests and usually are most abundant in the lowlands. Noisily aggressive birds and usually bellicose toward interlopers, they are not likely to be overlooked.

CASSIN KINGBIRD. *Tyrannus vociferans.*—8. Crown, hind-neck, and chest grayish or pale slate, the first with a concealed patch of red or orange; auriculars dusky; back and scapulars grayish olive; upper tail-coverts and tail black, the latter narrowly brown-tipped and having the outermost feathers edged with same; wings dusky, margined with whitish; throat white, shading to deep gray on forebreast; underparts otherwise mainly bright yellow, the crissum much paler than abdomen; breast and sides tinged with olive.

Distribution.—Western and central Mexico south to Guerrero, ranging southward in winter.

Races.—*T. v. vociferans* (as above, exclusive of Guerrero). *T. v. xenopterum* (Guerrero).

Remarks.—Cassin Kingbirds and the two that follow are very similar, but have distinctive tails. This species and the Western Kingbird have black tails, but the latter's rectrices are conspicuously margined with white. Tropical Kingbirds are distinguished by their dusky *brownish* tails. All three occur principally in rather open country and are most abundant in the lowlands. Their noisily restless habits and bright yellow underparts can hardly fail to attract attention. *See* Thick-billed Kingbird.

WESTERN KINGBIRD. *Tyrannus verticalis.*—7½–8. Similar to a Cassin Kingbird, but head and forebreast somewhat paler, and outer webs of the outermost rectrices *white*, not pale brownish.

Distribution.—Northern Baja California and northwestern Mexico (Sonora and Chihuahua), ranging southward in winter.

Remarks.—Also known as Arkansas Kingbird. *See* Cassin Kingbird.

TROPICAL KINGBIRD. *Tyrannus melancholicus* (Illus. p. 342).—
8–8½. Resembles a Cassin Kingbird superficially, but bill larger and broader
at base; back, scapulars, and rump usually brighter and more greenish, or
sometimes distinctly tinged with gray; upper tail-coverts and tail mainly
dusky brown, the latter narrowly margined with paler, or with dull olive;
throat more extensively white, and breast distinctly tinged with greenish
olive.

Distribution.—Coastal lowlands and southern Mexico, including the
Yucatán Peninsula.

Races.—*T. m. occidentalis* (Pacific slope from Sinaloa to Guerrero).
T. m. couchii (Caribbean slope from Nuevo León and Tamaulipas to Puebla

TROPICAL KINGBIRD

and Veracruz). *T. m. chloronotus* (Oaxaca and southern Veracruz southward).

Remarks.—Also known as Melancholy Kingbird. *See* Cassin Kingbird.

**GRAY KINGBIRD. *Tyrannus dominicensis dominicensis.*—8–9.
Above mainly gray or dusky, the crown with a concealed patch of orange or
reddish; lores and auriculars dusky; wings, upper tail-coverts, and tail dark
grayish brown, the feathers usually margined with whitish or pale brownish
gray; underparts white, the breast, sides, and flanks more or less tinged
with gray.

Distribution.—Casual on Cozumel Island, off the coast of Quintana
Roo. Winters principally beyond the Mexican area.

Remarks.—A large gray-and-white flycatcher not likely to be mistaken for any other. Gray Kingbirds barely reach our area (Cozumel
Island) and have not been recorded on the mainland.

THICK-BILLED KINGBIRD. *Tyrannus crassirostris.*—9. Above dark grayish brown, or crown and sides of head deep brownish, the back, scapulars, and rump paler and tinged with olive—in either case, with a concealed yellow patch in median crown; wings and tail dusky brown; throat and malar area white, shading to pale gray on breast, the underparts otherwise pale yellow or yellowish white tinged with grayish olive on sides and flanks.

Distribution.—Western and southwestern Mexico, chiefly in lowland areas.

Races.—*T. c. sequestratus* (northern Sonora). *T. c. pompalis* (southern Sonora and Chihuahua). *T. c. crassirostris* (Pacific slope from Sinaloa southward).

Remarks.—This common flycatcher has the pugnacious habits of all kingbirds, but lacks the *rich golden-yellow* underparts of the Cassin, Western, and Tropical. Where other kingbirds also occur the Thick-billed will be known by its *whitish* (not gray or grayish olive) *breast,* and *pale* yellow belly.

PIRATIC FLYCATCHER. *Legatus leucophaius variegatus.*—6½. *Adult:* Crown and sides of head dark brown, the former bordered laterally by a conspicuous white band virtually extending across the hind-neck; a concealed yellow patch in center of crown; back and scapulars paler than crown, dusky tinged with olive; rump, upper tail-coverts, and tail dusky, the feathers narrowly edged with cinnamon; malar area and throat white; underparts otherwise bright yellow, the breast and sides boldly streaked with dusky olive, and flanks tinged with same; bill black, rather short, and very broad at base. *Immature:* Similar, but superciliary stripes yellowish or buff, continuous behind; feathers of crown and wings margined with cinnamon; back more distinctly olivaceous.

Distribution.—Caribbean lowlands from San Luis Potosí and Veracruz southward.

Remarks.—Also known as Striped Flycatcher. Smallest and least common of the three flycatchers with bold streaks on the underparts. Its *short bill,* broad white superciliary stripes, and *immaculate throat* are excellent field marks. Noisy and conspicuous.

**SULPHUR-BELLIED FLYCATCHER. *Myiodynastes luteiventris* (Illus. p. 344).—7½–8½. Forehead, superciliaries, and malar area whitish; crown, back, and scapulars pale olive and buff, conspicuously streaked with brown; a concealed yellow patch in center of crown; rump, upper tail-coverts, and tail mainly cinnamon-rufous; wings dusky, the feathers edged with pale yellow, whitish, or grayish brown; lores, auriculars, chin, and submalar area dusky, the throat white, narrowly streaked with dusky; underparts otherwise pale yellowish or sulphur-colored, the breast, sides, and flanks broadly streaked with dusky; bill decidedly large, mainly black.

Distribution.—Virtually country-wide in summer, wintering to the southward.

Races.—*M. l. swarthi* (breeds in Sonora; migratory southward). *M. l. luteiventris* (breeds extensively, exclusive of Sonora, wintering south of Mexico).

SULPHUR-BELLIED FLYCATCHER

Remarks.—Over much of the country this is the only *streaked* fly-catcher likely to be seen, and then only in summer or during migration. In southeastern Mexico, where Streaked Flycatchers also occur, the Sulphur-bellied can be distinguished by its all-black bill, *white* super-ciliary stripes, and *distinctly yellowish underparts*.

STREAKED FLYCATCHER. *Myiodynastes maculatus insolens.*—$8\frac{1}{2}$. Resembles a Sulphur-bellied Flycatcher superficially, but superciliaries and malar area *yellowish:* upperparts distinctly buff or cinnamon buff, conspicuously streaked with dusky; wing-coverts and remiges broadly margined with cinnamon-buff; underparts, including chin and submalar area, mainly whitish, the breast, flanks, and crissum often faintly tinged with pale yellow and narrowly streaked with dusky; bill decidedly large, the under portion mainly pale.

Distribution.—Southeastern Mexico from southern Tamaulipas south through the Yucatán Peninsula, Oaxaca, and Chiapas.

Remarks.—*See* Sulphur-bellied Flycatcher.

BOAT-BILLED FLYCATCHER. *Megarhynchus pitangua.*—9. Forehead and superciliaries white, the ends of the latter extending across the hind-neck; crown dusky brown, the median portion with a concealed chestnut or yellow patch; back, scapulars, and rump dull olive or grayish olive; wings and tail brownish, the feathers of both narrowly margined with buff or cinnamon; throat white, passing *abruptly* into bright lemon-yellow on breast and posterior underparts; bill black, very large, and with a distinctly curved ridge.

Distribution.—Pacific and Caribbean slopes and south-central Mexico southward.

Races.—*M. p. tardiusculus* (southeastern Sinaloa west of the main Sierra Madre south, at moderate elevations, to western Nayarit). *M. p. caniceps* (Jalisco). *M. p. mexicanus* (Caribbean slope from southern Tamaulipas and San Luis Potosí southward, including the Yucatán Peninsula).

Remarks.—A large, rather phlegmatic, yellow-bellied flycatcher with a notably *broad, thick bill* and a conspicuous white border around the crown. This common species resembles a Kiskadee superficially but has a much heavier bill and very little cinnamon on its wings and tail. Although ranging from sea-level to an altitude of about 5,000 feet, it is most abundant at moderate elevations in fairly open country. *See* Great Kiskadee.

VERMILION-CROWNED FLYCATCHER. *Myiozetetes similis* (Illus. p. 346).—7–7½. Forehead and superciliary stripes white or faintly yellowish; crown and sides of head dusky, the former with a concealed patch of vermilion; back, scapulars, and rump uniform olive or brownish olive; wings and tail dusky, the feathers often narrowly edged with olive; throat white or faintly yellowish, passing abruptly into bright lemon-yellow on the breast and posterior underparts; bill black and rather small.

Distribution.—Pacific and Caribbean slopes north to Sinaloa and southern Tamaulipas.

Races.—*M. s. primulus* (Sonora). *M. s. texensis* (as above, exclusive of Sonora).

Remarks.—Also known as Social Flycatcher. This noisily conspicuous flycatcher avoids heavy forests and higher mountains, but is very abundant elsewhere. While much like a Boat-billed Flycatcher *in plumage*, it is smaller and has proportionately a *decidedly smaller bill.* Chiefly lowlands, but ranging locally to an altitude of about 6,000 feet.

Vermilion-crowned Flycatcher

GREAT KISKADEE. *Pitangus sulphuratus* (Illus. p. 346).—9–9½. Crown and sides of head black, the former bordered by a conspicuous white band, and with a partly concealed chrome-yellow patch; upperparts other-

Great Kiskadee

wise mainly brownish olive; the feathers of the wings and tail margined with cinnamon-rufous; throat white, passing *abruptly* into bright lemon-yellow on breast and posterior underparts; bill black, decidedly large.

Distribution.—Virtually country-wide, from sea-level to medium elevations.

Races.—*P. s. palliatus* (southern Sonora south, in the coastal belt, to Nayarit). *P. s. derbianus* (central and southwestern Mexico from Zacatecas south, in the interior, to the Isthmus of Tehuantepec). *P. s. texanus* (Nuevo León, Tamaulipas, northern and central Veracruz). *P. s. guatimalensis* (southern Veracruz and the Isthmus of Tehuantepec southward).

Remarks.—Also known as Derby Flycatcher. This abundant and noisily irritable flycatcher might easily be mistaken for a Boat-billed, except for its slenderer bill, much more extensive crown-patch, and the conspicuous cinnamon on its wings and tail. While mainly insectivorous like their relatives, Kiskadees also commonly catch small fish and often can be seen perched, sentinel-like, beside ponds and streams. *See* Boat-billed Flycatcher.

*GREAT-CRESTED FLYCATCHER. *Myiarchus crinitus.*—8. Above usually uniform dull olive, the crown moderately crested, sometimes darker than back and somewhat brownish; wings mainly dusky, the coverts and secondaries broadly edged with pale buffy olive or whitish; outer webs of primaries narrowly edged with cinnamon, the inner webs broadly so; tail brownish, the inner webs of the lateral feathers extensively cinnamon-rufous; sides of head dusky gray, shading to clear ash gray on throat and chest (sometimes entire breast), the underparts otherwise mainly yellowish; sides and flanks tinged with grayish olive; bill blackish, rather large, and strongly hooked.

Distribution.—Winters commonly in the eastern and southern portions of the country.

Remarks.—Seven species of this genus occur in Mexico. All have erectile crests, more or less *cinnamon* on the inner webs of their primaries and rectrices, immaculate *grayish* throats and breasts, and *pale* yellowish abdomens. They are essentially solitary, often noisily aggressive birds of second-growth or more open woodlands, and characteristically perch on exposed branches well above the ground. All apparently nest in cavities, either natural or those excavated by woodpeckers, and have very similar habits. They differ considerably in size, richness of coloring, and the extent of cinnamon on their tails, but most are difficult, if not impossible, to distinguish in the field.

ASH-THROATED FLYCATCHER. *Myiarchus cinerascens.*—7½–8. Similar to a Great-crested Flycatcher, but bill smaller, upperparts browner (less olive) and underparts notably paler, the throat and abdomen sometimes almost white.

Distribution.—Baja California and the northern portion of the country, ranging southward extensively in winter.

Races.—*M. c. pertinax* (southern Baja California and San Esteban Island, Gulf of California). *M. c. cinerascens* (northern Baja California and Mexico, wintering southward over the central and southern portions of the country).

Remarks.—*See* Great-crested Flycatcher.

PALE-THROATED FLYCATCHER. *Myiarchus nuttingi.*—7. Similar to the Ash-throated Flycatcher, but much smaller, and upperparts usually browner, the two not readily separable in the field and possibly conspecific.

Distribution.—Western, central, and southern portions of the country, exclusive of the Yucatán Peninsula.

Races.—*M. n. inquietus* (Sonora and Chihuahua south through western and central Mexico). *M. n. nuttingi* (southern Mexico, exclusive of the Yucatán Peninsula).

Remarks.—Also known as Nutting Flycatcher. *See* Great-crested Flycatcher.

OMETEPE FLYCATCHER. *Myiarchus brachyurus.*—7½–8. Similar to a Pale-throated Flycatcher, but somewhat larger and with a proportionately shorter tail.

Distribution.—Arid lowlands of Chiapas.

Remarks.—The occurrence in Mexico of this widespread Central American species is questioned by some authorities. It cannot be identified with certainty in the field and may be conspecific with the Brown-crested Flycatcher.

BROWN-CRESTED FLYCATCHER. *Myiarchus tyrannulus* (Illus. p. 349).—8½–9¼. Similar to a Great-crested Flycatcher, but notably larger, bill proportionately longer and slenderer, and underparts somewhat paler.

Distribution.—Virtually country-wide, exclusive of Baja California.

Races.—*M. t. magister* (western Mexico, including the Tres Marías Islands). *M. t. nelsoni* (Coahuila, Nuevo León, and Tamaulipas south through eastern and southern Mexico).

Remarks.—Also known as Wied Flycatcher. *See* Great-crested Flycatcher.

BROWN-CRESTED FLYCATCHER

YUCATÁN FLYCATCHER. *Myiarchus yucatanensis.*—7. Similar to a Pale-breasted Flycatcher, but crown deep rich brown (rather distinct from the olive back), and with the cinnamon-rufous of the lateral tail feathers limited to less than half the inner webs.

Distribution.—Campeche, Yucatán, and Cozumel Island. ENDEMIC.

Remarks.—*See* Great-crested Flycatcher.

DUSKY-CAPPED FLYCATCHER. *Myiarchus tuberculifer.*—6¼–7. Very similar to a Yucatán Flycatcher, the two usually not separable in areas occupied by both. Crown dark sooty brown, or sometimes concolor with the back and scapulars; tail extensively brown, the cinnamon-rufous portion of the inner webs usually being reduced to a narrow margin, or sometimes absent; outer webs of lateral rectrices often conspicuously edged with cinnamon.

Distribution.—Virtually country-wide, exclusive of Baja California.

Races.—*M. t. tresmariae* (Tres Marías Islands, off the coast of Tepic). *M. t. olivascens* (western Mexico, from Sonora and Chihuahua south to Oaxaca). *M. t. querulus* (southwestern Mexico, from southern Sinaloa south to Oaxaca, where not occupied by *olivascens*). *M. t. lawrenceii* (eastern and southern portions of the country, exclusive of the Yucatán Peninsula). *M. t. platyrhynchus* (eastern Tabasco and the Yucatán Peninsula; Cozumel Island).

Remarks.—Also known as Olivaceous Flycatcher. Under ideal conditions this common flycatcher can be distinguished from other members of the genus by its smaller size, reduction (sometimes absence) of the cinnamon on the inner webs of its lateral rectrices, and relatively conspicuous cinnamon margin on the outer webs. For general characteristics of the genus see Great-crested Flycatcher.

FLAMMULATED FLYCATCHER. *Deltarhynchus flammulatus.*—6–6¼. Above grayish olive, faintly tinged with greenish posteriorly; upper tail-converts brownish, broadly edged with cinnamon; wings dusky, the coverts tipped and remiges margined with cinnamon-buff; tail dark grayish brown, the lateral feathers more or less conspicuously edged with cinnamon; lores and orbital ring whitish, the sides of the head otherwise grayish olive; throat whitish, shading to pale gray on the breast, where broadly (but indistinctly) streaked with white and pale yellow, the underparts otherwise pale yellowish.

Distribution.—Southwestern and southern portions of the country (Jalisco, Guerrero, Oaxaca, and Chiapas). ENDEMIC.

Remarks.—This flycatcher resembles birds of the *Myiarchus* group superficially, but has a much shorter and broader bill, and lacks rufous on the inner webs of its tail. Its *vaguely streaked* breast and cinnamon-barred upper tail-coverts are its best field marks.

** OLIVE-SIDED FLYCATCHER. *Nuttallornis borealis.*—6½–7. Above mainly grayish olive, the crown usually somewhat darker than back; wings and tail dusky, the wing-coverts edged with paler and tips of secondaries usually with whitish on outer webs; auriculars, sides of breast, and flanks dusky grayish olive, the median underparts white or pale yellowish white, in sharp contrast with the adjacent parts; bill black above, paler below, rather large, and decidedly broad at base.

Distribution.—Breeds in northern Baja California, occurring extensively elsewhere (exclusive of the Yucatán Peninsula) during migration.

Remarks.—At a distance this flycatcher might be mistaken for an out-sized Wood Pewee with sharply *contrasting underparts*. A conspicuous *white patch* on each side of the rump is a good field character when the bird is perched.

*EASTERN WOOD PEWEE. *Contopus virens.*—5½–6. Above dull grayish olive, the feathers of the crown somewhat long and with dark centers; wings and tail dusky, the middle and greater wing-coverts edged with grayish (or buff in immature birds), the outer webs of the secondaries rather broadly margined with whitish; underparts pale yellowish white, the breast, sides, and flanks more or less tinged with grayish olive; bill dusky above, pale below.

Distribution.—Migratory in the eastern and southern portions of the country, including the Yucatán Peninsula and Cozumel Island; winters to the southward.

Remarks.—Birds of this genus resemble the *Empidonax* flycatchers superficially, but are somewhat larger and have darker, less greenish olive backs, much *grayer* underparts, relatively inconspicuous wing-bars, and no perceptable eye-ring. They usually select exposed perches from which to dart on short flights when feeding. A good field character is the proportionately long wing, the tip of which extends beyond the middle of the tail in pewees, as compared with about one-third the length in *Empidonax*. Wood pewees might be confused with Eastern Phoebes, but the latter has a *black bill*, very *dark* crown, barless wings, and habitually twitches its tail while perched.

WESTERN WOOD PEWEE. *Contopus richardsonii.*—5½–6. Similar to the migratory Eastern Wood Pewee, but upperparts less olivaceous, underparts duskier and more extensively grayish olive, and bill usually darker below; the two not readily separable in the field.

Distribution.—Breeds in Baja California and northern Mexico, and in the southern portion of the country from Guerrero and Veracruz southward, exclusive of the Yucatán Peninsula. Winters on the Pacific slope south to Oaxaca; widespread elsewhere during migration.

Races.—**C. r. richardsonii* (breeds in northern Baja California and across the northern tier of states, occurring southward in migration). *C. r. peninsulae* (breeds in southern Baja California; winters on Pacific slope to Oaxaca). **C. r. placens* (breeds in the foothills and mountains of eastern Sonora and western Chihuahua, migrating southward through Chiapas). **C. r. sordidulus* (breeds in southern Mexico north to Guerrero, Tabasco, and Veracruz; southward in winter).

Remarks.—*See* Eastern Wood Pewee.

TROPICAL PEWEE. *Contopus cinereus brachytarsus.*—5–5½. Resembles the migratory Eastern Wood Pewee, but smaller and with a proportionately larger bill.

Distribution.—Southeastern Mexico north to Oaxaca, southern Veracruz, and Yucatán.

Remarks.—Field identification of this common resident is likely to be uncertain in fall and spring when Eastern Wood Pewees appear in southeastern Mexico as migrants. Tropicals are the only pewees likely to be found on the southern Caribbean slope at other seasons.

GREATER PEWEE. *Contopus pertinax.*—7–7½. Above dull olive, or decidedly grayish olive, the occipital feathers forming an erectile crest; wings and tail dusky, the wing-coverts and secondaries margined with pale gray or buffy grayish, but without pronounced bars; underparts extensively dull olive or grayish olive, lightening posteriorly, where more or less tinged with dingy yellowish or buff; abdomen sometimes whitish, but never sharply delineated, as with the Olive-sided Flycatcher.

Distribution.—Highlands generally.

Races.—*C. p. pallidiventris* (south to Durango, Chihuahua, and Tamaulipas, chiefly at medium elevations). *C. p. pertinax* (mountains of the central and southern portions of the country).

Remarks.—Also known as Coues Pewee. A large, *grayish*, highland flycatcher, somewhat like an Olive-sided Flycatcher in general appearance, but much more uniform below.

*YELLOW-BELLIED FLYCATCHER. *Empidonax flaviventris.*—5–5½. Sides of head and upperparts mainly greenish olive, the wing-coverts with two pale yellow bars; secondaries broadly edged with yellow; a distinct yellowish eye-ring; throat, breast, and sides dull olivaceous, the abdomen and crissum uniformly pale yellow; bill dusky above, pale below.

Distribution.—Migratory in the eastern portion of the country, wintering casually from central Tamaulipas southward.

Remarks.—This species is the most brightly colored of the Empidonaces, but even it so closely resembles several related flycatchers that its identification in winter often cannot be assured. As a general rule, specific designation of *Empidonax* flycatchers (other than *flavescens*, *albigularis*, and *fulvifrons*) seen in Mexico is best avoided unless their distinctive calls are heard.

*ACADIAN FLYCATCHER. *Empidonax virescens.*—5–5½. Above mainly olive-green, the wing-coverts with two pale buff or buffy yellowish bars; secondaries broadly edged with pale yellow; lores whitish, the eye-ring pale yellow; throat pale yellowish white, the breast and sides rather abruptly grayish olive; abdomen pale yellowish white; bill dusky above, pale below.

Distribution.—Migratory in eastern and southern Mexico, wintering to the southward.

Remarks.—As with most *Empidonax* flycatchers, the Acadian is virtually indistinguishable by sight alone, especially during migration and winter. It is nearest the Yellow-bellied, Traill, and Least Flycatchers in appearance, but the four are separable (with certainty) in the field only by voice and choice of breeding habitat.

**TRAILL FLYCATCHER. *Empidonax traillii.*—5–5½. Similar to an Acadian Flycatcher, but upperparts darker and more brownish, the crown sometimes distinctly brown; wing-bars buffy olive or pale grayish olive; lores and eye-ring pale yellowish olive; throat white or whitish, contrasting distinctly with the grayish olive of breast and sides; tail rounded, or but slightly forked. Field identification uncertain unless verified by the distinctive call—a single emphatic phrase accented on the penultimate syllable.

Distribution.—Breeds in northwestern Mexico, including the northern portion of Baja California; migratory southward and in eastern Mexico. Winters in Central and South America.

Races.—***E. t. brewsteri* (as above, except eastern Mexico). **E. t. traillii* (migratory in the eastern and southern portion of the country).

Remarks.—Also known as Alder Flycatcher. *See* Acadian Flycatcher and Least Flycatcher.

*LEAST FLYCATCHER. *Empidonax minimus.*—4½–4¾. Similar to Traill Flycatchers, but smaller and usually paler and more grayish, the underparts mainly whitish, with little or no yellow posteriorly; eye-ring and wing-bars whitish; breast often tinged with brownish and tail slightly forked; these characters of little value under field conditions unless corroborated by the distinctive call—an emphatic "che-béc" not likely to be heard during migration or winter.

Distribution.—Migratory in eastern Mexico and the southern portion of the central plateau (Guanajuato to Nayarit), wintering from Tamaulipas (?), Morelos, and Guerrero southward. A rare straggler in Sonora and Sinaloa.

Remarks.—*See* Traill Flycatcher and Hammond Flycatcher.

*HAMMOND FLYCATCHER. *Empidonax hammondii.*—4¾–5. Resembles a Least Flycatcher, but bill proportionately smaller, tail more deeply notched, and underparts somewhat darker, the throat, breast, sides, and flanks being almost uniformly grayish olive (palest on throat), fading to dull yellowish on the abdomen and crissum.

Distribution.—Winters in the western mountains and on the central plateau, and more or less migratory in the northern portion.

Remarks.—*See* Least Flycatcher and Wright Flycatcher.

*WRIGHT FLYCATCHER. *Empidonax oberholseri.*—5. Nearest a Hammond Flycatcher, but very variable and usually not separable from other Empidonaces in winter.

Distribution.—Western and central Mexico southward, during migration and winter only.

*GRAY FLYCATCHER. *Empidonax wrightii.*—5–5½. Resembles both Wright and Hammond Flycatchers, but usually considerably grayer than either, especially above, and with conspicuously whitish wing-bars and eyering. Not distinguishable with certainty while in Mexico.

Distribution.—Migratory in Baja California, northwestern Mexico, and the central plateau, wintering south to Nayarit, Michoacán, and Puebla.

PINE FLYCATCHER. *Empidonax affinis.*—5–5½. Similar to a Wright Flycatcher, but decidedly variable, both geographically and seasonally. Like most Empidonaces, not usually separable under field conditions by sight alone.

Distribution.—Highlands generally, especially in pine and oak growth.

Races.—*E. a. pulverius* (pinelands of northwestern Mexico, in Sonora (?), Chihuahua, Durango, Zacatecas, and Jalisco). *E. a. trepidus* (pinelands of Tamaulipas and Sierra Guadalupe, Coahuila). *E. a. affinis* (southern portion of the central plateau). *E. a. bairdi* (Sierra Madre del Sur, Guerrero, and probably southward in the Pacific highlands). *E. a. vigensis* (Veracruz, in the vicinity of Las Vigas).

Remarks.—Also known as Allied Flycatcher. *See* Wright Flycatcher and Hammond Flycatcher.

WESTERN FLYCATCHER. *Empidonax difficilis* (Illus. p. 355).— 5–5¼. Similar to a Yellow-bellied Flycatcher, but upperparts usually less greenish (more olivaceous), breast more buffy olive or brownish, and abdomen not so purely yellow; wing-bars grayish, grayish buff, or brownish.

Distribution.—Northern and western portions of the country (including Baja California) southward, principally in highland areas.

Races.—*E. d. cineritus* (cape district of Baja California). *E. d. difficilis* (northern Sonora, and probably foothills of eastern Sinaloa, south in migration at least to southern Sinaloa; migratory in Baja California). *E. d. culia-*

cani (arid lowlands of Sinaloa south, in migration, to Durango and Michoacán). **E. d. hellmayri* (winters from north-central Mexico to Durango). *E. d. immodulatus* (higher mountains of western Chihuahua south, in winter, to Nayarit). *E. d. bateli* (high mountains of western Durango, southeastern Sinaloa, and Nayarit, chiefly on the western side of the Sierra Madres; winter range unknown). *E. d. occidentalis* (southern portion of the central plateau, from northeastern Guanajuato southward). *E. d. immemoratus* (recorded only from east-central Veracruz).

WESTERN FLYCATCHER

Remarks.—A Yellow-bellied flycatcher with *grayish* or *grayish buff* wing-bars. No other *Empidonax* flycatcher of its area has the underparts notably yellow at all seasons; a characteristic shared by *flaviventris* of eastern Mexico.

YELLOWISH FLYCATCHER. *Empidonax flavescens.*—5. Above greenish olive, darkest on crown; wings and tail dusky, edged with olive, the wing-coverts with two very conspicuous buffy olive bars; eye-ring pale yellowish; underparts extensively yellowish or greenish yellow, the sides of the throat, breast, and flanks more or less strongly tinged with grayish olive, yellowish olive, or buffy olive.

Distribution.—Volcán San Martín, Veracruz, and highlands of Chiapas.

Races.—*E. f. imperturbans* (Volcán San Martín, Sierra de Tuxtla, Veracruz). *E. f. salvini* (mountains of Chiapas).

Remarks.—This distinctive flycatcher was long considered a race of the Western. Its decidedly conspicuous, *buffy olive wing-bars* and *rich yellowish and olive underparts* are characters shared by no other Mexican *Empidonax*.

WHITE-THROATED FLYCATCHER. *Empidonax albigularis.*—4¾–5. Above, including sides of head, olive-green or brownish olive, the crown usually darker than back, and tail often faintly grayish olive; wing-coverts with two distinct brownish buff bars, the secondaries edged with grayish buff; edge of wing near bend, under wing-coverts and thighs pale buff; throat dull whitish; breast and sides pale brownish olive, or tinged with buff; abdomen and crissum pale yellow or yellowish buff.

Distribution.—Western, south-central, and southern Mexico, exclusive of the Yucatán Peninsula. Migratory in the north.

Races.—*E. a. timidus* (highlands of southwestern Chihuahua and Durango south, in winter, to Guerrero, and possibly Oaxaca). *E. a. subtilis* (coastal plains of Sinaloa to an altitude of about 1,000 feet). *E. a. axillaris* (Veracruz, Mexico, and Puebla). *E. a. albigularis* (Chiapas).

Remarks.—Under exceptional conditions the distinctive *buff-colored* thighs and under wing-coverts may be seen. While there is little to distinguish this flycatcher from other Empidonaces of its area, most do not occur in Mexico in summer. *See,* especially, Traill, Pine, and Western Flycatchers.

BUFF-BREASTED FLYCATCHER. *Empidonax fulvifrons.*—4½–4¾. Above brownish or grayish brown, the crown sometimes much darker than back, the tail usually more grayish; remiges narrowly edged with grayish, the coverts with two very conspicuous gray or grayish buff bars; eye-ring white or buffy white; underparts mainly tawny buff or buffy white, the throat (sometimes abdomen) usually paler than breast, often whitish, but always tinged with buff.

Distribution.—Highlands of northern and western Mexico.

Races.—*E. f. fulvifrons* (known only from the unique type, believed to have come from the mountains of northeastern Mexico). *E. f. pygmaeus* (Sonora, Chihuahua, and Durango, wintering south to Michoacán and Morelos). *E. f. rubicundus* (southern portion of the central plateau south to Guerrero, Oaxaca, and Chiapas). *E. f. fusciceps* (highlands of Chiapas).

Remarks.—Also known as Fulvous Flycatcher and Ruddy Flycatcher. The only *Empidonax* with distinctly *buffy or tawny underparts*. The most richly colored race (*fusciceps*) resembles a Tufted Flycatcher superficially, but has much paler underparts, conspicuous *whitish* eye-rings, and lacks a crest. It is one of the three Mexican Empidonaces that can be distinguished in the field with reasonable certainty by sight alone, the others being *flavescens* and *albigularis*.

TUFTED FLYCATCHER. *Mitrephanes phaeocercus.*—5–5¼. Above brownish olive, the crown tufted, often darker than back and more purely brown, or tinged with ochraceous; wing-coverts with two distinct cinnamon or buff-colored bars, the secondaries usually edged with same; sides of head and underparts mainly reddish or tawny ochraceous, palest medially, where sometimes buffy.

Distribution.—Highlands of western and southern Mexico, principally in oak forests.

Races.—*M. p. tenuirostris* (Sonora and Chihuahua south to Jalisco and Guerrero). *M. p. hidalgensis* (mountains of northern Hidalgo). *M. p. phaeocercus* (Michoacán, Mexico, Morelos, Veracruz, and Oaxaca).

Remarks.—The only Mexican flycatcher with conspicuously *tawny or cinnamon underparts*. The tufted crown is often a good field character. Characteristic of oak forests, where quite abundant locally at altitudes exceeding 4,000 feet.

PILEATED FLYCATCHER. *Aechmolophus mexicanus.*—5½. Upperparts essentially dusky brown, palest on lower back and rump; a pointed crest, the longer feathers lanceolate; two white wing-bars; throat white, faintly tinged with yellow; a dull, vague breast-band; abdomen, flanks, and under tail-coverts pale yellow.

Distribution.—Known only from Cuernavaca, Morelos, and Chilpancingo, Guerrero. ENDEMIC.

Remarks.—A small drab flycatcher with *white wing-bars* and a *pointed crest*. Belted Flycatchers are also crested, but have *buffy* wing-bars and a very conspicuous pectoral band. Except for its crest, the Pileated might be mistaken for a Traill Flycatcher or even a Western Wood Pewee.

BELTED FLYCATCHER. *Xenotriccus callizonus.*—5. Crown dusky, the occipital feathers very long, forming a conspicuously *pointed* crest; sides of head and hind-neck grayish olive, becoming brownish olive on back, scapulars, and rump; wing-coverts with two buffy bars, the secondaries narrowly edged with same; lores and eye-ring whitish; throat grayish, faintly tinged with yellow; a broad and very conspicuous cinnamon band across the breast, the posterior underparts pale yellowish.

Distribution.—Reported only in the vicinity of Ocosingo and at Chichimá, both in the highlands of Chiapas.

Remarks.—Also known as Cinnamon-breasted Flycatcher. An extremely rare and little-known species, of which there are but three Mexican records. Its *pointed crest* and broad, *cinnamon pectoral band* are unmistakable.

SULPHUR-RUMPED FLYCATCHER. *Myiobius sulphureipygius sulphureipygius.*—4¾–5. *Male:* Crown, back, and scapulars greenish olive, the first with a large, partly concealed yellow patch; rump pale yellow; sides of head and throat grayish, the latter tinged with yellow; chest, sides, and flanks tawny or yellowish cinnamon, the underparts otherwise mainly pale yellow; bill black above, pale below, and rather broad; rictal bristles notably long and curved, extending to or beyond the tip of the bill. *Female:* Similar to male, but usually without a crown-patch.

Distribution.—Caribbean lowlands from Veracruz southward, including the Yucatán Peninsula and Cozumel Island.

Remarks.—A small flycatcher with a conspicuous *yellow rump-patch.* The very long, curved rictal bristles and *yellow crown-patch* of the male can often be seen at a distance. Sulphur-rumped Flycatchers prefer the undergrowth of dense tropical forests and are rather uncommon in Mexico.

NORTHERN ROYAL-FLYCATCHER. *Onychorhynchus mexicanus mexicanus* (Illus. p. 358).—6½. *Male:* Forehead and median crown orange-vermilion, the occipital feathers very long, violet-tipped, and with a black

NORTHERN ROYAL-FLYCATCHER

subterminal spot, the whole forming a very prominent fan-shaped crest when raised and spread in display; sides of head and upperparts olive brown, the wing-coverts minutely buff-tipped and tertials edged with same, the latter with a narrow, black, subterminal band; upper tail-coverts yellowish, the tail tawny ochraceous, shading to dusky toward tips; throat pale buff, shading to ochraceous yellow posteriorly, the breast and sides often tinged or streaked with olive-brown; bill and rictal bristles about an inch long, the former decidedly broad and flattened. *Female:* Similar to male, but with an ochraceous crest.

Distribution.—Lowland forests of Veracruz, Oaxaca, Tabasco, Campeche, and Yucatán.

Remarks.—The only Mexican flycatcher with a brightly colored, fan-shaped crest; conspicuous even when lowered. Undergrowth and lower branches (usually) of dense tropical forests, especially near streams.

WHITE-THROATED SPADE-BILL. *Platyrinchus mystaceus cancrominus* (Illus. p. 359).—3¾–4. Above brownish olive, the posterior crown often with a small ochraceous patch; superciliaries whitish; lores, postocular

WHITE-THROATED SPADE-BILL

streak, and malar area dusky; wings and tail dusky, the latter decidedly short; throat and chest white; breast, sides, and flanks buffy olive, the abdomen and crissum yellowish; bill remarkably broad and flattened, the rictal bristles extending to or beyond the tip.

Distribution.—Lowland forests of Veracruz, Tabasco, Chiapas, Yucatán, and Quintana Roo.

Remarks.—Also known as Stub-tailed Spade-bill and White-throated Flat-bill. The notably *flattened bill* and *stubby tail* are unmistakable. In common with true flat-bills, this very distinctive flycatcher inhabits forest undergrowth or low branches and is not easily found. Some authorities consider the Mexican representative a distinct species.

YELLOW-OLIVE FLYCATCHER. *Tolomomyias sulphurescens cinereiceps.*—5. Crown, hind-neck, and sides of head grayish, the first sometimes tinged with olive; eye-ring and line above lores white; back, scapulars, and rump greenish; wings and tail grayish brown, the feathers edged with greenish; throat and chest grayish white, the latter tinged with greenish olive, and this passing into pale yellowish posteriorly; bill very broad and rather flattened; iris whitish.

Distribution.—Lowland forests of southeastern Mexico, including the Yucatán Peninsula.

Remarks.—Also known as Sulphury Flat-bill. A rather nondescript flycatcher that might be mistaken for one of the brighter Empidonaces except for its much *broader bill, white iris,* and lack of wing-bars. No similar flycatcher has a *gray crown* and contrasting *greenish back.*

EYE-RINGED FLAT-BILL. *Rhynchocyclus brevirostris brevirostris.*—6. Above olive-green, the wings and tail dusky, broadly edged with olive-green; lores and auriculars grayish, the eye-ring white; underparts mainly pale olive-green, vaguely streaked, the abdomen and crissum yellow; bill rather short and notably broad, the ridge (culmen) distinctly curved.

Distribution.—Lowland forests of southeastern and southern Mexico, including the Yucatán Peninsula.

Remarks.—Also known as Short-billed Flat-bill. A rather stocky, olive-green flycatcher with a very *broad bill* (about $\frac{1}{2}$ inch at base) and *conspicuous eye-rings.* From below the breast and sides appear vaguely (but broadly) streaked—a useful character in combination with the conspicuous eye-rings.

COMMON TODY-FLYCATCHER. *Todirostrum cinereum finitimum* (Illus. p. 361).—$3\frac{3}{4}$–$4\frac{1}{4}$. Crown and sides of head black, becoming paler, more grayish on back, scapulars, and rump, where faintly tinged with olive;

wing-coverts and remiges conspicuously edged with yellow; tail black, decidedly graduated, the lateral feathers white-tipped; malar area and underparts bright yellow; bill mainly black, long and flattened, but scarcely tapered; iris white.

Distribution.—Lowlands of southeastern Mexico, including the Yucatán Peninsula.

Remarks.—Also known as White-tipped Tody-Flycatcher. Tody-flycatchers are distinguished by their small size, long, *flattened bills*, and notably rounded tails. Both Mexican species inhabit thickets and forest undergrowth and usually are found within a few feet of the ground.

COMMON TODY-FLYCATCHER

They are very active birds, vireo- or warbler-like in movements, and characteristically hold their tails erect. This species is *wholly yellow below* and has *white eyes*. *See* Slate-headed Tody-Flycatcher.

SLATE-HEADED TODY-FLYCATCHER. *Todirostrum sylvia schista-ceiceps.*—3¾. Crown and hind-neck slate gray, the back, scapulars, lesser wing-coverts, and rump olive-green; middle and greater wing-coverts, remiges, and bend of wing more or less conspicuously edged with yellow or greenish; tail blackish, the lateral feathers notably graduated; sides of head pale gray, fading to white on throat, the lores dusky and with a whitish streak above; breast gray, fading to white on belly, the sides, flanks, and crissum faintly tinged with yellow; bill black, rather long, and, unlike *T. cinereum*, tapered toward tip.

Distribution.—Lowlands of southern Mexico (Veracruz, Tabasco, and Oaxaca).

Remarks.—A diminutive thicket inhabitant resembling a Bent-bill below, but with a *flat bill, yellow-tipped wing-coverts, and slaty crown.* Much less common in Mexico than *T. cinereum,* from which it differs most strikingly in color of underparts. Note the somewhat tapered bill and lack of white tail-spots.

NORTHERN BENT-BILL. *Oncostoma cinereigulare* (Illus. p. 362).— $3\frac{3}{4}$–4. Top and sides of head grayish, the crown dimly streaked with darker; back, scapulars, and rump olive-green, the feathers of wings and tail narrowly edged with same; throat and breast pale gray, vaguely streaked with

NORTHERN BENT-BILL

darker, the abdomen and crissum tinged with yellow; bill mainly dusky, moderately long, the ridge (culmen) decidedly high and decurved; iris white.

Distribution.—Lowland forests of southeastern and southern Mexico.

Races.—*O. c. cinereigulare* (Caribbean slope north to Veracruz). *O. c. pacifica* (Pacific lowlands from the Isthmus of Tehuantepec southward).

Remarks.—No other small flycatcher has a prominent bill that appears *bent* in the middle. While very similar to a Slate-headed Tody-Flycatcher below, it lacks the latter's conspicuous wing-bars and flattened bill.

YELLOW-BELLIED ELAENIA. *Elaenia flavogaster subpagana* (Illus. p. 363).—6. Above brownish olive, the crown usually darkest, and with a partly concealed, white median patch; an erectile crest; two pale wing-bars; primaries and feathers of tail edged with olive; throat pale gray, passing into brownish gray or grayish olive on chest, the underparts otherwise yellow; bill mainly dusky, rather short, the ridge somewhat arched.

Distribution.—Caribbean lowlands, from Veracruz southward.

Remarks.—Elaenias have rather *short, high-ridged bills,* erectile crests, and a *partly concealed crown-patch.* The Yellow-bellied is not very common in Mexico, but occurs locally, both in open woodlands and in villages. It is considerably larger than Greenish Elaenias, much duller (less olive) above, and has a *white* (not yellow) *crown-patch* and pale wing-bars.

YELLOW-BELLIED ELAENIA

CARIBBEAN ELAENIA. *Elaenia martinica remota.*—6. Similar to a Yellow-bellied Elaenia, but browner above, and underparts (except chest) essentially whitish.

Distribution.—Islands off the Yucatán Peninsula.

Remarks.—The only Mexican representative of a very abundant and widely distributed West Indian species. In common with Yellow-bellied Elaenias, the Caribbean has a *white crown-patch*, a character found in no other Mexican flycatcher.

GREENISH ELAENIA. *Elaenia viridicata.*—5–5¾. Above olive-green, the crown dullest, somewhat grayish olive, and with a partly concealed, median yellow patch; sides of head grayish, the lores and postocular streak dusky; throat and (sometimes) chest dull grayish, passing into grayish olive on breast and sides, these obscurely streaked with yellow; abdomen and crissum clear yellow; bill mainly black, moderately long, and rather slender.

Distribution.—Tres Marías Islands, off the coast of Jalisco, and lowland forests of southern Mexico.

Races.—*E. v. minima* (María Madre Island, Tres Marías Islands). *E. v. jaliscensis* (Jalisco, straggling to the Tres Marías Islands in winter). *E. v. pacifica* (Pacific lowlands of southeastern Chiapas). *E. v. placens* (southeastern Mexico north to southern Tamaulipas).

Remarks.—The bright *yellow crown-patch*, usually visible even when the bird is at rest, distinguishes Greenish Elaenias from all other small Mexican flycatchers except the distinctive Sulphur-rumped Flycatcher.

It prefers dense woodlands and is usually found among the lower branches or in undergrowth. *See* Yellow-bellied Elaenia.

NORTHERN BEARDLESS FLYCATCHER. *Camptostoma imberbe imberbe.*—4. Above grayish olive, the crown usually darkest; middle and greater wing-coverts broadly tipped with pale brown (or buff), the resulting bars rather inconspicuous; throat and breast pale gray, very faintly tinged with yellow, the abdomen and crissum pale yellowish white; bill notably small, rather narrow and compressed laterally, the culmen distinctly arched.

Distribution.—Virtually country-wide in arid lowlands.

Remarks.—Also known as Beardless Tyrannulet. This trim little flycatcher appears uniformly gray above and very pale below, with little or no yellow on its underparts. Its small size, *diminutive bill*, and *pale brownish wing-bars* are good field characters. Likely to be seen on an exposed perch well above the ground. *See* Verdin (immature).

PALTRY TYRANNULET. *Tyranniscus vilissimus vilissimus.*—4¾. Crown dusky gray; forehead and line above eye dull white; upperparts mainly olive-green, the wing-coverts and remiges edged with pale yellow; throat and breast ashy gray, shading to white on abdomen; sides and flanks pale greenish yellow, obscurely streaked with darker; bill notably small.

Distribution.—Chiapas southward.

Remarks.—The diminutive bill and contrasting crown and back are the best field characters. No similar flycatcher has a pale border around the forepart of its crown. Much like a Greenish Elaenia below, but with a paler belly. Both appear *vaguely striped*. Paltry Tyrannulets barely reach Mexico, although common in the lowlands of Central America.

YELLOW-BELLIED TYRANNULET. *Ornithion semiflavum semiflavum* (Illus. p. 364).—3–3¼. Crown, hind-neck, and lores slate gray, the auriculars dark olive; a conspicuous white superciliary streak; back, scapulars, and rump olive-green; tail notably short, the feathers narrowly

YELLOW-BELLIED TYRANNULET

edged with greenish; underparts bright yellow, the throat, breast, and sides faintly streaked with pale olive; bill black, compressed laterally, the culmen distinctly arched.

Distribution.—Lowlands of southern Veracruz, Tabasco, and Chiapas.

Remarks.—Smallest of Mexican flycatchers. A brightly colored tropical species with no close relatives north of Costa Rica. Best distinguished by its slate-colored head, contrasting olive back, *conspicuous superciliaries*, and strikingly *short tail*.

SEPIA-CAPPED FLYCATCHER. *Leptopogon amaurocephalus pileatus.*—5. Crown, hind-neck, and auriculars brownish or dark olive-brown, the upperparts otherwise extensively olive-green; wing-coverts with two olive-buff bars; lores, malar area, and throat grayish olive; breast, sides, and flanks greenish olive, passing into dull greenish yellow on the abdomen, where sometimes vaguely olive-streaked; bill mainly blackish, moderately long, and rather slender.

Distribution.—Humid lowlands of southern Veracruz, Tabasco, and Chiapas.

Remarks.—Also known as Brown-capped Leptopogon. A very rare bird, of which little is known. In good light the *contrasting* brownish head and olive-colored back is a useful field character. Note the two wing-bars and *slender black bill*.

OCHRE-BELLIED FLYCATCHER. *Pipromorpha oleaginea assimilis.*—5. Above greenish olive; sides of head, chin, and forepart of throat grayish, shading to grayish olive on chest and sides of breast; underparts otherwise dull ochraceous or yellowish buff, faintly streaked with olive on breast and sides; bill mainly blackish, moderately long, and rather slender.

Distribution.—Caribbean lowlands north to southern Veracruz.

Remarks.—Also known as Oleaginous Pipromorpha. A greenish olive flycatcher with *ochraceous underparts*. Quite unlike any other Mexican species. Thickets and forest undergrowth, usually within a few feet of the ground.

Family ALAUDIDAE. Larks

HORNED LARK. *Eremophila alpestris* (Illus. p. 366).—7–8. *Male (summer)*: Forehead, line over eye, auriculars, and throat yellow; a black band bordering forepart of crown, terminating in tufted "horns"; a conspicuous black stripe extending below eye from base of bill; median crown, hind-neck, and upper wing-coverts pinkish brown, the upperparts otherwise grayish brown streaked with darker; tail black, the outer webs of the outermost feathers usually whitish; underparts mainly white, the chest with a conspicuous black shield and sides tinged with pinkish brown; (*winter*): Similar, but duller and without horns. *Female:* Similar to male, but smaller and much duller. *Immature:* Brown above, where heavily spotted with white; below white, the chest usually tinged with buff, or brown-spotted.

Distribution.—Virtually country-wide, exclusive of wooded areas and the southeastern lowlands.

Races.—*E. a. leucolaema* (winters in northern Baja California, Sonora and Chihuahua). *E. a. enertera* (Baja California south to Magdalena

HORNED LARK

Bay). *E. a. baileyi* (San Benito Island, off Baja California). *E. a. occidentalis* and *E. a. adusta* (winters in Sonora and Chihuahua). *E. a. ammophila* (winters in Sonora). *E. a. leucansiptila* (northeastern Baja California and Sonora). *E. a. aphrastus* (Chihuahua, Coahuila, and Durango). *E. a. giraudi* (northeastern Tamaulipas). *E. a. diaphorus* (southern Tamaulipas and Hidalgo, wintering to Oaxaca). *E. a. chrysolaema* (southern portion of the central plateau from Veracraz to eastern Jalisco). *E. a. oaxacae* (southern Oaxaca).

Remarks.—Bare fields, grasslands, and beaches are the habitats of Horned Larks, the species ranging extensively on the central plateau and in the western portion of the country. Eight of the twelve races recorded in Mexico are residents, while four breed to the northward.

All nest on the ground, and in winter usually forage in flocks. While the "horns" are often obscure (lacking in winter), Horned Larks will always be known by their distinctive face pattern. In flight, they appear light below with a *black* tail.

Family HIRUNDINIDAE. Swallows

KEY TO THE SPECIES

11*a*. Above glossy purple, the underparts grayish brown and white
Gray-breasted Martin (male), p. 369

  b. Above dark brownish, more or less glossed with purple
Purple Martin (female), p. 368
Gray-breasted Martin (female), p. 369

**PURPLE MARTIN. *Progne subis* (Illus. p. 368).—7–8. *Male:* Dark
glossy purplish black; or mainly purplish, but with a white abdomen; wings
and tail black, the latter moderately forked. *Female and immature:* Above

PURPLE MARTIN (*above*); GRAY-BREASTED MARTIN (*below*)

dark brown, more or less glossed with purplish; often with a grayish nuchal
collar; forehead, throat, breast, and sides grayish brown, becoming white on
the abdomen and crissum.

Distribution.—Breeds in Baja California, northwestern Mexico, and
the central plateau south at least to Guanajuato; widespread elsewhere in
migration.

Races.—*P. s. subis* (breeds south at least to Jalisco and Veracruz;
winters in Brazil). *P. s. hesperis* (breeds in Baja California, Sonora, and
probably the western portion of the central plateau; winters south of
Mexico). *P. s. sinaloae* (breeds in Sinaloa; reported from Guatemala in
migration).

Remarks.—Martins are larger and more compact than other
swallows, and appear less graceful in flight. Adult male Purple Martins

are unmistakable: either wholly purplish black, or (*sinaloae*) with *contrasting white belly and crissum.* Females and immature birds are virtually indistinguishable from Gray-breasted Martins of the same sex and age, without direct comparison of size. Under ideal conditions *subis* sometimes shows a grayish nuchal collar that is lacking in *chalybea.*

GRAY-BREASTED MARTIN. *Progne chalybea* (Illus. p. 368).—6½. *Male:* Above glossy bluish purple, appearing black at a distance; sides of head, throat, breast, and sides grayish brown, becoming white on the abdomen and crissum. *Female and immature:* Similar to male, but upperparts essentially brownish, more or less glossed with purple.

Distribution.—Caribbean slope from Coahuila and Tamaulipas southward.

Remarks.—Also known as White-bellied Martin. Most abundant in the coastal lowlands, but also found in the interior (locally) up to an altitude of about 4,000 feet. Adult males in fresh breeding plumage resemble no other Mexican swallow. Females and immature birds are usually indistinguishable from Purple Martins of similar sex and age, except by size. *See* Purple Martin.

**CLIFF SWALLOW. *Petrochelidon pyrrhonota* (Illus. p. 369).—5–5½. *Adult:* Forehead pale buff or whitish, the crown and back deep glossy

C‍ʟɪꜰꜰ S‍ᴡᴀʟʟᴏᴡ

blue; a grayish nuchal collar; rump cinnamon-buff; sides of neck and throat rich chestnut, the latter with a dusky median patch; underparts extensively whitish, the breast and sides usually tinged with buff. *Immature:* Similar to adult, but upperparts mainly dark brown, and throat dusky, not chestnut.

Distribution.—Breeds extensively south to Oaxaca and Veracruz, occurring southward in migration. Winters in Central and South America.

Races.—*P. p. minima* (Sonora). *P. p. pyrrhonota* (Pacific slope from Sinaloa to Nayarit). *P. p. melanogaster* (western portion of the central plateau south to Oaxaca). *P. p. tachina* (northeastern Mexico south to Veracruz).

Remarks.—The *pale forehead*, distinct rump-patch, and *dark chestnut throat* are unmistakable. The Cave Swallow, a common resident species, has a similar pattern, but is distinguished by its much darker forehead and paler (pinkish buff) throat. Both are highly gregarious, particularly while breeding, and construct conspicuous globular nests with mud pellets.

CAVE SWALLOW. *Petrochelidon fulva.*—5½. Similar to a Cliff Swallow, but forehead *dark chestnut*, and throat, sides of neck, and nuchal collar cinnamon-buff.

Distribution.—Northeastern portion of the country and Yucatán.

Races.—*P. f. pallida* (Coahuila and Tamaulipas). *P. f. citata* (Yucatán).

Remarks.—Also known as Buff-throated Cliff Swallow. *See* Cliff Swallow.

ROUGH-WINGED SWALLOW. *Stelgidopteryx ruficollis.*—4½–5¼. Above dusky or grayish brown, darkest on wings and tail; throat, breast, and sides pale brownish gray, shading to dull whitish on the abdomen; crissum white, the feather-tips sometimes black.

Distribution.—The Pacific slope and southeastern Mexico from central Veracruz southward, chiefly at lower elevations, occurring elsewhere in migration.

Races.—**S. r. serripennis* (widespread migrant and winter visitant). *S. r. psammochrous* (Pacific slope south to Guerrero, ranging to Chiapas in migration). *S. r. fulvipennis* (Guerrero and central Veracruz southward at moderate elevations). *S. r. stuarti* (southern Veracruz and Tabasco east of the mountains). *S. r. ridgwayi* (northern Yucatán).

Remarks.—No other brown-backed swallow has a *uniform grayish throat and breast*. Rough-winged Swallows nest in holes dug in banks or in crevices, and in summer usually are found in small breeding colonies near water. The Bank Swallow, a common migrant, is very similar, but has a *distinct pectoral band* and much whiter underparts.

BLACK-CAPPED SWALLOW. *Notiochelidon pileata.*—5. Top and sides of head glossy black; back grayish brown, shading to deep sooty brown on the wings, rump, and tail, the last conspicuously forked; throat and median underparts white, the former often flecked with dusky; sides, flanks, and crissum dusky brown.

Distribution.—Highlands of Chiapas.

Remarks.—A small white-bellied swallow with a *deeply forked tail*. The *black cap* and contrasting *brown back* can be seen at a distance under favorable conditions.

*BANK SWALLOW. *Riparia riparia riparia.*—5. Above grayish brown or dusky; below mainly white, the chest with a distinct brownish band.

Distribution.—Migratory, wintering in South America.

Remarks.—The only Mexican swallow with a *distinct breast-band*. Rough-winged Swallows, while also brownish above, have *uniformly* dingy throats and breasts. Immature Tree Swallows often have an *incomplete* breast-band.

BARN SWALLOW. *Hirundo rustica erythrogaster* (Illus. p. 371).—5½–6½. *Adult:* Above glossy steel-blue, the forehead chestnut; wings and tail blackish, the latter deeply forked and with a white band across the inner

BARN SWALLOW

web of each feather; underparts rich buff or chestnut, darkest on throat, the chest sometimes with an *incomplete* blue collar. *Immature:* Similar to adult, but less glossy above and much paler below; tail moderately forked.

Distribution.—Breeds south to Jalisco, occurring extensively elsewhere during migration and winter.

Remarks.—The most graceful of swallows, and one of the most vocal. Barn Swallows are distinguished by their *brightly colored under-*

parts and scissor-like tails. Black-capped Swallows (Chiapas) also have forked tails, but are *white* below.

*TREE SWALLOW. *Iridoprocne bicolor.*—5–5½. *Adult:* Above glossy steel-blue, the wings and tail sooty black; below immaculate white. *Immature:* Brownish above, white below, the breast sometimes with an *incomplete* dusky band.

Distribution.—Abundant and widespread in winter.

Remarks.—Of the three swallows having immaculate *white* underparts, this species alone is uniformly colored above. Mangrove Swallows have a conspicuous white rump-patch. Violet-greens are less glossy above and have violet rumps. Immature Tree Swallows resemble Bank Swallows, but the breast-band is lacking or incomplete medially.

MANGROVE SWALLOW. *Iridoprocne albilinea* (Illus. p. 372).—5. *Adult:* Above mainly glossy green, with steel-blue reflections, the rump white; wings and tail blackish, glossed with greenish; underparts white.

MANGROVE SWALLOW

Immature: Grayish brown above, the rump dull white; below white, the chest tinged with pale brown; tertials edged with white.

Distribution.—Mainly coastwise, from southern Sonora and southern Tamaulipas southward.

Races.—*I. a. rhizophorae* (southern Sonora south at least to Nayarit), *I. a. albilinea* (both coasts, except where occupied by the preceding).

Remarks.—Mangrove Swallows are most abundant in the vicinity of coastal lagoons and tidal rivers, but have been reported some distance inland along rivers of the Caribbean lowlands. No other swallow of our area has a conspicuous *white rump-patch*. Not to be confused with the Violet-green Swallow, which, in flight, shows a white patch on each *side of the rump.*

VIOLET-GREEN SWALLOW. *Tachycineta thalassinus* (Illus. p. 373). —4½–5. *Male:* Crown greenish, the forehead and nape bronze-tinted; back velvety green, this often tinged with bronze; rump deep violet or purplish, the wings and tail blackish; sides of head and underparts white, this extending over sides of rump, where usually conspicuous in flight. *Female:* Similar to male, but duller. *Immature:* Grayish brown above, darkest on back, where glossed with purplish or bronze; below essentially white, the chest often tinged with brown; a white patch on each side of rump.

Violet-green Swallow

Distribution.—Baja California, coastal Sonora, and the central plateau, ranging southward during migration.

Races.—*T. t. brachyptera* (southern half of Baja California and the coast of Sonora in the vicinity of Guaymas). *T. t. thalassinus* (Sonora and Chihuahua south to Oaxaca, Puebla, and Veracruz). **T. t. lepida* (widespread migrant and common winter visitant).

Remarks.—The *varicolored*, greenish, and violet upperparts distinguish the Violet-green from all other white-bellied swallows. In flight a white patch shows on each *side* of the rump, not on the rump itself, as with Mangrove Swallows. *See* White-throated Swift.

Family CORVIDAE. Crows, Jays

Key to the Species

1*a*. Wholly black 2
  b. Not as in 1*a*. 5

2a. More than 20 inches 3

  b. Less than 18 inches 4

3a. Larger (24–26 inches). Feathers of neck dusky at base
Common Raven, p. 375

  b. Smaller (20–22 inches). Feathers of neck white at base
White-necked Raven, p. 375

4a. Larger (16–18 inches). Plumage lightly glossed with greenish and
purple (northern Baja California) . . . .   Common Crow, p. 375

  b. Smaller (15–16 inches). Plumage highly glossed with greenish and
purple . . . . Fish Crow, p. 376

5a. Upperparts green . . . . Green Jay, p. 378

  b. Upperparts not green 6

6a. Pale gray above and below, the wings and tail extensively black
Clark Nutcracker, p. 376

  b. Not as in 6*a*. 7

7a. Upperparts dusky brown 8

  b. Upperparts not dusky brown 9

8a. Tail broadly tipped with white . . White-tipped Brown Jay, p. 378

  b. Tail without white . . . . Plain-tailed Brown Jay, p. 378

9a. Body essentially white or whitish below 10

  b. Underside of body not white 13

10a. Conspicuously crested 11

  b. Not crested 12

11a. Crest erect, tufted . . . . Tufted Jay, p. 378

  b. Crest not tufted, the feathers long, narrow, and often recurved
Magpie-Jay, p. 376

12a. Back brownish, contrasting with head, wings, and tail; throat and
breast obscurely striped . . . . Scrub Jay, p. 381

  b. Back grayish, showing little contrast with adjacent parts; throat
and breast not striped . . . . Gray-breasted Jay, p. 383

13a. Underparts wholly black 14

  b. Underparts not wholly black 15

14a. Larger (16 inches). Above (except head) *deep* bluish purple or
hyacinth-blue . . . . Purplish-backed Jay, p. 380

  b. Smaller (12–13½ inches). Above (except head) *bright* blue
Black-and-Blue Jay, p. 379

15a. Mainly blue; crown or throat with a conspicuous color-patch . . 16

  b. Mainly blue; crown and throat without a distinct color-patch . . 18

COMMON RAVEN. *Corvus corax sinuatus.*—24–26. Entirely black, with a purplish gloss.

Distribution.—Western portion of the country, including the central plateau, and various offshore islands.

Remarks.—Ravens are considerably larger than crows, but the two are not always separable at a distance. This form prefers semiarid mountain regions, but it also occurs commonly at sea-level. Birds of the Revilla Gigedo group (off the Pacific Coast) and islands in the Gulf of California possibly constitute a distinct race (*clarionensis*).

WHITE-NECKED RAVEN. *Corvus cryptoleucus.*—20–22. Similar to a Common Raven, but smaller, and with a relatively shorter and heavier bill; concealed basal half of neck feathers white.

Distribution.—Deserts and plains south to Guanajuato.

Remarks.—White-necked Ravens closely resemble Common Ravens, and the two may be found together. The former is more partial to deserts and usually is found in flocks at all seasons. Common Ravens are more likely to occur singly or in pairs, especially in summer.

COMMON CROW. *Corvus brachyrhynchos hesperis.*—16–18. Wholly black, dullest below, the upperparts somewhat glossed with purple.

Distribution.—Northern Baja California; recorded in northern Sonora (lower Colorado River, March 14, 1894), where probably casual.

Remarks.—Crows are much smaller than ravens, and usually more gregarious. They prefer cultivated areas interspersed with woodlands, rather than dry wastelands, and are not so characteristic of the Mexican fauna. Except in Baja California, any crow seen is almost certainly a Fish Crow.

FISH CROW. *Corvus ossifragus imparatus.*—15–16. Glossy black, the upperparts appearing purplish in strong light, the underparts glossed with greenish.

Distribution.—Northern portion of the country south to Colima, San Luis Potosí, and southern Tamaulipas.

Remarks.—Fish Crows range widely in Mexico, but are most abundant in the humid lowlands, especially river valleys. They are much glossier below than Common Crows and have a different call.

CLARK NUTCRACKER. *Nucifraga columbiana.*—11–12½. Head, neck, and body pale gray, lightest on forehead and throat; wings glossy black, the secondaries and tertials conspicuously white-tipped; tail mainly white, the middle feathers black.

Distribution.—Northern Baja California (Sierra San Pedro Mártir) and at least casually elsewhere in the higher mountains of northern Mexico (Cerro de Potosí, Nuevo León).

Remarks.—The contrasting black and white (or pale gray) plumage is unmistakable. A bird of the higher mountains, and likely to be found only at or near timberline.

PIÑON JAY. *Gymnorhinus cyanocephalus.*—10½–11½. Mainly dull grayish blue, brightest and darkest on crown and cheeks, the throat streaked with white; inner webs of remiges blackish.

Distribution.—Northern Baja California (Sierra Juárez and Sierra San Pedro Mártir); a single record for Chihuahua (17 miles east of La Junta).

Remarks.—An undistinguished, bluish jay with a *white-striped throat*. Pine and juniper forests of mountainous areas are the habitat of this jay, which, in many of its actions, suggests a crow.

MAGPIE-JAY. *Calocitta formosa* (Illus. p. 377).—20–28. Forehead black, several or many of the feathers greatly elongated, forming a prominent crest; crown, and upperparts generally, bright blue or tinged with gray or purplish; sides of head and underparts either white, the throat bordered posteriorly by a narrow black band, or underparts mainly white, the throat and sides of head black, and with a bluish white malar streak; underside of tail black, the middle feathers notably long, the four outer feathers much shorter and conspicuously white-tipped.

Distribution.—Arid lowlands of the Pacific slope and south-central Mexico.

Races.—*C. f. arguta* (southeastern Sonora, southwestern Chihuahua, and northern Sinaloa). *C. f. colliei* (southern Sinaloa to Jalisco). *C. f. formosa* (Colima to Puebla and Oaxaca). *C. f. azurea* (Chiapas).

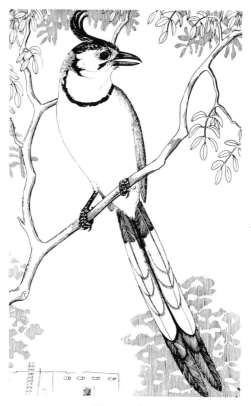

MAGPIE-JAY

Remarks.—The black-throated northern races (*arguta* and *colliei*) are considered a distinct species (*colliei*) by some authorities. In any case, Magpie-Jays are unmistakable, and all are alike in habits. Bold and inquisitive birds, they have a variety of unmusical whistles and calls and often are decidedly abundant.

PLAIN-TAILED BROWN JAY. *Psilorhinus morio.*—16–18. Head and mantle blackish, shading to dusky brown posteriorly; throat and breast intense dusky brown, becoming pale brownish gray or white on the abdomen and crissum; bill black or bright yellow, the latter probably indicating immaturity.

Distribution.—Nuevo León and Tamaulipas south to northern Tabasco. ENDEMIC.

Races.—*P. m. palliatus* (Nuevo León, Tamaulipas, and southeastern San Luis Potosí). *P. m. morio* (Veracruz and Tabasco).

Remarks.—Brown jays are distinguished by their essentially uniform, dusky, or brownish upperparts. This species is sometimes as pale below as the following, but has no white on its tail. Both are noisy, aggressive birds and have been found together in Veracruz. It has been suggested with some justification that the White-tipped is but a color-phase of this species.

WHITE-TIPPED BROWN JAY. *Psilorhinus mexicanus.*—16–18. Similar to *P. morio*, but abdomen and crissum white or cream-colored, and lateral rectrices conspicuously white-tipped.

Distribution.—Eastern and southeastern Mexico.

Races.—*P. m. mexicanus* (Tamaulipas [?], Veracruz, and probably Oaxaca). *P. m. cyanogenys* (Tabasco and Quintana Roo). *P. m. vociferus* (Yucatán).

Remarks.—*See* Plain-tailed Brown Jay.

TUFTED JAY. *Cyanocorax dickeyi.*—14½–15. Forehead and anterior portion of crown glossy black, the feathers forming a conspicuous, stiffly erect crest; throat and a broad band passing behind the white malar area and eye also black, but less glossy; posterior crown, neck, and underparts immaculate white; back, scapulars, wings, and basal portion of the lateral rectrices deep rich blue, the middle tail feathers white-tipped.

Distribution.—Sierra Madre of southeastern Sinaloa. ENDEMIC.

Remarks.—Also known as Dickey Jay. A magnificent, *black-crested* jay with no near relative in Mexico and few north of South America. It has a remarkably limited range and appears to be restricted to pine and oak forests above 4,000 feet in elevation.

GREEN JAY. *Xanthoura yncas* (Illus. p. 379).—9½–10½. Crown and malar area bright blue, the forehead white; throat, sides of neck, and stripe extending above eye to bill, black; back, wings, and the four inner tail feathers (above) bright green, becoming bluish toward tips; lateral rectrices bright yellow; underparts pale green, greenish yellow, or bright yellow.

Distribution.—Virtually country-wide, exclusive of Baja California and northwestern Mexico.

Races.—*X. y. speciosa* (Jalisco). *X. y. vivida* (Colima and Michoacán south to Chiapas). *X. y. luxuosa* (Nuevo León and Tamaulipas south to Guanajuato, Puebla, and Veracruz). *X. y. centralis* (Tabasco). *X. y. maya* (Yucatán Peninsula). *X. y. cozumelae* (Cozumel Island).

Remarks.—The only Mexican jay with *green* plumage. Essentially a woodland bird, and most abundant in the lowlands, it ranges to an altitude of about 6,000 feet in the mountains. Unmistakable.

GREEN JAY

BLACK-AND-BLUE JAY. *Cissilopha san-blasiana* (Illus. p. 380).— 12–13½. Head, hind-neck, and entire underparts black, the crissum and thighs tinged with blue; upperparts extensively bright blue, the tail sometimes purplish; a modified frontal crest, this best developed in western races; bill black (adult) or yellow (immature).

Distribution.—Coastal slopes from Guerrero and Yucatán north at least to Nayarit and Tabasco. ENDEMIC.

Races.—*C. s. san-blasiana* (Guerrero). *C. s. nelsoni* (Nayarit, Jalisco, Colima). *C. s. rivularis* (Tabasco and Campeche). *C. s. yucatanica* (Yucatán; Meco and Mujeres Islands).

Remarks.—Also known as San Blas Jay. The only jay in southern Mexico with *wholly black underparts*. Birds of the Caribbean slope are assigned to a separate species (*yucatanica*) by some authorities, and are known as Yucatán Jays. There is very little difference between any of the races.

BLACK-AND-BLUE JAY

PURPLISH-BACKED JAY. *Cissilopha beecheii.*—16. Head, hindneck, and entire underparts black, the crissum and thighs glossed with hyacinth; upperparts mainly glossy bluish purple (hyacinth); bill black (adult) or yellow (immature).

Distribution.—Lowlands and foothills of southeastern Sonora and Sinaloa. ENDEMIC.

Remarks.—Also known as Beechey Jay. The only jay of its area with *wholly black underparts*. Patterned like a Black-and-Blue Jay, but much larger, glossier, and decidedly *purplish above*.

AZURE-HOODED JAY. *Cyanolyca cucullata.*—11–12. Mainly dull purplish blue, the forepart of crown, sides of head, and throat black; hindpart of crown and nape pale blue, this separated from the black by a narrow white line extending behind the auriculars.

Distribution.—Humid mountain forests of southeastern Mexico, chiefly on the Caribbean slope.

Races.—*C. c. mitrata* (southeastern San Luis Potosí and Veracruz south to the Isthmus of Tehuantepec). *C. c. guatemalae* (Caribbean slopes of the mountains of interior Chiapas).

Remarks.—The only Mexican corvid with a conspicuous *pale blue occipital patch.* A silvery white line bordering the crown usually shows clearly even at a distance. Mountain forests, but rather uncommon.

WHITE-THROATED JAY. *Cyanolyca mirabilis.*—9–10. *Adult:* Head (except throat), neck, mantle, and breast black, abruptly restricted posteriorly; a narrow white band across forepart of the crown, this continuing along the sides of the crown, behind the auriculars, and extending downward as a fine stripe to the throat; throat white; plumage above and below otherwise dull grayish blue, more or less tinged with greenish. *Immature:* Similar to adult, but upperparts dull greenish or bluish slate, the body slate color below.

Distribution.—Oak forests of the Sierra Madre del Sur, Guerrero. ENDEMIC.

Remarks.—Also known as Omilteme Jay.

DWARF JAY. *Cyanolyca nana* (Illus. p. 381).—8–9. Mainly deep dull blue, palest on forehead and abdomen, where grayish blue; a conspicuous

DWARF JAY

black mask; throat pale bluish white, this bordered behind by a narrow band of blue much darker than adjacent parts.

Distribution.—Mountain forests of Veracruz, Mexico, and Oaxaca.

Remarks.—A diminutive *masked* jay with a *pale bluish throat-patch.*

BLACK-THROATED JAY. *Cyanolyca pumilo pumilo.*—9½–10½. Forehead, sides of head, and throat black, the latter tinged with dark blue; crown bordered anteriorly and laterally by a narrow white line, the plumage otherwise deep, rich blue tinged with purplish on crown, neck, and breast.

Distribution.—Mountain forests of Chiapas (Tumbalá).

Remarks.—Also known as Strickland Jay. Least distinguished of the smaller jays. It is apparently uncommon and occurs principally in oak forests 7,000–8,000 feet above sea-level. The *black face and throat* and *narrow* white stripe bordering the crown are its best field marks.

SCRUB JAY. *Aphelocoma coerulescens* (Illus. p. 382).—11–13. Above mainly blue, the back and scapulars dull grayish brown; white superciliaries; below gray, lightening on throat and chest where vaguely streaked; a dark, more or less pronounced, pectoral collar, this usually incomplete medially.

SCRUB JAY

Distribution.—Mountains of Baja California (to sea-level in cape region), western and eastern Mexico south to Guerrero and Oaxaca, occurring chiefly in oak or pine forests at altitudes exceeding 4,500 feet.

Races.—*A. c. obscura* (northwestern Baja California south in the Sierra San Pedro Mártir to latitude 30°). *A. c. cana* (extreme northern Baja California on eastern slope of the Sierra Juárez). *A. c. cactophila* (central part of Baja California south on the Pacific side at least to latitude 26°). *A. c. hypoleuca* (cape region of Baja California). *A. c. nevadae* (northeastern Sonora). *A. c. grisea* (Sierra Madre Occidental from central Chihuahua to northern Durango). *A. c. cyanotis* (mountains of east-central Mexico from Coahuila south to Hidalgo, Mexico, and Distrito Federal). *A. c. sumichrasti* (southeastern portion of central plateau from Tlaxcala and west-central Veracruz south to Oaxaca). *A. c. remota* (Sierra Madre del Sur, Guerrero).

Remarks.—A blue-and-gray jay with a *contrasting* brownish back, obscurely *streaked throat*, and (usually) a more or less distinct pectoral collar. Note the white superciliaries, lacking in the following species. Likely to be mistaken only for a Gray-breasted Jay, which also occurs commonly in pine and oak forests bordering the central plateau.

GRAY-BREASTED JAY. *Aphelocoma ultramarina.*—$11\frac{1}{2}$–$12\frac{1}{2}$. Head, wings, and tail dull blue, becoming somewhat gray on back and scapulars; no superciliary line; below essentially gray, usually palest on throat and lower abdomen, the chest sometimes distinctly tinged with brown.

Distribution.—Mountains of western and eastern Mexico, and southern part of the plateau, chiefly in oak and pine woods at altitudes exceeding 5,000 feet.

Races.—*A. u. arizonae* (Sierra Madre Occidental of Sonora and Chihuahua). *A. u. wollweberi* (southeastern Sonora and southwestern Chinuahua south to western Zacatecas and adjacent parts of northern Jalisco). *A. u. gracilis* (Nayarit and northern Jalisco). *A. u. colimae* (northeastern Colima to south-central Jalisco). *A. u. couchii* (Coahuila, southern Nuevo León, and west-central Tamaulipas). *A. u. sordida* (east-central Mexico south to central Hidalgo). *A. u. ultramarina* (southern part of plateau).

Remarks.—Also known as Mexican Jay and Ultramarine Jay. Much like a Scrub Jay, but virtually uniform above and without white superciliaries or throat-streaks. Some birds show a dim pectoral band, but usually the throat and breast are essentially alike.

UNICOLORED JAY. *Aphelocoma unicolor.*—$12\frac{1}{2}$–14. Above and below deep blue or purplish blue, the throat sometimes lightly streaked with gray; lower mandible of immature birds largely yellow.

Distribution.—Humid mountain forests (chiefly) from Guerrero, Mexico, and Veracruz southward.

Races.—*A. u. concolor* (eastern Mexico, Puebla, and west-central Veracruz). *A. u. guerrerensis* (vicinity of Omilteme, Guerrero). *A. u. oaxacae* (central highlands of Oaxaca; apparently rare). *A. u. unicolor* (Chiapas).

Remarks.—One of several characteristic mountain "cloud-forest" jays in southern Mexico, but often found in pine forests at high altitudes. Unicolored Jays are *wholly* blue; the others partly black and usually with conspicuous pale markings or patches on head or throat.

STELLER JAY. *Cyanocitta stelleri* (Illus. p. 384).—11–13. Mainly or extensively blue (grayish cerulean to purplish blue), the head, throat, and upper back of some races either entirely, or in part, dusky brown or blackish; a conspicuous crest, the forehead usually streaked; a distinct white spot often above and below eye; chin and forepart of throat sometimes paler than breast or vaguely streaked; wing-coverts and secondaries clearly black-barred, the tail similarly barred, but less distinctly.

Distribution.—Northwestern Baja California and mountainous portions of the country generally.

Races.—*C. s. frontalis* (northwestern Baja California). *C. s. macrolopha* (Sonora and Chihuahua south to Jalisco). *C. s. coronata* (Colima, Guerrero, and Oaxaca). *C. s. azteca* (Veracruz to Michoacán). *C. s. ridgwayi* (Chiapas).

Remarks.—The races of this jay vary considerably, especially in color of head and upper back, but the species is readily identified by its very *prominent crest* and regular *wing-barring*. A noisy and aggressive

STELLER JAY

bird, often found in flocks, it can hardly be overlooked in mountain pine and oak forests.

Family PARIDAE. Titmice

KEY TO THE SPECIES

5a. Crown and throat black 6

   b. Not as in 5*a.*; sides of head sometimes black or brown; tail notably long . . . . Bushtit, p. 388

6a. With conspicuous white superciliary stripes
                            Mountain Chickadee, p. 385

   b. Superciliaries not white . . . . Gray-sided Chickadee, p. 385

GRAY-SIDED CHICKADEE. *Parus sclateri.*—5. Not crested. Crown, throat, and chest black; upperparts mainly olive-gray; sides of head, median breast, and abdomen whitish, this shading to gray on the sides, flanks, and crissum.

Distribution.—Sonora, Chihuahua, and northwestern Durango south in the mountains to Oaxaca.

Races.—*P. s. eidos* (Sonora, Chihuahua, and northwestern Durango). *P. s. sclateri* (highlands of south-central Mexico from Zacatecas to Michoacán, Morelos, and Puebla). *P. s. rayi* (extreme southwestern Jalisco, the vicinity of Volcán de Colima, and the Sierra Madre del Sur, Guerrero, eastward into Oaxaca).

Remarks.—Also known as Mexican Chickadee. A *black-capped* chickadee with a very extensive bib and *dark gray sides.* Black-capped Chickadees (*P. atricapillus*) show much *less contrast below* and do not occur in Mexico. Chiefly coniferous forests, where abundant locally.

MOUNTAIN CHICKADEE. *Parus gambeli atratus.*—5. Not crested. Similar to a Gray-sided Chickadee, but with conspicuous white superciliary stripes and paler sides.

Distribution.—Mountains of northern Baja California (Sierra San Pedro Mártir and Sierra Juárez).

Remarks.—The only Mexican *chickadee* with white superciliaries and a *black eye-streak.* No similar bird occurs in Baja California. *See* Gray-sided Chickadee.

BLACK-CRESTED TITMOUSE. *Parus atricristatus atricristatus* (Illus. p. 386).—5½–6. Forehead, sides of head, and underparts whitish or pale gray, the flanks tinged with rufous; a pointed black crest, the upperparts otherwise grayish olive.

Distribution.—Coahuila, Nuevo León, and Tamaulipas south to San Luis Potosí and Veracruz.

Remarks.—The Mexican counterpart of the northern Tufted Titmouse (*P. bicolor*), but with a *black crest*. Juniper, pine, and scrub-oak woods of arid lowlands and foothills. *See* Plain Titmouse.

BLACK-CRESTED TITMOUSE

PLAIN TITMOUSE. *Parus inornatus.*—5–5½. Crested. Above dull grayish brown; sides of head and underparts pale gray or whitish.

Distribution.—Baja California.

Races.—*P. i. murinus* (northwestern Baja California south to latitude 30°). *P. i. cineraceus* (cape region of Baja California).

Remarks.—The least distinguished of the titmice, but readily identified by its *uniformly drab* (mouse-colored) plumage and *conspicuous crest*. Oak and juniper woods at moderate elevations. *See* Black-crested Titmouse.

BRIDLED TITMOUSE. *Parus wollweberi* (Illus. p. 387).—4¾–5. Throat, border of crown, and long occipital feathers black, the last forming a conspicuous crest; sides of head and superciliary stripes whitish, the auriculars bordered behind by a black "bridle" mark; median crown gray; back and scapulars grayish olive, the underparts mainly grayish white, faintly tinged with yellow on the abdomen.

Distribution.—Mountains of northern and western Mexico south to Veracruz and Oaxaca.

Races.—*P. w. phillipsi* (Sonora and western Chihuahua). *P. w. wollweberi* (mountains of eastern and southern Mexico, except where occupied by the following). *P. w. caliginosus* (mountains of Guerrero and Oaxaca).

Remarks.—A widespread inhabitant of mountain oak forests. The black-fringed crest and "bridled" cheeks are unmistakable.

BRIDLED TITMOUSE

VERDIN. *Auriparus flaviceps.*—3½–4. *Adult:* Head bright yellow or yellowish olive; body ashy gray, darkest above, the wings brownish; a patch of chestnut at band of wing. *Immature:* Similar to adult, but head gray, wings without chestnut, and bill yellow at base.

Distribution.—Baja California, northern and western Mexico south to Durango.

Races.—*A. f. flaviceps* (cape region of Baja California and San Estebán Island, Sonora). *A. f. acaciarum* (Baja California south to latitude 31°; northwestern Sonora). *A. f. fraterculus* (central and southern Sonora). *A. f. ornatus* (eastern Sonora to Tamaulipas, south to Durango).

Remarks.—Diminutive, grayish birds of brush-grown arid districts. Yellow-headed adults are unmistakable. Immature birds resemble Bushtits, but have shorter tails and occupy a different habitat. They also suggest Northern Beardless Flycatchers of the same region, but have partly yellow bills and different actions.

BUSHTIT. *Psaltriparus minimus* (Illus. p. 388).—$3\frac{3}{4}$–$4\frac{1}{4}$. above uniform dull grayish, or crown and cheeks pale buffy brown; sides of head either with conspicuous black (or pale brown), or concolor with back; underparts ashy gray, the lower abdomen sometimes tinged with buff; tail notably long. Females of black-faced races have light brown cheeks and usually show black only above the auriculars.

Distribution.—Arid foothills and mountains of Baja California and western Mexico south over the central plateau to Chiapas.

Races.—*P. m. melanurus* (Baja California south to latitude 30°). *P. m. grindae* (cape district of Baja California). *P. m. plumbeus* (Sonora, locally). *P. m. cecaumenorum* (northwestern Sonora). *P. m. lloydi* (northeastern

BUSHTIT (BLACK-EARED)

Sonora and northern Chihuahua). *P. m. dimorphicus* (Sierra Madre of southeastern Sonora and southwestern Chihuahua). *P. m. iulus* (western and central Mexico except where occupied by other races). *P. m. melanotis* (southern portion of the central plateau south through Oaxaca and Chiapas).

Remarks.—Some Bushtits resemble immature Verdins, but have proportionately longer tails. They frequent wooded areas, whereas Verdins prefer more open, arid lowlands. Their nests are bulky, pouch-like structures of moss, with an entrance on one side near the top. Notably active little birds, they range the woods in loose flocks when not breeding, and can be identified from a distance by their gentle *high-pitched, twittering notes.* The black-faced races (*lloydi, dimorphicus, iulus,* and *melanotis*) form a well-marked group commonly known as Black-eared Bushtit. While considered a distinct species (*melanotis*) by some authorities, the intermediate characters of *dimorphicus* favor the present treatment.

Family **SITTIDAE.** Nuthatches

KEY TO THE SPECIES

2*a*. Larger (5½ inches); sides of head and underparts white
White-breasted Nuthatch, p. 389

b. Smaller (4 inches); underparts buff or pale rufous; a dark eye-streak . . . . Red-breasted Nuthatch, p. 390

WHITE-BREASTED NUTHATCH. *Sitta carolinensis* (Illus. p. 389).—
5½. Crown and band across mantle glossy black, the upperparts otherwise mainly bluish gray; tail black, the lateral feathers white-tipped and partly white on outer webs; sides of head and underparts white, the thighs and crissum chestnut; bill rather long and slightly upturned.

WHITE-BREASTED NUTHATCH

Distribution.—Baja California, northern and western Mexico south in the highlands to Oaxaca.

Races.—*S. c. aculeata* (northern Baja California). *S. c. alexandrae* (pine belt of the Sierra San Pedro Mártir, Baja California). *S. c. lagunae* (Cape San Lucas district, Baja California). *S. c. nelsoni* (Sonora and northern Chihuahua). *S. c. oberholseri* (Coahuila). *S. c. umbrosa* (southeastern Sonora and southern Chihuahua south through western Zacatecas to northern Jalisco). *S. c. mexicana* (southern Chihuahua south to Oaxaca). *S. c. kinneari* (Guerrero).

Remarks.—Pine and oak forests of the highlands are the preferred habitat of nuthatches. The *black* cap and *white* underparts distinguish this common species from the Pygmy Nuthatch, a much smaller bird of the same area. Both have similar habits. When feeding, they characteristically descend tree-trunks head-foremost and prowl the underside of the branches with assurance.

RED-BREASTED NUTHATCH. *Sitta canadensis canadensis.*—4. Resembles a White-breasted Nuthatch above, but middle rectrices bluish gray like back, the remainder black with a white bar near tips; a conspicuous black stripe through the eye; underparts buffy or pale reddish.

Distribution.—Formerly resident on Guadalupe Island, off Baja California; present status uncertain.

PYGMY NUTHATCH. *Sitta pygmaea* (Illus. p. 390).—$3\frac{3}{4}$–$4\frac{1}{4}$. Crown and superciliary area grayish brown, the upperparts otherwise mainly bluish gray; nape often with a grayish patch; middle rectrices concolor with back,

PYGMY NUTHATCH

the remainder black, the outermost with white near tips; underparts whitish, faintly tinged with buff; bill rather short.

Distribution.—Mountains of northern Baja California, northern and western Mexico south in the highlands to Morelos and Puebla.

Races.—*S. p. leuconucha* (Sierra Juárez and Sierra San Pedro Mártir, northern Baja California). *S. p. melanotis* (northern Sonora). *S. p. chihuahuae* (eastern Sonora and Chihuahua). *S. p. flavinucha* (southern portion of the central plateau).

Remarks.—The only *brown-capped* nuthatch. Highland pine forests, where rather common and sometimes found in small companies. Its call is quite unlike that of a White-breasted Nuthatch, the only other "upside-down bird" on the mainland.

Family CERTHIIDAE. Creepers

BROWN CREEPER. *Certhia familiaris* (Illus. p. 391).—5–5½. Above dark brown, the crown and back finely streaked with white, the wings spotted with white and tawny; below wholly white or faintly tinged with buff; bill black, very slender, and somewhat decurved; tail rather long, the rectrices pointed and stiffened terminally.

Distribution.—Higher mountains generally (exclusive of Baja California), chiefly in coniferous forests.

BROWN CREEPER

Races.—*C. f. albescens* (Sonora, Chihuahua, and Tamaulipas south to northern Jalisco). *C. f. jaliscensis* (high mountains of southern Jalisco). *C. f. guerrerensis* (Sierra Madre del Sur, Guerrero). *C. f. alticola* (Michoacán Hidalgo, and Veracruz southward at high altitudes).

Remarks.—Brown Creepers are much smaller than most Dendrocolaptids (woodcreepers) and will be known by their *boldly streaked* upperparts and very *slender, decurved bills*. Their tails are somewhat stiffened, but not spine-tipped. Essentially solitary, and usually found scouting the bark of tree-trunks for food.

Family CHAMAEIDAE. Wrentits

WRENTIT. *Chamaea fasciata canicauda* (Illus. p. 392).—6–6½. Above slaty gray, darkening on the tail, this disproportionately long and notably graduated; below pale cinnamon-buff, the median abdomen whitish; throat and breast vaguely streaked; iris white; bill and legs black.

Distribution.—Northwestern Baja California south to latitude 30°.

WRENTIT

Remarks.—Wrentits, adept at skulking in low bushes and under-brush, are much more likely to be heard than seen. Their usual song, a series of staccato notes ending in a trill without change of pitch, is delivered in a loud ringing voice. With persistence, one may see the shy songster, a drab, sparrow-sized bird with *white* eyes and a *long, up-tilted tail*. Some Bushtits are very similar, even to the pale eye, but all are readily distinguished by their smaller size and conspicuously gregarious habits.

Family CINCLIDAE. Dippers

NORTH AMERICAN DIPPER. *Cinclus mexicanus mexicanus* (Illus. p. 393).—6½–7. *Summer:* Head and neck dull brown, darkest on the crown; plumage otherwise slate-colored, darkest on wings and tail; bill black; legs yellowish. *Winter:* As in summer, but feathers of wings and tail often white-tipped, and underparts obscurely barred with white; bill brownish.

Distribution.—Mountains of Chihuahua south in the highlands to Veracruz and Oaxaca.

NORTH AMERICAN DIPPER

Remarks.—Dippers are restricted to the immediate vicinity of mountain streams and are not likely to be found below an altitude of about 4,500 feet. They are quite at home in the water, entering readily to feed among the rocks at the bottom. On land they bob and "teeter" in the manner of Spotted Sandpipers. The nest—a bulky, domed structure of moss, with the entrance at one side—is usually placed on a rock ledge just above the water.

Family TROGLODYTIDAE. Wrens

KEY TO THE SPECIES

1a. Underparts more or less conspicuously spotted, streaked, or barred   2

  b. Underparts not spotted, streaked, or barred 9

2a. Markings below limited to the throat, breast, and upper abdomen   3

  b. Not as in 2a. 5

3a. More than 7 inches; upperparts conspicuously barred

                                     Band-backed Wren, p. 397

  b. Less than 6 inches; upperparts not barred   4

4a. Throat, breast, and upper abdomen *boldly* spotted
Spot-breasted Wren, p. 404

b. Throat and breast *lightly* spotted or streaked　. . Rock Wren, p. 409

5a. Upperparts conspicuously spotted, streaked, or barred 6

b. Crown and back uniform brown . . . . . . 　Banded Wren, p. 402

6a. Spots and bars of the underparts gray; not sharply defined
Gray-barred Wren, p. 397

b. Spots and bars of the underparts black 7

7a. Crown black; underparts sparsely spotted and barred
Rufous-naped Wren (adult), p. 398

b. Crown dark brown; underparts profusely spotted, streaked, or barred 8

8a. Chin and throat unmarked; a conspicuous black malar streak
Spotted Wren, p. 401

b. Chin (usually) and throat profusely spotted . . 　Cactus Wren, p. 399

9a. Sides of head and neck streaked or spotted, the markings sometimes obscure　. 10

b. Sides of head and neck not streaked or spotted　. 14

10a. Tail notably short; upperparts deep reddish brown 11

b. Tail not notably short; upperparts brown, cinnamon, or bright rufous 12

11a. Throat and breast essentially white; not streaked
White-breasted Wood-Wren (adult), p. 408

b. Throat and breast dusky gray; obscurely streaked
Gray-breasted Wood-Wren, p. 408

12a. Below tawny buff; sides of head boldly streaked
Happy Wren, p. 403

b. Below white; sides of head lightly streaked; under tail-coverts barred 13

13a. Brown above . . . . Bar-vented Wren, p. 402

b. Bright rufous above . . . . Rufous-and-White Wren, p. 402

14a. Upper back black, conspicuously streaked with white 15

b. Upper back not black, not white-streaked　. 16

15a. Crown obscurely spotted or streaked; crissum buffy
Sedge Wren, p. 396

b. Crown not spotted or streaked; crissum whitish
Marsh Wren, p. 397

16a. Crown black or chestnut, not concolor with back　. 17

b. Crown not black, but virtually concolor with back 20

17a. Crown and hind-neck chestnut; back spotted or barred

 b. Crown black . . . .

18a. Back uniform chestnut or cinnamon-rufous . .

 b. Back conspicuously streaked or spotted . . . .

19a. Back streaked with black; superciliaries buffy

 b. Back spotted with cinnamon; superciliaries whitish

20a. Throat and chest white, the breast and abdomen deep chestnut

 b. Underparts without deep chestnut or sharply contrasting colors

21a. Above and below mainly dusky, dark brown, or dark reddish brown

 b. Below white, grayish, buffy, or cinnamon, this distinctly lighter
   than the upperparts . . . .

22a. Tail notably short; throat whitish or dusky

 b. Tail not notably short; throat pale brown

23a. Superciliaries white, and usually very conspicuous . . . .

 b. Superciliaries sometimes pale buff or cinnamon, never white . .

24a. Underparts mainly buffy or tawny ochraceous . . . .

 b. Underparts not essentially buffy or ochraceous . . . .

25a. Superciliaries very conspicuous; tail without white

 b. Superciliaries rather obscure; tail white-tipped (Socorro Island)

26a. Below pale grayish, the flanks often tinged with buff; tail rather
   long and rounded, the lateral feathers white-tipped

 b. Below extensively white; flanks and sometimes abdomen pale
   brown or chestnut . . . .

27a. Outer rectrices barred and tipped with white

 b. Tail not white-tipped and without white bars . . . .

28a. Less than 4 inches. Tail rather short; flanks brownish

 b. More than 5 inches. Tail moderately long; flanks and crissum
   cinnamon or chestnut . . . .

29*a*. Flanks and lower abdomen conspicuously barred 30
   b. Flanks and lower abdomen not conspicuously barred
                                 House-Wren (spp.), pp. 405–6
30*a*. Throat and breast rich ochraceous buff, this contrasting with the
     abdomen . . . . Rufous-browed Wren, p. 407
   b. Below pale buff or cinnamon . . . . Brown-throated Wren, p. 407

SEDGE WREN. *Cistothorus platensis* (Illus. p. 396).—3¾–4¼. Crown sooty brown, finely streaked with buff, the back and scapulars black, liberally streaked with white; rump and upper tail-coverts cinnamon; wings and tail barred with buff or cinnamon; below whitish, the breast, flanks, and under tail-coverts tinged with pale buffy brown.

SEDGE WREN

Distribution.—Southern Mexico, locally, in grassy swamps and wet meadows.

Races.—*C. p. tinnulus* (western Michoacán). *C. p. elegans* (Veracruz and Chiapas).

Remarks.—Also known as Short-billed Marsh Wren. This species and the following are distinguished by their small size and black, *white-streaked* backs. Sedge Wrens have streaked (or spotted) crowns, and lack conspicuous superciliaries. Both frequent tangles of sedge and grass, especially in or near marshes, and are notably adept at avoiding observation.

*MARSH WREN. *Telmatodytes palustris.*—$4\frac{1}{2}$–$5\frac{1}{4}$. Similar to a Sedge Wren but crown unstreaked and superciliaries conspicuous; underparts tinged with brown, the crissum usually whitish.

Distribution.—Winters in Baja California and northern Mexico south to Jalisco, Zacatecas, and Veracruz.

Races.—*T. p. paludicola* (Baja California and northwestern Sonora). *T. p. aestuarinus* (Baja California and Sonora, possibly breeding locally). *T. p. plesius* (Baja California and south to Sinaloa and Tamaulipas). *T. p. dissaëptus* (northern Mexico south to Jalisco, Zacatecas, and Veracruz).

Remarks.—Also known as Long-billed Marsh Wren. *See* Sedge Wren.

GRAY-BARRED WREN. *Campylorhynchus megalopterus.*—$6\frac{1}{2}$–$7\frac{3}{4}$. *Adult:* Crown grayish brown, finely spotted or streaked with black, the hind-neck broadly streaked with black and white; back, wings, and tail liberally barred, the darker portions appearing dull at a distance; below dull whitish, this sometimes tinged with buff posteriorly; throat and breast profusely spotted with black or grayish brown, the flanks and abdomen heavily barred with same. *Immature:* Crown black, the upperparts otherwise dark brown, streaked and barred with buff; superciliaries buff or tawny, and quite prominent; below buffy white, obscurely barred with grayish brown posteriorly.

Distribution.—Southern portion of the Mexican plateau. ENDEMIC.

Races.—*C. m. megalopterus* (Michoacán, Morelos, and Mexico). *C. m. nelsoni* (Oaxaca and Veracruz).

Remarks.—Also known as Gray Cactus Wren and Gray Wren. In this form the streaks, spots, and bars are more profuse and much less distinct (grayer) than in related wrens. It also differs from most similar wrens in having little or no buff or reddish on the underparts.

BAND-BACKED WREN. *Campylorhynchus zonatus* (Illus. p. 398).— 7–$7\frac{3}{4}$. Very similar to a Gray-barred Wren above, but with much darker and more distinct bars and streaks, and the pale areas buff rather than white; rump and tail (above) buffy cinnamon; throat and breast white, profusely spotted with black, the posterior underparts bright cinnamon or rich buff, and virtually immaculate.

Distribution.—Oaxaca, Puebla, and Veracruz southward, occurring principally in pinelands 3,000–7,000 feet above sea-level.

Races.—*C. z. zonatus* (Puebla and Veracruz). *C. z. restrictus* (Tabasco and Campeche). *C. z. impudens* (isthmus of Tehuantepec, Oaxaca). *C. z. vulcanus* (Chiapas).

Remarks.—Also known as Banded Wren. The *brightly colored, immaculate belly* and flanks distinguish this common species from other barred and spotted wrens. *See* Cactus Wren.

BAND-BACKED WREN

RUFOUS-NAPED WREN. *Campylorhynchus rufinucha.*—5½–6. Crown black, or the feathers chestnut with black centers; nape and hind-neck chestnut or cinnamon-rufous; superciliaries buff or whitish; a black or brown postocular stripe; back and scapulars dull chestnut, this either streaked with black and whitish, or brown-spotted; wings and tail black or brown, evenly barred with buff or grayish; below usually immaculate whitish, the breast sometimes finely dotted, and the flanks moderately barred with dark brown.

Distribution.—Arid portions of southern Mexico, exclusive of the Yucatán Peninsula.

Races.—*C. r. rufinucha* (Veracruz and northern Oaxaca). *C. r. humilis* (southwestern Mexico, from Colima south to southern Oaxaca). *C. r. nigricaudatus* (arid lowlands of southern Chiapas).

Remarks.—Smallest of its genus. A useful field character is the conspicuously *reddish* coloring of the nape and hind-neck. The spots and bars of the underparts (when present) are never very prominent. *See* Giant Wren.

GIANT WREN. *Campylorhynchus chiapensis* (Illus. p. 399).—7½–8. Crown, nape, and postocular streak black; back, rump, and scapulars uniform chestnut or dark cinnamon-rufous; wings dark brown, with numerous buff or pale chestnut bars; tail mainly black, but tipped with white or dusky, and sometimes obscurely barred with buff; outer webs of the outer rectrices white-barred; superciliaries and underparts uniformly white, the lower abdomen and under tail-coverts sometimes faintly tinged with buff.

GIANT WREN

Distribution.—Humid lowland forests of southern Chiapas.

Remarks.—Also known as Chiapas Wren. No other Mexican wren has both the clear whitish underparts and *uniform rich chestnut* back and scapulars of this species. Common locally in wooded areas of low elevation. *See* Rufous-naped Wren.

CACTUS WREN. *Campylorhynchus brunneicapillus* (Illus. p. 400).— 7–8. *Adult:* Crown and hind-neck dark brown or grayish brown; back and scapulars similar to crown, but usually paler and grayer, and either narrowly streaked with white and black or more or less white-spotted; wings spotted and barred with white, gray, or buff; lateral rectrices black, spotted and barred with whitish, and usually with a white subterminal band; below grayish or pale buff, the posterior underparts sometimes rich buff, the whole liberally spotted with black, the flanks and under tail-coverts sometimes black-barred. *Immature:* Similar to adult, but smaller and paler, the upperparts vaguely spotted (not streaked), the spots below usually minute.

Distribution.—Dry lowlands and foothills (chiefly) south to Jalisco, Hidalgo, and Mexico; also the Yucatán Peninsula.

Races.—*C. b. couesi* (northern Baja California and Sonora eastward to Tamaulipas). *C. b. bryanti* (Pacific slope of northwestern Baja California). *C. b. purus* (middle portion of.Baja California). *C. b. affinis* (cape district of Baja California). *C. b. seri* (Tiburón Island, Gulf of California). *C. b. brunnei-*

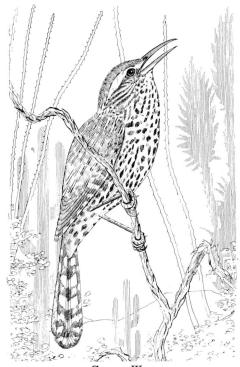

CACTUS WREN

capillus (coastal areas of southern Sonora). *C. b. guttatus* (central portion of the plateau from Durango and Tamaulipas south to Jalisco and Mexico). *C. b. yucatanensis* (Yucatán Peninsula).

Remarks.—The wren most likely to be seen in Mexico. Grayish brown above, where *narrowly streaked*, and very *profusely spotted below*. Rufous-naped and Giant Wrens are *reddish* above and have virtually *immaculate* bellies. *See* Spotted Wren.

SPOTTED WREN. *Campylorhynchus jocosus.*—6¼–7. *Adult:* Crown and nape brown or grayish brown, the superciliaries whitish or buff; a prominent black malar streak; hind-neck and upper back black, streaked and spotted with white, the lower back and scapulars variegated with buff; wings spotted or barred with buff or whitish; lateral rectrices grayish brown, usually white-tipped, and more or less barred with buff or white; below whitish, or tinged with buff posteriorly, the throat immaculate, but elsewhere liberally spotted with black. *Immature:* Crown, postocular streak, and malar streak black, the superciliaries buffy; upperparts mainly cinnamon-brown, the hind-neck and upper back black-streaked, the wings and tail barred with same; underparts immaculate, the throat whitish, this shading to buff posteriorly.

Distribution.—Northern and western Mexico south to Oaxaca, Puebla, and western Tamaulipas. ENDEMIC.

Races.—*C. j. gularis* (northern and western Mexico south to Michoacán, Querétaro, and western Tamaulipas). *C. j. jocosus* (Guerrero, Morelos, and Puebla south to Oaxaca).

Remarks.—The uniformly *brown* (not black or variegated) crown, *immaculate* whitish throat, *prominent malar stripe,* and evenly spotted underparts distinguish adults. Immature birds are quite different, but unmistakable—*wholly* whitish below, reddish brown above, and with a *contrasting black cap. See* Cactus Wren.

CAROLINA WREN. *Thryothorus ludovicianus.*—5–5½. Above dull brown or rufous, the lower back often with concealed white spots or streaks; wings and tail obscurely barred with black, the primaries notched with white; superciliaries white, this bordered above by a fine black line; a brownish postocular stripe; throat whitish, the underparts otherwise either buffy, darkening posteriorly, or mainly tawny ochraceous; flanks and crissum usually more or less barred with dusky.

Distribution.—Northern Mexico (west to eastern Chihuahua) south to San Luis Potosí.

Races.—*T. l. berlandieri* (northeastern Chihuahua, Nuevo León, and western Tamaulipas). *T. l. lomitensis* (northern Tamaulipas). *T. l. tropicalis* (Sierra Madre Oriental, San Luis Potosí).

Remarks.—No other Mexican wren with very *prominent white superciliaries* has *immaculate* buffy or tawny underparts. Ranges at least to 7,000 feet above sea-level. *See* White-browed Wren.

PLAIN WREN. *Thryothorus modestus pullus.*—5–5½. Above grayish brown, shading to russet or cinnamon on the rump and tail, the latter barred with black; superciliaries white, but less prominent than in a

Carolina Wren; a brown postocular streak; sides of head, throat, breast, and abdomen white or dusky (immature), the flanks and crissum buffy, cinnamon, or (rarely) chestnut.

Distribution.—Arid lowlands and foothills of Chiapas.

Remarks.—Much like a Bar-vented Wren, but grayer above and with an *immaculate* (reddish) *crissum.* The wings (remiges) are very obscurely, if at all, barred. *See* Rufous-and-White Wren.

BAR-VENTED WREN. *Thryothorus sinaloa.*—5–5½. Similar to a Plain Wren above, but browner (less grayish), and wings as well as tail black-barred; sides of head below the eye-stripe narrowly brown-streaked, appearing squamate at a distance; below mainly white, the *crissum barred* with black; flanks pale brownish, not buffy or cinnamon, as in a Plain Wren.

Distribution.—Lowlands and foothills of northwestern and western Mexico. ENDEMIC.

Races.—*T. s. cinereus* (Sonora, Chihuahua, and Durango). *T. s. sinaloa* (Pacific slope from Sinaloa to Jalisco). *T. s. russeus* (known only from Acahuitzotla, Guerrero).

Remarks.—Also known as Sinaloa Wren. The reddish tail, variegated cheeks, and white underparts are distinctive in combination. Open woodlands, thickets, and brush, especially along small streams. *See* Rufous-and-White Wren and Plain Wren.

RUFOUS-AND-WHITE WREN. *Thryothorus rufalbus transfinis.*—5½. Above bright rufous, the wings and tail liberally barred with black; white superciliaries; a rufous postocular stripe; cheeks dull white, vaguely streaked with dusky; underparts mainly immaculate white; flanks brownish; under tail-coverts boldly barred with black.

Distribution.—Extreme southwestern Chiapas in the vicinity of Jalapa, Escuintla.

Remarks.—Patterned like a Bar-vented Wren, but with *bright rufous upperparts.* Plain Wrens are much duller (grayish brown) above and lack bars on their under tail-coverts. This form, the northernmost representative of the species, is not likely to be mistaken for any other wren of its area.

BANDED WREN. *Thryothorus pleurostictus.*—5–5½. *Adult:* Resembles a Bar-vented Wren above, but wings and tail more distinctly barred; a conspicuous brown postocular streak; sides of neck broadly streaked with black and white; below white, the breast black-streaked, the abdomen, flanks, and crissum heavily barred with same. *Immature:* Similar to adult above, but underparts virtually immaculate, the median portion white, the sides and flanks brownish; lower throat usually faintly streaked with dusky.

Distribution.—Arid lowlands and foothills of southwestern and southern Mexico.

Races.—*T. p. pleurostictus* (Morelos and Guerrero). *T. p. oaxacae* (Oaxaca). *T. p. acaciarum* (Chiapas).

Remarks.—The very *heavily barred underparts* are distinctive. Grasslands and undergrowth. Common locally. *See* Bar-vented Wren.

WHITE-BROWED WREN. *Thryothorus albinucha albinucha.*—5–5¼. Similar to a Carolina Wren above, but tail mainly blackish, the outer feathers conspicuously barred with white; throat and crissum white, the latter barred with black; breast, flanks, and lower abdomen tinged with pale brown.

Distribution.—Yucatán and eastern Quintana Roo.

Remarks.—Also known as Cabot Wren. Much like the better-known Carolina Wren of northern and eastern Mexico, but lacking its buffy reddish underparts. Possibly a race of *ludovicianus*.

HAPPY WREN. *Thryothorus felix* (Illus. p. 403).—5–5½. Above cinnamon-brown, brightest on crown and tail, the latter usually barred; superciliaries white; sides of head very conspicuously streaked with black and

HAPPY WREN

white; a prominent black submalar streak; throat white; underparts mainly ochraceous buff, brightest on the flanks and lower abdomen; crissum distinctly barred with black.

Distribution.—Tres Marías Islands and western Mexico from southern Sonora south to Oaxaca. ENDEMIC.

Races.—*T. f. lawrencii* (María Madre Island). *T. f. magdalenae* (María Magdalena Island). *T. f. sonorae* (extreme southern Sonora). *T. f. pallidus* (Sinaloa, extreme western Durango, Nayarit, and northwestern Michoacán). *T. f. grandis* (Morelos). *T. f. felix* (Jalisco to Oaxaca).

Remarks.—The conspicuously *striped cheeks* and immaculate *white throat* are excellent field characters. No similar wren has *reddish underparts*.

SPOT-BREASTED WREN. *Thryothorus rutilus* (Illus. p. 404).—5–5½. *Adult:* Crown and hind-neck chestnut-brown, the upperparts otherwise dull olive-brown; tail usually brighter than the back and conspicuously barred with black; superciliaries, chin, and upper throat immaculate white; sides of head, lower throat, and breast to middle of abdomen white, generously streaked or minutely spotted with black; flanks and lower abdomen grayish

SPOT-BREASTED WREN

brown or dull grayish chestnut. *Immature:* Similar to adult, but anterior underparts grayish or brownish, and with smaller, less distinct spots; sides of head less conspicuously striped, and crissum without bars.

Distribution.—Lowlands of eastern and southeastern Mexico. Common.

Races.—*T. r. microstictus* (southern Tamaulipas). *T. r. maculipectus* (Veracruz, Puebla, and adjacent parts of Oaxaca). *T. r. canobrunneus* (Yucatán, Campeche, and Quintana Roo). *T. r. umbrinus* (Tabasco).

Remarks.—No other Mexican wren with *thickly spotted underparts* (lower throat, breast, and upper abdomen) is virtually *immaculate above*. Note the boldly barred tail and eye-streak.

BEWICK WREN. *Thryomanes bewickii.*—5–5½. *Adult:* Above plain brown, grayish brown, or olive-brown; wings similar, but obscurely barred; tail rather long, tipped with white or grayish, and barred with black; superciliaries white; a brown postocular streak; underparts pale gray (usually) or brownish, lightest on the throat; crissum conspicuously barred. *Immature:* Similar to adult, but breast feathers edged with dusky; crissum brownish, with few bars.

Distribution.—Cedros and Guadalupe Islands, Baja California, and Mexico generally, south to Oaxaca and southwestern Veracruz. Chiefly semiarid districts.

Races.—*T. b. charienturus* (northwestern Baja California). *T. b. cerroensis* (Cedros Island and Baja California between latitudes 25° and 30°). *T. b. atricauda* (middle portion of Baja California). *T. b. magdalensis* (coastal plain around Magdalena Bay, southwestern Baja California). *T. b. brevicauda* (formerly Guadalupe Island, Baja California; now probably extinct). *T. b. eremophilus* (northwestern Mexico south to Durango and central Zacatecas). *T. b. cryptus* (Tamaulipas and Nuevo León). *T. b. murinus* (south-central Mexico). *T. b. bairdi* (Oaxaca, southwestern Veracruz, and southern Puebla). *T. b. percnus* (Jalisco and southern Zacatecas).

Remarks.—The conspicuous *white* superciliaries and relatively *long, white-tipped tail* are the best field characters. Brown above, grayish below, and with a *barred crissum and tail.*

SOCORRO WREN. *Thryomanes sissonii.*—5–5½. Similar to a Bewick Wren, but tail shorter, and without broad white tips; superciliaries more restricted; underparts washed with ochraceous (not gray or brownish), and crissum spotted, not barred.

Distribution.—Socorro Island, Revilla Gigedo group, off western Mexico. ENDEMIC.

Remarks.—*See* Bewick Wren.

NORTHERN HOUSE-WREN. *Troglodytes aëdon.*—5. *Adult:* Upperparts, including sides of head and neck, dull brown or grayish brown, the rump usually brightest; wings and tail barred with black; below grayish, the breast and flanks darkest, and often washed with buff or brownish in winter, when usually obscurely barred; crissum whitish, barred with dusky. *Immature:* Similar to adult, but browner below, and feathers of the lower throat and breast edged with dusky.

Distribution.—Breeds in northern Baja California (San Pedro Mártir mountains). Winters extensively south to Oaxaca, Puebla, and Veracruz.

Races.—*T. a. aëdon* (winters casually in Tamaulipas). *T. a. parkmanii* (northern Baja California, wintering commonly south to Oaxaca, Puebla, and Veracruz).

Remarks.—A small, extremely active wren with no conspicuous field marks. The common resident house-wren (*T. musculus*) is similar, but has fairly *distinct buffy superciliaries* and more richly colored underparts. In this form the ground color of the crissum is *whitish*. It will not be found in summer except in northern Baja California. *See* Southern House-Wren.

CLARIÓN ISLAND WREN. *Troglodytes tanneri.*—5¼. Similar to a house-wren, but upperparts more grayish, and the bars on wings, tail, and crissum less distinct; below tinged with pale buff, not mainly grayish as in *T. aëdon.*

Distribution.—Clarión Island, Revilla Gigedo group, off western Mexico. ENDEMIC.

Remarks.—Taxonomic status uncertain, but probably a resident race of the Northern House-Wren.

SOUTHERN HOUSE-WREN. *Troglodytes musculus* (Illus. p. 406).—4¼–4¾. Above plain brown or grayish brown, the rump and upper tail-coverts sometimes chestnut-brown; superciliaries buffy; wings and tail

SOUTHERN HOUSE-WREN

more or less distinctly barred; below whitish, or tinged with dull cinnamon-buff, the crissum paler and usually prominently barred.

Distribution.—Eastern and southern Mexico; Cozumel Island, off Yucatán.

Races.—*T. m. peninsularis* (Caribbean slope from southern Tamaulipas to Yucatán). *T. m. beani* (Cozumel Island). *T. m. intermedius* (Yucatán, Oaxaca, and Chiapas).

Remarks.—This species replaces *T. aëdon*, a closely related bird, as the resident house-wren of eastern and southern Mexico. It is distinguished from the Northern House-Wren by its more richly colored underparts, *buffy* (not grayish) *crissum*, and fairly *distinct superciliaries*. Any *rufescent* house-wren probably is this species or the following. Sea-level to an altitude of about 8,000 feet. Very common.

BROWN-THROATED WREN. *Troglodytes brunneicollis.*—$4\frac{1}{4}$–5. Above plain brown, grayish brown, or chestnut-brown, the feathers of the crown often with darker centers; wings, tail, and sometimes the back distinctly barred; superciliaries buffy; below either rich cinnamon-buff, palest on the abdomen, or uniformly pale buff; throat and breast often lightly mottled, the flanks, lower abdomen, and crissum usually distinctly barred.

Distribution.—Wooded mountains (principally) of the Mexican plateau south to Oaxaca.

Races.—*T. b. cahooni* (western portion of the plateau south to Jalisco). *T. b. compositus* (Coahuila, Tamaulipas, and San Luis Potosí). *T. b. culequita* (southern Zacatecas, Hidalgo, Mexico, Tlaxcala, Morelos, and Puebla). *T. b. colimae* (Sierra Nevada de Colima, extreme southern Jalisco, south to Patzcuaro, Michoacán). *T. b. guerrerensis* (Sierra Madre del Sur, Guerrero). *T. b. brunneicollis* (Oaxaca and southern Veracruz).

Remarks.—Brown-throated Wrens resemble the most richly colored of the Southern House-Wrens (*T. m. intermedius*) but are distinguished by their *barred flanks* and considerably darker underparts. They are most abundant at high altitudes, whereas Southern House-Wrens are essential birds of the lowlands and foothills, although ranging to about 8,000 feet locally. *See* Southern House-Wren.

RUFOUS-BROWED WREN. *Troglodytes rufociliatus chiapensis.*—4. Upperparts and postocular stripe deep, rich brown, the back, wings, and tail more or less distinctly barred; superciliaries reddish buff; sides of the head, throat, and breast ochraceous-buff or tawny, the upper abdomen buffy; lower abdomen, flanks, and crissum either whitish, or pale brown heavily barred with blackish.

Distribution.—High mountains of Chiapas (San Cristobal).

Remarks.—The richly colored throat and breast and heavily barred abdomen and flanks are the best field marks. Likely to be found feeding in clumps of epiphytes some distance above the ground.

WHITE-BREASTED WOOD-WREN. *Henicorhina leucosticta prostheleuca* (Illus. p. 408).—3¾–4¼. *Adult:* Crown dark brown, the sides bordered with black; upperparts otherwise chestnut-brown, brightest on the rump; wings and tail distinctly barred, the latter notably short; upper wing-coverts usually white-tipped; superciliaries white, the postocular stripe black; sides of head and neck boldly streaked with black and white; throat white, this shading into pearl gray on the breast and upper abdomen; lower

White-breasted Wood-Wren

abdomen, flanks, and crissum russet or cinnamon. *Immature:* Similar to adult, but crown dull black; throat and breast dusky grayish; posterior underparts duller, less rufescent than in adults.

Distribution.—Puebla, Veracruz, Tabasco, Campeche, and Quintana Roo southward, chiefly in lowland forests.

Remarks.—A remarkable songster, much more likely to be heard than seen. Undergrowth of humid lowland forests. *See* Gray-breasted Wood-Wren.

GRAY-BREASTED WOOD-WREN. *Henicorhina leucophrys.*—3½–4. Similar to a White-breasted Wood-Wren, but upperparts dark reddish brown, the crown sometimes sooty gray; wings and tail inconspicuously barred; throat whitish, shading to dusky gray on the breast and upper abdomen, where often lightly scalloped; flanks, lower abdomen, and crissum dull russet or ochraceous buff.

Distribution.—Humid mountain forests from Michoacán and Veracruz southward.

Races.—*H. l. festiva* (Michoacán and Guerrero). *H. l. mexicana* (Puebla, Veracruz, and northern Oaxaca). *H. l. capitalis* (Pacific slope of Chiapas).

Remarks.—Also known as White-browed Wood-Wren. This woodwren replaces the White-breasted in the southern highlands. Both inhabit rank forest undergrowth and are very furtive, although quite vocal. A *stubby* tail and *dusky breast* are combined in no other Mexican wren. Note the *white* (not buffy) *superciliaries. See* White-breasted Wood-Wren.

WHITE-BELLIED WREN. *Uropsila leucogastra.*—$3\frac{1}{2}$–4. Above grayish brown; wings and tail obscurely barred, the latter rather short; a grayish brown postocular stripe; superciliaries, sides of head, and underparts white, the sides and flanks tinged with pale brown or buff; crissum white or buffy, this sometimes barred with dusky.

Distribution.—Wooded portions of central, eastern, and southern Mexico.

Races.—*U. l. pacificus* (Colima and Guerrero). *U. l. grisescens* (San Luis Potosí). *U. l. leucogastra* (Tamaulipas south to northern Oaxaca). *U. l. musicus* (Tabasco and northern Chiapas). *U. l. brachyurus* (Yucatán Peninsula).

Remarks.—A small, pale wren with no striking plumage pattern, but distinguished by its rather *short tail* and virtually *all-white* underparts. Wood-wrens have much *stubbier* tails and contrasting colors below. Common locally, in thickets and second-growth timber. The clear, sweet song has surprising volume for so small a bird.

ROCK WREN. *Salpinctes obsoletus* (Illus. p. 410).—5–$5\frac{3}{4}$. Above mainly pale grayish brown, minutely streaked and speckled with black and white, the rump cinnamon or pale chestnut; upper tail-coverts and tail obscurely barred, the lateral rectrices with a conspicuous subterminal black band; below whitish, the flanks and lower abdomen tinged with buff; throat and breast minutely streaked or speckled with brown, the crissum often heavily barred; bill long, slender, and slightly curved.

Distribution.—Guadalupe, San Benedicto, and San Benito Islands, Baja California, and the arid parts of Mexico generally.

Races.—*S. o. guadeloupensis* (Guadalupe Island, off Baja California). *S. o. tenuirostris* (San Benito Islands, off Baja California). *S. o. exsul* (San

Benedicto Island, Revilla Gigedo group). *S. o. obsoletus* (northern and western Mexico south to Zacatecas and San Luis Potosí). *S. o. notius* (southern portion of the Mexican plateau). *S. o. sollicitus* (Chiapas).

Remarks.—Rock Wrens prefer arid, barren regions and are most abundant in the highlands. No other *pale*, open-country wren has lightly *speckled plumage*.

ROCK WREN

CAÑON WREN. *Catherpes mexicanus* (Illus. p. 411).—$5\frac{1}{4}$–$5\frac{3}{4}$. Above grayish brown or deep sepia brown, shading to chestnut on the rump; crown and back obscurely barred with black, and minutely dotted with white or buff; wings dark brown, the outer webs barred with chestnut; tail chestnut or cinnamon-rufous, this distinctly barred with black; throat and upper breast immaculate white, the underparts otherwise deep chestnut, minutely spotted with black and white; bill long, slender, and virtually straight.

Distribution.—Baja California, northern and western Mexico south to Oaxaca.

Races.—*C. m. conspersus* (Baja California and Sonora). *C. m. meliphonus* (Sonora and Chihuahua). *C. m. albifrons* (Coahuila and Nuevo León south to Aguascalientes). *C. m. mexicanus* (central and southern portion of the Mexican plateau).

Remarks.—This distinctive wren will be known by its immaculate *white* throat and breast and *contrasting chestnut abdomen*. It frequents steep mountainsides and rocky canyons, a preference reflected by its vernacular name. Its characteristic song, a series of liquid musical notes, is unmistakable.

CAÑON WREN

SLENDER-BILLED WREN. *Hylorchilus sumichrasti.*—5½–6. Above rich brown or sooty; throat pale brown, shading through tawny brown to sooty, the abdomen sparsely dotted with white; tail moderately long, but less than twice the length of the bill; bill long, slender, and almost straight.

Distribution.—Lowland forests of Veracruz (Mato Bejuco, Motzorongo, Presidio). ENDEMIC.

Remarks.—Also known as Sumichrast Wren. While suggesting a Cañon Wren, this species is more drably colored, and lacks a white throat and contrasting abdomen. Heavily wooded canyons, usually among rocks and undergrowth. Apparently rare and decidedly local.

NIGHTINGALE WREN. *Microcerculus philomela philomela.*—3¾–4¼. *Adult:* Above dark rufescent brown, the remiges and tail black; chin and throat white, shading to gray on the breast and abdomen; sides, flanks, and under tail-coverts rich rufescent brown. *Immature:* Similar to adult, but darker and less rufescent above, the feathers of the crown and back obscurely edged with black; below darker and duskier, with little gray and no white, the feathers distinctly edged, and squamate in appearance.

Distribution.—Recorded in recent years from Ocosingo, Chiapas, and probably occurring elsewhere southward in humid forests at moderate elevations.

Remarks.—A small, dark forest wren with a notably short tail. Its song has many high notes and is remarkably melodious. Nightingale Wrens frequent dense forest undergrowth and are usually overlooked except when singing. *See* Wood-Wren.

Family MIMIDAE. Thrashers, Mockingbirds

KEY TO THE SPECIES

1*a*. Underparts spotted or mottled 2

  b. Underparts not spotted or mottled 8

2*a*. Spots dark brown or black; conspicuous 3

  b. Spots pale brown, often indistinct; underparts sometimes obscurely mottled 7

3*a*. Bill rather short, thrushlike; plumage above grayish brown
Sage Thrasher, p. 420
Socorro Thrasher, p. 419

  b. Bill long, distinctly curved; plumage above brown or rufescent . 4

4*a*. Outer rectrices usually white-tipped; posterior underparts distinctly buffy 5

  b. Outer rectrices not white-tipped; underparts whitish, with little or no buff 6

5*a*. If in Baja California . . . . Gray Thrasher, p. 414

  b. If in south-central Mexico . . . . . . Ocellated Thrasher, p. 414

6*a*. More than 10 inches; upperparts brown or dull cinnamon-rufous
Long-billed Thrasher, p. 413

  b. Less than 10 inches; upperparts bright cinnamon-rufous
Cozumel Thrasher, p. 414

7*a*. Spots small; upperparts pale brownish . . Bendire Thrasher, p. 414

  b. Spots large, or underparts mottled; plumage above brownish gray
Curve-billed Thrasher, p. 415

8*a*. Bill conspicuously long and curved; plumage above brown or grayish brown 9

  b. Bill not conspicuously long and curved; plumage above not brown or grayish brown 11

9*a*. Upperparts dark brown, with little gray 10

  b. Upperparts very pale grayish brown, the tail darker
Desert Thrasher, p. 416

LONG-BILLED THRASHER. *Toxostoma longirostre* (Illus. p. 413).—
10–11. Above dull cinnamon-rufous, the forehead (sometimes) and sides
of the head grayish; wings conspicuously barred; below whitish or pale

LONG-BILLED THRASHER

buffy white, the breast, sides, and flanks boldly streaked and spotted with
black; tail decidedly long, the feathers graduated and sometimes buff-tipped;
bill rather long and slender and moderately curved.

Distribution.—Lowlands and foothills of eastern Mexico south to
Puebla and Veracruz.

Races.—*T. l. sennetti* (northeastern Mexico south to central Nuevo
León and San Luis Potosí). *T. l. longirostre* (states of Querétaro, Veracruz,
Mexico, and Puebla).

Remarks.—Much like a Brown Thrasher (*T. rufum*), but less reddish above, and with *black* (not brown) *streaks*. Reports of Brown Thrashers in northeastern Mexico (winter) need confirmation. Ocellated Thrashers are also black-streaked but have *white-tipped* tails and much duller upperparts. Curve-billed Thrashers are much paler above, and *lightly spotted* (not boldly streaked) *below*, especially on the breast.

COZUMEL THRASHER. *Toxostoma guttatum.*—9–10. Similar to a Long-billed Thrasher, but smaller, bill *black* and less gray on sides of head.

Distribution.—Cozumel Island, off Quintana Roo. ENDEMIC.

Remarks.—Thrushes lack a thrasher's *slender* bill and *long graduated tail*. No other streaked or spotted mimid occurs on Cozumel Island. *See* Long-billed Thrasher.

OCELLATED THRASHER. *Toxostoma ocellatum.*—$10\frac{1}{2}$–$11\frac{1}{2}$. Above deep olive-brown, the lateral rectrices white-tipped and usually with a dusky subterminal bar; two indistinct wing-bars; superciliaries white or buffy, but usually obscure; below whitish, shading to dull buff posteriorly, the breast, sides, and flanks boldly spotted with black; bill dusky above, paler below, rather long and distinctly curved.

Distribution.—South-central Mexico, in the states of Puebla, Mexico, and Oaxaca. ENDEMIC.

Remarks.—A very dark, *brown-backed* thrasher with a *white-tipped tail*. *See* Long-billed Thrasher.

GRAY THRASHER. *Toxostoma cinereum.*—9–10. Above dark grayish brown, the rump usually brightest; sides of head dull whitish or buffy, this more or less streaked; two indistinct wing-bars; lateral rectrices usually with pale tips, but these often obscure; below whitish, or tinged with buff, the breast, sides, and flanks marked with black *triangular* spots; bill rather long and distinctly curved.

Distribution.—Baja California. ENDEMIC.

Races.—*T. c. mearnsi* (Pacific slope of northern Baja California). *T. c. cinereum* (Baja California south of latitude 28°).

Remarks.—Also known as Ash-colored Thrasher. No other *long-billed* thrasher of Baja California has conspicuous *black* spots. The Sage Thrasher, a winter visitor, is thrushlike in length of bill and tail.

BENDIRE THRASHER. *Toxostoma bendirei.*—9–10. Above pale grayish brown; two indistinct wing-bars; outer rectrices with pale tips; below pale buffy white, shading to brownish buff posteriorly; sides of throat, breast, and sides liberally marked with faint grayish brown spots; iris yellow; bill rather short and slightly curved.

Distribution.—Sonora, wintering to Tiburón Island and northern Sinaloa.

Races.—*T. b. bendirei* (northern Sonora, wintering south in deserts to northern Sinaloa). *T. b. candidum* (vicinity of Guaymas, Sonora; uncommon). *T. b. rubricatum* (southeastern Sonora; in winter northward to Tiburón Island).

Remarks.—Much like a Curved-billed Thrasher in paleness of spotting, but with a *shorter, straighter bill.* The song is a continuous musical warble without the phrasing of other thrashers.

CURVE-BILLED THRASHER. *Toxostoma curvirostre* (Illus. p. 415).—9½–11. Above brownish gray, the lateral rectrices white-tipped; two pale wing-bars; below whitish, usually more or less tinged with buff, the breast, upper abdomen, sides, and flanks mottled or faintly spotted with brownish gray; iris pale orange; bill long, slender, and decidedly curved.

CURVE-BILLED THRASHER

Distribution.—Islands of the Gulf of California and arid portions of the mainland south to Oaxaca, Puebla, and Veracruz.

Races.—*T. c. insularum* (San Estebán Island [formerly] and Tiburón Island, Gulf of California). *T. c. palmeri* (northern Sonora and northern Chihuahua). *T. c. maculatum* (southern Sonora, southwestern Chihuahua, and northern Sinaloa). *T. c. occidentale* (Sinaloa, Durango, and Nayarit). *T. c. oberholseri* (northeastern Mexico). *T. c. celsum* (central plateau, east of the Sierra Madre Occidental, south to northwestern Guanajuato and extreme northeastern Jalisco). *T. c. curvirostre* (arid lowlands of southern Mexico south to Oaxaca, Puebla, and Veracruz).

Remarks.—With the exception of the Bendire Thrasher, this is the only Mexican species with a *dimly spotted or mottled* breast. Where both occur together, note the length and shape of the bill—long and curved in this species; straight and almost thrushlike in the Bendire. Long-billed Thrashers are darker above and have *boldly streaked* underparts.

CALIFORNIA THRASHER. *Toxostoma redivivum redivivum.*—11–11½. Above dark grayish brown; inconspicuous grayish superciliaries; no wingbars; sides of head dark brown, finely streaked with buff; chin and upper throat buffy white; lower throat, breast, and sides pale grayish brown, the abdomen bright buff, crissum cinnamon; iris brown (adult) or whitish (immature); bill decidedly long, slender, and curved.

Distribution.—Baja California south of latitude 30° N.

Remarks.—Three unspotted thrashers with long, curved bills occur in Baja California. This species will be known by its *bright* cinnamon-buff abdomen and *pale superciliaries.* Crissal Thrashers are much darker (browner) below, and have *chestnut* under tail-coverts. Desert Thrashers are very pale above, with dark tails. Crissal and Desert Thrashers lack pale superciliary streaks.

DESERT THRASHER. *Toxostoma lecontei.*—10–10¾. Above pale grayish brown, darkening on the tail; no wing-bars; throat and median line of abdomen whitish, the breast, sides, and flanks pale buffy gray; iris dark (adult) or whitish (immature); bill long, slender, and decidedly curved.

Distribution.—Middle portion of the Pacific Coast of Baja California and drier parts of northwestern Sonora.

Races.—*T. l. arenicola* (Pacific side of Baja California between latitudes 26° and 29° N.). *T. l. lecontei* (northwestern Sonora).

Remarks.—Also known as Leconte Thrasher. A very *pale*, sickle-billed thrasher with a *dark tail.* Chiefly deserts. *See* California Thrasher and Crissal Thrasher.

CRISSAL THRASHER. *Toxostoma dorsale* (Illus. p. 417).—10½–11½. Above dull grayish brown, the tail darkest and usually obscurely tipped with buff; no wing-bars; chin and upper throat whitish, the malar streaks dusky; below much like upperparts, but paler and grayer; lower abdomen and under tail-coverts chestnut-rufous; iris dark (adult) or whitish (immature); bill notably long, slender, and curved.

Distribution.—Northern Baja California and Sonora east to Coahuila. Hidalgo locally.

Races.—*T. d. trinitatis* (Trinidad Valley, northern Baja California). *T. d. dorsale* (northeastern Baja California and Sonora east to Coahuila). *T. d. dumesum* (known from one specimen collected at Portezuelo, Hidalgo).

CRISSAL THRASHER

Remarks.—Darkest of the three unspotted, sickle-billed thrashers. No similar bird has *chestnut under tail-coverts. See* California Thrasher and Desert Thrasher.

BLUE MOCKINGBIRD. *Melanotis caerulescens* (Illus. p. 418).—9½–10½. *Adult:* Either mainly dull grayish blue (or bluish slate), becoming duskier on the lower belly, or grayish blue above, the throat, breast, and abdomen immaculate white (*hypoleucus*). Sides of head black or dusky in both plumages. If wholly bluish, the crown, throat, and breast lightly streaked. Bill moderately long and sturdy, the ridge slightly cruved. *Immature:* Essentially blackish, the upperparts lightly tinged with blue.

Distribution.—Tres Marías Islands, off the Pacific Coast; widespread on the mainland, chiefly below an altitude of 5,000 feet.

Races.—*M. c. longirostris* (Tres Marías Islands). *M. c. effuticius* (western Mexico from Sonora and Chihuahua south to Guerrero). *M. c. caerulescens*

(Veracruz, Mexico, Morelos, Puebla, and Oaxaca). *M. c. hypoleucus* (a white-bellied Central American form reported only at Ocosingo, Chiapas).

Remarks.—Blue Mockingbirds are notable songsters and often mimic other birds. They frequent thickets and second-growth woods and are quite common locally. No other Mexican thrasher-like bird is wholly or largely blue. The southern race (*hypoleucus*) is considered a

BLUE MOCKINGBIRD

distinct species by some authorities and is known as Blue-and-White Mockingbird.

BLACK CATBIRD. *Melanoptila glabrirostris.*—8. Wholly glossy blue-black; bill rather slender and thrushlike.

Distribution.—Cozumel Island, coastal Yucatán, and probably coastal Quintana Roo.

Remarks.—Thickets, brush, and forest edge. Similar to a Common Catbird in size, form, and actions, but *uniform glossy black.*

SOCORRO THRASHER. *Mimodes graysoni.*—10–11. *Adult:* Above grayish brown, the wings, wing-coverts, and rectrices with indistinct pale edgings; lores dusky; auriculars vaguely streaked with brown and whitish; a dusky submalar streak; below dingy whitish, the sides, flanks, and crissum streaked with grayish brown; bill shorter than head and rather stout. *Immature:* Similar, but brighter above, and wings with two buffy bars; chest vaguely spotted with grayish brown.

Distribution.—Socorro Island, Revilla Gigedo group, off the Pacific Coast. ENDEMIC.

Remarks.—The rather *short, heavy bill* suggests a thrush more than a thrasher. Liberally *streaked below,* and with two pale wing-bars. No similar bird is likely to be found on Socorro Island.

*COMMON CATBIRD. *Dumetella carolinensis carolinensis.*—7½–8. Mainly dull slate gray, lightest below, the crown and tail dull black; chestnut under tail-coverts.

Distribution.—Winters in eastern and southern Mexico, including the Yucatán Peninsula.

COMMON MOCKINGBIRD. *Mimus polyglottos leucopterus.*—8½–9¾. Above mainly brownish gray, the middle rectrices blackish; pale superciliaries; two white wing-bars and a conspicuous white patch at base of primaries; tail long and slender, the lateral feathers notably graduated and mainly white; below whitish, the breast more or less tinged with gray; bill rather short, the ridge curved.

Distribution.—Baja California and Mexico generally, south to Oaxaca and Veracruz. Also Tres Marías and Santa Barbara Islands, off the Pacific Coast. Accidental on Guadalupe Island.

Remarks.—This mockingbird occurs commonly both at sea-level and on the plateau. Its white wing- and tail-patches are especially conspicuous in flight. Tropical Mockingbirds of southeastern Mexico show much less white at all times.

TROPICAL MOCKINGBIRD. *Mimus gilvus.*—9–10. Similar to a Common Mockingbird, but grayer above and with much less white on the wings and tail. Wings and middle rectrices essentially black; wing-coverts usually white-tipped, but base of flight feathers without a white patch; outer rectrices with broad white tips, the outermost wholly white on the outer web.

Distribution.—Oaxaca and southern Veracruz southward, from sea-level to an altitude of about 5,000 feet.

Races.—*M. g. gracilis* (southern Veracruz south through Oaxaca and Chiapas). *M. g. clarus* (Tabasco, Yucatán Peninsula, and adjacent islands).

Remarks.—Also known as Graceful Mockingbird. The representative mockingbird of extreme southern Mexico. While much like a Common Mockingbird in habits and general appearance, it lacks a white wing-patch. The lateral rectrices are broadly *white-tipped*, not wholly white on the inner webs, as with *polyglottos*.

*SAGE THRASHER. *Oreoscoptes montanus.*—8. Above pale grayish brown, the head and back lightly streaked with darker; whitish superciliaries; two pale wing-bars; tail rather short, the lateral feathers white-tipped; below buffy white, more or less liberally marked with brownish streaks and triangular spots; bill rather short and thrushlike.

Distribution.—Winters in Baja California, Chihuahua, and Tamaulipas. Casual on Guadalupe Island.

Remarks.—The thrushlike bill and rather *short, white-tipped tail* are good field marks. Thrushes with spots or streaks lack wing-bars and white tail-tips. Other spotted thrashers have much longer bills and tails.

Family TURDIDAE. Thrushes

7a. Back and wings mainly olive-brown or russet

> Brown-backed Solitaire, p. 426

b. Upperparts uniform 8

8a. Slate gray above . . . . Slate-colored Solitaire, p. 427

b. Brownish gray above . . . . Townsend Solitaire, p. 426

9a. Wholly black or dark olive-brown . . . . . . Black Robin, p. 425

b. Not as in 9a. 10

10a. Underparts uniform ochraceous buff; throat obscurely streaked

> Clay-colored Robin, p. 424

b. Not as in 10a. 11

11a. A distinct chestnut or buffy nuchal collar

> Rufous-collared Robin, p. 422

b. No nuchal collar 12

12a. Underparts mainly pale buff, cinnamon-rufous, or tawny ochraceous 13

b. Not as in 12a. 14

13a. Head black, or crown and back concolor . American Robin, p. 422

b. Head not black; crown and back not concolor

> Rufous-backed Robin, p. 423

14a. More than 9 inches long 15

b. Less than 8 inches long 16

15a. Throat and abdomen white, the former boldly streaked

> White-throated Robin, p. 424

b. Without white below; throat very obscurely streaked

> Black-billed Robin, p. 425

16a. Sides of throat and breast distinctly spotted or streaked 17

b. Underparts not spotted; throat sometimes vaguely streaked . . . 21

17a. Upperparts bright russet or cinnamon-brown 18

b. Upperparts not russet or cinnamon-brown 19

18a. Breast, sides, and flanks liberally spotted with black

> Wood Thrush, p. 428

b. Sides of throat and chest (only) lightly spotted or streaked

> Veery, p. 429

19a. Tail cinnamon-brown or rufous, not concolor with back

> Hermit Thrush, p. 428

b. Upperparts virtually uniform 20

AMERICAN ROBIN. *Turdus migratorius.*—9–10. *Male (summer)*:
Crown and sides of head either black, unlike back, or pale grayish brown;
eye-ring and spot before eye white, or with a white eye-ring and conspicuous
superciliaries; back variable: either dark gray (unlike head), shading to
blackish on wings and tail, or pale grayish brown, like head; outer rectrices
sometimes white-tipped; throat white, streaked with black or brown;
underparts mainly cinnamon-rufous or pale buff, the lower abdomen and
crissum white; bill yellow; *(winter)*: As in summer, but tinged with olive
above and underparts paler, the feathers usually white-tipped; bill dusky.
Female: Similar to male, but paler and duller. *Immature:* Similar to female,
but browner above and paler below, the underparts liberally spotted.

   Distribution.—Common resident. Especially abundant and widespread in migration and winter.

   Races.—*T. m. confinis* (cape district of Baja California). **T. m. migratorius* (winters in Nuevo León). *T. m. propinquus* (south to Oaxaca and
[?] Veracruz; winters through Chiapas). *T. m. phillipsi* (southern Tamaulipas
and mountains of Veracruz). *T. m. permixtus* (mountains of Guerrero).

   Remarks.—The resident form of Baja California lacks a black head
and has very pale or white underparts. All other races are essentially
like our well-known northern birds.

   RUFOUS-COLLARED ROBIN. *Turdus rufitorques.*—9–10. *Male:*
Mainly black, the hind-neck, chest, and breast bright rufous; throat dusky,
or streaked with black and rufous; bill yellow. *Female:* Upperparts dark
brown, the collar and breast tawny or buffy cinnamon; throat streaked with
brown and white; belly buffy gray; bill yellow.

   Distribution.—Mountains of Chiapas.

Remarks.—The black-and-rufous males are unmistakable. Females usually have a suggestion of their *pattern*. They might be mistaken for Black-billed Robins, but have *yellow bills*, and are *purer brown* (less olive) *above*.

RUFOUS-BACKED ROBIN. *Turdus rufo-palliatus* (Illus. p. 423).— 9–9½. *Male:* Top of head and hind-neck gray; back, scapulars, and wing-coverts reddish brown, the upperparts otherwise brownish gray; throat white, streaked with dark brown; breast and sides tawny brown, shading to rufous on flanks; belly and crissum white; bill mainly yellow. *Female:* Similar to male, but much paler and duller. *Immature:* Above buff-streaked,

RUFOUS-BACKED ROBIN

the underparts boldly spotted with black; throat immaculate white; bill dusky.

Distribution.—Western Mexico from southern Sonora to Oaxaca; Tres Marías Islands, off the Pacific Coast. ENDEMIC.

Races.—*T. r. grisior* (southern Sonora and Sinaloa). *T. r. rufo-palliatus* (Durango south at least to Oaxaca). *T. r. graysoni* (Tres Marías Islands).

Remarks.—A reddish-backed thrush with *bright underparts*. No similar thrush has a *white throat with conspicuous streaks*.

WHITE-THROATED ROBIN. *Turdus assimilis* (Illus. p. 424).—9½.
Adult: Above bright olive, buffy olive, or deep gray tinged with olive; wings
and tail similar to back, but darker and browner; throat white, very liberally striped with deep brown or black, the whole sharply distinct from chest;
breast, sides, and flanks pale brown or grayish brown, shading to white on
belly and crissum; bill yellowish or dusky. *Immature:* Above like adult, but
more or less streaked and spotted with buff; below mainly buffy, boldly
spotted (breast) and barred (flanks) with brown.

Distribution.—Western and eastern Mexico, chiefly in wooded areas
below an altitude of 5,000 feet. Not reported in Baja California and the
Yucatán Peninsula.

W<small>HITE-THROATED</small> R<small>OBIN</small>

Races.—*T. a. calliphthongus* (southeastern Sonora and northeastern
Sinaloa on western slope of the Sierra Madre). *T. a. renominatus* (Durango
south to western Oaxaca). *T. a. assimilis* (San Luis Potosí and southern
Tamaulipas south to Puebla and Oaxaca). *T. a. leucauchen* (Chiapas).

Remarks.—The throats of some individuals are so heavily streaked
as to appear virtually black. However, even these have an immaculate
white crescent across the lower throat. Whether heavily streaked or not,
the contrast between throat and chest is a good field mark.

CLAY-COLORED ROBIN. *Turdus grayi* (Illus. p. 425).—9–9½. *Adult:*
Above buffy olive or olive-gray, darkest on wings and tail; throat pale buff,
lightly streaked with brownish olive; below tawny or cinnamon-buff, darkening on flanks; bill dull yellowish. *Immature:* Similar to adult, but darker and
richer brown (less olive) above, the wing-coverts with buff spots.

Distribution.—Eastern and southwestern Mexico from central Tamaulipas and Nuevo León southward.

Races.—*T. g. tamaulipensis* (arid coastal plains from central Tamaulipas and Nuevo León to Yucatán). *T. g. microrhynchus* (south-central San Luis Potosí). *T. g. grayi* (Guerrero, Mexico, and Veracruz southward, except where occupied by *tamaulipensis*).

Remarks.—No other Mexican robin has virtually *uniform tawny underparts*. Throat-streaks usually inconspicuous. Lowlands and foothills to an altitude of about 4,000 feet. Common in villages and cultivated country. *See* Black Robin (female).

CLAY-COLORED ROBIN

BLACK-BILLED ROBIN. *Turdus ignobilis differens.*—10. Mainly dull olive-brown, palest below, the throat faintly streaked; belly and under tail-coverts tinged with buff; bill blackish.

Distribution.—Mountains of Chiapas.

Remarks.—Mexican and Middle American birds are also known as Mountain Robins and may represent a distinct species (*plebejus*).

BLACK ROBIN. *Turdus infuscatus.*—8½–9. *Male:* Plumage wholly grayish black; bill and legs bright yellow. *Female:* Above rich olive-brown, darkest on wings and tail; throat buffy white streaked with dusky; below tawny or pale brownish gray, the median abdomen sometimes whitish; bill and legs dull yellowish.

Distribution.—Highlands of southwestern Tamaulipas, Veracruz, Oaxaca, and Chiapas.

Remarks.—Also known as Black Ouzel. No other Mexican robin is *wholly black*, or notably dark with a *yellow bill*. Females resemble Clay-colored Robins superficially, but are distinctly darker and lack any suggestion of cinnamon-buff. This robin is a mountain species; the Clay-colored is essentially a lowland bird.

*VARIED THRUSH. *Ixoreus naevius meruloides.*—8½–9½. *Male:* Above slate gray, becoming black on sides of head and tail, the latter white-tipped (outer feathers); postocular stripe; wing-bars and patches and underparts tawny cinnamon; a broad black chest-band; lower belly and crissum white. *Female:* Patterned like male, but brown above and duller below; a grayish chest-band, this often obscure.

Distribution.—Winters in northern Baja California; casual on Guadalupe Island.

Remarks.—No other thrush or thrushlike bird in Baja California has conspicuously *patterned wings*. Robin-like below, but with a *black or dusky collar*. Unmistakable.

TOWNSEND SOLITAIRE. *Myadestes townsendi calophonus.*—8. *Adult:* Above brownish gray, darkest on crown; white eye-ring; a tawny buff wing-patch; tail rather long, the outer feathers edged and tipped with white; below uniform gray; bill black, decidedly short. *Immature:* Similar to adult, but liberally spotted with white or buff.

Distribution.—Mountains of Chihuahua south to Muertocito, Durango; accidental in Baja California.

Remarks.—Solitaires have short, black bills and rather long, white-edged tails that convey an impression of trimness. All three Mexican species have white eye-rings and are wholly gray below. This species will be known by its *tawny wing-patches* and *dull grayish* (not slate or reddish brown) *upperparts*. Dense mountain forests at high altitudes. *See* Brown-backed Solitaire.

BROWN-BACKED SOLITAIRE. *Myadestes obscurus* (Illus. p. 427).— 7½–8. *Adult:* Head and underparts essentially gray, the throat and belly whitish; white eye-ring; back and scapulars olive-brown, brightening perceptibly on the wing-coverts and outer webs of the remiges; middle rectrices grayish, the lateral feathers black tipped with white; bill black, decidedly short. *Immature:* Buff-spotted above; throat, breast, and flanks buffy, barred and spotted with black.

Distribution.—Tres Marías Islands and heavily wooded mountains of the mainland.

Races.—*M. o. insularis* (Tres Marías Islands, off the Pacific Coast). *M. o. occidentalis* (Sonora and Chihuahua south to western Oaxaca). *M. o. obscurus* (Nuevo León and central Tamaulipas south to Chiapas).

Remarks.—A gray-headed solitaire with *bright olive-brown* back and wings. Widely known as "guarda-barranca." Unsurpassed as a songster, with an indescribable medley of clear, ringing notes. Heavily wooded mountains and ravines. *See* Townsend Solitaire and Slate-colored Solitaire.

BROWN-BACKED SOLITAIRE

SLATE-COLORED SOLITAIRE. *Myadestes unicolor unicolor.*—$7\frac{1}{2}$–8. Almost wholly gray, palest below; white eye-ring; obscure olive-gray wing-patches; outer rectrices pale, with white tips.

Distribution.—Wooded mountains of Veracruz and San Luis Potosí southward at high altitudes.

Remarks.—No other Mexican solitaire is distinctly *slate-gray* above. Townsend Solitaires are more or less tinged with brown and have *tawny wing-patches*. They do not range beyond the Sierra Madre Occidental.

*WOOD THRUSH. *Hylocichla mustelina.*—7–7½. Crown, hind-neck, and upper back bright cinnamon-brown or russet, shading to light olive on wings, rump, and tail; white eye-ring; sides of head lightly streaked; below essentially white, the malar area, breast, sides, and flanks very boldly spotted with black; legs yellowish.

Distribution.—Widespread in migration, wintering from Puebla southward.

Remarks.—A heavily spotted thrush with a bright reddish head and *contrasting olive back*. Likely to be confused only with other Hylocichlas, none of which has contrasting crown and back, or such conspicuous spots below.

HERMIT THRUSH. *Hylocichla guttata* (Illus. p. 428).—6. Above mainly grayish brown or dull olive-brown, the upper tail-coverts and tail bright cinnamon or russet; whitish eye-ring; throat and chest creamy buff,

HERMIT THRUSH

shading to white posteriorly, the sides of throat and breast spotted with brown; flanks lightly mottled; legs yellowish.

Distribution.—Breeds in mountains of southern Baja California. Widespread elsewhere in migration and winter.

Races.—*H. g. auduboni* (Sierra de la Laguna, cape district of Baja California; winters southward over Mexican plateau to Chiapas). **H. g. guttata* (winters in Baja California and northern Mexico). **H. g. nana* (winters in

Baja California). *H. g. slevini* (winters in Baja California and Sonora). *H. g. sequoiensis* (winters in northern Mexico).

Remarks.—The bright *reddish tail* is the hallmark of the Hermit. Wood Thrushes show contrast between head and back. All other Hylocichlas are virtually uniform above.

*SWAINSON THRUSH. *Hylocichla ustulata.*—6½–7. Above uniform olive-brown or reddish brown; eye-ring and lores pale buff; sides of head pale olive-brown; throat and breast tinged with buff, the latter boldly marked with triangular spots; abdomen white; sides and flanks pale olive-brown; legs pale brown.

Distribution.—Common winter visitant.

Races.—*H. u. ustulata* (widespread in winter). *H. u. swainsoni* (winters commonly in the south).

Remarks.—Also known as Olive-backed Thrush. Much like a Gray-cheeked Thrush, but with *buffy lores and eye-rings.* Gray-cheeks have been reported only on Cozumel Island during migration. Wood Thrushes and Hermit Thrushes have contrasting reddish heads *or* tails, and the Veery is uniformly tawny cinnamon above. *See* Gray-cheeked Thrush.

*GRAY-CHEEKED THRUSH. *Hylocichla minima aliciae.*—6½–7. Above uniform olive or grayish olive; sides of head grayish, the eye-ring inconspicuous; below mainly white, the breast more or less tinged with pale buff and boldly spotted with dusky; sides and flanks pale olive-brown; legs pale brown.

Distribution.—Casual or accidental on Cozumel Island during migration. To be expected on the adjacent coast as an occasional transient.

Remarks.—*See* Swainson Thrush.

*VEERY. *Hylocichla fuscescens.*—7. Above uniform tawny or cinnamon-brown; throat white, shading to pale buff on chest, where lightly spotted or streaked; breast, abdomen, and crissum immaculate white, the sides and flanks tinged with gray; legs pale brown.

Distribution.—Recorded only in Veracruz and Yucatán as a migrant.

Races.—*H. f. fuscescens* (Yucatán). *H. f. salicicola* (Veracruz).

Remarks.—Most lightly spotted of the Hylocichlas, and with *uniform tawny upperparts.* Gray-cheeked and Swainson Thrushes are wholly *olive-brown* above. Hermit and Wood Thrushes have *contrasting* reddish tails *or* heads.

SPOTTED NIGHTINGALE-THRUSH. *Catharus dryas ovandensis.*—7. Sides of head and crown black, eyelids orange; upperparts (except head) grayish olive-brown; below white, more or less tinged with pale buffy yellow, the breast spotted with pale olive-brown; bill and legs orange.

Distribution.—Humid forests on the upper slopes of Mount Ovando, Chiapas.

BLACK-HEADED NIGHTINGALE-THRUSH. *Catharus mexicanus mexicanus* (Illus. p. 430).—6. *Adult:* Crown dull black, shading to dusky gray on the sides; upperparts otherwise uniform olive; throat whitish, obscurely streaked with pale gray; chest, sides, and flanks pale olive, the lower breast and belly white; bill and eyelids bright yellow; legs dull yellow. *Im-*

BLACK-HEADED NIGHTINGALE-THRUSH

mature: Top of head and back concolor, the upperparts olive-brown streaked with buff; below grayish, the feathers edged with olive; bill black.

Distribution.—Tamaulipas, Veracruz, and state of Mexico.

Remarks.—A small olive-backed forest bird with a *black cap* and *grayish olive chest-band.* Its song suggests that of a Hermit Thrush.

RUSSET NIGHTINGALE-THRUSH. *Catharus occidentalis.*—6–6½. *Adult:* Above deep russet, brightest on head, rump, and tail, the back often tinged with olive; sides of head olive-brown or buffy olive; throat whitish or pale buff, often obscurely streaked with dusky olive; breast pale grayish olive, often mottled and lightly streaked or spotted with darker; abdomen and crissum white, the sides and flanks grayish olive; bill dusky above, dull yellowish below; legs dark. *Immature:* Similar to immature *C. mexicanus.*

Distribution.—Highlands of Chihuahua and Tamaulipas south in mountain forests to Chiapas.

Races.—*C. o. olivascens* (Chihuahua and Durango). *C. o. fulvescens* (Tamaulipas, Hidalgo, Mexico, Jalisco, Michoacán, Guerrero, and Morelos). *C. o. occidentalis* (Veracruz, Puebla, and Oaxaca). *C. o. alticola* (mountains of Chiapas).

Remarks.—Russet and Orange-billed Nightingale-Thrushes are much alike, but the former is *less uniform above*, and its back is usually tinged with olive. The Orange-billed has *orange eyelids* and a much brighter bill. Both birds frequent dense forests, chiefly at high altitudes, and are exceptional songsters.

ORANGE-BILLED NIGHTINGALE-THRUSH. *Catharus aurantiirostris.*—6–6½. *Adult:* Above *uniform* tawny olive or cinnamon-rufous; eyelids orange; throat and abdomen white, the former usually obscurely streaked with gray; breast, sides, and flanks pale gray or pale olive-brown; bill wholly yellow, or dusky above and orange below; legs dull orange. *Immature:* Brown above, more or less streaked with ochraceous; breast grayish olive spotted with buff; throat and abdomen white, the sides and flanks pale buff.

Distribution.—Mountain forests of central and southern Mexico.

Races.—*C. a. aenopennis* (southwestern Chihuahua to east-central Sinaloa on the western slope of the Sierra Madre). *C. a. clarus* (central and western highlands from Chihuahua to Guerrero and Puebla). *C. a. melpomene* (Veracruz, Oaxaca, and Chiapas).

Remarks.—Except when singing, nightingale-thrushes are likely to be overlooked in the heavy forest growth that forms their usual habitat. The song of this species suggests that of a Slaty Vireo (*Neochloe brevipennis*), but is longer and more varied. Its higher pitch and tinkling quality are distinctive. *See* Russet Nightingale-Thrush.

AZTEC THRUSH. *Ridgwayia pinicola* (Illus. p. 432).—8–8½. *Male:* Head, neck, breast, and upperparts deep sooty brown, the crown, hindneck, and back with pale shaft-streaks; wings and tail blackish, the former boldly patterned with pale buff and white, the tail white-tipped and with white upper coverts; abdomen and crissum white; a brown bar on each flank. *Female:* Patterned like male, but decidedly paler (grayish brown) and with more conspicuous buffy shaft-streaks.

Distribution.—High mountains from southern Chihuahua and northwestern Durango south to Guerrero, Oaxaca, and Veracruz. ENDEMIC.

Remarks.—A large dark thrush with a white belly and *white rump-patch*. No similar bird has *white-patterned wings*. Widespread at high altitudes, but rather uncommon.

AZTEC THRUSH

COMMON BLUEBIRD. *Sialia sialis.*—6–6½. *Male:* Above uniform bright blue, becoming duller on sides of head; throat, breast, sides, and flanks dull cinnamon-rufous or chestnut; abdomen and crissum white. *Female:* Similar to male, but much paler. *Immature:* Above essentially brownish, the back and scapulars spotted with buff; wings and tail bluish; below whitish, the throat, breast, and sides scalloped with brown.

Distribution.—Northern and eastern Mexico south in the highlands to Chiapas.

Races.—*S. s. fulva* (western portion of the plateau south to Jalisco; winters south to Chiapas). *S. s. episcopus* (lowlands of northern Tamaulipas). *S. s. guatemalae* (southern Tamaulipas and southern San Luis Potosí southward in the highlands).

Remarks.—Two of the three bluebirds found in Mexico are largely reddish below. Both are widespread in the highlands and may be found together. This species is distinguished by its *reddish throat* and *uniformly blue upperparts*. The Western has a blue or pale grayish throat, and may have a chestnut or brownish back. It is limited to the highlands; the Common Bluebird also occurs in the lowlands.

WESTERN BLUEBIRD. *Sialia mexicana* (Illus. p. 433).—6–6½. *Male:* Above bright blue or violaceous, the back and scapulars sometimes chestnut; sides of head and throat bright blue or pale grayish blue; breast, sides, and flanks chestnut-rufous; abdomen and crissum pale grayish blue. *Female:* Similar to male, but much paler and duller, the back and scapulars sometimes brownish but never chestnut; throat pale grayish or faintly tinged with blue; breast and sides grayish brown. *Immature:* Much like immature Common Bluebirds, but wings and tail more violaceous.

WESTERN BLUEBIRD

Distribution.—Mountains of northern Baja California and highlands generally south to Michoacán, Puebla, and Veracruz.

Races.—*S. m. anabelae* (northern Baja California). **S. m. occidentalis* (winters in extreme northern Baja California). *S. m. amabile* (high mountains of Chihuahua south to north-central and southwestern Durango). *S. m. bairdi* (western highlands south to Durango and Zacatecas). *S. m. mexicana* (northeastern portion of Mexican plateau). *S. m. australis* (southern portion of Mexican plateau).

Remarks.—The characteristic bluebird of the Mexican highlands. While varying considerably as to the extent of chestnut or brown on its back, this species can always be distinguished from a Common Bluebird by its *blue or pale grayish throat.*

*MOUNTAIN BLUEBIRD. *Sialia currucoides.*—6½. *Male:* Above uniform bright cerulean or turquoise-blue, the throat, breast, and sides similar, but much duller and paler; abdomen, flanks, and crissum whitish or faintly tinged with blue. *Female:* Mainly pale grayish brown, lightest below, the abdomen and crissum whitish; wings, rump, and tail dull bluish. *Immature:* Similar to female, but white below, the throat, breast, and sides scalloped with pale brown; upperparts more or less white-streaked.

Distribution.—Winters on Guadalupe Island(?), and in Baja California, Sonora, and Chihuahua.

Remarks.—Bluest of the bluebirds. Females might be confused with some female Western Bluebirds, but are much *duller brown* (less cinnamon-buff) *below,* and have distinctly *cerulean blue* rumps and tails.

Family SYLVIIDAE. Gnatcatchers, Gnatwrens

Key to the Species

1*a.* Bill longer than head and very slender; underparts buff or cinnamon
Long-billed Gnatwren, p. 437

  b. Bill not longer than head; underparts white or *pale* bluish gray . . 2

2*a.* Crown and back concolor at all seasons; forehead and sides of crown (male) edged with black . . . . Blue-gray Gnatcatcher, p. 434

  b. Crown sometimes black; when concolor with back, the forehead and crown not edged with black 3

3*a.* Tail white-tipped, the outer vanes only of outermost feathers wholly white . . . . Black-tailed Gnatcatcher, p. 437

  b. White of tail not restricted to tips and outer vanes of outermost feathers . . . . White-lored Gnatcatcher, p. 435
Black-capped Gnatcatcher, p. 436
Tropical Gnatcatcher, p. 436

BLUE-GRAY GNATCATCHER. *Polioptila caerulea.*—4–4½. *Male:* Upperparts mainly grayish blue, the crown brightest and darkest; forehead (usually) and border of crown to region of eye (often) black; wings slate colored, the tertials usually edged with whitish; tail mainly black, but the outermost feathers entirely white, those adjacent with the terminal half white and the third pair conspicuously white-tipped; sides of head pale bluish gray; underparts white, the throat, breast, and sides washed with pale bluish gray. *Female:* Similar to male, but less bluish (sometimes pale grayish brown) above; forehead and crown never bordered with black.

Distribution.—A widespread resident; the Caribbean slope in winter.

Races.—**P. c. caerulea* (eastern Mexico, in winter only). *P. c. amoenissima* (northwestern Mexico, including Baja California north of the Cape San Lucas region). *P. c. obscura* (Cape San Lucas region, Baja California). *P. c. gracilis* (Sierra Madre foothills, extreme southeastern Sonora; probably adjacent parts of Chihuahua and Sinaloa). *P. c. mexicana* (southeastern Mexico, locally, from southern San Luis Potosí southward). *P. c. cozumelae* (Cozumel Island, off Yucatán). *P. c. deppei* (Yucatán). *P. c. nelsoni* (Oaxaca and Chiapas).

Remarks.—This species lacks a black cap at all seasons. Males are distinguished by the inconspicuous black marks, like an inverted U, that crosses the forehead and extends along each side of crown to the eye. Females resemble the females of *albiloris* and *nigriceps* (and winter males of *nigriceps*), but lack conspicuous superciliaries. They usually have the sides of their heads delicately shaded, not abruptly distinct from the crown.

WHITE-LORED GNATCATCHER. *Polioptila albiloris* (Illus. p. 435). —4–4½. *Male:* Crown black; lores and superciliaries either black (summer) or white (winter); back and rump grayish blue; wings blackish slate or dusky brown, the tertials broadly edged with whitish; tail as in *caerulea*, but second and third (from outermost) feathers with more white, and the fourth white-

WHITE-LORED GNATCATCHER (SUMMER)

tipped; auriculars, malar region, and underparts either wholly white, or breast, sides, and flanks washed with pale bluish gray. *Female:* Similar to male, but crown concolor with back; lores and superciliaries white, usually conspicuous.

Distribution.—Southern Mexico locally, and Pacific lowlands south of Nayarit, chiefly in arid lowlands.

Races.—*P. a. vanrossemi* (interior of southern Mexico and the Pacific lowlands from Nayarit southward). *P. a. albiventris* (northern Yucatán; Cozumel Island?).

Remarks.—The only common Mexican gnatcatcher with a black crown (males only) throughout the year. Males have white lores and superciliaries in winter only. These are usually conspicuous in females at all seasons—an excellent field character. This species is characteristic of arid lowlands and is not likely to be found above an altitude of about 3,500 feet.

TROPICAL GNATCATCHER. *Polioptila plumbea superciliaris.*—4. *Male:* Crown glossy black; lores and superciliaries white; back, scapulars, wings, and rump bluish gray; middle tail feathers black, the lateral rectrices white-tipped, the two outermost wholly white; auriculars, malar area, and underparts white, faintly tinged with bluish gray on breast and sides. *Female:* Similar to male, but without black cap.

Distribution.—Southern Quintana Roo and possibly extreme southeastern Campeche.

Remarks.—Tropical Gnatcatchers, unlike male White-lored Gnatcatchers, have white lores and superciliaries throughout the year. Their ranges overlap in various parts of Central America, but apparently not in Mexico.

BLACK-CAPPED GNATCATCHER. *Polioptila nigriceps.*—4½. *Male:* Crown, lores, and superciliary area black (summer) or concolor with back (winter); back and rump bluish gray; wings brownish slate, the tertials edged with whitish; tail and underparts as in *albiloris. Female:* Similar to male, but without black crown, and upperparts more grayish.

Distribution.—Western Mexico south to Nayarit, or possibly Jalisco. ENDEMIC.

Races.—*P. n. restricta* (Sonora and extreme northern Sinaloa). *P. n. nigriceps* (Sinaloa south at least to Nayarit).

Remarks.—Also known as Black-headed Gnatcatcher. Males in summer closely resemble male White-lored Gnatcatchers in having all-black crowns, lores, and superciliaries. Winter males have no black on heads, and both sexes lack distinct superciliary streaks at all seasons.

BLACK-TAILED GNATCATCHER. *Polioptila melanura.*—3¾–4¼. *Male:* Crown and lores either entirely black (summer) or with black restricted principally to forehead (winter); back and rump dull bluish gray; wings brownish slate, the secondaries broadly edged with whitish; tail mainly black, the three outer feathers white-tipped, and the outermost (only) with white outer vane; underparts whitish or pale bluish gray. *Female:* Similar to male, but crown concolor with back; upperparts duller, sometimes grayish brown.

Distribution.—Baja California and arid districts of northwestern Mexico south to Durango.

Races.—*P. m. californica* (northwestern Baja California). *P. m. pontilis* (middle portion of Baja California). *P. m. margaritae* (Cape San Lucas region, Baja California, and adjacent islands). *P. m. curtata* (Tiburón Island, Gulf of California). *P. m. lucidae* (northeastern Baja California, Sonora, and Chihuahua south to Durango).

Remarks.—Also known as Plumbeous Gnatcatcher. The white-tipped tail, with only the *outer vane of the outermost feather wholly white,* distinguishes the Black-tailed from the three other gnatcatchers of Mexico. Each of these is much more conspicuously white-tipped.

LONG-BILLED GNATWREN. *Ramphocaenus rufiventris* (Illus. p. 437).—4¾–5. *Adult:* Bill slender, straight, and notably long (about 1 inch); crown and hind-neck bright olive-brown; upperparts otherwise grayish

LONG-BILLED GNATWREN

olive or slate, the remiges sometimes edged with cinnamon; tail blackish, the three outer feathers tipped with white; sides of head cinnamon; throat whitish, usually with a dusky or black-and-white spotted center; underparts otherwise buff or cinnamon, richest on breast and sides, and often shading to white on abdomen; flanks sometimes dusky. *Immature:* Similar to adult, but grayish brown above and paler below.

Distribution.—Lowlands of southeastern Mexico.

Races.—*R. r. rufiventris* (Veracruz, Tabasco, Oaxaca, and Chiapas). *R. r. ardeleo* (Yucatán).

Remarks.—A small wrenlike bird, with an extremely *long, slender bill.* Gnatwrens are very active and usually are found in shrubs or among the lower branches of trees. Their song is a soft, trilled whistle rendered entirely in the same key (Griscom).

Family REGULIDAE. Kinglets

KEY TO THE SPECIES

1*a*. Superciliaries conspicuous; a yellow or orange crown-patch
Golden-crowned Kinglet, p. 438

  b. Without distinct superciliaries; sometimes with a small red crown-
patch . . . . Ruby-crowned Kinglet, p. 438

GOLDEN-CROWNED KINGLET. *Regulus satrapa* (Illus. p. 438).—
3¾. *Male:* Forehead and superciliaries whitish; center of crown bright orange
fringed with yellow, the whole bordered laterally by two conspicuous black
stripes; hind-neck grayish, passing into olive or greenish olive on back and

RUBY-CROWNED KINGLET (*left*); GOLDEN-CROWNED KINGLET (*right*)

rump; wings and tail dusky, edged with yellowish, the former with two yellowish bars; sides of head and underparts dull grayish or buffy olive.
Female: Similar to male, but center of crown without orange.

Distribution.—Mountains of Michoacán, Mexico, Hidalgo, and Veracruz southward at high altitudes; highlands generally in winter.

Races.—*R. s. satrapa* (winters in Tamaulipas). *R. s. amoenus* (winters
extensively in the highlands). *R. s. clarus* (mountain forests of southern
Mexico).

Remarks.—The conspicuous superciliary streaks and *black-bordered*
orange or yellow crown-patch distinguish this kinglet from the Ruby-
crowned. Both have shorter tails and smaller bills than warblers of
comparable size. Mountains generally, chiefly at high altitudes.

RUBY-CROWNED KINGLET. *Regulus calendula* (Illus. p. 438).—
3¾–4. *Male:* Center of crown (from level of eyes) with a more or less con-

cealed vermilion patch; above mainly dull grayish olive or greenish olive, brightest posteriorly; wings and tail dusky, narrowly edged with yellowish olive, the inner secondaries usually broadly edged with whitish; two pale wing-bars; white eye-rings; sides of head olive, the underparts pale grayish olive or buffy olive. *Female:* Similar to male, but without a crown-patch.

Distribution.—Guadalupe Island, off Baja California; common elsewhere in winter.

Races.—*R. c. calendula* (virtually country-wide in winter). *R. c. cineraceus* (winters in Baja California and Sonora). *R. c. obscurus* (Guadalupe Island).

Remarks.—Females might be mistaken for various bar-winged warblers in winter plumage, but have shorter tails than any species of comparable size. The vermilion crown-patch of males is diagnostic, but often not visible. Both sexes have conspicuous eye-rings, but lack superciliary streaks, differing in this respect from Golden-crowns.

Family MOTACILLIDAE. Wagtails, Pipits

KEY TO THE SPECIES

1a. Conspicuously streaked or spotted above . . Sprague Pipit, p. 440
  b. Upperparts virtually uniform . . . . Water Pipit, p. 439

*PIED WIGTAIL. *Motacilla alba ocularis.*

Remarks.—Also known as White Wagtail. A widespread European and Asiatic species recorded occasionally in the Aleutians and Alaska, and once in Baja California (La Paz, January 9, 1882).

*WATER PIPIT. *Anthus spinoletta* (Illus. p. 440).—6. Above brownish olive (winter) or grayish olive (summer), the feathers of the crown, back, and scapulars with obscure darker streaks; wings dusky, the tertials and coverts conspicuously edged with pale gray or grayish buff; tail mainly dusky or blackish, the outermost feathers largely white and the adjacent pair white-tipped; superciliaries and underparts buffy white (winter) or dull cinnamon-buff (summer); sides of throat, breast, sides, and flanks streaked with dark brown (less conspicuous in summer); bill mainly dusky (summer), or with light-colored mandible (winter); legs brownish.

Distribution.—Widespread in winter.

Races.—*A. s. rubescens* (common winter visitant). *A. s. pacificus* (winters in Sonora).

Remarks.—Also known as American Pipit. At first glance, pipits might be mistaken for Horned Larks in winter plumage. Both occupy the same habitat—bare fields and grasslands—but pipits lack the yellow-and-black pattern of the lark's head and throat. They are rather slender in appearance and customarily pump their tails up and down when standing—a characteristic that eliminates all sparrows. Pipits show much more white on their outer tail feathers than larks, and their flocks are usually more loosely formed. This species is much darker and more uniform above than the Sprague, and has rather boldly streaked underparts.

*RED-THROATED PIPIT. *Anthus cervinus.*

Remarks.—A common Asiatic species recorded once in Baja California (San José del Cabo, January 26, 1883). Only one other record for the Western Hemisphere: St. Michael, western Alaska, 1867.

*SPRAGUE PIPIT. *Anthus spragueii* (Illus. p. 440).—6. Upperparts pale buff, broadly and conspicuously streaked and spotted with dusky brown; wings edged with grayish buff, the middle and greater coverts

WATER PIPIT (*left*); SPRAGUE PIPIT (*right*)

tipped with same; tail mainly dusky or blackish, the inner feathers edged with grayish buff; outermost rectrices wholly white, the adjacent pair virtually so; superciliaries, sides of head, and underparts whitish, more or less tinged with pale buff; chest narrowly streaked with brown; bill dusky above, paler below; legs pale brown.

Distribution.—Winters in central Mexico south to Michoacán, Puebla, and Veracruz.

Remarks.—At a distance Water Pipits appear almost uniform above, whereas this species is very conspicuously streaked or spotted.

Sprague Pipits are paler below, and their chest-streaks are quite narrow, or sometimes almost obsolete. *See* Water Pipit.

Family BOMBYCILLIDAE. Waxwings

*CEDAR WAXWING. *Bombycilla cedrorum* (Illus. p. 441).—6. Head, neck, and breast mainly velvety cinnamon or fawn color, the lores, chin, and eye-patch black; a conspicuous occipital crest; back, scapulars, and wing-coverts darker than head and tinged with gray, this passing into pure gray on rump; wings slate gray, the secondaries washed with brown and termi-

CEDAR WAXWING

nating (usually) in minute scarlet projections; tail slaty gray, broadly tipped with yellow; abdomen pale yellow; crissum white.

Distribution.—Widespread in winter.

Remarks.—Cedar Waxwings can hardly be confused with any other Mexican species. Wintering birds range the countryside in compact flocks, feeding on both insects and berries. They like to perch in treetops and often sit quietly for long periods with their heads raised and crests extended. Immature birds are more or less striped, but will be recognized by their crests and *yellow-tipped tails*.

Family PTILOGONATIDAE. Silky-flycatchers

KEY TO THE SPECIES

1a. Glossy black or grayish brown; if black, the primaries with white patches; a pointed crest . . . . Phainopepla, p. 442

b. Mainly bluish gray or brown; wings and tail black, the lateral rectrices with a broad white median bar; conspicuous yellow under tail-coverts . . . . Gray Silky-flycatcher, p. 442

GRAY SILKY-FLYCATCHER. *Ptilogonys cinereus* (Illus. p. 442).—
7–8½. *Male:* Crown, occipital crest, and sides of head pale gray or tinged with
brown; a white eye-ring; back, scapulars, rump, and upper tail-coverts
bluish gray; wings and tail black, the lateral rectrices with a broad white
median patch; throat and breast gray, the belly white; flanks and crissum
golden-olive and bright yellow. *Female:* Patterned like male, but with brown
replacing the gray above and below.

Distribution.—High mountains of western, central, and southern
Mexico.

Races.—*P. c. otofuscus* (southwestern Chihuahua and Durango). *P. c.
cinereus* (central and southern highlands, except where occupied by the

GRAY SILKY-FLYCATCHER

following). *P. c. pallescens* (Guerrero). *P. c. molybdophanes* (recorded from
Ocosingo, Chiapas).

Remarks.—Also known as Mexican Ptilogonys. The smooth, well-
groomed plumage, characteristic postures, and general appearance of
silky-flycatchers usually suggest waxwings. However, they have much
longer tails than waxwings and appear rather slender by comparison.
The white tail-patches show as a broad bar from below, and even
brown females have bright yellow under tail-coverts. Like waxwings,
silky-flycatchers often pose alertly with raised crests on exposed
perches. Virtually unmistakable at any distance.

PHAINOPEPLA. *Phainopepla nitens.*—7–7½. *Male:* Glossy black, the
inner webs of the primaries with a broad white patch; feathers of crown

elongated, forming a conspicuous pointed crest. *Female:* Mainly dusky grayish brown, darkening on wings and tail, where faintly glossed with greenish; wing-coverts, secondaries, and crissum narrowly edged with white; feathers of occipital crest glossy black.

Distribution.—Baja California and dry portions of northern Mexico south to Puebla and Veracruz.

Races.—*P. n. lepida* (Baja California, Sonora, and Chihuahua). *P. n. nitens* (Coahuila and Durango south to Puebla and Veracruz).

Remarks.—A slender, *glossy black* bird with a pointed crest and *white wing-patches*. The dusky females have similar crests, but lack wing-patches. Cedar Waxwings are brownish, and have yellow-tipped tails. No large flycatcher with uniform dusky plumage has a conspicuously *pointed crest.*

Family LANIIDAE. Shrikes

LOGGERHEAD SHRIKE. *Lanius ludovicianus* (Illus. p. 443).—7½–9. *Adult:* Crown, hind-neck, and back pale slate gray, fading to whitish on rump and upper tail-coverts, the latter sometimes abruptly white; scapulars

LOGGERHEAD SHRIKE

pale gray or white; wings black, the secondaries more or less broadly white-tipped; a white patch near base of primaries; tail black, the lateral feathers white-tipped, the outermost sometimes wholly white; a broad black band extending from bill to auriculars; underparts immaculate white or pale grayish. *Immature:* Similar to adult, but brownish above and liberally barred or vermiculated with darker.

Distribution.—Baja California; northern and eastern Mexico south to the Isthmus of Tehuantepec, especially in dry open country.

Races.—*L. l. grinnelli* (northern Baja California). *L. l. nelsoni* (central and southern Baja California, including Cedros and Margarita Islands). **L. l. gambeli* (winters in Baja California and western Mexico south to Morelos). *L. l. sonoriensis* (northwestern Mexico south to Mazatlán). *L. l. mexicanus* (central and southern Mexico). **L. l. excubitorides* (winters in eastern and central Mexico south to the Isthmus of Tehuantepec).

Remarks.—Shrikes resemble mockingbirds (*Mimus polyglottos*) superficially, but have strong, *hooked beaks*, *black masks*, and relatively short tails. Tropical Mockingbirds of the south have little white on their wings, but show white tail-tips.

Family CYCLARHIDAE. Pepper-shrikes

RUFOUS-BROWED PEPPER-SHRIKE. *Cyclarhis gujanensis* (Illus. p. 444).—6–6½. Forehead, sides of crown, and superciliaries rufous; median crown gray or tinged with brown; hind-neck and area below eye pale gray,

RUFOUS-BROWED PEPPER-SHRIKE

the upperparts otherwise olive-green; below mainly pale yellow, the belly sometimes white; bill very stout and strongly hooked.

Distribution.—Lowlands and foothills of southeastern and southern Mexico; also Meco and Cozumel Islands, off the Yucatán coast.

Races.—*C. g. flaviventris* (southern Tamaulipas and Mexico south to Oaxaca, except where occupied by the following). *C. g. yucatanensis* (Yucatán Peninsula and Meco Island). *C. g. insularis* (Cozumel Island). *C. g. nicaraguae* (Chiapas).

Remarks.—A stocky, green-backed bird with a gray head and *conspicuous rufous superciliaries.* No similar bird has a *powerful, hooked bill.* Pepper-shrikes frequent thickets and forest edge from sea-level to an altitude of about 4,000 feet. They usually prefer good cover within a few feet of the ground, but often select an exposed perch for singing. The song is rather weak, but fairly varied and musical.

Family VIREOLANIIDAE. Shrike-vireos

1a. Mainly greenish, the underparts strongly tinged with yellow; crown and hind-neck blue . . . .   Green Shrike-vireo, p. 446

 b. Buffy white below; a reddish chest-band; conspicuous yellow superciliaries . . . .   Chestnut-sided Shrike-vireo, p. 445

CHESTNUT-SIDED SHRIKE-VIREO. *Vireolanius melitophrys* (Illus. p. 445).—6¾. *Male:* Crown, hind-neck, and broad eye-stripe slate gray; a black rictal streak; conspicuous yellow superciliaries; back, rump, wings,

CHESTNUT-SIDED SHRIKE-VIREO

and tail olive-green; malar area and underparts whitish tinged with buff; a prominent reddish chest-band; sides and flanks often tawny. *Female:* Similar to male, but much paler and duller.

Distribution.—Mountain forests of south-central Mexico. To be expected elsewhere to the southward at high altitudes.

Races.—*V. m. goldmani* (Michoacán, Morelos, and Mexico). *V. m. melitophrys* (mountains of southern Veracruz).

Remarks.—Strongly patterned, but totally unlike any other Mexican species. The bright yellow superciliaries and *black rictal streaks* are conspicuous at a distance. From below look for the *reddish chest-band* on a whitish background. Little known and apparently restricted to oak forests at high altitudes.

GREEN SHRIKE-VIREO. *Smaragdolanius pulchellus.*—5½–6. Crown and hind-neck wholly blue, or with a green median patch; sides of head, back, rump, wings, and tail uniform rich green; below mainly pale yellowish green, the throat and crissum bright yellow.

Distribution.—Veracruz and Chiapas. Apparently rare, but to be expected elsewhere in forests of the south.

Races.—*S. p. pulchellus* (Veracruz). *S. p. verticalis* (Chiapas).

Remarks.—Also known as Greenlet. A small green-and-yellow forest bird with a heavy, shrikelike, bluish gray bill. Blue-crowned Chlorophonias are also blue-crowned, but have notably short tails and bills, and (males) a narrow pectoral band. Both birds live in the forest crown, where their plumage blends perfectly with the foliage. *See* Blue-crowned Chlorophonia.

Family VIREONIDAE. Vireos

Key to the Species

1a. With wing-bars 2

  b. Without wing-bars 10

2a. Crown and sides of head black, slate gray, or grayish; eye-ring and loral area white 3

  b. Crown and sides of head sometimes grayish; never black or slate gray 4

3a. Less than 4½ inches. Crown black or slate-colored; wing-bars yellowish . . . . Black-capped Vireo, p. 448

  b. More than 4½ inches. Crown grayish; wing-bars usually whitish
                                   Solitary Vireo, p. 451

4a. Eye-ring and loral area bright yellow 5

  b. Eye-ring and loral area not bright yellow 6

5a. Underparts uniform whitish or pale yellow
                            White-eyed Vireo, p. 448

*BLACK-CAPPED VIREO. *Vireo atricapillus* (Illus. p. 448).—4¼. *Adult:* Crown, hind-neck, and sides of head black or slate gray; eye-ring and lores white; upperparts mainly olive-green; two pale yellowish green wing-bars; underparts essentially white, the sides and flanks tinged with pale yellowish olive. *Immature:* Similar to adult, but crown grayish brown (not black); upperparts browner (less greenish), the underparts tinged with pale buff.

Distribution.—Winters in Sinaloa, Mexico, and Tamaulipas; perhaps elsewhere in northern Mexico.

Remarks.—No other vireo with prominent wing-bars has a *conspicuous black or slaty cap.* Solitary Vireos are essentially gray-crowned,

BLACK-CAPPED VIREO

especially in summer, but show much less contrast between head and back. Their wing-bars are essentially *white*, not yellowish.

COZUMEL VIREO. *Vireo bairdi.*—4½. Eye-ring and lores white; upperparts grayish brown, shading to cinnamon on cheeks and sides of breast; two white or pale yellowish wing-bars; underparts immaculate white shading to olive on flanks.

Distribution.— Cozumel Island, off Quintana Roo. ENDEMIC.

Remarks.—Also known as Baird Vireo. A brown-and-white vireo with *cinnamon cheeks*, incomplete eye-rings, and conspicuous wing-bars. Unmistakable.

WHITE-EYED VIREO. *Vireo griseus* (Illus. p. 449).—4¼-4¾. *Adult:* Eye-ring and loral area bright yellow; upperparts greenish olive or grayish olive, lightest on sides of head; two white or pale yellowish wing-bars; underparts either uniform pale yellow, or mainly white, with breast, sides, and flanks more or less washed with yellowish; iris white. *Immature:* Similar to adult, but eye-ring and lores whitish or pale brownish; plumage above duller and browner; underparts pale gray or brownish gray.

Distribution.—Both coastal slopes.

Races.—*V. g. palluster* (lowlands of southwestern Sonora and northwestern Sinaloa). *V. g. ochraceus* (mangrove swamps of Sinaloa, and probably southward locally). *V. g. noveboracensis (winters in Veracruz). *V. g. griseus (winters in eastern Mexico). V. g. micrus (eastern Coahuila, Nuevo León, and Tamaulipas south to northern Hidalgo). V. g. perquisitor (lowlands of northern Veracruz). V. g. semiflavus (Yucatán Peninsula; also Holbox and Mujeres Islands).

Remarks.—The Slaty Vireo, a very distinct species, also has white eyes. Only the White-eyed has both a white iris and a conspicuous *yellow eye-ring.* Its underparts may be either uniform pale yellowish, or essentially white with some yellow on the breast and sides. The affinities of several races are doubtful. The Veracruz Vireo (*perquisitor*) may represent a distinct species. Some authorities consider *palluster.*

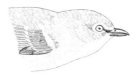

WHITE-EYED VIREO

ochraceus, and *semiflavus* conspecific with the Mangrove Vireo (*V. pallens*) of Central America.

HUTTON VIREO. *Vireo huttoni.*—$4\frac{1}{2}$–$4\frac{3}{4}$. *Adult:* Eye-ring (incomplete) and loral area whitish; above dull olive or grayish olive, shading to greenish olive on rump and upper tail-coverts; two prominent white wing-bars; underparts dull buffy olive, the abdomen paler, sometimes whitish. *Immature:* Similar to adult, but grayer above and much paler below; eye-ring and lores less distinct.

Distribution.—Mountains (chiefly) of Baja California and Mexico locally south to Oaxaca.

Races.—*V. h. huttoni* (northwestern Baja California). *V. h. cognatus* (cape district of Baja California). *V. h. carolinae* (southern Coahuila and southwestern Tamaulipas). *V. h. stephensi* (Sonora and Chihuahua south to Nayarit and Zacatecas). *V. h. mexicanus* (highlands of central and southern Mexico from San Luis Potosí to Oaxaca and Veracruz).

Remarks.—A decidedly nondescript vireo, with dull olive or dingy underparts and two very prominent white wing-bars. The *incomplete eye-ring* and pale lores distinguish the Hutton from similar vireos.

GOLDEN VIREO. *Vireo hypochryseus.*—5–$5\frac{1}{2}$. Above uniformly bright olive-green; wings and tail grayish olive narrowly edged with yellowish olive; superciliaries bright yellow; sides of head and neck dull yellowish olive, becoming bright yellow on underparts; throat, breast, and flanks sometimes tinged with olive.

Distribution.—Tres Marías Islands; western Mexico south to Oaxaca. ENDEMIC.

Races.—*V. h. sordidus* (Tres Marías Islands, off western Mexico). *V. h nitidus* (southern Sonora). *V. h. hypochryseus* (southern Sinaloa, and Chihuahua south to Oaxaca).

Remarks.—One of the most colorful vireos. No other species without wing-bars is *wholly yellow below*. Note the *yellow* superciliaries. *See* Yellow-throated Vireo.

GRAY VIREO. *Vireo vicinior.*—5. Eye-ring and loral area whitish; upperparts dull gray, the lower back, rump, and upper tail-coverts lightly washed with greenish; a single rather indistinct wing-bar; underparts mainly white, the throat and breast sometimes washed with very pale gray.

Distribution.—Northwestern Baja California (possibly wintering to cape district), Sonora, and Durango.

Remarks.—A decidedly drab *dry-country* vireo with a *narrow white eye-ring*. The single wing-bar is very obscure and may not show. Gray Vireos could be confused with Bell Vireos, but the two occupy different habitats. *See* Bell Vireo and Dwarf Vireo.

DWARF VIREO. *Vireo nelsoni.*—4. Very similar to a Gray Vireo, but much smaller and with *two* narrow, but rather distinct, wing-bars.

Distribution.—Known only from Querendaro, Michoacán. ENDEMIC.

Remarks.—Only one specimen of this diminutive vireo is known to science. Its relationships are uncertain, and nothing is known of its habits. *See* Gray Vireo and Bell Vireo.

BELL VIREO. *Vireo bellii.*—4–4¼. Eye-ring (narrow) and loral area whitish; crown and hind-neck dull gray, grayish brown, or brownish gray, shading to dull olive or grayish olive on the rump and upper tail-coverts; two rather indistinct whitish wing-bars; underparts dull white, the breast, sides, flanks, and crissum faintly tinged with grayish olive.

Distribution.—Breeds in northern Baja California, northwestern and north-central Mexico south to Guanajuato; winters in southern Baja California and extensively elsewhere.

Races.—*V. b. pusillus* (Baja California, wintering in southern portion). *V. b. arizonae* (Sonora and Chihuahua). *V. b. medius* (Coahuila and Durango south to Guanajuato). *V. b. bellii* (Tamaulipas; southward in winter).

Remarks.—Also known as Least Vireo. Nearest a Warbling Vireo in general appearance, but considerably smaller and with *two indistinct wing-bars*. Gray Vireos usually appear barless or have a *single vague wing-bar*. Note the very narrow pale eye-ring. Other vireos with wing-bars have much more conspicuous eye-rings. Very active and usually found in thickets or bushes near water. *See* Warbling Vireo, Gray Vireo, and Solitary Vireo.

*YELLOW-THROATED VIREO. *Vireo flavifrons* (Illus. p. 451).—5. Eye-ring and loral area bright yellow; crown, sides of head, hind-neck, and back uniform yellowish olive, shading to grayish or slate on rump and upper tail-coverts; two very prominent white wing-bars; throat, breast, and upper abdomen bright yellow, the posterior underparts immaculate white.

Yellow-throated Vireo

Distribution.—Winters in eastern and southern Mexico.

Remarks.—A white-bellied vireo with a bright yellow throat and breast. Golden Vireos are *wholly* yellow below and lack wing-bars. Sometimes confused with male Pine Warblers in spring plumage, but distinguished by its *thicker bill*, brighter, *unstreaked* breast, and unpatterned tail.

SOLITARY VIREO. *Vireo solitarius*.—4¾–5. *Adult:* Crown, hind-neck, and sides of head grayish or slate, the eye-ring and lores white; upperparts dull gray, grayish olive, or olive-green, brightest posteriorly; two conspicuous white or pale yellowish wing-bars; below white, the breast (sometimes), sides, and flanks tinged with gray or yellowish olive. *Immature:* Similar to adult, but duller (grayish brown) above.

Distribution.—Mountains (chiefly) of Baja California, western and north-central Mexico southward. Occurs extensively elsewhere in winter.

Races.—*V. s. lucasanus* (Cape San Lucas district of Baja California). *V. s. cassinii* (northern Baja California; winters extensively in western Mexico). *V. s. pinicolus* (mountains of southern Sonora and southwestern Chihuahua). *V. s. repetens* (western Mexico from southern Jalisco south to Oaxaca). *V. s. plumbeus* (Chihuahua—except southwestern portion—and Coahuila south to Veracruz; winters south to Oaxaca). **V. s. solitarius* (winters in eastern and southern Mexico).

Remarks.—Also known as Blue-headed Vireo. A gray-headed vireo with notably conspicuous white eye-rings and wing-bars. These are very obscure in Bell Vireos. Hutton Vireos have *incomplete* eye-rings and lack the gleaming white underparts of the Solitary. The latter is sometimes gray above, but always shows some contrast between crown and back. Gray Vireos have *narrow* eye-rings and a *single obscure wing-bar*.

**RED-EYED VIREO. *Vireo olivaceus* (Illus. p. 452).—5–5¼. Superciliaries dull white bordered with black; a dusky eye-streak; crown and hind-neck dull gray, the upperparts otherwise uniform olive-green; below

RED-EYED VIREO

either wholly dull white, or sides of breast, flanks, and crissum tinged with pale yellowish green; iris reddish.

Distribution.—Tres Marías Islands (María Madre and María Magdalena) and northern Mexico southward on the Pacific and Caribbean slopes in summer. Occurs commonly elsewhere during migration.

Races.—*V. o. hypoleucus* (east-central Sonora south to southern Sinaloa and Nayarit; apparently winters south of Mexico). *V. o. olivaceus* (breeds in northern Coahuila; winters in South America). *V. o. flavoviridis* (breeds on both coastal slopes, except where occupied by *hypoleucus*; winters south of Mexico). *V. o. forreri* (Tres Marías Islands, off western Mexico; winter range unknown).

Remarks.—The only gray-capped, green-backed Vireo without wing-bars. Under favorable conditions the dusky eye-streak is a good field mark. Note the reddish iris. Some authorities consider *flavoviridis* a distinct species. It is known as Yellow-green Vireo, and can be distinguished from other Red-eyes by its brighter coloring, especially the *yellowish* sides, flanks, and under tail-coverts. Their songs are virtually identical.

YUCATÁN VIREO. *Vireo magister magister.*—5¾. Upperparts dull grayish olive, the superciliaries yellowish buff; a dusky olive eye-streak; median underparts yellowish (or yellowish white), shading to grayish olive on sides of breast and flanks; bill decidedly large.

Distribution.—Coast of the Yucatán Peninsula and Holbox, Mujeres, and Cozumel Islands.

Remarks.—Also known as Belize Vireo. While vaguely suggesting a Red-eye, this common resident vireo will be recognized by its larger size (especially bill), *yellowish* superciliaries, dull *yellowish-and-olive* (not white) underparts, and virtually *uniform upperparts*. Not likely to be mistaken for any other vireo of its area.

*PHILADELPHIA VIREO. *Vireo philadelphicus.*—4½. *Adult:* Crown gray, sometimes tinged with olive, the upperparts otherwise uniform grayish olive-green; no wing-bars; auriculars and malar region pale olive, the area below the eye sometimes white; a dusky eye-streak; superciliaries whitish; underparts mainly pale greenish yellow, the throat and abdomen sometimes whitish. *Immature:* Similar to adult, but crown like back, and underparts more distinctly yellow.

Distribution.—Winters on Cozumel Island, off Quintana Roo. To be expected elsewhere in eastern Mexico as a transient.

Remarks.—Much like a Warbling Vireo, but paler above and much *yellower below*, especially on the breast. Both lack wing-bars, but have distinct whitish superciliaries. Several warblers are very similar, particularly the Orange-crowned, fall Tennessee, and female Black-throated Blue. Vireos are much less active than warblers and have *thicker* (not needle-like) *bills* with a curved ridge.

WARBLING VIREO. *Vireo gilvus.*—4½-5. Superciliaries dull white, usually distinct; lores and eye-streak pale brown, darker than auriculars; upperparts dull gray, somewhat tinged with olive posteriorly; below essentially white, the sides and flanks more or less tinged with pale greenish olive.

Distribution.—Mountains of Baja California, Sonora, and Chihuahua; widespread elsewhere in winter.

Races.—*V. g. swainsonii* (migratory in Baja California and Sonora; southward in winter). *V. g. victoriae* (Victoria Mountains, southern Baja California). *V. g. brewsteri* (mountains of southeastern Sonora and Chihuahua; winter range uncertain). *V. g. eleanorae* (wooded mountains of southern Tamaulipas and northern Hidalgo). *V. g. connectens* (Sierra Madre del Sur, Guerrero). *V. g. gilvus* (common migrant, wintering in Guatemala).

Remarks.—Decidedly nondescript, lacking both eye-rings and wing-bars. Such a vireo with virtually *uniform grayish upperparts* is likely to be this species. Red-eyes have their superciliaries bordered with black, and usually show some contrast between the crown and back. Philadelphia Vireos are darker (more olive) above, yellower below—especially on the breast—and have a *dark loral spot. See* Bell Vireo and Gray Vireo.

BROWN-CAPPED VIREO. *Vireo leucophrys.*—4½. Superciliaries dull white; auriculars and sides of neck pale brown, the latter sometimes tinged with buff; crown sooty brown, the upperparts otherwise brownish olive; wings and tail brown or dusky, the feathers usually narrowly edged with olive; below dull white, the breast, flanks, and crissum often washed with pale yellowish olive.

Distribution.—Wooded mountains of Veracruz and Chiapas.

Races.—*V. l. amauronotus* (Veracruz). *V. l. strenuus* (Chiapas).

Remarks.—Possibly conspecific with the Warbling Vireo, but *browner* (less grayish) *above* and with a distinctly *brown cap* of a darker shade than the back. No eye-ring or wing-bars, but with whitish superciliaries. The song is much like that of a Warbling Vireo.

SLATY VIREO. *Neochloe brevipennis* (Illus. p 455).—4¾. Top of head, wings, and tail bright olive-green; elsewhere mainly slaty gray, the chin, lower breast, abdomen, and under tail-coverts white; iris white.

Distribution.—Mountains of southern Veracruz and southwestern Guerrero. ENDEMIC.

Races.—*N. b. brevipennis* (Orizaba and Jalapa, Veracruz). *N. b. browni* (Guerrero).

Remarks.—Also known as Green-winged Vireo. A rare and little-known species, suggesting a warbler in boldness of pattern. No other Mexican vireo has bright olive-green and slaty gray plumage conspicuously combined. Its song, according to Loetscher, consists of three to five notes and suggests that of a White-eyed Vireo, but is shorter and has less volume. Emphasis is on either the third or the fourth note.

SLATY VIREO

Orange-billed Nightingale-Thrushes have a longer and more varied song that is pitched higher and has a tinkling quality.

TAWNY-CROWNED GREENLET. *Hylophilus ochraceiceps ochraceiceps* (Illus. p. 456).—4¼. Crown tawny olive, brightest on forehead; upperparts otherwise rich olive-brown, shading to russet on tail and wings; throat grayish; breast and sides tawny, becoming pale greenish yellow on flanks, belly, and crissum.

Distribution.—Wooded lowlands of Veracruz, Tabasco, Campeche, and Oaxaca. To be expected elsewhere in southeastern Mexico.

Remarks.—Greenlets have relatively long, slender bills as compared to other vireos. They lack both wing-bars and conspicuous eye-rings, and are rather undistinguished in appearance. This species is essentially tawny above and below, with a brighter forehead and gray throat. *See* Gray-headed Greenlet.

GRAY-HEADED GREENLET. *Hylophilus decurtatus decurtatus* (Illus. p. 456).—4¼. Crown and hind-neck gray, lightening on sides of head; upperparts otherwise bright olive-green; below dull white, the sides, flanks, and crissum yellowish green.

Distribution.—Wooded lowlands of Veracruz, Tabasco, Oaxaca, Yucatán, and Quintana Roo.

Tawny-crowned Greenlet (*above*); Gray-headed Greenlet (*below*)

Remarks.—This greenlet resembles a Tennessee Warbler, but has a heavier bill and shorter tail. The warbler is wholly white below; the greenlet uniformly greenish on sides, flanks, and under tail-coverts. Both Mexican greenlets are vireo-like in actions. They are not so likely to be found in treetops as are wintering warblers. *See* Tawny-crowned Greenlet.

Family COEREBIDAE. Honeycreepers

Key to the Species

1*a*. Bill slightly upturned and conspicuously hooked
Cinnamon-bellied Flower-piercer, p. 457

   b. Bill slender, slightly decurved, and with a pointed tip 2

2*a*. Blackish above, yellow below, the superciliaries white

Bananaquit, p. 459

  b. Not as in 2*a*. 3

3*a*. Underparts either glossy bluish green, or bright yellowish green; bill yellowish below . . . . Green Honeycreeper, p. 457

  b. Underparts either rich purplish blue, or dull olive, faintly streaked with yellowish; bill wholly black . . Red-legged Honeycreeper, p. 458

CINNAMON-BELLIED FLOWER-PIERCER. *Diglossa baritula* (Illus. p. 457).—$4\frac{1}{4}$–$4\frac{1}{2}$. *Male:* Sides of head and crown slaty black, becoming bluish slate on back, scapulars, and rump; wings and tail sooty; underparts uniform cinnamon or russet, the throat or chin (and malar area) blackish,

CINNAMON-BELLIED FLOWER-PIERCER

like cheeks; mandible upturned, and tip of bill conspicuously hooked. *Female:* Above dull olive, the wings and tail dusky edged with buffy olive; throat and chest olive-buff, shading to cinnamon-buff posteriorly; bill as in male.

Distribution.—Mountain forests of southern Mexico.

Races.—*D. b. baritula* (Colima, Guanajuato, and Veracruz south to Oaxaca). *D. b. montana* (Chiapas).

Remarks.—Also known as Cinnamon-bellied Diglossa. No other small Mexican bird has an *upturned, hooked bill*. At a distance males appear black above, and *rich cinnamon below*. Females have similar bills, but are dull olive above and rather dingy below.

GREEN HONEYCREEPER. *Chlorophanes spiza guatemalensis* (Illus. p. 458).—5–$5\frac{1}{2}$. *Male:* Top and sides of head velvety black, the plumage otherwise mainly glossy bluish green; remiges and lateral rectrices sooty, more or less broadly edged with bluish green; bill rather long, slightly decurved, dusky above and yellow below. *Female:* Glossy yellowish green, palest and brightest (more yellowish) below.

Distribution.—Reported only from Campeche, Oaxaca, and Chiapas. To be expected elsewhere in lowland forests of southern Mexico.

Remarks.—A common Central American honeycreeper occasionally found in the southern part of our area. Males are unlike any other

Mexican bird. Females can be distinguished from other wholly yellow-ish green species by their rather *long, decurved bills*. In both sexes the bill is dusky above and conspicuously *yellow* below.

GREEN HONEYCREEPER

RED-LEGGED HONEYCREEPER. *Cyanerpes cyaneus* (Illus. p. 458). —4½. *Male:* Mainly glossy purplish blue, the median crown bright turquoise-blue; stripe through eye, back, wings, and tail black; underside of the wings bright yellow; bill black, rather slender, and slightly decurved; legs bright red. *Female:* Above olive-green, the underparts dull yellowish, vaguely streaked with olive; legs reddish.

Distribution.—Lowland forests of southern Mexico.

Races.—*C. c. carneipes* (Veracruz, Yucatán, and Oaxaca southward, except where occupied by the following). *C. c. striatipectus* (Pacific slope of Chiapas).

Remarks.—Also known as Blue Honeycreeper. Males, deep purplish blue patterned with black, and with a turquoise crown-patch and

RED-LEGGED HONEYCREEPER

vermilion legs, are among the most beautiful of resident birds. Females are drab by comparison—olive-green above, with lightly streaked olive-and-yellow underparts. Female Green Honeycreepers are decidedly brighter above and below, and have *dusky* (not reddish) *legs*. Their bills are *yellow below*, not wholly black as with this species.

BANANAQUIT. *Coereba flaveola* (Illus. p. 459).—4–4½. Sides of head and upperparts mainly sooty black, darkest on crown, the superciliaries white; rump golden-olive; a small white patch at base of outer primaries; lateral rectrices white-tipped on inner webs; throat pale gray; breast and

BANANAQUIT

abdomen bright yellow, the lower belly and under tail-coverts dingy white; bill black, moderately long, and slightly decurved.

Distribution.—Lowlands of southeastern Mexico. Also Holbox and Cozumel Islands, off the coast of Quintana Roo.

Races.—*C. f. mexicana* (Veracruz and Oaxaca). *C. f. caboti* (Holbox and Cozumel Islands).

Remarks.—A representative tropical American species with more than thirty races in the West Indies and tropical Central and South America. Bananaquits are characteristic of lowland forests, but may also be found in trees near houses. They feed among the outer twigs and foliage like warblers, but are easily distinguished by their needle-pointed, *curved bills* and relatively short tails. At a distance Bananaquits appear black above and bright yellow below, with a *gray throat* and very conspicuous *white superciliaries*. The white wing-patch is usually obscure.

Family PARULIDAE. Wood Warblers

KEY TO THE SPECIES (ADULTS ONLY)

I. Either with conspicuous bright red, or breast, abdomen, and flanks uniform pinkish orange; if the latter, the outer rectrices white-tipped.
See page 460

II. Throat alone, or throat and breast, yellow, yellowish, orange, or tawny
ochraceous; this either immaculate or more or less streaked, but usually
contrasting sharply with the white, pale yellowish white, or buffy white
of the belly. If the throat alone is yellow, the chest and breast are sometimes black or grayish.   *See* page 461

III. Underparts, *including throat* (except one species with a rufous head),
wholly or mainly yellow or yellowish, this either streaked or immaculate.
Belly and under tail-coverts sometimes white, whitish, or buffy, but
not contrasting sharply with the yellow of the breast as with birds of
Category II. One species, blackish above, and with a white-tipped tail,
has a tawny brownish chest and olive flanks.   *See* page 462

IV. Throat and chest black, blackish, gray, or chestnut, this *contrasting
sharply* with the white or yellow of the breast and belly. Without red
below, but one species with bright orange patches on wings, tail, and
sides of breast.   *See* page 464

V. Underparts *(including throat)* wholly or mainly white, whitish, gray,
or pale buff, this either streaked or immaculate. Throat and breast sometimes faintly tinged with yellow. Sides of head never bright yellow. One
species with chest and sides wholly black, the throat and belly white.
                                                          See page 465

Category I

1a. Above and below extensively red, the head sometimes silvery pink   2
 b. Upperparts without red   3
2a. Head and breast silvery pink . . . .   Pink-headed Warbler, p. 499
 b. Head and breast bright red; a silvery ear-patch   Red Warbler, p. 498
3a. Face and throat red, the breast and abdomen white
                                           Red-faced Warbler, p. 495
 b. Head and throat without red   4
4a. Mainly black or blackish, the wing-coverts and outer rectrices white
                                           Painted Redstart, p. 496
 b. Wings without white 5
5a. Throat white; mainland races with a black chest-band
                                    Red-breasted Chat (male), p. 492
 b. Throat gray or slaty black; no chest-band   6
6a. Breast, median abdomen, and crissum bright red, the flanks white;
a white spot above auriculars (Caribbean lowlands)
                                 Gray-throated Chat (male), p. 493
 b. Breast, abdomen, and flanks bright red or pinkish orange; a
chestnut crown-patch; outer rectrices with broad white tips
(western and southern mountains)
                              Slate-throated Redstart (male), p. 497

Category II

1a. Underparts more or less liberally streaked, the markings often confined to the sides and flanks, and in winter sometimes sparse or obscure. Wings barred, and tail (outer rectrices) with white patches. One species with black breast and sides 2

  b. Not streaked below. Wings and tail with or without white markings. One species with a dingy chest-patch 8

2a. Throat (or upper portion) alone yellow, this bordered behind with white, black, or vague dusky streaks 3

  b. Throat and chest (sometimes breast) yellow, yellowish, or orange, this bordered behind with white. In one species the belly faintly tinged with yellow 4

3a. Sides of head bright yellow; a dark eye-streak; chest white, or with more or less black . . . . Golden-cheeked Warbler (female), p. 482

  b. Sides of head not yellow; breast black, or vaguely streaked; a yellow patch on rump and sides of breast . . Audubon Warbler, p. 480

4a. Lower throat, chest, and breast liberally streaked; auriculars chestnut or dusky; rump conspicuously yellowish
                                        Cape May Warbler, p. 479

  b. Not as in 4a. 5

5a. Throat, chest, and superciliaries bright orange (male), or orange-yellow (female); a bright patch on forepart of crown; back black, or liberally streaked . . . . Blackburnian Warbler, p. 483

  b. Not as in 5a. Back greenish olive or gray, this sometimes streaked; abdomen white, contrasting sharply with yellow of breast . . . 6

6a. Above greenish olive; lores and auriculars dull olive, conspicuously bordered with bright yellow
                            Townsend Warbler (female and fall male), p. 481

  b. Above bluish gray, the back sometimes striped or tinged with brown; auriculars black or gray, the superciliaries white or yellow 7

7a. Superciliaries white, the auriculars black; sides and flanks very boldly striped; a white patch behind auriculars
                                      Yellow-throated Warbler, p. 483

  b. Superciliaries yellow, the auriculars gray; yellow of throat and breast not conspicuously bordered with black   Grace Warbler, p. 484

8a. Wings barred; outer rectrices with white patches on inner webs . 9

  b. Wings and tail without white markings 12

9a. Head, throat, and breast dull yellowish or tawny ochraceous; back gray; a black or dusky eye-patch . . . . . Olive Warbler, p. 476

  b. Not as in 9a. 10

10a. Upperparts (except wings and tail) uniform olive-green; throat, breast, and upper abdomen bright yellow . . . Pine Warbler, p. 485

   b. Sides of head bright yellow, or upperparts mainly grayish blue . 11

11a. Forehead, sides of head, and chin bright yellow, the underparts almost wholly white . . . . Hermit Warbler (female), p. 482

   b. Sides of head and upperparts blue or grayish blue (tinged with olive in winter), the back with a distinct greenish patch; chest sometimes tawny ochraceous or with a dusky patch
Northern Parula Warbler, p. 474
Tropical Parula Warbler, p. 474

12a. Larger (7 inches). Above uniform grayish olive-green; eye-ring, stripe above lores, and malar stripe (at least anteriorly) white
Yellow-breasted Chat, p. 492

   b. Smaller ($4\frac{1}{2}$–$5\frac{1}{4}$ inches). Cheeks and top of head rufous or bluish gray, unlike the back, or with a conspicuous black mask 13

13a. Sides of head and crown rufous, the superciliary and malar stripes white . . . . Rufous-capped Warbler, p. 500

   b. Head without rufous 14

14a. With a black mask, this bordered behind with white; belly white or yellow . . . . Common Yellowthroat (male), p. 489

   b. Above bluish gray, the back and rump bright olive-green; superciliaries white; a brownish crescentic chest-patch
Crescent-chested Warbler, p. 473

CATEGORY III

1a. Underparts more or less streaked or spotted, the markings sometimes confined to the sides and flanks (often obscure in winter), or forming a distinct chest-band 2

   b. Underparts without streaks or spots 6

2a. White wing-bars or a white wing-patch; a yellow rump-patch; tail (outer feathers) white, broadly tipped with black
Magnolia Warbler, p. 478

   b. Wings without white; usually without a distinct rump-patch; tail not as in 2a. 3

3a. Streaks below reddish; tail patterned with yellow; head or crown sometimes rufous . . . . Yellow Warbler (male), p. 477

   b. Streaks (or spots) below black or dusky olive; tail uniform or patterned with white 4

4a. Crown chestnut, the superciliaries yellow; belly much duller than breast and under tail-coverts; rump greenish
Palm Warbler (spring), p. 486

   b. Not as in 4a. 5

5a. Gray above; wings and tail uniform; a distinct pectoral band of black or dusky spots . . . . Canada Warbler, p. 495

b. Greenish above; white tail-patches; wings uniform or with yellow bars; sides streaked, the breast immaculate . Prairie Warbler, p. 486

6a. With white wing-bars and white tail-patches 7

b. Wings without white; tail usually unpatterned, but four species with conspicuous white or yellow patches on the outer feathers . 9

7a. Greenish above 8

b. Blue or bluish gray above, the back with a greenish patch; lower belly and crissum white; throat and breast sometimes tawny
Tropical Parula Warbler, p. 474

8a. Larger (5 inches). Top of head bright olive-green like back; lower belly and crissum white; sides of breast sometimes obscurely streaked with olive . . . . Pine Warbler, p. 485

b. Smaller (4½ inches). Forehead or entire crown bright yellow, contrasting with the nape and back; a black eye-streak; underparts (except crissum) wholly bright yellow
Blue-winged Warbler, p. 469

9a. Tail patterned, the outer feathers white-tipped, or with white or yellow patches on the inner webs 10

b. Tail virtually uniform; with one exception, the upperparts distinctly greenish or olive 13

10a. Tail-patches yellow; wholly yellow below, or head and throat rufous
Yellow Warbler, p. 477

b. Tail white-tipped, or with white patches on the outer feathers . 11

11a. Blackish above; a yellow crown-patch; breast tawny, the throat and belly bright yellow . . . . Fan-tailed Warbler, p. 498

b. Greenish above, the head and hind-neck sometimes bright golden-yellow 12

12a. Head and underparts wholly bright golden-yellow; wings and rump bluish slate . . . . Prothonotary Warbler, p. 468

b. Forehead and sides of head bright yellow, the mid-crown and sides of crown with more or less black; wings and rump greenish
Hooded Warbler (female), p. 494

13a. Above slaty gray, sometimes tinged with olive; a yellow stripe through middle of crown, this bordered with black
Golden-crowned Warbler, p. 499

b. Upperparts greenish or olive, the crown or sides of head often with conspicuous black or chestnut 14

14a. Head with conspicuous black or chestnut 15

b. Not as in 14a. 18

15a. Cheeks and middle of crown chestnut, the superciliaries bright yellow . . . . Golden-browed Warbler, p. 500

   b. Head without chestnut 16

16a. A black cap (reduced or sometimes lacking in females); forehead, superciliaries, and sides of head bright yellow

                                     Pileolated Warbler, p. 494

   b. With a conspicuous black mask, this modified in one species by yellow superciliaries. Black of mask often bordered behind with white or yellow, or sometimes covering most of the crown 17

17a. Superciliaries bright yellow; forepart of crown black like the lores and cheeks . . . . Kentucky Warbler, p. 488

   b. Without yellow superciliaries; black of mask usually very prominent, but in one species (*C. poliocephala*) confined to the forehead and loral area . . . . Yellowthroat spp. (male), pp. 489–91

18a. Sides and top of head distinctly gray, contrasting with the back; white eye-rings; an obscure chestnut crown-patch

                                  Nashville Warbler, p. 470

   b. Not as in 18a. 19

19a. Below dingy olive yellowish, the breast and sides vaguely streaked with darker; rump brighter than back; a concealed reddish crown-patch . . . . Orange-crowned Warbler, p. 470

   b. Not as in 19a. 20

20a. Smaller (4¾ inches). Superciliaries and wing-bars pale yellowish; below pale yellowish white, or mainly greenish yellow, the abdomen and under tail-coverts white

                      Tennessee Warbler (female and fall male), p. 47

   b. Larger (5–5½ inches). Without wing-bars or distinct superciliaries; underparts wholly bright yellow, or throat, breast, and crissum bright yellow, the belly whitish, buffy white, or yellowish buff

                      Yellowthroat spp. (female), pp. 489–91

CATEGORY IV

1a. Yellow below 2

   b. White below 4

2a. Head and chest uniform gray; white eye-rings; no wing-bars or tail patches . . . . MacGillivray Warbler, p. 488

   b. Not as in 2a. 3

3a. With a black hood; forehead and cheeks bright yellow; no wing-bars

                              Hooded Warbler (male), p. 494

   b. Not hooded, but head with conspicuous black; superciliary and malar stripes bright yellow; white wing-bars; sides and flanks heavily streaked . . . . . Townsend Warbler (spring male), p. 481

4a. Throat, sides, and flanks chestnut; forehead and sides of head black; white wing-bars and tail-patches

Bay-breasted Warbler (spring male), p. 484

   b. Without chestnut; throat and chest (at least) black or blackish .   5

5a. Head, and sometimes wings, with conspicuous yellow   6

   b. Without yellow; one species with bright orange wing- and tail-patches   9

6a. Crown and wing-coverts yellow; sides of head black; a white malar stripe . . . . . . Golden-winged Warbler (male), p. 469

   b. Sides of head (at least) yellow; white wing-bars   7

7a. Top of head, back, and rump uniform bright olive-green

Black-throated Green Warbler (spring), p. 481

   b. Not as in 7a.   8

8a. Top of head, back, and rump wholly black; a black eye-streak ·

Golden-cheeked Warbler (spring), p. 482

   b. Forehead, forepart of crown, and sides of head bright yellow; no eye-streak; back gray, or striped with black

Hermit Warbler (male), p. 482

9a. Above and below heavily striped with black and white; a white stripe through middle of crown

Black-and-White Warbler (male), p. 468

   b. Not as in 9a. 10

10a. Sides of breast, wings, and tail with bright orange patches

American Redstart (male), p. 496

   b. Without orange patches 11

11a. White superciliary and malar stripes; two broad white wing-bars; sides boldly striped . Black-throated Gray Warbler (spring), p. 480

   b. Without superciliary or malar stripes; a conspicuous white wing-patch; throat, sides, and flanks wholly black

Black-throated Blue Warbler (male), p. 479

CATEGORY V

1a. Underparts with more or less conscious streaks or spots, these often sparse or dim in winter, and sometimes confined to the breast, or to the sides and flanks. [Species with decidedly obscure markings are repeated under 1b.]   2

   b. Underparts virtually immaculate, or with very obscure streaks or spots 10

2a. White or whitish wing-bars and tail-patches   3

   b. Without wing-bars or tail-patches; heavily streaked or spotted below   8

3a. Under tail-coverts bright yellow; breast and sides faintly streaked; superciliaries whitish; rump greenish . . . Palm Warbler (fall), p. 486

   b. Under tail-coverts white like belly 4

4a. Blue above; a bluish band across chest
Cerulean Warbler (male), p. 482

   b. Not blue above; no pectoral band 5

5a. Upperparts boldly striped with black and white, the underparts sometimes similar . . . . Black-and-White Warbler, p. 468

   b. Not as in 5a. 6

6a. A yellow patch on rump and sides of breast; chest and sides sometimes wholly black . . . . Myrtle Warbler, p. 480

   b. Without yellow patches 7

7a. Top of head wholly black, unlike back, or crown and back dull olive-green, liberally streaked with black
Blackpolled Warbler, p. 485

   b. Sides of head and upperparts gray; conspicuous white superciliary and malar stripes; a white or yellow spot above lores
Black-throated Gray Warbler (female and winter male), p. 480

8a. Above greenish; crown tawny orange bordered with black
Ovenbird, p. 486

   b. Not greenish above; crown and back uniform 9

9a. Upperparts dull grayish olive; white superciliaries; throat immaculate white; breast and belly *pale creamy buff*
Louisiana Waterthrush, p. 487

   b. Upperparts dull brownish olive; pale buff superciliaries; throat usually lightly speckled; breast and belly *pale yellowish*
Northern Waterthrush, p. 487

10a. With white or yellow wing-bars and tail-patches. Wing-bars of one species represented by a white or yellow patch at the base of the primaries or secondaries 11

   b. Without wing-bars. Three species with white tail-patches 19

11a. Wing-bars or wing-patch yellow 12

   b. Wing-bars or wing-patch white 15

12a. Sides and flanks with more or less chestnut; above bright greenish yellow, or back heavily striped with black
Chestnut-sided Warbler, p. 484

   b. Without chestnut; upperparts not streaked, the back essentially gray, brownish, or dull olive 13

13a. Wings, tail, and sides of breast with very conspicuous yellow patches . . . . American Redstart (female), p. 496

   b. Not as in 13a. 14

14a. Forepart of crown and wing-coverts bright yellow; cheeks blackish; throat, chest, and sides gray, the belly white
Golden-winged Warbler (female), p. 469

   b. Upperparts uniform dull olive or olive-gray; below whitish or pale yellowish white; wing-bars inconspicuous; inner webs of outer rectrices edged with yellow . . . . Yellow Warbler (female), p. **477**

15a. Below white or whitish, the breast and sides sometimes lightly streaked 16

   b. Below pale buffy yellowish, without streaks 18

16a. Gray above; sides of head blackish, the superciliaries and malar area gleaming white; a white spot above lores
Black-throated Gray Warbler (fall), p. 480

   b. Not as in 16a. 17

17a. Above uniform bluish, or bluish olive-green; distinct whitish superciliaries . . . Cerulean Warbler (female and fall male), p. 482

   b. Above dull olive-green, liberally streaked with black; no distinct superciliary line; breast and sides usually lightly streaked
Blackpolled Warbler (female and fall male), p. 485

18a. Two conspicuous wing-bars; above bright olive-green, or crown with more or less chestnut; sides and flanks sometimes tinged with reddish . . . . Bay-breasted Warbler (female and fall male), p. 484

   b. A small white patch at base of primaries; white eyelids; above uniform dull olive-gray Black-throated Blue Warbler (female), p. 479

19a. Outer rectrices white-tipped, or with white patches 20

   b. Tail without white 22

20a. Gray above; breast, sides, and line above auriculars buffy . . . 21

   b. Brownish above, the rump greenish; underparts tinged with yellow, the crissum bright yellow; breast sometimes lightly streaked
Palm Warbler (fall), p. 486

21a. Tail long and fanlike, the outer feathers with conspicuous white patches; under tail-coverts bright red or pink (Pacific slope)
Red-breasted Chat (female), p. 492

   b. Not as in 21a (Caribbean lowlands)
Gray-throated Chat (female), p. 493

22a. Sides of head, throat, and breast gray; under tail-coverts ochraceous; a large chestnut crown-patch . . . . Colima Warbler, p. 472

   b. Not as in 22a. 23

23a. Crown bordered with black, the median stripe, superciliaries, and cheeks yellowish buff . . . . Worm-eating Warbler, p. 469

   b. Not as in 23a. 24

*BLACK-AND-WHITE WARBLER. *Mniotilta varia.*—4½–5. *Male:*
Above and below boldly striped with black and white, the belly immaculate;
a broad white crown-stripe and two white wing-bars; lateral rectrices white-
tipped. *Female:* Similar above, but somewhat duller; below mainly white,
the sides and flanks striped with dusky.

Distribution.—Migratory in Baja California and on both coasts.
Winters in southern Baja California, and from Colima and Nuevo León
southward.

Remarks.—The *black-and-white striped plumage* is unmistakable.
Females are essentially white below, although boldly marked above. A
conspicuous white stripe through the median crown at once eliminates
the Blackpolled and all similar warblers.

*PROTHONOTARY WARBLER. *Protonotaria citrea.*—5¼. *Male:*
Head, neck, and underparts bright golden-yellow; back and scapulars
yellowish olive-green; wings and rump bluish slate; no wing-bars; tail black,
the lateral feathers with conspicuous white on the inner webs. *Female:*
Similar, but much duller; olive-green of back extending over the crown; below tinged with olive.

Distribution.—Winters casually in Campeche, apparently migrating
across the Gulf.

Remarks.—A bright yellow warbler with uniform *bluish* wings and
a *white patterned* tail. Blue-winged and Yellow Warblers are also conspicuously yellow, but the former has white wing-bars; the latter yellowish wings and a yellow-patterned tail.

*SWAINSON WARBLER. *Limnothlypis swainsonii.*—5. Above uniform olive-brown; superciliaries yellowish buff or whitish; a brown eye-streak; no wing-bars or tail-patches; below pale yellowish white, the sides and flanks tinged with olive; bill light brownish; legs pale flesh color.

Distribution.—Migratory in Tamaulipas and Veracruz; winters casually in Quintana Roo.

Remarks.—Much like a Worm-eating Warbler, but without black crown-stripes. Waterthrushes are similar above, but have boldly streaked underparts.

*WORM-EATING WARBLER. *Helmitheros vermivorus.*—5. Sides of crown and postocular stripe black, the median crown and superciliaries yellowish buff; upperparts dull olive-green; no wing-bars or tail-patches; below buffy, palest on the throat and abdomen, the breast, sides, and flanks more or less tinged with tawny; bill and legs pale brownish or flesh color.

Distribution.—Migratory in eastern Mexico, wintering at least casually in the extreme south (Quintana Roo, Cozumel Island, and Chiapas).

Remarks.—No other warbler with *black crown-stripes* has a *buffy* head and breast.

*GOLDEN-WINGED WARBLER. *Vermivora chrysoptera* (Illus. p. 471).—4½. *Male:* Forehead and crown bright yellow, this more or less replaced by olive-green in winter; sides of head, throat, and chest black, the throat bordered laterally with white; posterior superciliaries white; upperparts mainly gray, this tinged with olive in winter; a patch of bright yellow on the upper wing; inner webs of lateral rectrices largely white; below (except throat) white, the flanks tinged with gray. *Female:* Similar, but yellow of crown reduced, and the black of the cheeks and throat replaced with gray.

Distribution.—Migratory in eastern Mexico, wintering casually in the south.

Remarks.—A small grayish warbler with bright *yellow crown and wing-patches*. Males have black cheeks and a *black bib.*

*BLUE-WINGED WARBLER. *Vermivora pinus.*—4½. *Male:* Head and underparts bright golden-yellow, this shading to bright olive-green on the hind-neck, back, scapulars, and rump; a black eye-stripe; wings and tail bluish gray, the wing-coverts and inner webs of the rectrices largely white. *Female:* Similar, but somewhat duller, and with less white on the wings; crown often olive-green like the back.

Distribution.—Migratory in eastern Mexico, wintering in the south.

Remarks.—A bright yellow warbler with a *black eye-stripe* and *white wing-bars*. Yellow Warblers lack wing-bars and have *yellow* (not white) *patches* on the tail. Prothonotaries have *unpatterned bluish wings*.

*TENNESSEE WARBLER. *Vermivora peregrina.*—4¾. *Male* (*spring*): Crown and hind-neck gray, the back, scapulars, and rump bright olive-green; superciliaries white; no wing-bars or tail-patches; below mainly white, the sides and flanks tinged with gray; (*fall*): Similar, but gray of head, sides, and flanks more or less tinged with olive-green; white of belly sometimes tinged with yellow. *Female:* Essentially like fall male, but more extensively greenish, and with pale yellowish wing-bars.

Distribution.—Migratory in eastern Mexico, wintering casually in the south.

Remarks.—The *gray* crown and contrasting *greenish* back serve to distinguish males in spring. Females and males in fall plumage are largely yellowish below and greenish above. The slender, warbler-type bill is unlike that of any yellow-and-greenish vireo. Similar warblers have *yellow* (not white) under tail-coverts. Female Canadas, while yellow-bellied and white-vented, have distinctly *gray* upperparts. *See* Warbling Vireo and Philadelphia Vireo.

ORANGE-CROWNED WARBLER. *Vermivora celata.*—4½–5. *Adult* (*spring*): Above dull greenish olive or bright olive-green, brightest on the rump; a tawny crown-patch, this usually obscure, and in females often lacking; superciliaries and underparts dingy olive-yellowish, the breast and sides vaguely streaked with darker; no wing-bars or tail-patches; (*fall*): Similar, but much duller; crown-patch obscure or lacking.

Distribution.—Resident on Todos Santos Islands, off northwestern Baja California. Widespread elsewhere in migration and winter.

Races.—*V. c. sordida* (Todos Santos Islands, Baja California). **V. c. orestera* (winters in Baja California and south to Guerrero, Puebla, and Tamaulipas). **V. c. lutescens* (winters in southern Baja California, and from Chihuahau southward). **V. c. celata* (winters south to Hidalgo and southern Veracruz).

Remarks.—An undistinguished, dingy greenish warbler with *vaguely streaked underparts*. The orange crown-patch is likely to be seen only under exceptional conditions. *See* Philadelphia Vireo.

*NASHVILLE WARBLER. *Vermivora ruficapilla.*—4½. *Male:* Crown, hind-neck, and sides of head gray, the first with a chestnut patch; a conspicuous white eye-ring; upperparts mainly olive-green, brightest on the rump; no wing-bars or tail-patches; below bright golden-yellow, the lower

MALE WOOD WARBLERS

GOLDEN-WINGED WARBLER
(p. 469)

TOWNSEND WARBLER
(p. 481)

MAGNOLIA WARBLER
(p. 478)

BLACK-THROATED GREEN
WARBLER (p. 481)

MYRTLE WARBLER
(p. 480)

GOLDEN-CHEEKED WARBLER
(p. 482)

BLACK-THROATED GRAY
WARBLER (p. 480)

BLACKPOLLED WARBLER
(p. 485)

abdomen white. *Female:* Similar to male, but somewhat duller, and usually without chestnut on the crown. *Immature:* Much like adult female, but even duller; gray of head replaced with grayish brown.

Distribution.—Widespread in migration and winter.

Races.—*V. r. ridgwayi* (migratory in Baja California; winters in western Mexico south to Oaxaca and Puebla). *V. r. ruficapilla* (migratory in eastern Mexico, wintering from Veracruz southward).

Remarks.—Also known as Gray-capped Warbler. The only gray-headed, olive-backed warbler with wholly yellow underparts. Look for the white eye-ring, and note the absence of wing-bars and tail-patches. MacGillivray Warblers are somewhat similar, but have *gray* throats and breasts.

*VIRGINIA WARBLER. *Vermivora virginiae.*—4½. *Adult:* Above grayish, the rump and tail-coverts bright yellowish olive-green; a chestnut crown-patch, this concealed in winter and often obscure in females; a white eye-ring; no wing-bars or tail-patches; below dingy whitish, the median breast usually with a yellow patch, this sometimes extending over the throat; crissum bright lemon-yellow. *Immature:* Similar, but without a crown-patch, and median underparts pale buffy, the chest sometimes faintly tinged with yellow.

Distribution.—Winters in western Mexico south to Guerrero and Morelos.

Remarks.—A small, pale-bellied, grayish warbler with *yellowish* under tail-coverts and rump. No similar bird has yellow on the breast. Unfortunately, this character is sometimes obscure. Virginia Warblers could be confused with either the Colima or the Lucy, both of which lack yellow on the breast. The former, a highland resident, is *brownish olive* (not gray) *above*, and has distinctly *tawny* under tail-coverts. Lucy Warblers have *chestnut* rumps and *white* under tail-coverts. While all three possess a chestnut crown-patch, this character usually is conspicuous only in the Colima Warbler.

COLIMA WARBLER. *Vermivora crissalis.*—5¼. Above brownish olive, the rump yellowish olive-green; a large chestnut crown-patch; eye-ring white; no wing-bars or tail-patches; below mainly gray, the flanks tinged with olive, the crissum bright ochraceous buff.

Distribution.—Recorded in the mountains of Coahuila (Sierra Guadalupe; Diamante Pass), western Tamaulipas (Miquihuana), Michoacán (Patamba), Colima (Sierra Nevada), and Guerrero (Tepoxtepec).

Remarks.—This representative Mexican warbler breeds locally, and in some abundance, in the Chisos Mountains of southwestern

Texas. It resembles a Virginia Warbler, but is darker (less grayish)
above, lacks a yellow breast-patch, and has *tawny* (not bright yellow)
under tail-coverts. Pine and oak forests at high altitudes.

LUCY WARBLER. *Vermivora luciae.*—4. *Adult:* Above mainly gray,
the upper tail-coverts rich chestnut; a chestnut crown-patch, this concealed
in winter, and sometimes obscure in females; no wing-bars or tail-patches;
lores, eye-ring, and underparts essentially white, the breast, sides, and flanks
very faintly tinged with buff. *Immature:* Similar to adult, but without a
crown-patch, and chestnut of the rump replaced with ochraceous buff; two
pale wing-bars.

Distribution.—Northern Baja California, wintering also in western
Mexico south to Jalisco.

Remarks.—Much like a Virginia Warbler, but *white-vented*, and
with a *chestnut* rump. Adult Virginias usually have at least a smudge of
yellow on the breast, while this species is virtually uniform below.

CRESCENT-CHESTED WARBLER. *Vermivora superciliosa* (Illus. p.
473).—4½. Crown, hind-neck, and sides of head gray, this tinged with olive
in subadult birds; superciliaries white; back, scapulars, and rump bright
olive-green; wings and tail uniform gray; throat, breast, and sides bright
golden-yellow, the posterior underparts whitish; a transverse chestnut patch

CRESCENT-CHESTED WARBLER

on the lower throat, this usually crescentic, but variable and sometimes obsolete.

Distribution.—Wooded highlands, chiefly above an altitude of 5,000 feet.

Races.—*V. s. sodalis* (mountains of southwestern Chihuahua south through western Durango and eastern Sinaloa to the vicinity of Tepec, Nayarit). *V. s. palliata* (Sierra Madre del Sur, Guerrero, north in the mountains to Jalisco). *V. s. mexicana* (highlands of eastern Mexico south to Oaxaca). *V. s. superciliosa* (mountains of Chiapas).

Remarks.—Also known as Hartlaub Warbler and Mexican Warbler. A common mountain resident, occurring principally in oak and pine forests. No other bluish warbler with a yellow throat and breast has conspicuous *white superciliaries*. A *sharply defined crescentic patch* usually shows at the base of the throat. Both Parulas have white wing-bars. The Northern often has a conspicuous, but *ill-defined*, chest-patch, quite unlike that of this species.

*NORTHERN PARULA WARBLER. *Parula americana pusilla* (Illus. p. 475).—4–4½. *Male:* Sides of head and upperparts mainly dull grayish blue, the back and scapulars yellowish olive; lateral rectrices with a white patch; two conspicuous white wing-bars; throat and breast bright yellow, the median chest usually with a blackish and tawny patch; posterior underparts white. *Female:* Similar to male, but much duller, especially below; chest but faintly tinged with tawny, and usually without a dusky patch. *Immature:* Much like an adult, but gray of upperparts tinged with olive, the back-patch relatively indistinct; throat and breast uniformly bright yellow, the belly faintly tinged with buff.

Distribution.—Winters in eastern and southern Mexico.

Remarks.—A small *bluish* warbler, with conspicuous *white wing-bars*, and a yellow throat and breast. Adults in breeding plumage have a blackish band or smudge on the breast. Tropical Parulas have *clear* yellow or tawny breasts, and usually show some yellow on the abdomen. Both species have yellowish olive backs. Winter females are often virtually indistinguishable. *See* Crescent-chested Warbler.

TROPICAL PARULA WARBLER. *Parula pitiayumi* (Illus. p. 476).—4–4½. *Male:* Above mainly bluish gray, grayish blue, or dull indigo-blue, these sometimes tinged with olive; a large triangular yellowish olive patch on the back; sides of head grayish or virtually black; two conspicuous white wing-bars; inner webs of lateral tail feathers with a white patch; underparts mainly or extensively yellow, this becoming buffy or white on the lower abdomen; lower throat and breast sometimes more or less tinged with orange

MALE WOOD WARBLERS

NORTHERN PARULA WARBLER
(p. 474)

COMMON YELLOWTHROAT
(p. 489)

HERMIT WARBLER
(p. 482)

HOODED WARBLER
(p. 494)

OVENBIRD
(p. 486)

PILEOLATED WARBLER
(p. 494)

MacGILLIVRAY WARBLER
(p. 488)

GOLDEN-BROWED WARBLER
(p. 500)

or tawny. *Female:* Similar to male, but usually much duller above and below.

Distribution.—Socorro Island, Todos Santos Islands, southern Baja California, the Pacific slope south to Jalisco, and northeastern Mexico south to San Luis Potosí. Also the mountains of Chiapas.

Races.—*P. p. graysoni* (Socorro Island, Revilla Gigedo group; also casually in southern Baja California). *P. p. insularis* (Tres Marías Islands and the Pacific Coast from Labrados, Sinaloa, to San Blas, Nayarit). *P. p. pulchra* (Pacific slope from southern Sonora and Chihuahua to Jalisco). *P. p. nigrilora* (Nuevo León, Tamaulipas, and San Luis Potosí). *P. p. inornata* (mountains of Chiapas).

TROPICAL PARULA WARBLER

Remarks.—Also known as Olive-backed Warbler and Pitiayumi Warbler. Much like the Northern Parula in general appearance, but without a dark breast-band, and usually more extensively yellow below. Eastern males have *blackish* cheeks, and *rich tawny* (not bright yellow) *breasts*. Socorro Island birds may represent a distinct species.

OLIVE WARBLER. *Peucedramus taeniatus* (Illus. p. 477).—5. *Male:* Head, neck, throat, and breast rich tawny ochraceous, the sides of the head with a broad black band; back, scapulars, and rump gray, this sometimes tinged with olive; wings and tail sooty, the former with two conspicuous white bars, the inner webs of the outer rectrices largely white; belly white.

Female: Similar to male in pattern, but top of head yellowish olive-green, this shading to dull yellow on the neck, throat, and breast; black of face-patch replaced with dusky.

Distribution.—High mountains, chiefly in pine forest.

Races.—*P. t. arizonae* (Chihuahua, Durango, and Tamaulipas). *P. t. taeniatus* (mountains of southern Mexico, from Jalisco to Veracruz and Oaxaca). *P. t. aurantiacus* (pine forests of Chiapas).

Remarks.—A *rich tawny head and breast* (olive and yellowish in females), and black or dusky eye-patch are found in no other gray-backed, white-bellied warbler. Females possibly could be confused with

OLIVE WARBLER

female Townsend or Hermit Warblers. The former usually shows some streaks below; the latter has a *white* breast.

YELLOW WARBLER. *Dendroica petechia.*—4½–5. *Male (type A):* Above yellowish olive-green, brightest on the forehead; wings and tail dusky, the wing-coverts and remiges edged with yellow, the inner webs of the rectrices largely yellow; sides of head and underparts bright yellow or greenish yellow, the breast, sides, and flanks more or less streaked with reddish; *(type B):* Essentially like type A, but head chestnut, or with a conspicuous chestnut crown-patch. *Female:* Similar to males of type A, but somewhat duller, and usually without ventral streaks; in winter often tinged above with gray, and very pale below.

Distribution.—Widespread, especially in winter and during migration. Several races, either chestnut-headed or chestnut-capped, are largely restricted to mangrove swamps and brackish estuaries.

Races.—(*Type A*): *D. p. aestiva (migratory in eastern Mexico, wintering from Yucatán southward). *D. p. morcomi (winters in western Mexico). *D. p rubiginosa (migratory in Baja California, wintering southward in western Mexico). D. p. brewsteri (breeds in northern Baja California south to latitude 30°; winters casually in southern Baja California, and southward in western Mexico). D. p. sonorana (breeds in northeastern Baja California, Sonora, and Chihuahua, ranging southward in winter). **D. p. inedita (breeds in mountains of western Tamaulipas; migratory southward). D. p. dugesi (Guanajuato, Tlaxcala, Michoacán, and Morelos). (*Type B*): D. p. hueyi (San Ignacio and Pond lagoons on the Pacific Coast of central Baja California). D. p. castaneiceps (coasts of southern Baja California north to Magdalena Bay on the Pacific side, and to San Lucas an the Gulf). D. p. rhizophorae (mangrove swamps and brackish estuaries of southern Sonora, and probably northern Sinaloa). D. p. bryanti (mangrove swamps and brackish estuaries from Tampico, Tamaulipas southward). D. p. rufivertex (Cozumel Island, off Quintana Roo).

Remarks.—This common warbler appears virtually all-yellow in the field, and usually will not be mistaken for any other species. In case of doubt, look for the *yellow* patches on the tail. Adult males in breeding plumage often have *chestnut streaks below*. The brown-headed coastal races are called Mangrove Warblers and may represent a distinct species. Yellow Warblers of the interior are most likely to be found in willows and cottonwoods bordering streams.

*MAGNOLIA WARBLER. *Dendroica magnolia* (Illus. p. 471).—4½–5. *Male (spring)*: Crown bluish gray; a white line behind eye; sides of head, back, scapulars, upper tail-coverts, and middle rectrices black, the lateral rectrices white basally, but very broadly black-tipped; rump yellow; wings black, the coverts largely white; below bright yellow, the breast, sides, and flanks very heavily streaked with black. *Female (spring)*: Similar to summer male, but pattern less sharply defined, and the colors duller; black of back much reduced. *Immature and adults in fall:* Similar to summer female, but crown and sides of head ashy; back greenish, this sometimes intermixed with black; two white wing-bars; below yellow, the flanks sometimes spotted or streaked.

Distribution.—Migratory in eastern Mexico. Winters from Puebla southward, but as yet unrecorded in the Yucatán Peninsula.

Remarks.—One of several boldly patterned warblers with *heavily streaked, yellow underparts*. Adults in breeding plumage have *gray* crowns and *black* backs. From below the Magnolia's tail is always distinctive; white basally, the *terminal half black*.

*CAPE MAY WARBLER. *Dendroica tigrina.*—4½–5. *Male (spring)*: Crown essentially black; superciliaries and sides of neck yellow, the auriculars chestnut; back and scapulars olive-green, spotted or streaked with black; rump yellowish olive; wing-coverts largely white; tail blackish, the inner webs of the lateral feathers with a large white patch near tips; throat and breast yellow, shading to white on the abdomen and crissum, the breast and sides black-streaked. *Female (spring)*: Above essentially grayish olive-green, the crown black-spotted, the rump bright yellowish olive; superciliaries yellow, the cheeks dusky; a reduced white wing-patch; tail as in male; below mainly ʸellowish streaked with dusky, the abdomen and crissum immaculate white. *Immature and adults in fall:* Similar to female, or much grayer and more uniform above, and with white underparts liberally streaked with dusky.

Distribution.—Winters at least casually in Yucatán and Quintana Roo. A single winter record for Chinchorro Bank off the coast of Quintana Roo.

Remarks.—Males in breeding plumage are unmistakable—bright yellow below, where liberally streaked with black, and with *chestnut cheeks*. Females and fall males are rather undistinguished and might be confused with several other species, especially Myrtle, Palm, and Pine Warblers. Cape Mays always have a *yellow patch* (suffused and vague in fall) *behind the auriculars*. Fall birds are *uniformly grayish olive* (not brownish) *above*. Note the *white* (not yellow) *crissum*.

*BLACK-THROATED BLUE WARBLER. *Dendroica caerulescens.*— 5. *Male:* Above uniform grayish blue, the back often black-spotted; a large white patch at base of primaries; inner webs of the lateral rectrices with a white patch near the tips; sides of head, throat, chest, sides, and flanks black, the underparts otherwise white. *Female:* Above uniform dull olive-gray; a pale incomplete eye-ring; a small white patch at base of primaries; tail usually tinged with bluish, the lateral feathers faintly patterned as in male; below uniform buffy yellowish.

Distribution.—Casual or accidental (two records) in winter on Cozumel Island, off Quintana Roo.

Remarks.—Adult males are notably distinctive: bluish above, black-throated, and with immaculate white breast and belly. Females and immature birds resemble Philadelphia Vireos and fall Tennessee Warblers superficially, but have conspicuously *dusky cheeks* and a small *white wing-patch* that is diagnostic. *See* Orange-crowned Warbler.

MYRTLE WARBLER. *Dendroica coronata* (Illus. p. 471).—5½. *Male (spring)*: Above bluish gray, streaked with black, the median crown, rump, and sides of breast bright yellow; two white wing-bars; inner webs of outer rectrices with a white patch near tips; throat, abdomen, and crissum white, the breast and upper belly mainly black. *Female (spring)*: Similar, but browner above, yellow patches less conspicuous, and breast black-streaked. *Immature and adults in fall:* Above essentially brownish, the crown-patch usually obscure, the rump yellow; below dingy whitish, the breast, sides, and flanks dimly streaked with dusky; a yellowish patch on each side of breast.

Distribution.—Widespread in winter.

Races.—*D. c. hooveri* (winters south at least to Baja California and Veracruz). *D. c. coronata* (widespread in winter).

Remarks.—Much like the following, but with a *white* throat. Both species have a *conspicuous yellow rump-patch* at all seasons, and usually at least a suggestion of yellow on the crown, and on each side of the breast. Winter birds are essentially *brown* (not gray) above. *See* female Cape May Warbler.

AUDUBON WARBLER. *Dendroica auduboni.*—5. Similar to a Myrtle Warbler in comparable plumage, but with a yellow (not white) throat, bluish gray (not black) cheeks, and a large white wing-patch. Winter birds have two white wing-bars.

Distribution.—Mountains of northwestern Mexico (Chihuahua and Durango), occurring extensively elsewhere in winter.

Races.—*D. a. auduboni* (widespread in winter). *D. a. nigrifrons* (breeds in the mountains of Chihuahua and Durango, ranging southward in winter).

Remarks.—*See* Myrtle Warbler.

BLACK-THROATED GRAY WARBLER. *Dendroica nigrescens* (Illus. p. 471).—4½–4¾. *Male (spring)*: Crown, sides of head, and throat black, the superciliaries and broad malar stripe white; a small yellow spot above the lores; upperparts otherwise mainly bluish gray, the back streaked with black; inner webs of the lateral rectrices white; two broad white wing-bars; underparts (except throat) white, the sides and flanks broadly streaked with black. *Female (spring)*: Essentially like the male, but crown usually grayish like back, and throat usually white, more or less intermixed with black. *Immature and adults in fall:* Similar to adults in spring, but much duller, the upperparts tinged with brown, and the black streaks obscure or lacking; below whitish, the throat, sides, and flanks sometimes with more or less black.

Distribution.—Breeds in the mountains of northern Baja California, wintering in southern Baja California, and in western Mexico from Durango southward.

Remarks.—A white-bellied warbler with a black crown, cheeks, and throat. Females are gray above, white below, and usually have little black on the throat. Both sexes have conspicuous white superciliaries and wing-bars. A small *yellowish* spot above the lores is good corroborative evidence.

*TOWNSEND WARBLER. *Dendroica townsendi* (Illus p. 471).—$4\frac{1}{2}$–$4\frac{3}{4}$. *Male (spring)*: Crown, sides of head, and throat black, the superciliaries, sides of neck, and broad malar stripe bright yellow; back, scapulars, and rump greenish olive, streaked or spotted with black; two white wing-bars; tail blackish, the inner webs of the lateral feathers white; breast yellow, the sides streaked with black; belly and crissum white. *Female (spring)*: Essentially like male, but duller, the black of the crown much intermixed with olive, the cheeks dusky olive (not black), the throat mainly yellow. *Immature and adults in fall:* Similar to summer females, but crown, back, rump, and auriculars uniform greenish olive; throat and breast yellow, the sides and flanks sometimes vaguely streaked.

Distribution.—Winters in the Tres Marías Islands, Baja California, and southward over western and central Mexico.

Remarks.—Patterned like a Black-throated Gray Warbler, but with *green* replacing the gray of the upperparts, and with *bright yellow* replacing the white of the head and breast. Note the *white belly*. The sides of the breast usually are more or less streaked at all seasons.

*BLACK-THROATED GREEN WARBLER. *Dendroica virens virens* (Illus. p. 471).—$4\frac{1}{2}$. *Male (spring)*: Above bright olive-green, the sides of the head bright yellow; wings and tail blackish, the former with two broad white bars; inner webs of the outer rectrices white-tipped, the outer webs white at base; throat and breast black; abdomen and crissum white, the flanks streaked with black. *Female (spring)*: Similar to male, but the black of the throat and breast much intermixed with yellow. *Immature and adults in fall:* Throat and breast pale yellow, this sometimes intermixed with black.

Distribution.—Winters in eastern Mexico from Nuevo León southward, including the Yucatán Peninsula and Cozumel Island.

Remarks.—A white-bellied, *green-backed* warbler with *yellow cheeks*. Males in breeding plumage have a black bib that extends over the sides of the breast. Females and fall males resemble female Golden-cheeked Warblers, but usually lack a distinct eye-streak, and are faintly tinged with yellow below.

*GOLDEN-CHEEKED WARBLER. *Dendroica chrysoparia* (Illus. p. 471).—4½–5. *Male* (*spring*): Upperparts, throat, and breast black; sides of head bright yellow, the eye-streak black; two broad white wing-bars; inner webs of outer rectrices mainly white; lower breast, abdomen, and crissum white, the sides and flanks heavily streaked with black. *Female* (*spring*): Similar to summer male, but the black of the upperparts replaced with olive-green, this finely streaked with black; throat yellow like sides of head, the chest usually with more or less black. *Immature and adults in fall:* Either essentially like summer plumage of the respective adults, or similar to adult female, but with white throat and breast.

Distribution.—Migratory in eastern Mexico, wintering in the southern highlands.

Remarks.—Spring males, black above and black-throated, are unmistakable. Females, and males in winter, might be mistaken for Black-throated Green Warblers. However, Golden-cheeks are whiter below and, under favorable conditions, usually show a *distinct eye-streak*. *See* Hermit Warbler.

*HERMIT WARBLER. *Dendroica occidentalis* (Illus. p. 475).—*Male:* Top and sides of head bright yellow, the throat black; back, scapulars, and rump olive-gray, very broadly streaked with black, this intensified on the hind-neck and often spotting the crown; two broad white wing-bars; tail black, the three outer feathers largely white; breast and posterior underparts immaculate white. *Female:* Similar to male, but top of head black-spotted, back obscurely streaked, and the black of the throat replaced with yellow. *Immature:* Much like adult female, but top of head with less yellow, and throat essentially white like breast.

Distribution.—Winters in Baja California and south over the Mexican plateau, occurring casually elsewhere.

Remarks.—Adults in breeding plumage appear yellow-headed. While possible to confuse with Black-throated Green and Golden-cheeked Warblers, the black bib of the male Hermit is *rounded posteriorly* and does not extend over the sides of the breast. Females are much like Townsend, Black-throated Green, and Golden-cheeked Warblers. Note the *white underparts* (throat alone faintly tinged with yellow), the absence of ventral streaking, and the lack of a distinct eye-streak.

*CERULEAN WARBLER. *Dendroica cerulea.*—4½. *Male:* Above bright blue, the back streaked with black; wings and tail blackish edged with blue, the former with two white bars, the outer rectrices white-spotted near tips of the inner webs; below white, the breast with a bluish band, and sides striped with same. *Female:* Above uniform bluish olive-green; superciliaries pale; wings and tail patterned as in male; below white, faintly tinged with yellow. *Immature:* Similar to adult female, but greener above, and more yellowish below.

Distribution.—Migratory, wintering in northern South America.

Remarks.—A white-bellied, bluish warbler with a dark collar. Females and immature birds lack the collar, and may be *greenish* above, and tinged with yellow below. Note the *two white wing-bars*, and *white-patterned tail. See* Tennessee Warbler and Black-throated Blue Warbler.

*BLACKBURNIAN WARBLER. *Dendroica fusca.*—5. *Male:* Above mainly black, the crown with an orange patch, the back sometimes white-streaked; superciliaries, sides of neck, throat, and breast bright orange, the cheeks black; wings and tail black, the wing-coverts and inner webs of the lateral rectrices mainly white; abdomen pale yellowish, the sides and flanks streaked with black. *Female:* Similar to male, but with yellow replacing the orange markings, and upperparts essentially dull olive-green, more or less streaked with black and whitish; two white wing-bars. *Immature:* Essentially like female, but even duller, the yellow markings quite pale, and the crown-patch often lacking; streaks on sides and flanks dusky and obscure.

Distribution.—Migratory in eastern Mexico, wintering casually from Yucatán southward.

Remarks.—The only warbler with a *bright orange throat.* Females are patterned somewhat like males, but have *yellow* throats and dimly streaked sides. The wing-bars are usually very conspicuous. Note the yellowish crown-patch and superciliaries. *See* female Grace Warbler.

*YELLOW-THROATED WARBLER. *Dendroica dominica albilora.*— *Adult:* Above bluish gray, the forehead and sides of head black; superciliaries white; wings and tail sooty, the former with two white bars, the inner webs of the lateral rectrices white-tipped; throat and median breast bright yellow, this bordered with black laterally; sides of breast and posterior underparts white, the sides and flanks broadly streaked with white. *Immature:* Similar to adult, but more or less tinged with brown, especially above, and with obscure streaks below.

Distribution.—Winters from Colima, Puebla, and Yucatán southward. Also on Cozumel, Mujeres, and Holbox Islands.

Remarks.—No other gray-backed warbler with a conspicuous yellow bib has *white superciliaries* and *black cheeks.* The heavily barred

sides and white patch behind the auriculars are also good characters.
Grace Warblers are less boldly patterned, and have *yellow* superciliaries
and *gray* cheeks.

GRACE WARBLER. *Dendroica graciae.*—4½–5. *Male:* Upperparts and
sides of head gray, the crown and back streaked with black; superciliaries,
throat, and breast bright yellow; two white wing-bars; tail blackish, the
inner webs of the outer feathers extensively white; abdomen white, the sides
and flanks streaked with black. *Female:* Similar to male, but duller, and
tinged with brown above, the dorsal stripes usually obscure or absent.
Immature: Essentially like female, but brownish above, virtually unstreaked
below, and abdomen usually tinged with buff.

Distribution.—Breeds in the mountains of Sonora, Chihuahua, Oaxaca,
and Chiapas, wintering extensively elsewhere in the highlands.

Races.—*D. g. graciae* (mountains of Sonora and Chihuahua, ranging
south to Nayarit, Jalisco, and Michoacán in winter). *D. g. decora* (Oaxaca
and Chiapas).

Remarks.—*See* Yellow-throated Warbler.

*CHESTNUT-SIDED WARBLER. *Dendroica pensylvanica.*—4½–5.
Spring: Crown bright greenish yellow, bordered with black; auriculars and
sides of neck white, the forepart of the face and stripe bordering throat
black; back, scapulars, and rump greenish olive, more or less extensively
striped with black; two yellowish white wing-bars, the remiges black edged
with greenish; tail black, the lateral feathers white toward tips; below white,
the sides of the breast and flanks with more or less chestnut. *Fall:* Above
bright yellowish olive-green, the back sometimes obscurely streaked with
black; sides of head gray; wing-bars pale yellowish; below white, the sides of
adults usually streaked with chestnut.

Distribution.—Casual or accidental in southern Mexico during migration. Winters to the southward.

Remarks.—The *yellowish crown* and *chestnut sides* distinguish
adults when in breeding plumage. Fall and winter birds are yellowish
green above, and either wholly white below, or with a few chestnut
streaks on the sides. Note the *gray* cheeks and *pale yellow wing-bars*
of this plumage.

*BAY-BREASTED WARBLER. *Dendroica castanea.*—5–5½. *Male*
(*spring*): Forehead, sides of head, and chin black, the crown chestnut;
throat, chest, sides, and flanks chestnut-rufous, the lower breast, abdomen,
and crissum *buffy* whitish; a buffy patch on each side of neck; back and
rump grayish, the former streaked with black; two white wing-bars; tail
black, the outer feathers white near tips. *Female* (*spring*): Above essentially

like male, but crown dull olive-green, more or less streaked with black and suffused with chestnut; sides of head and underparts buffy whitish, the sides and flanks tinged with reddish. *Fall:* Above bright olive-green, dimly streaked with black; wings and tail as in summer; below buffy yellowish; crown and flanks sometimes with traces of chestnut.

Distribution.—Casual or accidental migrant. Recorded once each in Oaxaca (Tehuantepec) and Quintana Roo (Chetumal).

Remarks.—Fall birds are often confused with fall Blackpolled Warblers. The smaller Blackpolled is paler below, and has *white* (not buffy) under tail-coverts. Its breast and sides may be dimly streaked. Bay-breasted has *dark legs;* those of the Blackpolled are *pale yellowish. See* female and immature Pine Warbler.

*BLACKPOLLED WARBLER. *Dendroica breviunguis* (Illus. p. 471).— $4\frac{3}{4}$. *Male (spring)*: Crown and hind-neck black; sides of head white; back and rump grayish, streaked with black; two white wing-bars; tail blackish, the outer feathers white near tips; below white, the sides of the throat, sides of breast, and flanks streaked with black; legs pale yellow. *Female (spring)*: Above dull olive-green, liberally streaked with black; wings and tail as in male; below white, faintly tinged with greenish, the sides and flanks more or less streaked with black. *Fall:* Similar to female in spring, but brighter above, the dorsal streaks dim or absent; below more yellowish, and but faintly streaked.

Distribution.—Casual migrant.

Remarks.—Males in breeding plumage suggest Black-and-White Warblers, but have *solid black caps.* The paler underparts, lightly streaked breast, white under tail-coverts, and *pale yellowish legs* distinguish fall birds from fall Bay-breasted Warblers. *See* female and immature Pine Warbler.

*PINE WARBLER. *Dendroica pinus pinus.*—5. *Male:* Above bright olive-green; wings and tail sooty, the former with two white bars, the inner webs of the outer rectrices white toward tips; below bright yellow, shading to white on the lower belly and crissum, the breast very obscurely streaked with olive. *Female:* Similar to male, but much duller, the upperparts sometimes tinged with brown or gray; throat and breast pale yellowish, or underparts entirely whitish. *Immature:* Above brownish olive; below buffy whitish.

Distribution.—Winters in Tamaulipas.

Remarks.—Spring males suggest Yellow-throated Vireos, but have much thinner bills, *vaguely streaked* breasts, and white tail-spots. Females and immature birds are decidedly nondescript and are easily con-

fused with fall Blackpolled and Bay-breasted Warblers. These, however, are more or less *streaked* above and have either pale *yellowish*
legs (Blackpolled) or *buffy* under tail-coverts (Bay-breasted).

*PRAIRIE WARBLER. *Dendroica discolor discolor.*—4–4¼. *Male:*
Above bright greenish olive, the back more or less conspicuously spotted
with chestnut-rufous; two yellowish wing-bars; inner webs of outer rectrices
broadly tipped with white; dusky eye-streak, the superciliaries and area
below eye bright yellow; a black crescentic malar stripe; underparts bright
yellow, the sides and flanks broadly streaked with black. *Female:* Similar to
male, but somewhat duller, the black markings of the head replaced with
dusky, the chestnut of the back very obscure or lacking. *Immature:* Above
uniform grayish olive-green, the cheeks ashy, the wings without bars; below
yellow, the sides very dimly streaked.

Distribution.—Winters casually on Cozumel Island off the coast of
Quintana Roo.

Remarks.—A small olive-and-yellow warbler with conspicuously
streaked sides and flanks. No similar bird has *two distinct face-stripes,*
one through the eye and one below the auriculars. Immature birds are
pale yellow below, virtually without streaks, and lack wing-bars. As
with Palm Warblers, this species habitually flicks its tail while standing.

*PALM WARBLER. *Dendroica palmarum palmarum.*—5. *Adult*
(spring): Crown bright chestnut; superciliaries yellow; hind-neck, back, and
scapulars brownish olive, obscurely streaked with darker, the rump yellowish olive; no distinct wing-bars; tail sooty, the inner webs of the outer
feathers white-tipped; throat, breast, and crissum bright yellow, this becoming dingy yellowish white on the abdomen; breast and sides lightly
streaked with chestnut. *Fall:* Similar to spring plumage, but crown usually
with little, if any, chestnut; superciliaries and eye-ring white (not yellow);
underparts whitish, very faintly tinged with yellow, the streaks dusky.
Immature: Similar to adults in fall, but browner above, and with less distinct superciliaries; below pale buffy yellowish white, the crissum bright
yellow, the breast dimly streaked with dusky.

Distribution.—Winters in Yucatán.

Remarks.—A rather nondescript brownish warbler with a pale,
lightly streaked breast, and bright *yellow under tail-coverts.* Adults in
breeding plumage have yellowish throats and superciliaries; the male a
chestnut crown. Palm Warblers spend much time on the ground and
habitually flick the tail in the manner of a Prairie Warbler.

*OVENBIRD. *Seiurus aurocapillus* (Illus. p. 475).—5½–5¾. Median
portion of crown dull orange, bordered laterally with black; superciliaries,

hind-neck, and upperparts generally olive-green; no wing-bars or tail-patches; malar area white; a narrow black rictal stripe; underparts white, the breast, sides, and flanks streaked or spotted with black; bill brownish above, pale below; legs pale pinkish.

Distribution.—Migratory in western Mexico. Winters in the eastern and southern parts of the country.

Races.—*S. a. cinereus* (migratory on the Pacific slope, occurring also in the Tres Marías Islands). *S. a. aurocapillus* (winters in eastern and southern Mexico).

Remarks.—A small, thrushlike ground warbler with a *black-bordered, orange stripe* through the center of the crown. Note the pale *flesh-colored legs.* Frequents woodlands, where usually found on or near the ground.

*LOUISIANA WATERTHRUSH. *Seiurus motacilla.*—5½–6. Above uniform grayish olive, the superciliaries white; no wing-bars or tail-patches; below white; the breast, sides, and flanks faintly tinged with creamy buff, and heavily streaked with brown; bill brownish, palest below; legs pale flesh color.

Distribution.—Winters extensively in eastern, western, and southern Mexico.

Remarks.—Waterthrushes are superficially alike, but need not confuse even the novice. The Louisiana will be recognized by its *white superciliaries, immaculate throat,* and virtually *white* underparts. It is considerably larger than the Northern, and distinctly grayer above. The latter is washed with *pale yellow below,* and usually has *yellowish superciliaries.* Its throat is lightly spotted. Both species habitually teeter in the manner of a Least Sandpiper and prefer moist woods near streams.

*NORTHERN WATERTHRUSH. *Seiurus noveboracensis* (Illus. p. 488).—5¼–5¾. Above uniform brownish olive, the superciliaries pale buff; no wing-bars or tail-patches; below pale yellowish, or sometimes virtually white, the throat dotted, the remainder liberally striped with sooty olive; bill and legs brownish.

Distribution.—Widespread during migration and in winter.

Races.—*S. n. limnaeus* (winters in Baja California, and probably southward through western Mexico). *S. n. notabilis* (as above). *S. n. noveboracensis* (winters from the valley of Mexico southward).

Remarks.—Also known as Small-billed Waterthrush. *See* Louisiana Waterthrush.

NORTHERN WATERTHRUSH

*KENTUCKY WARBLER. *Oporornis formosus.*—5½. *Adult:* Above olive-green, the forehead and anterior crown black; a black patch extending from lores to auriculars and sides of neck; superciliaries and underparts bright yellow; no wing-bars or tail-patches; bill brown above, pale below; legs flesh color. *Immature:* Similar to adult, but duller, more brownish above, the forehead and crown concolor with the back; lores dusky, the cheeks like upperparts.

Distribution.—Winters from Oaxaca, Tabasco, and Campeche southward.

Remarks.—The conspicuous *yellow superciliaries* at once distinguish this warbler from other species with black face-patches and *wholly yellow underparts.* Immature birds can be confused with some female yellowthroats; the Kentucky, however, is usually much brighter below, and has a *yellow eye-ring* and *dusky lores.* Female Hooded Warblers have white on the tail. Canada Warblers are *gray above*, have *white* under tail-coverts, and show at least a trace of streaks on the breast.

*MacGILLIVRAY WARBLER. *Oporornis tolmiei* (Illus. p. 475).— 5. *Male:* Head, throat, and breast gray, the last more or less flecked with white, the lores and band above bill black; an incomplete white eye-ring; upperparts otherwise uniform olive-green; no wing-bars or tail-patches; abdomen and crissum bright yellow, the sides and flanks tinged with olive. *Female:* Similar to male, but head without black; throat and breast uniform ashy gray.

Distribution.—Winters in Baja California and over Mexico generally.

Remarks.—The only olive-backed, yellow-bellied warbler with a *gray hood* covering the entire head, throat, and chest. Note the white spot on the upper and lower eyelids. Nashville Warblers resemble MacGillivrays superficially, but have *yellow* throats and breasts.

COMMON YELLOWTHROAT. *Geothlypis trichas* (Illus. p. 475).— $4\frac{1}{2}$–$5\frac{1}{4}$. *Male:* Forehead and sides of head black, bordered behind with a pale gray band, this sometimes more or less suffused over the crown; upperparts olive-green or brownish olive; no wing-bars or tail-patches; throat and breast bright yellow, the belly either whitish or yellow; sides and flanks tinged with olive or brownish; crissum yellow. *Female:* Sides of head and upperparts uniform olive-green or brownish olive; throat and breast yellow, the latter often tinged with buff; belly buffy white; crissum yellowish.

Distribution.—Resident in the western side of northern Baja California, northwestern Mexico south to Colima, and in the states of Veracruz, Guanajuato, Tlaxcala, Mexico, Puebla, and Oaxaca. Winters in Baja California and in both coastal slopes.

Races.—*G. t. scirpicola* (western Baja California south to latitude 30°). *G. t. chryseola* (north-central Sonora and northern Chihuahua). *G. t. riparia* (Mayo and Yaqui River valleys, extreme southern Sonora). *G. t. modesta* (coastal marshes from southern Sonora to Jalisco and Colima; accidental in southern Baja California). *G. t. melanops* (south-central Mexico). *G. t. occidentalis* (winters in Baja California and western Mexico). *G. t. brachidactyla* (winters in eastern and southern Mexico). *G. t. typhicola* (winters in eastern Mexico, the southern limits uncertain).

Remarks.—The black mask, with its whitish posterior border, is the hallmark of this yellowthroat. Most of the races have *whitish bellies*, but some are wholly yellow below. Females lack the distinctive face-patch and are likely to be difficult. The creamy white belly (sometimes entire underparts) is a useful character. Swamps, marshes, and underbrush, especially near water and in dense cover.

PENINSULAR YELLOWTHROAT. *Geothlypis beldingi.*—$5\frac{1}{2}$. *Male:* Forehead and sides of head either black, bordered behind with a narrow band of yellow (*beldingi*), or crown mainly grayish, the black mask not bordered with yellow (*goldmani*); upperparts essentially yellowish olive-green, this sometimes tinged with brownish or gray; no wing-bars or tail-spots; below either uniform bright yellow (*beldingi*), or lower abdomen white (*goldmani*); flanks buffy olive or grayish; crissum dull yellow. *Female:* Essentially like male, but without a black mask, the face and upperparts virtually uniform.

Distribution.—Middle and southern Baja California south of latitude 28°. ENDEMIC.

Races.—*G. b. goldmani* (middle portion of Baja California from latitude 26° to 28°; accidental in winter in the Cape San Lucas region). *G. b. beldingi* (cape district of Baja California).

Remarks.—Also known as Belding Yellowthroat. The only yellowthroat of its area, although a resident race of *trichas* occurs in northwestern Baja California. Males have either a *yellow border* behind the black mask, or a mask without a distinct border. Yellowthroats of the first type also occur locally in Jalisco and in the coastal marshes of southern Tamaulipas and northern Veracruz. These are now considered distinct species but may prove to be but races of *beldingi*.

YELLOW-CROWNED YELLOWTHROAT. *Geothlypis flavovelata.*—5. Similar to *G. b. beldingi* of southern Baja California, but crown, hind-neck, and sides of neck sometimes (male in summer) extensively yellow.

Distribution.—Coastal marshes of southern Tamaulipas (Altamira, near Tampico) and northern Veracruz. ENDEMIC.

Remarks.—Also known as Altamira Yellowthroat. Possibly conspecific with *beldingi* and *chapalensis*, the males of all three having more or less *yellow* behind the mask. Common Yellowthroats that winter in eastern Mexico have *gray-bordered masks* and *white bellies*.

CHAPALA YELLOWTHROAT. *Geothlypis chapalensis.*—5½. Resembles the Yellow-crowned Yellowthroat of the Atlantic Coast, but much larger. In both, the black mask of the male is bordered behind by a distinct yellow band, or the entire crown (except forehead) and sides of neck are yellow.

Distribution.—Jalisco, in fresh-water marshes along lower Lerma River and the eastern border of Lake Chapala (La Barca to Ocotlán). ENDEMIC.

Remarks.—Chapala Yellowthroats resemble both Peninsulars and Yellow-crowns and may represent an evolutionary link between the two. While the three possibly are conspecific, detailed field studies are needed to establish their relationship with any degree of finality.

BLACKPOLLED YELLOWTHROAT. *Geothlypis speciosa.*—5–5¼. *Male:* Forehead and sides of head dull black, this shading gradually through dusky (crown) to yellowish olive-green on the hind-neck and upperparts generally; no wing-bars or tail-patches; throat, breast, abdomen, and crissum deep golden-yellow, brightest anteriorly, the flanks tinged with brown; bill slender, blackish. *Female:* Similar to male, but greener above, and without black on the head. Sides of head olive-brown, mottled with yellow spots, the median underparts pale yellow, more or less tinged with buff.

Distribution.—Highland marshes in the states of Michoacán, Mexico (Lake Chalco), Puebla (near San Mateo), and Veracruz (vicinity of Orizaba). ENDEMIC.

Remarks.—Easily recognized as a yellowthroat, but with a blackish crown that *shades* into the olive back. Males are intensely golden-yellow or *deep chrome below*, with *brown flanks*. Hooded Yellowthroats, while somewhat similar, have more or less *gray* on the crown, brighter underparts, and *olive flanks*. The females are virtually indistinguishable in the field.

HOODED YELLOWTHROAT. *Geothlypis nelsoni.*—5. *Male:* Sides of head, forehead, and (usually) forepart of crown black, bordered behind by a grayish (or grayish olive) band, this sometimes quite broad, or even suffused over the mid-crown; upperparts otherwise deep olive-green or grayish olive; no wing-bars or tail-patches; below bright yellow, palest on the abdomen, the sides, flanks, and crissum tinged with olive-green. *Female:* Above uniform yellowish olive; below bright yellow, the breast often tinged with ochraceous.

Distribution.—Mountains of eastern San Luis Potosí and southern Tamaulipas south to eastern Oaxaca (Mount Zempoaltepec). ENDEMIC.

Races.—*G. n. nelsoni* (southeastern San Luis Potosí, southern Tamaulipas, Veracruz, and Hidalgo). *G. n. karlenae* (Distrito Federal and Puebla south to eastern Oaxaca).

Remarks.—*See* Blackpolled Yellowthroat.

GRAY-CROWNED YELLOWTHROAT. *Chamaethlypis poliocephala.*—5–5½. *Male:* Loral area black; crown and hind-neck grayish, the upperparts otherwise olive-green; a white or yellowish patch on each eyelid; no wing-bars or tail-patches; below mainly bright yellow, the abdomen sometimes buffy whitish; sides and flanks tinged with buffy olive; bill rather thick, brownish above, pale below. *Female:* Similar to male, but somewhat duller; black of head replaced with dusky, and crown virtually concolor with back.

Distribution.—Lowlands generally, and at moderate elevations locally, chiefly in marshes and brushy meadows.

Races.—*C. p. poliocephala* (northern and central Mexico, south probably to Michoacán and Morelos). *C. p. pontilis* (Pacific watershed of Morelos and Michoacán). *C. p. ralphi* (northeastern Mexico; extent of range unknown). *C. p. palpebralis* (Caribbean slope from central Veracruz southward). *C. p. caninucha* (southern Chiapas).

Remarks.—Also known as Thick-billed Yellowthroat. No other yellowthroat has so restricted a face-patch. Note the *grayish cap* (male), and decidedly thick (vireo-like) bill, the latter quite *pale below*. Females are best distinguished from other yellowthroats that occur in the same area by their bills and essentially *yellow* (not whitish) underparts.

YELLOW-BREASTED CHAT. *Icteria virens.*—7. Above grayish olive-green; superciliaries, eye-ring, and malar stripe white, the latter sometimes much abbreviated; no wing-bars or tail-patches; throat, breast, and sides bright yellow, the posterior underparts mainly white; flanks tinged with buffy brown.

Distribution.—Breeds in Baja California and western Mexico south to Jalisco, Guanajuato, and Mexico, wintering extensively elsewhere.

Races.—*I. v. auricollis* (western Mexico except where occupied by the following; winters on the tableland, and south to Oaxaca). *I. v. tropicalis* (arid lowlands of southern Sonora, north in the Bavispe River Valley to latitude 30°30'). **I. v. virens* (winters in eastern and southeastern Mexico).

Remarks.—Largest of our warblers, suggesting a thrush in size and general proportions. No other bird of this character has a bright yellow throat and breast and white belly. The migrant race is distinguished by its relatively short malar stripe and greener (less grayish) upperparts. Both have similar habits and frequent undergrowth and brushy places.

RED-BREASTED CHAT. *Granatellus venustus* (Illus. p. 493).—5½–6. *Male:* Above mainly bluish gray; sides of crown, lores, and auriculars black, the last bordered above by a white stripe; hind-neck sometimes (*francescae*) with an obscure white collar; wings uniform, or with two narrow white bars; tail notably long and fanlike, mainly black, the outermost feathers white, the adjacent pairs white-tipped; throat and flanks white, the breast, median abdomen, and crissum vermilion. Mainland birds have a conspicuous black chest-band. *Female:* Above as in male, but duller, the tail dusky and usually with less white; auriculars grayish, bordered above by a buffy stripe; wings sometimes with two buffy bars; below essentially whitish, the breast and abdomen more or less tinged with buff; crissum usually pink.

Distribution.—María Madre Island of the Tres Marías group, and the Pacific slope from southern Sinaloa to Oaxaca. ENDEMIC.

Races.—*G. v. francescae* (María Madre Island, Tres Marías group). *G. v. melanotis* (southern Sinaloa south at least to Guerrero). *G. v. venustus* (Pacific slope of Chiapas and possibly Oaxaca).

Remarks.—The only red-breasted warbler with a *white* throat. Males of both mainland races have a conspicuous *black chest-band*. Females, slaty above and buffy white below, differ from all similar birds in having a very long fanlike tail with white outer feathers.

RED-BREASTED CHAT

GRAY-THROATED CHAT. *Granatellus sallaei* (Illus. p. 494).—5. *Male:* Top of head and upperparts bluish slate, this shading to gray on the throat and chest; a white patch behind the eye; no wing-bars; tail mainly black, the outermost feathers white-tipped; breast, median abdomen, and crissum vermilion, the sides and flanks mainly white. *Female:* Above uniform gray or bluish slate, the wings and tail as in male; sides of head buffy brown, the auriculars bordered above by a creamy or tawny stripe; throat, abdomen, and crissum pale buffy white, the breast, sides, and flanks deep buff.

Distribution.—Caribbean lowlands from Veracruz and the Yucatán Peninsula southward.

Races.—*G. s. sallaei* (Veracruz south to Oaxaca, exclusive of the Yucatán Peninsula). *G. s. boucardi* (Yucatán Peninsula).

Remarks.—Much like the Red-breasted Chat of the Pacific slope, but with a *gray throat* and decidedly shorter tail. No other warbler with red plumage is to be expected in the eastern and southern *lowlands*. Females are rather undistinguished: gray above, buff and whitish below, with a *tawny stripe above the auriculars*.

GRAY-THROATED CHAT

*HOODED WARBLER. *Wilsonia citrina* (Illus. p. 475).—5¼. *Male:* Forepart of crown and sides of head bright yellow, the posterior crown, sides of neck, throat, and chest black; upperparts mainly olive-green, the inner webs of the outer rectrices broadly tipped with white; no wing-bars; breast and posterior underparts bright yellow. *Female:* Similar, but virtually without black, the hood usually represented by a blackish band across the mid-crown and by a dark border above the auriculars; underparts uniform bright yellow, or sometimes with a dusky chest-band.

Distribution.—Winters in eastern Mexico.

Remarks.—A black-headed warbler with bright *yellow forehead and cheeks.* Note the olive back, and *immaculate* yellow breast and belly. Females usually show a trace of the hood on top of the head, but lack the black throat and chest of males. Olive above and bright yellow below, they suggest out-sized Pileolated Warblers, but have *white tail-patches.*

*PILEOLATED WARBLER. *Wilsonia pusilla* (Illus. p. 475).—4½. *Male:* Forehead, sides of head, and underparts bright yellow, the last sometimes tinged with olive; crown black, the upperparts otherwise bright olive-green; no wing-bars or tail-patches. *Female:* Similar to male, but black crown-patch usually obsolete or restricted, and sometimes wholly replaced with olive-green.

Distribution.—Virtually country-wide in migration and winter.

Races.—*W. p. chryseola* (winters in southern Baja California, and in western Mexico south at least to Nayarit). *W. p. pileolata* (winters from Durango and Nuevo León southward). *W. p. pusilla* (winters in southern Mexico, north casually to Michoacán).

Remarks.—This species includes the well-known Wilson Warbler. A small, olive-and-gold warbler with a *round black crown-patch.* Immature birds and some females are wholly olive-green above and have *yellow superciliaries.* They resemble female Hooded Warblers, but are much smaller and have no white on their tails. Nashville Warblers are gray-cheeked and show some white on the lower abdomen. Yellow Warblers have yellow tail-patches.

*CANADA WARBLER. *Wilsonia canadensis.*—5¼. *Male:* Forehead black, the crown more or less liberally spotted, the upperparts otherwise uniform gray; no wing-bars or tail-patches; a white eye-ring; streak above lores, malar region, and underparts mainly bright yellow; a broad band of spots across the breast; crissum white. *Female:* Sides of head and upperparts gray, the back and crown often tinged with olive; a white eye-ring; line above lores and underparts bright yellow, the breast obscurely spotted and streaked with olive or dusky; crissum white.

Distribution.—Migratory in eastern Mexico.

Remarks.—The *gray upperparts* and bright yellow ventral plumage are good characters in combination, especially if the breast is crossed by a band of black (or dusky) spots. Note the *white crissum,* and unmarked wings and tail.

RED-FACED WARBLER. *Cardellina rubrifrons* (Illus. p. 496).—5. *Adult:* Forepart of head, throat, chest, and sides of neck bright red, the crown and auriculars black; a white nuchal collar and rump-patch; back, wings, and tail uniform gray; no wing-bars or tail-patches; body white below, the breast tinged with pink. *Immature:* Similar to adults, but much duller; vermilion of head replaced with flesh color; nuchal collar and underparts tinged with buff.

Distribution.—Highlands generally, chiefly in pine forests.

Remarks.—The only gray-and-white warbler with a bright red (adult) or pink (immature) face and chest. Note the black-patterned head. Widespread on the tableland south to Oaxaca and Veracruz.

Red-faced Warbler

*AMERICAN REDSTART. *Setophaga ruticilla.*—5. *Male:* Mainly black, the belly, flanks, and crissum white; sides of breast, base of remiges, and basal half of lateral rectrices bright orange. *Female:* Sides of head and upperparts essentially grayish brown; below whitish, the sides of the breast yellow; wings and tail patterned as in male, but with *yellow* (not orange) patches.

Distribution.—Winters from southern Baja California and central Mexico (Puebla) southward, occurring extensively elsewhere in migration.

Remarks.—A white-bellied, black warbler with *bright orange patches* on its wings, tail, and sides. The brown-backed females are white below, with *yellow patches* where males have orange. One of our more active warblers, and quite unlike any other in pattern.

PAINTED REDSTART. *Setophaga picta.*—5¼. *Adult:* Mainly black, the median breast and median abdomen blood-red; wing-coverts and outer rectrices white. *Immature:* Above blackish, the wing-coverts and outer rectrices white; below dusky brownish, the belly sometimes white; breast obscurely spotted or streaked.

Distribution.—Tableland and higher mountains south through Chiapas, occurring principally in pine and oak forests.

Races.—*S. p. picta* (as above, exclusive of Chiapas). *S. p. guatemalae* (mountains of Chiapas).

Remarks.—The only red-bellied warbler with white wing-patches. Immature birds usually lack any trace of red, but otherwise resemble adults. *See* Slate-throated Redstart.

SLATE-THROATED REDSTART. *Myioborus miniatus* (Illus. p. 497). —5. *Male:* Sides of head and upperparts deep slate, the median crown chestnut; forehead, superciliaries, and throat black; tail black, the outer feathers white-tipped; breast and abdomen vermilion or pinkish orange. *Female:* Similar to male, but black of head replaced with slate, and underparts

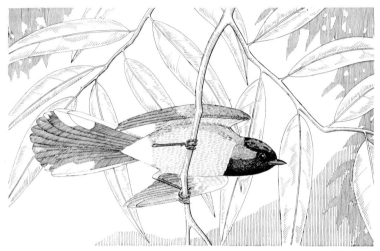

SLATE-THROATED REDSTART

somewhat paler. *Immature:* Head and upperparts sooty slate, the wings and tail essentially as in adults; median breast and abdomen dull chestnut or cinnamon.

Distribution.—Southern Sonora and Chihuahua southward at high altitudes.

Races.—*M. m. miniatus* (southern Sonora and Chihuahua south to Veracruz, Puebla, and Oaxaca). *M. m. molochinus* (Volcán San Martín, Veracruz, and probably adjacent highlands). *M. m. intermedius* (mountains of Chiapas).

Remarks.—Much like a Painted Redstart, but without a wing-patch, and with less white on the tail. Underparts *bright orange* to vermilion, not blood-red as in *S. picta*. In good light the back appears bluish slate, and the *chestnut crown-patch* may be visible.

FAN-TAILED WARBLER. *Euthlypis lachrymosa* (Illus. p. 498).—5¾.
Forehead, sides of crown, and lores black, the first with a white spot at each
side; a yellow crown-patch; a white patch on each eyelid; sides of head
and upperparts dull slate, the back often tinged with olive; no wing-bars;
tail black, the lateral feathers graduated and white-tipped; throat and abdomen yellow, more or less tinged with buff, the breast tawny; sides and
flanks olive; crissum white.

Distribution.—Lowlands and foothills, ranging from Sonora, Chihuahua, and southern Tamaulipas south through western Chiapas. Casual
or accidental in Baja California (a December record for Santo Domingo).

FAN-TAILED WARBLER

Races.—*E. l. tephra* (western Mexico from Sonora and Chihuahua
south to Jalisco; apparently casual in Baja California). *E. l. lachrimosa*
(eastern Mexico from southern Tamaulipas south to Guerrero, Oaxaca, and
Veracruz). *E. l. schistacea* (western Chiapas).

Remarks.—Fan-tails frequent thickets and the lower branches of
trees. They are conspicuous birds of restless activity, and have a habit

of flicking the tail in the manner of redstarts. No other warbler with a *yellow crown-patch* is essentially *tawny below*. Note the white eye-spots.

RED WARBLER. *Ergaticus ruber* (Illus. p. 499).—5. *Adult:* Mainly rich red, brightest below, the auriculars silvery white or grayish black; wings and tail sooty brown, tinged and margined with reddish. *Immature:* Cinnamon-brown, the auriculars grayish.

Distribution.—Mountain forests of Sinaloa, southwestern Chihuahua, and Durango south at high altitudes to Veracruz and Oaxaca. ENDEMIC.

Races.—*E. r. melanauris* (breeds on the upper slopes of Mount Mohinora, extreme southwestern Chihuahua; winters at lower elevations in the mountains of southwestern Sinaloa, and probably southern Durango). *E. r. ruber* (high mountains of south-central Mexico south to Oaxaca).

Remarks.—Totally unlike any other warbler except the Pink-headed of Chiapas. Both are virtually all-red. This species has whitish

RED WARBLER

cheeks; the latter a pinkish head and chest that appear silvery in certain light. Both inhabit forests at high altitudes.

PINK-HEADED WARBLER. *Ergaticus versicolor.*—5. Mainly rich red, brightest below, the head and breast silvery pink; wings and tail sooty brown, tinged and margined with reddish.

Distribution.—High mountains of Chiapas.

Remarks.—*See* Red Warbler.

GOLDEN-CROWNED WARBLER. *Basileuterus culicivorus.*—5–5¼. Sides of crown black, the broad median stripe yellow, this usually tinged with olive-green posteriorly; sides of head, and upperparts otherwise deep olive-gray, the eye-ring and line above lores pale yellow; no wing-bars or tail-patches; below rich yellow, more or less tinged with greenish, the sides and flanks olive-green.

Distribution.—Jalisco, and eastern Mexico from Nuevo León and central Tamaulipas southward, chiefly in wooded areas of moderate elevation.

Races.—*B. c. flavescens* (mountains of western Jalisco). *B. c. brasherii* (Nuevo León, Tamaulipas, San Luis Potosí, and northern Veracruz). *B. c. culicivorus* (southern Veracruz and Puebla south through Oaxaca and Chiapas).

Remarks.—Unlike numerous other warblers with yellow underparts, this common resident has a *broad yellow* (or yellowish) *stripe* through the center of the crown. Fan-tailed Warblers also show yellow on top of the head, but they are distinctly *tawny below* (not bright greenish yellow), and have white tail-tips.

GOLDEN-BROWED WARBLER. *Basileuterus belli* (Illus. p. 475).—$5\frac{1}{4}$. *Adult:* Above mainly olive-green, the forepart of the crown and auriculars chestnut; forehead and sides of crown black, the superciliaries bright yellow; no wing-bars or tail-patches; below bright yellow, shading to yellowish olive-green on the sides and flanks. *Immature:* Above deep brown, the wings with two buffy cinnamon bars; no distinct superciliary stripes; sides of head, throat, and chest olive, the sides and flanks tawny olive; abdomen and crissum pale yellow.

Distribution.—Mountains of southeastern Sinaloa and southern Tamaulipas southward, chiefly at high altitudes.

Races.—*B. b. bateli* (southeastern Sinaloa south through Jalisco and Michoacán to the mountains bordering the valley of Mexico). *B. b. belli* (southwestern Tamaulipas and San Luis Potosí south to Mount Zempoaltepec, eastern Oaxaca). *B. b. clarus* (Guerrero). *B. b. scitulus* (Chiapas).

Remarks.—The *chestnut cheeks* and *yellow superciliaries* in combination are diagnostic. Under favorable conditions a chestnut patch is visible on the forepart of the crown. Rufous-capped Warblers of the same region have *white* superciliaries, and the entire crown *uniform reddish brown.* Most Rufous-caps (except *salvini*) are white-bellied; the Golden-browed is wholly yellow below. Both species frequent thickets and forest undergrowth and may be found with Golden-crowned Warblers.

RUFOUS-CAPPED WARBLER. *Basileuterus rufifrons.*—$4\frac{3}{4}$–5. *Adult:* Crown and sides of head rufous, the superciliaries and malar stripes white; upperparts mainly brownish olive; no wing-bars or tail-patches; below either wholly bright yellow (*B. r. salvini*), or throat and breast yellow, the abdomen and flanks essentially white. *Immature:* Auriculars and upperparts brownish olive, the wings and tail edged with yellowish olive-green; two buffy wing-bars; a whitish or buffy streak above auriculars; below essentially buffy, more or less tinged with olive laterally.

Distribution.—Highlands generally, occurring at lower elevations in winter.

Races.—*B. r. caudatus* (Sonora, Chihuahua, and Sinaloa). *B. r. dugesi* (Jalisco and Nayarit south to Oaxaca). *B. r. jouyi* (southern Tamaulipas and San Luis Potosí south to Hidalgo, northern Puebla, and northern Veracruz). *B. r. rufifrons* (Puebla and central Veracruz, northern Oaxaca, and Chiapas). *B. r. salvini* (southern Veracruz, Tabasco, and Chiapas).

Remarks.—*See* Golden-browed Warbler.

Family PLOCEIDAE. Weaver Finches

HOUSE SPARROW. *Passer domesticus domesticus.*—5½–6. *Male:* Crown and rump grayish, darkening on tail; postocular stripe, hind-neck, back, and scapulars bright chestnut, the back streaked with black; a white wing-bar; sides of head and underparts dingy white, the throat and breast black. *Female:* Sides of head and upperparts pale grayish brown, the back broadly streaked with black; a pale wing-bar; superciliaries and underparts dingy white.

Distribution.—South, locally, at least to Guerrero.

Remarks.—Also known as English Sparrow. An introduced species, virtually restricted to the vicinity of human dwellings, and quite unlike any native Mexican species. Males will be recognized by their thick bills, black bibs, and *chestnut-and-black* backs. Females are rather nondescript finches, with broadly streaked backs and whitish underparts. Note the pale superciliaries and wing-bar.

Family ICTERIDAE. Blackbirds, Troupials, and Allies

KEY TO THE SPECIES

1a. Plumage partly yellow, yellowish, or orange 2
  b. Plumage without yellow, yellowish, or orange 30
2a. More than 10 inches long. Yellow restricted to tail, or to tail, rump, and wings 3
  b. Less than 10 inches long. Yellow (or orange) not restricted to tail, rump, and wings 5

3a. Wing-coverts, rump, and outer rectrices yellow

Yellow-winged Cacique, p. 507

  b. Outer rectrices alone yellow 4

4a. Larger (15–19 inches). Mainly rufous, the head black; bill black tipped with orange . . . . Montezuma Oropendola, p. 506

  b. Smaller (11–14 inches). Mainly blackish, the head chestnut; bill pale greenish, the base flattening over forehead

Chestnut-headed Oropendola, p. 506

5a. Black, the head and breast yellow, or deep sooty brown with dingy yellowish superciliaries, throat, and breast (marshes)

Yellow-headed Blackbird, p. 520

  b. Not as in 5a. 6

6a. Brown-striped above and bright yellow below; a black crescentic chest-patch and white outer rectrices (grasslands)

Meadowlark (spp.), pp. 520–21

  b. Not as in 6a. 7

7a. Head and throat wholly or mainly black, this sometimes extending over the back and breast; sides of head or posterior crown sometimes orange or yellow 8

  b. Head not black; often with a black bib 14

8a. Back bright olive-yellow 9

  b. Back black 10

9a. Larger (8–9 inches). Head and chest wholly black (highlands)

Black-headed Oriole, p. 515

  b. Smaller (7–7½ inches). Hindpart of crown concolor with back (southeastern lowlands)

Black-cowled Oriole (immature male), p. 513

10a. Outer rectrices with conspicuous orange or lemon-yellow; white wing-patches or a white wing-bar 11

  b. Tail wholly black; wings without white, the lesser coverts yellow 13

11a. Underparts and lateral rectrices bright orange; wings white-patterned 12

  b. Belly and basal half of lateral rectrices lemon-yellow; a white wing-bar . . . . Scott Oriole (male), p. 514

12a. Head wholly black; lesser wing-coverts bright orange like rump and underparts . . . . Baltimore Oriole (male), p. 511

  b. Sides of head, rump, and underparts bright orange, or auriculars, rump, and flanks black; wing-coverts white

Bullock Oriole (male), p. 511

13a. Tail-coverts (above and below) black (highlands)

  b. Tail-coverts yellow (southeastern lowlands)

14a. Back black or boldly striped with black; head, rump, and underparts (except throat) yellow or orange . . . .

  b. Back not black or boldly striped with black . . . .

15a. Back boldly streaked; wings white-patterned and lateral rectrices
gray-tipped . . . .

  b. Back wholly black, sharply contrasting with head and rump. . .

16a. Sides of breast spotted with black; head, rump, and belly bright
orange . . . .

  b. Breast not spotted . . . .

17a. Outer rectrices yellow or yellow-tipped, the tail appearing wholly
yellow below (southeastern lowlands) .

  b. Tail wholly black, the outer feathers sometimes narrowly white-
tipped . . . .

18a. Larger ($8\frac{1}{2}$–10 inches). Lesser wing-coverts yellow or orange; secondaries conspicuously edged with white

  b. Smaller (7–8 inches). Lesser wing-coverts black; a white wing-bar

19a. Crown, back, and rump uniform yellow or orange-yellow; wings and
tail *conspicuously black*—not olivaceous, grayish, or dusky . . .

  b. Wings and tail essentially olivaceous, grayish, or dusky—not conspicuously black; back usually grayish or olive, the crown and
rump sometimes similar . . . .

20a. Larger (8–$8\frac{1}{2}$ inches). Wings, including lesser coverts, wholly black;
yellow of plumage either tinged with ocher, or underparts pale
lemon-yellow and without a black bib (southeastern lowlands)

  b. Smaller ($7\frac{1}{2}$ inches). Lesser wing-coverts yellow; a white wing-bar;
plumage extensively orange-yellow (Yucatán)

21a. With a black bib or crescentic chest-patch . . . . :

  b. Without a black bib; two white wing-bars . . . .

22a. Crown and back spotted or streaked with dusky; rump olive-yellow

  b. Crown and back unmarked . . . .

23a. Forehead and sides of head black; crown, back, and rump olive-green or greenish yellow . . Black-vented Oriole (immature), p. 514

Hooded Oriole (immature), p. 518

 b. Not as in 23a. 24

24a. Head bright yellow, not concolor with back; a yellow wing-patch and black crescentic chest-patch

Yellow-tailed Oriole (immature), p. 514

 b. Not as in 24a. 25

25a. Top of head, back, and rump grayish olive, virtually uniform; below pale greenish yellow . . Orchard Oriole (immature male), p. 512

Hooded Oriole (female), p. 518

 b. Not as in 25a. Sides of head and underparts usually orange-yellow 26

26a. Larger (8½–10 inches). Head and rump much brighter than back (eastern and southern lowlands)

Black-throated Oriole (female), p. 517

 b. Smaller (7½ inches). Yellowish olive above, orange-yellow below; a white wing-bar (Yucatán) . . . . . . Orange Oriole (female), p. 515

27a. Larger (7–8 inches) 28

 b. Smaller (6–6½ inches). Olive above, brightest on rump, yellowish below . . . . Orchard Oriole (female), p. 512

28a. Breast and rump tinged with orange

Baltimore Oriole (female), p. 511

 b. Not as in 28a. 29

29a. Underparts virtually white, the breast sometimes yellowish

Bullock Oriole (female), p. 511

 b. Underparts uniform dull greenish yellow

Scott Oriole (female), p. 514

Hooded Oriole (female), p. 518

30a. Wholly or mainly glossy (usually) black; rump and underparts (except throat) sometimes chestnut 31

 b. Essentially grayish or dusky, especially below; underparts sometimes brownish or heavily streaked with black 41

31a. Rump and underparts chestnut . . . Orchard Oriole (male), p. 512

 b. Rump and underparts wholly black 32

32a. Wing-coverts red and white or red and tawny

Tricolored Blackbird or Red-winged Blackbird, p. 519

 b. Without bright wing-coverts or epaulets 33

33a. Larger (13–18 inches). Wholly glossy black, with purplish or greenish reflections; tail notably long and rounded, or with a conspicuous neck-ruff 34

b. Smaller (6–12 inches). Largest species not notably glossy, and without prow-shaped tails or neck-ruffs 35

34*a.* Tail notably long and rounded, appearing keel-like when spread
Boat-tailed Grackle (male), p. 509

b. Tail not as in 34*a*. With a neck-ruff or mantle
Giant Cowbird (male), p. 508

35*a.* Bill pale greenish white . . . . Yellow-billed Cacique, p. 507

b. Bill black 36

36*a.* Head, neck, and chest dull brown, contrasting with glossy breast and back; bill finchlike . . . Brown-headed Cowbird (male), p. 508

b. Not as in 36*a*. 37

37*a.* Head, neck, and body bronzy green; a neck-ruff; iris reddish
Bronzed Cowbird (male), p. 508

b. Not as in 37*a*. 38

38*a.* Larger (10–12 inches). Uniform glossy black or deep sooty brown, appearing wholly black at a distance 39

b. Smaller (7–9 inches). Head with purplish reflections or wholly dull black 40

39*a.* Glossy black . . . . Melodious Blackbird, p. 510

b. Deep sooty brown or dull black . . Giant Cowbird (female), p. 508

40*a.* Bill finchlike; mainly dull black, the wings and tail lightly glossed
Brown-headed Cowbird (female), p. 508

b. Bill not finchlike; glossy greenish black, the head purplish; iris pale yellow . . . . Brewer Blackbird (male), p. 510

41*a.* Throat and breast, or entire underparts liberally streaked 42

b. Not streaked 43

42*a.* Essentially dusky, the throat and breast (only) streaked
Tricolored Blackbird (female), p. 519

b. Essentially brownish, the back and underparts boldly streaked
Red-winged Blackbird (female), p. 519

43*a.* Larger (11–13 inches). Tail long, expansive, and notably rounded; underparts dingy brownish
Boat-tailed and Slender-billed Grackles (females), p. 509

b. Smaller (5½–9 inches). Tail not as in 43*a*. 44

44*a.* Bill finchlike; essentially gray, palest below
Brown-headed Cowbird (female), p. 508

b. Bill not finchlike; head and breast brownish
Brewer Blackbird (female), p. 510

CHESTNUT-HEADED OROPENDOLA. *Zarhynchus wagleri* (Illus. p. 506).—Male 14; female 11. Bill pale greenish, the base of the culmen rounded and expanding over the entire forehead; wings, back, belly, and middle rectrices glossy black; head, breast, rump, and posterior underparts chestnut; lateral rectrices bright yellow.

Distribution.—Lowlands of Veracruz and Chiapas.

Remarks.—Also known as Wagler Oropendola. A yellow-tailed, chestnut-and-black troupial, with a *conspicuous frontal shield.* Montezuma Oropendolas are much larger and mainly chestnut-rufous, with a black head and bare cheeks. Their bills are quite different. Both are noisily gregarious when breeding. Their long pendulant grass-and-fiber nests are often suspended by the dozen in a single tree.

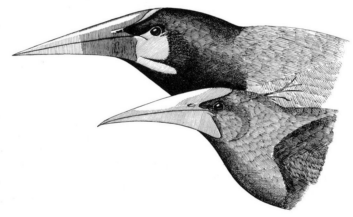

MONTEZUMA OROPENDOLA (*above*)
CHESTNUT-HEADED OROPENDOLA (*below*)

MONTEZUMA OROPENDOLA. *Gymnostinops montezuma* (Illus. p. 506).—Male 20; female 17. Bill black, broadly tipped with orange; bare skin at base of bill pink; head, hind-neck, and breast black, the plumage otherwise mainly chestnut-rufous, darkening below; lateral rectrices bright yellow, the tail appearing wholly yellow below.

Distribution.—Lowlands of southern Tamaulipas, Veracruz, Oaxaca, Tabasco, and Quintana Roo.

Remarks.—One of the largest of all troupials. Its bare face and orange-tipped black bill are diagnostic. Both Mexican oropendolas are colonial species with very similar habits. The Montezuma has a remarkable variety of liquid whistles and rasping or gurgling notes quite unlike those of any other bird of its area. *See* Chestnut-headed Oropendola.

YELLOW-BILLED CACIQUE. *Amblycercus holosericeus holosericeus.*—8–9½. Wholly dull black, the bill pale yellow or greenish; iris white or pale yellow.

Distribution.—Southeastern Mexico north to Puebla and southern Tamaulipas.

Remarks.—Also known as Prevost Cacique. No other wholly black icterid of our area has a *pale greenish yellow bill.* This species frequents undergrowth, usually singly or in pairs, and ranges from sea-level to an altitude of about 4,500 feet. Its calls include both harsh and liquid notes, but are weaker than those of oropendolas.

YELLOW-WINGED CACIQUE. *Cassiculus melanicterus* (Illus. p. 507). —10–11½. *Male:* Mainly black, the wing-coverts, rump, lateral rectrices, and tail-coverts bright yellow; bill yellowish white; occipital feathers narrow

YELLOW-WINGED CACIQUE

and elongated, forming a crest. *Female:* Patterned like male, but much smaller and with black plumage replaced with olive-slate and dusky gray.

Distribution.—Extreme southern Sonora south on the Pacific slope to the vicinity of Tonalá, Chiapas. ENDEMIC.

Remarks.—Also known as Mexican Cacique. No other yellow-tailed, black icterid has a yellow wing-patch, yellow rump, and *pale bill.*

This troupial is colonial in habits and occurs commonly both in woods and in the vicinity of villages. Its pendulant grass-and-fiber nests, often suspended in clusters, are a characteristic feature of the Pacific lowlands.

GIANT COWBIRD. *Psomocolax oryzivorus impacifus.*—11½–14. *Male:* Glossy purplish black; feathers of neck form a distinct ruff or mantle; bill black, rather short and thick; iris red. *Female:* Much smaller and duller than male, and without a ruff or mantle.

Distribution.—Caribbean slope from Veracruz southward.

Remarks.—Also known as Rice Grackle. Glossy males might be mistaken for male Boat-tailed Grackles, but have much sturdier bills and *shorter*, untroughed tails, with only *slightly rounded tips*. Boat-tails lack the cowbird's conspicuous *erectile màntle*. Female Giant Cowbirds resemble Melodious Blackbirds, but are larger and duller, and have heavier bills.

BRONZED COWBIRD. *Tangavius aeneus.*—7–8½. *Male:* Mainly bronzy black, the wing-coverts and rump glossy purplish; remiges and tail glossed with green; a conspicuous erectile ruff; bill black, decidedly sturdy; iris reddish. *Female:* Sooty black, the wings and tail lightly glossed with green; smaller than male and without a ruff.

Distribution.—Both coastal slopes, chiefly in the lowlands.

Races.—*T. a. milleri* (Sonora and Sinaloa to Nayarit). *T. a. assimilis* (Jalisco south to the Pacific lowlands of Oaxaca). *T. a. aeneus* (Caribbean slope).

Remarks.—Also known as Red-eyed Cowbird. Cowbirds will be recognized as *thick-billed* blackbirds with shorter tails than other blackbirds of comparable size. They walk with their tails held well above the ground. Males of both Mexican species are notably glossy, but the Bronzed is virtually uniform (not brown-headed), and has a prominent mantle that is displayed with much posturing and strutting during the breeding season. Females are relatively dull, but *wholly black*, not distinctly grayish, as with female Brown-headed Cowbirds. Both species parasitize the nests of other birds and may be found together in flocks when not breeding.

BROWN-HEADED COWBIRD. *Molothrus ater.*—5½–7½. *Male:* Head, hind-neck, throat, and chest deep brown, the plumage otherwise glossy greenish black with violet reflections; bill black, short and conical; iris brown. *Female:* Above grayish brown, lightening below to brownish gray; wings and tail faintly glossed.

Distribution.—Los Coronados Islands, Baja California, and Mexico generally south to Oaxaca and Veracruz.

Races.—*M. a. californicus* (casual on Los Coronados Islands, off Baja California). *M. a. obscurus* (northern Baja California [winters south to Cape District] and Mexico south to Oaxaca and Veracruz). **M. a. ater* (winters in northeastern Mexico). **M. a. artemisiae* (winters south to Michoacán and Veracruz).

Remarks.—Also known as Common Cowbird. *See* Bronzed Cowbird.

BOAT-TAILED GRACKLE. *Cassidix mexicanus.*—Male 16–18; female 12–13. *Male:* Mainly deep glossy purplish black, the wings and tail glossed with green; tail notably long and fanlike, and usually with a median trough or keel when spread; bill black, moderately long and sturdy. *Female:* Sides and top of head brownish, shading to black on back, wings, and tail, where lightly glossed with green; superciliaries and underparts tawny brown, the flanks and crissum sooty; tail fanlike, but not notably long.

Distribution.—Virtually country-wide, exclusive of Baja California.

Races.—*C. m. nelsoni* (coastal area of Sonora). *C. m. graysoni* (coastal area of Sinaloa; accidental on María Madre, Tres Marías Islands). *C. m. obscurus* (coastal area of southwestern Mexico from Nayarit and Colima to Guerrero). *C. m. monsoni* (Chihuahua). *C. m. prosopidicola* (Coahuila, Nuevo León, and Tamaulipas). *C. m. mexicanus* (tableland and lowlands of eastern and southern Mexico generally, except where occupied by other races).

Remarks.—Also known as Great-tailed Grackle. A large, glossy, purplish or brownish blackbird with a *long wedge-shaped tail*. Males are much larger than females, and their tails proportionately longer, with a conspicuous keel-like crease down the middle when spread. Likely to be confused only with the Slender-billed Grackle, a smaller species restricted to marshes near Mexico City.

SLENDER-BILLED GRACKLE. *Cassidix palustris.*—Male 13–15; female 11–12. *Male:* Similar to a Boat-tailed Grackle, but much smaller and with a relatively slender bill; plumage more or less glossed with violet. *Female:* Above dusky brown, darkest on wings, rump, and tail; superciliaries rich buff; below tawny cinnamon, the throat and abdomen pale buff.

Distribution.—Marshes near Mexico City. ENDEMIC.

Remarks.—*See* Boat-tailed Grackle.

*RUSTY BLACKBIRD. *Euphagus carolinus.*

Remarks.—Accidental in Baja California (Valladeres), December 12, 1888.

BREWER BLACKBIRD. *Euphagus cyanocephalus.*—8–9. *Male:* Glossy black, the head and chest with purplish violet reflections, the plumage elsewhere glossed with green; bill black, moderately long, and thick; iris white or pale yellowish. *Female:* Grayish brown, palest on throat; wings and tail glossy black with green reflections.

Distribution.—Breeds in northern Baja California, and probably elsewhere in northern Mexico. Virtually country-wide in winter, exclusive of the Yucatán Peninsula.

Remarks.—Males appear wholly black at a distance, and females dingy brown or grayish. Cowbirds are similar, but have much heavier bills and proportionately shorter tails. Cowbirds walk with their tails raised well above the ground, a characteristic not shared with other blackbirds and grackles. The Brewer's *white eyes* (males only) are diagnostic. A male Bronzed Cowbird can usually be distinguished by its neck-ruff. Melodious Blackbirds are much larger than either.

MELODIOUS BLACKBIRD. *Dives dives dives* (Illus. p. 510).—10–11. *Male:* Wholly black, lightly glossed with green; tail slightly rounded but not troughed. *Female:* Similar to male, but smaller and duller.

MELODIOUS BLACKBIRD

Distribution.—Southern Tamaulipas and Mexico southward, including the Yucatán Peninsula. Chiefly dry districts.

Remarks.—Also known as Sumichrast Blackbird. A common blackbird of town and country, ranging from sea-level to an altitude of about 4,000 feet. Both sexes are wholly black and rather undistinguished in appearance. Even males are much less glossy than cowbirds and grackles. At a distance they might be mistaken for Brewer Blackbirds, although considerably larger. The song has a pleasing liquid quality.

*BALTIMORE ORIOLE. *Icterus galbula.*—7–8. *Male:* Head, neck, throat, and back black; rump, upper tail-coverts, shoulders, and underparts (except throat) bright orange; wings black, the greater coverts and remiges edged with white; lateral rectrices mainly orange. *Female:* Above grayish olive, brightest on head and rump; crown and back lightly spotted or mottled; two white wing-bars; below dull yellowish orange, the throat sometimes spotted.

Distribution.—Migrates through eastern Mexico. Winters in the south.

Remarks.—A black-headed, black-backed oriole with *bright orange* underparts. The white wing-markings and *orange tail-patches* eliminate all similar species. Females suggest female Bullock Orioles, but are brighter (more yellowish) below and less grayish above. They usually have a suggestion of orange on breast and rump.

BULLOCK ORIOLE. *Icterus bullockii* (Illus. p. 512).—7–8. *Male:* Top of head, throat, back, and middle rectrices black; a black eye-streak, or (*abeillei*) with black auriculars; wings black, the coverts and edgings of secondaries white; sides of head, rump, lateral rectrices, and underparts (except throat) bright orange except in *abeillei*, which has black auriculars, rump, upper tail-coverts, and flanks. *Female:* Above grayish olive, brightest on head and tail; two white wing-bars; below dull yellow, the abdomen usually whitish.

Distribution.—Northern Baja California and northwestern Mexico south over the southern portion of the plateau. Elsewhere in winter.

Races.—*I. b. parvus* (breeds in northern Baja California; winter range unknown, but migratory in southern Sonora). *I. b. bullockii* (Sonora, Sinaloa, and northern Durango; widespread in winter). *I. b. abeillei* (southern portion of Mexican plateau from San Luis Potosí to Jalisco and Puebla).

Remarks.—Bright orange and black, with very conspicuous white wing-markings. The only yellow-faced oriole with a black crown and back. Resident birds in the southern portion of the plateau (*abeillei*) differ from other Bullock Orioles in having *black* (not orange) *auriculars*, rumps, upper tail-coverts, and flanks. Some authorities consider them a distinct species, best known as Black-backed Oriole. Female Bullocks resemble female Baltimore Orioles, but are much grayer above and below. Female Baltimores usually have a suggestion of *orange* on the rump and breast.

BULLOCK ORIOLE

ORCHARD ORIOLE. *Icterus spurius.*—6–6½. *Male* (*adult*): Head, chest, back, wings, and tail black; shoulders, rump, and underparts (except throat and chest) deep chestnut or pale brown; (*immature*): Grayish olive above, yellowish below, the throat black. *Female:* Similar to immature male, but without a black bib; two white wing-bars.

Distribution.—Breeds in southern Tamaulipas; recorded in Jalisco and Oaxaca in June and July, but not known to breed on the Pacific slope. Widespread as a migrant, wintering in southern Mexico.

Races.—*I. s. spurius* (common migrant, wintering in the south). *I. s. fuertesi* (southern Tamaulipas to southern Veracruz and Guerrero).

Remarks.—Chestnut-bellied (tawny in *fuertesi*) adult males are unlike any other oriole. Females resemble immature Scott and Hooded Orioles, but are much smaller than either. Except for size, immature males might be mistaken for female Hooded Orioles in intermediate plumage. The little-known Ochre Oriole of southern Tamaulipas (*fuertesi*), treated here as a resident race of the Orchard, is considered a distinct species by some authorities. It is also known as Fuertes Oriole.

BLACK-COWLED ORIOLE. *Icterus prosthemelas prosthemelas* (Illus. p. 513).—7–8. *Adult:* Mainly black, the shoulders (middle and lesser coverts) lower back, rump, and posterior underparts bright yellow; upper abdomen usually with an indistinct chestnut patch or band. *Immature:* Forehead, sides of head, throat, breast, wings (except shoulders), and tail black; hind-crown, back, and rump bright yellowish olive, the wing-coverts, belly, and

BLACK-COWLED ORIOLE

under tail-coverts canary yellow. Sometimes essentially like adult, but black of back intermixed with olive, and without a chestnut patch below.

Distribution.—Veracruz, Oaxaca, and Yucatán southward, chiefly in humid lowland forests.

Remarks.—Also known as Strickland Oriole. The only oriole in the *southeastern lowlands* with a wholly black head, back, breast, and tail. Scott Orioles range east to the mountains of Veracruz in winter, but are readily distinguished by their yellow-and-black tails. Black-vented Orioles are highland birds; the Black-cowled a representative lowland species with *yellow* (not black) *under tail-coverts*. Black-faced, olive-backed immature birds are virtually unmistakable. Their wings and tails are conspicuously *black*, not grayish as with other subadult orioles.

SCOTT ORIOLE. *Icterus parisorum* (Illus. p. 516).—7½–8. *Male:* Mainly black, the shoulders, rump, basal half of lateral rectrices, and posterior underparts bright yellow; a white wing-bar. *Female:* Above essentially grayish olive, brightest on head, the rump and tail usually bright yellowish olive; crown and back more or less streaked or spotted; two white wing-bars; below greenish yellow, brightest on belly; throat and breast sometimes blotched or wholly black.

Distribution.—Baja California and western portion (chiefly) of the Mexican plateau south to Michoacán, Hidalgo, and the mountains of Veracruz. Extent of breeding range uncertain.

Remarks.—A common highland species resembling a Black-vented Oriole, but with a *yellow* crissum and yellow-and-black tail. Females have white-barred, grayish wings and olive tails. They may be either *wholly greenish yellow* below, or have a black bib like immature males. Female Bullocks have *whitish* (not lemon-yellow) bellies, and female Baltimore Orioles are usually tinged with orange. Orchard Orioles are much smaller than Scotts.

BLACK-VENTED ORIOLE. *Icterus wagleri.*—7½–8½. Similar to a Black-cowled Oriole, but larger, much brighter (essentially orange color in adults), and with *black tail-coverts.*

Distribution.—Northern Mexico (except Tamaulipas) southward in the highlands.

Races.—*I. w. castaneopectus* (Sonora and Chihuahua). *I. w. wagleri* (Coahuila, Nuevo León, and Tepic southward in the highlands).

Remarks.—Also known as Wagler Oriole. The common black-headed oriole of the plateau and mountains. Much like the Black-cowled Oriole of the southeastern lowlands, and possibly only an altitudinal representative. *See* Scott Oriole.

YELLOW-TAILED ORIOLE. *Icterus mesomelas mesomelas.*—8½. *Adult:* Mainly bright yellow, the loral area, throat, median chest, back, wings (except coverts), and four inner rectrices black. *Immature:* Above yellowish olive, brightening on crown and forehead; wings and tail dusky olive, the former with a more or less conspicuous yellow patch; sides, of head and underparts bright golden-yellow, the throat or median chest usually with a black or olive patch.

Distribution.—Lowlands of southeastern Mexico north to Oaxaca and Veracruz.

Remarks.—A conspicuous yellow-headed oriole with *broadly yellow-tipped outer rectrices*. Adults are unmistakable. Olive-backed immature birds have dusky wings with yellow patches, and olive or dingy yellowish tails. Their plumage, especially of the head and underparts, is usually much brighter (golden-yellow) than that of other immature orioles. Most subadult Yellow-tails have a vague, crescentic olive (or black) chest-patch.

YELLOW-BACKED ORIOLE. *Icterus chrysater* (Illus. p. 516).—8½–9. *Adult:* Mainly rich yellow, the loral area, forepart of face, throat, wings, and tail *wholly* black; underparts or border of throat-patch sometimes strongly tinged with brownish orange. *Immature:* Similar to adult, but much duller (yellowish olive above, lemon-yellow below), and usually without black on face and throat; wings and tail sometimes dusky olive; throat sometimes flecked with black.

Distribution.—Lowlands of southeastern Mexico north to Oaxaca and Veracruz.

Races.—*I. c. chrysater* (as above, except northern part of Yucatán Peninsula). *I. c. mayensis* (northern part of Yucatán Peninsula).

Remarks.—Also known as Lesson Oriole. Yellow-backed and diminutive Orange Orioles of Yucatán and Meco Island are patterned alike, but the latter is much richer in color (distinctly orange-yellow) and has *white wing-edgings*. Most adult Yellow-backs are tinged below with *brownish orange*, this being especially conspicuous just below the black throat-patch.

ORANGE ORIOLE. *Icterus auratus.*—7½. *Male:* Mainly rich orange-yellow, the loral area, throat, wings, and tail black; lesser wing-coverts white-tipped, and remiges edged with white. *Female:* Similar to male, but much duller (less orange), the crown and back tinged with yellowish olive; back sometimes black-streaked; tail dusky above, olive below.

Distribution.—Campeche, Yucatán, and Meco Island. ENDEMIC.

Remarks.—A bright orange or yellow oriole with *white-marked black wings*. Hooded Orioles are similar, but have black backs. Yellow-backed Orioles are much larger and have *wholly black wings* and a narrow black band across the forehead. They are much less brilliant (more purely yellow) than Orange Orioles and often are tinged with brown below.

BLACK-HEADED ORIOLE. *Icterus graduacauda* (Illus. p. 516).—8–9. Head, throat to median breast, wings, and tail black; elsewhere bright lemon-yellow; wing-coverts and remiges usually edged with white; black of breast often with scalloped border.

Distribution.—Northeastern Mexico (in winter southward at least to San Luis Potosí) and the southern portion of the Mexican plateau southward in highland areas.

 SPOT-BREASTED ORIOLE (p. 517)

 BLACK-THROATED ORIOLE (p. 517)

 STREAK-BACKED ORIOLE (p. 519)

 SCOTT ORIOLE (p. 514)

 YELLOW-BACKED ORIOLE (p. 515)

 BLACK-HEADED ORIOLE (p. 515)

Races.—*I. g. audubonii* (Nuevo León and Tamaulipas; winters south to San Luis Potosí). *I. g. nayaritensis* (Nayarit, in the vicinity of Tepic). *I. g. dickeyae* (Sierra Madre of Guerrero). *I. g. richardsoni* (Oaxaca, in the vicinity of Chimalapa, Tehuantepec). *I. g. graduacauda* (Jalisco, southern San Luis Potosí and Veracruz southward in the highlands, except where occupied by other races).

Remarks.—Also known as Audubon Oriole. No other yellow-backed Mexican species has a *wholly black head*. Back and belly are *lemon-yellow*, with no suggestion of orange. Wings usually with narrow white markings. Chiefly highlands, where widespread and common.

SPOT-BREASTED ORIOLE. *Icterus pectoralis pectoralis* (Illus. p. 516).—8–8½. *Adult:* Lores, throat to median breast, wings, back, and tail black; breast and sides of chest black-spotted; base of primaries white, the secondaries edged with same; above and below (including lesser wing-coverts) otherwise bright orange. *Immature:* Similar to adult, but much duller and without breast-spots; back and tail dingy olive.

Distribution.—Arid lowlands of Colima, Guerrero, Oaxaca, and Chiapas.

Remarks.—A bright orange, black-backed oriole with conspicuous spots bordering its bib. Adults are unmistakable. Olive-backed immature birds are much more brightly colored (orange) than most other subadult orioles and have *white wing-markings*.

BLACK-THROATED ORIOLE. *Icterus gularis* (Illus. p. 516).—8½–10. *Adult:* Rich yellow or flaming orange (females duller), the lores, throat and median chest, back, wings, and tail black; lesser wing-coverts yellow, greater coverts white-tipped, secondaries edged with white. *Immature:* Head, rump, and underparts wholly yellow, this often tinged with ochraceous; back and tail dusky olive; wings brownish edged with paler.

Distribution.—Eastern and southern Mexico (both coastal slopes), chiefly in arid lowlands.

Races.—*I. g. tamaulipensis* (San Luis Potosí and central Tamaulipas south to Puebla and western Campeche). *I. g. yucatanensis* (Yucatán Peninsula and Cozumel Island). *I. g. gularis* (arid lowlands of Guerrero, Oaxaca, and extreme western Chiapas).

Remarks.—Also known as Altamira Oriole and Lichtenstein Oriole. Largest of the yellow-headed, black-backed orioles. Individuals vary in brilliance, but most are distinctly orange-yellow (not lemon-yellow) or bright reddish orange. Spot-breasted and Hooded Orioles are similar, but much smaller. The former is distinguished by its breast-spots; the latter by its *black* shoulders and white wing-bar.

HOODED ORIOLE. *Icterus cucullatus* (Illus. p. 518).—7–8 *Male* (*adult*): Loral area, throat, upper back, wings, and tail black; hood, lower back, rump, and underparts (except throat) bright lemon-yellow or rich orange-yellow; a white wing-bar; remiges usually narrowly edged with white; (*immature*): Similar to female, but with a black throat. *Female:* Above dingy olive, brightening on head and rump; two white wing-bars; below dull greenish yellow, the sides and flanks tinged with olive.

Distribution.—Baja California and Mexico generally, including islands of the Yucatán Peninsula.

Races.—*I. c. trochiloides* (southern Baja California north to about latitude 27°). *I. c. californicus* (Baja California, breeding in the northern

HOODED ORIOLE

half). *I. c. nelsoni* (northern Sonora and northwestern Chihuahua). *I. c. restrictus* (extreme southern Sonora and possibly northern Sinaloa). *I. c. sennetti* (northern Coahuila, Nuevo León, and Tamaulipas; southward in winter to Guerrero and Morelos). *I. c. cucullatus* (eastern and southern Mexico from southern Nuevo León and Tamaulipas south to Colima, Guerrero, and Veracruz). *I. c. igneus* (northern parts of the Yucatán Peninsula). *I. c. masoni* (southeastern Quintana Roo). *I. c. duplexus* (Mujeres, Holbox, and Meco Islands). *I. c. cozumelae* (Cozumel Island).

Remarks.—Only three other yellow-hooded, black-backed orioles occur in Mexico. The Yellow-tailed has conspicuous yellow outer rectrices. Spot-breasted and Black-throated Orioles have *yellow shoulders;* not black shoulders and a white wing-bar. Both are considerably larger than the Hooded. Female (and immature male) Hooded and Orchard Orioles are alike except in size. Both are much smaller than a Scott or Bullock, and lack the latter's white belly.

STREAK-BACKED ORIOLE. *Icterus pustulatus* (Illus. p. 516).—$7\frac{1}{2}$–8. *Male:* Loral area, throat, wings, and tail black, the wing-coverts and remiges edged with white, and outer rectrices gray-tipped; head and breast orange-red (duller on crown) shading to orange-yellow posteriorly; back and scapulars boldly striped with black. *Female:* Similar to male, but much duller; back gray or olive, streaked as in male. *Immature:* Similar to female, but without black bib.

Distribution.—Western and southern lowlands and foothills, chiefly in arid districts. Also Tres Marías Islands, off the Pacific Coast. ENDEMIC.

Races.—*I. p. microstictus* (Sonora and Chihuahua south to Nayarit and Jalisco). *I. p. pustulatus* (lowlands of Colima, Guerrero, Mexico, Morelos, Puebla, and Veracruz). *I. p. formosus* (arid lowlands of Oaxaca and Chiapas). *I. p. graysonii* (Tres Marías Islands).

Remarks.—Also known as Flame-headed Oriole and Scarlet-headed Oriole. The only Mexican oriole with a *streaked back*. Birds of Oaxaca and Chiapas (*formosus*) are so liberally striped as to appear virtually black-backed. Some authorities consider these to be conspecific with *sclateri*, a common Central American oriole.

TRICOLORED BLACKBIRD. *Agelaius tricolor.*—$7\frac{1}{2}$–$8\frac{1}{2}$. *Male:* Glossy black, the lesser wing-coverts deep red, the middle coverts either abruptly white (summer) or tinged with tawny. *Female:* Sides of head and upperparts deep sooty, the crown, hind-neck, and back liberally speckled or streaked with gray; pale superciliaries; a whitish wing-bar; throat and breast dull white, conspicuously streaked with sooty; abdomen, flanks, and crissum wholly sooty.

Distribution.—Marshes of northwestern Baja California.

Remarks.—Also known as Tricolored Red-wing. Summer males are distinguished from Red-winged Blackbirds by their sharply contrasting *red-and-white epaulets*. Females have sooty, *unstreaked bellies*, quite unlike the boldly marked underparts of *phoeniceus*. In fall and winter the Tricolored's epaulets are usually tinged with buff, but the red is of a deeper hue than in *phoeniceus*. Females have *unstreaked, sooty bellies*, and are decidedly duskier (less brownish) than female Red-winged Blackbirds.

RED-WINGED BLACKBIRD. *Agelaius phoeniceus.*—7–9. *Male:* Glossy black, the lesser wing-coverts bright vermilion, scarlet, or orange, the middle coverts distinctly tawny or buff. *Female:* Above dusky brown, more or less conspicuously streaked with grayish brown, buff, and rufous; pale superciliaries; below dull white, boldly streaked with black; throat and chest sometimes tinged with pink.

Distribution.—Virtually country-wide in marshes.

Races.—*A. p. neutralis* (Pacific slope of Baja California south to latitude 30°). *A. p. sonoriensis* (northeastern Baja California [winters south to Cape San Lucas], Sonora, Chihuahua, and Sinaloa). **A. p. nevadensis* (winters in Chihuahua). *A. p. nayaritensis* (coastal plains of Nayarit). *A. p. megapotamus* (Coahuila, Nuevo León, and Tamaulipas south to northern Veracruz). *A. p. gubernator* (highlands of Durango and Zacatecas south to Oaxaca). *A. p. richmondi* (Caribbean slope from Veracruz southward; also Cozumel Island). *A. p. matudae* (Tabasco and Campeehe, in the valley of the Río Usumacinta).

Remarks.—This handsome blackbird occurs abundantly in marshes throughout the country. Males are virtually unmistakable, but might be confused with Tricolored Blackbirds in northwestern Baja California. Females suggest heavily streaked sparrows, but are larger than most similar fringillids and have very broad, *sharply defined markings. See* Tricolored Blackbird.

YELLOW-HEADED BLACKBIRD. *Xanthocephalus xanthocephalus.*— 8–9½. *Male:* Head, neck, and breast yellow, the crown and hind-neck more or less dusky in winter; above and below uniform sooty black; a white wing-patch. *Female:* Mainly uniform dusky brown, the superciliaries, malar stripes, throat, and breast dingy yellowish; a conspicuous submalar stripe.

Distribution.—Marshes of northern Baja California and northern Mexico, wintering south at least to Jalisco, Michoacán, and Puebla.

Remarks.—Yellow-headed Blackbirds, like Red-wings, breed almost exclusively in marshes but may be found elsewhere in winter. Both sexes are totally unlike any other Mexican species.

COMMON MEADOWLARK. *Sturnella magna.*—7½–9½. Upperparts deep sooty brown, very liberally streaked with tawny buff; secondaries and inner rectrices barred or notched with tawny, the outer rectrices immaculate white; a distinct white crown-stripe; malar area, auriculars, and posterior part of superciliaries dull white; a dark postocular stripe; forepart of superciliaries, throat, breast, and belly bright yellow, the flanks and crissum buffy white streaked with black; a prominent black crescentic chest-patch.

Distribution.—Virtually country-wide in grassy districts.

Races.—*S. m. lilianae* (northern plateau region of Sonora and Chihuahua). *S. m. auropectoralis* (Sinaloa and Durango south to Michoacán). *S. m. hoopesi* (northern Tamaulipas). *S. m. alticola* (highlands from western Veracruz and Puebla southward). *S. m. mexicana* (lowlands of Veracruz and Tabasco). *S. m. griscomi* (northern Yucatán in the vicinity of Progreso and Río Lagartos).

Remarks.—Stocky, short-tailed icterids with bright yellow underparts and a *black crescentic breast-patch*. Meadowlarks are restricted to grasslands and are essentially terrestrial in habits. When in flight, their white outer rectrices show clearly, and are useful supplementary field marks. No similar bird alternates rapid wing-beats with periods of sailing. Common and Western Meadowlarks are virtually indistinguishable in the field except by song. Westerns sing in a lower pitch than Common Meadowlarks, and their song has a more liquid quality.

WESTERN MEADOWLARK. *Sturnella neglecta.*—8½–9. Similar to a Common Meadowlark, but with yellow of throat encroaching on the malar area.

Distribution.—Northwestern Baja California (south to the cape district in winter) and northern Mexico generally. Winters south to Jalisco and Guanajuato.

Remarks.—*See* Common Meadowlark.

Family THRAUPIDAE. Tanagers

KEY TO THE SPECIES

1a. Wholly or partly red or reddish, this usually conspicuous but sometimes restricted to forepart of head or rump 2

  b. Without red or reddish 14

2a. Underparts wholly or mainly black 3

  b. Underparts not black 4

3a. Wholly black below, the rump and upper tail-coverts red
                          Scarlet-rumped Tanager (male), p. 530

  b. Not wholly black below; breast and under tail-coverts red
                          Crimson-collared Tanager, p. 530

4a. Bright yellow below, the throat (or entire head) red or reddish . . 5

  b. Not yellow below 6

5a. Back, wings, and tail black; two wing-bars; forepart of head (at least) red . . . . Western Tanager (male), p. 533

  b. Upperparts essentially yellowish olive, the head and neck bright red . . . . Red-headed Tanager (male), p. 535

6a. Uniform slaty gray above, or with dull red crown, wings, and tail 7

  b. Not as in 6a. 8

7a. Thrushlike. Superciliaries, throat, breast, and median abdomen
rose-red . . . . Rose-breasted Thrush-Tanager, p. 538

b. Sparrowlike. Throat pale rose-red, the breast and belly gray
Rose-throated Tanager (male), p. 532

8a. Dull red, palest below; a crimson crown-patch 9

b. Bright red or orange-red, the wings and tail sometimes black; no
crown-patch 10

9a. Throat much brighter than breast; crown-patch not bordered with
black . . . . Red-throated Ant-Tanager (male), p. 536

b. Throat and breast virtually concolor; crown-patch bordered with
black . . . . Red-crowned Ant-Tanager (male), p. 535

10a. Wings and tail black or blackish 11

b. Wings and tail not black or blackish 13

11a. Wings barred; bill black 12

b. Wings not barred; bill pale . . Scarlet Tanager (spring male), p. 532

12a. Larger (7 inches). Back boldly streaked; outer rectrices white-
tipped . . . . Flame-colored Tanager (male), p. 534

b. Smaller (5½ inches). Back not streaked; face black
White-winged Tanager (male), p. 532

13a. Wholly bright red; bill pale . . . . Summer Tanager (male), p. 531

b. Wings and back grayish brown or dusky, more or less tinged with
red; auriculars dingy; bill black . . Hepatic Tanager (male), p. 531

14a. Wholly or partly blue, bright purple, or glossy purplish blue. Birds
of the last category are notably small and have bright yellow or
tawny rufous underparts 15

b. Not as in 14a. 22

15a. Pale grayish blue, darkest on back; epaulets lilac-blue
Blue-gray Tanager, p. 529

b. Not pale grayish blue 16

16a. Head and neck alone purplish blue; yellow wing-patches
Yellow-winged Tanager, p. 529

b. Not as in 16a. 17

17a. Blue-capped, or with a blue crown-patch. If the latter, plumage
mainly glossy green, the breast and median abdomen sometimes
bright yellow 18

b. Not as in 17a. 19

18a. Crown and hind-neck wholly bright blue
Blue-hooded Euphonia, p. 525

b. A bright blue crown-patch . . . Blue-crowned Chlorophonia, p. 524

30a. Smaller (3½–4 inches). Bill stubby; tail notably short 31
 b. Larger (5½–8 inches). Bill and tail not as in 30a. 33
31a. Upperparts bronzy olive, the forehead bright yellow or dingy chestnut; abdomen and crissum sometimes rufous
Olive-backed Euphonia, p. 527
 b. Not as in 31a. 32
32a. Above uniform olive-green; below essentially bright greenish yellow . . . . Yellow-throated Euphonia (female), p. 527
 b. Sides of head, crown, and back essentially gray; below pale yellow
Scrub Euphonia (female), p. 526
33a. Two white or pale yellow wing-bars 34
 b. Without wing-bars 36
34a. Back broadly streaked . . Flame-colored Tanager (female), p. 534
 b. Back not streaked 35
35a. Larger (6½–7 inches). Back dusky; bill pale yellowish brown
Western Tanager (female), p. 533
 b. Smaller (5½ inches). Back yellowish olive; bill black
White-winged Tanager (female), p. 532
36a. Throat (sometimes entire head) gray or dusky 37
 b. Throat and head not gray or dusky 39
37a. Back, wings, and tail rich brown; bill conspicuously hooked
Black-throated Shrike-Tanager (female), p. 537
 b. Not as in 37a. 38
38a. Breast and rump bright orange-olive; tail sooty black
Scarlet-rumped Tanager (female), p. 530
 b. Olive-green above, bright yellow below, the head wholly gray
Gray-headed Tanager, p. 537
39a. Bill black; cheeks, back, and wings dusky
Hepatic Tanager (female), p. 531
 b. Bill pale yellowish brown; cheeks and back not dusky 40
40a. Upperparts olive-green, the wings and tail blackish
Scarlet Tanager (female), p. 532
 b. Upperparts essentially yellowish olive
Summer Tanager (female), p. 531

BLUE-CROWNED CHLOROPHONIA. *Chlorophonia occipitalis occipitalis* (Illus. p. 525).—5½. *Male:* Mainly bright green, the breast, median line of abdomen, and crissum bright yellow; a *narrow* brown band bordering green of chest; crown-patch and narrow nuchal band pale blue. *Female:*

Similar to male, but green of underparts shading to yellow on belly and crissum.

Distribution.—Wooded mountains of Veracruz and Chiapas.

Remarks.—A stocky, *short-tailed* green and yellow tanager with a blue patch in middle of crown. Males are sharply patterned below and have a *dark band* dividing the green and yellow of chest and breast. Females are almost wholly green below and lack a chest-band. Look for

BLUE-CROWNED CHLOROPHONIA

Chlorophonias in the treetops, especially those with berrying mistletoe. *See* Green Shrike-vireo.

BLUE-HOODED EUPHONIA. *Tanagra musica* (Illus. p. 526).—4½. *Male:* Crown, nape, and sides of neck bright blue; throat, sides of head, and upperparts (except crown) glossy purplish blue, appearing black at a distance; forehead, breast, and posterior underparts tawny rufous; bill very short and broad at base. *Female:* Mainly olive-green, palest below, the throat tawny; crown and hind-neck bright blue; forehead chestnut.

Distribution.—Wooded mountains of western and southern Mexico.

Races.—*T. m. rileyi* (extreme southeastern Sonora below an altitude of about 5,000 feet). *T. m. elegantissima* (Sinaloa, Guanajuato, and Veracruz southward in mountains).

Remarks.—Euphonias are diminutive short-tailed tanagers with broad stubby bills. Males of all four Mexican species are very colorful and have bold, distinctive patterns. This species alone has a conspicuous *blue crown* (both sexes), and rufous underparts. Females are *pale olive* below. *See* females of other euphonias.

BLUE-HOODED EUPHONIA

SCRUB EUPHONIA. *Tanagra affinis* (Illus. p. 527).—3½–4. *Male:* Head (except forepart of crown), throat, and upperparts glossy purplish blue, appearing black at a distance; forehead (to level of eyes) and underparts (except throat) clear bright yellow; white tail-patches. *Female:* Above essentially grayish olive, the forehead, rump, and upper tail-coverts bright olive-green; below dull yellowish olive, brightening posteriorly; under tail-coverts yellow or white.

Distribution.—Both coastal slopes, chiefly in dry districts.

Races.—*T. a. godmani* (Sonora south at least to Nayarit and Colima). *T. a. esperanza* (Chiapas). *T. a. affinis* (Caribbean slope north to southern Tamaulipas).

Remarks.—Also known as Lesson Euphonia. Birds of the Pacific slope (*godmani*) have *white* under tail-coverts, and may represent a distinct species, the Pale-vented Euphonia. Yellow-throated Euphonias (males) of the Caribbean slope are also yellow-fronted like male Scrub

SCRUB EUPHONIA

Euphonias, but have *wholly* yellow underparts. Their females, olive-green above and greenish yellow below, are conspicuously brighter than female Scrub Euphonias.

YELLOW-THROATED EUPHONIA. *Tanagra lauta lauta.*—4. *Male:* Forehead and underparts bright golden-yellow; sides of head and upperparts (except forehead) glossy purplish blue; white tail-patches. *Female:* Uniform olive-green above, the underparts bright greenish yellow more or less intermixed with white.

Distribution.—Caribbean slope north to southern Tamaulipas.

Remarks.—Also known as Bonaparte Euphonia. The only diminutive Mexican tanager with *wholly yellow underparts*. Scrub Euphonias are somewhat similar, but males have dark throats and females are much duller, with essentially grayish (not olive) upperparts. Males of both species have white tail-patches that show from below and in flight.

OLIVE-BACKED EUPHONIA. *Tanagra gouldi gouldi.*—3¾. *Male:* Above bronzy olive lightly glossed with blue, the forehead bright yellow; throat and breast dull olive-green; sides and flanks yellow flecked with olive; belly and under tail-coverts tawny rufous. *Female:* Similar to male, but forehead dusky chestnut and rufous of underparts limited to under tail-coverts.

Distribution.—Caribbean lowlands north to Oaxaca, Quintana Roo, and Veracruz.

Remarks.—Also known as Gould Euphonia. The only notably small Mexican tanager with very glossy, *deep olive* upperparts. Females suggest female Yellow-throated Euphonias, but have *rufous* (not bright yellow) under tail-coverts and dingy chestnut foreheads. Yellow-fronted males show rufous on belly and crissum.

MASKED TANAGER. *Tangara nigro-cincta larvata* (Illus. p. 528).—$5\frac{1}{4}$. Forehead, malar area, and auriculars bright purple, fringed behind with pale blue; a black band extending from chin and base of bill through eyes; crown (except forepart), hind-neck, and sides of neck glossy golden-buff, darkening on throat; back, scapulars, chest, and breast black; wings and

MASKED TANAGER

tail mainly black; wing-coverts purple and blue, the remiges edged with green; rump and upper tail-coverts pale blue; sides purplish blue, the median abdomen and under tail-coverts white.

Distribution.—Humid lowland forests of Chiapas and Tabasco.

Remarks.—The Mexican form is also known as Golden-masked Tanager. This representative tropical American genus barely reaches Mexico, although widespread and abundant to the south. It includes many notably colorful and boldly patterned species, of which this is a good example. No other black-breasted Mexican bird has a golden-buff head and bright purplish blue face. Look for it in treetops.

AZURE-RUMPED TANAGER. *Tangara cabanisi.*—5¾. *Subadult:* Crown and hind-neck greenish blue or grayish blue, the feathers with black centers; back and rump greenish; wings and tail black, edged with blue; sides of head greenish yellow or dusky; below pale greenish blue, shading to white on abdomen; breast sometimes spotted with black.

Distribution.—Recorded once (August 29, 1937) on Mount Ovando, near Escuintla, Chiapas.

Remarks.—Also known as Cabanis Tanager. Only two specimens, both in subadult plumage, are known to science. The first was collected many years ago at Costa Cuca, in the arid lowlands of western Guatemala.

BLUE-GRAY TANAGER. *Thraupis virens diaconus.*—6½. Pale bluish gray, darkening on back and rump; wings edged with light blue, the lesser coverts bright lilac-blue.

Distribution.—Lowlands of southern Veracruz, Tabasco, and Quintana Roo.

Remarks.—A very pale bluish gray tanager with *bright blue epaulets.* In certain light the back, wings, and rump appear lightly tinged with green. Forest-edge and cultivated districts.

YELLOW-WINGED TANAGER. *Thraupis abbas.*—7. Head purplish blue, lightening to grayish blue on throat and chest, where shading into olive of breast and posterior underparts; back and rump grayish olive, the former blotched with black; wings mainly black, the remiges bright yellow basally, the coverts olive; tail black.

Distribution.—Lowlands of southeastern Mexico north to Oaxaca, San Luis Potosí and southern Tamaulipas.

Remarks.—Also known as Abbot Tanager. A blue-headed, olive-and-black tanager with *bright yellow wing-patches.* Quite handsome, although lacking the brilliant plumage of many relatives. Wooded districts, chiefly in treetops.

STRIPE-HEADED TANAGER. *Spindalis zena benedicti.*—6–6½. *Male:* Superciliaries and malar stripes white; crown, broad band through eye, and throat black, the last with a yellow median patch; hind-neck, sides of neck, and breast chestnut, the last conspicuously bordered behind with bright yellow; sides, lower abdomen, and crissum white; back olive-brown, the lower portion golden-olive; rump chestnut; wings and tail black, boldly patterned with white. *Female:* Above dull grayish olive, lightening on throat, breast, and flanks; abdomen dull white; wing-coverts and secondaries edged with white.

Distribution.—Cozumel Island, off the coast of Quintana Roo.

Remarks.—Also known as Spindalis. Sole Mexican representative of a common West Indian genus. Sparrow-like in form, but very colorful and with a white-striped head and chestnut-and-yellow breast. Females are quite drab—dull olive above, pale below, and with *whitish wing-markings.* Female Rose-throated Tanagers have *pale yellow throats* and *unpatterned* wings.

SCARLET-RUMPED TANAGER. *Ramphocelus passerinii passerinii.*—6¾. *Male:* Velvety black, the lower back, rump, and upper tail-coverts bright scarlet; bill pale bluish gray. *Female:* Head and neck brownish gray; elsewhere essentially orange-olive, brightest on rump and breast; remiges and tail sooty black.

Distribution.—Tabasco, and probably elsewhere in humid lowland forests of southeastern Mexico.

Remarks.—Also known as Velvet Tanager and Passerini Tanager. Probably more widespread than present records indicate. Males are very conspicuous and totally unlike any other Mexican species. Females are dusky-headed, with golden-olive breasts and rumps. The swollen, *pale bluish bill* is a useful supplementary character.

CRIMSON-COLLARED TANAGER. *Phlogothraupis sanguinolenta sanguinolenta* (Illus. p. 530).—7½. Mainly glossy black, the crown, neck, breast, and tail-coverts (above and below) deep red; bill pale grayish blue; iris red.

CRIMSON-COLLARED TANAGER

Distribution.—Humid lowlands of Veracruz, Tabasco, Oaxaca, and Quintana Roo.

Remarks.—A bright red-and-black tanager of spectacular appearance. While most abundant in lowland rain forests, it ranges locally to an altitude of about 4,000 feet. Unmistakable wherever found.

SUMMER TANAGER. *Piranga rubra.*—7. *Male:* Wholly bright red, palest below; bill yellowish brown. *Female:* Uniform olive above, the underparts dull yellow; no wing-bars; bill as in male.

Distribution.—Northeastern Baja California and northern Mexico south to northern Durango and Nuevo León; southward in winter.

Races.—*P. r. cooperi* (as above, wintering south to Guerrero and Morelos). *P. r. rubra* (breeds in northeastern Mexico; winters from central Mexico and Yucatán southward).

Remarks.—The only wholly *bright red* tanager with a *pale* bill. Male Hepatics are much duller above and below, and have both a dark bill and *dusky cheeks.* Female Summer Tanagers can usually be distinguished from similar olive-and-yellow tanagers by their pale bills, unbarred wings, and virtually *uniform dull olive upperparts.* No other tanager has all of these characters.

HEPATIC TANAGER. *Piranga flava.*—7–7½. *Male:* Wholly red (or reddish), brightest on crown and underparts, the auriculars, back, scapulars, and wings more or less tinged with grayish brown; bill black. *Female:* Upperparts dusky, brightening to yellowish olive on crown, tail-coverts, and tail; no wing-bars; cheeks dusky; throat, chest, and under tail-coverts bright yellow, lightening on abdomen; bill black.

Distribution.—Highlands generally.

Races.—*P. f. zimmeri* (Sonora, on western slope of the Sierra Madre, and southwestern Chihuahua; winters south to Jalisco). *P. f. hepatica* (highlands generally, west of the Sierra Madre del Oriente). *P. f. dextra* (highlands of eastern Nuevo León, Tamaulipas, Veracruz, northern Puebla, eastern Oaxaca, and Chiapas).

Remarks.—Hepatic Tanagers are essentially highland birds and can hardly be confused with any other Mexican species except a Summer Tanager. Both sexes have *black* bills; the Summer's bill is distinctly yellowish brown. Male Hepatics have dusky cheeks and are much duller than Summer Tanagers. Female Hepatics are duskier and less uniform above than female Summer Tanagers. Their brighter, sometimes orange-yellow, throat and breast corroborate other field marks. *See* female Summer Tanager.

ROSE-THROATED TANAGER. *Piranga roseo-gularis* (Illus. p. 532).
—6. *Male:* Essentially gray, palest below, the crown, wings, and tail dull red; throat, chest, and under tail-coverts rose-red or pink; bill brown above, pale below. *Female:* Patterned like male, but red of crown, wings, and tail replaced with yellowish olive; throat and under tail-coverts pale yellow.

Distribution.—Yucatán Peninsula and offshore islands.

Races.—*P. r. roseo-gularis* (Yucatán, extreme northern Quintana Roo, and Meco Island). *P. r. tincta* (Campeche and most of Quintana Roo). *P. r. cozumelae* (Cozumel and Mujeres Islands).

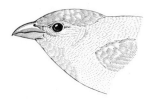

ROSE-THROATED TANAGER

Remarks.—A gray finchlike tanager with *dull red* or *yellowish olive* crown, wings, and tail. The red or pale yellow *throat-patch* eliminates all similar birds in its area.

***SCARLET TANAGER.** *Piranga olivacea.*—6½–7. *Male (spring):* Bright scarlet, with wholly black wings and tail; bill pale brown; *(fall):* Similar to female, but with black wings and tail. *Female:* Uniform olive-green above, the wings and tail dusky; underparts greenish yellow, more or less tinged with olive on sides and flanks; bill pale brown.

Distribution.—Casual migrant in southeastern Mexico.

Remarks.—Scarlet Tanagers winter in northwestern South America and migrate chiefly through the West Indies and eastern Central America. Although rare in our area, they can be expected as occasional transients in the southeastern lowlands. Males, whether in breeding or in blotchy transition plumage, are unmistakable. Females and males in fall plumage resemble female Summer Tanagers, but have *blackish wings* and brighter green (less olive) upperparts. Both species have *pale bills* and lack wing-bars. This combination of characters eliminates other olive-and-yellow tanagers and orioles.

WHITE-WINGED TANAGER. *Piranga leucoptera leucoptera* (Illus. p. 533).—5½. *Male:* Mainly bright red, the forehead, orbital region, bill, wings, and tail black; two broad white wing-bars. *Female:* Yellowish olive above, rich golden-yellow below, the wings and tail blackish; two broad white wing-bars.

Distribution.—Southern Tamaulipas and state of Mexico south through Veracruz, Puebla, and Chiapas.

Remarks.—A medium-sized red-and-black or olive-and-yellow tanager with very *conspicuous white wing-bars*. Males are unmistakable. Females resemble female Western Tanagers but are much smaller, brighter below, and have *black* bills. Their wing-bars are conspicuously

WHITE-WINGED TANAGER

white, not pale yellowish. This distinctive little tanager frequents the tops of trees and is most abundant between 2,000 and 4,000 feet above sea-level.

WESTERN TANAGER. *Piranga ludoviciana* (Illus. p. 534).—6½–7. *Male (summer):* Forepart of head red, shading to orange posteriorly; neck, underparts (except throat and chest), rump, and upper tail-coverts bright yellow; back, wings, and tail black; two *pale yellow* wing-bars; bill pale brown; *(winter)*: Similar to summer plumage, but head mainly yellowish olive, the forehead and chin alone red. *Female:* Crown, hind-neck, rump, and upper tail-coverts yellowish olive; back, wings, and tail dusky; two pale yellow or whitish wing-bars; underparts wholly yellow; bill pale brown.

Distribution.—Breeds in northern Baja California and northern Sonora. Winters extensively elsewhere, chiefly in the highlands.

Remarks.—A red-faced, *black-backed* (dusky in females) tanager with prominent wing-bars. Male Red-headed Tanagers lack wing-bars and are olive-backed. Female Westerns resemble White-winged and Flame-colored Tanagers but have *brownish* (not black) bills and *yellowish* wing-bars. The White-winged is a much smaller bird and *bidentata*

WESTERN TANAGER

has a striped back. Female orioles have sharply pointed bills and brighter cheeks.

FLAME-COLORED TANAGER. *Piranga bidentata* (Illus. p. 534).—7. *Male:* Head, neck, and underparts bright red or orange-red; auriculars dusky reddish, bordered behind with black; back and scapulars dull reddish, broadly striped with black; wings and tail sooty black, the outer rectrices

FLAME-COLORED TANAGER

white-tipped; two pinkish white wing-bars; bill black. *Female:* Patterned like male, but the red replaced with yellowish olive above and rich yellow below; top of head and hind-neck finely streaked; white wing-bars; bill dusky.

Distribution.—Tres Marías Islands, off the Pacific Coast, and the Sierra Madres southward at high altitudes.

Races.—*P. b. flammea* (María Madre and María Magdalena Islands, Tres Marías group). *P. b. bidentata* (mountains of the Pacific slope from Sinaloa to Mexico). *P. b. sanguinolenta* (mountains of eastern Mexico from central Nuevo León and Tamaulipas southward).

Remarks.—Also known as Swainson Tanager. The only Mexican species with a boldly *striped back*. Only two other tanagers, the White-winged and Western, have wing-bars. Most males have a *distinct ear-patch* bordered behind with black. Their white tail-tips are not likely to be seen.

RED-HEADED TANAGER. *Piranga erythrocephala.*—6. *Male:* Head and neck bright red, lightening on throat; upperparts uniform yellowish olive; below bright yellow, palest on belly, the sides and flanks tinged with olive. *Female:* Top of head yellowish olive, shading to olive-green posteriorly; sides of head essentially gray; below dull yellow, tinged with pale brown on flanks, the under tail-coverts tawny buff.

Distribution.—Western and south-central Mexico south to Oaxaca. ENDEMIC.

Races.—*P. e. candida* (southeastern Sonora and Chihuahua south to Jalisco). *P. e. erythrocephala* (Guanajuato, Mexico, Guerrero, and Oaxaca).

Remarks.—The only olive-backed tanager with a red head. Male Westerns are yellow-necked and have *black* backs, wings, and tails. Their heads are never wholly red. Female Red-headed Tanagers lack wing-bars and have *buffy under tail-coverts*.

RED-CROWNED ANT-TANAGER. *Habia rubica* (Illus. p. 536).— 6½–7. *Male:* Dull reddish brown, brightening on throat and chest; breast, abdomen, and crissum dull pinkish brown; a conspicuous bright red crown-patch, bordered laterally with black. *Female:* Dull olive-brown, lightening on median underparts; a conspicuous tawny crown-patch.

Distribution.—Pacific and Caribbean slopes from Nayarit and southern Tamaulipas southward.

Races.—*H. r. rosea* (coastlands of Nayarit). *H. r. affinis* (Pacific slope of Oaxaca and possibly Guerrero). *H. r. holobrunnea* (humid mountain forests of Veracruz). *H. r. rubicoïdes* (lowlands of southern Tamaulipas, eastern Veracruz, northern Oaxaca, Tabasco, and Campeche). *H. r. nelsoni* (Yucatán and adjacent parts of Campeche and Quintana Roo).

Remarks.—Also known as Red Ant-Tanager. Ant-tanagers frequent underbrush and lower branches of thick woods and are quite common locally. Both Mexican species are very similar and may be found together in the Caribbean lowlands. Males of this species are paler below than Red-throated Ant-Tanagers, and their scarlet crown-patches have black borders. Female Red-crowns are *olive-brown*, not deep chocolate-

RED-CROWNED ANT-TANAGER

brown. Their tawny crown-patch is diagnostic. Female Red-throated Ant-Tanagers lack a crown-patch, but have rather conspicuous *buffy yellow* throats.

RED-THROATED ANT-TANAGER. *Habia gutturalis.*—7–8. *Male:* Above dull reddish brown, shading to dull pinkish brown below, where brightening on throat; a bright red crown-patch. *Female:* Upperparts deep chocolate-brown, lightening on breast, sides, and flanks; throat buffy yellow in contrast to brown of chest; abdomen and under tail-coverts tawny.

Distribution.—Caribbean lowlands north to southern Tamaulipas. Meco and Mujeres Islands, off the coast of Quintana Roo.

Races.—*H. g. littoralis* (coastal forests of southern Tamaulipas, Tabasco, and northern Chiapas). *H. g. salvinii* (southern Veracruz, Oaxaca, and Chiapas). *H. g. peninsularis* (northern part of Yucatán Peninsula). *H. g. rooensis* (Quintana Roo). *H. g. insularis* (Meco and Mujeres Islands).

Remarks.—Two very similar ant-tanagers occur commonly in the Caribbean lowlands. While not always separable in the field, each has field marks that can be seen under favorable conditions. Males of this species are distinctly redder (less pinkish) below than male Red-crowns, and their throats conspicuously brighter than their chests. The scarlet crown-patch lacks a black border. Female Red-throats have no crown-patch. They are rich woods brown (not olive-brown), and have *yellowish buff throats* that contrast with their chests.

BLACK-THROATED SHRIKE-TANAGER. *Lanio aurantius auran-*
tius (Illus. p. 537).—7½–8. *Male:* Head, neck, wings, and tail black; lesser
wing-coverts white; back, rump, and underparts (except throat) bright yellow; the median chest usually tinged with brown; bill heavy, very strongly
hooked, and with a notch on edge of upper mandible. *Female:* Head gray,
the crown tinged with olive; upperparts otherwise mainly rich olive-
brown, the rump bright tawny olive; breast, sides, and flanks olive-green,
the abdomen bright yellow; under tail-coverts tawny buff; bill as in male.

BLACK-THROATED SHRIKE-TANAGER

Distribution.—Humid lowland forests of Veracruz, Tabasco, Oaxaca,
and Quintana Roo.

Remarks.—Yellow-and-black males are patterned like Black-
headed Orioles of the plateau. No oriole of the Caribbean lowlands has a
black head and yellow back. In any case, the *strongly hooked bill* eliminates all icterids and similar birds. Gray-headed females have *bright
tawny rumps* that contrast with their deep-brown backs and tails.

GRAY-HEADED TANAGER. *Eucometis penicillata pallida* (Illus. p.
538).—6½. Head and neck gray; above otherwise bright olive-green, the
underparts (except throat) rich yellow, tinged with olive on sides and flanks.

Distribution.—Lowlands of southern Veracruz and Yucatán Peninsula.
Also Meco Island, off Quintana Roo.

GRAY-HEADED TANAGER

Remarks.—A bright olive-and-yellow, sparrow-like tanager with a *gray head*. Unmistakable. Chiefly dry, open country, and especially abundant in the peninsula coastlands.

ROSE-BREASTED THRUSH-TANAGER. *Rhodinocichla rosea schistacea* (Illus. p. 538).—8. *Male:* Mainly slaty gray, the superciliaries, throat, breast, median line of abdomen, and under tail-coverts bright rose-red; bill thrushlike. *Female:* Patterned like male, but red replaced by tawny rufous; posterior half of superciliaries white.

ROSE-BREASTED THRUSH-TANAGER

Distribution.—Wooded lowlands of southern Sinaloa, Nayarit, Jalisco, and Colima.

Remarks.—A slaty, *thrushlike* tanager, with red or tawny rufous superciliaries, throat, and breast. Wholly unlike any other Mexican bird.

Thrush-Tanagers frequent dense woods and are best found by tracing the rich, melodious song.

COMMON BUSH-TANAGER. *Chlorospingus opthalmicus* (Illus. p. 539).—5½. Top and sides of head sooty brown; eyelids and spot behind eye white; upperparts (except head) uniform greenish olive; throat and abdomen dull white or grayish, the chest, sides, flanks, and under tail-coverts bright yellowish olive.

Distribution.—Mountains of southern Mexico.

COMMON BUSH-TANAGER

Races.—*C. o. albifrons* (Guerrero). *C. o. postocularis* (Pacific slope of Chiapas). *C. o. wetmorei* (southern Veracruz). *C. o. opthalmicus* (Puebla and Oaxaca). *C. o. dwighti* (Atlantic slope of Chiapas).

Remarks.—Also known as Brown-headed Chlorospingus. A small dusky-capped, olive-backed bird with a conspicuous *yellowish pectoral band*. The white postocular stripe, a good field mark, can usually be seen at a distance. Chiefly underbrush and thickets at high altitudes.

Family FRINGILLIDAE. Grosbeaks, Finches, Buntings

Finches and their allies occur abundantly in all parts of Mexico. They account for more than a tenth of the entire bird fauna, and a score or more resident species may be found in a single locality. Although a diverse group, varying considerably in color, pattern, and size, most fringillids are readily distinguished from other birds by their thick, more or less conelike bills. All but two Mexican species meet the specifications of one or more of the six arbitrary categories listed below, and appear in their respective keys. The two exceptions, Five-lined Sparrow (*Aimophila quinquestriata*) and Sage Sparrow (*Amphispiza belli*), both of western Mexico, are illustrated and described in the text.

KEY TO THE SPECIES (ADULTS ONLY)

I. Notably large or very small fringillids. Includes several colorful species, and some with remarkably thick, conelike bills. *See* page 540

II. Small and medium-sized species (i.e., less than 7 inches) with notably colorful plumage, or with more or less conspicuous patches of red, yellow, or blue. If with yellow, this sometimes restricted to the head or breast, or showing only as wing-patches. *See* page 544

III. Tail with more or less white; this usually restricted to the outer feathers, or to the feather-tips, and often inconspicuous except in flight. *See* page 547

IV. Crown (or crown-patch) uniform rufous or chestnut, or top of head with a pale (sometimes immaculate white), more or less conspicuous median stripe. Species with streaked underparts are not treated in this section. *See* page 549

V. More or less liberally streaked, the markings sometimes restricted to the upperparts. Tail and top of head without white, but the crown often with a pale, usually ill-defined median stripe. Plumage generally drab and undistinguished, but some species with yellow or yellowish superciliaries, yellow wing-patches, or bright yellow (sometimes pink) wing-linings. This section includes many of the small, furtive species often referred to as "grass sparrows" or "field sparrows" by the novice. Only adult plumages are considered. *See* page 551

VI. Small and medium-sized finches (4–6½ inches) with unpatterned black, slaty, or brownish plumage. Either virtually uniform above and below, or underparts essentially buffy white or pale buffy brown.

CATEGORY I

1*a*. More than 6½ inches long (at least as large as a Rose-breasted Grosbeak, Green-tailed Towhee, or Fox Sparrow) 2

  b. Less than 4½ inches long (not larger than a Pine Siskin or goldfinch) 26

2*a*. Conspicuously colorful, or with brightly colored patches. Birds with olive-green upperparts or chestnut crowns are not treated here 3

14a. Above mainly yellowish olive-green 15

   b. Above not olive-green 19

15a. Crown uniform chestnut, or with a chestnut patch, this sometimes
     limited to the hinder portion 16

   b. Crown and nape without chestnut 18

16a. Forehead and sides of head black; a black band across the chest . 17

   b. Forehead, sides of head, and chest pale gray, the white throat
     sharply defined . . . . Green-tailed Towhee, p. 580

17a. Crown and hind-neck wholly chestnut, the forehead partly black;
     a narrow black chest-band . . Chestnut-capped Brush-Finch, p. 577

   b. Posterior part of crown alone chestnut, the forehead and anterior
     crown black; a black chest-band, this sometimes spreading over
     most of the throat . . . . Collared Towhee, p. 581

18a. Throat white or tawny, bordered with black, this forming a con-
     spicuous band across the chest . . . . Black-headed Saltator, p. 555
                           Buff-throated Saltator, p. 555

   b. Throat white, the chest slate gray; crown striped with black and
     olive-yellow . . . . Striped Brush-Finch, p. 578

19a. Underparts very boldly spotted . . . . Fox Sparrow, p. 604

   b. Not as in 19a. 20

20a. Above virtually uniform gray or brown, the crown sometimes
     brighter than the back, but without a pale median stripe 21

   b. Above not uniform, the crown with a pale median stripe, and back
     often somewhat streaked; throat sometimes black 24

21a. With very conspicuous white superciliaries; a black stripe on each
     side of the white throat . . . . Grayish Saltator, p. 556

   b. Not as in 21a. 22

22a. Lores and chin dusky, the underparts uniform tawny ochraceous
                             Abert Towhee, p. 584

   b. Not as in 22a. 23

23a. Throat tawny, bordered with small triangular spots
                           Brown Towhee, p. 582

   b. Throat and chest white, the first with a buffy transverse band
                      White-throated Towhee, p. 583

24a. Throat black; a conspicuous white ear-patch and black breast-spot
               White-eared Ground-Sparrow, p. 585

   b. Not as in 24a. 25

25a. Head boldly striped with black and white, the back brown-streaked
               Stripe-headed Sparrow, p. 592

    b. Sides of crown chestnut, the median stripe grayish; a conspicuous black submalar stripe . . . . Rusty Sparrow, p. 593

26*a.* With conspicuous yellow, or bright olive-green, this sometimes limited to the head, wings, or underparts 27

    b. Not as in 26*a.* 34

27*a.* Head and breast extensively black or dusky, the forehead and throat sometimes yellow or yellowish 28

    b. Below mainly or entirely yellow or olive-green, the throat sometimes black, like the crown and lores 29

28*a.* Head and breast uniform black or dusky; a yellow wing-patch
                             Black-headed Siskin, p. 573

    b. Forehead, superciliaries, and throat golden-yellow, or throat and spot about lores pale yellow; wings uniform olive-green
                         Yellow-faced Grassquit, p. 564

29*a.* Crown, lores, and throat black, the breast golden-yellow, or head and throat grayish brown, the breast dull yellowish
                        Lawrence Goldfinch, p. 574

    b. Underparts uniform bright yellow, yellowish, or dull olive-green . 30

30*a.* Above liberally streaked, the underparts either bright yellow, or dingy whitish, faintly tinged with yellow
                      Yellow-breasted Grass-Finch, p. 576

    b. Above not streaked 31

31*a.* Bright yellow or yellowish below 32

    b. Dull olive-green below, the crown, wings, and tail (male) mainly black . . . . Black-capped Siskin, p. 572

32*a.* Back and scapulars bright yellow or brownish olive
                        American Goldfinch, p. 574

    b. Sides of head and upperparts black, or crown, wings, and tail black, the back and rump olive-green (male); in either case, the female dull olive above, with blackish wings and tail
                      Dark-backed Goldfinch, p. 574

33*a.* Boldly streaked above and below; a yellow wing-patch; tail deeply notched . . . . Pine Siskin, p. 572

    b. Not as in 33*a.* 34

34*a.* Rump and underparts cinnamon-rufous
                  Ruddy-breasted Seedeater (male), p. 570

    b. Not as in 34*a.* 35

35*a.* Wholly glossy black, or black above, the underparts buffy white or tawny 36

    b. Without conspicuous black, the wings and tail sometimes dusky . 38

36a. Wholly black 37

   b. Below tawny or buff, the chest black

                        White-collared Seedeater (male), p. 569

37a. Bill notably stout; a small white patch at base of primaries

                        Black Seedeater (male), p. 570

   b. Bill not notably stout; wings without white patch

                        Blue-black Grassquit (male), p. 571

38a. Dull brownish olive, palest below; no suggestion of wing-bars or ventral streaks . . . . Black Seedeater (female), p. 570

   b. Not as in 38a. 39

39a. Below uniform yellowish buff or buffy white; bill notably stout

                     White-collared Seedeater (female), p. 569

                     Ruddy-breasted Seedeater (female), p. 570

   b. Below not uniform, the breast, sides, and flanks more or less streaked; bill not notably stout Blue-black Grassquit (female), p. 571

Category II

1a. With conspicuous red or reddish purple 2

   b. Usually without red or purplish. If partly red and pink below, the plumage elsewhere blue 6

2a. Above and below essentially uniform: either dull red or mainly reddish purple 3

   b. Not as in 2a. If uniform red below, the head purplish blue, and back yellowish green 4

3a. Larger ($5\frac{1}{2}$–$6\frac{1}{2}$ inches). Dull red or brownish red; tips of bill crossed

                       Red Crossbill (male), p. 575

   b. Smaller ($4\frac{1}{2}$–5 inches). Mainly reddish purple, the nape and eyelids bright red; lores and chin black . . . Varied Bunting (male), p. 562

4a. Either bright red below, with a purplish head and green back, or uniform bright green above and yellowish below

                       Painted Bunting, p. 563

   b. Not as in 4a. 5

5a. Head and back black; median breast bright red or pink

                  Rose-breasted Grosbeak (summer male), p. 559

   b. Without black. Head and breast essentially red and pinkish, the abdomen white . . . . *Carpodacus* spp. (male), pp. 566–67

6a. Mainly blue or purplish blue. Sometimes partly red and pink below, but never with yellow 7

   b. With more or less yellow or yellowish, this sometimes much localized (throat, breast, wings, etc.), but usually conspicuous 11

7*a.* Underparts essentially like back, and virtually unmarked 8

  b. Underparts not uniform, and not like back 10

8*a.* Larger (6–6½ inches). Mainly rich purplish blue; wing-coverts chestnut . . . . Blue Grosbeak (male), p. 560

  b. Smaller (4½–5½ inches). Purplish or bluish; wing-coverts not chestnut 9

9*a.* Deep purplish blue, appearing black at a distance; forehead, lesser wing-coverts, and rump bright azure-blue

Blue Bunting (male), p. 561

  b. Mainly cerulean blue, sometimes with bluish green reflections; head and median underparts purplish blue   Indigo Bunting (male), p. 561

10*a.* Above cerulean blue, the breast and abdomen scarlet and pink

Rose-bellied Bunting (male), p. 563

  b. Throat and upperparts turquoise-blue; breast and sides tawny ochraceous, the belly white . . . . . Lazuli Bunting (male), p. 562

11*a.* Extensively yellow, bright greenish yellow, or yellowish olive . . 12

  b. With isolated patches of yellow or bright greenish yellow, these restricted to the head, breast, or wings 22

12*a.* Larger (6½–7 inches). Bill notably large and conelike, or crown with a broad white median stripe 13

  b. Smaller (3¾–5¾ inches). Bill not notably large, but often conelike and with a sharp tip 16

13*a.* A white crown-stripe; underparts bright yellow

White-naped Brush-Finch, p. 577

  b. Crown not striped; head or face black, or above and below essentially dingy yellowish olive; bill conelike 14

14*a.* Face and throat black, the plumage otherwise bright golden-yellow

Black-faced Grosbeak, p. 557

  b. Head wholly black, or forehead bright yellow, the plumage otherwise essentially dingy yellowish olive; wings and tail black, the tertials pale gray or white; a pale conelike bill 15

15*a.* Head black; tertials pale gray . . . Hooded Grosbeak (male), p. 565

  b. Forehead and superciliaries bright yellow, the plumage otherwise dingy yellowish olive; tertials white

Evening Grosbeak (male), p. 565

16*a.* With conspicuous black, this sometimes restricted to the head, wings, and tail. 17

  b. Without black 20

17*a*. Throat or entire head black; a conspicuous yellow wing-patch, or remiges and coverts edged with greenish yellow 18

  b. Below wholly bright yellow; a white wing-patch or wing-bar . . 19

18*a*. Head and chest black; a large yellow wing-patch
                                        Black-headed Siskin, p. 573

  b. Crown, lores, and median throat black, the cheeks pale gray; a greenish yellow breast-patch . . Lawrence Goldfinch (male), p. 574

19*a*. Bright yellow, the crown, wings, and tail black
                                    American Goldfinch (male), p. 574

  b. Sides of head and upperparts glossy black, or greenish olive above, the wings and tail black . . Dark-backed Goldfinch (male), p. 574

20*a*. Above mainly bright blue or uniform grayish green, the underparts bright yellow . . . . Orange-breasted Bunting, p. 563

  b. Upperparts not as in 20*a*. 21

21*a*. Larger (5¾ inches). Crown chestnut, the dorsal plumage otherwise olive-brown . . . . Rufous-capped Brush-Finch, p. 576

  b. Smaller (4½ inches). Crown and back yellowish olive-green, liberally streaked with dusky . . Yellow-breasted Grass-Finch (male), p. 576

22*a*. Throat bright yellow, in sharp contrast with the breast 23

  b. Throat varied, but never bright yellow, and sometimes concolor with the breast 24

23*a*. Larger (6½–6¾ inches). Breast and abdomen white; a white crown-stripe . . . . Yellow-throated Brush-Finch, p. 577

  b. Smaller (4 inches). Breast black or blackish; superciliaries yellow, like upper throat . . . . Yellow-faced Grassquit, p. 564

24*a*. Throat white; yellow restricted to the superciliaries (anterior portion), shoulders, or middle of breast 25

  b. Throat either black, pale olive-green, or pale grayish; when not black, the throat and breast virtually uniform 27

25*a*. Bend of wing (shoulder) bright yellow; a black chest-band; bill orange . . . . Orange-billed Sparrow, p. 579

  b. Not as in 25*a*. Back brownish or reddish, liberally streaked with darker 26

26*a*. Breast bright yellow, the median chest sometimes black; wing-coverts usually rufous . . . . Dickcissel, p. 564

  b. Yellow restricted to forepart of superciliaries; a conspicuous white or pale crown-stripe; chest pale gray, throat white
                                  White-throated Sparrow, p. 603

27*a.* Throat black; a white ear-patch bordered above and behind with greenish yellow; a black breast-spot

White-eared Ground-Sparrow, p. 585

  b. Not as in 27*a.* 28

28*a.* Larger (6½ inches). Throat and breast pale grayish; a bright olive-yellow crown-patch, this bordered laterally with black

Golden-crowned Sparrow, p. 602

  b. Smaller (4½ inches). Throat and breast pale olive-green; crown sometimes black; wings and tail black with yellow markings

Black-capped Siskin, p. 572

CATEGORY III

1*a.* With bright plumage, the underparts at least having more or less yellow, orange, red, cinnamon, or rufous 2

  b. Not notably colorful, but often boldly patterned, and sometimes with chestnut or rufous on the cheeks, hind-neck, back, or shoulders 9

2*a.* More than 7 inches long 3

  b. Less than 4½ inches long 7

3*a.* Head wholly or mainly black 4

  b. Head without black 6

4*a.* Breast bright red or washed with pink; if pink, the head with more or less white . . . . Rose-breasted Grosbeak, p. 559

  b. Without red or pink 5

5*a.* Sides and flanks cinnamon, rufous, or tawny; upperparts mainly black, sooty brown, brownish olive, or olive; sometimes spotted above . . . . Red-eyed Towhee, p. 582

  b. Underparts and nuchal collar buffy cinnamon, the head and back mainly black . . . . Black-headed Grosbeak (male), p. 560

6*a.* Head and underparts bright yellow or orange

Yellow Grosbeak (male), p. 558

  b. Head and underparts dingy, the throat white bordered with black streaks; sides of breast and wing-linings yellowish olive

Evening Grosbeak (female), p. 565

7*a.* Underparts wholly yellow or yellowish 8

  b. Yellow of underparts restricted to breast and upper abdomen; throat black or pale grayish . . . . . Lawrence Goldfinch, p. 574

8*a.* Back bright yellow, like underparts, or brownish olive above, the wings and tail blackish, patterned with white

American Goldfinch, p. 574

  b. Upperparts wholly black, or crown black, the back dull olive

Dark-backed Goldfinch (male), p. 574

9a. More or less streaked above, the streaks often dim or inconspicuous 10

  b. Not streaked above; back sometimes distinctly reddish (or brown),
     in sharp contrast with adjacent plumage 15

10a. More or less streaked below, at least on the chest, sides, and flanks 11

  b. Not streaked below; white of tail usually very conspicuous in flight 12

11a. A band of streaks across the breast; lesser wing-coverts dull rufous;
     outermost rectrices white, the others dusky   Vesper Sparrow, p. 589

  b. Underparts heavily streaked, or chin and median abdomen black;
     lateral rectrices white-tipped; a buff or buffy white wing-bar
                        Lark Bunting (female and winter male), p. 586

12a. Below wholly white; sides of crown and auriculars chestnut; a con-
     spicuous black submalar streak . . . . . .   Lark Sparrow, p. 589

  b. Not as in 12a. Underparts with more or less black or pale buff . . 13

13a. Below partly black, this sometimes very extensive 14

  b. Without black below
                     Chestnut-collared Longspur (female and winter male), p. 606
                          McCown Longspur (female and winter male), p. 606

14a. Breast and abdomen black; a chestnut nuchal collar
                          Chestnut-collared Longspur (summer male), p. 606

  b. A black band across breast; shoulders chestnut
                                McCown Longspur (summer male), p. 606

15a. Mainly black; a very conspicuous white wing-patch
                                Lark Bunting (summer male), p. 586

  b. Not as in 15a. 16

16a. Below pale gray or whitish; flanks sometimes pinkish 17

  b. Throat and breast (sometimes entire head) black or slate-gray, the
     abdomen white; back sometimes reddish brown or rufous, the
     flanks pinkish 18

17a. Sides and flanks pinkish or cinnamon (southern Baja California)
                                          Oregon Junco, p. 598

  b. Sides and flanks not pink or cinnamon .   Yellow-eyed Junco, p. 599

18a. Above grayish, the throat and chest black; conspicuous white
     superciliary and malar stripes; outer rectrices white-tipped
                               Black-throated Sparrow, p. 596

  b. Superciliaries and malar area not white; upperparts uniform slate
     gray, or back brown or reddish; outer rectrices almost wholly
     white 19

19a. Above uniform slate gray . . . .   Slate-colored Junco, p. 598

  b. Above not uniform, the back distinctly browner or rustier than
     crown and rump . . . . Oregon Junco, p. 598

12a. Throat black; a white ear-patch bordered above and behind with
bright olive-yellow . . . . . . White-eared Ground-Sparrow, p. 585

   b. Throat white 13

13a. A broad black pectoral band; bend of wing bright yellow; bill
orange . . . . Orange-billed Sparrow, p. 579

   b. Pectoral band incomplete medially; sides of neck bright rufous;
back boldly streaked . . . . Rufous-collared Sparrow, p. 603

14a. Crown-stripe essentially white or whitish 15

   b. Crown-stripe not essentially white or whitish 19

15a. Throat or entire underparts bright yellow; uniform dark slate
above 16

   b. Without yellow below; back streaked; superciliaries prominent . 17

16a. Underparts wholly yellow . . . White-naped Brush-Finch, p. 577

   b. Throat yellow, the breast and abdomen pale gray
Yellow-throated Brush-Finch, p. 577

17a. Superciliaries immaculate white, at least posteriorly; a white or
pale gray crown-stripe; cheeks pale gray 18

   b. Crown-stripe, superciliaries, and throat creamy white; cheeks
blackish . . . . Stripe-headed Sparrow, p. 592

18a. Superciliaries bright yellow anteriorly; white of throat sharply
defined . . . . White-throated Sparrow, p. 603

   b. Superciliaries wholly white; throat and breast virtually concolor
White-crowned Sparrow, p. 602

19a. Upperparts mainly brown, the back and scapulars broadly striped 20

   b. Upperparts mainly greenish olive; back and scapulars not striped 22

20a. Sides of head black, the superciliaries pale buffy white
Striped Sparrow, p. 585

   b. Sides of head and superciliaries pale brownish gray 21

21a. Sides of crown black, the median stripe bright olive-yellow anteriorly . . . . Golden-crowned Sparrow, p. 602

   b. Sides of crown rufous, the median stripe grayish; a black postocular
and submalar streak . . . . Rusty Sparrow, p. 593

22a. Crown-stripe, superciliaries, and hind-neck with more or less
conspicuous yellowish olive; sides of head black
Striped Brush-Finch, p. 578

   b. Not as in 22a. 23

23a. Sides of crown black, the pale gray median stripe contrasting with
the back . . . . Green-backed Sparrow, p. 580

   b. Sides of crown reddish brown, the olive median stripe and back
virtually concolor . . . . Olive Sparrow, p. 579

Category V

1a. Underparts more or less streaked 2

  b. Underparts not streaked 10

2a. Larger (7–8 inches). Wing-linings bright yellow or pinkish; bill
decidedly large 3

  b. Smaller ($4\frac{1}{2}$–$6\frac{1}{4}$ inches). Plumage and bill not as in 2a. 4

3a. Wing-linings bright yellow; breast (at least) tawny-buff
Black-headed Grosbeak (female), p. 560

  b. Wing-linings pinkish; underparts white
Rose-breasted Grosbeak (female), p. 559

4a. Superciliaries yellowish, or with a yellow patch at base of primaries   5

  b. Not as in 4a. 6

5a. Larger (5–$5\frac{3}{4}$ inches). Superciliaries and bend of wing yellowish;
sometimes with a pale crown-stripe (prairies and fields)
Savannah Sparrow, p. 586

  b. Smaller ($4\frac{1}{2}$–$4\frac{3}{4}$ inches). Liberally streaked above and below;
base of tail and wing-patch bright yellow; tail notched
Pine Siskin, p. 572

6a. Hind-neck and sides of head tawny buff, or with a streaked buffy
band across the chest 7

  b. Not as in 6a. 8

7a. Median crown, hind-neck, and sides of head tawny buff, the throat
and breast sometimes similar . . . . . . Baird Sparrow, p. 587

  b. A buffy chest-band streaked with black   . Lincoln Sparrow, p. 604

8a. Underparts very conspicuously streaked; above either unpatterned,
or broadly striped; bill decidedly large
Carpodacus spp. (female), pp. 566–67

  b. Throat and abdomen immaculate white or whitish, the breast and
sides liberally streaked with dusky, black, or reddish; sometimes
with a breast-spot 9

9a. Notably small (4 inches). Above uniform olive-brown; breast
broadly streaked with dusky   Blue-black Grassquit (female), p. 571

  b. Medium-sized ($5\frac{1}{4}$–$6\frac{1}{4}$ inches). Conspicuously streaked above and
below . . . . Sierra Madre Sparrow (highlands only), p. 588
Song Sparrow, p. 605

10a. Throat black, or with a black chest-band, this sometimes more or
less disrupted medially 11

  b. Without black below; sometimes with a black submalar streak   . 14

11a. Throat black; head uniform gray, or with white malar stripes . . 12

   b. Throat white, the chest or breast with conspicuous black 13

12a. Smaller (5¼ inches). Head and breast clear slate gray, the lores, chin, and upper throat black; bill pinkish
Black-chinned Sparrow (male), p. 601

   b. Larger (6 inches). Crown black-streaked; scapulars, rump, and flanks reddish; a prominent white malar stripe
Bridled Sparrow, p. 591

13a. Chest, or sides of chest black, the nape and sides of neck bright rufous; crown-stripe gray, bordered with black; back heavily streaked . . . . Rufous-collared Sparrow, p. 603

   b. Pectoral band and submalar stripe black, the first notably broad and conspicuous; a black stripe on each side of crown; back reddish, lightly streaked with black . . . . . Black-chested Sparrow, p. 591

14a. Top of head gray, reddish, or chestnut, this virtually uniform, and usually with no suggestion of a pale median stripe 15

   b. Top of head liberally streaked, or with a more or less distinct pale median stripe 18

15a. Head, throat, and breast uniform gray; bill pinkish
Black-chinned Sparrow (female), p. 601

   b. Head, throat, and breast not uniform gray, the crown (at least) distinctly rufous or chestnut 16

16a. Crown bright rufous, unlike the hind-neck and back; bill black
Chipping Sparrow, p. 599

   b. Not as in 16a. 17

17a. Larger (5½–6¼ inches). Top of head and broad stripes on back dull reddish; a prominent black submalar stripe; below grayish buff
Rufous-crowned Sparrow, p. 594

   b. Smaller (5¼ inches). Top of head essentially reddish, the median part sometimes gray; sides of head pale gray, the eye-ring sometimes white; back streaked with dusky; two pale wing-bars; bill pinkish . . . . Field Sparrow, p. 601
Worthen Sparrow, p. 601

18a. Larger (6¼–7½ inches). Lores and auriculars black, or with a prominent submalar stripe; top of head deep chestnut, the pale median stripe usually conspicuous 19

   b. Smaller (4½–5¾ inches). Top of head liberally streaked, and sometimes with a pale median stripe; sides of crown blackish, this often streaked with paler 21

19*a*. Sides of head black; a grayish crown-stripe and conspicuous whitish superciliaries; striped above; whitish below

Striped Sparrow, p. 585

  b. Sides of head not black; a conspicuous submalar stripe 20

20*a*. Superciliaries whitish; chestnut of crown streaked with paler; tail reddish above; bill pale below . .   Cinnamon-tailed Sparrow, p. 593

  b. Superciliaries gray; chestnut of crown virtually uniform or streaked with black; tail brown above; bill wholly black

Rusty Sparrow, p. 593
Oaxaca Sparrow, p. 593

21*a*. Top of head uniformly streaked 22

  b. Top of head not uniformly streaked; a pale crown-stripe, this sometimes lightly streaked, but always distinct 24

22*a*. Bend of wing (edge) pale yellow . . . . . Botteri Sparrow, p. 595

Yellow-carpalled Sparrow, p. 595
Cassin Sparrow, p. 596

  b. Bend of wing (edge) white 23

23*a*. Upperparts uniformly streaked with black; a pale wing-bar; bill brown above, pale below . . . .   Brewer Sparrow, p. 600

  b. Top of head streaked with chestnut; shoulders reddish; a dusky submalar streak; bill cinnamon above, pale below

Rufous-winged Sparrrow, p. 592

24*a*. Crown-stripe and superciliaries pale grayish; back reddish brown, broadly streaked with black; breast dingy grayish brown

Swamp Sparrow, p. 605

  b. Crown-stripe, superciliaries, and breast dull whitish or buffy . . 25

25*a*. Underparts dull white; a pale gray nuchal collar; auriculars buff, margined above and below with dusky

Clay-colored Sparrow, p. 600

  b. Sides of head, throat, and breast buffy, the abdomen white; hindneck liberally streaked with reddish; edge of wing near bend pale yellow . . . .   Grasshopper Sparrow, p. 587

Category VI

1*a*. Wholly black, glossy blue-black, or bluish slate, the wing-linings sometimes white 2

  b. Deep chocolate-brown, olive-brown, or brownish above, with buffy white underparts 5

2*a*. Smaller (4–5 inches). Black 3

  b. Larger (5–6½ inches). Glossy blue-black or bluish slate 4

3a. Bill notably thick and conelike; a small white patch at base of
primaries . . . . Black Seedeater (male), p. 570
Thick-billed Seed-Finch (male), p. 571

  b. Bill moderately thick; glossy blue-black; a concealed white patch
on sides of chest; no wing-patch
Blue-black Grassquit (male), p. 571

4a. Larger (6–6½ inches). Deep bluish black, the forehead, sides of
crown, and shoulders distinctly bluish; bill notably large and thick
Blue-black Grosbeak (male), p. 561

  b. Smaller (5–5¼ inches). Bluish slate; bill not notably large, but
either very thick or with a sharp tip
Slate-blue Seedeater (male), p. 570
Slaty Finch (male), p. 576

5a. Mainly deep chocolate-brown or brownish olive; no wing-bars;
bill notably thick and conelike 6

  b. Above grayish brown or olive-brown; below pale buff, the throat
and abdomen whitish 8

6a. Chocolate-brown 7

  b. Brownish olive, palest below, the wing-linings white
Black Seedeater (female), p. 570

7a. Larger (6–6½ inches). Bill wholly black
Blue-black Grosbeak (female), p. 561

  b. Smaller (4½–5½ inches). Bill pale below
Blue Bunting (female), p. 561
Thick-billed Seed-Finch (female), p. 571

8a. Wings barred 9

  b. Wings not barred 10

9a. Larger (6–6½ inches). Bill notably large and thick
Blue Grosbeak (female), p. 560

  b. Smaller (4½–5½ inches). Bill not notably large
Lazuli Bunting (female), p. 562
Varied Bunting (female), p. 562

10a. Wings, tail, and rump faintly tinged with bluish; chest and flanks
very lightly streaked . . . . . . Indigo Bunting (female), p. 561

  b. Not as in 10a. 11

11a. Larger (5¼ inches). Underparts pale buffy brown (highlands of
Guerrero) . . . . Slate-blue Seedeater (female), p. 570

  b. Smaller (4–4½ inches). Underparts pale buffy white (coastal slopes)
White-collared Seedeater (female), p. 569

BLACK-HEADED SALTATOR. *Saltator atriceps* (Illus. p. 555).—
10. Head mainly black, the sides partly gray; upperparts bright yellowish
olive-green; sides of throat and band across chest black, the throat itself
white (usually) or brown (*S. a. suffuscus*); breast and abdomen uniformly
gray, the crissum tawny.

Distribution.—Lowland forests of southeastern and southern Mexico.

Races.—*S. a. atriceps* (southern Tamaulipas, Veracruz, and Puebla
southward, except where occupied by the following). *S. a. suffuscus* (southern Tamaulipas, from Tres Zapotes across to Paso Nuevo, and coastward).
S. a. raptor (Yucatán and Quintana Roo). *S. a. flavicrissus* (Guerrero). *S. a.
peeti* (Pacific slope of Chiapas, from Tonalá to Finca Juárez).

BLACK-HEADED SALTATOR

Remarks.—A very large *black-headed* grosbeak with bright olive-
green upperparts and a black chest-band. The throat may be either
white or brown. Buff-throated Saltators are considerably smaller. They
have a conspicuously *tawny* throat, and often little or no black on top
of the head. Both species inhabit woodlands, especially in humid areas
of low altitude.

BUFF-THROATED SALTATOR. *Saltator maximus.*—8–8½. Crown
black or dusky olive, the sides of the head gray; white superciliaries; upperparts bright yellowish olive-green; sides of throat and band across chest
black; throat tawny buff, the chin white; breast and abdomen gray, the sides
and flanks sometimes tinged with olive; crissum tawny.

Distribution.—Lowland forests of southeastern and southern Mexico.

Races.—*S. m. gigantodes* (Veracruz, Tabasco, and Oaxaca). *S. m.
magnoides* (Chiapas, Campeche, and Quintana Roo).

Remarks.—*See* Black-headed Saltator.

GRAYISH SALTATOR. *Saltator coerulescens* (Illus. p. 556).—$7\frac{1}{2}$–$8\frac{1}{2}$. Above ashy gray or olive-gray; superciliaries and throat white, the latter bordered laterally with black; breast grayish, this becoming whitish, or more or less buffy posteriorly, the crissum often tawny cinnamon.

Distribution.—Wooded portions of both coastal slopes, from sea-level to an altitude of about 5,000 feet.

Races.—*S. c. vigorsii* (Sinaloa, Durango, and Nayarit). *S. c. richardsoni* (Jalisco, south through Colima and Guerrero to Oaxaca). *S. c. grandis* (southern Tamaulipas southward, exclusive of the Yucatán Peninsula). *S. c. yucatanensis* (Yucatán Peninsula).

GRAYISH SALTATOR

Remarks.—A large *grayish* grosbeak with white superciliaries, and a white throat bordered laterally with black. No similar bird has a grayish, *unpatterned chest*, and buffy abdomen.

CRIMSON-COLLARED GROSBEAK. *Rhodothraupis celaeno.*—8–$8\frac{1}{2}$. *Male:* Mainly black, the hind-neck, upper back, abdomen, sides, and flanks dull red, more or less intermixed with black. *Female:* Similar to the male in pattern, but with the red plumage replaced by yellowish olive-green; wing-coverts and crissum often tipped with pale yellow.

Distribution.—Southern Nuevo León and central Tamaulipas south through eastern San Luis Potosí to Veracruz and Puebla. ENDEMIC.

Remarks.—The only black-headed grosbeak with *red* or *dull yellowish olive* underparts. Male Hooded Grosbeaks, while black-headed, have *bright yellow* underparts, and *contrasting black wings and tails*. Common locally in brushy woods at moderate elevations. Usually avoids exposed perches while singing.

BLACK-FACED GROSBEAK. *Caryothraustes poliogaster poliogaster* (Illus. p. 557).—6½-7. Lores, area below eyes, and throat black, the plumage otherwise mainly bright yellowish olive; scapulars, rump, and upper tail-coverts gray, the posterior underparts similar, but paler.

Distribution.—Humid lowland forests of Veracruz, Tabasco, and Oaxaca.

Remarks.—Also known as Bishop Grosbeak. A common fruit-eating grosbeak of dense lowland forests. The black face and bright yellowish olive plumage are distinctive. Frequents the tops of trees, often in flocks.

BLACK-FACED GROSBEAK

COMMON CARDINAL. *Richmondena cardinalis.*—7½-8½. *Male:* Conspicuously crested. Throat and area bordering bill black; crown, sides of head, and underparts bright red or vermilion, the upperparts dull red, often intermixed with gray on back and scapulars; bill reddish orange. *Female:* Crest, wings, and tail red, as in male, but duller; throat and area bordering bill grayish, dusky, or black; back, scapulars, and rump grayish olive or buffy gray, the underparts buffy brown, tawny, or ochraceous.

Distribution.—Baja California, lowlands and foothills of the Pacific and Atlantic slopes, and various offshore islands.

Races.—*R. c. mariae* (Tres Marías Islands). *R. c. seftoni* (central Baja California, in the vicinity of Santa Gertrudis). *R. c. ignea* (cape district or Baja California north to latitude 27°). *R. c. townsendi* (Tiburón Island, Gulf of California). *R. c. superba* (northern and central Sonora). *R. c. affinis* (eastern and southern Sonora and southwestern Chihuahua). *R. c. sinaloensis* (southern Sinaloa). *R. c. carnea* (Pacific Coast from Colima to Oaxaca). *R. c. canicauda* (eastern Mexico south to Michoacán and Puebla). *R. c. coccinea* (Caribbean slope of Veracruz and Oaxaca). *R. c. littoralis* (coastal plains of extreme southeastern Veracruz). *R. c. yucatanica* (Yucatán Peninsula). *R. c. flammigera* (southern Quintana Roo). *R. c. saturata* (Cozumel Island).

Remarks.—Males, bright red except for the black throat and fore-part of head, are virtually unmistakable. Females might be confused with female Pyrrhuloxias where their ranges overlap. Widespread, chiefly in the lowlands.

PYRRHULOXIA. *Pyrrhuloxia sinuata.*—7–8. *Male:* Above pale grayish brown, the occipital crest, lesser wing-coverts, primaries, and tail deep red; area bordering bill, and median underparts bright red or vermilion; bill yellowish. *Female:* Similar to male, but without conspicuous red on the face and underparts, the latter mainly grayish buff.

Distribution.—Baja California and the drier parts of northern and western Mexico south to Puebla.

Races.—*P. s. peninsulae* (arid lowlands of Baja California north to about latitude 27°). *P. s. fulvescens* (arid lowlands and foothills of Sonora, Sinaloa, and western Durango south to Nayarit). *P. s. sinuata* (north-central and northeastern Mexico south to Guanajuato and Puebla).

Remarks.—To the novice, Pyrrhuloxias usually suggest Cardinals, the females especially being much alike. However, they have notably stubby, *yellow* (not reddish) *bills, grayish upperparts* (both sexes), and lack black on the head and throat. Male Pyrrhuloxias are essentially *gray* above, with bright *red median underparts*.

YELLOW GROSBEAK. *Pheucticus chrysopeplus* (Illus. p. 559).—8–9. *Male:* Bright orange or lemon-yellow, the wings, scapulars, and tail mainly black, the first white-spotted, and the lateral rectrices with broad white tips. *Female:* Essentially like male, but much duller above; head, back, and scapulars liberally streaked; wings and tail mainly grayish brown.

Distribution.—Western Mexico, chiefly in the foothills and highlands. Migratory in northern part of range.

Races.—*P. c. dilutus* (southern Sonora, southwestern Chihuahua, and northern Sinaloa). *P. c. chrysopeplus* (southern Sinaloa and Durango south to Guerrero). *P. c. rarissimus* (Puebla). *P. c. aurantiacus* (foothills and highlands of Chiapas).

Remarks.—Also known as Orange-colored Grosbeak. The notably thick, stubby bill at once eliminates all orioles of similar color and pattern.

YELLOW GROSBEAK

*ROSE-BREASTED GROSBEAK. *Pheucticus ludovicianus.*—7–8. *Male (summer)*: Head, back, wings, and tail black, the wings boldly patterned with white, and the three outer rectrices mainly white on their inner webs; rump, upper tail-coverts, and posterior underparts white, the breast and median abdomen bright red; (*winter*): Wings and tail as in summer; head and back broadly streaked, the median crown with a pale stripe; superciliaries and malar area whitish; underparts essentially buff or whitish, the breast and sides narrowly streaked; breast usually tinged with pink. *Female:* Similar to male in winter plumage, but wings and tail brownish, the latter without white, and the white of the wings much reduced; below whitish, liberally streaked with olive-brown; wing-linings pink in both sexes.

Distribution.—Winters in southeastern and southern Mexico. Migratory in the east.

Remarks.—The distinctive male breeding plumage is not often seen in Mexico. Winter and migrant males are less colorful, but have much the same over-all pattern, and usually show some *pink* on the breast. Females, while drab and heavily streaked, like various sparrows, will be known by their large size, notably thick bills, *white-patterned wings*, and very *conspicuous whitish superciliaries*.

BLACK-HEADED GROSBEAK. *Pheucticus melanocephalus.*—7–8. *Male:* Head, back, scapulars, wings, and tail mainly black, the wings conspicuously patterned with white, the lateral rectrices white-tipped; hindneck, rump, and underparts rich tawny cinnamon, the chin (sometimes upper throat) black; median abdomen and wing-linings lemon-yellow. *Female:* Above grayish brown or brownish olive, conspicuously streaked with paler, the median crown with a single pale stripe; superciliaries and malar area white; wing-bar and white patch at base of primaries much reduced, the wing-linings bright yellow; tail usually without white; throat and breast ochraceous buff, the abdomen whitish; sides and flanks brown-streaked, the breast virtually immaculate.

Distribution.—Breeds in the mountains (chiefly) of northern Baja California and northern and western Mexico south to Oaxaca and Veracruz, wintering extensively elsewhere.

Races.—*P. m. melanocephalus* (Coahuila, Nuevo León, and Tamaulipas, wintering south to Guerrero, and Puebla). *P. m. maculatus* (northern Baja California, south in western Mexico to Oaxaca and Veracruz; winters in southern Baja California and state of Mexico).

Remarks.—The only large black fringillid with *tawny cinnamon underparts.* Females resemble female Rose-breasted Grosbeaks superficially, but have *tawny* breasts with little or no streaking. When in flight the *yellow wing-linings* often flash conspicuously.

BLUE GROSBEAK. *Guiraca caerulea.*—6–6½. *Male (summer):* Deep purplish blue, the middle wing-coverts chestnut; *(winter):* Similar, but plumage extensively edged with buff or whitish. *Female:* Above olive-brown, the crown and hind-neck tawny, the back and scapulars obscurely streaked; wings with two tawny bars; tail dusky, narrowly edged with bluish; underparts pale brownish buff, the throat and abdomen often whitish.

Distribution.—Resident in Baja California, western and southern Mexico, occurring extensively elsewhere in winter.

Races.—*G. c. salicaria* (Baja California south to latitude 31°, wintering in the cape district and in northwestern Mexico). *G. c. interfusa* (northwestern Mexico, wintering southward). *G. c. deltarhyncha* (southern Sonora south to Guerrero). *G. c. eurhyncha* (southern Mexico, from San Luis

Potosí and Guanajuato to Oaxaca and Chiapas). *G. c. caerulea (winters in the eastern portion of the country).

Remarks.—A deep-blue finch with two *reddish brown wing-bars.* Males appear all-black at a distance, and might then be mistaken for a cowbird. The brownish females are distinguished from similar fringillids by their conspicuous *buff-colored* wing-bars. *See* Blue Bunting and Blue-black Grosbeak.

BLUE BUNTING. *Cyanocompsa parellina.*—5–5½. *Male:* Forehead, malar area, lesser wing-coverts, and rump bright azure-blue; elsewhere deep purplish blue; bill dusky, notably thick. *Female:* Above rich chocolate-brown, the underparts paler, approaching cinnamon or ochraceous.

Distribution.—Pacific and Atlantic lowlands north to Sinaloa, Nuevo León, and central Tamaulipas.

Races.—*C. p. indigotica* (Pacific Coast from Sinaloa south to Oaxaca). *C. p. beneplacita* (Nuevo León, Tamaulipas, and possibly San Luis Potosí). *C. p. lucida* (lowlands of southern interior Tamaulipas). *C. p. parellina* (lowlands of southeastern Mexico, from Puebla and Veracruz southward, including the Yucatán Peninsula and offshore islands).

Remarks.—Not to be confused with the Blue-black Grosbeak of Veracruz, Tabasco, and Oaxaca, a considerably larger and much darker species with virtually *uniform* plumage. Under favorable conditions male Blue Buntings show *bright blue patches*, and females are much paler above and below than female Blue-blacks. Note the grayish *horn-colored* (not black) *bill.* Common in brushy fields; the Blue-black prefers forest undergrowth.

BLUE-BLACK GROSBEAK. *Cyanocompsa cyanoides-concreta.*—6–6¼. *Male:* Deep blue-black, the forehead, sides of crown, and lesser wing-coverts brightest, but appearing wholly black at a distance; bill black, notably thick. *Female:* Above deep chocolate-brown, the underparts somewhat paler.

Distribution.—Lowlands of Veracruz, Tabasco, and Chiapas, chiefly in forest undergrowth.

Remarks.—*See* Blue Bunting and Blue Grosbeak.

*INDIGO BUNTING. *Passerina cyanea.*—4½–5. *Male:* Head and median underparts purplish blue, the plumage elsewhere mainly cerulean blue with bluish green reflections in certain lights. *Female:* Above olive-brown, the back sometimes lightly streaked; primaries and tail dusky, narrowly edged with greenish, the greater wing-coverts and secondaries edged with cinnamon-buff; below buffy white, the breast, sides, and flanks tinged with brown, this usually faintly streaked.

Distribution.—Winters in eastern and southern Mexico.

Remarks.—Indigo Buntings suggest diminutive Blue Grosbeaks, but have smaller bills and lack obvious wing-bars. While males are virtually unmistakable, females closely resemble female Varied Buntings. The very *dim chest-streaks and vague wing-bars* are the female Indigos' best field marks. *See* female Blue-black Grassquit.

LAZULI BUNTING. *Passerina amoena.*—5½. *Male:* Head, throat, rump, and upper tail-coverts bright cerulean or turquoise-blue, the back and scapulars dusky bluish; wings and tail blackish, the former with two white bars; breast and sides tawny ochraceous, the abdomen and flanks white. *Female:* Above rich brown, the rump and upper tail-coverts paler and tinged with greenish blue, the primaries and tail narrowly edged with same; two buffy or whitish wing-bars; throat and breast tawny buff, the abdomen whitish.

Distribution.—Breeds in northwestern Baja California and possibly northern Sonora, wintering southward to the cape district, Durango, and south-central Mexico.

Remarks.—No other blue-headed, tawny-breasted bird of our area has prominent *white wing-bars*. A female might be mistaken for a female Blue Grosbeak, but the Lazuli is much the smaller of the two, and has a proportionately smaller bill and paler wing-bars. *See* Western Bluebird.

VARIED BUNTING. *Passerina versicolor.*—4½–5. *Male* (*summer*): Area bordering bill black; forepart of crown, auriculars, hind-neck, and rump pale bluish purple; posterior portion of crown, nape, and eyelids bright red; back and underparts dusky purplish, the throat and breast strongly tinged with purplish red; (*winter*): Duller, the plumage more or less extensively intermixed with grayish or buff. *Female:* Above grayish olive-brown, the wings and tail dusky, faintly glossed with bluish; no wing-bars; below pale buff, the throat and abdomen sometimes whitish.

Distribution.—Widespread, chiefly in dry lowlands.

Races.—*P. v. pulchra* (breeds in the cape district of Baja California; migratory in Sonora). *P. v. dickeyae* (north-central Sonora and western Chihuahua south on the Pacific Coast to Nayarit; casual in Jalisco). *P. v. purpurascens* (arid lowlands of Guerrero and Morelos). *P. v. versicolor* (eastern portion of the country south to Veracruz, wintering west to Sonora, Jalisco, and Guerrero).

Remarks.—One of several richly colored finches that appear dusky or black at a distance. In good light the males' *reddish purple* plumage is unmistakable. Females are drab by comparison, and quite undistinguished. *See* Indigo Bunting, female Rose-bellied Bunting, and female White-collared Seedeater.

ROSE-BELLIED BUNTING. *Passerina rositae.*—5½. *Male:* Bright cerulean blue, the chest, breast, and upper abdomen more or less intermixed with scarlet, this fading to salmon-pink posteriorly. *Female:* Above dull grayish brown, the crown, rump, upper tail-coverts, and tail distinctly tinged with bluish; below buffy brown, palest on the abdomen, where usually pinkish buff.

Distribution.—Pacific slope of Oaxaca and Chiapas. ENDEMIC.

Remarks.—Also known as Rosita Bunting. Males suggest oversized Indigo Buntings, but have *scarlet breasts* and *pinkish* abdomens. Females are relatively drab: mainly brownish, the head, rump, and tail more or less tinged with blue. *See* female Varied Bunting.

PAINTED BUNTING. *Passerina ciris.*—5¼. *Male:* Head (except throat) and hind-neck purplish blue, the lores and chin greenish; back and scapulars bright yellowish green; rump and upper tail-coverts deep red, the eye-ring, throat, and underparts bright scarlet. *Female:* Above greenish, brightest on the back and scapulars; below dull yellow or yellowish white, the breast, sides, and flanks more or less tinged with olive.

Distribution.—Breeds in northwestern Mexico and (probably) northern Tamaulipas. Widespread elsewhere in migration and winter.

Races.—*P. c. ciris* (winters in Yucatán, apparently migrating across the Gulf of Mexico). *P. c. pallidior* (northern Chihuahua and Coahuila, wintering extensively from northern Mexico southward; reported in Veracruz in July).

Remarks.—Our most colorful finch, blue-headed, yellow-backed, and with bright red underparts. The greenish females and first-year males are unlike any other Mexican fringillid except the female Orange-breasted Bunting. It is duller (less greenish) above, decidedly yellow below, with a suggestion of blue on its wings and tail. *See* female Dark-backed Goldfinch and female Orange-breasted Bunting.

ORANGE-BREASTED BUNTING. *Passerina leclancherii.*—5. *Male:* Crown bright yellowish green; sides of head and upperparts cerulean or turquoise-blue, the wings and tail mainly dusky; lores, eye-ring, and underparts bright lemon-yellow, the breast usually tinged with orange. *Female:* Sides of head and upperparts dull grayish green, the wings, upper tail-coverts, and tail faintly tinged with bluish; lores, eye-ring, and underparts bright yellow, the breast and sides washed with olive.

Distribution.—Dry lowlands of southwestern Mexico south to Oaxaca. ENDEMIC.

Races.—*P. l. leclancherii* (Colima, Guerrero, and probably Puebla). *P. l. grandior* (Oaxaca).

Remarks.—Also known as Leclancher Bunting. A blue-and-yellow finch with a *bright green crown.* Females are less distinctive: greenish above, bright yellow below, and with *yellow eye-rings. See* female Painted Bunting.

YELLOW-FACED GRASSQUIT. *Tiaris olivacea* (Illus. p. 564).—4. *Male:* Superciliaries and upper throat bright golden-yellow; above dull olive, the crown (especially anteriorly) and sides of the head often blackish; lower

YELLOW-FACED GRASSQUIT

throat, breast, and upper abdomen black, the posterior underparts grayish olive. *Female:* Similar, but the yellow and black areas duller, and much reduced or obsolescent.

Distribution.—Lowlands of southeastern Mexico, and various offshore islands.

Races.—*T. o. pusilla* (Atlantic coastal lowlands from southern Tamaulipas southward). *T. o. intermedia* (Holbox and Cozumel Islands, off the coast of Quintana Roo).

Remarks.—The bright yellow head markings of males are conspicuous at any distance. Females are more obscurely patterned, but usually have at least a suggestion of yellow on the upper throat, and some black on the chest. Common in brushy fields and pastures.

*DICKCISSEL. *Spiza americana.*—5¾–6½. *Male:* Crown, hind-neck, and auriculars gray, the superciliaries pale yellowish; upperparts extensively grayish brown, the back and scapulars black-streaked; wing-coverts chestnut; throat white, a black bib covering the lower portion; breast bright yellow, this usually extending to the median abdomen, the underparts otherwise white. *Female:* Similar to male, but crown and auriculars brownish, the superciliaries mainly white; chestnut wing-patch reduced or absent; black bib of male replaced by narrow black streaks; bill bluish.

Distribution.—Migratory on both coastal slopes, wintering to the southward. Accidental in Baja California.

Remarks.—The black bib of the male is obscure or lost in the fall. The *yellow* (or yellowish) *breast* (on a *white* background) and *rusty shoulders* are useful field marks for both sexes at all seasons. Females resemble female House Sparrows, but have *bluish* bills, yellow-tinged breasts, and much *whiter* superciliaries.

EVENING GROSBEAK. *Hesperiphona vespertina montana.*—7. *Male:* Forehead and superciliaries golden-yellow; crown, tail, and wings black, the last with a very prominent white patch; back, sides of head, and throat dusky yellowish olive, this becoming much brighter on the scapulars, rump, and posterior underparts; crissum lemon-yellow; bill pale yellowish green. *Female:* Above grayish, the hind-neck tinged with yellowish olive; wings and tail black, the former boldly patterned with white, the inner webs of the lateral tail feathers white-tipped; median throat and median abdomen dull whitish, the breast, sides, and flanks pale buffy grayish; a black stripe on each side of throat.

Distribution.—Interior mountains south to Puebla, Veracruz, and Oaxaca.

Remarks.—A large, dingy yellowish finch, with a notably thick, *pale bill* and white-patterned wings. The Hooded Grosbeak, which occurs in the same region, has a *jet-black head and chest*, and bright yellow underparts (male); the female a *black crown*. Flight undulating, and white wing-patches notably conspicuous.

HOODED GROSBEAK. *Hesperiphona abeillei* (Illus. p. 566).—6½. *Male:* Head, wings, and tail black, the inner remiges (tertials) pale gray; back yellowish olive, becoming bright chrome-yellow on the rump; breast and posterior underparts bright olive-yellow; bill grayish olive. *Female:* Crown and area bordering bill black; back, scapulars, and rump dull olive-green; wings and tail dull black, the outermost rectrices white-tipped; throat pale grayish, becoming yellowish olive posteriorly, where more or less tinged with brown.

Distribution.—Highland forests (chiefly) or northwestern and southeastern Mexico.

Races.—*H. a. pallida* (Chihuahua). *H. a. abeillei* (southern Tamaulipas, Veracruz, Puebla, and Oaxaca).

Remarks.—Also known as Abeille Grosbeak. *See* Evening Grosbeak.

HOODED GROSBEAK

PURPLE FINCH. *Carpodacus purpureus californicus.*—5½. *Male:* Above deep red or purplish red, brightest on the head, the back and scapulars broadly streaked with brown; throat and breast bright purplish red, fading to pink on the sides and flanks, where somewhat blotchy; abdomen and crissum immaculate white. *Female:* Above olive-greenish, dimly streaked with darker; superciliaries and malar area whitish, the auriculars forming a distinct dark patch; below white, the throat, breast, sides, and flanks liberally streaked with dusky olive, but this not sharply defined, as in the following two species.

Distribution.—Baja California, breeding south to the Sierra Juárez, and wintering south to about latitude 30°41′.

Remarks.—In Baja California one may well be confused by the three resident species of this genus. Males of each have red or reddish heads and breasts, and the females are rather drab, brownish, or dull olive birds with boldly streaked white underparts. On closer examination several specific characters become obvious. Purple and Cassin

Finches differ from House Finches in having distinctly *notched* tails, and males are *unstreaked below*. The females are either prominently streaked above (*C. cassinii*), *or* the ground color of the upperparts is distinctly olive-greenish (*C. purpureus*). By contrast, female House Finches are *brownish* above, with little or no apparent streaking. While Purple and Cassin Finches are much alike, male Cassins have a *distinct red crown-patch*, with very little reddish suffusion on the hind-neck and back. Female Cassins will be known by their boldly striped upperparts, and sharply defined ventral streaking. The females of all three species can usually be distinguished from other streaked sparrows by their large bills.

CASSIN FINCH. *Carpodacus cassinii.*—6. *Male:* Crown bright red, the hind-neck, back, and scapulars grayish brown, broadly streaked with dusky, the whole sometimes *faintly* tinged with reddish; auriculars brownish, the superciliaries, malar area, throat, and breast dull rose-pink, fading to white posteriorly; lower flanks (sometimes) and under tail-coverts obscurely streaked. *Female:* Above grayish brown, liberally streaked with darker; below white, very conspicuously streaked with brown, this well-defined and in sharp contrast with the ground color.

Distribution.—Mountains of northern Baja California, wintering on the Mexican plateau south to the valley of Mexico and Veracruz (Mirador, Mount Orizaba).

Remarks.—In Mexico proper, Cassin Finches are likely to be confused only with House Finches. Both can be confused with Purple Finches in Baja California, where all three occur. Their respective field characters are discussed under the latter.

HOUSE FINCH. *Carpodacus mexicanus* (Illus. p. 568).—5–5¾. *Male:* Very variable, especially as to the pattern, extent, and shade of red, but usually as follows: Crown (or forehead and sides of crown), hind-neck, malar area, throat, breast—or the anterior portion—and rump bright red, purplish red, or pinkish; elsewhere, the upperparts grayish brown, often tinged with reddish, the back and scapulars obscurely streaked; abdomen, sides, and flanks white, more or less conspicuously streaked with brown. *Female:* Above grayish brown, sometimes *obscurely streaked* with darker; below whitish, very liberally streaked with dusky.

Distribution.—Baja California, various offshore islands, and Mexico generally, exclusive of the eastern and southeastern lowlands. [Ranges of the races listed below, based in part on Moore's revision of the species (*Condor*, 1939, pp. 177–205), include only those areas in which the racial characters are best developed. Areas not designated may be occupied by House Finches with intermediate characters.]

Races.—*C. m. mcgregori* (San Benito Island, off Baja California; casual on Cedros Island). *C. m. amplus* (Guadalupe Island, off Baja California). *C. m. clementis* (Los Coronados Islands, off Baja California). *C. m. grinnelli* (Baja California south to about latitude 28°). *C. m. ruberrimus* (southern half of Baja California, south-central and southwestern Sonora, and extreme northern Sinaloa). *C. m. rhodopnus* (central third of Sinaloa, from the coast

HOUSE FINCH

to an altitude of 3,000 feet). *C. m. altitudinus* (higher mountains on the eastern boundary of Sinaloa). *C. m. coccineus* (mountains of Tepic and Guadalajara south to Colima and Michoacán). *C. m. griscomi* (Sierra Madre del Sur of Guerrero). *C. m. roseipectus* (Oaxaca). *C. m. potosinus* (northeastern Chihuahua, Coahuila, and Nuevo León south to San Luis Potosí). *C. m. centralis* (Guanajuato and northern Michoacán). *C. m. nigrescens* (vicinity of Miquihuana, southern Tamaulipas). *C. m. mexicanus* (southern portion of the Mexican plateau).

Remarks.—Chiefly arid open country, where very abundant, and likely to be confused only with the two preceding species. *See* Purple Finch for a discussion of field characters.

WHITE-COLLARED SEEDEATER. *Sporophila torqueola* (Illus. p. 569).—4–4½. *Male:* Sides of head and upperparts mainly black, the rump cinnamon or tawny buff; a small white patch at base of primaries; below tawny or buffy white, the chest either with a broad black band or black

WHITE-COLLARED SEEDEATER

mottling, this sometimes extending over the throat. *Female:* Above pale olive-brown, the wings usually with two pale bars; below dull buff or ochraceous, the abdomen often whitish.

Distribution.—Pacific and Atlantic coastal slopes, in open brushy country.

Races.—*S. t. torqueola* (Pacific slope from southern Sinaloa southward). *S. t. sharpei* (Nuevo León, Tamaulipas, and San Luis Potosí). *S. t. morelleti* (Atlantic slope from Veracruz southward).

Remarks.—The only small *buff-bellied* finch with a white wing-patch. Females lack this patch, but have two pale wing-bars. They are not easily distinguished from female Ruddy-breasted Seedeaters in areas occupied by both. *See* female Varied Bunting.

BLACK SEEDEATER. *Sporophila aurita corvina.*—4½. *Male:* Glossy black, the wing-linings and spot at base of primaries white. *Female:* Brownish olive, palest below, the wing-linings white; lower abdomen and crissum usually tawny buff.

Distribution.—Lowlands of Veracruz and Oaxaca, chiefly in clearings and brushy fields.

Remarks.—Also known as Variable Seedeater. Three small finches with jet-black males inhabit much of the lowlands. This species and Thick-billed Seed-Finches alone have a distinct white patch at the base of the primaries, and immaculate white wing-linings. Both have decidedly thicker bills than Blue-black Grassquits, and their plumage lacks the latter's bluish reflections. Black Seedeaters will be known by their normal finchlike bills and jet-black (male) or uniform brownish olive (female) plumage; the Thick-billed Seed-Finch (both sexes) by its grotesque bill. Female Blue-black Grassquits differ from most other small finches in being whitish below, with distinct streaks on the breast.

RUDDY-BREASTED SEEDEATER. *Sporophila minuta parva.*—3¾. *Male:* Sides of head and upperparts mainly ash-gray, the rump and underparts cinnamon-rufous; a small white patch at base of primaries. *Female:* Above buffy brown or pale olive-brown, the wings with two pale bars; below pale buff, darkest on the breast and sides.

Distribution.—Arid lowlands of Nayarit, Oaxaca, and Chiapas.

Remarks.—Also known as Lesser Seedeater and Minute Seedeater. Smallest of the Mexican fringillids, known both by its diminutive size and by the uniform dull rufous underparts of the male. Females resemble female White-collared Seedeaters, both being very small, undistinguished finches with *two pale wing-bars.*

SLATE-BLUE SEEDEATER. *Amaurospiza relictus* (Illus. p. 571).—5¼. *Male:* Bluish slate or dull slate-blue, the lores, wings, and tail black; bill blackish, decidedly thick, the lower mandible abruptly paler toward tip. *Female:* Above uniform grayish olive-brown, the underparts paler and somewhat buffy.

Distribution.—Guerrero, where recorded only from Chilpancingo and in the vicinity of Omilteme at an altitude of 8,200 feet. ENDEMIC.

Remarks.—Also known as Guerrero Blue Seedeater. This rare finch will be known by the *uniformity* of its plumage, either dull blue (or bluish slate) in males or brownish in females. Males resemble Slaty Finches (Veracruz and possibly Chiapas), but have thicker bills and, in favorable light, appear much bluer. Originally described as a new genus (*Amaurospizopsis*), it may prove to be conspecific with the Blue Seedeater (*A. concolor*) of southern Central America.

SLATE-BLUE SEEDEATER

THICK-BILLED SEED-FINCH. *Oryzoborus funereus* (Illus. p. 571).— 4½–5. *Male:* Glossy black, the wing-linings white; a small white spot at base of primaries; bill notably thick and conelike. *Female:* Above deep chocolate-brown or olive-brown; below brownish cinnamon, brightest on the abdomen.

Distribution.—Lowlands of Veracruz, Tabasco, and Oaxaca.

Remarks.—Also known as Lesser Rice Grosbeak. The grotesquely thick bill, forming almost a right angle at the tip, distinguishes this

THICK-BILLED SEED-FINCH

species from all other small finches. Clearings, and the edges of heavy forest. *See* Black Seedeater.

BLUE-BLACK GRASSQUIT. *Volatinia jacarina splendens.*—4. *Male:* Glossy blue-black, the sides of the chest with a concealed white patch. *Female:* Above dull olive-brown; throat and abdomen whitish, the breast, sides, and flanks more or less streaked with dusky.

Distribution.—Open and brushy lowlands, to an altitude of about 5,000 feet, from southern Sinaloa and southern Tamaulipas southward.

Remarks.—The *glossy black* males are quite conspicuous, and often show a patch of white on the sides of the chest. Females, lightly streaked below, suggest the immature plumage of various sparrows, but are smaller than most, and likely to be found with the black males. Grassquits are especially abundant in weedy and brush-grown fields. *See* Black Seedeater and female Indigo Bunting.

PINE SISKIN. *Spinus pinus.*—4½–4¾. *Adult:* Above grayish or grayish buff, very conspicuously streaked with dusky, the rump sometimes tinged with yellowish; a patch of yellow at base of remiges, the primaries narrowly edged with same; tail deeply notched, the basal portion (usually concealed) bright yellow; underparts whitish, boldly streaked with dusky; bill conical, sharply pointed. *Immature:* Similar to adult, but wing-coverts buff-tipped, and underparts usually tinged with yellow.

Distribution.—Resident in the mountains of northern Baja California and highlands of western Mexico south through Zacetecas to Veracruz and Chiapas; winters extensively in the northern portion of the country.

Races.—*S. p. pinus* (winters in Baja California, northern Sonora, Chihuahua, northwestern Durango, and Tamaulipas). *S. p. macropterus* (mountains of northern Baja California and Sonora south through Zacatecas and Michoacán to Mexico, Puebla, and Veracruz). *S. p. perplexus* (mountains of Chiapas).

Remarks.—The only heavily streaked finch with a yellow wing-patch (male), or a flash of yellow on the wings and tail. Immature Black-capped Siskins (Chiapas) are similar, but can be distinguished by the *pale yellowish* ground color of their underparts. Female Purple and House Finches, also prominently streaked, have much thicker bills and lack yellow on the wings and tail. Chiefly pine woods at medium altitudes.

BLACK-CAPPED SISKIN. *Spinus atriceps.*—4½. *Male:* Crown black, the upperparts otherwise extensively dark olive-green; wings black, the coverts and base of remiges partly yellow; tail notched, yellow basally, where concealed by the coverts, the terminal half black; below pale olive-green, the upper throat often tinged with black; bill sharply pointed. *Female:* Similar to male, but crown without black. *Immature:* Above and below streaked with black, the former mainly dull olive-green, the underparts yellowish; wings black, the greater coverts buff-tipped.

Distribution.—Mountains of Chiapas.

Remarks.—Also known as Guatemalan Pine Siskin. *See* Pine Siskin.

BLACK-HEADED SISKIN. *Spinus notatus* (Illus. p. 573).—$4\frac{1}{4}$-$4\frac{3}{4}$. *Male:* Head, chest, wings, and tail black, the lateral rectrices yellow basally; a very conspicuous yellow wing-bar; back and scapulars dingy yellowish olive, this sometimes obscurely spotted; rump and underparts bright golden-olive. *Female:* Similar to male, but duller, and with much less yellow on wings and tail. *Immature:* Resembles the female, but with two yellowish wing-bars and without black on the head and chest.

BLACK-HEADED SISKIN

Distribution.—Pine and oak forests (chiefly) in the highlands of western, southeastern, and southern Mexico.

Races.—*S. n. forreri* (northeastern Sonora, Chihuahua, and Durango). *S. n. griscomi* (Nayarit and Zacatecas south through Jalisco to Guerrero). *S. n. notatus* (Veracruz, Puebla, Mexico, Oaxaca, and Chiapas).

Remarks.—A small *black-headed* finch with yellowish olive underparts, and a very prominent *yellow wing-patch*. Note the conical bill and notched tail. Flight undulating as with goldfinches.

AMERICAN GOLDFINCH. *Spinus tristis.*—4½. *Male (summer):* Bright lemon-yellow, the crown, wings, and tail black, the flight feathers and rectrices patterned with white; *(winter):* Resembles the female. *Female:* Somewhat like male, but much duller, the upperparts (including crown) brownish olive, and black of the wings and tail replaced with sooty brown. *Immature:* Resembles the female, but duller; plumage tinged with buff, and with cinnamon replacing the white of the wings.

Distribution.—Resident in northwestern Baja California, wintering also in northeastern Mexico south to Veracruz.

Races.—*S. t. salicamans* (northwestern Baja California). **S. t. pallida* (winters in Coahuila, Nuevo León, Tamaulipas, and Veracruz).

Remarks.—Yellow-and-black summer males are unmistakable. Females resemble female Dark-backed Goldfinches, but are much brighter and show considerable *white* on the tail. Both have undulating flight and are likely to be found together in winter.

DARK-BACKED GOLDFINCH. *Spinus psaltria.*—3¾–4¼. *Male:* Sides of head and upperparts variable: either wholly black above, or crown black, the sides of the head, hind-neck, back, and rump dull greenish olive (*S. p. hesperophilus*); in either case, wings and tail mainly black, the former conspicuously patterned with white; inner webs of the lateral rectrices sometimes mainly white; underparts bright lemon-yellow or golden-yellow. *Female:* Dull olive-green or grayish olive, the underparts palest; wings and tail dusky brown, the white pattern like that of the male, but much restricted. *Immature:* Similar to female, but duller, the upperparts tinged with buff, and white of the wings replaced with buff.

Distribution.—Virtually country-wide.

Races.—*S. p. hesperophilus* (Baja California and northern Sonora). *S. p. psaltria* (virtually country-wide, exclusive of the extreme northwestern and southeastern portions). *S. p. jouyi* (Yucatán and Mujeres Island). *S. p. colombianus* (southwestern Chiapas).

Remarks.—Also known as Lesser Goldfinch and Green-backed Goldfinch. The geographical varieties of this goldfinch are notably different, but all have bright *lemon-yellow* underparts and *white-patterned* wings. The back may be either jet-black or dull olive, but never lemon-yellow as with male American Goldfinches. Females resemble female *S. tristis*, but are much duller (more olivaceous), especially below. *See* female American Goldfinch.

LAWRENCE GOLDFINCH. *Spinus lawrencei.*—4¼. *Male:* Forepart of crown, lores, and throat black; sides of head, hind-neck, and back gray, the last often tinged with olive; rump and breast bright yellowish olive; wings and tail black, the former patterned with yellowish olive, the inner webs of the lateral rectrices with a large white patch; abdomen and flanks whitish. *Female:* Similar to male, but much duller; yellow of breast less distinct, and head without black.

Distribution.—Resident in northern Baja California, wintering also in Sonora.

Remarks.—A grayish goldfinch with a *black forehead and throat,* and a bright yellow breast. Females lack black on the head. Both sexes are without the *distinct* wing-patches of other goldfinches, but show a *broad expanse of yellowish olive* on the wings at all seasons.

RED CROSSBILL. *Loxia curvirostra* (Illus. p. 575).—5½–6½. *Male:* Deep red or brownish red, brightest below, the back and scapulars sometimes obscurely spotted with darker; wings and tail blackish, faintly tinged

RED CROSSBILL

with reddish; tail distinctly notched; tips of the bill conspicuously crossed in adults of both sexes. *Female:* Grayish olive, more or less tinged with yellowish, the upperparts obscurely streaked or spotted with dusky; wings, tail, and bill as in male. *Immature:* Broadly striped above and below; bill as in adult.

· **Distribution.**—Coniferous mountain forests of northern Baja California and eastern Mexico southward.

Races.—*L. c. bendirei* and *L. c. grinnelli* (casual in Baja California, and on Guadalupe Island, where possibly breeding). *L. c. stricklandi* (Sierra San Pedro Mártir and Sierra Juárez, Baja California, and the mountains of eastern Mexico southward at high altitudes).

Remarks.—No other Mexican bird has a bill with crossed tips. At a distance the bill appears longer and thinner than that of other finches, and the *brick-red or dingy olive* plumage quite unlike that of any other highland bird. Immature Crossbills suggest out-sized Pine Siskins, but have no yellow on their wings.

YELLOW-BREASTED GRASS-FINCH. *Sicalis luteola.*—4½. *Male:* Above dull yellowish olive-green, brightest on rump, the crown, back, and scapulars streaked with dusky; wings and tail dusky, the feathers edged with paler; superciliaries and underparts bright golden-yellow, the breast and sides tinged with olive. *Female:* Similar, but much duller, the upperparts browner, and below dingy whitish, more or less washed with yellow medially.

Distribution.—Caribbean slope of southern Veracruz and Chiapas, and the Pacific watershed of central Mexico.

Races.—*S. l. chrysops* (southern Veracruz and the Caribbean slope of Chiapas). *S. l. mexicana* (Morelos and Puebla).

Remarks.—Also known as Yellow Finch. A boldly striped finch with bright yellow underparts. Females appear *dingy yellowish below,* and are rather nondescript. They will be known by their *striped upperparts* and thick, *conical bills,* this combination of characters eliminating all similar birds. Brushy places and grasslands, chiefly in dry districts.

SLATY FINCH. *Spodiornis rusticus uniformis* (Illus. p. 576).—5. *Male:* Uniform dark slate, the underparts palest; bill sharply pointed, conical, black above, bluish below. *Female:* Unknown, but probably brownish olive

Slaty Finch

above, the crown and nape (at least) obscurely streaked with dusky, and underparts probably brownish and buff.

Distribution.—The Mexican form is known from a single male collected at Jalapa, in the highlands of Veracruz. An unidentified finch, possibly the female of this rare bird, has since been reported from Chiapas (Chiquihuite), at an altitude of about 8,000 feet.

Remarks.—No other fringillid in our area is *uniformly dull slate-colored.* The Slate-blue Seedeater of Guerrero (*Amaurospiza relictus*) is superficially similar, but its plumage has a distinctly *bluish* tone, and its bill is much more finchlike. *See* Slate-blue Seedeater.

RUFOUS-CAPPED BRUSH-FINCH. *Atlapetes pileatus.*—5¾. Crown and nape rufous, the upperparts otherwise dull olive-brown or olive-gray;

lores and malar area black, shading to gray on the auriculars and sides of neck; throat and abdomen yellow, the breast, sides, flanks, and crissum strongly tinged with brownish olive.

Distribution.—Mexican plateau, chiefly at high altitudes in pine and oak forests. ENDEMIC.

Races.—*A. p. dilutus* (Chihuahua, San Luis Potosí, and Tamaulipas). *A. p. pileatus* (middle and southern portion of the Mexican plateau). *A. p. canescens* (high mountains of Guerrero).

Remarks.—Also known as Rufous-capped Atlapetes. A brownish sparrow with a *rufous* cap and *dingy yellowish underparts*. Essentially terrestrial, and fairly common locally at altitudes above 7,000 feet.

WHITE-NAPED BRUSH-FINCH. *Atlapetes albinucha.*—7. *Adult:* Forehead, sides of head, and crown black, the latter with a very conspicuous white median stripe, the upperparts otherwise uniform dark slate; below bright golden-yellow, the sides and flanks tinged with olive. *Immature:* Above sooty brown, the crown-stripe usually indistinct; below pale yellowish, the breast, sides, and flanks more or less streaked.

Distribution.—Highlands of Veracruz, Puebla, Oaxaca, and Chiapas.

Remarks.—Also known as White-naped Atlapetes. One of the more characteristic birds of the southern mountains. The *bright yellow underparts* and very prominent *white crown-stripe* are distinctive. A related species in Chiapas (*A. gutturalis*) is similar above, but has a *white breast and abdomen*. Both spend much time on the ground, and are most likely to be found in brush or thickets.

YELLOW-THROATED BRUSH-FINCH. *Atlapetes gutturalis griseipectus.*—6½–6¾. Similar to the White-naped Brush-Finch, but throat alone bright yellow, the breast and posterior underparts dull whitish, tinged with gray laterally.

Distribution.—Mountain forests of southern Chiapas (Niquivil, Volcán de Tacaná).

Remarks.—Also known as Yellow-throated Atlapetes. *See* White-naped Brush-Finch.

CHESTNUT-CAPPED BRUSH-FINCH. *Atlapetes brunnei-nucha brunnei-nucha* (Illus. p. 578).—7½. *Adult:* Forehead, sides of head, and band across chest black; a white spot above the lores; crown chestnut, bordered laterally with bright tawny, the upperparts otherwise dull greenish olive; throat and median underparts (except pectoral band) white, the sides, flanks, and crissum grayish olive. *Immature:* Crown deep brown; sides of head dusky; upperparts brownish olive-green; below brownish, more or less streaked with yellow and yellowish white.

Distribution.—Humid mountain forests of San Luis Potosí, Veracruz, Mexico, Guerrero, Oaxaca, and Chiapas.

Remarks.—Also known as Chestnut-capped Atlapetes. Some Collared Towhees, especially the race in Guerrero, are much like this species. The absence of white superciliaries, the narrower pectoral band, and the less conical bill of the brush-finch are useful field characters. Common locally in heavy mountain forests, usually on or near the ground. *See* Collared Towhee and Plain-breasted Brush-Finch.

CHESTNUT-CAPPED BRUSH-FINCH

PLAIN-BREASTED BRUSH-FINCH. *Atlapetes apertus.*—7. Similar to a Chestnut-capped Brush-Finch, but without a black band across the chest, and without a pale line bordering the sides of the crown.

Distribution.—Higher portions of Volcán San Martín and Cerro de Tuxtla, southern Veracruz. ENDEMIC.

Remarks.—Also known as San Martín Atlapetes. *See* Chestnut-capped Brush-Finch and Collared Towhee.

STRIPED BRUSH-FINCH. *Atlapetes torquatus.*—7½. *Adult:* Superciliaries and broad stripe through the median crown bright yellowish olive, the forehead, sides of crown, and sides of head black; upperparts (except head) greenish olive; throat and median abdomen white, the breast and sides decidedly gray, this more or less tinged with greenish olive posteriorly. *Immature:* Above olive-brown, the bright stripes (head) of the adult replaced by dingy yellowish; below olive-brown, the throat and abdomen liberally streaked with dull yellowish.

Distribution.—Mountains (locally) of southeastern Sinaloa, Jalisco, and south-central portion of the Mexican plateau.

Races.—*A. t. verecundus* (mountain tops forming the boundary between southeastern Sinaloa and Durango). *A. t. colimae* (Volcán de Colima, Jalisco). *A. t. virenticeps* (south-central Mexico, in the states of Michoacán, Morelos, Puebla, Mexico, and Guanajuato).

Remarks.—The Mexican representatives of this common tropical American ground sparrow are distinguished by their conspicuous *yellowish olive* superciliaries and crown-stripe. Some authorities assign them to a distinct species (*virenticeps*), usually known as Green-striped Brush-Finch or Atlapetes. In any case, they resemble Chestnut-capped Brush-Finches below, but have a broad *gray* (not black) *breast-band.*

ORANGE-BILLED SPARROW. *Arremon aurantiirostris saturatus.*—6–6½. Head mainly black, the crown with a gray median stripe; superciliaries and throat white; a broad black band across the breast; back, scapulars, rump, and upper tail-coverts olive-green, the lesser wing-coverts and edge of wing near bend bright yellow; abdomen white, the sides and flanks dusky olive; bill orange or orange-red.

Distribution.—Humid lowland forests of Oaxaca and Tabasco.

Remarks.—A rather large, black-headed, olive-colored forest sparrow with an *orange bill* and *bright yellow shoulders.*

OLIVE SPARROW. *Arremonops rufivirgatus.*—5½–6. *Adult:* Above brownish olive, becoming olive-green on wings and tail, the sides of the crown bordered with deep brown; superciliaries and sides of the head pale brownish gray; a dark-brown eye-stripe; edge of wing at bend bright yellow; underparts more or less extensively buffy brown or grayish buff, the abdomen white. *Immature:* Above uniform brownish, the wing-coverts edged and tipped with fulvous; below paler, the abdomen buffy.

Distribution.—Virtually country-wide (except Baja California), from sea-level to an altitude of about 6,000 feet locally.

Races.—*A. r. sinaloae* (southern Sinaloa south to Nayarit). *A. r. sumichrasti* (Colima, Guerrero, and Oaxaca). *A. r. chiapensis* (valley of the Chiapas River, Chiapas). *A. r. rufivirgatus* (Nuevo León, Tamaulipas, northern Veracruz, and San Luis Potosí, except where occupied by the following). *A. r. ridgwayi* (southeastern San Luis Potosí, Hidalgo, and probably adjacent parts of Tamaulipas and Veracruz). *A. r. crassirostris* (Veracruz,

Puebla, and Oaxaca). *A. r. verticalis* (Campeche and northern Yucatán, including Meco Island).

Remarks.—An olive-backed sparrow with a prominent *brown eye-streak*, and two *dull brown crown-stripes*. A strip of bright yellow on the edge of the wing helps verify the identification. In the southeastern lowlands one must also consider the following species, which is best distinguished by its *grayish* head and *black* head-stripes.

GREEN-BACKED SPARROW. *Arremonops conirostris chloronotus.*— 5½. Similar to an Olive Sparrow, but much greener (less brownish) above, and with *black* (not brown) stripes bordering the crown, the area between *clear gray*. Underparts extensively whitish; crissum pale yellowish.

Distribution.—Lowlands of Tabasco, the Yucatán Peninsula, and Chiapas.

Remarks.—*See* Olive Sparrow.

*GREEN-TAILED TOWHEE. *Chlorura chlorura* (Illus. p. 580).—6¾–7. *Adult:* Crown bright cinnamon-rufous, the forehead, superciliaries, and sides of head grayish; upperparts extensively grayish olive, this becoming bright

GREEN-TAILED TOWHEE

olive-green on wings and tail; edge of wing at bend bright yellow; throat and abdomen white, the former distinctly outlined by the gray of the breast; flanks and crissum buffy. *Immature:* Above pale olive or grayish brown streaked with dusky; remiges and tail olive-green, the wing-coverts buff-tipped; below whitish, the breast and sides more or less streaked.

Distribution.—Winters in Baja California, and from northern Mexico south to Guanajuato.

Races.—*C. c. zapolia* (winters in Baja California, Sonora, and Sinaloa). *C. c. chlorura* (winters in Baja California, and south to Guanajuato and Michoacán).

Remarks.—A rufous-capped, olive-backed sparrow with *gray cheeks and breast*. The *clearly defined white throat* suggests a White-throated Sparrow. Weedy fields and brush, usually on or near the ground.

COLLARED TOWHEE. *Pipilo ocai* (Illus. p. 581).—8–8½. *Adult:* Head and throat variable, the usual patterns as follows: Forehead (or forepart of crown) and sides of head black, the former often with a white median stripe; crown from level of eyes (or posterior portion only) chestnut; superciliaries white, or lacking; upperparts uniform olive-green; below variable, the throat and breast either white, with a conspicuous black band across the chest, or both mainly black, the median throat with a white patch; in both

COLLARED TOWHEE

types the lower breast and abdomen white, the flanks brownish, shading to buff on the crissum. *Immature:* Above dull olive-brown, the primaries and tail often yellowish olive; median throat and abdomen pale yellowish, the breast and sides brown-streaked.

Distribution.—Highlands of southwestern and southern Mexico. ENDEMIC.

Races.—*P. o. alticola* (western Jalisco south at least to Volcán de Colima). *P. o. nigrescens* (Michoacán, from Cerro San Andrés west to Mount Tancítaro). *P. o. guerrerensis* (Sierra Madre del Sur, Guerrero, at least west of Chilpancingo). *P. o. ocai* (mountains of eastern Puebla and western Veracruz). *P. o. brunnescens* (highlands of Oaxaca, chiefly from Cerro San Felipe to Mount Zempoaltepec).

Remarks.—Brushy fence rows, thickets, and coniferous forests at higher altitudes are the usual habitats of Collared Towhees. The races vary considerably as to head pattern, but all have more or less white on the throat, and at least a small patch of chestnut on the crown. Hybridization with Red-eyed Towhees occurs locally, but generally the two remain distinct. *See* Chestnut-capped Brush-Finch.

RED-EYED TOWHEE. *Pipilo erythrophthalmus.*—7½–8. *Male:* Head, throat, and upper breast black or sooty brown, the upperparts either similar, or the back (at least) distinctly olive, grayish olive-brown, or brownish olive —in any case, the back and scapulars more or less streaked and spotted with white or yellowish; tail usually black, the lateral feathers broadly white-tipped; lower breast and abdomen white, the sides, flanks, and crissum cinnamon-rufous or tawny. *Female:* Similar, but somewhat duller, the black areas usually replaced with brown.

Distribution.—Baja California and the Mexican plateau locally south to the highlands of Chiapas; also Socorro and Guadalupe Islands, off the Pacific Coast.

Races.—*P. e. consobrinus* (Guadalupe Island, off Baja California; probably extinct). *P. e. socorroensis* (Socorro Island, Revilla Gigedo group). *P. e. megalonyx* (extreme northwestern Baja California). *P. e. umbraticola* (northwestern Baja California south to latitude 30°). *P. e. magnirostris* (mountains of the Cape district of Baja California). *P. e. montanus* (northern portion of the Sierra Madre Occidental south to about 29° N. latitude). *P. e. griseipygius* (mountains of central Chihuahua south to southern Durango and northern Nayarit). *P. e. macronyx* (mountains of the Michoacán border east to the western side of the valley of Mexico). *P. e. vulcanorum* (mountains forming the southeastern side of the valley of Mexico). *P. e. orientalis* (northern portion of the Sierra Madre Oriental south to about 22° N. latitude). *P. e. maculatus* (east-central highlands in the states of Hidalgo, Veracruz, and Puebla). *P. e. oaxacae* (highlands of Oaxaca). *P. e. chiapensis* (highlands of north-central Chiapas). *P. e. repetens* (Volcán de Tacaná, Chiapas).

Remarks.—The *black* head, throat, and chest, *tawny or rufous sides*, and *white-tipped* tail are the hallmark of this towhee. The spot-backed races, and those with greenish backs, are known respectively as Spotted and Olive-backed Towhees. They hybridize to some extent, but were long considered distinct species. All frequent thickets, underbrush, or grassy fields and are essentially terrestrial in habits.

BROWN TOWHEE. *Pipilo fuscus* (Illus. p. 583).—7½–8¼. Above grayish brown, the crown sometimes distinctly reddish brown; throat pale buff or tawny, conspicuously bordered with dusky triangular spots; a dusky pectoral patch (lacking in Baja California races); median breast and abdomen more or less extensively grayish or white; flanks grayish buff, deepening to tawny or cinnamon-buff on under tail-coverts; iris brown.

Distribution.—Baja California, Tiburón Island, and drier portions of the elevated interior.

Races.—*P. f. senicula* (Pacific side of Baja California south to latitude 29°). *P. f. aripolius* (middle portion of Baja California from Playa María Bay south to Guajademí, latitude 26°35′). *P. f. albigula* (cape region of

Baja California north to Guajademí). *P. f. jamesi* (Tiburón Island, off Sonora). *P. f. mesoleucus* (northern Sonora and northern Chihuahua south to latitude 30°). *P. f. intermedius* (central Sonora south to northern Sinaloa). *P. f. perpallidus* (Chihuahua, Durango, and Zacatecas, in the Sierra Madre Occidental and its eastern foothills). *P. f. potosinus* (eastern and central Mexico). *P. f. compoi* (Hidalgo). *P. f. fuscus* (southwestern highlands from Nayarit to extreme north-central Guerrero, ranging east to Mexico, Morelos, and Distrito Federal). *P. f. toroi* (Tlaxcala and adjacent parts of Veracruz south through eastern Puebla to central Oaxaca).

Remarks.—A large drab sparrow with a *buffy throat bordered with triangular spots*. White-throated Towhees are very similar in general appearance, but have white-tipped middle wing-coverts, and essentially

BROWN TOWHEE

white throats bordered behind by a *narrow dusky band*. Both are distinguished from thrashers by their thick bills. *See* White-throated Towhee.

WHITE-THROATED TOWHEE. *Pipilo rutilus.*—7½. Similar to a Brown Towhee, but throat essentially white, the anterior third usually dull orange, the posterior edge bordered with a *narrow dusky band;* middle wing-coverts white-tipped; white of abdomen often mottled with gray.

Distribution.—Dry mountains of Puebla, Guerrero (Chilpancingo), and Oaxaca, mainly from 5,200–6,200 feet above sea-level. ENDEMIC.

Races.—*P. r. rutilus* (Puebla and Oaxaca, chiefly in the drainages of the Río Salado and Río Atoyac; one record for Chilpancingo, central Guerrero). *P. r. parvirostris* (vicinity of Mount Zempoaltepec, Oaxaca).

Remarks.—Also known as Sclater Towhee. While obviously closely related to the Brown Towhee, this species is distinguished by a continuous *dark band* (not spots) bordering its *white* throat behind. The forepart of its throat is usually ochraceous, and most individuals have a distinct *pale wing-bar*. Mesquite scrub and brush near cultivated fields. *See* Brown Towhee.

ABERT TOWHEE. *Pipilo aberti dumeticolus.*—8½–9. Above pale grayish brown, shading to tawny ochraceous on the underparts, where more or less tinged with vinaceous; lores and chin dusky, the throat often streaked with same.

Distribution.—Dry lowlands and foothills of northeastern Baja California and northwestern Sonora.

Remarks.—A shy, thrasher-sized sparrow, brownish above and *buffy below*, with a *black* area bordering its bill. Common locally, frequenting dense cover, especially mesquite, arrowweed, or willows in the vicinity of water.

RUSTY-CROWNED GROUND-SPARROW. *Melozone kieneri* (Illus. p. 584).—6–6½. Middle and hind-portion of crown and posterior border of auriculars chestnut, the upperparts otherwise uniform olive-brown or gray-

RUSTY-CROWNED GROUND-SPARROW

ish olive; lores and eye-ring usually white; underparts white, the median breast often with a distinct black spot; sides and flanks olive-brown; crissum tawny buff.

Distribution.—Foothills and highlands of western and southern Mexico.

Races.—*M. k. grisior* (extreme southeastern Sonora, northeastern Sinaloa, and probably adjacent portions of Chihuahua). *M. k. kieneri* (southern Sinaloa and southwestern Durango south to Nayarit). *M. k. rubricatum* (southern portion of the Mexican plateau, in the states of Morelos, Puebla, Guerrero, and Oaxaca). *M. k. hartwegi* (highlands of Chiapas).

Remarks.—The only *chestnut-topped* sparrow with white lores and a *black breast-spot*. Thickets and brush, chiefly at high altitudes.

WHITE-EARED GROUND-SPARROW. *Melozone leucotis occipitalis.* —6½–7. Sides of crown, sides of hind-neck, and throat black, the median crown grayish; lores and auriculars white, the latter bordered above by a bright olive-yellow stripe, this extending behind the auriculars and becoming suffused over the hind-neck; back, rump, wings, and tail brown; breast and abdomen white, the former with a conspicuous black patch; crissum tawny.

Distribution.—Highlands of Chiapas.

Remarks.—A *black-throated* sparrow with very conspicuous *white auriculars*. Forest undergrowth, usually on or near the ground.

STRIPED SPARROW. *Oriturus superciliosa* (Illus. p. 585).—6–7. *Adult:* Sides of crown deep chestnut, the median stripe grayish, the whole streaked with black; superciliaries whitish or buffy, the lores and auriculars black;

STRIPED SPARROW

back, scapulars, and rump pale gray intermixed with reddish, the whole conspicuously streaked with black; wings and tail sooty, the feathers broadly edged with buff or gray; underparts dingy gray; bill wholly black. *Immature:* Similar, but below buffy white, the chest narrowly streaked with dusky.

Distribution.—Northwestern Sonora, northern Chihuahua, and Durango south over the tableland to Michoacán, Puebla, and Veracruz. ENDEMIC.

Races.—*O. s. palliata* (mountains of extreme eastern Sonora and Chihuahua). *O. s. superciliosa* (central and southern portion of the Mexican tableland).

Remarks.—This common highland species will be known by its sturdy, *jet-black bill*, conspicuous *black face-band*, and boldly streaked, reddish brown upperparts. Its crown is essentially chestnut, not white bordered with black as in Stripe-headed Sparrows. The underparts and superciliaries are quite dingy as compared with those of *A. ruficauda*.

*LARK BUNTING. *Calamospiza melanocorys.*—6½. *Male (summer)*: Mainly black, the wing-coverts white, the innermost remiges margined with same; lateral rectrices white-tipped on inner webs, the outermost narrowly edged with white; *(winter)*: Similar to female, but chin and upper throat black; belly usually with a black patch. *Female:* Above grayish brown streaked with dusky, the wing-coverts broadly buff-tipped; superciliaries and malar stripe pale buff; below whitish, liberally streaked with dusky, the breast, sides, and flanks often tinged with buff.

Distribution.—Winters in Baja California and locally on the central plateau, where recorded from Durango, Zacatecas, Guanajuato, and Mexico.

Remarks.—Lark Buntings inhabit open country, a preference that helps to eliminate other species resembling the striped females and winter males. These, in any case, have a *white* or pale *buffy wing-patch* that is usually conspicuous in flight. *See* female Purple Finch and related species.

SAVANNAH SPARROW. *Passerculus sandwichensis.*—5–5¾. Superciliaries and bend of wing yellow or whitish; above pale grayish brown, liberally streaked with black, the back, scapulars, and rump often with more or less reddish brown; crown usually with a distinct pale median stripe; wing-coverts and remiges sometimes broadly edged with tawny; below white, the breast, sides, and flanks liberally streaked; tail distinctly notched, the feathers rather pointed; legs pale pink.

Distribution.—Tidal marshes of Baja California (including various offshore islands), the coasts of Sonora and Sinaloa, and grasslands of the Mexican tableland southward at medium and high altitudes.

Races.—*P. s. sanctorum* (San Benito Islands, off Baja California). *P. s. beldingi* (Todos Santos Islands and the Pacific Coast of northwestern Baja California south to about latitude 30°). *P. s. anulus* (Pacific Coast of central

Baja California). *P. s. guttatus* (Pacific Coast of Baja California in the vicinity of Pond and San Ignacio lagoons; ranges south to the cape district in winter). *P. s. magdalenae* (Magdalena Bay, southwestern Baja California, wintering south to the cape district). *P. s. rostratus* (mouth of the Colorado River south along the coast of Sonora to Puerto Lobos; winters south at least to northern Sinaloa, along both coasts of Baja California, and on most offshore islands except the San Benitos and Guadalupe). *P. s. atratus* (coast of Sinaloa, wintering also in the cape region of Baja California). **P. s. anthinus* (winters casually in northern Baja California and Sonora). **P. s. nevadensis* (winters in northern Baja California and northern Mexico). *P. s. rufofuscus* (Chihuahua, wintering southward to Jalisco). *P. s. brunnescens* (tablelands of the interior). **P. s. savanna* (winters in northeastern Mexico).

Remarks.—Savannah Sparrows resemble Song Sparrows superficially, but have relatively *short* tails, pale or *yellowish superciliaries*, a more or less *distinct pale crown-stripe*, and *pinkish legs*. They prefer open country, occurring commonly both in tidal marshes and in the grasslands of the interior highlands. *See* Song Sparrow, Sierra Madre Sparrow, and Baird Sparrow.

GRASSHOPPER SPARROW. *Ammodramus savannarum.*—4½–4¾. Sides of crown sooty, the median stripe pale grayish buff; hind-neck streaked with chestnut; back and scapulars much intermixed with pale gray, reddish, and black; edge of wing at bend and lores (usually) bright yellow; tail rather short, the feathers somewhat pointed; sides of head, throat, breast, and flanks distinctly buffy, the abdomen white.

Distribution.—Resident in the unforested portions of southern Mexico, occurring extensively elsewhere in migration and winter.

Races.—**A. s. perpallidus* (winters in Baja California, and western Mexico southward). **A. s. pratensis* (winters in eastern and southern Mexico). *A. s. bimaculatus* (southern Mexico in the states of Mexico, Veracruz, Oaxaca, and Chiapas).

Remarks.—A common short-tailed sparrow of weedy fields and open prairies. The *immaculate* underparts, *buff-tinged throat and breast*, and pale median crown-stripe are distinctive, as is the male's song, a long, *high-pitched buzz* following several short notes. *See* Cassin Sparrow and related species.

*BAIRD SPARROW. *Ammodramus bairdii.*—5. Above liberally streaked with sooty brown, the median stripe of the crown, superciliaries, and hind-neck buffy or tawny; below mainly white (tawny buff in immature birds), the chest with a narrow band of fine blackish streaks.

Distribution.—Winters in northwestern Mexico.

Remarks.—Like the Savannah Sparrow, a bird of grassy open country, the two not always separable in the field. Baird Sparrows are less profusely streaked below, and more boldly streaked above. The Baird's distinctly *tawny* (or buffy) *head coloring* is perhaps its best field character. Note the breast-band of minute black streaks. *See* Savannah Sparrow.

SIERRA MADRE SPARROW. *Xenospiza baileyi* (Illus. p. 588).—5. Above essentially reddish brown, much streaked (crown and hind-neck) and spotted (back and scapulars) with black; inner remiges mainly blackish; superciliaries and stripe through median crown grayish; edge of wing at bend pale yellow; below dull white, the sides of the throat, breast, and sides broadly streaked with black, the flanks tinged with buff.

Distribution.—Mountains of southern Durango, northern Jalisco, and Distrito Federal. ENDEMIC.

SIERRA MADRE SPARROW

Races.—*X. b. baileyi* (southern Durango and northern Jalisco, at high altitudes). *X. b. sierrae* (known only from the vicinity of La Cima, in the high mountains near Mexico City, D.F.).

Remarks.—Also known as Bailey Sparrow. A little-known species, resembling both a Savannah and a Song Sparrow superficially. It is distinguished by its darker, extensively chestnut upperparts, very conspicuous *black streaking* on the breast, sides, and flanks, and the pale *yellow* on the bend of the wing. The absence of yellow on the sides of its head helps to eliminate the Savannah Sparrow. Sierra Madre Sparrows occur both in grassy, open pine woods at high altitudes and locally in mountain marshes. The song has been described as consisting of seven or eight short syllables followed by two melodic notes.

*VESPER SPARROW. *Pooecetes gramineus.*—$5\frac{1}{2}$–6. Above pale grayish brown generously streaked with sooty, this most conspicuously on crown and back; lesser wing-coverts cinnamon or tawny chestnut, the middle and greater coverts tipped with whitish; tail dusky, the outer half of the outermost feathers white; auriculars buffy brown; underparts whitish, or buffy white, the sides of the throat, breast, sides, and flanks streaked with dusky.

Distribution.—Widespread in winter, preferring open country, fence rows, and brushy fields.

Races.—*P. g. affinis* (winters in northern Baja California). *P. g. confinis* (winters in Baja California, and western Mexico southward). *P. g. gramineus* (winters casually in Yucatán, probably occurring elsewhere in eastern Mexico at that season).

Remarks.—The *white outer tail feathers*, usually conspicuous in flight, distinguish Vespers from other *streaked* sparrows. The *rusty shoulder patch* is a useful corroborative character. Lark Sparrows, while streaked above, have *white-tipped* tails. Pipits, streaked above and with white outer rectrices, have *thin* bills and habitually *walk* (not hop) when on the ground. *See* Song Sparrow.

LARK SPARROW. *Chondestes grammacus* (Illus. p. 590).—6–$6\frac{1}{4}$. Crown and auriculars chestnut, the former with a conspicuous pale median stripe, the auriculars bordered above and below with white or whitish; a broad black submalar stripe; hind-neck, back, and rump pale grayish brown, the back and scapulars boldly streaked; tail fanlike, mainly sooty, the lateral feathers with broad white tips, these progressively broader toward the outermost feather, where occupying the terminal half; below white, the median breast usually with a black spot.

Distribution.—Northern portion of the central plateau (Chihuahua, Coahuila, Durango), wintering in Baja California, and from northern and eastern Mexico southward in open country.

Races.—*C. g. strigatus* (as above, except eastern and southern Mexico). **C. g. grammacus* (winters in eastern and southern Mexico).

Remarks.—The boldly patterned head, *chestnut auriculars*, and *white-tipped, rounded tail* are the best field characters. Immature birds

LARK SPARROW

are essentially like adults but are finely streaked below and lack a median breast-spot. Brushy fields and grassy open country. *See* Sage Sparrow and Vesper Sparrow.

FIVE-STRIPED SPARROW. *Aimophila quinquestriata* (Illus. p. 590). —5½–5¾. Above dusky brownish, the back and outer webs of secondaries tinged with dull reddish; superciliaries and malar stripe white; sides of throat black, the chin, median throat, and abdomen white; chest, sides, and flanks dull slate-gray, the median breast with a black patch.

FIVE-STRIPED SPARROW

Distribution.—Lowlands and foothills of western Mexico. ENDEMIC.

Races.—*A. q. septentrionalis* (Sonora, Chihuahua, Sinaloa, and probably northern Durango). *A. q. quinquestriata* (Jalisco).

Remarks.—A drab, unstreaked sparrow with slaty gray underparts, and a black patch in the center of the breast. No similar bird has a *pale median throat-stripe bordered on each side with black.*

BRIDLED SPARROW. *Aimophila mystacalis* (Illus. p. 591).—6. *Adult:* Crown, hind-neck, and sides of head grayish, the first black-streaked; spot above the lores and malar stripe white; upper throat black, the chin usually white; back brownish, broadly streaked with black, the scapulars and rump extensively rufous; wings and tail dusky; two narrow wing-bars; chest and breast ash gray, shading to whitish on abdomen, the flanks and

BRIDLED SPARROW

crissum pale cinnamon. *Immature:* Essentially like adult, but wing-bars and white of head yellowish; throat whitish, bordered with black, the median portion flecked with dusky; chest whitish, streaked with dusky.

Distribution.—Mountains of southern Veracruz, Puebla, and Oaxaca. ENDEMIC.

Remarks.—A *black-chinned, rufous-rumped,* highland sparrow with a very *conspicuous white malar stripe.* Note the two wing-bars, white in adults and yellowish or buffy in immature birds.

BLACK-CHESTED SPARROW. *Aimophila humeralis* (Illus. p. 591).— 5¾–6. Crown, hind-neck, and rump (sometimes) dull grayish brown, this becoming dusky on sides of head; malar stripe and spot above lores white; a

BLACK-CHESTED SPARROW

black submalar stripe; back, scapulars, and shoulders cinnamon-rufous, the first sometimes with a few black streaks; no wing-bars; underparts white, the chest crossed by a very broad black band; flanks and crissum tinged with pale buff.

Distribution.—Southern portion of the Mexican plateau. ENDEMIC.

Races.—*A. h. humeralis* (highlands of Guerrero, Michoacán, Morelos, and Puebla). *A. h. asticta* (Colima).

Remarks.—Also known as Ferrari-Perez Sparrow.

STRIPE-HEADED SPARROW. *Aimophila ruficauda* (Illus. p. 592).—$6\frac{1}{2}$–7. Head very conspicuously patterned: stripe through median crown, superciliaries, and throat white, the sides of the crown, lores, and auriculars

STRIPE-HEADED SPARROW

black; upperparts mainly cinnamon-brown, sometimes tinged with grayish, the back and scapulars broadly striped with sooty; below white, the flanks and crissum grayish buff or tawny ochraceous, the breast and sides sometimes distinctly mottled with gray; bill black above, pale below.

Distribution.—Arid lowlands and foothills of southwestern Mexico.

Races.—*A. r. nayaritensis* (vicinity of Tepic, Nayarit). *A. r. acuminata* (Durango, Jalisco, and Colima east to Morelos and Puebla). *A. r. guerrerensis* (Guerrero). *A. r. lawrencii* (Oaxaca).

Remarks.—Also known as Russet-tailed Sparrow. The boldly patterned black-and-white head, and especially the conspicuous *white median crown-stripe* (not shown in illustration), eliminates most reddish-backed sparrows with spotted or streaked upperparts. Some Stripe-headed Sparrows are virtually immaculate below, while others have dingy breasts. Note the two-toned bill. *See* Striped Sparrow and White-crowned Sparrow.

RUFOUS-WINGED SPARROW. *Aimophila carpalis*.—$5\frac{1}{2}$. Crown rufous-streaked, or rufous laterally, with a pale gray median stripe; superciliaries and sides of head pale gray; a rufous postocular stripe; upperparts mainly pale grayish brown, the back and scapulars streaked with dark brown; shoulders rufous; below grayish white, the malar area bordered above and below by a narrow dusky streak.

Distribution.—Dry lowlands and foothills of Sonora and Sinaloa.

Races.—*A. c. carpalis* (northern and western parts of Sonora). *A. c. bangsi* (southern Sonora, and northern Sinaloa south to the Sinaloa River). *A. c. cohaerens* (Sinaloa, from the Sinaloa River south to Elota, south-central Sinaloa).

Remarks.—Much like a Chipping Sparrow, but with a *brownish bill and rufous shoulders*. The dusky streaks bordering the pale malar stripe are corroborative. The flight of a "chippy" is more direct; that of a Rufous-winged Sparrow periodically dips a little.

CINNAMON-TAILED SPARROW. *Aimophila sumichrasti.*—6½. Similar to the Rufous-winged Sparrow of Sonora and Sinaloa, but much larger and browner above (less grayish), with heavier *blackish* markings on the head, and with distinctly rufescent (not brownish gray) tail and coverts. Lower abdomen and crissum pale tawny buff. Taxonomic status uncertain, and possibly only a race of *A. carpalis*.

Distribution.—Arid lowlands of Oaxaca. ENDEMIC.

Remarks.—Also known as Sumichrast Sparrow. While probably more closely related to the smaller Rufous-winged Sparrow of northwestern Mexico, this species also resembles a Rusty Sparrow, three races of which occur in Oaxaca. The latter is considerably larger, has a *blackish* (not brown) *bill,* and lacks a dusky streak *above* the pale malar stripe. Cinnamon-tailed Sparrows have *black* streaks on their crowns, rather boldly striped backs as compared with Rusty Sparrows, and tawny rufous tails. *See* Rufous-winged Sparrow.

OAXACA SPARROW. *Aimophila notosticta.*—6¼. Similar to a Rusty Sparrow, but somewhat smaller, bill uniformly black, chestnut of the crown without appreciable black, and tail distinctly grayish brown, with little or no reddish.

Distribution.—*Oaxaca* (Cerro San Felipe, Ejutla) and possibly adjacent parts of Puebla. ENDEMIC.

Remarks.—*See* Rusty Sparrow.

RUSTY SPARROW. *Aimophila rufescens* (Illus. p. 594).—6¾–7½. Crown mainly chestnut, much intermixed with black (especially posteriorly), the median portion usually with a more or less conspicuous grayish stripe; superciliaries, auriculars, and sides of neck grayish, the malar stripe buffy; a prominent black submalar stripe; a sooty postocular stripe; upperparts mainly reddish brown, the back and scapulars sparsely streaked with black; below dingy whitish, palest on throat and abdomen, the remainder usually strongly tinged with buff; bill dusky above, pale below.

Distribution.—Dry foothills and mountains of western and southeastern Mexico.

Races.—*A. r. antonensis* (Sierra de San Antonio, north-central Sonora). *A. r. mcleodii* (southern Sonora, Chihuahua, and Durango). *A. r. pallida* (southwestern portion of Mexican plateau from southern Sinaloa to Michoacán). *A. r. rufescens* (arid highlands of southeastern Mexico from San Luis Potosí to Morelos, northern Oaxaca, and Veracruz). *A. r. subvespera* (Pacific slope of Guerrero and Oaxaca). *A. r. cinerea* (Cerro de la Gineta, Chiapas) *A. r. gigas* (interior southern Chiapas).

Rusty Sparrow

Remarks.—One of the larger sparrows, whitish below, dull reddish brown above (where more or less black-streaked), and with a grayish stripe through the median portion of the chestnut crown. The black submalar stripe is notably conspicuous. Bushes and grassy open woods on mountainsides, where usually found on or near the ground. *See* Cinnamon-tailed Sparrow.

RUFOUS-CROWNED SPARROW. *Aimophila ruficeps.*—5½–6¼. Crown rufous, the median portion sometimes lightly streaked with gray, but without a well-defined median stripe; upperparts mainly pale grayish, the hind-neck, back, and scapulars broadly striped with rufous; superciliaries gray, the anterior portion (above lores) usually whitish; a rufous postocular stripe; malar area buffy white; a conspicuous black submalar stripe; throat and abdomen dull whitish, the breast, flanks, and crissum tinged with buff or buffy gray.

Distribution.—Dry foothills and mountains generally; also the Todos Santos Islands, off the Pacific Coast of northern Baja California.

Races.—*A. r. sanctorum* (Todos Santos Islands). *A. r. canescens* (northern Baja California south to latitude 30°30′). *A. r. sororia* (cape district of Baja California). *A. r. scottii* (northern Sonora and northern Chihuahua). *A. r. simulans* (southern Sonora and southern Chihuahua south to northwestern Durango and Nayarit). *A. r. eremoeca* (winters from Tamaulipas south to Puebla and Veracruz). *A. r. boucardi* (southeastern Coahuila, southern Tamaulipas, and San Luis Potosí south to Mexico, Puebla, and Veracruz). *A. r. fusca* (southwestern portion of the highlands, from Jalisco to Guerrero). *A. r. australis* (Oaxaca).

Remarks.—The only Mexican sparrow having both the entire crown and the streaks of the back and scapulars *uniform* rufous or reddish brown. Its conspicuous *black submalar stripe* is a fine supplementary character. Dry, open country, especially grassy and brushy hillsides.

BOTTERI SPARROW. *Aimophila botterii.*—5¾. Above extensively reddish, the feathers narrowly edged with gray or buff; back usually black-streaked; edge of wing at bend pale yellow; lores pale; an obscure dusky submalar stripe; throat and abdomen white, the breast, flanks, and crissum tinged with buff or pale tawny.

Distribution.—Highlands of western and southeastern Mexico; extreme northeastern Tamaulipas near mouth of the Rio Grande.

Races.—*A. b. goldmani* (southern Sinaloa to southern Nayarit). *A. b. botterii* (highlands of Colima, Guanajuato, and Veracruz south to the Pacific slope of Chiapas). *A. b. texana* (coastal prairies near mouth of the Rio Grande, extreme northeastern Tamaulipas).

Remarks.—This undistinguished sparrow resembles a Cassin, but is browner (less grayish) above, and has a quite different song that has been described (Peterson) as a "constant tinkling and 'pitting,' sometimes running into a dry rattle." Cassins are much more musical. Their song consists of a high trill following two opening notes, and ending with two lower notes. Both birds occur principally in fairly open country, or grassy pinelands at high altitudes, and may be found together in some areas. *See* Cassin Sparrow and Yellow-carpalled Sparrow.

YELLOW-CARPALLED SPARROW. *Aimophila petenica petenica.*—5¼. Similar to a Botteri Sparrow, but somewhat darker (less reddish) above, the crown (usually), back, and scapulars broadly streaked with black; lores dusky.

Distribution.—Pine ridges of the Caribbean lowlands of Veracruz and Chiapas.

Remarks.—Also known as Petén Sparrow. The taxonomic relationships of this species are uncertain; it may yet prove to be but a geographical representative of the Botteri Sparrow. The yellow carpals (coverts near bend of wing) are usually conspicuous. While not diagnostic, they nevertheless serve to eliminate many other small obscure sparrows. *See* Botteri Sparrow.

CASSIN SPARROW. *Aimophila cassinii.*—$5\frac{1}{2}$-$5\frac{3}{4}$. Above pale gray, liberally striped with reddish brown, the feathers often with a blackish subterminal spot; sometimes with an obscure dusky submalar stripe; lores pale; secondaries dusky, broadly margined with whitish, the edge of the wing near bend pale yellow; outermost rectrices sooty, tipped with grayish, the inner feathers dark medially, broadly edged with grayish; below dull white, the breast and flanks more or less tinged with gray or buff.

Distribution.—Northern Sonora, wintering south to southern Sinaloa, Nuevo León, and Tamaulipas.

Remarks.—A notably undistinguished "grass-sparrow" with liberally streaked, grayish upperparts and dingy whitish underparts. *No markings below,* but with some yellow on the edge of the wing near bend. *See* Botteri Sparrow and Grasshopper Sparrow.

BLACK-THROATED SPARROW. *Amphispiza bilineata* (Illus. p. 596).—5-$5\frac{1}{2}$. Above immaculate grayish, the back and scapulars tinged with pale brown; superciliaries and malar stripes white; auriculars pale gray;

BLACK-THROATED SPARROW

tail mainly sooty black, the lateral feathers broadly white-tipped, the two outermost with white outer webs; lores, throat, chest, and median breast black, the underparts otherwise mainly white, tinged with grayish buff on the flanks and crissum.

Distribution.—Baja California, islands of the Gulf of California, and arid parts of northern Mexico south to northern Sinaloa, Durango, and Hidalgo.

Races.—*A. b. deserticola* (northern Baja California south to latitude 27° northern Sonora south to about 29°, and northern Chihuahua). *A. b. bangsi* (Baja California and adjacent islands north to latitude 27°). *A. b. tortugae* (Tortuga Island, Gulf of California). *A. b. cana* (San Estebán Island, Gulf of California). *A. b. carmenae* (Carmen Island, Gulf of California). *A. b. pacifica* (arid lowlands of southern Sonora and northern Sinaloa). *A. b. confinis* (deserts of central Chihuahua). *A. b. grisea* (southern Chihuahua south through Durango and San Luis Potosí to Hidalgo). *A. b. bilineata* (Coahuila, Nuevo León, and Tamaulipas).

Remarks.—Also known as Desert Sparrow. In flight, note the *blackish tail*; its white tips show only when fully spread. *See* Black-throated Gray Warbler.

SAGE SPARROW. *Amphispiza belli* (Illus. p. 597).—$5\frac{1}{4}$–$5\frac{3}{4}$. Sides of head and upperparts pale grayish brown, the back and scapulars more or less obscurely streaked with dusky; spot above lores, eye-ring, and malar

SAGE SPARROW

stripe white, the last bordered below by a conspicuous black submalar stripe or broken line; wings and tail sooty, the wing-coverts and secondaries broadly margined with buff; below white, the breast usually with a black median spot; flanks usually tinged with buff, and sometimes lightly streaked.

Distribution.—Baja California, wintering also in the northern parts of Sonora and Chihuahua.

Races.—*A. b. belli* (Baja California south to latitude 30°). *A. b. xerophilus* (Pacific Coast of Baja California, in the vicinity of Santa Catarina Landing, latitude 29°30′). *A. b. cinerea* (middle part of Baja California, from latitude 29° to latitude 26°). **A. b. canescens* (winters in the Colorado delta district, extreme northwestern Baja California). **A. b. nevadensis* (winters in the northern parts of Sonora and Chihuahua).

Remarks.—Also known as Bell Sparrow. A grayish brown sparrow, white below, with a black spot in the center of the breast, and with a conspicuous black stripe on each side of the throat. Lark Sparrows are somewhat similar, but have conspicuously white-tipped tails and *chestnut* auriculars.

*SLATE-COLORED JUNCO. *Junco hyemalis cismontanus.*—5½–6.
Male: Mainly slate gray, darkest on the head, the lower breast, abdomen,
and crissum immaculate white; tail black, the two outer pairs of feathers
white; bill pinkish; iris reddish brown. *Female:* Similar, but much duller,
the gray portions more or less tinged with brown.

Distribution.—Winters casually in Baja California and Chihuahua.

Remarks.—Slaty gray sparrows with white bellies and conspicuously white outer tail feathers. Most Oregon and Yellow-eyed Juncos have
more or less contrasting hoods and backs, the last usually distinctly
brown or reddish. This junco is *uniform above* and lacks rusty coloring
on its flanks. Likely to be found with flocks of other juncos in winter.
All are essentially terrestrial. *See* Oregon Junco.

OREGON JUNCO. *Junco oreganus.*—5¼–5¾. *Adult:* Head, neck, chest,
and (sometimes) breast black, slaty, or grayish, this usually more or less distinct from the adjacent plumage; back and scapulars reddish brown, cinnamon, or rufous; outermost rectrices white, the adjacent feather usually white,
the next often with considerable white on the inner web; lower breast and
abdomen whitish, the sides and flanks grayish, or strongly tinged with cinnamon or pinkish buff; bill pinkish or yellow; iris brown or yellow. *Immature:*
Above grayish brown, lightly streaked with dusky, the back and scapulars
usually somewhat brighter than the adjacent parts; tail as in adult; throat,
breast, and sides buffy brown, more or less streaked with dusky.

Distribution.—Guadalupe Island and Baja California, wintering also in
northwestern Mexico.

Races.—*J. o. insularis* (Guadalupe Island, off Baja California). *J. o.
pontilis* (Sierra Juárez, northern Baja California). *J. o. townsendi* (Sierra San
Pedro Mártir, Baja California). *J. o. bairdi* (Victoria Mountains, cape district of Baja California). **J. o. shufeldti* (winters in northwestern Baja California, Sonora, and Chihuahua). **J. o. thurberi* (winters in Baja California
south to latitude 30°). **J. o montanus* (winters in Chihuahua). **J. o.
mearnsi* (winters in Sonora and Chihuahua). **J. o. caniceps* (winters in
Sonora, Chihuahua, and northwestern Durango).

Remarks.—Also known as Pink-sided Junco. The races of this
junco vary considerably, especially as to the color and distinctness of
the "hood." In some the head, throat, and breast are black or gray, in
sharp contrast with the back and abdomen. Other forms are virtually
uniform above, and almost wholly white below. All the races have
white outer tail feathers. Most, unlike typical Slate-colored Juncos, show
some pink or rusty coloring on their sides and flanks. Some authorities
consider *caniceps*, treated here as a race of *oreganus*, a distinct species,

usually known as Gray-headed Junco. It has a rusty back, grayish sides, and dark eyes—characters held in common with several other forms. Juncos interbreed freely where their ranges meet, and their relationships are not yet fully known. In Mexico, where so many migrants and residents mingle in winter, there is little point in attempting to sort out the "species" in the field. *See* Slate-colored Junco and Yellow-eyed Junco.

YELLOW-EYED JUNCO. *Junco phaeonotus.*—6. *Adult:* Sides of head, crown, and hind-neck grayish slate, the lores and orbital area usually blackish; back and scapulars either olive-brown, tinged with rusty, or bright cinnamon-rufous; outermost rectrices white, the adjacent pair largely so; underparts pale grayish, fading to white on the abdomen, the sides and flanks brownish olive or gray; bill dusky above, pinkish or yellow below; iris brown or yellow. *Immature:* Essentially like adult, but duller, and more or less streaked, especially on the throat, breast, and sides.

Distribution.—Highland areas exclusive of Baja California.

Races.—*J. p. dorsalis* (winters in Sonora and Chihuahua). *J. p. palliatus* (mountains of Sonora, Chihuahua, and probably western Durango). *J. p. phaeonotus* (southern Chihuahua, San Luis Potosí, and Tamaulipas south in high mountains to Oaxaca). *J. p. colimae* (Sierra Nevada de Colima, at high altitudes). *J. p. australis* (Sierra Madre of Guerrero). *J. p. fulvescens* (highlands of Chiapas).

Remarks.—Also known as Red-backed Junco and Mexican Junco. A gray-headed, *chestnut-backed* junco with virtually *uniform grayish white underparts.* In the north this species might be confused with certain wintering Oregon Juncos (especially *caniceps*), but these have gray throats and breasts that contrast with their white abdomens. Moreover, the lores of Yellow-eyed Juncos are *black,* and distinctly darker than the adjacent plumage, a condition not usually found among Oregon Juncos. Note the *gray or brownish olive sides and flanks. See* Oregon Junco.

CHIPPING SPARROW. *Spizella passerina* (Illus. p. 600).—5–5¼. Crown chestnut-rufous, this sometimes streaked with black; superciliaries, auriculars, and hind-neck pale gray, the last often black-streaked; a dusky eye-streak; back and scapulars tawny or reddish, conspicuously streaked with black, the rump grayish; tail notched; below dull grayish white, the breast and flanks darkest and sometimes tinged with buff; bill black.

Distribution.—Mountains of northern Baja California (wintering to the cape district), and northwestern Mexico southward on the tableland to Chiapas; winters also in northeastern Mexico.

Races.—*S. p. arizonae* (Sierra San Pedro Mártir, Baja California, wintering south to the cape district, and on the Mexican tableland; casual on Guadalupe Island, off Baja California). *S. p. atremaeus* (highlands of eastern Sinaloa, southwestern Chihuahua, and northwestern Durango). *S. p. mexicana* (highlands of southern Mexico, from Nayarit, Jalisco, Michoacán, Tlaxcala, and Veracruz south to Chiapas). *S. p. passerina (winters in northeastern Mexico).

Remarks.—A small chestnut-capped sparrow with a *black bill*, pale superciliaries, and *whitish underparts*. The Rufous-winged Sparrow of Sonora and Sinaloa is superficially similar, but has a *brownish bill and*

CHIPPING SPARROW

rusty shoulders. See Rufous-crowned Sparrow, Clay-colored Sparrow, and Field Sparrow.

*CLAY-COLORED SPARROW. *Spizella pallida.*—4¾–5. Sides of crown tawny, streaked with black, the median stripe conspicuously paler; hind-neck (usually) and sides of neck pale gray; superciliaries and malar area whitish, the latter bordered by an obscure submalar stripe; auriculars and back pale buffy brown, the former sharply outlined with darker, the back and scapulars black-streaked; below immaculate, essentially whitish.

Distribution.—Winters in Baja California and over the Mexican plateau to the southern portion of the country.

Remarks.—The only small, white-breasted, open-country sparrow with a pale stripe through the median crown, and *sharply defined, tawny auriculars*. Immature and fall Chipping Sparrows are very similar, but lack a dark border above and below the ear-patch. Young Clay-colored Sparrows have *brownish* (not gray) rumps.

*BREWER SPARROW. *Spizella breweri breweri.*—5–5¼. Above *pale grayish brown*, very evenly streaked with black; greater wing-coverts tipped with buffy white, this forming an indistinct wing-bar; a pale superciliary stripe; sides of head pale buffy brown, the auriculars sometimes bordered above and below with darker; underparts dull whitish.

Distribution.—Winters in Baja California, and in the northwestern portion of the Mexican plateau south to Jalisco.

Remarks.—The only clear-breasted, open-country sparrow having its entire crown, hind-neck, back, and scapulars *uniformly streaked*. Note the pale superciliaries and *buffy* auriculars.

*FIELD SPARROW. *Spizella pusilla arenacea.*—5¼. Crown reddish brown, the median portion (stripe) often grayish; superciliaries and sides of head pale gray; an *obscure* eye-ring and reddish eye-streak; back and scapulars grayish or reddish brown, very conspicuously streaked with black; rump immaculate gray; two pale wing-bars; underparts dull whitish; bill pink.

Distribution.—Winters in northeastern Mexico (Nuevo León and Tamaulipas).

Remarks.—Of the small sparrows with *pink* bills, only the Field and Worthen are likely to be confused. Field Sparrows will be recognized by their relatively long tails, and *distinct eye-streak*. Worthens have conspicuous white eye-rings and virtually no eye-streak. Chipping Sparrows are *dark-billed* and have wholly rufous caps.

WORTHEN SPARROW. *Spizella wortheni.*—5¼. Similar to a Field Sparrow, but with a shorter tail, rather obscure wing-bars, *conspicuous white eye-rings*, and uniform gray auriculars, the postocular stripe being absent.

Distribution.—Northern Tamaulipas, wintering southward to Veracruz and southern Puebla.

Remarks.—*See* Field Sparrow.

BLACK-CHINNED SPARROW. *Spizella atrogularis* (Illus. p. 602).—5¼. *Male:* Head, hind-neck, and breast gray, the lores, chin, and upper throat black; back and scapulars rusty brown or cinnamon, liberally streaked with black; rump and upper tail-coverts gray; abdomen grayish white; bill pinkish. *Female:* Similar to male, but usually much duller; black of the throat restricted or replaced with gray.

Distribution.—Baja California south to latitude 30° (wintering to the cape district), northeastern Sonora, and the eastern and southern portions of the Mexican plateau.

Races.—*S. a. cana* (breeds in northern Baja California, ranging to Cape San Lucas in winter). *S. a. evura* (northeastern Sonora, probably wintering extensively in northwestern Mexico). *S. a. atrogularis* (southern Coahuila south over the plateau to Jalisco, Guerrero, and Puebla).

Remarks.—A common gray-headed, *pink-billed* sparrow with a *black chin and upper throat*. Females and immature birds lack the black patch, but will be known by their *contrasting* gray heads and reddish brown backs.

BLACK-CHINNED SPARROW

*WHITE-CROWNED SPARROW. *Zonotrichia leucophrys.*—6–6¼. Stripe through median crown, nape, and superciliaries white, the sides of the crown and a conspicuous stripe from eye to hind-neck black; back, scapulars, and rump pale grayish brown, the first very broadly striped with rusty brown; two white wing-bars; lores, auriculars, breast, and sides clear gray, fading to white on throat and abdomen, the flanks brownish; bill cinnamon-brown or pinkish.

Distribution.—Winters in Baja California, and from northern Mexico south over the plateau to Sinaloa, Jalisco, and Guanajuato.

Races.—*Z. l. leucophrys* (winters in southern Baja California, and over the Mexican plateau to Sinaloa, Durango, Jalisco, and Guanajuato). *Z. l. gambelii* (winters in Baja California, and northern Mexico south to Sinaloa and San Luis Potosí).

Remarks.—The strikingly patterned black-and-white crown and superciliaries of the adult are distinctive. In immature birds the head has a similar pattern, but the black and white are replaced with reddish brown and pale buffy brown. Birds in this plumage sometimes resemble Golden-crowned Sparrows, but the latter lacks a buffy line over the eye. The two races that range into Mexico can be distinguished by the extent of their white superciliary stripes. In *gambelii* these originate at the *base* of the bill, not above the eye, as with *leucophrys*. *See* Golden-crowned Sparrow, White-throated Sparrow, and Stripe-headed Sparrow.

*GOLDEN-CROWNED SPARROW. *Zonotrichia atricapilla.*—6½. Sides of crown and superciliaries black; stripe through median crown two-toned, the anterior portion bright olive-yellow, the posterior half usually pale gray; upperparts mainly grayish brown, the back and scapulars broadly striped with deep brown; two conspicuous white wing-bars; lores, auriculars, throat, and breast grayish, often more or less tinged with pale brown, the abdomen dull white; flanks pale buffy brown.

Distribution.—Winters in Baja California, and casually on Guadalupe Island.

Remarks.—The *olive-yellow crown-patch* is distinctive. Otherwise much like the White-crowned Sparrow, but without white superciliaries. Immature White-crowns might be confused with this species in Baja California.

*WHITE-THROATED SPARROW. *Zonotrichia albicollis.*—6. Sides of crown and postocular stripe black; a well-defined white or pale grayish stripe through the median crown; anterior portion of superciliaries greenish yellow, the remainder white; upperparts reddish brown, the back and scapulars broadly streaked with black; two white wing-bars; throat and abdomen white, the former rather sharply defined by the gray of the auriculars and chest.

Distribution.—Winters in northeastern Mexico; casual on Guadalupe Island, off Baja California.

Remarks.—Much like a White-crowned Sparrow, but with a *well-defined white throat-patch*, and a conspicuous *yellow* stripe above the lores. In White-crowns the white of the throat *shades* imperceptibly into the pearl-gray breast, and the crown appears quite *puffy*, not slightly rounded as in White-throats and Golden-crowns. *See* Stripe-headed Sparrow.

RUFOUS-COLLARED SPARROW. *Zonotrichia capensis septentrionalis* (Illus. p. 604).—5¾. Sides of crown black, the median stripe, superciliaries, and auriculars pale gray; hind-neck and sides of neck bright rufous, this sometimes extending to sides of chest; upperparts mainly grayish brown, the back and scapulars broadly streaked with black; two vague wing-bars; throat and malar area white, this bordered behind by a more or less discontinuous black collar; lower breast pale grayish, fading to dull white on abdomen.

Distribution.—Mountains of Chiapas (San Cristobal; Pinabete, near Comitán), chiefly in open, grassy pinelands.

Remarks.—A characteristic tropical American species with more than a dozen varieties south of Mexico. While vaguely suggesting a White-throat, it has *gray* (not white) head stripes, a more or less complete chest-band, and considerable rufous on the sides of its neck.

RUFOUS-COLLARED SPARROW

*FOX SPARROW. *Passerella iliaca.*—6–7¼. Above uniform dark brown or brownish slate, the wings, upper tail-coverts, and tail somewhat rufescent; below white, very liberally and conspicuously spotted and streaked with dusky brown, this often forming a patch in the center of the breast.

Distribution.—Winters commonly in northern Baja California.

Races.—*P. i. altivagans; P. i. unalaschcensis; P. i. sinuosa; P. i. schistacea; P. i. fulva; P. i. megarhyncha; P. i. canescens; P. i. monoensis.*

Remarks.—A large *plain-backed* sparrow with very *boldly streaked underparts.* In winter several races are likely to be found together, but these are virtually indistinguishable in the field.

*LINCOLN SPARROW. *Melospiza lincolnii.*—5–5½. Sides of crown rusty brown, the median stripe pale gray, the whole liberally streaked with black; superciliaries pale gray; auriculars and malar area buffy, the latter bordered above and below by a narrow black stripe; a narrow eye-ring and fine postocular stripe; above pale grayish brown, the back and scapulars very broadly streaked with black; a pale buffy band across the chest, this narrowly streaked with black; throat and abdomen white, the sides and flanks pale buffy-brown, more or less streaked with dusky.

Distribution.—Widespread as a transient and winter visitor.

Races.—*M. l. lincolnii* (Baja California, and probably northern Mexico southward). *M. l. gracilis* (northern Baja California and Sonora; eastern and southern limits of winter range uncertain). *M. l. alticola* (northern and eastern Mexico southward).

Remarks.—While resembling some races of Song Sparrow above, Lincoln Sparrows are much less profusely streaked below. Its *buffy chest-band* is virtually diagnostic. Note the *narrow eye-ring*. Thickets and weedy places. *See* Swamp Sparrow and Song Sparrow.

*SWAMP SPARROW. *Melospiza georgiana.*—5¼. Crown essentially chestnut, much intermixed with black, the median stripe, lores, superciliaries, and hind-neck grayish; a dusky postocular stripe; auriculars buffy brown; an obscure submalar stripe; upperparts extensively reddish brown, the back and scapulars very broadly striped with black; wing-coverts and outer webs of remiges russet, the inner secondaries mainly black margined with whitish; *no wing-bars;* throat and abdomen dull white, the breast tinged with pale brown; flanks distinctly tawny.

Distribution.—A winter visitor, ranging south at least to Jalisco and Tamaulipas.

Remarks.—Swamp Sparrows are rather undistinguished. They are darker than Song Sparrows above, where more heavily streaked, and show considerable rufous on their wings. Their dingy underparts are unmarked (adults) and may be strongly tinged with buff. Immature Swamp and Lincoln Sparrows are much alike, but the latter has very *sharp, fine* (not dull) *streaks* below. Thickets, weedy fields, and brush, especially in wet places. *See* Song Sparrow and Lincoln Sparrow.

SONG SPARROW. *Melospiza melodia.*—5¼–6¼. Sides of crown reddish brown, sometimes narrowly streaked with black, the paler (grayish) median portion often forming an ill-defined stripe; lores, superciliaries, and auriculars grayish; a brown or reddish postocular and submalar stripe; upperparts mainly grayish brown, the back and scapulars broadly streaked with rufous or dusky brown; wing-coverts and outer webs of remiges largely russet; below white, the breast and sides liberally streaked with black, brown, or russet, this sometimes forming a distinct patch in the center of the breast; flanks tawny or brownish.

Distribution.—Baja California, Los Coronados Islands, and northern Mexico south over the plateau to Michoacán and Puebla.

Races.—*M. m. coronatorum* (Los Coronados Islands, Baja California). *M. m. cooperi* (Baja Califoria south to latitude 30°). *M. m. saltonis* (Colorado delta of northeastern Baja California, and northern Sonora). *M. m. rivularis* (south-central Baja California from San Ignacio to Comondú). **M. m. montana* (winters in Sonora and Chihuahua). *M. m. goldmani* (mountains of western Durango). *M. m. adusta* (highlands of Michoacán). *M. m. pectoralis* (Hidalgo south to Puebla, in highland areas).

Remarks.—Song Sparrows vary a great deal in size and in general coloration, but all are more or less heavily streaked below, and *adults* usually have a *dark patch* in the center of the breast. Savannah Sparrows, also streaked, lack a breast-spot and have yellow above the eyes. Moreover, the Savannah's tail is conspicuously notched. Immature birds are much like Lincoln Sparrows, but the Song Sparrow characteristically pumps its tail while in flight. *See* Sierra Madre Sparrow, Vesper Sparrow, Lincoln Sparrow, and Swamp Sparrow.

*McCOWN LONGSPUR. *Rhynchophanes mccownii.*—5¾. *Male (summer)*: Crown, submalar streak, and crescent-shaped band across chest black; nape and hind-neck pale gray, this becoming pale buffy brown on the back and scapulars, where broadly streaked with dusky; middle and lesser wing-coverts bright chestnut, the wings otherwise brownish; tail essentially white, the middle feathers dusky, the others black-tipped; underparts white, the chest (or breast) with a crescentic collar; *(winter)*: Similar to summer plumage, but without black, the crown buffy brown, the chest tinged with buff. *Female:* Above pale buffy brown, liberally streaked with dusky; a rufous patch on wing-coverts; tail as in male; below dingy whitish, the breast and flanks more or less tinged with buff.

Distribution.—Winters in Chihuahua and northwestern Durango.

Remarks.—In flight, the pattern of the tail—*white, with a conspicuous black or dusky* T—distinguishes this species in all plumages. Chestnut-collared Longspurs show a *black* V-*shaped patch* on the white tail. Males of both species are unmistakable when in breeding plumage. Bare fields and grassy plains. *See* Chestnut-collared Longspur.

*CHESTNUT-COLLARED LONGSPUR. *Calcarius ornatus.*—5½. *Male (summer)*: Crown, postocular stripe, posterior border of auriculars, breast, and abdomen black; superciliaries white; throat and auriculars pale buff or whitish; a bright chestnut band across hind-neck; upperparts mainly grayish buffy brown, the back and scapulars broadly streaked with sooty; lateral rectrices extensively white, tipped and edged with dusky, the two outermost virtually immaculate; *(winter)*: Essentially like female, but breast and abdomen often mottled with black, and hind-neck usually reddish. *Female:* Above pale grayish or buffy brown, liberally streaked with dusky; tail as in summer male; throat whitish, this rather sharply defined, the breast buffy brown fading to buffy white posteriorly.

Distribution.—Winters in the northern portion of the country (south to Veracruz in the east), exclusive of Baja California.

Remarks.—*See* McCown Longspur.

INDEX

Page numbers in boldfaced type refer to illustrations and are placed only after the approved English names of species.